# COCOMO II.2000 Scale Factors and Efforts Multipliers

| Drivers | Symbol | XL | VL | L | N | H | VH | XH | Productivity Range[1,2] |
|---|---|---|---|---|---|---|---|---|---|
| **Scale Factors** | | | | | | | | | |
| PREC | SF1 | | 6.20 | 4.96 | 3.72 | 2.48 | 1.24 | 0.00 | 1.33 |
| FLEX | SF2 | | 5.07 | 4.05 | 3.04 | 2.03 | 1.01 | 0.00 | 1.26 |
| RESL | SF3 | | 7.07 | 5.65 | 4.24 | 2.83 | 1.41 | 0.00 | 1.39 |
| TEAM | SF4 | | 5.48 | 4.38 | 3.29 | 2.19 | 1.10 | 0.00 | 1.29 |
| PMAT | SF5 | | 7.80 | 6.24 | 4.68 | 3.12 | 1.56 | 0.00 | 1.43 |
| **Post-Architecture Effort Multipliers** | | | | | | | | | |
| RELY | EM1 | | 0.82 | 0.92 | 1.00 | 1.10 | 1.26 | | 1.54 |
| DATA | EM2 | | | 0.90 | 1.00 | 1.14 | 1.28 | | 1.42 |
| CPLX | EM3 | | 0.73 | 0.87 | 1.00 | 1.17 | 1.34 | 1.74 | 2.38 |
| RUSE | EM4 | | | 0.95 | 1.00 | 1.07 | 1.15 | 1.24 | 1.31 |
| DOCU | EM5 | | 0.81 | 0.91 | 1.00 | 1.11 | 1.23 | | 1.52 |
| TIME | EM6 | | | | 1.00 | 1.11 | 1.29 | 1.63 | 1.63 |
| STOR | EM7 | | | | 1.00 | 1.05 | 1.17 | 1.46 | 1.46 |
| PVOL | EM8 | | | 0.87 | 1.00 | 1.15 | 1.30 | | 1.49 |
| ACAP[†] | EM9 | | 1.42 | 1.19 | 1.00 | 0.85 | 0.71 | | 2.00 |
| PCAP[†] | EM10 | | 1.34 | 1.15 | 1.00 | 0.88 | 0.76 | | 1.76 |
| PCON | EM11 | | 1.29 | 1.12 | 1.00 | 0.90 | 0.81 | | 1.51 |
| APEX | EM12 | | 1.22 | 1.10 | 1.00 | 0.88 | 0.81 | | 1.51 |
| PLEX | EM13 | | 1.19 | 1.09 | 1.00 | 0.91 | 0.85 | | 1.40 |
| LTEX | EM14 | | 1.20 | 1.09 | 1.00 | 0.91 | 0.84 | | 1.43 |
| TOOL | EM15 | | 1.17 | 1.09 | 1.00 | 0.90 | 0.78 | | 1.50 |
| SITE | EM16 | | 1.22 | 1.09 | 1.00 | 0.93 | 0.86 | 0.80 | 1.53 |
| SCED | EM17 | | 1.43 | 1.14 | 1.00 | 1.00 | 1.00 | | 1.43 |
| **Early Design Effort Multipliers** | | | | | | | | | |
| RCPX | EM1 | 0.49 | 0.60 | 0.83 | 1.00 | 1.33 | 1.91 | 2.72 | 5.55 |
| RUSE | EM2 | | | 0.95 | 1.00 | 1.07 | 1.15 | 1.24 | 1.31 |
| PDIF | EM3 | | | 1.00 | 1.00 | 1.00 | | | 1.00 |
| PERS | EM4 | 2.12 | 1.62 | 1.26 | 1.00 | 0.83 | 0.63 | 0.50 | 4.24 |
| PREX | EM5 | 1.59 | 1.33 | 1.12 | 1.00 | 0.87 | 0.74 | 0.62 | 2.56 |
| FCIL | EM6 | 1.43 | 1.30 | 1.10 | 1.00 | 0.87 | 0.73 | 0.62 | 2.31 |
| SCED | EM7 | | 1.43 | 1.14 | 1.00 | 1.00 | 1.00 | | 1.43 |

**For Effort Calculations:**

Multiplicative constant A = 2.94;

Exponential constant B = 0.91

**For Schedule Calculations:**

Multiplicative constant C = 3.67;

Exponential constant D = 0.28

[1]**For Scale Factors:**

$$PR_{SF_n} = \frac{(100)^{0.91 + (0.01 \times SF_{n_{MAX}})}}{(100)^{0.91}}$$

[2]**For Effort Multipliers:**

$$PR_{EM_n} = \frac{EM_{n_{MAX}}}{EM_{n_{MIN}}}$$

[†]PR for Personnel/team capability shown on the front cover is determined as a combination of ACAP and PCAP:

$$PR_{Personnel/team\ capacity} = \frac{ACAP_{MAX} \times PCAP_{MAX}}{ACAP_{MIN} \times PCAP_{MIN}}$$

"One of the most significant software technology accomplishments of the last quarter of this century is the increasing usage of software parametric models for resource estimation and project management. There is an especially wide familiarity of the COCOMO model across a range of academia, industry and government. The publication in 1981 of the original COCOMO model in *Software Engineering Economics* remains the one technical reference that everyone involved in this field of endeavor has on their bookshelf and is still in continous usage. The development of the COCOMO II model encompasses key advances in software technology. This new textbook on COCOMO II as we enter this next millennium will fill the same crucial niche and should be a must as a companion volume on every bookshelf."

—Marilee Wheaton
Director, Office of Cost Estimation
TRW Systems & Information Technology Group

"This book is the culmination of five years of partnering between the USC Center for Software Engineering and industrial experts in the field of software cost estimation. While not a replacement for Dr. Boehm's classic *Software Engineering Economics,* consider it a valuable and timely supplement focusing upon today's software products and processes."

—Gary Thomas
Engineering Fellow
Raytheon

" ...Barry Boehm's team-produced book is not simply about cost estimation, but a comprehensive and state-of-the-art view of the software engineering process. A great strength of the new book is Chapter 3, which presents detailed application examples. In the first example, Boehm revisits the Transaction Process System case study from the '81 *Software Engineering Economics* book and, while applying the new COCOMO II model, gives a practical, concise view of the last 20 years' progress in software engineering methodology. Another example, the Airborne Radar System design, demonstrates that the methods and tools taught are highly applicable to and useful in designing large, complex, real-time embedded systems as well."

—Dr. Peter Hantos
Principal Scientist
Xerox Corporation

"Barry Boehm and his colleagues address the wide range of modern software development practices in their COCOMO II family of estimation models described in this book. The focus is primarily on estimating size, effort, and schedule. A quality model has also been included. This book is a 'must have' for every software estimator and cost analyst. Managers and instructors will also find it interesting and useful."

—Richard D. Stutzke
Vice President
Science Applications International Corp.

# Software Cost Estimation with COCOMO II

Barry W. Boehm, Chris Abts, A. Winsor Brown,
Sunita Chulani, Bradford K. Clark, Ellis Horowitz,
Ray Madachy, Donald J. Reifer, and Bert Steece

PH
PTR

Prentice Hall PTR
Upper Saddle River, New Jersey 07458
www.phptr.com

ISBN 0-13-026692-2

90000

9 780130 266927

**Library of Congress Cataloging-in-Publication Data**

Software cost estimation with Cocomo II / by Barry W. Boehm . . . [et al.].
     p.  cm.
   Includes bibliographical references and index.
   ISBN 0-13-026692-2
   1.  Computer software--Costs.   I.  Boehm, Barry W.
  QA76.76.C73 S64 2000
005.3'068'1--dc21                     00–032644

Acquisitions editor: *Paul Petralia*
Cover designer: *Talar Agasyan*
Cover design director: *Jerry Votta*
Manufacturing manager: *Alexis Heydt*
Buyer: *Maura Goldstaub*
Marketing manager: *Bryan Gambrel*
Editorial assistant: *Justin Somma*
Project coordinator: *Anne Trowbridge*
Compositor/Production services: *Pine Tree Composition, Inc.*

© 2000 by Prentice Hall PTR
Prentice-Hall, Inc.
Upper Saddle River, New Jersey 07458

Prentice Hall books are widely used by corporations and government agencies for training, marketing, and resale.

The publisher offers discounts on this book when ordered in bulk quantities. For more information contact:

Corporate Sales Department
Phone: 800-382-3419
Fax: 201-236-7141
E-mail: corpsales@prenhall.com

Or write:

Prentice Hall PTR
Corp. Sales Dept.
One Lake Street
Upper Saddle River, New Jersey 07458

Printed in the United States of America
10  9  8  7  6

ISBN: 0-13-026692-2

Prentice-Hall International (UK) Limited, *London*
Prentice-Hall of Australia Pty. Limited, *Sydney*
Prentice-Hall Canada Inc., *Toronto*
Prentice-Hall Hispanoamericana, S.A., *Mexico*
Prentice-Hall of India Private Limited, *New Delhi*
Prentice-Hall of Japan, Inc., *Tokyo*
Pearson Education Asia Pte Ltd.
Editora Prentice-Hall do Brasil, Ltda., *Rio de Janeiro*

# Contents

# List of Figures

## Chapter 5

# List of Tables

## Chapter 3

## Chapter 4

## Appendix E

# Foreword

I predict that *Software Cost Estimation with COCOMO II* will be a best-seller among a certain class of people in the software industry. These won't be the programming whizzes, marketing geniuses, technology experts, or software architects. The book's success won't be centered in the process groups or among toolsmiths, quality assessors, or project managers. It will be most popular with a narrow band of people that crosses all these audiences but is not easily discernible in most organizations: the "professional" software engineers, those behind-the-scenes working stiffs who care about building useful products within the context of a profitable business.

COCOMO II is an objective cost model for planning and executing software projects. It is an important ingredient for managing software projects or software lines of business. A cost model provides a framework for communicating business decisions among the stakeholders of a software effort. COCOMO II supports contract negotiations, process improvement analyses, tool purchases, architecture changes, component make/buy tradeoffs, and several other return-on-investment decisions with a credible basis of estimate. This book demonstrates how COCOMO II can be used to support such analyses and how credible the results will be.

COCOMO II was pioneered and championed by Dr. Barry Boehm, one of the most influential, often-quoted professionals in the software industry. His classic 1981 book, *Software Engineering Economics,* introduced COCOMO. It provided a well-defined, open "engineering" basis for reasoning about the cost and schedule implications of a software solution, and was a minor breakthrough in the software industry. COCOMO rapidly became the most popular software cost model.

Over the past several years, usage of COCOMO has required a little bending and adaptation to accommodate the dramatic shifts in software life cycles, technologies, components, tools, notations, and organizational cultures. Dr. Boehm and USC's Center for Software Engineering have invested more than four years in a COCOMO update that better accommodates the modern trends in software engineering. This book is the product of that investment. COCOMO II incorporates several field-tested improvements to both broaden its applicability and improve its estimating accuracy for modern software development approaches. It is the result of many software economics experts using COCOMO for countless hours in field applications and in research laboratories across a wide spectrum of software domains and organizations.

COCOMO II includes two underlying information models. The first is a framework for describing a software project, including models of the process, culture, stakeholders, methods, tools, teams, and the size/complexity of the software product. The second is an experience base that can be used to estimate the likely resources (effort and time) of a project from historical precedents. COCOMO II includes significant updates to COCOMO to improve its applicability to modern processes, methods, tools, and technologies. It also includes a much larger, more pertinent database of modern precedents and improves the adaptability of the model so it can be optimized across a broad spectrum of domains and project circumstances. This book captures the results of this work and presents the information in a way that will satisfy its many audiences: COCOMO experts, cost model newcomers, COCOMO users, and COCOMO toolsmiths. Multiple perspectives are covered with thorough examples and thoughtful commentary.

Rampant hyperbole has infected the software industry over the past 10 years. The biased presentations of various process improvements, new techniques, and new technologies are symptoms of an industry with ambiguous benchmarks of performance and little accountability. With an ever-increasing demand for improving time to market, shortcuts and clean-it-up-later approaches win out more often than they should. The COCOMO II product captured in this book is a shining counter-example to our rush-to-market mentality. COCOMO II is a thorough engineering model based on sound mathematics, pre-eminent industry expertise, and broad, modern project experience. As a USC affiliate, Rational Software Corporation has openly supported and invested in the development of COCOMO II. Software cost modeling, and particularly the COCOMO II alignment with modern iterative processes, architecture-first life cycles, and UML-based analysis and design methods are discriminating advantages needed to succeed in software development projects.

Twenty years ago, I enrolled in UCLA's first Software Engineering Economics class, a graduate course offered by the Computer Science Department and taught by Barry Boehm. Most of the class, including me, did not understand 10 percent of what it took to deliver software products successfully. Most of us also failed to appreciate that the context and decision-making for most software development projects were predominantly driven by business concerns rather than technical concerns. This course had a profound impact on my views of project management and on the entire software industry. While much of this original COCOMO material is still pertinent in today's software management discipline, this new book incorporates substantial updates for the lessons learned over the past 20 years. More than ever before, software project decisions are influenced by their business context. The COCOMO II model sets a new standard for modern software project management and provides an economic framework for assessing the next generation of process, methods, and tool improvements within the software industry.

Walker Royce,
Vice President
Rational Software Corporation

# Preface

"We are becoming a software company" is an increasingly repeated phrase in organizations as diverse as finance, transportation, aerospace, electronics, and manufacturing firms. Competitive advantage increasingly depends on developing software for smart, tailorable products and services, and on the ability to develop and adapt these products and services more rapidly than competitors' adaptation times. These trends highlight the need for strong capabilities to accurately estimate software cost and schedules, and to support tradeoff, risk, sensitivity, and business case analyses for software decisions.

Concurrently, a new generation of software processes and products is changing the way organizations develop software. These new approaches—evolutionary, risk-driven, and collaborative software processes; fourth-generation languages and application generators; commercial off-the-shelf (COTS) and reuse-driven software approaches; fast-track software development approaches; software process maturity initiatives—lead to significant benefits in terms of improved software quality and reduced software cost, risk, and cycle time.

However, although some of the existing software cost models have initiatives addressing aspects of these issues, these new approaches have not to date been strongly matched by complementary new models for estimating software costs and schedules. This makes it difficult for organizations to conduct effective planning, analysis, and control of projects using the new approaches.

These concerns have led the authors of this book to formulate a new version of the Constructive Cost Model (COCOMO) for software effort, cost and schedule estimation. The original COCOMO 81 [Boehm 1981] and its specialized Ada COCOMO successor [Boehm and Royce 1989] were reasonably well matched to the classes of software projects that they modeled: largely custom, built-to-specification software [Miyazaki and Mori 1985; Goudy 1987]. Although Ada COCOMO added a capability for estimating the costs and schedules for incremental software development, COCOMO 81 encountered increasing difficulty in estimating the costs of software created via spiral or evolutionary development models, or of software developed largely via commercial off-the-shelf (COTS) applications-composition capabilities.

## SOFTWARE ESTIMATION STATE OF THE PRACTICE

A number of commercial software estimation models continue to pass the market test for value added to users. And quite a few organizations do a good job of software project planning, estimating, and control. However, a very large number of organizations do not: in the 1995 Standish Group study, over 53% of the software projects were overrun by more than 50% in both budget and schedule [Standish 1995].

Some recent collections of software failure case studies provide more detail on the reasons for such overruns. Table P1 summarizes the results from six such projects. The first three are from [Flowers 1996]; the second three are from [Glass 1998].

## MODEL CLASHES AND MBASE

We have analyzed the projects in Table P1, and have found that many of their problems result from model clashes [Boehm-Port 1999b]. Model clashes involve incompatibilities among the primary models being used to define and manage the project. These include product models (requirements, architecture, design, etc.); process models (waterfall, spiral, maturity models, etc.); property models (cost, schedule, performance, etc.), and success models (business case, stakeholder win-win, IKIWISI: I'll know it when I see it, etc.).

The projects in Table P1 all had a number of model clashes contributing to their failure. Several model clashes involved cost and schedule property models. For example, the London Ambulance project established a $2.25M cost baseline from misreading a consultant's report giving a best-possible cost if an (unavailable) packaged product solution could be found. The low bidder's $1.5M bid was based on a very sketchy build-from-scratch product model.

At the USC Center for Software Engineering (USC-CSE), we have been developing an approach called Model-Based (System) Architecting and Software

**Table P1   Software Overrun Case Studies**

| Project | First; Last Estimate | | Status at Completion |
|---------|-------------|-------------------|----------------------|
|         | Cost ($M)   | Schedule (Months) |                      |
| PROMS (Royalty collection) | 12; 21+ | 22; 46 | Cancelled, Month 28 |
| London Ambulance | 1.5; 6+ | 7; 17+ | Cancelled, Month 17 |
| London Stock Exchange | 60–75; 150 | 19; 70 | Cancelled, Month 36 |
| Confirm (Travel reservations) | 56; 160+ | 45; 60+ | Cancelled, Month 48 |
| FAA Advanced Automation System | 3700; 7000+ | 48; 96 | Cancelled, Month 70 |
| Master Net (Banking) | 22; 80+ | 9; 48+ | Cancelled, Month 48 |

Engineering (MBASE), for endowing a project with a consistent and mutually supportive set of product, process, property, and success models [Boehm-Port 1999a; see also http://sunset.usc.edu/research/MBASE]. It uses stakeholder success models as the critical project drivers, and a stakeholder win-win variant of the spiral model to determine a compatible set of product, process, property, and success models for the system. It also integrates software engineering with system engineering, and provides a strong framework for transitioning to the new Integrated Capability Maturity Model (CMM I).

## MBASE AND COCOMO II

Our research on MBASE includes research on success models (win-win; expectations management); process models (WinWin Spiral Model, anchor points, requirements negotiation); product models (domain models, software architectures); and property models (primarily COCOMO II and its extensions). The concurrent research on these component models helps to strengthen their relationships and to ground them in software practices. For example, our anchor point process research began with an effort to define a set of common life-cycle milestones upon which to base COCOMO II cost and schedule estimates. In collaboration with Rational, Inc., we have integrated the MBASE phases and milestones with those of the Rational Unified Process, and have provided MBASE/RUP phase and activity distribution estimators for COCOMO II in Appendix A.

Also, we try to apply MBASE to our own projects. Thus, in scoping CO-COMO II, we used the MBASE principles of identifying stakeholders, gathering their objectives in using software estimation models, and determining their principal needs for improvement over the existing COCOMO 81 capability. Thus, Chapter 1 of this book begins with a summary of COCOMO II user objectives, followed by a set of COCOMO II model objectives in terms of desired improvements over COCOMO 81, followed by a set of COCOMO II development and evolution strategies for achieving the objectives.

One of the stakeholder objectives was to avoid basing COCOMO II on a single process model such as the waterfall model assumed in COCOMO 81. Thus, we have developed interpretations of COCOMO II to cover the waterfall model, MBASE/RUP, and incremental development.

## CONTENT OF BOOK CHAPTERS

Chapter 1 provides the overall context and framework for COCOMO II, including its model of future software practices and resulting choice of a three-stage model tailorable to the major future software practices. Chapter 2 presents the specific definitions of COCOMO II quantities, estimating equations, cost driver and scale factor definitions and rating scales, and guidance in interpreting the definitions in special situations.

The final section of Chapter 2 shows how to use COCOMO II to perform quick manual analyses for a number of the objectives established in Chapter 1: making investment decisions, performing tradeoff and risk analyses, tailoring models to project practices.

Chapter 3 shows how you can use the USC COCOMO II tool to perform more extensive cost estimates and tradeoff analyses, using two representative examples: a transaction processing system and an aircraft radar system.

Chapter 4 summarizes the COCOMO II Bayesian calibration process and results, and provides guidelines for organizations to produce their own calibrated version of the model.

Chapter 5 describes some emerging extensions of the central COCOMO II model. The Applications Composition model is still considered to be an emerging extension, as its calibration and counting rules are not yet robust. Others address the problems of estimating the cost of software COTS integration (COCOTS); phase distribution of schedule and effort (COPSEMO); rapid application development effort and schedule adjustments (CORADMO); quality in terms of delivered defect density (COQUALMO); and the effects of applying software productivity strategies (COPROMO).

Chapter 6 projects future software trends and how they are likely to affect software cost estimation and COCOMO II.

Six appendices provide A) COCOMO II definitions, assumptions, and phase/activity distribution estimates, B) an incremental development estimation model, C) data collection forms for COCOMO II and emerging extensions to better calibrate the model to your organization, D) information on the USC-CSE COCOMO II and other Affiliate programs, E) a Software Reference Manual for the USC COCOMO II tool, and forms and guidelines for COCOMO II data collection, and F) information on the content and use of the accompanying CD-ROM.

This CD provides you a current copy of a COCOMO II estimating software package developed by USC-CSE, and demonstration copies of three commercial COCOMO II packages. We have also put the examples used within the book as files on the CD so that you can generate the results we've come up with using the package. This is important because it shows you how to effectively employ the package—and the COCOMO II model—to develop estimates, make tradeoffs and perform various kinds of cost analyses.

The CD also provides you with a number of additional resources. It contains briefings, reports, manuals and amplifying details on the COCOMO II package so that you will understand its history and how it was derived. Our goal is to update the CD every two years as we publish updates to this book.

## MAPPING OF CHAPTERS ONTO READER INTERESTS

If you are a software manager, analyst, or developer wishing to make and use software estimates, read Chapters 1, 2, and 3, and Appendix E in concert with use of the USC COCOMO II tool.

If you are a software estimation specialist for your organization, read the entire book.

If you are a software metrics and models researcher, read Chapters 1, 2, 4, 5, 6 and Appendices A, B, and C.

If you want a general understanding of COCOMO II and its uses, read Chapters 1, 2, and 3.

## RELATION TO 1981 SOFTWARE ENGINEERING ECONOMICS BOOK

About 30 % of the 1981 *Software Engineering Economics* book [Boehm 1981] is superseded by the contents of this book. Here is a chapter-by-chapter assessment of the 1981 book as it relates to the contents of this COCOMO II book—remember, the chapters listed below are those found in the original 1981 book:

Chapters 1 and 2. These chapters are still timely and useful as a motivation for the human-economics approach to software engineering.

Chapter 3. The GOALS approach has evolved into MBASE and the stakeholder win-win approach. The material here and in Appendix B is good for background and examples, but not for operational guidance.

Chapter 4. COCOMO II has been structured to produce cost and schedule estimates consistent with the Waterfall Model milestones in this chapter. The Work Breakdown Structure framework is also still applicable.

Chapters 5–9. The material on Basic and Intermediate COCOMO 81 has been replaced by the COCOMO II Applications Composition, Early Design, and Post-Architecture series of models. Portions of Chapters 6 and 7 on Waterfall-model phase and activity distributions are still relevant.

Chapters 10–20. The material on software microeconomics is still valid as a framework for using COCOMO II estimates.

Chapters 21 and 22. The seven-step approach and comparison of software estimation techniques are still valid. The COCOMO II book complements this material by providing example-based guidance on using COCOMO II for various estimation, tradeoff analysis and life-cycle estimation purposes (in Chapters 2 and 3).

Chapter 23. This material is specific to COCOMO 81. Including phase-sensitive cost drivers is a downstream COCOMO II goal.

Chapters 24–27. Some of the cost driver experience discussions are dated (Turnaround Time, Tool Use, Modern Programming Practices, Schedule stretchout effects). The others are still useful. We plan to provide updates and coverage of the new cost drivers in some future editions.

Chapter 28. Personnel Continuity and Documentation are now COCOMO II cost drivers. Their effects were significant in the latest COCOMO II data analysis. Requirements Volatility is now being treated as a size modifier via the breakage parameter, REVL. Other parts of the chapter are largely specific to COCOMO 81.

Chapter 29. The material in this chapter is largely superseded by Chapter 4 of the COCOMO II book.

Chapter 30. The maintenance data trends are still relevant. The maintenance model for COCOMO II has been updated to include the Software Understanding and Personnel Unfamiliarity factors.

Chapter 31. The material on estimating conversion, computer, installation, training and documentation costs is largely out of date. The business case in Section 31.8 is still highly useful.

Chapter 32. The planning and control techniques are still valid. Earned value techniques are now more frequently used for software. The primary trend not captured is the use of other progress tracking metrics such as those in the *Practical Software Measurement* handbook [McGarry et al. 1998]

Chapter 33. The coverage of COTS and Very High Level Languages was very good for 1981, but much more is known now; see the COCOTS discussion in Section 5.4 of this book. The discussions of product, platform, and people productivity factors are still useful. COCOMO II has more process productivity options in its scale factors, and a stronger treatment of reuse.

Appendix A. Superseded by current Appendix C.

Appendix B. Good for background, as discussed for Chapter 3.

## BOTTOM LINE

Most of the 1981 book is still useful and relevant. The parts that are mostly outdated or superseded by this book are Chapters 5–9, 23, 28–29, 31 (except Section 31.8), and Appendices A and B.

# ACKNOWLEDGMENTS

The development of the COCOMO II book has been a collaborative team effort by all of the authors. Most of the chapters have been worked on by several authors over the several years since 1995, and the chapters have been extensively cross-reviewed to ensure consistency. However, we would like to particularly acknowledge the lead authorship responsibilities for each of the chapters and sections: Chapter 1 (Barry Boehm); Chapter 2 (Brad Clark); Chapter 3 (Don Reifer for the Transaction Processing System example; Ray Madachy for the Airborne Radar System example); Chapter 4 (Sunita Chulani and Bert Steece); Chapter 5 (Barry Boehm for Applications Composition; Winsor Brown and Barry Boehm for COPSEMO, CORADMO, and COPROMO; Chris Abts for COCOTS and overall book integration; Sunita Chulani for COQUALMO; Ray Madachy for Expert CO-COMO and Dynamic COCOMO); Chapter 6 (Barry Boehm); Appendix A (Barry Boehm); Appendix B (Brad Clark); Appendix C (Don Reifer, Winsor Brown, Sunita Chulani, Chris Abts, Brad Clark); Appendix D (Winsor Brown); Appendix E (Ellis Horowitz); and Appendix F (Winsor Brown).

We would also like to thank the following organizations and individuals without whose support and efforts this book, the COCOMO II model itself, and its emerging extensions would not have become a reality:

The USC-CSE Affiliates, past and present: Aerospace Corporation, Air Force Cost Analysis Agency, Allied Signal, AT&T, Bellcore, Boeing, C-bridge, DARPA, DISA, Draper Labs, EDS, E-Systems, FAA, Fidelity, GDE Systems, Hughes, IBM, Iconix, IDA, JPL, Litton, Lockheed Martin, Loral, Lucent, MCC, MDAC, Microsoft, Motorola, Northrop Grumman, ONR, Rational, Raytheon, Rockwell, SAIC, SEI, SPC, Sun, TASC, Teledyne, TI, TRW, USAF Rome Lab, US Army Research Lab, US Army TACON, Xerox.

Past COCOMO research group principals Rick Selby and Chris Westland; the many USC computer science graduate students who created and still maintain the USC COCOMO II software and CD, in particular Jongmoon Baik and Heechul Kwon; Cyrus Fakharzadeh; other contributors and supporters Vic Basili, Larry Bernstein, George Bozoki, Anita Carleton, Marvin Carr, Betsy Bailey Clark, Adrian Cowderoy, Rich DeMillo, Brad Donald, Tim Ellis, Tom Frazier, John Gaffney, Stuart Glickman, Wolf Goethert, Verna Griffin, Jack Gruczka, Gary Hafen, Peter Hantos, Jairus Hihn, Morton Hirschberg, Walt Johnson, Tony Jordano, Marc Kellner, Ray Kile, Charles Leinbach, Alex Lubashevsky, Steve

Lucks, Jack McGarry, Lloyd Mosemann, Hillel Myers, Charity Nosse, Rhoda Novak, Arnold Pittler, Leitha Purcell, Art Pyster, Sarala Ravishankar, Dan Richard, Michael Saboe, John Salasin, Lita Schulte, Anca-Juliana Stoica, Greg Stratton, Sherry Stukes, Mike Sweeney, Iva Voldase, Ralph Wachter, Tony Wasserman, Marilee Wheaton, Jean Whitaker, Douglas White;

The employers of researchers on the COCOMO II team: IBM for Sunita Chulani, Litton Guidance and Control Systems and C-bridge Internet Solutions for Ray Madachy;

The proprietors of other software estimation models who shared information on their models with us—Dan Galorath, Randy Jensen, Capers Jones, Rob Park and Howard Rubin;

The many members of the professional communities, particularly those of the International Society of Parametric Analysts (ISPA) and the Society of Cost Estimating and Analysis (SCEA), who have critiqued and encouraged our research;

A special and deeply felt thanks goes to our manuscript reviewers, Dan Ligett, Walter Royce, Dick Stutzke and Gary Thomas. Their wise comments and suggestions greatly improved the clarity and value of this work.

Finally we would like to honor the memory of three wonderful people who profoundly influenced COCOMO's evolution: Tom Bauer, Paul Rook and Winston Royce. Their constructive spirit and seminal contributions live on after them.

# About the Authors

Barry Boehm received his bachelor at Harvard University, his doctorate at the University of California, Los Angeles, and an honorary doctorate from the University of Massachusetts. He is currently TRW Professor of Software Engineering in the department of computer science and director of the Center for Software Engineering at the University of Southern California.

Chris Abts received his bachelor at the Georgia Institute of Technology and his master's in industrial and systems engineering at the University of Southern California. He has fifteen years' experience as a software engineer and consultant.

A. Winsor Brown received his bachelor in engineering science at Rensselaer Polytechnic Institute and his master's in electrical engineering at the California Institute of Technology. He is currently the assistant director of the Center for Software Engineering at the University of Southern California and has over thirty years' experience as a consultant and software engineer.

Sunita Chulani received her bachelor from Bombay University, Bombay, India, and her doctorate in computer science at the University of Southern California. She is currently with IBM Almaden Research Center in San Jose, CA.

Brad Clark received his bachelor at the University of Florida and his doctorate in computer science at the University of Southern California. He is currently a Visiting Scientist at the Software Engineering Institute at Carnegie Mellon University and a principal of the consulting firm Software Metrics, Inc. near Washington, D.C.

Ellis Horowitz received his bachelor at Brooklyn College and his doctorate at the University of Wisconsin, Madison. He is currently Director, Distance Education and Information Technology in the school of engineering and Professor and *Chairman Emeritus* of the department of computer science at the University of Southern California.

Ray Madachy received his bachelor in mechanical engineering at the University of Dayton and his doctorate in industrial and systems engineering at the University of Southern California. He is a managing principal at C-bridge Internet Solutions (previously he was manager of the Software Engineering Process Group at Litton Guidance and Control Systems when most of the book was written); and an Adjunct Assistant Professor in the department of computer science at the University of Southern California.

Don Reifer received his bachelor at New Jersey Institute of Technology and his master's degree at the University of Southern California. He is the founder and president of the consulting firm Reifer Consultants, Inc. in Torrance, CA, and has thirty years' experience as a software engineer, program manager and management consultant.

Bert Steece received both his bachelor and doctorate degrees at the University of Southern California. He is currently deputy dean of academic programs and a professor specializing in statistics in the information and operations management department in the Marshall School of Business at the University of Southern California.

# 1

# Introduction
# to COCOMO II

## 1.1 COCOMO II USER OBJECTIVES

COCOMO II is a model to help you reason about the cost and schedule implications of software decisions you may need to make. In the last eighteen years of answering phone calls and email messages from users of the original COCOMO ([Boehm, 1981]; here called COCOMO 81), we have found many different types of COCOMO 81 users and uses. Perhaps the most unexpected were the occasional calls from Internal Revenue Service auditors. After quickly assuring us that our tax returns were not being audited, they would ask us about how to use COCOMO 81 to validate someone's software tax write-off claim.

Here is a list of the major decision situations we have determined that you might want to use COCOMO II for in the future:

1. *Making investment or other financial decisions involving a software development effort.* A business case or return-on-investment analysis involving software development needs either an estimate of the software development cost or a life-cycle software expenditure profile.

2. *Setting project budgets and schedules as a basis for planning and control.* For example, how many people should you assign to the early, middle, and late

stages of a software project? How much of the effort, cost, and schedule should be expended to reach the major project milestones?

3. *Deciding on or negotiating tradeoffs among software cost, schedule, functionality, performance or quality factors.* For example, to what extent can one say, "Quality is free?" Is it actually cheaper to build life-critical software than to build, say, inventory control software?

4. *Making software cost and schedule risk management decisions.* You will have unavoidable uncertainties about many of the factors influencing your project's cost and schedule. Some example uncertainties are the amount of software your project will develop and reuse. Cost models can help you perform sensitivity and risk analyses covering your sources of uncertainty.

5. *Deciding which parts of a software system to develop, reuse, lease, or purchase.* A good cost model can help you understand, for example, when it is cheaper to build a component than to rework an existing component.

6. *Making legacy software inventory decisions: what parts to modify, phase out, outsource, etc.* For example, the model can help you develop and periodically update a multi-year plan indicating how many of the highest-priority capabilities can be developed in each legacy system upgrade.

7. *Setting mixed investment strategies to improve your organization's software capability, via reuse, tools, process maturity, outsourcing, etc.* Here, the model can help you develop and periodically update a multi-year technology investment plan. For example, COCOMO II has capabilities both to estimate the additional investment required to produce reusable software, and the resulting savings accruing from its reuse.

8. *Deciding how to implement a process improvement strategy,* such as that provided in the SEI Capability Maturity Model [Paulk et al. 1995]. For Level 2, how should you combine software cost models such as COCOMO II with other methods of sizing, estimating, planning, and tracking software projects' cost, schedule, and effort? For Level 3, how do you assess the benefits of training in terms of improvements in such cost drivers as application, platform, language, and tool experience? For Level 4, how can frameworks such as COCOMO II help you set up an effective quantitative software management program? For Level 5, how can you evolve this framework to accommodate such new practices as product lines, rapid application development, and commercial-off-the-shelf (COTS) software integration?

As a bottom line, a software estimation model can be much more than a facility to plug in cost driver ratings and receive budget and schedule estimates. Helping you realize these additional decision support capabilities has determined a number of COCOMO II's objectives and strategies, as discussed next.

## 1.2   COCOMO II MODEL OBJECTIVES

As discussed in the Preface, we will relate the COCOMO II model objectives to the feedback we have received over the years on the strong points and capabilities needing improvement in COCOMO 81:

1. *Provide accurate cost and schedule estimates for both current and likely future software projects.* COCOMO 81 is built on the 1970s' "waterfall" process framework (sequentially progressing through requirements, design, code, and test). Many organizations are evolving toward mixes of concurrent, iterative, incremental, and cyclic processes. COCOMO II provides a framework for tailoring a version of the model to your desired process, including the waterfall.

2. *Enable organizations to easily recalibrate, tailor, or extend COCOMO II to better fit their unique situations.* Recalibration enables your organization to fit COCOMO II to your collected project data, with its own special interpretations of project endpoints, product definitions, labor definitions, and organizational practices. Tailoring and extensibility enable you to orchestrate COCOMO II variants to fit your organization's product, process, and personnel practice variants. COCOMO 81 provided recalibration, but tailoring was available only within the assumptions of the waterfall model.

3. *Provide careful, easy-to-understand definitions of the model's inputs, outputs, and assumptions.* Without such definitions, it is easy to create "million-dollar mistakes" when different people use different interpretations of the model's estimates. COCOMO 81 was generally satisfactory here; COCOMO II provides some additional definition assistance for the cost driver rating scales.

4. *Provide a constructive model,* in which the job of cost and schedule estimation helps people better understand the nature of the project being estimated. This was a major objective for COCOMO 81, and continues to be for COCOMO II. The primary improvements in this direction have been to add further cost drivers to help understand the effects of project decisions in the reuse and economy-of-scale areas.

5. *Provide a normative model,* which allocates the resources necessary for effective software development or maintenance; which highlights unrealistic cost and schedule objectives; and which identifies management controllables for improving current or future projects. Software cost models calibrated to data generally do well on being normative, because very few poorly-managed projects collect data for calibration. As discussed with the previous objective, COCOMO II identifies further management controllables in the reuse and economy-of-scale areas.

6. *Provide an evolving model,* which adds new capabilities to address new needs (e.g., COTS integration, rapid application development), and maintains relevance to evolving software practices. The COCOMO 81 effort did not plan for model evolution. COCOMO II is a continuing project, both for refining the main project cost-schedule estimation model and for providing extensions (discussed primarily in Chapter 5).

## 1.3    COCOMO II DEVELOPMENT AND EVOLUTION STRATEGIES

Developing a model to satisfy all of the above objectives would be difficult even in a relatively stable software arena. It is even more difficult in the current and foreseeable future situation, in which new generations of products and processes are changing the way organizations develop software.

Our strategies in developing and evolving COCOMO II have reflected this climate of rapid change and limited foreseeability. The three primary strategies pursued to date have been:

1. *Proceed incrementally,* addressing the estimation issues of most importance and tractability with respect to modeling, data collection and calibration. Our primary initial focus has been on developing a solid model for overall project cost and schedule estimation. We have also initially addressed some further areas where we have had a reasonable combination of experience and data, such as software maintenance. We have proceeded more cautiously in areas where we had less experience and data. These areas are discussed in Chapter 5: applications composition, COTS integration, rapid application development, detailed effort and schedule breakdowns by stage and activity.

2. *Test the models and their concepts to gain first-hand experience.* We use COCOMO II in our annual series of USC Digital Library projects. These involve the architecting of fifteen to twenty potential products, and the selection, development and transition of five to six products annually. We have found the need to modify COCOMO II somewhat to adapt it to our two-semester, fixed-team-size projects. But the experience has given us numerous insights, particularly in the development of the COCOMO II extensions for COTS integration and rapid applications development.

3. *Establish a COCOMO II Affiliates' program,* enabling us to draw on the prioritized needs, expertise and calibration data of leading software organizations. This has given us access to the large-project experience unavailable in a university setting. We have been fortunate to have a good mix of commercial software developers, government software contractors, and government software acquisition organizations from whom we have acquired a

balanced set of project data points for calibrating COCOMO II. Also, the Affiliate connections have provided us with access to many of the leading software cost estimation and metrics practitioners. A list of the COCOMO II Affiliates is provided in the acknowledgements appearing after the Preface.

The Affiliates' prioritized needs and available expertise and data have led to six additional strategies:

4. *Provide an externally and internally open model*, enabling users to fully understand and deal with its inputs, outputs, internal models, and assumptions. The only hidden aspect of COCOMO II is its database of Affiliates' project effort and schedule data. We have developed a set of safeguards and procedures that have prevented any leakage of Affiliates' sensitive data.

5. *Avoid unnecessary incompatibilities with COCOMO 81*, which most Affiliates have still found largely useful and relevant. There were a few exceptions to this strategy, where subsequent trends and insights had made the original COCOMO 81 approach obsolete. These included eliminating the Turnaround Time cost driver, rebaselining the Software Tools rating scale, eliminating the schedule-stretchout penalty, replacing the linear reuse model with a nonlinear one, and replacing development modes by exponential scale factors.

6. *Experiment with a number of model extensions*, prioritizing their pursuit based on Affiliates' needs and available data. These have included some extensions of the main COCOMO II project cost and schedule model, such as adding multiplicative cost drivers addressing development for reuse and personnel continuity, and adding exponential scale factors for process maturity and team cohesion. They also include the experimental extensions discussed in Chapter 5, covering estimators for COTS integration and rapid development effects, and for delivered software quality (defect density).

7. *Balance expert-determined and data-determined modeling*, most effectively via Bayesian analysis techniques. The Bayesian calibration approach has been our most significant methodological improvement. Section 1.6 provides an overview, and Chapter 4 provides the full approach and results.

8. *Develop a sequence of increasingly accurate models*, based on the increasingly detailed and accurate input data available to estimators as they progress through succeeding stages of the software life cycle. We have done this via the Applications Composition, Early Design, and Post-Architecture sequence of models discussed in the next two sections.

9. *Key the COCOMO II models to projections of future software life-cycle practices.*

Our projection of future software practices and associated set of COCOMO II models is discussed next.

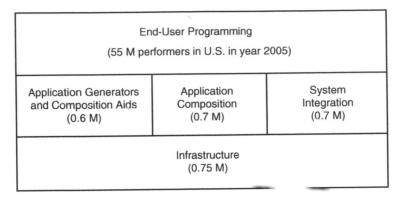

**Figure 1.1**   Future software practices marketplace model

## 1.4   FUTURE SOFTWARE PRACTICES MARKETPLACE MODEL

Figure 1.1 summarizes the model of the future software practices marketplace that we developed in 1994 to guide the development of COCOMO II [Boehm et al. 1995]. It includes a large upper "end-user programming" sector with an estimated size of roughly fifty-five million practitioners in the United States by the year 2005; a lower "infrastructure" sector with roughly 750,000 practitioners; and three intermediate sectors, involving the development of application generators and composition aids (600,000 practitioners), the development of systems by applications composition (700,000), and system integration of large-scale and/or embedded software systems (700,000).[1]

*End-user programming* will be driven by increasing computer literacy and competitive pressures for rapid, flexible, and user-driven information processing solutions. These trends will push the software marketplace toward having users develop most information processing applications themselves via application generators. Some example application generators are spreadsheets, extended query systems, and simple, specialized planning or inventory systems. They en-

---

[1]These figures are judgment-based extensions of the Bureau of Labor Statistics moderate-growth labor distribution scenario for the year 2005 [CSTB, 1993; Silvestri and Lukasiewicz, 1991]. The fifty-five million End-User programming feature was obtained by applying judgment-based extrapolations of the 1989 Bureau of the Census data on computer usage fractions by occupation [Kominski, 1991] to generate end-user programming fractions by occupation category. These were then applied to the 2005 occupation-category populations (e.g., 10% of the 25M people in "Service Occupations"; 40% of the 17M people in "Marketing and Sales Occupations"). The 2005 total of 2.75M software practitioners was obtained by applying a factor of 1.6 to the number of people traditionally identified as "Systems Analysts and Computer Scientists" (0.829M in 2005) and "Computer Programmers" (0.882M). The expansion factor of 1.6 to cover software personnel with other job titles is based on the results of a 1983 survey on this topic [Boehm 1983]. The 2005 distribution of the 2.75M software developers is a judgment-based extrapolation of current trends.

able users to determine their desired information processing application via domain-familiar options, parameters, or simple rules. A major new source of such applications could be called "Webmaster" applications. Every enterprise from Fortune 100 companies to small businesses and the U.S. government will be involved in this sector.

Typical *infrastructure* sector products will be in the areas of operating systems, database management systems, user interface management systems, and networking systems. Increasingly, the infrastructure sector will address "middleware" solutions for such generic problems as distributed processing and transaction processing. Representative firms in the Infrastructure sector are Microsoft, Netscape, Oracle, Sybase, 3Com, Novell, and the major computer vendors.

In contrast to end-user programmers, who will generally know a good deal about their applications domain and relatively little about computer science, the infrastructure developers will generally know a good deal about computer science and relatively little about applications. Their product lines will have many reusable components, but the pace of technology (new processor, memory, communications, display, and multimedia technology) will require them to build many components and capabilities from scratch.

### 1.4.1   Intermediate Sectors

Performers in the three *intermediate sectors* in Figure 1.1 will need to know a good deal about computer science-intensive infrastructure software and also one or more application domains. Creating this talent pool is a major national challenge.

The *application generators* sector will create largely prepackaged capabilities for user programming. Typical firms operating in this sector are Microsoft, Netscape, Lotus, Novell, Borland, and vendors of computer-aided planning, engineering, manufacturing, and financial analysis systems. Their product lines will have many reusable components but will also require a good deal of new-capability development from scratch. *Application composition aids* will be developed both by the above firms and by software product-line investments of firms in the applications composition sector.

The *applications composition* sector deals with applications that are too large or diversified to be fully handled by prepackaged solutions, but which are sufficiently simple or mature to be rapidly composable from interoperable components. Typical components will be graphic user interface (GUI) builders, database or object managers, middleware for distributed processing or transaction processing, hypermedia handlers, smart data finders, and domain-specific components such as financial, medical, or industrial process control packages.

Most large firms will have groups to compose such applications, but a great many specialized software firms will provide composed applications on contract. These range from large, versatile firms such as Andersen Consulting and EDS, to small firms specializing in such specialty areas as decision support or transaction processing, or in such application domains as finance or manufacturing.

The *system integration* sector deals with large-scale, highly embedded, or un-precedented systems. Portions of these systems can be developed with application composition capabilities, but their demands generally require a significant amount of up-front systems engineering and custom software development. Aerospace firms operate within this sector, as do major system integration firms such as EDS and Andersen Consulting, large firms developing software-intensive products and services (telecommunications, automotive, financial, and electronic products firms), and firms developing very large-scale corporate information systems or manufacturing support systems.

### 1.4.2   1999 Model Assessment

In a 1999 assessment of the model, it appeared that its predictions were reasonably on track. The fifty-five million figure for end-user programming performers in 2005 may be somewhat high. But the trend is toward a very high number, particularly with the emergence of large numbers of practitioners in the "Webmaster" category—although such categories are blurring the distinction between what might or might not be called end-user programming.

The 1998 U.S. population of software developers has been estimated by [Jones 1998] and [Rubin 1999] to be roughly two million. Given a rough trend of a 5 percent cumulative annual growth rate in software developers, this would yield a 2005 population of roughly 2.8 million, fairly close to the 2.75 million estimated in the 1994 model.

The distribution of software developers across the sectors is more difficult to compare, given the blurring of distinctions among the sectors. As another example, it is hard to distinguish which Web application support capabilities should be called "application generators" and which "infrastructure."

## 1.5   RESULTING FAMILY OF COCOMO II MODELS

To support the software practices marketplace sectors above, COCOMO II provides a family of increasingly detailed software cost estimation models, each tuned to the sectors' needs and type of information available to support software cost estimation.

### 1.5.1   COCOMO II Models for the Software Marketplace Sectors

*The user programming sector does not need a COCOMO II model.* Its applications are typically developed in hours to days, so a simple activity-based estimate will generally be sufficient.

*The COCOMO II model for the application composition sector is based on object points.* Object points are a count of the screens, reports and third-generation language modules developed in the application, each weighted by a three-level (simple, medium, difficult) complexity factor [Banker et al. 1994; Kauffman-Kumar 1993]. This is commensurate with the level of information generally known about an application composition product during its planning stages, and the corresponding level of accuracy needed for its software estimates (such applications are generally developed by a small team in a few weeks to months).

The COCOMO II capability for estimation of *application generator, system integration*, or *infrastructure* developments is based on a tailorable mix of the application composition model (for early prototype efforts) and two increasingly detailed estimation models for subsequent portions of the life cycle.

The rationale for providing this tailorable mix of models rests on three primary premises:

*First*, unlike the initial COCOMO 81 situation in the late 1970s, in which there was a single, preferred software life-cycle model (the waterfall model), current and future software projects will be tailoring their processes to their particular process drivers. These process drivers include COTS or reusable software availability; degree of understanding of architectures and requirements; market window or other schedule constraints; and required reliability (see [Boehm 1989, pp. 436–437] for an example of such tailoring guidelines).

*Second*, the granularity of the software cost estimation model used needs to be consistent with the granularity of the information available to support software cost estimation. In the early stages of a software project, very little may be known about the size of the project to be developed, the nature of the target platform, the nature of the personnel to be involved in the project, or the detailed specifics of the process to be used.

Figure 1.2, extended from [Boehm 1981, p. 311], indicates the effect of project uncertainties on the accuracy of software size and cost estimates. In the very early stages, one may not know the specific nature of the product to be developed to better than a factor of 4. As the life cycle proceeds, and product decisions are made, the nature of the product and its consequent size are better known, and the nature of the process and its consequent cost drivers are better known. The earlier "completed programs" size and effort data points in Figure 1.2 are the actual sizes and efforts of seven software products built to a partially-defined specification [Boehm et al. 1984].[2] The later "USAF/ESD proposals" data points are from five proposals submitted to the U.S. Air Force Electronic Systems Division in response to a fairly thorough specification [Devenny 1976].

*Third*, given the situation in the first and second premises, COCOMO II enables projects to furnish coarse-grained cost driver information in the early project stages, and increasingly fine-grained information in later stages. Consequently, COCOMO II does not produce point estimates of software cost and ef-

---

[2]These seven projects implemented the same algorithmic version of the Intermediate COCOMO 81 cost model, but with the use of different interpretations of the other product specifications: produce a "friendly user interface" with a "single-user file system."

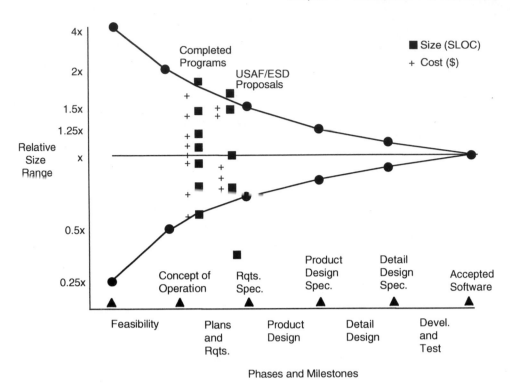

**Figure 1.2**    Software costing and sizing accuracy versus phase

fort, but rather range estimates tied to the degree of definition of the estimation inputs. The uncertainty ranges in Figure 1.2 are used as starting points for these estimation ranges.

### 1.5.2   Tailoring COCOMO II Estimation Models to Process Strategies

With respect to *process strategy*, application generator, system integration, and infrastructure software projects will involve a mix of three major process models. The appropriate sequencing of these models will involve a mix of three major process models. The appropriate sequencing of these models will depend on the project's marketplace drivers and degree of product understanding.

The *early prototyping* stage involves prototyping efforts to resolve potential high-risk issues such as user interfaces, software/system interaction, performance, or technology maturity. The costs of this type of effort are best estimated by the application composition model.

The *early design* stage involves exploring alternative software/system architectures and concepts of operation. At this stage, not enough is generally known to support fine-grain cost estimation. The corresponding COCOMO II capability involves the use of function points (or lines of code where available) and a small number of additional cost drivers.

The post-architecture stage involves the actual development and maintenance of a software product. This stage proceeds most cost-effectively if a software life-cycle architecture has been developed; validated with respect to the system's mission, concept of operation, life-cycle plan and risk; and established as the framework for the product. The corresponding COCOMO II model has about the same granularity as the previous COCOMO 81 and Ada COCOMO models. It uses source instructions and/or function points for sizing, with modifiers for reuse and software breakage; a set of seventeen multiplicative cost drivers; and a set of five factors determining the project's scaling exponent. These factors replace the development modes (Organic, Semidetached, or Embedded) in the original COCOMO 81 model, and refine the four exponent-scaling factors in Ada COCOMO.

To summarize, COCOMO II provides the following three-model series for estimation of Application Generator, System Integration and Infrastructure software projects contained in our marketplace model:

1. The earliest phases or spiral cycles will generally involve prototyping, using Application Composition capabilities. The COCOMO II Application Composition model supports these phases, and any other prototyping activities occurring later in the life cycle.

2. The next phases or spiral cycles will generally involve exploring architectural alternatives or incremental development strategies. To support these activities, COCOMO II provides an early estimation model. This uses function points (or lines of code where available) for sizing, and a coarse-grained set of seven cost drivers (e.g., two cost drivers for Personnel Capability and Personnel Experience in place of the six current Post-Architecture model cost drivers covering various aspects of personnel capability, continuity and experience). Again, this level of detail is consistent with the general level of information available and the general level of estimation accuracy needed at this stage.

3. Once the project is ready to develop and sustain a fielded system, it should have a life-cycle architecture, which provides more accurate information on cost driver inputs and enables more accurate cost estimates. To support this stage of development COCOMO II provides a model whose granularity is roughly equivalent to the current COCOMO 81 and Ada COCOMO models. It can use either source lines of code or function points for a sizing parameter, five exponential scale factors as a refinement of the COCOMO 81 development modes, and seventeen multiplicative cost drivers.

# 2

# COCOMO II
# Model Definition

## 2.1 INTRODUCTION

### 2.1.1 Overview

This chapter presents two models, the Post-Architecture and Early Design models. Recall from Chapter 1 that these two models are used in the development of application generator, system integration, or infrastructure developments. The Post-Architecture is a detailed model that is used once the project is ready to develop and sustain a fielded system. The system should have a life-cycle architecture package, which provides detailed information on cost driver inputs, and enables more accurate cost estimates. The Early Design model is a high-level model that is used to explore architectural alternatives or incremental development strategies. This level of detail is consistent with the general level of information available and the general level of estimation accuracy needed.

The Post-Architecture and Early Design models use the same approach for product sizing (including reuse) and for scale factors. These will be presented first. Then, the Post-Architecture model will be explained followed by the Early Design model. The chapter ends with a discussion and example of using the models for the eight decision analysis situations introduced in Section 1.1.

### 2.1.2  Nominal-Schedule Estimation Equations

Both the Post-Architecture and Early Design models use the same functional form to estimate the amount of effort and calendar time it will take to develop a software project. These nominal-schedule (NS) formulas exclude the Cost Driver for Required Development Schedule (SCED). The full formula is given in Section 2.3. The amount of effort in person-months, $PM_{NS}$, is estimated by the formula:

$$PM_{NS} = A \times \text{Size}^E \times \prod_{i=1}^{n} EM_i \qquad \text{Eq. 2.1}$$

$$\text{where } E = B + 0.01 \times \sum_{j=1}^{5} SF_j$$

The amount of calendar time, $TDEV_{NS}$, it will take to develop the product is estimated by the formula:

$$TDEV_{NS} = C \times (PM_{NS})^F \qquad \text{Eq. 2.2}$$

$$\text{where } F = D + 0.2 \times 0.01 \times \sum_{j=1}^{5} SF_j$$

$$= D + 0.2 \times (E - B)$$

The value of $n$ is 16 for the Post-Architecture model effort multipliers, $EM_i$, and 6 for the Early Design model, the number of $SF_j$ stands for exponential scale factors. The values of $A$, $B$, $EM_1$, ..., $EM_{16}$, $SF_1$, ..., and $SF_5$ for the COCOMO II.2000 Post-Architecture model are obtained by calibration to the actual parameters and effort values for the 161 projects currently in the COCOMO II database. The values of $C$ and $D$ for the COCOMO II.2000 schedule equation are obtained by calibration to the actual schedule values for the 161 projects currently in the COCOMO II database.

The values of $A$, $B$, $C$, $D$, $SF_1$, ..., and $SF_5$ for the Early Design model are the same as those for the Post-Architecture model. The values of $EM_1$, ..., and $EM_6$ for the Early Design model are obtained by combining the values of their 16 Post-Architecture counterparts; the specific combinations are given in Section 2.3.2.2.

The subscript $NS$ applied to $PM$ and $TDEV$ indicates that these are the nominal-schedule estimates of effort and calendar time. The effects of schedule compression or stretch-out are covered by an additional cost driver, Required Development Schedule. They are also included in the COCOMO II.2000 calibration to the 161 projects. Its specific effects are given in Section 2.4.

The specific milestones used as the endpoints in measuring development effort and calendar time are defined in Appendix A, as are the other definitions and assumptions involved in defining development effort and calendar time. Size is expressed as thousands of source lines of code (SLOC) or as unadjusted function points (UFP), as discussed in Section 2.2. Development labor cost is obtained by multiplying effort in $PM$ by the average labor cost per $PM$. The values of $A$, $B$, $C$, and $D$ in the COCOMO II.2000 calibration are:

$$A = 2.94 \quad B = 0.91$$
$$C = 3.67 \quad D = 0.28$$

Details of the calibration are presented in Chapter 4, which also provides formulas for calibrating either $A$ and $C$ or $A$, $B$, $C$, and $D$ to one's own database of projects. It is recommended that at least $A$ and $C$ be calibrated to the local development environment to increase the model's accuracy.

As an example, let's estimate how much effort and calendar time it would take to develop an average 100 KSLOC-sized project. For an average project, the effort multipliers are all equal to 1.0. $E$ will be set to 1.15 reflecting an average, large project. The estimated effort is $PM_{NS} = 2.94(100)^{1.15} = 586.61$.

Continuing the example, the duration is estimated as $TDEV_{NS} = 3.67(586.6)^{(0.28+0.2\times(1.15-0.91))} = 3.67(586.6)^{0.328} = 29.7$ months. The average number of staff required for the nominal-schedule development is $PM_{NS}\ /\ TDEV_{NS} = 586.6\ /\ 29.7 = 19.75$ or about 20 people. In this example, an average 100 KSLOC software project will take about thirty months to complete with an average of twenty people.

## 2.2  SIZING

A good size estimate is very important for a good model estimation. However, determining size can be challenging. Projects are generally composed of new code, code reused from other sources—with or without modifications—and automatically translated code. COCOMO II only uses size data that influences effort which is new code and code that is copied and modified.

For new and reused code, a method is used to make them equivalent so they can be rolled up into an aggregate size estimate. The baseline size in COCOMO II is a count of new lines of code. The count for code that is copied and then modified has to be adjusted to create a count that is equivalent to new lines of code. The adjustment takes into account the amount of design, code, and testing that was changed. It also considers the understandability of the code and the programmer familiarity with the code.

For automatically translated code, a separate translation productivity rate is used to determine effort from the amount of code to be translated.

The following sections discuss sizing new code and reused code.

### 2.2.1  Counting Source Lines of Code (SLOC)

There are several sources for estimating new lines of code. The best source is historical data. For instance, there may be data that will convert Function Points, components, or anything available early in the project to estimate lines of code. Lacking historical data, expert opinion can be used to derive estimates of likely, lowest-likely, and highest-likely size.

Code size is expressed in thousands of source lines of code (KSLOC). A source line of code is generally meant to exclude nondelivered support software such as test drivers. However, if these are developed with the same care as delivered software, with their own reviews, test plans, documentation, etc., then they should be counted [Boehm 1981, pp. 58–59]. The goal is to measure the amount of intellectual work put into program development.

Defining a line of code is difficult because of conceptual differences involved in accounting for executable statements and data declarations in different languages. Difficulties arise when trying to define consistent measures across different programming languages. In COCOMO II, the logical source statement has been chosen as the standard line of code. The Software Engineering Institute (SEI) definition checklist for a logical source statement is used in defining the line of code measure. The SEI has developed this checklist as part of a system of definition checklists, report forms and supplemental forms to support measurement definitions [Park 1992, Goethert et al. 1992].

Figure 2.1 shows the SLOC definition checklist as it is being applied to support the development of the COCOMO II model. Each checkmark in the "Includes" column identifies a particular statement type or attribute included in the definition, and vice versa for the excludes. Other sections in the definition clarify statement attributes for usage, delivery, functionality, replications, and development status. The full checklist is provided at the end of this chapter in Table 2.53.

Some changes were made to the line of-code definition that depart from the default definition provided in [Park 1992]. These changes eliminate categories of software, which are generally small sources of project effort. For example, not included in the definition are commercial-off-the-shelf software (COTS), government-furnished software (GFS), other products, language support libraries and operating systems, or other commercial libraries. Code generated with source code generators is handled by counting separate operator directives as lines of source code. It is admittedly difficult to count "directives" in a highly visual programming system. As this approach becomes better understood, we hope to provide more specific counting rules. For general source code sizing approaches, such as PERT sizing, expert consensus, analogy, top-down, and bottom-up, see Section 21.4 and Chapter 22 of [Boehm 1981].

### 2.2.2 Counting Unadjusted Function Points (UFP)

The function point cost estimation approach is based on the amount of functionality in a software project and a set of individual project factors [Behrens 1983; Kunkler 1983; IFPUG 1994]. Function points are useful estimators since they are based on information that is available early in the project life cycle. A brief summary of function points and their calculation in support of COCOMO II follows.

Function points measure a software project by quantifying the information processing functionality associated with major external data or control input, out-

# Definition Checklist for Source Statements Counts

Definition name: __Logical Source Statements__ Date:_____

_____ (basic definition) _____ Originator:_____

| Measurement unit: | | Physical source lines | | | | Includes | Excludes |
|---|---|---|---|---|---|---|---|
| | | Logical source statements | √ | | | | |
| Statement type | Definition | √ | Data Array | | | Includes | Excludes |
| *When a line or statement contains more than one type,* *classify it as the type with the highest precedence.* | | | | | | | |
| | | | | | | | |
| 1 Executable | Order of precedence | | | | 1 | √ | |
| 2 Nonexecutable | | | | | | | |
| 3 Declarations | | | | | 2 | √ | |
| 4 Compiler directives | | | | | 3 | √ | |
| 5 Comments | | | | | | | |
| 6 On their own lines | | | | | 4 | | √ |
| 7 On lines with source code | | | | | 5 | | √ |
| 8 Banners and non-blank spacers | | | | | 6 | | √ |
| 9 Blank (empty) comments | | | | | 7 | | √ |
| 10 Blank lines | | | | | 8 | | √ |
| 11 | | | | | | | |
| 12 | | | | | | | |
| How produced | Definition | √ | Data array | | | Includes | Excludes |
| 1 Programmed | | | | | | √ | |
| 2 Generated with source code generators | COCOMO II | | | | | | √ |
| 3 Converted with automated translators | | | | | | √ | |
| 4 Copied or reused without change | | | | | | √ | |
| 5 Modified | | | | | | √ | |
| 6 Removed | | | | | | | √ |
| 7 | | | | | | | |
| 8 | | | | | | | |
| Origin | Definition | √ | Data array | | | Includes | Excludes |
| 1 New work: no prior existence | | | | | | √ | |
| 2 Prior work: taken or adapted from | | | | | | | |
| 3 A previous version, build, or release | | | | | | √ | |
| 4 Commercial, off-the-shelf software (COTS), other than libraries | | | | | | | √ |
| 5 Government furnished software (GFS), other than reuse libraries | | | | | | | √ |
| 6 Another product | | | | | | | √ |
| 7 A vendor-supplied language support library (unmodified) | | | | | | | √ |
| 8 A vendor-supplied operating system or utility (unmodified) | | | | | | | √ |
| 9 A local or modified language support library or operating system | | | | | | | √ |
| 10 Other commercial library | | | | | | | √ |
| 11 A reuse library (software designed for reuse) | | | | | | √ | |
| 12 Other software component or library | | | | | | √ | |
| 13 | | | | | | | |
| 14 | | | | | | | |

**Figure 2.1** SLOC Checklist

put, or file types. Five user function types should be identified as defined in Table 2.1.

Each instance of these function types is then classified by complexity level. The complexity levels determine a set of weights, which are applied to their corresponding function counts to determine the Unadjusted Function Points (UFP) quantity. This is the Function Point sizing metric used by COCOMO II. The usual Function Point procedure, which is not followed by COCOMO II involves assessing the degree of influence (DI) of fourteen application characteristics on the software project determined according to a rating scale of 0.0 to 0.05 for each characteristic. The fourteen ratings are added together and then added to a base level of 0.65 to produce a general characteristic adjustment factor that ranges from 0.65 to 1.35.

Each of these fourteen characteristics, such as distributed functions, performance, and reusability, thus have a maximum of 5 percent contribution to estimated effort. Having, for example, a 5 percent limit on the effect of reuse is inconsistent with COCOMO experience; thus COCOMO II uses Unadjusted Function Points for sizing, and applies its reuse factors, cost drivers, and scale factors to this sizing quantity to account for the effects of reuse, distribution, etc. on project effort.

The COCOMO II procedure for determining Unadjusted Function Points follows the definitions in [IFPUG 1994]. This four step procedure, which follows, is used in both the Early Design and the Post-Architecture models.

**Table 2.1   User Function Types**

| Function Point | Description |
| --- | --- |
| External Input (EI) | Count each unique user data or user control input type that enters the external boundary of the software system being measured. |
| External Output (EO) | Count each unique user data or control output type that leaves the external boundary of the software system being measured. |
| Internal Logical File (ILF) | Count each major logical group of user data or control information in the software system as a logical internal file type. Include each logical file (e.g., each logical group of data) that is generated, used, or maintained by the software system. |
| External Interface Files (EIF) | Files passed or shared between software systems should be counted as external interface file types within each system. |
| External Inquiry (EQ) | Count each unique input-output combination, where input causes and generates an immediate output, as an external inquiry type. |

1. Determine function counts by type. The unadjusted function counts should be counted by a lead technical person based on information in the software requirements and design documents. The number of each of the five user function types should be counted [Internal Logical File (ILF), External Interface File (EIF), External Input (EI), External Output (EO), and External Inquiry (EQ)]. See [IFPUG 1994] for more detailed interpretations of the counting rules for those quantities.

2. Determine complexity levels. Classify each function count into Low-, Average- and High-complexity levels depending on the number of data element types contained and the number of file types referenced. Use the scheme in Table 2.2.

3. Apply complexity weights. Weight the number of function types at each complexity level using the scheme in Table 2.3 (the weights reflect the relative effort required to implement the function).

4. Compute Unadjusted Function Points. Add all the weighted functions counts to get one number, the Unadjusted Function Points.

### Table 2.2    FP Complexity Levels

**For Internal Logical Files and External Interface Files**

| Record Elements | Data Elements | | |
| --- | --- | --- | --- |
| | **1–19** | **20–50** | **51+** |
| 1 | Low | Low | Avg. |
| 2–5 | Low | Avg. | High |
| 6+ | Avg. | High | High |

**For External Output and External Inquiry**

| File Types | Data Elements | | |
| --- | --- | --- | --- |
| | **1–5** | **6–19** | **20+** |
| 0 or 1 | Low | Low | Avg. |
| 2–3 | Low | Avg. | High |
| 4+ | Avg. | High | High |

**For External Input**

| File Types | Data Elements | | |
| --- | --- | --- | --- |
| | **1–4** | **5–15** | **16+** |
| 0 or 1 | Low | Low | Avg. |
| 2–3 | Low | Avg. | High |
| 3+ | Avg. | High | High |

**Table 2.3   UFP Complexity Weights**

| Function Type | Complexity-Weight | | |
|---|---|---|---|
| | *Low* | *Average* | *High* |
| Internal Logical Files | 7 | 10 | 15 |
| External Interfaces Files | 5 | 7 | 10 |
| External Inputs | 3 | 4 | 6 |
| External Outputs | 4 | 5 | 7 |
| External Inquiries | 3 | 4 | 6 |

### 2.2.3   Relating UFPs to SLOC

Next, convert the Unadjusted Function Points (UFP) to Lines of Code. The unadjusted function points have to be converted to source lines of code in the implementation language (Ada, C, C++, Pascal, etc.). COCOMO II does this for both the Early Design and Post-Architecture models by using backfining tables to convert Unadjusted Function Points into equivalent SLOC. The current conversion ratios shown in Table 2.4 are from [Jones 1996]. Updates to these conversion ratios as well as additional ratios can be found at http://www.spr.com/library/0Langtbl.htm.

USR_1 through USR_5 are five extra slots provided by USC COCOMO II.2000 to accommodate user specified additional implementation languages. These ratios are easy to determine with historical data or with a recently completed project. It would be prudent to determine your own ratios for your local environment.

### 2.2.4   Aggregating New, Adapted, and Reused Code

A product's size discussed thus far has been for new development. Code that is taken from another source and used in the product under development also contributes to the product's effective size. Preexisting code that is treated as a black-box and plugged into the product is called reused code. Preexisting code that is treated as a white-box and is modified for use with the product is called adapted code. The effective size of reused and adapted code is adjusted to be its equivalent in new code. The adjusted code is called equivalent source lines of code (ESLOC). The adjustment is based on the additional effort it takes to modify the code for inclusion in the product. The sizing model treats reuse with function points and source lines of code the same in either the Early Design model or the Post-Architecture model.

**Table 2.4    Default UFP to SLOC Conversion Ratios**

| Language | SLOC / UFP | Language | SLOC / UFP |
|----------|-----------|----------|-----------|
| Access | 38 | Jovial | 107 |
| Ada 83 | 71 | Lisp | 64 |
| Ada 95 | 49 | Machine Code | 640 |
| AI Shell | 49 | Modula 2 | 80 |
| APL | 32 | Pascal | 91 |
| Assembly—Basic | 320 | PERL | 27 |
| Assembly—Macro | 213 | PowerBuilder | 16 |
| Basic—ANSI | 64 | Prolog | 64 |
| Basic—Compiled | 91 | Query—Default | 13 |
| Basic—Visual | 32 | Report Generator | 80 |
| C | 128 | Second Generation Language | 107 |
| C++ | 55 | Simulation—Default | 46 |
| Cobol (ANSI 85) | 91 | Spreadsheet | 6 |
| Database—Default | 40 | Third Generation Language | 80 |
| Fifth Generation Language | 4 | Unix Shell Scripts | 107 |
| First Generation Language | 320 | USR_1 | 1 |
| Forth | 64 | USR_2 | 1 |
| Fortran 77 | 107 | USR_3 | 1 |
| Fortran 95 | 71 | USR_4 | 1 |
| Fourth Generation Language | 20 | USR_5 | 1 |
| High Level Language | 64 | Visual Basic 5.0 | 29 |
| HTML 3.0 | 15 | Visual C++ | 34 |
| Java | 53 | | |

### 2.2.4.1   NONLINEAR REUSE EFFECTS

Analysis in [Selby 1988] of reuse costs across nearly three thousand reused modules in the NASA Software Engineering Laboratory indicates that the reuse cost function, relating the amount of modification of the reused code to the resulting cost to reuse, is nonlinear in two significant ways (see Figure 2.2). The effort required to reuse code does not start at zero. There is generally a cost of about 5 percent for assessing, selecting, and assimilating the reusable component.

Figure 2.2 shows the results of the NASA analysis as blocks of relative cost. A dotted line is superimposed on the blocks of relative cost to show increasing cost as more of the reused code is modified. (The solid lines are labeled AAM for Adaptation Adjustment Modifier. AAM is explained in Equation 2.4.) It can be

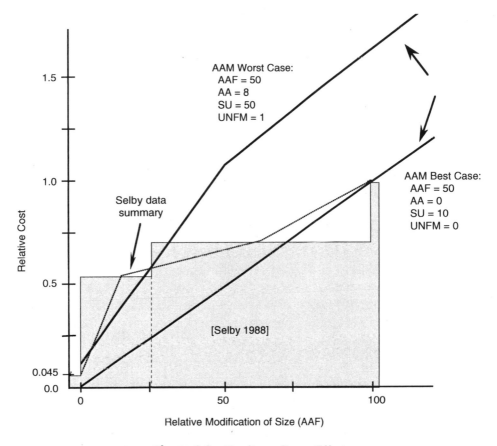

**Figure 2.2**   Nonlinear Reuse Effects

seen that small modifications in the reused product generate disproportionately large costs. This is primarily because of two factors: the cost of understanding the software to be modified, and the relative cost of checking module interfaces.

[Parikh-Zvegintzov 1983] contains data indicating that 47 percent of the effort in software maintenance involves understanding the software to be modified. Thus, as soon as one goes from unmodified (black-box) reuse to modified-software (white-box) reuse, one encounters this software understanding penalty. Also, [Gerlich-Denskat 1994] shows that, if one modifies $k$ out of $m$ software modules, the number of module interface checks required, $N$, is expressed in Equation 2.3.

$$N = k \times (m - k) + k \times \left( \frac{k - 1}{2} \right) \qquad \text{Eq. 2.3}$$

Figure 2.3 shows this relation between the number of modules modified $k$ and the resulting number, $N$, of module interface checks required for an example

For  *m* = 10

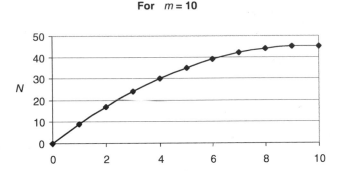

**Figure 2.3** Number of Module Interface Checks, *N*, vs. Modules Modified, *k*

of *m* = 10 modules. In this example, modifying 20 percent (2 of 10) of the modules required revalidation of 38 percent (17 of 45) of the interfaces.

The shape of this curve is similar for other values of *m*. It indicates that there are nonlinear effects involved in the module interface checking, which occurs during the design, code, integration, and test of modified software.

The size of both the software understanding penalty and the module interface-checking penalty can be reduced by good software structuring. Modular, hierarchical structuring can reduce the number of interfaces which need checking [Gerlich-Denskat 1994], and software that is well-structured, explained, and related to its mission will be easier to understand. COCOMO II reflects this in its allocation of estimated effort for modifying reusable software.

### 2.2.4.2   A REUSE MODEL

The COCOMO II treatment of software reuse uses a nonlinear estimation model, Equation 2.4. This involves estimating the amount of software to be adapted and three degree-of-modification factors: the percentage of design modified (*DM*), the percentage of code modified (*CM*), and the percentage of integration effort required for integrating the adapted or reused software (*IM*). These three factors use the same linear model as used in COCOMO 81, but COCOMO II adds some nonlinear increments to the relation of *Adapted KSLOC of Equivalent KSLOC* to reflect the non-linear tendencies of the model. These are explained next.

$$\text{Equivalent } KSLOC = \text{Adapted } KSLOC \times \left(1 - \frac{AT}{100}\right) \times AAM \qquad \text{Eq. 2.4}$$

where $\qquad AAF = (0.4 \times DM) + (0.3 \times CM) + (0.3 \times IM)$

$$AAM = \begin{cases} \dfrac{[AA + AAF(1 + (0.02 \times SU \times UNFM))]}{100} \text{, for } AAF \le 50 \\[4mm] \dfrac{[AA + AAF + (SU \times UNFM)]}{100} \text{, for } AAF > 50 \end{cases}$$

The Software Understanding increment (*SU*) is obtained from Table 2.5. *SU* is expressed quantitatively as a percentage. If the software is rated very high on structure, applications clarity, and self-descriptiveness, the software understanding and interface-checking penalty is 10 percent. If the software is rated very low on these factors, the penalty is 50 percent. *SU* is determined by taking the subjective average of the three categories.

The other nonlinear reuse increment deals with the degree of Assessment and Assimilation (*AA*) needed to determine whether a reused software module is appropriate to the application, and to integrate its description into the overall product description. Table 2.6 provides the rating scale and values for the assessment and assimilation increment. *AA* is á percentage.

The amount of effort required to modify existing software is a function not only of the amount of modification (*AAF*) and understandability of the existing software (*SU*), but also of the programmer's relative unfamiliarity with the software (*UNFM*). The *UNFM* factor is applied multiplicatively to the software understanding effort increment. If the programmer works with the software every

**Table 2.5   Rating Scale for Software Understanding Increment SU**

|  | Very Low | Low | Nominal | High | Very High |
|---|---|---|---|---|---|
| **Structure** | Very low cohesion, high coupling, spaghetti code. | Moderately-low cohesion, high coupling. | Reasonably well-structured; some weak areas. | High cohesion, low coupling. | Strong modularity, information hiding in data/control structures. |
| **Application Clarity** | No match between program and application world-views. | Some correlation between program and application. | Moderate correlation between program and application. | Good correlation between program and application. | Clear match between program and application world-views. |
| **Self-Descriptiveness** | Obscure code; documentation missing, obscure or obsolete. | Some code commentary and headers; some useful documentation. | Moderate level of code commentary, headers, documentation. | Good code commentary and headers; useful documentation; some weak areas. | Self-descriptive code; documentation up-to-date, well-organized, with design rationale. |
| **SU Increment to ESLOC** | 50 | 40 | 30 | 20 | 10 |

**Table 2.6    Rating Scale for Assessment and Assimilation Increment (AA)**

| AA Increment | Level of AA Effort |
|:---:|:---|
| 0 | None |
| 2 | Basic module search and documentation |
| 4 | Some module Test and Evaluation (T&E), documentation |
| 6 | Considerable module T&E, documentation |
| 8 | Extensive module T&E, documentation |

day, the 0.0 multiplier for *UNFM* will add no software understanding increment. If the programmer has never seen the software before, the 1.0 multiplier will add the full software understanding effort increment. The rating of *UNFM* is shown in Table 2.7.

**Table 2.7    Rating Scale for Programmer Unfamiliarity (UNFM)**

| UNFM Increment | Level of Unfamiliarity |
|:---:|:---|
| 0.0 | Completely familiar |
| 0.2 | Mostly familiar |
| 0.4 | Somewhat familiar |
| 0.6 | Considerably familiar |
| 0.8 | Mostly unfamiliar |
| 1.0 | Completely unfamiliar |

Equation 2.4 is used to determine an equivalent number of new source lines of code. The calculation of equivalent *SLOC* is based on the product size being adapted and a modifier that accounts for the effort involved in fitting adapted code into an existing product, called Adaptation Adjustment Modifier (*AAM*). The term $(1 - AT/100)$ is for automatically translated code and is discussed in Section 2.2.6. If there is no automatically translated code in a given development, however, this term disappears from the equation as AT goes to zero.

*AAM* uses the factors discussed above, Software Understanding (*SU*), Programmer Unfamiliarity (*UNFM*), and Assessment and Assimilation (*AA*) with a factor called the Adaptation Adjustment Factor (*AAF*). *AAF* contains the quantities *DM*, *CM*, and *IM* where:

- *DM* (Percent Design Modified) is the percentage of the adapted software's design which is modified in order to adapt it to the new objectives and environment. (This is necessarily a subjective quantity.)

- *CM* (Percent Code Modified) is the percentage of the adapted software's code which is modified in order to adapt it to the new objectives and environment.
- *IM* (Percent of Integration Required for Adapted Software) is the percentage of effort required to integrate the adapted software into an overall product and to test the resulting product as compared to the normal amount of integration and test effort for software of comparable size.

If there is no *DM* or *CM* (the component is being used unmodified) then there is no need for *SU*. If the code is being modified then *SU* applies.

The range of *AAM* is shown in Figure 2.2. Under the worst case, it can take twice the effort to modify a reused module than it takes to develop it as new (the value of *AAM* can exceed 100). The best case follows a one for one correspondence between adapting an existing product and developing it from scratch.

### 2.2.4.3  GUIDELINES FOR QUANTIFYING ADAPTED SOFTWARE

This section provides guidelines to estimate adapted software factors for different categories of code using COCOMO II. The *New* category refers to software developed from scratch. *Adapted* code is preexisting code that has some changes to it, while *reused* code has no changes to the preexisting source (i.e., used as-is). *COTS* is off-the-shelf software that is generally treated the same as reused code when there are no changes to it. One difference is that there may be some new glue code associated with it that also needs to be counted (this may happen with reused software, but here the option of modifying the source code may make adapting the software more attractive).

Since there is no source code modified in reused and *COTS*, *DM* = 0, *CM* = 0, and *SU* and *UNFM* don't apply. *AA* and *IM* can have non-zero values in this case. Reuse doesn't mean free integration and test. However in the reuse approach, with well-architected product-lines, the integration and test is minimal.

For adapted software, *CM* > 0, *DM* is usually > 0, and all other reuse factors normally have non-zero values. *IM* is expected to be at least moderate for adapted software, but can be higher than 100 percent for adaptation into more complex applications. Table 2.8 shows the valid ranges of reuse factors with additional notes for the different categories.

### 2.2.5  Requirements Evolution and Volatility (REVL)

COCOMO II uses a factor called *REVL*, to adjust the effective size of the product caused by requirements evolution and volatility caused by such factors as mission or user interface evolution, technology upgrades, or *COTS* volatility. It is the percentage of code discarded due to requirements evolution. For example, a project which delivers 100,000 instructions but discards the equivalent of an additional 20,000 instructions has an *REVL* value of 20. This would be used to

**Table 2.8   Adapted Software Parameter Constraints and Guidelines**

| Code Category | Reuse Parameters | | | | | |
|---|---|---|---|---|---|---|
| | *DM* | *CM* | *IM* | *AA* | *SU* | *UNFM* |
| **New**<br>all original<br>software | | | not<br>applicable | | | |
| **Adapted**<br>changes to<br>pre-existing<br>software | 0–100%<br>normally<br>> 0% | 0–100%<br>usually<br>> DM and<br>must be > 0% | 0–100+%<br>IM usually<br>moderate and<br>can be > 100% | 0–8% | 0–50% | 0–1 |
| **Reused**<br>unchanged<br>existing<br>software | 0% | 0% | 0–100%<br>rarely 0%,<br>but could be<br>very small | 0–8% | not applicable | |
| **COTS**<br>off-the-shelf<br>software (often<br>requires new<br>glue code as a<br>wrapper around<br>the COTS) | 0% | 0% | 0–100% | 0–8% | not applicable | |

adjust the project's effective size to 120,000 instructions for a COCOMO II esti-mation.

The use of *REVL* for computing size in given in Equation 2.5.

$$\text{Size} = \left(1 + \frac{REVL}{100}\right) \times \text{Size}_D \qquad \text{Eq. 2.5}$$

where

$\text{Size}_D$ is the reuse-equivalent of the delivered software.

## 2.2.6   Automatically Translated Code

The COCOMO II reuse model needs additional refinement to estimate the costs of software reengineering and conversion. The major difference in reengineering and conversion is the efficiency of automated tools for software restructuring. These can lead to very high values for the percentage of code modified (*CM* in the COCOMO II reuse model), but with very little corresponding effort. For example, in the NIST reengineering case study [Ruhl-Gunn 1991], 80 percent of the code

(13,131 COBOL source statements) was reengineered by automatic translation, and the actual reengineering effort, 35 person-months, was more than a factor of 4 lower than the COCOMO estimate of 152 person-months.

The COCOMO II reengineering and conversion estimation approach involves estimating an additional factor, *AT*, the percentage of the code that is reengineered by automatic translation. Based on an analysis of the project data above, the default productivity value for automated translation is 2400 source statements per person-month. This value could vary with different technologies and is designated in the COCOMO II model as another factor called ATPROD. In the NIST case study, *ATPROD* = 2400. Equation 2.6 shows how automated translation affects the estimated effort, $PM_{Auto}$.

$$PM_{Auto} = \frac{\text{Adapted } SLOC \times (AT/100)}{ATPROD} \qquad \text{Eq. 2.6}$$

The NIST case study also provides useful guidance on estimating the AT factor, which is a strong function of the difference between the boundary conditions (e.g., use of *COTS* packages, change from batch to interactive operation) of the old code and the reengineered code. The NIST data on percentage of automated translation (from an original batch processing application without *COTS* utilities) are given in Table 2.9 [Ruhl and Gunn 1991].

Automated translation is considered to be a separate activity from development. Thus, its *Adapted SLOC* are not included as *Size in Equivalent KSLOC*, and its $PM_{AUTO}$ are not included in $PM_{NS}$ in estimating the project's schedule. If the automatically translated *Adapted SLOC* count is included as Size in the Equivalent *KSLOC*, it must be backed out to prevent double counting. This is done by adding the term (1 – AT/100) to the equation for *Equivalent KSLOC*, Equation 2.4.

### 2.2.7  Sizing Software Maintenance

COCOMO II differs from COCOMO 81 in applying the COCOMO II scale factors to the size of the modified code rather than applying COCOMO 81 modes to the size of the product being modified. Applying the scale factors to a ten million SLOC product produced overlarge estimates as most of the product was not

**Table 2.9  Variation in Percentage of Automated Reengineering**

| Reengineering Target | AT (% automated translation) |
| --- | --- |
| Batch processing | 96% |
| Batch with SORT | 90% |
| Batch with DBMS | 88% |
| Batch, SORT, DBMS | 82% |
| Interactive | 50% |

being touched by the changes. COCOMO II accounts for the effects of the product being modified via its software understanding and unfamiliarity factors discussed for reuse in Section 2.2.4.2.

The scope of "software maintenance" follows the COCOMO 81 guidelines in [Boehm 1981, pp. 534–536]. It includes adding new capabilities and fixing or adapting existing capabilities. It excludes major product rebuilds changing over 50 percent of the existing software, and development of sizable (over 20 percent changed) interfacing systems requiring little rework of the existing system.

The maintenance size is normally obtained via Equation 2.7, when the base code size is known and the percentage of change to the base code is known.

$$(Size)_M = [(Base\ Code\ Size) \times MCF] \times MAF \qquad Eq.\ 2.7$$

The Maintenance Adjustment Factor (*MAF*) is discussed below. But first, the percentage of change to the base code is called the Maintenance Change Factor (*MCF*). The *MCF* is similar to the Annual Change Traffic in COCOMO 81, except that maintenance periods other than a year can be used. Conceptually the *MCF* represents the ratio in Equation 2.8:

$$MCF = \frac{Size\ Added + Size\ Modified}{Base\ Code\ Size} \qquad Eq.\ 2.8$$

A simpler version can be used when the fraction of code added or modified to the existing base code during the maintenance period is known. Deleted code is not counted.

$$(Size)_M = (Size\ Added + Size\ Modified) \times MAF \qquad Eq.\ 2.9$$

The size can refer to thousands of source lines of code (KSLOC), Function Points, or Application Points. When using Function Points or Application Points, it is better to estimate MCF in terms of the fraction of the overall application being changed, rather than the fraction of inputs, outputs, screens, reports, etc. touched by the changes. Our experience indicates that counting the items touched can lead to significant overestimates, as relatively small changes can touch a relatively large number of items. In some very large COBOL programs, we found ratios of 2 to 3 FP-touched/SLOC-changed as compared to 91 FP/SLOC for development.

The Maintenance Adjustment Factor (*MAF*), Equation 2.10, is used to adjust the effective maintenance size to account for software understanding and unfamiliarity effects, as with reuse. COCOMO II uses the Software Understanding (*SU*) and Programmer Unfamiliarity (*UNFM*) factors from its reuse model (discussed in Section 2.2.4.2) to model the effects of well or poorly structured/understandable software on maintenance effort.

$$MAF = 1 + \left( \frac{SU}{100} \times UNFM \right) \qquad Eq.\ 2.10$$

The use of $(Size)_M$ in determining maintenance effort, Equation 2.9, is discussed in Section 2.5.

## 2.3  EFFORT ESTIMATION

In COCOMO II effort is expressed as person-months (*PM*). A person-month is the amount of time one person spends working on the software development project for one month. COCOMO II treats the number of person-hours per person-month, *PH/PM*, as an adjustable factor with a nominal value of 152 hours/*PM*. This number excludes time typically devoted to holidays, vacations, and week-end time-off. The number of person-months is different from the time it will take the project to complete; this is called the development schedule or Time to Develop, *TDEV*. For example, a project may be estimated to require 50 *PM* of effort but have a schedule of eleven months. If you use a different value of *PH/PM*—say, 160 instead of 152—COCOMO II adjusts the *PM* estimate accordingly (in this case, reducing by about 5 percent). This reduced *PM* will result in a smaller estimate of development schedule.

The COCOMO II effort estimation model was introduced in Equation 2.1, and is summarized in Equation 2.11. This model form is used for both the Early Design and Post-Architecture cost models to estimate effort between the end-points of *LCO* and *IOC* for the MBASE/RUP and *SRR* and *SAR* for the Waterfall Models. The inputs are the Size of software development; a constant, *A*; an exponent, *E*; and a number of values called effort multipliers (*EM*). The number of effort multipliers depends on the model.

$$PM = A \times \text{Size}^E \times \prod_{i=1}^{n} EM_i \qquad \text{Eq. 2.11}$$

where $A = 2.94$ (for COCOMO II.2000)

The exponent *E* is explained in detail in Section 2.3.1. The effort multipliers are explained in Section 2.3.2. The constant, *A*, approximates a productivity constant in $(PM)/(KSLOC)$ for the case where $E = 1.0$. Productivity changes as *E* increases because of the nonlinear effects on Size. The constant *A* is initially set when the model is calibrated to the project database reflecting a global productivity average. The COCOMO model should be calibrated to local data which then reflects the local productivity and improves the model's accuracy. Chapter 4 discusses how to calibrate the model.

The Size is *KSLOC*. This is derived from estimating the size of software modules that will constitute the application program. It can also be estimated from unadjusted function points (*UFP*), converted to *SLOC*, then divided by one thousand. Procedures for counting *SLOC* or *UFP* were explained in Section 2.2, including adjustments for reuse, requirements evolution, and automatically translated code.

*Cost drivers* are used to capture characteristics of the software development that affect the effort to complete the project. A cost driver is a model factor that "drives" the cost (in this case *PM*) estimated by the model. All COCOMO II cost drivers have qualitative rating levels that express the impact of the driver on development effort. These ratings can range from Extra Low to Extra High. Each rating level of every cost driver has a value, called an *effort multiplier* (EM), associated with it. This scheme translates a cost driver's qualitative rating into a quantitative one for use in the model. The EM value assigned to a cost driver's nominal rating is 1.00. If a multiplicative cost driver's rating level causes more software development effort, then its corresponding EM is above 1.0. Conversely, if the rating level reduces the effort then the corresponding EM is less than 1.0.

The rating of cost drivers is based on a strong rationale that they would independently explain a significant source of project effort or productivity variation. The difference between the Early Design and Post-Architecture models are the number of multiplicative cost drivers and the areas of influence they explain. There are seven multiplicative cost drivers for the Early Design model and seventeen multiplicative cost drivers for the Post-Architecture model. Each set is explained with its model later in the chapter.

It turns out that the most significant input to the COCOMO II model is Size. Size is treated as a special cost driver in that it has an exponential factor, E. This exponent is an aggregation of five scale factors. These are discussed next.

What is not apparent in the model definition form given in Equation 2.11 is that there are some model drivers that apply only to the project as a whole. The scale factors in the exponent, E, are only used at the project level. Additionally, one of the cost drivers that is in the product of effort multipliers, Required Development Schedule (SCED) is only used at the project level. The other multiplicative cost drivers, which are all represented in the product of effort multipliers, and Size apply to individual project components. The model can be used to estimate effort for a project that has only one component or multiple components. For multicomponent projects the project-level cost drivers apply to all components, see Section 2.2.3.

### 2.3.1   Scale Factors

The exponent E in Equation 2.11 is an aggregation of five *scale factors (SF)* that account for the relative economies or diseconomies of scale encountered for software projects of different sizes [Banker et al. 1994a]. If $E < 1.0$, the project exhibits economies of scale. If the product's size is doubled, the project effort is less than doubled. The project's productivity increases as the product size is increased. Some project economies of scale can be achieved via project-specific tools (e.g., simulations, testbeds), but in general these are difficult to achieve. For small projects, fixed start-up costs such as tool tailoring and setup of standards and administrative reports are often a source of economies of scale.

If $E = 1.0$, the economies and diseconomies of scale are in balance. This linear model is often used for cost estimation of small projects.

If $E > 1.0$, the project exhibits diseconomies of scale. This is generally because of two main factors: growth of interpersonal communications overhead and growth of large-system integration overhead. Larger projects will have more personnel, and thus more interpersonal communications paths consuming over-head. Integrating a small product as part of a larger product requires not only the effort to develop the small product, but also the additional overhead effort to de-sign, maintain, integrate, and test its interfaces with the remainder of the product. See [Banker et al. 1994] for a further discussion of software economies and disec-onomies of scale.

Equation 2.12 defines the exponent, $E$, used in Equation 2.11. Table 2.10 pro-vides the rating levels for the COCOMO II scale factors. The selection of scale fac-tors is based on the rationale that they are a significant source of exponential variation on a project's effort or productivity variation. Each scale factor has a range of rating levels, from Very Low to Extra High. Each rating level has a weight. The specific value of the weight is called a *scale factor (SF)*. The project's scale factors, the selected scale factor ratings, are summed and used to determine a scale exponent, $E$, via Equation 2.12. The $B$ term in the equation is a constant that can be calibrated. Calibration is discussed in Chapter 4.

$$E = B + 0.01 \times \sum_{j=1}^{5} SF_j \qquad \text{Eq. 2.12}$$

where $B = 0.91$ (for COCOMO II.2000)

For example, scale factors in COCOMO II with an Extra High rating are each assigned a scale factor weight of (0). Thus, a 100 KSLOC project with Extra High ratings for all scale factors will have $\Sigma SFj = 0$, $E = 0.91$, and a relative effort of $2.94(100)^{0.91} = 194$ *PM*. For the COCOMO II.2000 calibration of scale factors in Table 2.10, a project with Very Low ratings for all scale factors will have $\Sigma SFj = 31.6$, $E = 1.226$, and a relative effort of $2.94(100)^{1.226} = 832$ *PM*. This represents a large variation, but the increase involved in a one-unit rating level change in one of the scale factors is only about 6 percent. For very large (1,000 *KSLOC*) prod-ucts, the effect of the scale factors is much larger, as seen in Figure 2.4.

The two scale factors, Precedentedness and Flexibility largely capture the differences between the Organic, Semidetached, and Embedded modes of the

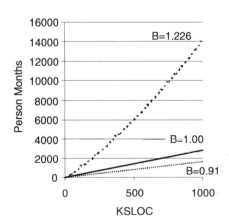

**Figure 2.4**   Diseconomies of Scale
Effect on Effort

**Table 2.10  Scale Factor Values $SF_j$ for COCOMO II Models**

| Scale Factors | Very Low | Low | Nominal | High | Very High | Extra High |
|---|---|---|---|---|---|---|
| PREC | thoroughly unprecedented | largely unprecedented | somewhat unprecedented | generally familiar | largely familiar | thoroughly familiar |
| $SF_j$: | 6.20 | 4.96 | 3.72 | 2.48 | 1.24 | 0.00 |
| FLEX | rigorous | occasional relaxation | some relaxation | general conformity | some conformity | general goals |
| $SF_j$: | 5.07 | 4.05 | 3.04 | 2.03 | 1.01 | 0.00 |
| RESL | little (20%) | some (40%) | often (60%) | generally (75%) | mostly (90%) | full (100%) |
| $SF_j$: | 7.07 | 5.65 | 4.24 | 2.83 | 1.41 | 0.00 |
| TEAM | very difficult interactions | some difficult interactions | basically cooperative interactions | largely cooperative | highly cooperative | seamless interactions |
| $SF_j$: | 5.48 | 4.38 | 3.29 | 2.19 | 1.10 | 0.00 |
| PMAT | --------- The estimated Equivalent Process Maturity Level (EPML) or --------- | | | | | |
| | SW-CMM Level 1 Lower | SW-CMM Level 1 Upper | SW-CMM Level 2 | SW-CMM Level 3 | SW-CMM Level 4 | SW-CMM Level 5 |
| $SF_j$: | 7.80 | 6.24 | 4.68 | 3.12 | 1.56 | 0.00 |

**Table 2.11   Precedentedness Rating Levels**

| Feature | Very Low | Nominal/High | Extra High |
|---|---|---|---|
| Organizational understanding of product objectives | General | Considerable | Thorough |
| Experience in working with related software systems | Moderate | Considerable | Extensive |
| Concurrent development of associated new hardware and operational procedures | Extensive | Moderate | Some |
| Need for innovative data processing architectures, algorithms | Considerable | Some | Minimal |

original COCOMO model [Boehm 1981]. Table 2.11 and Table 2.12 reorganize [Boehm 1981; Table 6.3] to map its project features onto the Precedentedness and Development Flexibility scales. These tables can be used as a more in depth explanation for the PREC and FLEX rating scales given in Table 2.10.

### 2.3.1.1   PRECEDENTEDNESS (PREC)

If a product is similar to several previously developed projects, then the precedentedness is high (Table 2.11).

### 2.3.1.2   DEVELOPMENT FLEXIBILITY (FLEX)

The PREC and FLEX scale factors are largely intrinsic to a project and uncontrollable. The next three scale factors identify management controllables by which projects can reduce diseconomies of scale by reducing sources of project turbulence, entropy, and rework.

**Table 2.12   Development Flexibility Rating Levels**

| Feature | Very Low | Nominal/High | Extra High |
|---|---|---|---|
| Need for software conformance with pre-established requirements | Full | Considerable | Basic |
| Need for software conformance with external interface specifications | Full | Considerable | Basic |
| Combination of inflexibilities above with premium on early completion | High | Medium | Low |

### 2.3.1.3    ARCHITECTURE / RISK RESOLUTION (RESL)

This factor combines two of the scale factors in Ada COCOMO, Design Thoroughness by Product Design Review (PDR) and Risk Elimination by PDR [Boehm and Royce 1989; Figures 4 and 5]. Table 2.13 consolidates the Ada COCOMO ratings to form a more comprehensive definition for the COCOMO II RESL rating levels. It also relates the rating level to the MBASE/RUP Life Cycle Architecture (LCA) milestone as well as to the waterfall PDR milestone. The RESL rating is the subjective weighted average of the listed characteristics.

### 2.3.1.4    TEAM COHESION (TEAM)

The Team Cohesion scale factor accounts for the sources of project turbulence and entropy because of difficulties in synchronizing the project's stakeholders: users, customers, developers, maintainers, interfacers, others. These difficulties may arise from differences in stakeholder objectives and cultures; difficulties in reconciling objectives; and stakeholders' lack of experience and familiarity in operating as a team. Table 2.14 provides a detailed definition for the overall TEAM rating levels. The final rating is the subjective weighted average of the listed characteristics.

### 2.3.1.5    PROCESS MATURITY (PMAT)

**2.3.1.5.1    Overall Maturity Levels.**    The procedure for determining PMAT is organized around the Software Engineering Institute's Capability Maturity Model (CMM). The time period for rating Process Maturity is the time the project starts. There are two ways of rating Process Maturity. The first captures the result of an organized evaluation based on the CMM, and it is shown in Table 2.15.

**2.3.1.5.2    Key Process Area Questionnaire.**    The second is organized around the eighteen Key Process Areas (KPAs) in the SEI Capability Maturity Model [Paulk et al., 1995]. The procedure for determining PMAT is to decide the percentage of compliance for each of the KPAs. If the project has undergone a recent CMM Assessment, then the percentage compliance for the overall KPA (based on KPA Key Practice compliance assessment data) is used. If an assessment has not been done, then the levels of compliance to the KPA's goals are used (with the Likert scale in Table 2.16) to set the level of compliance. The goal-based level of compliance is determined by a judgment-based averaging across the goals for each Key Process Area. See [Paulk et al. 1995] for more information on the KPA definitions, goals and activities.

An Equivalent Process Maturity Level (*EPML*) is computed as five times the average compliance level of all *n*-rated *KPAs* for a single project (Does Not Apply and Don't Know are not counted which sometimes makes *n* less than 18). After each *KPA* is rated, the rating level is weighted (100 percent for Almost Always, 75 percent for Frequently, 50 percent for About Half, 25 percent for Occasionally, 1 percent for Rarely if Ever). The *EPML* is calculated as in Equation 2.13.

**Table 2.13   RESL Rating Levels**

| Characteristic | Very Low | Low | Nominal | High | Very High | Extra High |
|---|---|---|---|---|---|---|
| Risk Management Plan identifies all critical risk items, establishes milestones for resolving them by PDR or LCA. | None | Little | Some | Generally | Mostly | Fully |
| Schedule, budget, and internal milestones through PDR or LCA compatible with Risk Management Plan. | None | Little | Some | Generally | Mostly | Fully |
| Percent of development schedule devoted to establishing architecture, given general product objectives. | 5 | 10 | 17 | 25 | 33 | 40 |
| Percent of required top software architects available to project. | 20 | 40 | 60 | 80 | 100 | 120 |
| Tool support available for resolving risk items, developing and verifying architectural specs. | None | Little | Some | Good | Strong | Full |
| Level of uncertainty in key architecture drivers: mission, user interface, COTS, hardware, technology, performance. | Extreme | Significant | Considerable | Some | Little | Very Little |
| Number and criticality of risk items. | > 10 Critical | 5–10 Critical | 2–4 Critical | 1 Critical | > 5 Non-Critical | < 5 Non-Critical |

**Table 2.14   TEAM Rating Components**

| Characteristic | Very Low | Low | Nominal | High | Very High | Extra High |
|---|---|---|---|---|---|---|
| Consistency of stakeholder objectives and cultures | Little | Some | Basic | Consid-erable | Strong | Full |
| Ability, willingness of stakeholders to accommo-date other stakeholders' objectives | Little | Some | Basic | Consid-erable | Strong | Full |
| Experience of stakeholders in operating as a team | None | Little | Little | Basic | Consid-erable | Exten-sive |
| Stakeholder teambuilding to achieve shared vision and commitments | None | Little | Little | Basic | Consid-erable | Exten-sive |

$$ EPML = 5 \times \left( \sum_{i=1}^{n} \frac{KPA\%_i}{100} \right) \times \frac{1}{n} \qquad \text{Eq. 2.13} $$

An *EPML* of 0 corresponds with a PMAT rating level of Very Low in the rating scales of Table 2.10 and Table 2.15.

The COCOMO II project is tracking the progress of the recent CMM Integration (CMM-I) activity to determine likely future revisions in the definition of PMAT.

**Table 2.15   PMAT Ratings for Estimated Process Maturity Level (EPML)**

| PMAT Rating | Maturity Level | EPML |
|---|---|---|
| Very Low | CMM Level 1 (lower half) | 0 |
| Low | CMM Level 1 (upper half) | 1 |
| Nominal | CMM Level 2 | 2 |
| High | CMM Level 3 | 3 |
| Very High | CMM Level 4 | 4 |
| Extra High | CMM Level 5 | 5 |

### 2.3.2   Effort Multipliers

#### 2.3.2.1   POST-ARCHITECTURE COST DRIVERS

This model is the most detailed. It is intended to be used when a software life-cycle architecture has been developed. This model is used in the development and maintenance of software products in the Application Generators, System Integration, or Infrastructure sectors discussed in Chapter 1.

**Table 2.16 KPA Rating Levels**

| Key Process Areas (KPA) | Almost Always[1] | Frequently[2] | About Half[3] | Occasionally[4] | Rarely if Ever[5] | Does Not Apply[6] | Don't Know[7] |
|---|---|---|---|---|---|---|---|
| **Requirements Management**<br>• System requirements allocated to software are controlled to establish a baseline for software engineering and management use.<br>• Software plans, products, and activities are kept consistent with the system requirements allocated to software. | ☐ | ☐ | ☐ | ☐ | ☐ | ☐ | ☐ |
| **Software Project Planning**<br>• Software estimates are documented for use in planning and tracking the software project.<br>• Software project activities and commitments are planned and documented.<br>• Affected groups and individuals agree to their commitments related to the software project. | ☐ | ☐ | ☐ | ☐ | ☐ | ☐ | ☐ |
| **Software Project Tracking and Oversight**<br>• Actual results and performances are tracked against the software plans<br>• Corrective actions are taken and managed to closure when actual results and performance deviate significantly from the software plans.<br>• Changes to software commitments are agreed to by the affected groups and individuals. | ☐ | ☐ | ☐ | ☐ | ☐ | ☐ | ☐ |
| **Software Subcontract Management**<br>• The prime contractor selects qualified software subcontractors.<br>• The prime contractor and the subcontractor agree to their commitments to each other.<br>• The prime contractor and the subcontractor maintain ongoing communications.<br>• The prime contractor tracks the subcontractor's actual results and performance against its commitments. | ☐ | ☐ | ☐ | ☐ | ☐ | ☐ | ☐ |
| **Software Quality Assurance (SQA)**<br>• SQA activities are planned.<br>• Adherence of software products and activities to the applicable standards, procedures, and requirements is verified objectively. | ☐ | ☐ | ☐ | ☐ | ☐ | ☐ | ☐ |

*(continued)*

**Table 2.16** *continued*

| Key Process Areas (KPA) | Almost Always[1] | Frequently[2] | About Half[3] | Occasionally[4] | Rarely if Ever[5] | Does Not Apply[6] | Don't Know[7] |
|---|---|---|---|---|---|---|---|
| • Affected groups and individuals are informed of software quality assurance activities and results.<br>• Noncompliance issues that cannot be resolved within the software project are addressed by senior management. | | | | | | | |
| **Software Configuration Management (SCM)**<br>• SCM activites are planned.<br>• Selected workproducts are identified, controlled, and available.<br>• Changes to identified work products are controlled.<br>• Affected groups and individuals are informed of the status and content of software baselines. | ☐ | ☐ | ☐ | ☐ | ☐ | ☐ | ☐ |
| **Organization Process Focus**<br>• Software process development and improvement activities are coordinated across the organization.<br>• The strengths and weaknesses of the software processes used are identified relative to a process standard.<br>• Organization-level process development and improvement activities are planned. | ☐ | ☐ | ☐ | ☐ | ☐ | ☐ | ☐ |
| **Organization Process Definition**<br>• A standard software process for the organization is developed and maintained.<br>• Information related to the use of the organization's standard software process by the software projects is collected, reviewed, and made available. | ☐ | ☐ | ☐ | ☐ | ☐ | ☐ | ☐ |
| **Training Program**<br>• Training activities are planned.<br>• Training for developing the skills and knowledge needed to perform software management and technical roles is provided.<br>• Individuals in the software engineering group and software-related groups receive the training necessary to perform their roles. | ☐ | ☐ | ☐ | ☐ | ☐ | ☐ | ☐ |
| **Integrated Software Management**<br>• The project's defined software process is a tailored version of the organization's standard software process.<br>• The project is planned and managed according to the project's defined software process. | ☐ | ☐ | ☐ | ☐ | ☐ | ☐ | ☐ |

| Key Process Areas (KPA) | Almost Always[1] | Frequently[2] | About Half[3] | Occasionally[4] | Rarely if Ever[5] | Does Not Apply[6] | Don't Know[7] |
|---|---|---|---|---|---|---|---|
| **Software Product Engineering**<br>• The software engineering tasks are defined, integrated, and consistently performed to produce the software<br>• Software work products are kept consistent with each other. | ☐ | ☐ | ☐ | ☐ | ☐ | ☐ | ☐ |
| **Intergroup Coordination**<br>• The customer's requirements are agreed to by all affected groups.<br>• The commitments between the engineering groups are agreed to by the affected groups.<br>• The engineering groups identify, track, and resolve intergroup issues. | ☐ | ☐ | ☐ | ☐ | ☐ | ☐ | ☐ |
| **Peer Reviews**<br>• Peer review activities are planned.<br>• Defects in the software work products are identified and removed. | ☐ | ☐ | ☐ | ☐ | ☐ | ☐ | ☐ |
| **Quantitative Process Management**<br>• The quantitative process management activities are planned.<br>• The process performance of the project's defined software process is controlled quantitatively.<br>• The process capability of the organization's standard software process is known in quantitative terms. | ☐ | ☐ | ☐ | ☐ | ☐ | ☐ | ☐ |
| **Software Quality Management**<br>• The project's software quality management activities are planned.<br>• Measurable goals of software product quality and their priorities are defined.<br>• Actual progress toward achieving the quality goals for the software products is quantified and managed. | ☐ | ☐ | ☐ | ☐ | ☐ | ☐ | ☐ |
| **Defect Prevention**<br>• Defect prevention activities are planned.<br>• Common causes of defects are sought out and identified.<br>• Common causes of defects are priortized and systematically eliminated. | ☐ | ☐ | ☐ | ☐ | ☐ | ☐ | ☐ |

(*continued*)

**Table 2.16**   *continued*

| Key Process Areas (KPA) | Almost Always[1] | Frequently[2] | About Half[3] | Occasionally[4] | Rarely if Ever[5] | Does Not Apply[6] | Don't Know[7] |
|---|---|---|---|---|---|---|---|
| **Technology Change Management**<br>• Incorporation of technology changes are planned.<br>• New technologies are evaluated to determine their effect on quality and productivity.<br>• Appropriate new technologies are transferred into normal practice across the organization. | ☐ | ☐ | ☐ | ☐ | ☐ | ☐ | ☐ |
| **Process Change Management**<br>• Continuous process improvement is planned.<br>• Participation in the organization's software process improvement activities is organization wide.<br>• The organization's standard software process and the project's defined software processes are improved continuously. | ☐ | ☐ | ☐ | ☐ | ☐ | ☐ | ☐ |

1. Check **Almost Always** when the goals are consistently achieved and are well established in standard operating procedures (over 90% of the time).
2. Check **Frequently** when the goals are achieved relatively often, but sometimes are omitted under difficult circumstances (about 60 to 90% of the time).
3. Check **About Half** when the goals are achieved about half of the time (about 40 to 60% of the time).
4. Check **Occasionally** when the goals are sometimes achieved, but less often (about 10 to 40% of the time).
5. Check **Rarely If Ever** when the goals are rarely if ever achieved (less than 10% of the time).
6. Check **Does Not Apply** when you have the required knowledge about your project or organization and the KPA, but you feel the KPA does not apply to your circumstances.
7. Check **Don't Know** when you are uncertain about how to respond for the KPA.

The seventeen Post-Architecture effort multipliers (*EM*) are used in the COCOMO II model to adjust the nominal effort, *PM*, to reflect the software product under development, see Equation 2.11. Each multiplicative cost driver is defined below by a set of rating levels and a corresponding set of effort multipliers. The Nominal level always has an effort multiplier of 1.00, which does not change the estimated effort. Off-nominal ratings generally do change the estimated effort. For example, a high rating of Required Software Reliability (RELY) will add 10 percent to the estimated effort, as determined by the COCOMO II.2000 data calibration. A Very High RELY rating will add 26 percent. It is possible to assign intermediate rating levels and corresponding effort multipliers for your project.

For example, the USC COCOMO II software tool supports rating cost drivers between the rating levels in quarter increments, e.g., Low +0.25, Nominal +0.50, High +0.75, etc. Whenever an assessment of a cost driver is halfway between quarter increments always round to the Nominal rating, e.g., if a cost driver rating falls halfway between Low +0.5 and Low +0.75, then select Low +0.75; or if a rating falls halfway between High +0.25 and High +0.5, then select High +0.25. Normally, linear interpolation is used to determine intermediate multiplier values, but nonlinear interpolation is more accurate for the high end of the TIME and STOR cost drivers and the low end of SCED.

The COCOMO II model can be used to estimate effort and schedule for the whole project or for a project that consists of multiple modules. The size and cost driver ratings can be different for each module, with the exception of the Required Development Schedule (SCED) cost driver and the scale factors. The unique handling of SCED is discussed in Section 2.3.2.1.4 and in 2.4.

**2.3.2.1.1  Product Factors.**    Product factors account for variation in the effort required to develop software caused by characteristics of the product under development. A product that is complex, has high-reliability requirements, or works with a large testing database will require more effort to complete. There are five product factors, and complexity has the strongest influence on estimated effort.

*Required Software Reliability (RELY)*    This is the measure of the extent to which the software must perform its intended function over a period of time. If the effect of a software failure is only slight inconvenience then RELY is very low. If a failure would risk human life then RELY is very high. Table 2.17 provides the COCOMO II.2000 rating scheme for RELY.

**Table 2.17    RELY Cost Driver**

| RELY Descriptors: | slight inconvenience | low, easily recoverable losses | moderate, easily recoverable losses | high financial loss | risk to human life | |
|---|---|---|---|---|---|---|
| **Rating Levels** | Very Low | Low | Nominal | High | Very High | Extra High |
| **Effort Multipliers** | 0.82 | 0.92 | 1.00 | 1.10 | 1.26 | n/a |

This cost driver can be influenced by the requirement to develop software for reusability, see the description for RUSE.

*Database Size (DATA)*    This cost driver attempts to capture the effect large test data requirements have on product development. The rating is determined by calculating $D/P$, the ratio of bytes in the testing database to SLOC in the program. The reason the size of the database is important to consider is because of the effort required to generate the test data that will be used to exercise the program. In other words, DATA is capturing the effort needed to assemble and maintain the data required to complete test of the program through IOC. See Table 2.18.

**Table 2.18　DATA Cost Driver**

| DATA*<br>Descriptors | | Testing $DB$<br>bytes/Pgm<br>$SLOC < 10$ | $10 \le D/P$<br>$< 100$ | $100 \le D/P$<br>$< 1000$ | $D/P$<br>$\ge 1000$ | |
|---|---|---|---|---|---|---|
| Rating Levels | Very Low | Low | Nominal | High | Very High | Extra High |
| Effort Multipliers | n/a | 0.90 | 1.00 | 1.14 | 1.28 | n/a |

*DATA is rated as Low if $D/P$ is less than 10 and it is very high if it is greater than 1000. $P$ is measured in equivalent source lines of code ($SLOC$), which may involve function point or reuse conversions.

*Product Complexity (CPLX)*　Complexity is divided into five areas: control operations, computational operations, device-dependent operations, data management operations, and user interface management operations. Using Table 2.19, select the area or combination of areas that characterize the product or the component of the product you are rating. The complexity rating is the subjective weighted average of the selected area ratings. Table 2.20 provides the COCOMO II.2000 effort multiplier for CPLX.

*Developed for Reusability (RUSE)*　This cost driver accounts for the additional effort needed to construct components intended for reuse on current or future projects. This effort is consumed with creating more generic design of software, more elaborate documentation, and more extensive testing to ensure components are ready for use in other applications. "Across project" could apply to reuse across the modules in a single financial applications project. "Across program" could apply to reuse across multiple financial applications projects for a single organization. "Across product line" could apply if the reuse is extended across multiple organizations. "Across multiple product lines" could apply to reuse across financial, sales, and marketing product lines. See Table 2.21.

Development for reusability imposes constraints on the project's RELY and DOCU ratings. The RELY rating should be at most one level below the RUSE rating. The DOCU rating should be at least Nominal for Nominal and High RUSE ratings, and at least High for Very High and Extra High RUSE ratings.

*Documentation Match to Life-Cycle Needs (DOCU)*　Several software cost models have a cost driver for the level of required documentation. In COCOMO II, the rating scale for the DOCU cost driver is evaluated in terms of the suitability of the project's documentation to its life cycle needs. The rating scale goes from Very Low (many life-cycle needs uncovered) to Very High (very excessive for life-cycle needs). See Table 2.22.

**Table 2.19  Component Complexity Ratings Levels**

| | Control Operations | Computational Operations | Device-dependent Operations | Data Management Operations | User Interface Management Operations |
|---|---|---|---|---|---|
| Very Low | Straight-line code with a few non-nested structured programming operators: DOs, CASEs, IF-THEN-ELSEs. Simple module composition via procedure calls or simple scripts. | Evaluation of simple expressions: e.g., $A = B + C*(D - E)$ | Simple read, write statements with simple formats. | Simple arrays in main memory. Simple COTS-DB queries, updates. | Simple input forms, report generators. |
| Low | Straightforward nesting of structured programming operators. Mostly simple predicates. | Evaluation of moderate-level expressions: e.g., $D = SQRT(B**2 - 4.*A*C)$ | No cognizance needed of particular processor or I/O device characteristics. I/O done at GET/PUT level. | Single file subsetting with no data structure changes, no edits, no intermediate files. Moderately complex COTS-DB queries, updates. | Use of simple graphic user interface (GUI) builders. |
| Nominal | Mostly simple nesting. Some intermodule control. Decision tables. Simple callbacks or message passing, including middleware-supported distributed processing. | Use of standard math and statistical routines. Basic matrix/vector operations. | I/O processing includes device selection, status checking and error processing. | Multi-file input and single file output. Simple structural changes, simple edits. Complex COTS-DB queries, updates. | Simple use of widget set. |

*(continued)*

**Table 2.19**   *continued*

|  | Control Operations | Computational Operations | Device-dependent Operations | Data Management Operations | User Interface Management Operations |
|---|---|---|---|---|---|
| High | Highly nested structured programming operators with many compound predicates. Queue and stack control. Homogeneous, distributed processing. Single processor soft real-time control. | Basic numerical analysis: multivariate interpolation, ordinary differential equations. Basic truncation, round-off concerns. | Operations at physical I/O level (physical storage address translations; seeks, reads, etc.). Optimized I/O overlap. | Simple triggers activated by data stream contents. Complex data restructuring. | Widget set development and extension. Simple voice I/O, multimedia. |
| Very High | Reentrant and recursive coding. Fixed-priority interrupt handling. Task synchronization, complex callbacks, heterogeneous distributed processing. Single-processor hard real-time control. | Difficult but structured numerical analysis: near-singular matrix equations, partial differential equations. Simple parallelization. | Routines for interrupt diagnosis, servicing, masking. Communication line handling. Performance-intensive embedded systems. | Distributed database coordination. Complex triggers. Search optimization. | Moderately complex 2D/3D, dynamic graphics, multimedia. |
| Extra High | Multiple resource scheduling with dynamically changing priorities. Microcode-level control. Distributed hard real-time control. | Difficult and unstructured numerical analysis: highly accurate analysis of noisy, stochastic data. Complex parallelization. | Device timing-dependent coding, micro-programmed operations. Performance-critical embedded systems. | Highly coupled, dynamic relational and object structures. Natural language data management. | Complex multimedia, virtual reality, natural language interface. |

**Table 2.20  CPLX Cost Driver**

| Rating Levels | Very Low | Low | Nominal | High | Very High | Extra High |
|---|---|---|---|---|---|---|
| Effort Multipliers | 0.73 | 0.87 | 1.00 | 1.17 | 1.34 | 1.74 |

**Table 2.21  RUSE Cost Driver**

| RUSE Descriptors: | | None | Across project | Across program | Across product line | Across multiple product lines |
|---|---|---|---|---|---|---|
| Rating Levels | Very Low | Low | Nominal | High | Very High | Extra High |
| Effort Multipliers | n/a | 0.95 | 1.00 | 1.07 | 1.15 | 1.24 |

Attempting to save costs via Very Low or Low documentation levels will generally incur extra costs during the maintenance portion of the life cycle. Poor or missing documentation will increase the *SU* increment discussed in Section 2.2.4.2. See Table 2.22.

**Table 2.22  DOCU Cost Driver**

| DOCU Descriptors: | Many life-cycle needs uncovered | Some life-cycle needs uncovered | Right-sized to life-cycle needs | Excessive for life-cycle needs | Very excessive for life-cycle needs | |
|---|---|---|---|---|---|---|
| Rating Levels | Very Low | Low | Nominal | High | Very High | Extra High |
| Effort Multipliers | 0.81 | 0.91 | 1.00 | 1.11 | 1.23 | n/a |

This cost driver can be influenced by the developed for reusability cost factor, see the description for RUSE.

**2.3.2.1.2  Platform Factors.**  The platform refers to the target-machine complex of hardware and infrastructure software (previously called the virtual machine). The factors have been revised to reflect this as described in this section. Some additional platform factors were considered, such as distribution, parallelism, embeddedness, and real-time operations. These considerations have been accommodated by the expansion of the Component Complexity rating levels in Table 2.19.

*Execution Time Constraint (TIME)*  This is a measure of the execution time constraint imposed upon a software system. The rating is expressed in terms of the percentage of available execution time expected to be used by the system or subsystem consuming the execution time resource. The rating ranges from nominal, less than 50 percent of the execution time resource used, to extra high, 95 percent of the execution time resource is consumed. See Table 2.23.

**Table 2.23    TIME Cost Driver**

| TIME Descriptors: | | | ≤ 50% use of available execution time | 70% use of available execution time | 85% use of available execution time | 95% use of available execution time |
|---|---|---|---|---|---|---|
| **Rating Levels** | Very Low | Low | Nominal | High | Very High | Extra High |
| **Effort Multipliers** | n/a | n/a | 1.00 | 1.11 | 1.29 | 1.63 |

*Main Storage Constraint (STOR)*    This rating represents the degree of main storage constraint imposed on a software system or subsystem. Given the remarkable increase in available processor execution time and main storage, one can question whether these constraint variables are still relevant. However, many applications continue to expand to consume whatever resources are available—particularly with large and growing *COTS* products—making these cost drivers still relevant. The rating ranges from nominal (less than 50 percent), to extra high (95 percent). See Table 2.24.

**Table 2.24    STOR Cost Driver**

| STOR Descriptors: | | | ≤ 50% use of available storage | 70% use of available storage | 85% use of available storage | 95% use of available storage |
|---|---|---|---|---|---|---|
| **Rating Levels** | Very Low | Low | Nominal | High | Very High | Extra High |
| **Effort Multipliers** | n/a | n/a | 1.00 | 1.05 | 1.17 | 1.46 |

*Platform Volatility (PVOL)*    "Platform" is used here to mean the complex of hardware and software (OS, DBMS, etc.) the software product calls on to perform its tasks. If the software to be developed is an operating system then the platform is the computer hardware. If a database management system is to be developed then the platform is the hardware and the operating system. If a network text browser is to be developed then the platform is the network, computer hardware, the operating system, and the distributed information repositories. The platform includes any compilers or assemblers supporting the development of the software system. This rating ranges from low, where there is a major change every twelve months, to very high, where there is a major change every two weeks. See Table 2.25.

**Table 2.25   PVOL Cost Driver**

| PVOL Descriptors: | | Major change every 12 mo.; Minor change every 1 mo. | Major change every 6 mo.; Minor change every 2 wk. | Major change every 2 mo.; Minor change every 1 wk. | Major change every 2 wk.; wk.; Minor: change every 2 days | |
|---|---|---|---|---|---|---|
| **Rating Levels** | Very Low | Low | Nominal | High | Very High | Extra High |
| **Effort Multipliers** | n/a | 0.87 | 1.00 | 1.15 | 1.30 | n/a |

**2.3.2.1.3   Personnel Factors.**   After product size, people factors have the strongest influence in determining the amount of effort required to develop a software product. The Personnel Factors are for rating the development team's capability and experience—not the individual. These ratings are most likely to change during the course of a project reflecting the gaining of experience or the rotation of people onto and off the project.

*Analyst Capability (ACAP)*   Analysts are personnel who work on requirements, high-level design, and detailed design. The major attributes that should be considered in this rating are analysis and design ability, efficiency and thoroughness, and the ability to communicate and cooperate. The rating should not consider the level of experience of the analyst; that is rated with APEX, LTEX, and PLEX. Analyst teams that fall in the fifteenth percentile are rated very low and those that fall in the ninetieth percentile are rated as very high. See Table 2.26.

**Table 2.26   ACAP Cost Driver**

| ACAP Descriptors: | 15th percentile | 35th percentile | 55th percentile | 75th percentile | 90th percentile | |
|---|---|---|---|---|---|---|
| **Rating Levels** | Very Low | Low | Nominal | High | Very High | Extra High |
| **Effort Multipliers** | 1.42 | 1.19 | 1.00 | 0.85 | 0.71 | n/a |

*Programmer Capability (PCAP)*   Current trends continue to emphasize the importance of highly capable analysts. However the increasing role of complex *COTS* packages, and the significant productivity leverage associated with programmers' ability to deal with these *COTS* packages, indicates a trend toward higher importance of programmer capability as well.

Evaluation should be based on the capability of the programmers as a team rather than as individuals. Major factors which should be considered in the rating are ability, efficiency and thoroughness, and the ability to communicate and cooperate. The experience of the programmer should not be considered here; that is rated with APEX, LTEX, and PLEX. A very low rated programmer team is in the fifteenth percentile and a very high rated programmer team is in the ninetieth percentile. See Table 2.27.

**Table 2.27   PCAP Cost Driver**

| PCAP Descriptors: | 15th percentile | 35th percentile | 55th percentile | 75th percentile | 90th percentile | |
|---|---|---|---|---|---|---|
| Rating Levels | Very Low | Low | Nominal | High | Very High | Extra High |
| Effort Multipliers | 1.34 | 1.15 | 1.00 | 0.88 | 0.76 | n/a |

*Personnel Continuity (PCON)*   The rating scale for PCON is in terms of the project's annual personnel turnover: from 3 percent, very high continuity, to 48 percent, very low continuity. See Table 2.28.

**Table 2.28   PCON Cost Driver**

| PCON Descriptors: | 48%/year | 24%/year | 12%/year | 6%/year | 3%/year | |
|---|---|---|---|---|---|---|
| Rating Levels | Very Low | Low | Nominal | High | Very High | Extra High |
| Effort Multipliers | 1.29 | 1.12 | 1.00 | 0.90 | 0.81 | |

*Applications Experience (APEX)*   The rating for this cost driver (formerly labeled AEXP) depends on the level of applications experience of the project team developing the software system or subsystem. The ratings are defined in terms of the project team's equivalent level of experience with this type of application. A very low rating is for application experience of less than two months. A very high rating is for experience of six years or more. See Table 2.29.

**Table 2.29   APEX Cost Driver**

| APEX Descriptors: | ≤ 2 months | 6 months | 1 year | 3 years | 6 years | |
|---|---|---|---|---|---|---|
| Rating Levels | Very Low | Low | Nominal | High | Very High | Extra High |
| Effort Multipliers | 1.22 | 1.10 | 1.00 | 0.88 | 0.81 | n/a |

*Platform Experience (PLEX)*   The Post-Architecture model broadens the productivity influence of platform experience, PLEX (formerly labeled PEXP), by recognizing the importance of understanding the use of more powerful platforms, including more graphic user interface, database, networking, and distributed middleware capabilities. See Table 2.30.

*Language and Tool Experience (LTEX)*   This is a measure of the level of programming language and software tool experience of the project team develop-

**Table 2.30   PLEX Cost Driver**

| PLEX Descriptors: | ≤ 2 months | 6 months | 1 year | 3 years | 6 years | |
|---|---|---|---|---|---|---|
| Rating Levels | Very Low | Low | Nominal | High | Very High | Extra High |
| Effort Multipliers | 1.19 | 1.09 | 1.00 | 0.91 | 0.85 | n/a |

ing the software system or subsystem. Software development includes the use of tools that perform requirements and design representation and analysis, configuration management, document extraction, library management, program style and formatting, consistency checking, planning and control, etc. In addition to experience in the project's programming language, experience on the project's supporting tool set also affects development effort. A low rating is given for experience of less than 2 months. A very high rating is given for experience of 6 or more years. See Table 2.31.

**Table 2.31   LTEX Cost Driver**

| LTEX Descriptors: | ≤ 2 months | 6 months | 1 year | 3 years | 6 years | |
|---|---|---|---|---|---|---|
| Rating Levels | Very Low | Low | Nominal | High | Very High | Extra High |
| Effort Multipliers | 1.20 | 1.09 | 1.00 | 0.91 | 0.84 | |

**2.3.2.1.4   Project Factors.**   Project factors account for influences on the estimated effort such as use of modern software tools, location of the development team, and compression of the project schedule.

***Use of Software Tools (TOOL)***   Software tools have improved significantly since the days of the 1970s era projects that were used to calibrate the 1981 version of COCOMO. The tool rating ranges from simple edit and code, very low, to integrated life cycle management tools, very high. A Nominal TOOL rating in COCOMO 81 is equivalent to a Very Low TOOL rating in COCOMO II. An emerging extension of COCOMO II is in the process of elaborating the TOOL rating scale and breaking out the effects of TOOL capability, maturity, and integration. See Table 2.32.

***Multisite Development (SITE)***   Given the increasing frequency of multisite developments, and indications that multisite development effects are significant, the SITE cost driver has been added in COCOMO II. Determining its cost driver rating involves assessing and judgement-based averaging two factors: site collocation (from fully collocated to international distribution) and communication support (from surface mail and some phone access to full interactive multimedia). See Table 2.33.

0

**Table 2.32    TOOL Cost Driver**

| TOOL Descriptors | edit, code, debug | simple, frontend, backend CASE, little integration | basic life-cycle tools, moderately integrated | strong, mature life-cycle tools, moderately integrated | strong, mature, proactive life-cycle tools, well integrated with processes, methods, reuse | |
|---|---|---|---|---|---|---|
| **Rating Levels** | Very Low | Low | Nominal | High | Very High | Extra High |
| **Effort Multipliers** | 1.17 | 1.09 | 1.00 | 0.90 | 0.78 | n/a |

For example, if a team is fully collocated, it doesn't need interactive multimedia to achieve an Extra High rating. Narrowband e-mail would usually be sufficient. See Table 2.33.

***Required Development Schedule (SCED)***    This rating measures the schedule constraint imposed on the project team developing the software. The ratings are defined in terms of the percentage of schedule stretch-out or acceleration with respect to a nominal schedule for a project requiring a given amount of effort. Accelerated schedules tend to produce more effort in the earlier phases to eliminate risks and refine the architecture, more effort in the later phases to accomplish more testing and documentation in parallel. In Table 2.34, a schedule compression of 75 percent is rated very low. A schedule stretch-out of 160 percent is rated

**Table 2.33    SITE Cost Driver**

| SITE: Collocation Descriptors: | International | Multi-city and Multi-company | Multi-city or Multi-company | Same city or metro. area | Same building or complex | Fully collocated |
|---|---|---|---|---|---|---|
| **SITE: Communications Descriptors:** | Some phone, mail | Individual phone, FAX | Narrow band e-mail | Wideband electronic communication | Wideband electronic communication, occasional video conf. | Interactive multimedia |
| **Rating Levels** | Very Low | Low | Nominal | High | Very High | Extra High |
| **Effort Multipliers** | 1.22 | 1.09 | 1.00 | 0.93 | 0.86 | 0.80 |

**Table 2.34 SCED Cost Driver**

| SCED Descriptors | 75% of nominal | 85% of nominal | 100% of nominal | 130% of nominal | 160% of nominal | |
|---|---|---|---|---|---|---|
| **Rating Level** | Very Low | Low | Nominal | High | Very High | Extra High |
| **Effort Multiplier** | 1.43 | 1.14 | 1.00 | 1.00 | 1.00 | n/a |

very high. Stretch-outs do not add or decrease effort. Their savings because of smaller team size are generally balanced by the need to carry project administrative functions over a longer period of time. The nature of this balance is undergoing further research in concert with our emerging CORADMO extension to address rapid application development (see Chapter 5).

SCED is the only cost driver that is used to describe the effect of schedule compression/expansion *for the whole project*. The scale factors are also used to describe the whole project. All of the other cost drivers are used to describe each module in a multiple module project. Using the COCOMO II Post-Architecture model for multiple module estimation is explained in Section 2.3.3.

SCED is also handled differently in the COCOMO II estimation of time to develop, TDEV. This special use of SCED is explained in Section 2.4.

### 2.3.2.2 EARLY DESIGN MODEL DRIVERS

This model is used in the early stages of a software project when very little may be known about the size of the product to be developed, the nature of the target platform, the nature of the personnel to be involved in the project, or the detailed specifics of the process to be used. This model could be employed in either Application Generator, System Integration, or Infrastructure development sectors. For discussion of these marketplace sectors see Chapter 1.

The Early Design model uses KSLOC or unadjusted function points (UFP) for size. UFPs are converted to the equivalent SLOC and then to KSLOC as dis-

**Table 2.35 Early Design and Post-Architecture Effort Multipliers**

| Early Design Cost Driver | Counterpart Combined Post-Architecture Cost Drivers |
|---|---|
| RCPX | RELY, DATA, CPLX, DOCU |
| RUSE | RUSE |
| PDIF | TIME, STOR, PVOL |
| PERS | ACAP, PCAP, PCON |
| PREX | APEX, PLEX, LTEX |
| FCIL | TOOL, SITE |
| SCED | SCED |

cussed in Section 2.2.3. The application of exponential scale factors is the same for Early Design and the Post-Architecture models and was described in Section 2.3.1. In the Early Design model a reduced set of multiplicative cost drivers is used as shown in Table 2.35. The Early Design cost drivers are obtained by combining the Post-Architecture model cost drivers. Whenever an assessment of a cost driver is halfway between the rating levels always round to the Nominal rating, e.g. if a cost driver rating is halfway between Very Low and Low, then select Low. The effort equation is the same as given in Equation 2.9 except that the number of effort multipliers is 7 ($n = 7$).

*Overall Approach*    The following approach is used for mapping the full set of Post-Architecture cost drivers and rating scales onto their Early Design model counterparts. It involves the use and combination of numerical equivalents of the rating levels. Specifically, a Very Low Post-Architecture cost driver rating corresponds to a numerical rating of 1, Low is 2, Nominal is 3, High is 4, Very High is 5, and Extra High is 6. For the combined Early Design cost drivers, the numerical values of the contributing Post-Architecture cost drivers are summed, and the resulting totals are allocated to an expanded Early Design model rating scale going from Extra Low to Extra High. The Early Design model rating scales always have a Nominal total equal to the sum of the Nominal ratings of its contributing Post-Architecture elements. An example is given below for the PERS cost driver.

*Product Reliability and Complexity (RCPX)*    This Early Design cost driver combines the four Post-Architecture cost drivers Required software reliability (RELY), Database size (DATA), Product complexity (CPLX), and Documentation match to life cycle needs (DOCU). Unlike the PERS components, the RCPX components have rating scales with differing width. RELY and DOCU range from Very Low to Very High; DATA ranges from Low to Very High, and CPLX ranges from Very Low to Extra High. The numerical sum of their ratings thus ranges from 5 (VL, L, VL, VL) to 21 (VH, VH, EH, VH).

Table 2.36 assigns RCPX ratings across this range, and associates appropriate rating scales to each of the RCPX ratings from Extra Low to Extra High. As with PERS, the Post-Architecture RELY, DATA CPLX, and DOCU rating scales discussed in Section 2.3.2.1.1 provide detailed backup for interpreting the Early Design RCPX rating levels.

*Developed for Reusability (RUSE)*    This Early Design model cost driver is the same as its Post-Architecture counterpart, which is covered in Section 2.3.2.1.2.

*Platform Difficulty (PDIF)*    This Early Design cost driver combines the three Post-Architecture cost drivers Execution time constraint (TIME), Main storage constraint (STOR), and Platform volatility (PVOL). TIME and STOR range from Nominal to Extra High; PVOL ranges from Low to Very High. The numerical sum of their ratings thus ranges from 8 (N, N, L) to 17 (EH, EH, VH).

**Table 2.36   RCPX Cost Driver**

| RCPX Descriptors: | | | | | | | |
|---|---|---|---|---|---|---|---|
| • Sum of RELY, DATA, CPLX, DOCU Ratings | 5, 6 | 7, 8 | 9–11 | 12 | 13–15 | 16–18 | 19–21 |
| • Emphasis on reliability, documentation | Very Little | Little | Some | Basic | Strong | Very Strong | Extreme |
| • Product complexity | Very simple | Simple | Some | Moderate | Complex | Very complex | Extremely complex |
| • Database size | Small | Small | Small | Moderate | Large | Very Large | Very Large |
| **Rating Levels** | Extra Low | Very Low | Low | Nominal | High | Very High | Extra High |
| **Effort Multipliers** | 0.49 | 0.60 | 0.83 | 1.00 | 1.33 | 1.91 | 2.72 |

Table 2.37 assigns PDIF ratings across this range, and associates the appropriate rating scales to each of the PDIF rating levels. The Post-Architecture rating scales in Tables 2.23, 2.24, 2.25 provide additional backup definition for the PDIF ratings levels.

*Personnel Capability (PERS) and Mapping Example*   An example will illustrate this approach. The Early Design PERS cost driver combines the Post-Architecture cost drivers Analyst capability (ACAP), Programmer capability (PCAP), and Personnel continuity (PCON). See Table 2.38. Each of these has a rating scale from Very Low (= 1) to Very High (= 5). Adding up their numerical ratings produces values ranging from 3 to 15. These are laid out on a scale, and the Early Design PERS rating levels assigned to them, as shown below. The associated effort multipliers are derived from the ACAP, PCAP, and PCON effort multipliers by averaging the products of each combination of effort multipliers associated with the given Early Design rating level.

**Table 2.37   PDIF Cost Driver**

| PDIF Descriptors: | | | | | |
|---|---|---|---|---|---|
| • Sum of TIME, STOR, and PVOL ratings | 8 | 9 | 10–12 | 13–15 | 16, 17 |
| • Time and storage constraint | ≤ 50% | ≤ 50% | 65% | 80% | 90% |
| • Platform volatility | Very stable | Stable | Somewhat volatile | Volatile | Highly volatile |
| **Rating Levels** | Low | Nominal | High | Very High | Extra High |
| **Effort Multipliers** | 0.87 | 1.00 | 1.29 | 1.81 | 2.61 |

**Table 2.38    PERS Cost Driver**

| PERS Descriptors: | | | | | | | |
|---|---|---|---|---|---|---|---|
| • Sum of ACAP, PCAP, PCON Ratings | 3, 4 | 5, 6 | 7, 8 | 9 | 10, 11 | 12, 13 | 14, 15 |
| • Combined ACAP and PCAP Percentile | 20% | 35% | 45% | 55% | 65% | 75% | 85% |
| • Annual Personnel Turnover | 45% | 30% | 20% | 12% | 9% | 6% | 4% |
| **Rating Levels** | Extra Low | Very Low | Low | Nominal | High | Very High | Extra High |
| **Effort Multipliers** | 2.12 | 1.62 | 1.26 | 1.00 | 0.83 | 0.63 | 0.50 |

The effort multipliers for PERS, like the other Early Design model cost drivers are derived from those of the Post-Architecture model by averaging the products of the constituent Post-Architecture multipliers (in this case ACAP, PCAP, PCON) for each combination of cost driver ratings corresponding with the Early Design rating level. For PERS = Extra High, this would involve four combinations: ACAP, PCAP, and PCON all Very High, or only one High and the other two Very High.

The Nominal PERS rating of 9 corresponds to the sum (3 + 3 + 3) of the Nominal ratings for ACAP, PCAP, and PCON, and its corresponding effort multiplier is 1.0. Note, however that the Nominal PERS rating of 9 can result from a number of other combinations, e.g. 1 + 3 + 5 = 9 for ACAP = Very Low, PCAP = Nominal, and PCON = Very High.

The rating scales and effort multipliers for PCAP and the other Early Design cost drivers maintain consistent relationships with their Post-Architecture counterparts. For example, the PERS Extra Low rating levels (20 percent combined ACAP and PCAP percentile; 45 percent personnel turnover) represent averages of the ACAP, PCAP, and PCON rating levels adding up to 3 or 4.

Maintaining these consistency relationships between the Early Design and Post-Architecture rating levels ensures consistency of Early Design and Post-Architecture cost estimates. It also enables the rating scales for the individual Post-Architecture cost drivers, Table 2.35, to be used as detailed backups for the top-level Early Design rating scales given above.

***Personnel Experience (PREX)***    This Early Design cost driver combines the three Post-Architecture cost drivers Application experience (APEX), Language and tool experience (LTEX), and Platform experience (PLEX). Each of these range from Very Low to Very High; as with PERS, the numerical sum of their ratings ranges from 3 to 15.

Table 2.39 assigns PREX ratings across this range, and associates appropriate effort multipliers and rating scales to each of the rating levels.

**Table 2.39 PREX Cost Driver**

| PREX Descriptors: | | | | | | | |
|---|---|---|---|---|---|---|---|
| • Sum of APEX, PLEX, and LTEX ratings | 3, 4 | 5, 6 | 7, 8 | 9 | 10, 11 | 12, 13 | 14, 15 |
| • Applications, Platform, Language and Tool Experience | ≤ 3 mo. | 5 months | 9 months | 1 year | 2 years | 4 years | 6 years |
| **Rating Levels** | Extra Low | Very Low | Low | Nominal | High | Very High | Extra High |
| **Effort Multipliers** | 1.59 | 1.33 | 1.22 | 1.00 | 0.87 | 0.74 | 0.62 |

*Facilities (FCIL)* This Early Design cost driver combines two Post-Architecture cost drivers: Use of software tools (TOOL) and Multisite development (SITE). TOOL ranges from Very Low to Very High; SITE ranges from Very Low to Extra High. Thus, the numerical sum of their ratings ranges from 2 (VL, VL) to 11 (VH, EH).

Table 2.40 assigns FCIL ratings across this range, and associates appropriate rating scales to each of the FCIL rating levels. The individual Post-Architecture TOOL and SITE rating scales in Section 2.3.2.1.4 again provide additional backup definition for the FCIL rating levels.

*Required Development Schedule (SCED)* This Early Design model cost driver is the same as its Post-Architecture counterpart, which is covered in Section 2.3.2.1.4.

### 2.3.3 Multiple Module Effort Estimation

Usually software systems are comprised of multiple subsystems or components. It is possible to use COCOMO II to estimate effort and schedule for multiple components. The technique described here is for one level of sub-components. For multiple levels of subcomponents see [Boehm 1981].

The COCOMO II method for doing this does not use the sum of the estimates for each component as this would ignore effort due to integration of the components. The COCOMO II multiple method for n number of modules has the following steps:

1. Sum the sizes for all of the components, $Size_I$, to yield to aggregate size.

$$Size_{Aggregate} = \sum_{i=1}^{n} Size_i$$

2. Apply the project-level drivers, the Scale Factors and the SCED Cost Driver, to the aggregated size to derive the overall basic effort for the total project,

**Table 2.40  FCIL Cost Driver**

| FCIL Descriptors: | | | | | | |
|---|---|---|---|---|---|---|
| • Sum of TOOL and SITE ratings | 2 | 3 | 4,5 | 6 | 7,8 | 9,10 | 11 |
| • TOOL support | Minimal | Some | Simple CASE tool collection | Basic life cycle tools | Good; moderately integrated | Strong; moderately integrated | Strong; well integrated |
| • Multisite conditions | Weak support of complex multisite (M/S) development | Some support of complex M/S development | Some support of moderately complex M/S development | Basic support of moderately complex M/S development | Strong support of moderately complex M/S development | Strong support of simple M/S development | Very strong support of collocated or simple M/S development |
| **Rating Levels** | Extra Low | Very Low | Low | Nominal | High | Very High | Extra High |
| **Effort Multipliers** | 1.43 | 1.30 | 1.10 | 1.0 | 0.87 | 0.73 | 0.62 |

$PM_{Basic}$. The scale factors are discussed in Section 2.3.1 and *SCED* is discussed in Section 2.3.2.1.

$$PM_{Basic} = A \times (Size_{Aggregate})^E \times SCED$$

3. Determine each component's basic effort, $PM_{Basic(i)}$, by apportioning the overall basic effort to each component based on its contribution to the aggregate size.

$$PM_{Basic(i)} = PM_{Basic} \times \left( \frac{Size_i}{Size_{Aggregate}} \right)$$

4. Apply the component-level Cost Drivers (excluding *SCED*) to each component's basic effort.

$$PM_i = PM_{Basic(i)} \times \sum_{j=1}^{16} EM_j$$

5. Sum each component's effort to derive the aggregate effort, $PM_{Aggregate}$, for the total project.

$$PM_{Aggregate} = \sum_{i-1}^{n} PM_i$$

6. The schedule is estimated by repeating steps 2 through 5 without the *SCED* Cost Driver used in step 2. Using this modified aggregate effort, the schedule is derive using Equation 2.14 in Section 2.4.

---

## 2.4   SCHEDULE ESTIMATION

The initial version of COCOMO II provides a simple schedule estimation capability similar to those in COCOMO 81 and Ada COCOMO. The initial baseline schedule equation for the COCOMO II Early Design and Post-Architecture stages is:

$$TDEV = \left[ C \times (PM_{NS})^{(D + 0.2 \times (E - B))} \right] \times \frac{SCED\%}{100} \qquad \text{Eq. 2.14}$$

where $C = 3.67, D = 0.28, B = 0.91$

In equation 2.14, C is a *TDEV* coefficient that can be calibrated, $PM_{NS}$ is the estimated *PM excluding* the *SCED* effort multiplier as defined in Equation 2.1, D is a *TDEV* scaling base-exponent that can also be calibrated, E is the effort scaling exponent derived as the sum of project scale factors and B as the calibrated scale factor base-exponent (discussed in Sections 2.1.2 and 2.3.1), and *SCED%* is the compression/expansion percentage in the SCED effort multiplier rating scale discussed in Section 2.3.2.1.4.

*Time to Develop, TDEV,* is the calendar time in months between the estimation endpoints of *LCO* and *IOC* for the MBASE/RUP Model and *SRR* and *SAR* for the Waterfall Models. For the waterfall model, this goes from the determination of a product's requirements baseline to the completion of an acceptance activity certifying that the product satisfies its requirements. For the MBASE/RUP model discussed in Appendix A, it covers the time span between LCO and IOC milestones.

As COCOMO II evolves, it will have a more extensive schedule estimation model, reflecting the different classes of process models a project can use. The effects of reusable and COTS software; the effects of applications composition capabilities; and the effects of alternative strategies such as Rapid Application Development are discussed in Chapter 5.

## 2.5   SOFTWARE MAINTENANCE

Software maintenance is defined as the process of modifying existing software while not changing its primary functions [Boehm 1981]. The assumption made by the COCOMO II model is that software maintenance cost generally has the same cost driver attributes as software development costs. Maintenance includes redesign and recoding of small portions of the original product, redesign and development of interfaces, and minor modification of the product structure. Maintenance can be classified as either updates or repairs. Product repairs can be further segregated into corrective (failures in processing, performance, or implementation), adaptive (changes in the processing or data environment), or perfective maintenance (enhancing performance or maintainability). Maintenance sizing is covered in Section 2.2.7.

There are special considerations for using COCOMO II in software maintenance. Some of these are adapted from [Boehm 1981].

- The SCED cost driver (Required Development Schedule) is not used in the estimation of effort for maintenance. This is because the maintenance cycle is usually of a fixed duration.
- The RUSE cost driver (Required Reusablity) is not used in the estimation of effort for maintenance. This is because the extra effort required to maintain a component's reusability is roughly balanced by the reduced maintenance effort due to the component's careful design, documentation, and testing.
- The RELY cost driver (Required Software Reliabilty) has a different set of effort multipliers for maintenance. For maintenance the RELY cost driver depends on the required reliability under which the product was developed. If the product was developed with low reliability it will require more effort to fix latent faults. If the product was developed with very high reliability, the

**Table 2.41    RELY Maintenance Cost Driver**

| RELY Descriptors: | slight inconvenience | low, easily recoverable losses | moderate, easily recoverable losses | high financial loss | risk to human life | |
|---|---|---|---|---|---|---|
| **Rating Levels** | Very Low | Low | Nominal | High | Very High | Extra High |
| **Effort Multipliers** | 1.23 | 1.10 | 1.00 | 0.99 | 1.07 | n/a |

effort required to maintain that level of reliability will be above nominal. Table 2.41 shows the effort multipliers for RELY.

- The scaling exponent, $E$, is applied to the number of changed *KSLOC* (added and modified, not deleted) rather than the total legacy system *KSLOC*. As discussed in Section 2.2.7, the effective maintenance size $(\text{Size})_m$ is adjusted by a Maintenance Adjustment Factor (*MAF*) to account for legacy system effects.

The maintenance effort estimation formula is the same as the COCOMO II Post-Architecture development model (with the exclusion of SCED and RUSE):

$$PM_M = A \times (\text{Size}_M)^E \times \prod_{i=1}^{15} EM_i \qquad \text{Eq. 2.15}$$

The COCOMO II approach differs from the COCOMO 81 maintenance effort estimation by letting you use any desired maintenance activity duration, TM. The average maintenance staffing level, FSPM, can then be obtained via the relationship:

$$FSPM = PM_M/TM \qquad \text{Eq. 2.16}$$

## 2.6    USING COCOMO II FOR SOFTWARE DECISIONS

In Section 1.1, we presented a number of software decision situations for which COCOMO II can provide help in reasoning about your options and decisions. Now that we have described the COCOMO II framework and cost driver values, we can use these to illustrate how you can use these for software decision analyses, even without exercising the full model.

Our example organization is an auto-parts company named UST, Inc. It has outsourced or acquired commercial packages for many of its business functions, but it retains a software engineering staff of about two hundred people to perform corporate success-critical software functions.

### 2.6.1   Making Investment Decisions and Business-Case Analyses

UST is considering developing a manufacturing control system (MCS) to support just-in-time manufacturing in its primary factory. UST expects that the reductions in inventory carrying costs (usually about 25 percent of the value of the inventory per year) will justify the expenditure (mostly software) to develop the MCS, but would like to do a return-on-investment (ROI) analysis to make sure. The analysis will make conservative assumptions, both for simplicity and to strengthen the conclusions.

Conservatively, UST estimates that the new system will reduce its current average manufacturing inventory value of $80 M by 20 percent. The corresponding savings in annual carrying costs (for investing control, property taxes, finances, etc.) is ($80M)(20%)(25%) = $4M/year.

A similar simple, conservative COCOMO II software cost analysis assumes that the MCS system will require 100 *KSLOC* of software, that all the cost driver and scale factor ratings will be nominal, and that the burdened cost of a UST software engineer is $8K/*PM*. The nominal effort multipliers are all set to 1.0. The nominal scale factors in Table 2.10 lead to a scaling exponent $E = 0.91+.01(3.72 +3.04+4.24+3.29+4.68) = 1.10$. The resulting estimated effort is $E = 2.94(100)^{1.10} = 466\ PM$. The corresponding estimated development cost is $(466)(\$8K) = \$3.728M$.

However, the development cost is not the full MCS project cost. For the MBASE/RUP spiral model being used for the MCS project, Table 2.42 indicates that an added 6 percent is needed for the project's Inception phase, and an added 12 percent is needed for the Transition phase. This extra 18 percent means that the estimated project cost will rise to $(1.18)(\$3.728M) = \$4.4M$.

For software maintenance, the ratings are again assumed to be nominal, and the annual amount of modified software, discussed in Section 2.2.7, is estimated to be 20 percent or 20 *KSLOC*. The estimated annual cost of software maintenance is $2.94(20)^{1.10}(\$8K) = \$635K$; the net savings per year is thus $\$4M - .635M = \$3.365M$. The annual return on investment is thus savings/project costs or $\$3.365M/\$4.4M = 76\%$. For five years of operation, the savings are $5 \times (\$3.365M) = \$16.8M$, and the ROI (5 years) is $16.8/4.4 =$ about 380%.

**Table 2.42   MCS Project Phase Distributions**

| | Effort | | Schedule | | Personnel | Cost @ |
|---|---|---|---|---|---|---|
| Phase | % | PM | % | Mo | P | $8K/PM |
| Inception | 6 | 28 | 12.5 | 3.25 | 8.6 | $224K |
| Elaboration | 24 | 112 | 37.5 | 9.75 | 11.5 | $896K |
| Construction | 76 | 354 | 62.5 | 16.25 | 21.8 | $2832K |
| Devel. Total | 100 | 466 | 100.0 | 26.00 | 17.9 | $3728K |
| Transition | 12 | 56 | 12.5 | 3.25 | 17.2 | $448K |
| Project Total | 118 | 550 | 125 | 32.5 | 16.9 | $4400K |

This is sufficiently high to justify the investment, even though we have not used a present-value analysis to reconcile present and future cash flows. Techniques for such analyses and more complete business-case analyses can be found in Chapters 14 and 31.8 of [Boehm 1981].

### 2.6.2 Setting Project Budgets and Schedules

The development schedule for the MCS is estimated to be $TDEV = 3.67$ $(MCS–PM)^{(0.28 + 0.2(E - 0.91))} = 3.67(466)^{0.318} = 26$ months. As the MCS project plans to use the MBASE/RUP spiral approach to development, we can use the phase schedule and effort percentages in Section 2.5 to calculate the schedule and effort within each phase. Once we have the estimated effort in $PM$ and the schedule in months (mo) for each phase, we can calculate the average personnel level for each phase as $P = PM/$Mo. These calculations are illustrated in Table 2.42.

Thus, if the MCS project were truly all-nominal with respect to its cost drivers and scale factors, its manager should expect, for example, to employ an average of 11.5 people during its Elaboration phase (between its Life-Cycle Objective and Life-Cycle Architecture milestones as defined in Table A.1 of Appendix A). The MCS manager should also plan for the Elaboration phase to take 9.75 months and to cost $896K.

### 2.6.3   Performing Tradeoff Analyses

The COCOMO II cost drivers can be used directly to analyze their effects on a project's cost and schedule. For example, we can use the Required Reliability (RELY) effort multipliers for software development and maintenance to analyze the effects of different RELY levels on software life-cycle costs of the MCS project. For projects such as MCS, a good planning factor is to assume that life-cycle maintenance costs will be about twice as high as the original project costs for a Nominal level of RELY.

The resulting analysis is shown in Table 2.43. For development, it appears that lower RELY levels can save money. But these lower RELY levels cause more

**Table 2.43   Effects of Reliability Level on MCS Life-Cycle Costs**

| RELY Rating | Very Low | Low | Nominal | High | Very High |
|---|---|---|---|---|---|
| **Development** | | | | | |
| Effort Multiplier | 0.82 | 0.92 | 1.0 | 1.10 | 1.26 |
| Cost | $3,608K | $4,048K | $4,400K | $4,840K | $5,544K |
| **Maintenance** | | | | | |
| Effort Multiplier | 1.35 | 1.15 | 1.0 | 0.98 | 1.10 |
| Cost (x2 for Nom.) | $11,880K | $10,120K | $8,800K | $8,624K | $9,680K |
| **Life-Cycle Cost** | $15,488K | $14,168K | $13,200K | $13,464K | $15,224K |

maintenance effort to be spent on debugging and error correction, making their life cycle costs higher than the Nominal level of required reliability. When the costs of operational failures are also included, the higher RELY levels will turn out to be lower-cost for high cost-of-failure systems.

### 2.6.4    Cost Risk Management

If there are uncertainties in key cost drivers, it can be a good idea to establish a risk management reserve to cover the resulting possibilities of cost growth [Edgar 1982]. For example, suppose that there is some chance that new developments will cause a 15 percent requirement evolution and volatility factor (REVL) in the amount of software to be developed. From Equation 2.5, this changes the effective size of the product to $(1.15)(100\ KSLOC) = 115\ KSLOC$, and the estimated cost to $(2.94)(115)^{1.1}\ (1.18)(\$8K) = \$5130K$, an increase of \$730K over the original \$4400K estimate. In such a case, the project's financial sponsor could establish a risk management reserve of \$730K to cover any added costs due to requirements evolution or volatility. Experience has shown that it is best to provide performance incentives such as award fees to encourage conserving as much as possible of the risk management reserve.

The project may have other common risks to assess. For example, the project may not get all the experienced people it has asked for. Rather than having overall Nominal ratings of Applications Experience (APEX) and Platform Experience (PLEX), the project personnel may average halfway between Nominal and Low for these cost drivers. Should this happen, the effort multipliers for APEX (1.05) and PLEX (1.045) would be halfway between the Nominal and Low values in Section 2.3.2.1.3. The resulting estimated cost would be $(\$4400K)(1.05)(1.045) = \$4828K$ and the resulting potential overrun risk would be \$428K. Further risk assessment guidance can be found in [Boehm 1989] or [Hall 1998].

### 2.6.5    Development vs. Reuse Decisions

Another way of dealing with cost-growth (or schedule-growth) risks is to reduce the costs. Many of the COCOMO II cost drivers provide opportunities to reduce costs; one of the most attractive is to reduce the effective product-development size via software reuse or commercial-off-the-shelf (COTS) products.

The COCOMO II reuse model, Section 2.2.4, includes a number of factors which help you to reason about reuse decisions. In the context of the MCS system, for example, suppose we find a 40 *KSLOC* component of a related project which we might reuse. However, it will need a good deal of redesign and recoding. It is also not well-structured or well-documented, and there are no people available for its modification who are familiar with its internals. (Note that in this example, there is no automatically translated code, so in this instance the term $(1 - AT/100)$ does not appear in the accompanying equation used to calculate ESLOC.)

We would evaluate the COCOMO II reuse factors as follows:

$$DM = 40 \quad (\% \text{ design modified})$$
$$CM = 50 \quad (\% \text{ code modified})$$
$$IM = 100 \quad (\% \text{ integration into new system required})$$
$$SU = 50 \quad (\text{poorly structured and documented})$$
$$UNFM = 1.0 \quad (\text{complete unfamiliarity with software})$$
$$AA = 5 \quad (\text{average assessment and adaptation effort})$$

The resulting equivalent size of the reuse component is:

$$ESLOC = \text{Adapted } SLOC \times \left( \left[ \frac{(0.4 \times DM + 0.3 \times CM + 0.3 \times IM)}{100} \right] \right.$$
$$\left. + \left[ \frac{AA + (SU \times UNFM)}{100} \right] \right)$$
$$= 40 \; KSLOC \times \left( \left[ \frac{(0.4 \times 40 + 0.3 \times 50 + 0.3 \times 100)}{100} \right] \right.$$
$$\left. + \left[ \frac{5 + (50 \times 1.0)}{100} \right] \right)$$
$$= 40 \; KSLOC \times (0.61 + 0.55)$$
$$= 46.4 \; KSLOC$$

Thus, for this situation, we can see that the reuse component would be a poor decision: its equivalent size, and thus its contribution to cost and schedule, is larger than the 40 *KSLOC* option of developing a new component. Experience has shown that this is the case for many hasty reuse decisions.

However, the COCOMO II reuse model also shows us which factors might be able to change the situation. We can't do much about the nature of the reused component, but if we could find people to modify it who were very familiar with its code and structure, we could reduce the unfamiliarity factor, *UNFM*, enough to reduce the equivalent size *ESLOC* below 40 *KSLOC*. However, we would still have some highly unmaintainable software, and a life cycle analysis would probably show that newly developed software with better *DM*, *CM*, *IM*, and *SU* factors would still be a better decision. A similar life-cycle decision situation, legacy software phaseout, is discussed next.

### 2.6.6  Legacy Software Phaseout Decisions

A separate program related to the MCS program is a corporate property value accounting system. It is an old 50 *KSLOC* COBOL program which is becoming increasingly difficult to maintain. Its key factors are:

Annual $MCF = 0.20$     (20% of the code—10 KSLOC—is changed each year)
$SU = 50$     (very poorly structured and documented)
$UNFM = 0.7$     (few people familiar with the code)

Thus, its equivalent size to be changed each year is:

$$10\ KSLOC \times \left[ \frac{(1 + (50 + 0.7))}{100} \right] = 13.5\ KSLOC/\text{Yr.}$$

If the program were redeveloped, it could use the same database management system and graphic user interface software as the MCS system is using, leaving only 20 $KSLOC$ of new applications software to be built. Conservatively, let us assume that the new software will reduce the SU penalty from 50 to 25, and that the $UNFM$ factor will be reduced from 0.7 to 0.4. Then the equivalent size to be changed each year is:

$$20\ KSLOC \times 0.20 \times \left( \frac{1 + (25 \times 0.4)}{100} \right) = 4 \times 1.1 = 4.4\ KSLOC/\text{Yr.}$$

If we add up the equivalent sizes of developing and maintaining the new software for, say, three years, we get:

$$20 + (3 \times 4.4) = 33.2\ KSLOC$$

Maintaining the old legacy software for three years generates a larger equivalent size of

$$3 \times 13.5 = 40.5\ KSLOC$$

Given that we will need to do property value accounting for at least three years, and that the size and cost reductions for the new software continue to improve after three years, it is a good decision to build the new system and phase out the old one.

### 2.6.7   Software Reuse and Product Line Decisions

Besides its primary factory in the United States, UST has two large foreign factories and several smaller factories. UST wishes to analyze whether it would pay off to develop an MCS to support just-in-time manufacturing in all of its factories. The product line would have particular challenges; due to the need to accommodate multiple-country supplier logistics, order-processing interfaces, and labor regulations. COCOMO II can support such an analysis via its Developed for Reusability (RUSE) and related cost drivers affecting the cost to develop suitably reusable software, and via the reused-software part of its sizing model.

In assessing the RUSE factor with respect to the rating scale in Section 2.3.2.1.1, UST conservatively judges that its multi-country factories have some aspects of multiple product lines, and assigns a RUSE rating halfway between Very

High and Extra High. Following the RUSE guidance that the RELY rating should be at most one level below the RUSE rating, RELY is rated halfway between High and Very High. Conservatively, UST also assigns a High rather than Nominal rating to the Documentation (DOCU) cost driver. With all the other ratings at Nominal, this leads to an Effort Adjustment Factor of $(RUSE)(RELY)(DOCU) = (1.195)(1.18)(1.11) = 1.565$. Applying this to the Nominal project cost estimate produces a develop-for-reuse cost estimate of $(\$4400K)(1.565) = \$6886K$.

In assessing the size adjustments caused by reused software, UST makes the following factor ratings, which are conservative for software developed to the product-line standards in the develop-for-reuse cost estimate (again, as in the example in Section 2.6.5, there is no automatically translated code here, so the term $(1 - AT/100)$ does not appear in the equivalent SLOC equations):

| | |
|---|---|
| New factory-specific software: | 40% |
| Black-box plug-and-play reuse: | 30% |
| Reuse with modifications: | 30% |
| Assessment and assimilation factor ($AA$): | 2 |
| Software understanding increment ($SU$): | 10 |
| Unfamiliarity factor ($UNFM$): | 0.3 |
| % design modified ($DM$): | 10% |
| % code modified ($CM$): | 20% |
| % integration redone ($IM$): | 20% |

With respect to the 100 $KSLOC$ MCS product, the equivalent size, $EKSLOC$, caused by reuse works out to:

$$EKSLOC_1 = 0.4 \times 100 \ KSLOC$$
$$= 40 \ KSLOC$$

$$EKSLOC_2 = 0.3 \times 100 \ KSLOC \times \left[ \frac{2 + 0 \times (1 + (0.02 \times 0 \times 0))}{100} \right]$$
$$= 0.6 \ KSLOC$$

$$EKSLOC_3 = 0.3 \times 100 \ KSLOC \times$$
$$\left[ \frac{2 + (0.4 \times 10 + 0.3 \times 20 + 0.3 \times 20) \times (1 + (0.02 \times 10 \times 0.3))}{100} \right]$$
$$= 5.7 \ KSLOC$$

$$EKSLOC = EKSLOC_1 + EKSLOC_2 + EKSLOC_3$$
$$= (40 + 0.6 + 5.7)KSLOC$$
$$= 46.3 \ KSLOC$$

Including the 18 percent additional effort for the Inception and Transition phases the resulting cost to reuse the software at each new factory is then:

$$\text{Cost} = 2.94 + 46.3^{1.1} \times 1.18 \times 1.565 \times \frac{\$8K}{PM}$$

$$= \$2951K$$

We can then compare the cost of redeveloping the MCS software for each new factory to the product line cost of developing-for-reuse plus the cost-to-reuse for each reuse instance, as summarized in Figure 2.5.

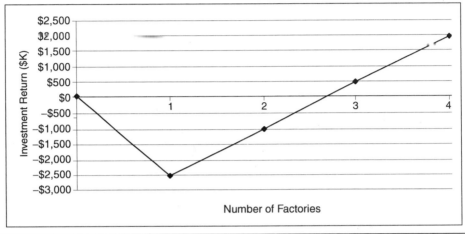

| Number of Factories | Redevelopment Cost | Product Line Cost | Investment Return |
|---|---|---|---|
| 1 | $4,400K | $6,886K | −$2,486K |
| 2 | $8,800K | 9,837K | −1,037K |
| 3 | 13,200K | 12,788K | 412K |
| 4 | 17,600K | 15,739K | 1,861K |

**Figure 2.5**   Reuse vs. Redevelopment Costs

The results are consistent with the empirical "Rule of Three" for software reuse: that it usually takes three instances of a product line to achieve a net pay-off. Given that UST has at least three large factories, and that its factor estimates have been conservative, a decision to invest in a product line appears reasonable. However, the decision should also consider other cultural circumstances critical to successful software reuse; see [Reifer 1997a; Jacobson et al. 1997; Poulin 1997].

### 2.6.8   Process Improvement Decisions

COCOMO II has several cost drivers and scale factors which can be used to evaluate candidate strategies for software process and productivity improvement. Besides the software process maturity scale factor (PMAT), the main COCOMO II factors include the reuse size factor we just discussed, the tool usage cost driver (TOOL), the architecture and risk resolution scale factor (RESL), and the project communications portion of the multisite development cost driver (SITE). As discussed in Chapter 4, the analysis of the 161 project data points in the current COCOMO II data base show a statistically significant correlation between improvements in these and most other COCOMO II cost drivers and reductions in software project effort.

Below, we show a simple return-on-investment analysis for improving software productivity based just on the improvements in the Software Engineering Institute Capability Maturity Model's (SEI-CMM's) 18 Key Process Areas included in the PMAT scale driver rating. The COCOMO II PMAT variable separates out such pure-process gains from complementary gains achievable via reuse, tools, project communications, personnel factors, etc. In practice, the PMAT analysis should be only a part of an overall product/process/personnel productivity improvement analysis addressing not just effort and cost reduction but other goals such as schedule reduction and quality improvement. An emerging COCOMO II extension called the Constructive Productivity Model (COPROMO) is discussed in Chapter 5 as a step in this direction.

The UST software organization has achieved Level 2 on the SEI-CMM rating scale, and wishes to perform a return-on-investment analysis for the investment required to achieve Level 3. UST's analysis of required investments identifies process definition and training as the major investment items. Process definition will be the main responsibility of a Software Engineering Process Group (SEPG) of three full-time people plus four quarter-time people from UST's major performer organizations. This cost over the normal two years required to go from Level 2 to Level 3 [Hayes-Zubrow, 1995] is estimated as (2 years)(4 persons)($96K/person-year) = $768K.

For training, UST has identified three one-week courses on Peer Reviews, Product Engineering, and Management and Organizational Factors to cover the seven Key Process Areas at Level 3. Conservatively, UST assumes that all two hundred software people will require the three weeks of training. This is 3/52 of their annual personnel cost of (200 persons)($8K/PM)(12 mo) = $19,200K, or $1,108K. The other main costs of learning, institutionalization, and evaluation will largely be done by the SEPG, but UST budgets another $124K for contingencies to make a total investment of $768K + $1,108K + $124K = $2,000K, or $2 million.

From the COCOMO II scale drivers in Table 2.10, we can see that the effect of going from Level 2 (Nominal) to Level 3 (High) involves reducting the scale factor from 4.68 to 3.12, or a reduction of .0156 in the exponent $E$ used to relate size to effort. For the typical 100 $KSLOC$, all-nominal UST project, the baseline exponent $E = 1.10$ yields an estimated effort of $2.94(100)^{1.10} = 466$ $PM$. The reduced exponent for Level 3 yields an estimated effort of $2.94(100)^{1.0844} = 434$ $PM$, roughly a 7% improvement in productivity. This percentage improvement will vary from about 4% for small projects (10 $KSLOC$) to about 11% for very large projects (2000 $KSLOC$).

As discussed above, the annual cost of UST's 200-person software organization is roughly $19.2 million. A 7 percent improvement in productivity corresponds with an annual savings of (.07)($19.2 million) = $1.344 million. This is an annual return of about 67 percent on the $2 million investment to achieve Level 3.

Even a conservative 4 percent productivity improvement would produce an annual return of about 38 percent. This conservative top-level analysis provides stronger support of the anecdotal evidence that investments in software process maturity are worthwhile. However, it is important to repeat that an organization's productivity strategies and analyses should not just look at the CMM, but should be driven by the organization's goals and priorities (e.g., for improving cost, schedule, or quality); should consider added improvement strategies such as reuse, staffing, and tool; and should be tailored to the organization's specific situation.

### 2.6.9   Decision Analysis Summary

This section showed how the elements of the COCOMO II model defined in Chapter 2 can support the eight decision analysis situations presented at the beginning of Chapter 1. Note that all of the analyses could be done by hand (and a hand calculator) via use of COCOMO II's open internal equations, tables, and definitions. One of the major advantages of COCOMO II is its ability to support such analyses, based on a full understanding of the underlying cost drivers and their effects, and to support reasoned discussion and negotiation of software cost and schedule tradeoffs, based on the project stakeholders' shared understanding of the underlying model.

## 2.7   COCOMO II MODEL SUMMARY AND VERSIONS

This section is a summary of the Early Design and Post-Architecture models discussed in this chapter.

### 2.7.1   Model Equations, Tables, and Driver-Rating Scales

#### 2.7.1.1   SIZING EQUATIONS

The Post-Architecture and Early Design models use the same sizing equations. Sizing is summarized below and discussed in Sections 2.2.4.2 and 2.2.5. Table 2.44 explains the acronyms.

$$\text{Size} = \left(1 + \frac{REVL}{100}\right) \times (\text{New } KSLOC + \text{Equivalent } KSLOC)$$

$$\text{Equivalent } KSLOC = \text{Adapted } KSLOC \times \left(1 - \frac{AT}{100}\right) \times AAM$$

$$AAM = \begin{cases} \dfrac{AA + AAF \times (1 + [0.02 \times SU \times UNFM])}{100} \text{, for } AAF \le 50 \\ \dfrac{AA + AAF + (SU \times UNFM)}{100} \text{, for } AAF > 50 \end{cases}$$

$$AAF = (0.4 \times DM) + (0.3 \times CM) + (0.3 \times IM)$$

**Table 2.44   Sizing Equation Symbol Descriptions**

| Symbol | Description |
|--------|-------------|
| *AA* | Percentage of Assessment and Assimilation |
| *AAF* | Adaptation Adjustment Factor |
| *AAM* | Adaptation Adjustment Modifier |
| *AT* | Percentage of the Adapted KSLOC that is re-engineered by automatic translation |
| *CM* | Percent Code Modified |
| *DM* | Percent Design Modified |
| *IM* | Percent of Integration Integration Required for the Adapted Software |
| *KSLOC* | Thousands of Source Lines of Code |
| *REVL* | Percentage of Requirements Evolution and Volatility |
| *SU* | Percentage of Software Understanding |
| *UNFM* | Programmer Unfamiliarity with Software |

### 2.7.1.2   POST-ARCHITECTURE MODEL EQUATIONS

This model is explained in Section 2.3, and Table 2.45 explains the acronyms.

$$PM = A \cdot \text{Size}^E \times \prod_{i=1}^{17} EM_i + PM_{\text{Auto}}$$

$$E = B + 0.01 \times \sum_{j=1}^{5} SF_j$$

$$PM_{\text{Auto}} = \frac{\text{Adapted } SLOC \times \left( \dfrac{AT}{100} \right)}{ATPROD}$$

**Table 2.45   Post-Architecture Model Symbol Descriptions**

| Symbol | Description |
|--------|-------------|
| *A* | Effort coefficient that can be calibrated, currently set to 2.94 |
| *AT* | Percentage of the adapted SLOC that is reengineered by automatic translation |
| *ATPROD* | Automatic translation productivity |
| *B* | Scaling base-exponent for effort that can be calibrated, currently set to 0.91 |
| *E* | Scaling exponent for effort described in Section 2.3.1 |
| *EM* | 17 Effort Multipliers discussed in Section 2.3.2.1 |
| *PM* | Person-Months effort from developing new and adapted code |
| *PM*<sub>Auto</sub> | Person-Months effort from automatic translation activities discussed in Section 2.2.6. |
| *SF* | 5 Scale Factors discussed in Section 2.3.1 |
| SLOC | Source Lines of Code |

**Table 2.46    Early Design Symbol Descriptions**

| Symbol | Description |
|---|---|
| $A$ | Effort coefficient that can be calibrated, currently set to 2.94 |
| $E$ | Scaling exponent for effort described in Section 2.3.1 |
| $EM$ | 7 Effort Multipliers discussed in Section 2.3.2.2 |
| $PM$ | Person-Months effort from developing new and adapted code |
| $PM_{Auto}$ | Person-Months effort from automatic translation activities discussed in Section 2.2.6. |
| $SF$ | 5 Scale Factors discussed in Section 2.3.1 |
| $SLOC$ | Source Lines of Code |

### 2.7.1.3    EARLY DESIGN MODEL EQUATIONS

This model is explained in Section 2.3. Table 2.46 explains the acronyms.

$$PM = A \cdot Size^E \times \prod_{i=1}^{7} EM_i + PM_{Auto}$$

### 2.7.1.4    TIME TO DEVELOP EQUATION

This equation is explained in Section 2.4. Table 2.47 explains the acronyms.

$$TDEV = [C \times (PM_{NS})^F] \times \frac{SCED\%}{100}$$

$$F = (D + 0.2 \times [E - B])$$

### 2.7.1.5    DRIVER-RATING SCALES

The driver-rating scales for the scaling Cost Drivers are given below in Table 2.48 and discussed in Section 2.3.1.

**Table 2.47    TDEV Equation Symbol Descriptions**

| Symbol | Description |
|---|---|
| $B$ | The scaling base-exponent for the effort equation, currently set to 0.91 |
| $C$ | Schedule coefficient that can be calibrated, currently set to 3.67 |
| $D$ | Scaling base-exponent for schedule that can be calibrated, currently set to 0.28 |
| $E$ | The scaling exponent for the effort equation |
| $F$ | Scaling exponent for schedule |
| $PM_{NS}$ | Person-Months estimated without the SCED cost driver (Nominal Schedule) and without $PM_{AUTO}$ |
| $SCED$ | Percentage of Required Schedule Compression |
| $TDEV$ | Time to Develop in calendar months |

**Table 2.48  Scale Factors for COCOMO II Models**

| Scale Drivers | Very Low | Low | Nominal | High | Very High | Extra High |
|---|---|---|---|---|---|---|
| PREC | thoroughly unprecedented | largely unprecedented | somewhat unprecedented | generally familiar | largely familiar | thoroughly familiar |
| FLEX | rigorous | occasional relaxation | some relaxation | general conformity | some conformity | general goals |
| RESL | little (20%) | some (40%) | often (60%) | generally (75%) | mostly (90%) | full (100%) |
| TEAM | very difficult interactions | some difficult interactions | basically cooperative interactions | largely cooperative | highly cooperative | seamless interactions |
| PMAT | SW-CMM Level 1 Lower | SW-CMM Level 1 Upper | SW-CMM Level 2 | SW-CMM Level 3 | SW-CMM Level 4 | SW-CMM Level 5 |

------------------------ or the estimated Equivalent Process Maturity Level (EPML) --------------------

**Table 2.49   Cost Driver Ratings for Post-Architecture Model**

| Cost Drivers | Very Low | Low | Nominal | High | Very High | Extra High |
|---|---|---|---|---|---|---|
| **RELY** | slight inconvenience | low, easily recoverable losses | moderate, easily recoverable losses | high financial loss | risk to human life | |
| **DATA** | | Testing $DB$ bytes/Pgm SLOC $<10$ | $10 \leq D/P < 100$ | $100 \leq D/P < 1000$ | $L/P > 1000$ | |
| **CPLX** | see Table 2.19 | | | | | |
| **RUSE** | | none | across project | across program | across product line | across multiple product lines |
| **DOCU** | Many life-cycle needs uncovered | Some life-cycle needs uncovered. | Right-sized to life-cycle needs | Excessive for life-cycle needs | Very excessive for life-cycle needs | |
| **TIME** | | | $\leq 50\%$ use of available execution time | 70% | 85% | 95% |
| **STOR** | | | $\leq 50\%$ use of available storage | 70% | 85% | 95% |
| **PVOL** | | major change every 12 mo.; minor change every 1 mo. | major: 6 mo.; minor: 2 wk. | major: 2 mo.; minor: 1 wk. | major: 2 wk.; minor: 2 days | |

| | 15th percentile | 35th percentile | 55th percentile | 75th percentile | 90th percentile | |
|---|---|---|---|---|---|---|
| **ACAP** | 15th percentile | 35th percentile | 55th percentile | 75th percentile | 90th percentile | |
| **PCAP** | 15th percentile | 35th percentile | 55th percentile | 75th percentile | 90th percentile | |
| **PCON** | 48%/year | 24%/year | 12%/year | 6%/year | 3%/year | |
| **APEX** | ≤ 2 months | 6 months | 1 year | 3 years | 6 years | |
| **PLEX** | ≤ 2 months | 6 months | 1 year | 3 years | 6 year | |
| **LTEX** | ≤ 2 months | 6 months | 1 year | 3 years | 6 year | |
| **TOOL** | edit, code, debug | simple, frontend, backend CASE, little integration | basic life-cycle tools, moderately integrated | strong, mature life-cycle tools, moderately-integrated | strong, mature, proactive life-cycle tools, well integrated with processes, methods, reuse | |
| **SITE: Collocation** | International | Multi-city and multi-company | Multi-city or multi-company | Same city or metro area | Same building or complex | Fully collocated |
| **SITE: Communication** | Some phone, mail | Individual phone, FAX | Narrow-band e-mail | Wide-band electronic communication | Wide-band electronic communication, occasional video conference | Interactive multimedia |
| **SCED** | 75% of nominal | 85% of nominal | 100% of nominal | 130% of nominal | 160% of nominal | |

The driver-rating scales for the Post-Architecture model cost drivers are given below in Table 2.49 and discussed in Section 2.3.2.1. The cost drivers for the Early Design model are discussed in Section 2.3.2.2

### 2.7.2    COCOMO II Version Parameter Values

#### 2.7.2.1    COCOMO II.2000 CALIBRATION

The following table, Table 2.50, shows the COCOMO II.2000 calibrated values for Post-Architecture scale factors and effort multipliers.

**Table 2.50    COCOMO II.2000 Post-Architecture Calibrated values**

Baseline Effort Constants:       $A = 2.94$;    $B = 0.91$
Baseline Schedule Constants:    $C = 3.67$;    $D = 0.28$

| Driver | Symbol | VL | L | N | H | VH | XH |
|---|---|---|---|---|---|---|---|
| **PREC** | $SF_1$ | 6.20 | 4.96 | 3.72 | 2.48 | 1.24 | 0.00 |
| **FLEX** | $SF_2$ | 5.07 | 4.05 | 3.04 | 2.03 | 1.01 | 0.00 |
| **RESL** | $SF_3$ | 7.07 | 5.65 | 4.24 | 2.83 | 1.41 | 0.00 |
| **TEAM** | $SF_4$ | 5.48 | 4.38 | 3.29 | 2.19 | 1.10 | 0.00 |
| **PMAT** | $SF_5$ | 7.80 | 6.24 | 4.68 | 3.12 | 1.56 | 0.00 |
| **RELY** | $EM_1$ | 0.82 | 0.92 | 1.00 | 1.10 | 1.26 | |
| **DATA** | $EM_2$ | | 0.90 | 1.00 | 1.14 | 1.28 | |
| **CPLX** | $EM_3$ | 0.73 | 0.87 | 1.00 | 1.17 | 1.34 | 1.74 |
| **RUSE** | $EM_4$ | | 0.95 | 1.00 | 1.07 | 1.15 | 1.24 |
| **DOCU** | $EM_5$ | 0.81 | 0.91 | 1.00 | 1.11 | 1.23 | |
| **TIME** | $EM_6$ | | | 1.00 | 1.11 | 1.29 | 1.63 |
| **STOR** | $EM_7$ | | | 1.00 | 1.05 | 1.17 | 1.46 |
| **PVOL** | $EM_8$ | | 0.87 | 1.00 | 1.15 | 1.30 | |
| **ACAP** | $EM_9$ | 1.42 | 1.19 | 1.00 | 0.85 | 0.71 | |
| **PCAP** | $EM_{10}$ | 1.34 | 1.15 | 1.00 | 0.88 | 0.76 | |
| **PCON** | $EM_{11}$ | 1.29 | 1.12 | 1.00 | 0.90 | 0.81 | |
| **APEX** | $EM_{12}$ | 1.22 | 1.10 | 1.00 | 0.88 | 0.81 | |
| **PLEX** | $EM_{13}$ | 1.19 | 1.09 | 1.00 | 0.91 | 0.85 | |
| **LTEX** | $EM_{14}$ | 1.20 | 1.09 | 1.00 | 0.91 | 0.84 | |
| **TOOL** | $EM_{15}$ | 1.17 | 1.09 | 1.00 | 0.90 | 0.78 | |
| **SITE** | $EM_{16}$ | 1.22 | 1.09 | 1.00 | 0.93 | 0.86 | 0.80 |
| **SCED** | $EM_{17}$ | 1.43 | 1.14 | 1.00 | 1.00 | 1.00 | |

**Table 2.51    COCOMO II.2000 Early Design Calibrated values**

| Baseline Effort Constants: | | $A = 2.94;$ | | $B = 0.91$ | | | |
|---|---|---|---|---|---|---|---|
| Baseline Schedule Constants: | | $C = 3.67;$ | | $D = 0.28$ | | | |

| Driver | Symbol | XL | VL | L | N | H | VH | XH |
|---|---|---|---|---|---|---|---|---|
| PERS | $EM_1$ | 2.12 | 1.62 | 1.26 | 1.00 | 0.83 | 0.63 | 0.50 |
| RCPX | $EM_2$ | 0.49 | 0.60 | 0.83 | 1.00 | 1.33 | 1.91 | 2.72 |
| PDIF | $EM_3$ | | | 0.87 | 1.00 | 1.29 | 1.81 | 2.61 |
| PREX | $EM_4$ | 1.59 | 1.33 | 1.12 | 1.00 | 0.87 | 0.74 | 0.62 |
| FCIL | $EM_5$ | 1.43 | 1.30 | 1.10 | 1.0 | 0.87 | 0.73 | 0.62 |
| RUSE | $EM_6$ | | | 0.95 | 1.00 | 1.07 | 1.15 | 1.24 |
| SCED | $EM_7$ | | 1.43 | 1.14 | 1.00 | 1.00 | 1.00 | |

Table 2.51 shows the COCOMO II.2000 calibrated values for Early Design effort multipliers. The scale factors are the same as for the Post-Architecture model.

### 2.7.2.2    COCOMO II.1997 CALIBRATION

Table 2.52 shows the COCOMO II.1997 calibrated values for scale factors and effort multipliers.

## 2.7.3    Logical Lines of Source Code Counting Rules

What is a line of source code? This checklist, Table 2.53, adopted from the Software Engineering Institute [Park 1992], attempts to define a *logical* line of source code. The intent is to define a logical line of code while not becoming too language specific for use in collection data to validate the COCOMO II model.

## 2.7.4    COCOMO Model comparisons

Since the 1981 publication of *Software Engineering Economics*, there have been upgrades and modifications to COCOMO. The latest upgrade to the model is presented in this chapter. Table 2.54 contrasts the differences of two major upgrades to the original COCOMO 1981 model: Ada COCOMO and COCOMO II.

**Table 2.52    COCOMO II.1997 Post-Architecture Calibrated values**

Baseline Effort Constants:     $A = 2.45$;      $B = 1.01$
Baseline Schedule Constants:    $C = 2.66$;      $D = 0.33$

| Driver | Symbol | VL | L | N | H | VH | XH |
|--------|--------|------|------|------|------|------|------|
| PREC | $SF_1$ | 4.05 | 3.24 | 2.43 | 1.62 | 0.81 | 0.00 |
| FLEX | $SF_2$ | 6.07 | 4.86 | 3.64 | 2.43 | 1.21 | 0.00 |
| RESL | $SF_3$ | 4.22 | 3.38 | 2.53 | 1.69 | 0.84 | 0.00 |
| TEAM | $SF_4$ | 4.94 | 3.95 | 2.97 | 1.98 | 0.99 | 0.00 |
| PMAT | $SF_5$ | 4.54 | 3.64 | 2.73 | 1.82 | 0.91 | 0.00 |
| RELY | $EM_1$ | 0.75 | 0.88 | 1.00 | 1.15 | 1.39 | |
| DATA | $EM_2$ | | 0.93 | 1.00 | 1.09 | 1.19 | |
| RUSE | $EM_3$ | | 0.91 | 1.00 | 1.14 | 1.29 | 1.49 |
| DOCU | $EM_4$ | 0.89 | 0.95 | 1.00 | 1.06 | 1.13 | |
| CPLX | $EM_5$ | 0.75 | 0.88 | 1.00 | 1.15 | 1.30 | 1.66 |
| TIME | $EM_6$ | | | 1.00 | 1.11 | 1.31 | 1.67 |
| STOR | $EM_7$ | | | 1.00 | 1.06 | 1.21 | 1.57 |
| PVOL | $EM_8$ | | 0.87 | 1.00 | 1.15 | 1.30 | |
| ACAP | $EM_9$ | 1.50 | 1.22 | 1.00 | 0.83 | 0.67 | |
| PCAP | $EM_{10}$ | 1.37 | 1.16 | 1.00 | 0.87 | 0.74 | |
| PCON | $EM_{11}$ | 1.24 | 1.10 | 1.00 | 0.92 | 0.84 | |
| APEX | $EM_{12}$ | 1.22 | 1.10 | 1.00 | 0.89 | 0.81 | |
| PLEX | $EM_{13}$ | 1.25 | 1.12 | 1.00 | 0.88 | 0.81 | |
| LTEX | $EM_{14}$ | 1.22 | 1.10 | 1.00 | 0.91 | 0.84 | |
| TOOL | $EM_{15}$ | 1.24 | 1.12 | 1.00 | 0.86 | 0.72 | |
| SITE | $EM_{16}$ | 1.25 | 1.10 | 1.00 | 0.92 | 0.84 | 0.78 |
| SCED | $EM_{17}$ | 1.29 | 1.10 | 1.00 | 1.00 | 1.00 | |

| Table 2.53    Definition Checklist for Source Statements Counts |
| --- |

**Definition Checklist for Source Statements Counts**

| Definition name: | Logical Source Statements (basic definition) | Date: _____ Originator: COCOMO II |
| --- | --- | --- |

| Measurement unit: | Physical source lines | |
| --- | --- | --- |
| | Logical source statements | ✓ |

| Statement type | Definition | ✓ | Data Array | | | Includes | Excludes |
| --- | --- | --- | --- | --- | --- | --- | --- |
| *When a line or statement contains more than one type, classify it as the type with the highest precedence.* | | | | | | | |
| 1 Executable | | | Order of precedence: | | 1 | ✓ | |
| 2 Nonexecutable | | | | | | | |
|   3 Declarations | | | | | 2 | ✓ | |
|   4 Compiler directives | | | | | 3 | ✓ | |
|   5 Comments | | | | | | | |
|     6 On their own lines | | | | | 4 | | ✓ |
|     7 On lines with source code | | | | | 5 | | ✓ |
|     8 Banners and non-blank spacers | | | | | 6 | | ✓ |
|     9 Blank (empty) comments | | | | | 7 | | ✓ |
|     10 Blank lines | | | | | 8 | | ✓ |

| How produced | Definition | ✓ | Data array | | Includes | Excludes |
| --- | --- | --- | --- | --- | --- | --- |
| 1 Programmed | | | | | ✓ | |
| 2 Generated with source code generators | | | | | | ✓ |
| 3 Converted with automated translators | | | | | ✓ | |
| 4 Copied or reused without change | | | | | ✓ | |
| 5 Modified | | | | | ✓ | |
| 6 Removed | | | | | | ✓ |

| Origin | Definition | ✓ | Data array | | Includes | Excludes |
| --- | --- | --- | --- | --- | --- | --- |
| 1 New work: no prior existence | | | | | ✓ | |
| 2 Prior work: taken or adapted from | | | | | | |
|   3 A previous version, build, or release | | | | | ✓ | |
|   4 Commercial, off-the-shelf software (COTS), other than libraries | | | | | | ✓ |
|   5 Government furnished software (GFS), other than reuse libraries | | | | | | ✓ |
|   6 Another product | | | | | | ✓ |
|   7 A vendor-supplied language support library (unmodified) | | | | | | ✓ |
|   8 A vendor-supplied operating system or utility (unmodified) | | | | | | ✓ |
|   9 A local or modified language support library or operating system | | | | | | ✓ |
|   10 Other commercial library | | | | | | ✓ |
|   11 A reuse library (software designed for reuse) | | | | | ✓ | |
|   12 Other software component or library | | | | | ✓ | |

| Usage | Definition | ✓ | Data array | | Includes | Excludes |
| --- | --- | --- | --- | --- | --- | --- |
| 1 In or as part of the primary product | | | | | ✓ | |
| 2 External to or in support of the primary product | | | | | | ✓ |

*(continued)*

**Table 2.53** *continued*

### Definition Checklist for Source Statements Counts

| Definition name: | Logical Source Statements (basic definition) | | Date: _____ Originator: COCOMO II | | | |

| Delivery | **Definition** ✓ | **Data array** [  ] | | **Includes** | **Excludes** |
|---|---|---|---|---|---|
| 1 Delivered: | | | | | |
| 2 Delivered as source | | | | ✓ | |
| 3 Delivered in compiled or executable form, but not as source | | | | | ✓ |
| 4 Not delivered: | | | | | |
| 5 Under configuration control | | | | | ✓ |
| 6 Not under configuration control | | | | | ✓ |

| Functionality | **Definition** ✓ | **Data array** [  ] | | **Includes** | **Excludes** |
|---|---|---|---|---|---|
| 1 Operative | | | | ✓ | |
| 2 Inoperative (dead, bypassed, unused, unreferenced, or unaccessible): | | | | | |
| 3 Functional (intentional dead code, reactivated for special purposes) | | | | ✓ | |
| 4 Nonfunctional (unintentionally present) | | | | | ✓ |

| Replications | **Definition** ✓ | **Data array** [  ] | | **Includes** | **Excludes** |
|---|---|---|---|---|---|
| 1 Master source statements (originals) | | | | ✓ | |
| 2 Physical replicates of master statements, stored in the master code | | | | ✓ | |
| 3 Copies inserted, instantiated, or expanded when compiling or linking | | | | | ✓ |
| 4 Postproduction replicates—as in distributed, redundant, or reparameterized systems | | | | | ✓ |

| Development status | **Definition** ✓ | **Data array** [  ] | | **Includes** | **Excludes** |
|---|---|---|---|---|---|
| *Each statement has one and only one status, usually that of its parent unit.* | | | | | |
| 1 Estimated or planned | | | | | ✓ |
| 2 Designed | | | | | ✓ |
| 3 Coded | | | | | ✓ |
| 4 Unit tests completed | | | | | ✓ |
| 5 Integrated into components | | | | | ✓ |
| 6 Test readiness review completed | | | | | ✓ |
| 7 Software (CSCI) tests completed | | | | | ✓ |
| 8 System tests completed | | | | ✓ | |

| Language | **Definition** ✓ | **Data array** [  ] | | **Includes** | **Excludes** |
|---|---|---|---|---|---|
| *List each source language on a separate line.* | | | | | |
| 1 Separate totals for each language | | | | ✓ | |

| Table 2.53   *continued* |
|---|

### Definition Checklist for Source Statements Counts

Definition name:   Logical Source Statements          Date: _____
                   (basic definition)               Originator: COCOMO II

| Clarifications | Definition | ✓ | Data array | | Includes | Excludes |
|---|---|---|---|---|---|---|
| *(general)* | | | | | | |
| 1  Nulls, continues, and no-ops | | | | | ✓ | |
| 2  Empty statements, e.g. ";;" and lone semicolons on separate lines | | | | | | ✓ |
| 3  Statements that instantiate generics | | | | | ✓ | |
| 4  Begin...end and {...} pairs used as executable statements | | | | | ✓ | |
| 5  Begin...end and {...} pairs that delimit (sub)program bodies | | | | | | ✓ |
| 6  Logical expressions used as test conditions | | | | | | ✓ |
| 7  Expression evaluations used as subprograms arguments | | | | | | ✓ |
| 8  End symbols that terminate executable statements | | | | | | ✓ |
| 9  End symbols that terminate declarations or (sub)program bodies | | | | | | ✓ |
| 10  Then, else, and otherwise symbols | | | | | | ✓ |
| 11  Elseif statements | | | | | ✓ | |
| 12  Keywords like procedure division, interface, and implementation | | | | | ✓ | |
| 13  Labels (branching destinations) on lines by themselves | | | | | | ✓ |
| **Clarifications** | **Definition** | ✓ | **Data array** | | **Includes** | **Excludes** |
| *(language specific)* | | | | | | |
| **Ada** | | | | | | |
| 1  End symbols that terminate declarations or (sub)program bodies | | | | | | ✓ |
| 2  Block statements, e.g. begin...end | | | | | ✓ | |
| 3  With and use clauses | | | | | ✓ | |
| 4  When (the keyword preceding executable statements) | | | | | | ✓ |
| 5  Exception (the keyword, used as a frame header) | | | | | ✓ | |
| 6  Pragmas | | | | | ✓ | |
| **Assembly** | | | | | | |
| 1  Macro calls | | | | | ✓ | |
| 2  Macro expansions | | | | | | ✓ |
| **C and C++** | | | | | | |
| 1  Null statement, e.g. ";" by itself to indicate an empty body | | | | | | ✓ |
| 2  Expression statements (expressions terminated by semicolons) | | | | | ✓ | |
| 3  Expression separated by semicolons, as in a "for" statement | | | | | ✓ | |
| 4  Block statements, e.g. {...} with no terminating semicolon | | | | | ✓ | |
| 5  ";", ";" or ";" on a line by itself when part of a declaration | | | | | | ✓ |
| 6  ";" or ";" on a line by itself when part of an executable statement | | | | | | ✓ |
| 7  Conditionally compiled statements (#if, #ifdef, #ifndef) | | | | | ✓ | |
| 8  Preprocessor statements other than #if, #ifdef, and #ifndef | | | | | ✓ | |

*(continued)*

**Table 2.53**  *continued*

### Definition Checklist for Source Statements Counts

| Definition name: | Logical Source Statements (basic definition) | Date: _____ Originator: COCOMO II | | | |
|---|---|---|---|---|---|

| Clarifications | Definition | ✓ | Data array | | Includes | Excludes |
|---|---|---|---|---|---|---|
| *(language specific)* | | | | | | |
| **CMS-2** | | | | | | |
| 1 Keywords like SYS-PROC and SYS-DD | | | | | ✓ | |
| **COBOL** | | | | | | |
| 1 "PROCEDURE DIVISION", "END DECLARATIVES", etc. | | | | | ✓ | |
| **FORTRAN** | | | | | | |
| 1 END statements | | | | | ✓ | |
| 2 Format statements | | | | | ✓ | |
| 3 Entry statements | | | | | ✓ | |
| **Pascal** | | | | | | |
| 1 Executable statements not terminated by semicolons | | | | | ✓ | |
| 2 Keywords like INTERFACE and IMPLEMENTATION | | | | | ✓ | |
| 3 FORWARD declarations | | | | | ✓ | |

### Summary of Statement Types

### Executable statements

Executable statements cause runtime actions. They may be simple statements such as assignments, goto's, procedure calls, macro calls, returns, breaks, exits, stops, continues, nulls, no-ops, empty statements, and FORTRAN's END. Or they may be structured or compound statements, such as conditional statements, repetitive statements, and "with" statements. Languages like Ada, C, C++, and Pascal have block statements [begin...end and {...}] that are classified as executable when used where other executable statements would be permitted. C and C++ define expressions as executable statements when they terminate with a semicolon, and C++ has a <declaration> statement that is executable.

### Declarations

Declarations are nonexecutable program elements that affect an assembler's or compiler's interpretation of other program elements They are used to name, define, and initialize; to specify internal and external interfaces; to assign ranges for bounds checking; and to identify and bound modules and sections of code. Examples include declarations of names, numbers, constants, objects, types, subtypes, programs, subprograms, tasks, exceptions, packages, generics, macros, and deferred constants. Declarations also include renaming declarations, use clauses, and declarations that instantiate generics. Mandatory begin...end and {...} symbols that delimit bodies of programs and subprograms are integral parts of program and subprogram declarations. Language superstructure elements that establish boundaries for different sections of source code are also declarations. Examples include terms such as PROCEDURE DIVISION, DATA DIVISION, DECLARATIVES, END DECLARATIVES, INTERFACE, IMPLEMENTATION, SYS-PROC and

| Table 2.53 *continued* |
| --- |

SYS-DD. Declarations, in general, are never required by language specifications to initiate run-time actions, although some languages permit compilers to implement them that way.

**Compiler Directives**

Compiler directives instruct compilers, preprocessors, or translators (but not runtime systems) to perform special actions. Some, such as Ada's pragma and COBOL's COPY, REPLACE, and USE, are integral parts of the source language. In other languages like C and C++, special symbols like # are used along with standardized keywords to direct preprocessor or compiler actions. Still other languages rely on nonstandardized methods supplied by compiler vendors. In these languages, directives are often designated by special symbols such as #, $, and {$}.

**Table 2.54  COCOMO Model Comparisons**

| | COCOMO 81 | Ada COCOMO | COCOMO II Early Design | COCOMO II Post-Architecture |
|---|---|---|---|---|
| Size | Delivered Source Instructions (DSI) or Source Lines of Code (SLOC) | DSI or SLOC | Function Points (FP) with Language or SLOC | FP with Language or SLOC |
| Reuse | Equivalent SLOC = Linear f(DM,CM,IM) | Equivalent SLOC = Linear f(DM,CM,IM) | Equivalent SLOC = nonlinear f(AA,SU,UNFM, DM,CM,IM) | Equivalent SLOC = nonlinear f(AA,SU,UNFM,DM, CM,IM) |
| Requirements Change | Requirements Volatility rating (RVOL) | RVOL rating | Change %: Requirements Evolution (REVL) | REVL |
| Maintenance | Annual Change Traffic (ACT) = (%added + % modified)/yr. | ACT | f(MCF, SU, UNFM) MCF = (% added + % modified) | f(MCF, SU, UNFM) |
| Scale Drivers, B, in $PM_{Nom} = A(Size)^B$ | Organic: 1.05 Semidetached: 1.12 Embedded: 1.20 | Embedded: 1.04–1.24 depending on the degree of: –early-risk elimination –solid architecture –stable requirements –Ada process maturity | B = 0.91–1.23[3] depending on the degree of: –precedentedness –development conformity –early architecture and risk resolution –team Cohesion –process maturity | B = 0.91–1.23[3] depending on the degree of: –predecentedness –development conformity –early architecture and risk resolution –team Cohesion –process maturity |
| Product Cost Drivers | RELY, DATA, CPLX | RELY[1], DATA, CPLX[1], RUSE | RCPX[1,2], RUSE[1,2] | RELY[1], DATA[1], DOCU[1,2], CPLX[1,2], RUSE[1,2] |
| Platform Cost Drivers | TIME, STOR, VIRT, TURN | TIME, STOR, VMVH, VMVT, TURN | Platform difficulty: PDIF[1,2] | TIME[1], STOR[1], PVOL[1] (=VIRT) |
| Personnel Cost Drivers | ACAP, AEXP, PCAP, VEXP, LEXP | ACAP[1], AEXP, PCAP[1], VEXP, LEXP | Personnel capability and experience: PERS[1,2], PREX[1,2] | ACAP[1], PCAP[1], PCON[1,2], APEX[1,2], LTEX[1,2], PLEX[1,2] |
| Project Cost Drivers | MODP, TOOL, SCED | MODP[1], TOOL[1], SCED, SECU | SCED[1], FCIL[1,2] | TOOL[1,2], SCED[1], SITE[1,2] |

[1]Different multipliers
[2]Different rating scale
[3]For COCOMO II.2000 calibration

# 3

# Application Examples

## 3.1 INTRODUCTION

This chapter provides a set of examples designed to show you how to use the COCOMO II model to develop estimates, perform trade studies, and do other useful work (justifying the purchase of software tools, performing risk analysis, etc.). The first example updates the problem used to illustrate model features and usage in the original COCOMO text published in 1981 [Boehm 1981]. The second example provides an in-depth look at the issues associated with estimating resources using the COCOMO II model for a real-time sensor system. Both examples are used to illustrate model usage in the remaining chapters of the book. Both examples are also included on the accompanying CD so that you can exercise the model to generate the results described as you read the book.

## 3.2 TRANSACTION PROCESSING SYSTEM (TPS) OVERVIEW

This section describes a transaction processing system that can be used to interactively process queries and perform a variety of user functions across a network. We will use this example to show how to use the COCOMO II model to develop estimates for a variety of purposes (cost the original system, perform tradeoffs, etc.).

### 3.2.1   Transaction Processing System (TPS) Description

The TPS is a client-server system developed to allow users to access information of interest from different hosts across wideband communications networks. The distinguishing features of the TPS are:

- Input transactions are generated by users on their client workstations at un-specified (unpredictable) times.
- Input transactions are processed by servers as quickly as possible within rel-atively short time periods (i.e., typically generate some form of response in seconds).
- Users may multiprocess as they wait for transactions to be processed (i.e., do other work on their workstations as they wait).
- The amount of processing involved in a transaction is not large.

The type of transactions being processed might involve airline reservations, financial transactions (e.g., stock purchases, account queries), library searches, and/or remote database browsing. The techniques used in this book to develop and refine estimates for an example TPS could pertain to any such system.

Figure 3.1 illustrates the basic configuration of the TPS we will use as our example. The basic node at your site links fifty workstations via a Local Area Network (LAN) to a machine whose primary function is to act as a file server. Other nodes that are geographically dispersed can be linked together via a

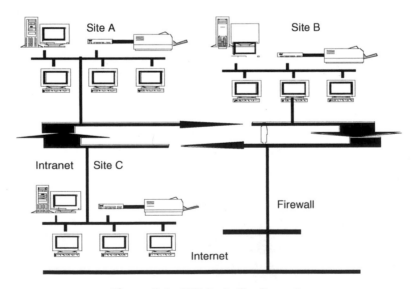

**Figure 3.1**   TPS Basic Configuration

privately-owned Intranet as either clients or servers. You can also link to the Internet to gain access to other servers after passing through a firewall.

### 3.2.2 Transaction Processing System (TPS) Software Functions

The software functions have been allocated to clients/servers in this configuration as shown in Table 3.1. Both clients and servers are connected together via the network. Transactions are communicated to/from clients and servers via the intra/internet interactively. The client workstation recognizes the query/command and generates a message to be sent to the appropriate client/server for action. The communications function determines the appropriate protocol and packages the message prior to initiating transmission. Servers respond to client requests for information based upon pre-established protocols with acknowledgements. Files (data, multimedia, etc.) or applets of information are transmitted back using prioritized conventions (e.g., acknowledge receipt or retransmit). Clients may manipulate the data received to generate a variety of user-defined or programmable textual/graphical reports using a variety of software applications developed for that purpose. Reports can be predefined or developed by the user interactively. User applications may be linked into the process using a variety of tools (templates, frameworks, etc.) provided for that purpose. Both client and server systems have authentication and security controls built-in to protect against unauthorized access. Both systems perform synchronization and status

**Table 3.1   TPS Software Capabilities**

| Client Software | Server Software |
| --- | --- |
| *Systems functions* | *Systems functions* |
| • Command processing | • Command processing |
| • Communications | • Communications |
| • Protocol conversion | • Protocol conversion |
| • Security and integrity controls | • Security and integrity controls |
| • Utilities | • Resource management |
| *User applications* | • Utilities/libraries |
| • Report generation | *Query processing* |
| • Screen processing | • Database management |
| • Transaction processing | • File management |
|   • Authentication | • Persistent database management |
|   • Receipt and display | *Status monitoring* |
| • User applications | • Checksum processing |
| *Fault diagnosis* | *Fault diagnosis* |
| • Built-in testing | • Built-in testing |
| • Fault isolation and recovery management | • Fault isolation and recovery management |

monitoring functions in order to make sure that requests for service are handled within appropriate time limits. Built-in test functions are performed to diagnose problems and isolate faults to the line replaceable unit.

### 3.2.3    Transaction Processing System (TPS) Software Development Organization

The organization developing software for the TPS is very talented and progressive. They have a young, educated, and motivated staff. Most of their programmers have at least four years of experience with client-server applications and are skilled in the use of the C/C++ programming language and the rich programming environment you have provided them. Getting equipment and software tools for your staff is not a problem because upper management understands the need to capitalize software. Each programmer assigned to the project has an average of 2.3 workstations available. Technical training is encouraged with on-site classes being offered in areas where new skills need to be built (Java, persistent databases, specialized tools, web programming, etc.). Management encourages technical people to take at least two weeks of training during office hours per year. Both university and internally taught classes are held on-site and there is ample opportunity for everyone to participate in them. In addition, your organization has recently launched a lunch-time seminar program which invites experts from the local community to speak on-site.

The organization also mounted an aggressive software process improvement effort two years ago. Best practices used in the past have been collected and a repeatable process has been inserted for everyone to use. Processes and best practices are available on-line along with examples that are designed to serve as models for new starts. Most programmers have bought into the process and it is being used extensively throughout most shops. Management is proud that they were rated a SEI Level 2 last year according to the Software Engineering Institute's Software Capability Maturity Model (CMM). An improvement effort is underway, and the organization will reach Level 3 by next year.

As expected, the organization does have some problems. Its first-level managers are chosen based upon their technical skills and the respect shown by their peers. Little training in management is provided, although new managers are exposed to good management practices through scheduled process initiative training. Many times, these good technical practitioners have difficulty making the transition into management. The process group has suggested a new supervisor-training program and a mentor relationship. Management is debating the issue and has yet to fund either of these training initiatives.

A second problem has emerged relative to the use of programming language. Some of your technical leaders argue for C/C++, while others demand Java. Upper management doesn't know which alternative to pursue. Work done using both technologies has been impressive. The company has purchased compilers and tools for both and is convinced that each alternative has advantages. At this time, both languages are being used because management cannot make up their minds about a language. Management has asked the process group to address their dilemma by using their metrics data to build a business case for or against Java/C++.

Another problem being experienced has to do with estimating. Effort and schedule estimates generated by technical teams tend to come in two flavors: overly optimistic and overly pessimistic. Management tries, but teams generating estimates most often believe the jobs will be simpler than they are. These same teams are highly motivated and try to deliver what they promise. As a result, they often work long hours and weekends to try to catch up when they get into trouble. Because they come close to burnout, they tend to overestimate the job the next time through. Management is bringing in estimating tools and training to try to improve the situation. Time will tell whether or not they will be successful in this venture.

The final problem deals with metrics. Major battles are being fought over which metrics should be collected and what their definitions are. Two camps have emerged: the lines of code versus the function point advocates. Both sides argue the merits of their cause. Both refuse to use the other measure of the work involved. Both quote the experts and are religious in their beliefs. As a consequence, estimates come in using different bases. The process team is upset because their efforts to create a consistent cost database seem stymied.

### 3.2.4   Transaction Processing System (TPS) Software Development Estimate

You have been asked to develop an estimate for the effort involved in developing TPS client-side software. Management has stated that the effort must be completed in eighteen months maximum because of commitments they have made to customers. In other words, the schedule is a given. You are lucky because the process group has devised the estimating process illustrated in Figure 3.2 for such use. The process calls for developing two estimates independently and comparing them to see where and why there are differences. Unfortunately, you have never used this process before. Your first attempt at developing an estimate will therefore be a learning experience.

The first stage in the process involves the development team working with the clients to determine the most essential software functions needed and their associated sizes. Table 3.2 summarizes the components identified by the team along with their associated sizes. Notice that both lines of code and function points have been provided for your use as size estimates. You will have to figure out how to relate the two as you use your estimating tool.

As the second stage in the process, the software development team will generate a set of estimates for each of their work tasks using the standard Work Breakdown Structure (WBS) developed for that purpose which is illustrated in Figure 3.3. The WBS represents the family tree of the work that your staff must

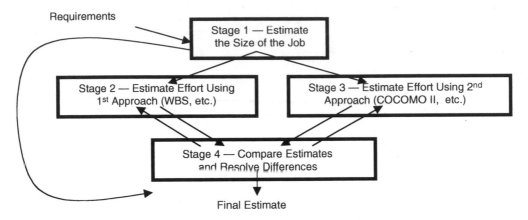

**Figure 3.2**    Estimating Process

perform to implement your tailored version of your organization's defined process. Your staff will justify their task estimates based upon past experience with similar projects and document their assumptions using worksheets. They will also document any exceptions that they need to satisfy the customer. The total effort for the project will be the sum of the individual task estimates.

In parallel with the team's effort, the process group will develop an independent estimate using the COCOMO II Post-Architecture model as Stage 3. The standard Work Breakdown Structure to be used to develop this model-based estimate is portrayed in Figure 3.3 and Section 3.2.4.3. Assumptions made by the team relative to model parameters will be explained in subparagraphs. You have

**Table 3.2    Size for Identified Functions**

| Component | Functions | Size | Notes |
|---|---|---|---|
| Systems software | • Communications driver<br>• Protocol converters<br>• Authentication module<br>• Class libraries (e.g., widgets, filters, active components) | 18KSLOC (new)<br>10KSLOC (reused) | Libraries are brought as-is from vendors. Extensions to the library and glue code included as new |
| User applications | • Screens and reports<br>• Interface for user-developed applications | 800 SLOC (new) | Human interface developed using a GUIbuilder and graphical 4GL (Visual Basic) |
| Fault diagnosis | • Built-in test<br>• Fault isolation logic<br>• Recovery management | 8K function points | Brand-new concept using neural nets to make determinations and findings |

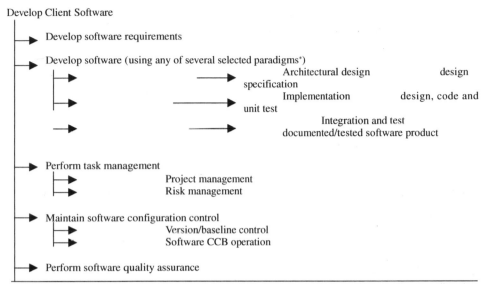

Develop Client Software

— ▶ Develop software requirements

— ▶ Develop software (using any of several selected paradigms*)
    ├ ▶      — ▶ Architectural design               design specification
    ├ ▶      — ▶ Implementation          design, code and unit test
     — ▶      — ▶ Integration and test documented/tested software product

— ▶ Perform task management
    ├ ▶ Project management
    ├ ▶ Risk management

— ▶ Maintain software configuration control
    ├ ▶ Version/baseline control
    ├ ▶ Software CCB operation

— ▶ Perform software quality assurance

*The tasks shown can be accomplished using the waterfall, phased, incremental, or other paradigm by defining the anchor points and phase activities using the MBASE/RUP model described in Chapter 2.

**Figure 3.3**   Standard Work Breakdown Structure

read several papers and have purchased this book on the COCOMO II model and are anxious to start using it. It sounds like it will help you get the job done with increased accuracy.

Differences between estimates will be examined and adjustments for risk and customer requirements will be made during the final stage of the process. These adjustments may force the estimating teams to generate additional estimates to address the "what-if" questions that are typically posed as the developers and clients resolve tradeoffs, address differing priorities and attempt to finalize their estimate.

Table 3.3 provides you with another way to look at the work included within the scope of a COCOMO II estimate. The activities listed are identified as either within or outside the scope of the estimate. This is an important consideration because the estimate needs to reflect the data upon which the model was calibrated. Several COCOMO packages allow the user to estimate the tasks outside the scope using a percentage of the estimated software development effort. For example, the requirements synthesis activity could be added by assuming a 6 to 10 percent delta cost for this activity.

We want to follow the standard process to develop our estimates. Let's agree to use the process illustrated in Figure 3.2. We will develop a WBS-based and COCOMO estimate as the basis of our final forecast. Then, we will compare the estimates and try to resolve the differences. Once this is accomplished, we

**Table 3.3   COCOMO Model Scope**

| Activity | In or Out of Scope |
|---|:---:|
| Requirements (RQ) | Out |
| Product Design (PD) | In |
| Implementation (IM) | In |
| Integration & Test (I&T) | In |
| Project Management (PM) | In |
| Project Configuration Management (CM) | In |
| Project Quality Assurance (QA) | In |
| Project Management activities done above the project level | Out |

will submit the estimate and see what management says relative to the acceptability of the costs.

### 3.2.4.1   STAGE 1—ESTIMATE THE SIZE OF THE JOB

The first thing we have to do is to check the reasonableness of the initially provided size estimates. We also have to convert them into equivalent new source lines of code (SLOC) using the formulas provided in earlier chapters of the book. Let's attack this task by component. We understand that we must develop conventions for and address the following four types of software in these estimates:

1. New
2. Modifed
3. Reused
4. COTS

The systems software component looks reasonable. It is neither large in size nor entirely new. Lots of libraries are utilized. However, we must convert the reused software to equivalent new lines. We will do this using the following formula:

$$AAF = 0.4(DM) + 0.3(CM) + 0.3(IM)$$

where

$DM$ = % Design Modified = 0%
$CM$ = % Code Modified = 0%
$IM$ = % Integration Modified = 50%

(Note: $IM$ is defined as "Percent of Integration Required for Modified Software." It assumes that integration activities are repeated, not modified.)

The reused libraries are vendor-supplied. They are neither design nor code modified. Reused software is by definition designed to be instantiated without change [Reifer, 1997a]. However, the libraries will be wrapped and integrated into the system software component and tested extensively. The libraries are extendable, and the user will probably add functionality as the software is developed. Any new library and glue software will be treated as new code. The *AAF* for the reused software is therefore computed a number between 0 and 100 as follows:

$$AAF = 0.4(0) + 0.3(0) + 0.3(50) = 15$$

This means that each line of reused code will be treated as 0.15 line of new code when we compute effort. We are not finished. We must factor in the effort needed to understand and assimilate the libraries into the build using the following formula:

$$ESLOC = \{ASLOC[AA + AAF(1 + 0.02(SU)(UNFM))]\}/100$$

when $$AAF \leq 50$$

This factor adds effort to understand what the reused software does and how to interface it to the rest of the system. Some systems are self-explanatory while others take a lot of effort to comprehend.

Using tables provided earlier in the text, we select the following values for the software understanding increment (*SU*), degree of assessment and assimilation (*AA*), and level of unfamiliarity (*UNFM*):

| Parameter | Value | Description |
|---|---|---|
| *SU* | 20 | High cohesion, good code |
| *AA* | 4% | Some module Test & Evaluation, documentation |
| *UNFM* | 0.8 | Mostly unfamiliar |

Plugging these values and the value of *AAF* into the *ESLOC* formula, we develop the following equivalent size (note that *SU* is set to zero when *DM* and *CM* = 0 per Chapter 2):

$$ESLOC = 10{,}000[.04 + 0.15(1 + 0.02(20)(0.0))] = 10{,}000[0.04 + 0.15]$$
$$= 10{,}000[.19] = 1{,}900 \ SLOC$$

The size of the system software component is therefore estimated to be 19,900 *SLOC* of equivalent new code (18,000 + 1,900). As previously noted, this size estimate includes glue code development and library extensions.

The size of the next component, user applications, takes some reflection. Although the GUI-builder will generate thousands of lines of code, we will write only 800 lines of new Visual Basic script. From a productivity point of view, we will like to take credit for those lines that we don't have to generate. But, from a costing viewpoint, all we have to generate is 800 lines.

The size of the final component, fault diagnosis, is in function points. Function points are a language independent measure that represents the volume of work we have to do to get the product out. As we've seen in earlier chapters, the COCOMO model converts unadjusted function point counts to equivalent new source lines of code using the following backfiring equation that assumes a specific language or language level:

$$ESLOC = FP \text{ (language conversion factor)}$$

Assuming an 80 SLOC/FP language conversion factor (i.e., we selected Third Generation language because it represented the midpoint for the backfiring conversion; i.e., between 53 to 128), our 8,000 function points converts to 640,000 source lines of code. This doesn't seem reasonable. The estimator must have made a mistake in counting. We must ask the estimator to look the estimate over to confirm that the size is as large as he thinks it is going to be.

After checking with the estimator, you learn that he did not count function points properly. Instead of counting each repeat input and output one time, he counted them every time. In a diagnosis system, there are a lot of repeat operations especially when dealing with neural nets. These neural networks remotely query the system to determine whether components are exhibiting potential failure patterns (i.e., remote failure diagnosis via local diagnostics at the component level). If they do, the neural networks trigger an alarm, make repairs and/or identify potential repair actions (i.e., if repairs cannot be made, fixes are suggested on the maintenance console). Many alarms are typically generated. Each of these was counted instead of each class of alarm. After recounting using the proper counting conventions, the estimator comes up with a total count of 300 function points. Using the same language conversion factor, this equates to 24,000 equivalent source lines of code. This count seems much more reasonable.

You have used a mixture of function points and SLOC to develop your size estimate. This isn't bad. COCOMO is a SLOC-based model. Function points are converted to SLOC using the backfiring tables. After some debate, both metrics will be carried forward because others have found it useful to keep function points to track their productivity and to keep SLOC to track their effort and costs.

### 3.2.4.2   STAGE 2—ESTIMATE EFFORT USING THE WBS APPROACH

Now that we have sized the job, let's look at developing our first cost estimate for the client-side software. To do this, we will estimate the cost of each of the tasks in the Work Breakdown Structure (WBS) shown in Figure 3.3 and sum them across all of the line items [Reifer, 1997b]. The results are summarized in Table 3.4.

#### 3.2.4.2.1   Task 1—Define Software Requirements.   There are several ways we could cost the requirements effort. The simplest approach is one where

**Table 3.4   Summary of WBS Estimate**

| WBS Task | Estimate (staff hours) | Basis of Estimate |
|---|---|---|
| 1. Develop software requirements | 1,600 | Mutiplied number of requirements by productivity figure |
| 2. Develop software | 22,350 | Multiplied source lines of code by productivity figure |
| 3. Perform task management | 2,235 | Assumed a 10 percent surcharge to account for the effort |
| 4. Maintain configuration control | 1,440 | Assumed a dedicated person assigned to the task |
| 5. Perform software quality assurance | 1,440 | Assumed a dedicated person assigned to the task |
| **TOTAL** | 29,065 | |

we use our experience to determine how long it would take a team composed of client-side experts to firm up the requirements. For example, let's assume that an Integrated Product Team composed of three full-time people and several part-timers over a period of twelve weeks accomplished the effort. To quantify the effort involved, we would have to make numerous assumptions. For example, we might assume that a rapid user-interface prototype would be developed for use as a tool to get the users to put their thoughts on the screen interfaces to paper. We would also have to assume that the right experts would be available when we need them to facilitate development of the requirements. Based upon these assumptions, we would estimate the effort at 1,680 hours assuming that you needed 3.5 people for the 12 weeks.

As an option, we might use rules of thumb developed based upon previous experience to develop our effort estimate. For example, we might estimate that there were 200 requirements. Based upon experience, we might estimate the effort based upon some heuristic like "it takes on average 8 hours/requirement to develop an acceptable work product." The resulting estimate for this task would then be 1,600 hours. The advantages of this approach are that it is simple and you could argue for additional budget every time there was growth in the requirements. If there is volatility, you could adjust the heuristic for breakage or volatility based upon some expected/assumed percentage of rework [i.e., 1.2 (8 hours/requirement) to account for an estimated 20% rework factor].

As a final alternative, you could estimate the effort associated with requirements using some percentage of the software development effort that you will derive for task 2. Based upon your experience, you might add from 6 to 12 percent of this effort in hours to compensate for the additional hours needed to develop a stable set of requirements. For example, you might add 7 percent when using the waterfall model for this activity.

When using MBASE/RUP model, you might add 6 percent in the Inception Phase to handle the requirements task (i.e., as noted in earlier chapters, the amount of effort in MBASE will vary as a function of phase/activity distribution).

When using Integrated Product Teams to define requirements, you should increase the team's effort to 10 or 12 percent to cover the participation of other disciplines in the activity. Ten to 12 percent might even be low when requirements are vague and a great deal of discovery has to be performed to figure out what the user truly wants from the system.

**3.2.4.2.2   Task 2—Develop Software.**   To quantify the effort associated with developing software, you will need some measure of the size of the job and some basis of estimate. For example, we might develop our estimate based upon a number of standard building blocks or modules. We could break each component into a number of parts and estimate each part based upon some standard metric. For example, we could assume the diagnostic component had 16 parts and each part took 100 hours to design, develop and test. The resulting estimate would be 1,600 hours for the fault diagnosis component. The estimate scope assumed would typically be from the requirements review until completion of software acceptance testing. The effort encompassed within this scope might include all of the programming effort needed to get the product out of the door assuming that best commercial practices were used.

To develop your estimate using this approach, you would break the client side components into their root-level components. Then, using historically based metrics (they could differ by component), you would then develop an estimate for the total job.

As an alternative, we could use a productivity figure like two source lines of code/staff hour or $50/deliverable source line of code as the basis of our estimate. Using the source lines of code size estimates we've previously derived, we would sum the source lines of code for the three components for our client side system to establish our basis of estimate as 44,700 equivalent new *SLOC*. Our estimate would then be computed as follows:

$$(44{,}700 \; SLOC)/(2 \; SLOC/\text{staff hour}) = 22{,}350 \text{ staff hours}$$

Independent of the approach we take, the key to developing an accurate estimate is understanding what effort it includes and what it doesn't. Normally, such decisions are framed by the accounting systems you use to bound your history and productivity figures of merit. Under most accounting systems, most engineering costs charged directly to past jobs are included based upon some known start and stop point in the process. Some management costs are also included and some aren't. Engineering documentation is normally included, marketing and sales literature is not. As a result, the costs that are part of your history can vary and can establish different bases for your productivity figures.

**3.2.4.2.3   Task 3—Perform Project Management.**   Sometimes, management is included as part of our software development scope. Sometimes, it is not.

If it were not, then you would probably estimate the effort required to manage the software teams and provide task direction as a level of effort task. This could be done by assuming there is one manager per so many people assigned to the job or by using some surcharge. Normally, many add a 10 percent surcharge to account for the labor involved in task management during software development. This assumption is predicated on the hypothesis that the first line supervisor both manages and technically contributes to the job. Based upon circumstances, this could be higher or lower. For example, international teams might take more effort to manage than the normal. In flat organizations where the task leader is also assigned development responsibilities, the effort might be less.

For the purpose of this estimate, we will add 10 percent to account for the management effort performed by task leaders. This will provide them with the hours necessary to plan, control, motivate, and direct personnel under their direct supervision.

### 3.2.4.2.4    Task 4—Maintain Configuration Control.

Like task management, configuration control is sometimes included as part of the software development scope. Sometimes, only part of the effort (i.e., version, not release and distribution control) is included. For the case where it is not included, you could again estimate the effort involved using either some fixed number of people or as a percentage level of effort. Typically, a 4 to 6 percent surcharge is added for the labor involved during software development, especially on large projects. Again, this estimate could vary based upon circumstances. For example, more effort might be needed to manage changes to reusable software components that are shared across product families and product lines (i.e., there are more people impacted by the changes).

For the purposes of this estimate, we will assume that we dedicate one person to the function half time throughout the eighteen months of the project. We will also assume that this person administers the software library and acts as system administrator for computational resources for the project.

### 3.2.4.2.5    Task 5—Perform Software Quality Assurance.

The final task in our WBS is software quality assurance. This function provides needed checks and balances to ensure standards are being adhered to and that the products generated are of the highest quality. When this is done by an organization outside the group, it is normally not included as part of the software development estimate. Under such circumstances, we estimate the effort involved using either a fixed number of people or percentage level of effort. Typically, the range of the estimate can be between 4 and 8 percent depending on the work performed.

Quality assurance personnel at the low end of this range perform audits to ensure software developers are adhering to their standards and the organization's defined software process. At the high end, these same personnel take on many more responsibilities and get more involved in the development. For example, they facilitate inspections and develop checklists of common defects for use during their conduct. They take the metrics data being generated and do root cause analysis. They evaluate products based upon predefined measures of goodness and determine their quality. Added effort on their part should result in increased quality.

For the purpose of this estimate, we will assume that one person is dedicated half time to the function for the eighteen months of the project. We will present this assumption and our corresponding track record of deliverable quality to the clients to see if they wish to okay a higher price for more quality assurance personnel.

### 3.2.4.3   STAGE 3—DEVELOP A COCOMO II ESTIMATE

We will now use the COCOMO II.2000 Post-Architecture model as the basis of our second estimate per the scenario shown in Figure 3.4. Step 1 in the figure, "Estimate Size," has already been done during Stage 1 of the estimating process as illustrated in Figure 3.2. For Step 2, we would rate the five scale and seventeen effort multiplier factors (cost drivers). Scale factors can be rated at the project level, while effort multipliers can be rated at either the project or component level. We would also agree with the assumptions upon which the Post-Architecture model estimates are based. These include that the requirements are stable and that the project is well managed.

Starting with the scale factors, we have summarized our ratings and the rationale behind them in Table 3.5. As you can see, we have made many assumptions based upon the limited information that was provided with the case. This is the normal case. To develop an estimate, you must know something about the job, the people, the platform, and the organization that will be tasked to generate the product. Once understood, we will press on to rate the cost drivers that comprise the effort multiplier.

The rating and rationale for each of the model's cost drivers is summarized in Tables 3.6, 3.7, 3.8 and 3.9 under the headings: product, personnel, platform, and project factors. We have elected to rate the effort multipliers at the project

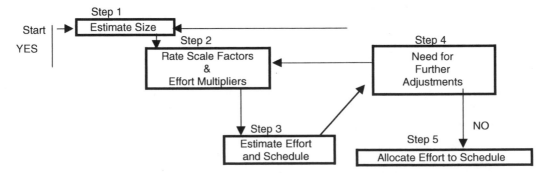

**Figure 3.4**   COCOMO II Estimate Development Scenario

**Table 3.5   Scale Factor Ratings and Rationale**

| Scale Factor | Rating | Rationale |
|---|---|---|
| PREC | High | The organization seems to understand the project's goals and have considerable experience in working related systems. |
| FLEX | High | Because this is an organization in the midst of a process improvement program, we have assumed that there is general conformity to requirements and a premium placed on delivering an acceptable product on time and within cost. |
| RESL | High | We assumed and checked that attention placed on architecture and risk identification and mitigation is consistent with a fairly mature process. |
| TEAM | Very High | This is a highly cooperative customer-developer team so far. It isn't distributed and seems to work well together. |
| PMAT | Norminal | A level 2 rating on the Software Engineering Institute's Capability Maturity Model (CMM) scale is nominal. |

**Table 3.6   Product Cost Driver Ratings and Rationale**

| Cost Drivers | Rating | Rationale |
|---|---|---|
| RELY | Nominal | Potential losses seem to be easily recoverable and do not lead to high financial losses. |
| DATA | Nominal | Because no database information was provided, we have assumed a nominal rating. We should check this with the client to make sure. |
| CPLX | Nominal | Based upon the guidelines in Table 2.19 and the available infrastructure software, we assume TPS software to be nominal with the exception of the fault diagnosis software. We would rate this module "high" because of the added complexity introduced by the neural network algorithms. |
| RUSE | Nominal | Again, we assumed nominal because we did not know how to rate this factor. |
| DOCU | Nominal | We assume the level of required documentation is right-sized to the life-cycle needs of the project. This seems to be an inherent characteristic of using the organization's preferred software process. |

**Table 3.7    Platform Cost-Driver Ratings and Rationale**

| Cost Drivers | Rating | Rationale |
|---|---|---|
| TIME | Nominal | Execution time is not considered a constraint. |
| STOR | Nominal | Main storage is not considered a constraint. |
| PVOL | Nominal | By its nature, the platform seems stable. The rating was selected because it reflects normal change characteristics of commercially available operating environments. |

**Table 3.8    Personnel Cost-Driver Ratings and Rationale**

| Cost Drivers | Rating | Rationale |
|---|---|---|
| ACAP | High | We have commitments to get some of the highest-ranked analysts available. However, the mix of personnel will be such that we can assume "high" as the norm for the project. |
| PCAP | Nominal | Unfortunately, we do not know who we will get as programmers. Therefore, we assumed a nominal rating. |
| PCON | High | Turnover in the firm averaged about 3% annually during the past few years. We have doubled this figure to reflect assumed project turnover, based on usual project experience of the firm. |
| APEX | High | Most of the staff in the organization will have more than 3 years of applications experience in transaction processing systems. |
| LTEX | Nominal | Because of the Java/C/C++ uncertainties, we will assume the experience level with languages & tools is between 1 and 2 years. |
| PLEX | High | The mix of staff with relevant platform experience is high as well based on the information given about the project (more than 3 years of experience). |

**Table 3.9    Project Cost-Driver Ratings and Rationale**

| Cost Drivers | Rating | Rationale |
|---|---|---|
| TOOL | High | We assume that we will have a strong, mature set of tools that are moderately integrated. |
| SITE | Low | Because we don't know how to rate this factor, we have conservatively assumed Low for now. |
| SCED | Nominal | We will adjust this factor to address the schedule desires of management after the initial estimates are developed. |

level because we wanted to develop our first estimate "quick and dirty." We could have just as well done this at the component level. Developing such ratings is relatively easy after the fact because all you have to do is change those factors that are different (i.e., the other factors remain as the default value). However, we decided to wait and see if there was any major difference between the COCOMO and the WBS estimates. If there is, we will probably refine both estimates and eliminate the shortcuts we've taken. Let's move ahead and start developing our estimate.

In order to rate each of the factors in this and the other tables, we have to make assumptions. Making assumptions is a natural part of your job when developing an estimate as not all of the information that is needed will be known. We recommend taking a pessimistic instead of optimistic view. This will lead to our discrepancies on the high side. Such errors will provide us with some margin should things go awry (and they probably will). The scale factor entries are pretty straightforward. They assume we will be in control of the situation and manage the project well. Many of the ratings refer you back to the descriptions about the organization and its level of process maturity that we provided earlier in the chapter. The COCOMO II.2000 Post-Architecture model is calibrated largely based upon making such assumptions. Again, we warn you not to be overly optimistic when you make these entries.

As we look at the product factors, we see several cost drivers we don't know anything about. For example, we don't know the reliability, RELY, or how complex the application will be, CPLX. Based upon our experience with similar applications, we could make an educated guess. However, we are reluctant to do so without having further knowledge of the specifics that will only come after we get started with the development. We recommend selecting a nominal rating under such circumstances because this represents what most experts and our data from past projects portray as the norm for the factor. We can either consult other parts of this book or the *COCOMO II Model Reference Manual* to determine ratings. Luckily, we can do this via "help" in the package because invoking this command provides immediate on-line access to the excerpts from the manual that we need to complete our task. Using this feature, it is relatively simple to review the guidelines and make a selection.

To rate the platform cost drivers, we have to make some assumptions about timing and storage constraints. Normally, such factors are not limitations in client-server systems because we can add more processors and memory when we encounter problems. We could also replace processors with ones that are more powerful when performance becomes a problem. We could also add communications channels should bandwidth become a limitation.

We also have to make some assumptions about the operating environment. For this factor, we select nominal because this reflects the normal state of affairs. Later, we can adjust the estimate if the operating system and environment constraints are identified during the process by the team defining the requirements.

Personnel factors are extremely tricky to rate. Many managers assume they will get the best people. Unfortunately, such assumptions rarely come true because the really good people are extremely busy and tend to be consumed on other jobs. We can assume in most firms that most analysts assigned to a project are capable. After all, only a few are needed to get the job done and those who are incapable have probably been motivated to seek employment elsewhere. However, we should check this and other personnel assumptions with respect to other projects' demands for staff. Also, we cannot make such an assumption when it comes to programmers. We must assume a nominal mix to be conservative.

We must also estimate potential turnover of personnel. From a project viewpoint, this includes people who are assigned to other projects prior to completing their tasks. Luckily, such statistics are readily available in most firms.

When rating personnel factors, remember that the selection should represent the average for the team. For example, a team with two experienced and two novice practitioners should probably be rated nominal.

The last sets of factors we will rate pertain to the project. Because we have a large capital budget for tools and new workstations, we will assume that we will have a very capable software environment either for Java or for C/C++. However, office space is at a premium. We are fighting to put our personnel at the development site in the same area. But, the situation is volatile and getting commitments for space is difficult. We really don't have any insight into whether or not we will be successful. In response, we have rated this driver low.

The final cost driver is SCED. Per the process shown in Figure 3.5, we first will generate our effort and duration estimates. Then, we will adjust the SCED driver to reflect the desired schedule. For example, this would adjust the effort if target delivery date for the release of the software is eighteen months versus let's say either a twelve-month or a twenty-four-month estimate from the model. Once all the scale factors and effort multipliers are rated, we can generate an initial effort and duration estimate. We do this by plugging our size estimates and the scale factors and cost driver ratings we've developed into the Post-Architecture model that is part of the USC COCOMO II package. Samples that illustrate the model's output for the nominal and schedule constrained cases are shown as Figures 3.5 and 3.6. As these screens illustrate, the most probable effort and duration estimates derived via the model are 92.4 person-months (PM) and 14.7 months. To accelerate the schedule to satisfy management's desire to shorten the schedule to 12 months, we must add about 13.0 PM, corresponding to a SCED rating of VL. The effort estimate translates to 14,044.8 hours of effort using a conversion factor of 152 hours/PM.

### 3.2.4.4   STAGE 4—COMPARE THE ESTIMATES AND RESOLVE THE DIFFERENCES

There is quite a difference between the two estimates. The WBS estimate assumed we can do the TPS job in 18 months for 29,065 hours of labor allocated as summarized in Table 3.3. However, the COCOMO II model suggests that the job

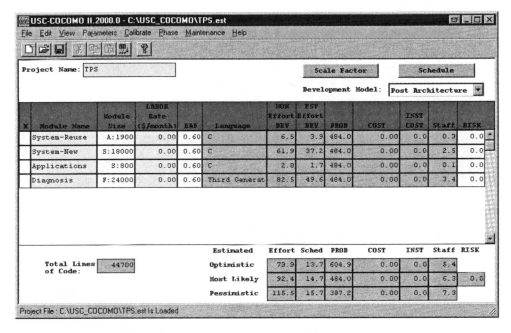

**Figure 3.5**   COCOMO II Nominal Output Screen

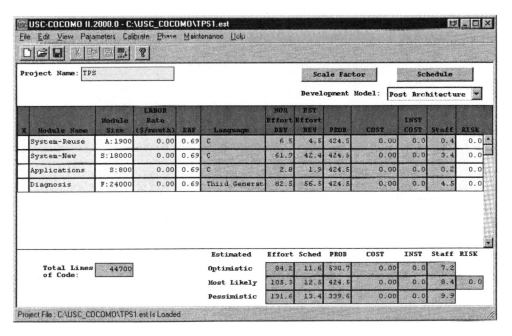

**Figure 3.6**   COCOMO II Schedule Constrained Output Screen

can be done in five-sixths the time (15 months) for about half the effort (14,045 staff hours). Why is there such a large difference? Which approach is correct? Can I trust either estimate? Which one of the estimates is right?

There are a number of simple explanations to the dilemma. First, the scope of the two estimates could be different. Second, the simplifying assumptions we made for either the WBS estimate or the COCOMO run could have caused a wide variation. Third, the difference could indicate that we might have to consider other factors. Let's investigate the situation.

The first problem that is readily apparent is that the two estimates have different scopes. The WBS estimate we developed included requirements definition, software development, management, configuration management, and quality assurance tasks. COCOMO by definition does not include the effort to define the requirements, although it does include the others. Therefore, the WBS estimate must be reduced by 1,600 hours to 27,465 hours to have a comparable scope with the COCOMO. In addition, the nominal eighteen-month schedule needs to be reduced by the amount of time you believe is needed to derive the requirements. Such a definition task could easily take four to six months to accomplish.

As a bit of advice, you might use the COCOMO II phase/activity distributions to provide the specific details of the allocations. To do this, you will have to decide whether to use the waterfall, spiral, incremental development, or MBASE/RUP model or some alternative. Then, you would use the phase distributions from the model that you selected to allocate the estimated effort to the prescribed schedule.

The second problem deals with the simplifying assumptions we made as we ran the model. There is no doubt that system software is more difficult than GUI or fault diagnosis software (i.e., with the exception of the neural net algorithms that are new and difficult). In addition, the relative experience and capabilities of the staff probably normally varies as a direct function of the type of software being developed. Just changing the system software to reflect its increased complexity to "High" and adjusting the analyst/programmer experience and capabilities to "Nominal" increases the estimate to 17,571.2 staff hours of effort (i.e., 115.6 staff months) and 15.7 months. This quickly narrows the gap between the two estimates. Things are starting to look better.

We probably should take a little more pessimistic view of our situation. After all, that is the norm and that is what the rules of thumb we used for our WBS estimate are based upon. Let's assume the architecture risks are not as well controlled as we initially thought and that there is some uncertainty associated with how we would handle the requirements. We really want to have our forecasts revolve around the most likely rather than the best case. To reflect this worsened state of affairs, we should set all of the scale factors to nominal. Our estimate would then become 21,933.6 staff months (i.e., 144.3 staff months) and have 17.8 months duration.

The third set of problems deals with other factors that might influence our estimate. For example, we assumed that the staff works 152 effective hours a month. Such an assumption takes vacation, sick leave and nonproductive time into account. However, many software professionals often put in fifty to sixty hours a week. They do whatever is necessary to get the job done. Under such circumstances, we may want to take this uncompensated overtime into account. However, this overtime will not affect the effort estimates. Your people still will work the same number of hours independent of whether or not you capture the uncompensated overtime charges. The required effort doesn't change.

The important thing that developing two estimates has forced you to do is question your assumptions. Whether you are optimistic or pessimistic in your estimates really doesn't matter so long as you make such decisions consciously. Just using a model like COCOMO to churn out numbers is not what estimating is all about. Estimating is about making choices, assessing risks, and looking at the impact of the many factors that have the potential to influence your costs and schedules. These are the topics that follow in the remainder of this chapter.

### 3.2.5   Bounding Risk

You can do a lot of useful things with the model once you have finished with your estimates. For example, you can quantify the impact of any risks you may have identified during the process using the cost and duration estimates you have developed. Using these numbers as your basis, you can then prioritize your risks and develop your risk mitigation plans.

Let's assume that we have developed the risk matrix for the project that appears as Table 3.10 as part of our planning process. This contains your "Top 10 list." As you can see, many of the facts that we discussed early in the chapter appear as risk items in the table. In addition, we have added several other items that are often considered risks for software projects like this one.

Now comes the difficult question: "Which of these items in Table 3.10 are the big swingers?" Let's look at how we would use the COCOMO II model to develop an answer using the information in the table to start with.

1.  *Managers are "techies:"* The COCOMO model assumes that your project is "well managed." The model does not take situations like having good technical people promoted to managerial positions into account normally. However, you could take into account the impact of this problem if you were overly concerned about it by adjusting the ACAP, PCAP, and TEAM ratings. ACAP and PCAP address developer-customer team as well as individual capabilities. For example, you could down-rate TEAM from the "Very High" rating we gave it to "Nominal" to assess the risk of degrading the current developer-customer relationship. By looking at the numbers, you will see that such a down-rating would cause your cost to go up by about 10 percent.

2.  *New programming language:* As noted in the table, new programming languages affect effort and duration estimates in a number of ways. First, you must

**Table 3.10 Risk Matrix**

| Risk | Priority | Description |
|---|---|---|
| 1. Managers are "techies" | ? | Managers are chosen based on their technical skills. This could lead to problems as new supervisors perfect their skills. Learning curves therefore must be addressed. |
| 2. New programming language | ? | The organization is deciding whether to go Java or C/C++. Learning curves again become a factor as does the negative potential impacts of new, immature compilers and tools. |
| 3. New processes | ! | The organization has made major investments in process improvement. New processes mean turmoil especially if you are the first to use them. Learning curves becomes a factor again as does the time needed to pilot and perfect processes. |
| 4. Lack of credible estimates | ? | The job is routinely under or over quoted. This process problem creates unrealistic expectations and leads to people burning the midnight oil trying to get the job done. |
| 5. New size metrics | ? | Either SLOC or function points will be chosen to measure the volume of work involved. Setting up processes for both would result in redundant work. |
| 6. Size growth | ? | The basis of our estimates is size. Unfortunately, size estimates may have large uncertainties and our estimates may be optimistic. Incorrect size estimates could have a profound impact on the cost as the effects are nonlinear. |
| 7. Personnel turnover | ? | Often, the really good people are pulled to work the high priority jobs. As a result, the experience mix may be less than expected or needed to get the job done and the experienced people spend more time mentoring the replacement people. |
| 8. New methods and tools | ? | Like new processes, new methods and tools create turmoil. Learning curves become a factor as does the maturity of the methods and tools. |
| 9. Volatile requirements | ? | Requirements are never stable. However, they become a major factor when changes to them are not properly controlled. Designs and other work done to date quickly become out-dated and rework increases as a direct result. |
| 10. Aggressive schedules | ? | Often, we tell management we will try to meet their schedule goals even when they are unrealistic. The alternative would be cancellation or descoping of the project. |

assess the effect of the learning curve. In COCOMO II, this is easily done through the use of the cost driver LTEX. For a programming language that is new for your people like Java, you would rate your experience lower than for languages that your staff had a lot of experience with. Second, you could adjust the TOOL and PVOL to assess the impact of related immature compilers and the accompanying less powerful run-time support platforms. We would recommend that you vary the settings of these three cost drivers incrementally to quantify the relative impact of this risk factor. Vary the settings and look at the combined effect on effort and duration throughout the entire length of the project.

**3.** *New processes:* Although new processes have a positive long-term effect on cost and productivity, there can be some turmoil in the short-term. The way to quantify this transient effect is through the scale factor PMAT and the cost driver DOCU. Again, you can assess the relative impact by looking at different ratings for these factors. You might also include RESL in the impact analysis if you were using new risk-management processes for the first time. Realize that you are looking at the combined effect of these factors across the full length of the project. Therefore, using a middle-of-the-road rating for each scale factor and cost driver would probably reflect the situation you'll be exposed to best.

**4.** *Lack of credible estimates:* The only way to improve the credibility of your estimates is to change perceptions. Using a defined estimating process and a calibrated cost model such as COCOMO II will improve your estimating accuracy tremendously in the future. However, it won't change opinions developed through past accuracy problems. The only way to change these perceptions is to generate better results. What you could do to assess the impact of this problem is to determine how far off your estimates were in the past. You could then adjust your estimates by this past standard error factor to determine for such key cost drivers as size and complexity the relative impact of poor estimating processes on your costs and schedules.

**5.** *New size metrics:* In the COCOMO II cost model, source lines of code (SLOC) are the basis for relating size to effort and cost. Function points are transformed to SLOC using conversion factors provided in this book. However, confusion and duplication of effort may result when the choice of the size metric is left open too long. You must make your selection early. Else, the lack of clear definitions and counting conventions could result in a wide variation in how your people come up with their size estimates.

**6.** *Size growth:* You could use the PERT sizing formula developed for use with the original COCOMO model to adjust the effective size of your product to reflect the possible growth:

$$Size = (a_i + 4m_i + b_i)/6 \qquad \Phi_i = (b_i - a_i)/6$$

Where $a_i$ = the smallest possible size for the software component

$m_i$ = the most likely size of the software component

$b_i$ = the largest possible size of the software component

$\Phi_i$ = the estimated standard deviation

For example, because of the potential risk, you might want to bound your potential size growth for the fault diagnosis component as follows using our user defined SLOC/function point conversion factor of 80:

$$\text{Size} = (22,\!400 + 4(24,\!000) + 28,\!000)/6 = 24,\!400 \text{ SLOC}$$

Where $a = 280$ function points (22,400 SLOC)

$m = 300$ function points (24,000 SLOC)

$b = 350$ function points (28,000 SLOC)

You could then assess the impact by using the effective size in the COCOMO II model as the basis for computing the delta cost and duration due to the growth of the requirements. As an alternative, you could use the RESL factor to estimate this factor directly.

**7.** *Personnel turnover:* Luckily, the COCOMO II model has a cost driver, Personnel Continuity or PCON, which takes annual personnel turnover into account. The impact of increased turnover can be computed by adjusting the rating for this factor. However, just looking at this one factor alone may not be sufficient. You probably should adjust the relative experience factor ratings, APEX, PLEX, and LTEX, to assess the effort and duration impacts caused by replacing experienced with less experienced personnel—i.e., PCON assumes the replacements have comparable background and experience—more realistically.

**8.** *New methods and tools:* The original COCOMO model had two parameters, MODP and TOOL, which you could adjust to look at the potential impacts of selected methods and tool approaches on effort and duration. However, the COCOMO II model has replaced MODP by Process Maturity, PMAT, and revamped the TOOL cost driver to reflect 1990s' technology. How do you look at the combined effects? Think about what "new" really means in terms of the model's usage. All it really means is that the learning curve and effective capability of the platform tools and methods are important factors. As already noted, there are cost drivers that deal directly with these factors in COCOMO II. For example, you can assess the impact of different tool experience levels by varying the settings of LTEX. The TOOL rating somewhat addresses the degree of integration and support for the tools (i.e., we are defining individual rating scales for tool-set capabilities, integration, and maturity and support). But, where do you treat your experience with and the maturity of your methods? This is one major difference between the current and past COCOMO models. In COCOMO II, you would address methodology as part of your process maturity scale factor rating, PMAT. This is logical because more mature organizations institutionalize their methods—both technical and managerial—systematically. They train their people in these methods and provide guidelines and examples so that they are easy to use.

**9.** *Volatile requirements:* COCOMO II uses a new factor called Requirements Evolution and Volatily, *REVL,* to adjust the effective size of your product to reflect the percentage of code you will have to throw away due to requirements instability. In our example, you would compensate for risk if you were concerned about fault diagnosis requirements that seemed to be constantly changing due to new and innovative neural net algorithms. Because these algorithms were being designed as you were developing your code, you might add 20 percent to the size ($REVL = 20$) to adjust the effective size to provide coverage for growth and volatility. You could then assess the impact by using the increased size in the COCOMO II model as the basis for computing the delta effort and duration due to the volatility of the requirements. You should note that you might have already taken this risk into account if you used the PERT-sizing formula to develop expected size estimates that reflect growth as we suggested in item 6. It is up to you to decide whether or not such double counting may or may not be appropriate.

**10.** *Aggressive schedules:* As its initial output, the COCOMO model gives you the most likely duration. As you saw in earlier chapters, effectively using the COCOMO model requires you to adjust the schedule, SCED, to reflect the desired endpoint. Don't be confused by what is meant by these statements. Often, you are asked to estimate the effort to get a job done within a specific time period. This desired duration might differ greatly from the most likely estimate that the COCOMO model generates. To compensate for shortened time periods, you must add effort. You do this using the SCED cost driver by adding effort based upon the percentage of time you need to shorten the schedule relative to the original estimate. Under certain circumstances, the SCED cost driver also tells you that it is not feasible to shorten the schedule even further. In other words, it proves Brooks' law which suggests that just because a woman can have a baby in nine months doesn't mean that nine women can give birth to the same baby in one month. You must realize that there are limitations to what can be done. Therefore, you must check the reasonableness of the estimate before you publish the numbers.

To perform your risk analysis, you can perform the parametric studies we have suggested either singly or in combination. The results can then be used to prioritize your risk management plan. Those items that have the greatest cost and schedule impacts should be addressed first. You can also go to management with the results to seek relief from unreasonable expectations. For example, you can show them that compressing schedules drives the cost up nonlinearly. You could suggest a spiral delivery approach which lets you reduce risk by incrementally delivering builds with differing capabilities. In other words, you can show them how to meet their customers' expectations in ways that reduce risk.

Always represent the results of a risk analysis as a range of numbers. When management asks how to realize the lower end of the range, get them to buy into your risk management plan.

### 3.2.6 Conducting Trade Studies

You can also perform a lot of useful trade studies once you have finished with your estimates. For example, you could look at the impact of using COTS software packages, different languages or different development paradigms on your estimated costs or schedules. Let's look at how we would perform these three trade studies using the COCOMO II model estimates as our basis:

### 3.2.6.1 COTS SOFTWARE TRADE STUDIES

Use of COTS software is attractive to most developers because of the apparent cost and schedule leverage. As noted in earlier chapters, COTS software is software that exists and is used "as-is" to perform functions in your application. You don't have to maintain COTS because it is provided by some third party. Instead, your efforts can be focused on figuring out how to integrate the package into your application and test it. If you require enhancements, you will have to pay the vendor to make them. This can be done as part of the standard release process or in a separate customized version of the product. Unfortunately, you lose many of the advantages when you have to modify COTS. You also have little control over the destiny of the package or its evolution. To assess the relative cost/benefits associated with the use of COTS, you might construct a spreadsheet like the one in Table 3.11 that follows for our case study.

Let's look at how the numbers for COTS were derived and what they mean. As noted above, the numbers assume that you would have to buy a one-time license that allows you to use the COTS software as part of your product. It also provides you with fifty run-time licenses that permit you to distribute the derived product to your clients on a machine-by-machine license basis (i.e., fifty such licenses priced at $1,000 each). We also assumed that the integration and test costs of COTS were 20 percent of the new development. This could be low if the COTS did not support your standard Application Program Interface (API) and the amount of glue code needed was larger than expected. Finally, we assumed that as annual versions of the COTS were released you would have to update the glue that bound the software to your products and retest it.

This trade study shows that it would be beneficial to use COTS if the following assumptions hold true:

- The maximum number of run-time licenses did not exceed fifty. If it did, the benefits of COTS would diminish quickly as the number of licenses required increases.

**Table 3.11  Case Study Spreadsheet 1**

| Factor | COTS | New |
|---|---|---|
| • Cost of acquiring software | $100,000 (license) | $924,000* |
| • Integration & test costs | 100,000 | Included |
| • Run-time license costs | 50,000 | Not applicable |
| • Maintenance costs (5-year) | $50,000 | 92,400 |
| Total | $300,000 | $1,016,400 |

*Assume cost of a staff-month = $10,000; therefore, the cost of 92.4 staff-months = $924,000.

- You don't need to modify the COTS to provide additional functionality or to satisfy any unique API or other interface requirement.
- The company that sold you the COTS is stable, provides you adequate support, and stays solvent. If not, you may have to take over maintenance of the COTS package to continue supporting your clients (this assumes that you have put a copy of the source code in escrow to guard against this contingency). This would quickly negate the advantage of using COTS. As part of your COTS licensing practices, you should make sure that the vendors you hire are going to be around for the long run.

This trade study looks at both the advantages and disadvantages of using COTS as part of your product development. As discussed in Chapter 5, the COCOMO II project is actively involved in developing a model called COCOTS that permits you to look at the many cost drivers that influence this decision. What was provided here was a brief discussion of some of the many factors that you might want to consider as you perform your analysis. As noted, licensing practices may have a large impact on what selection you will make. We therefore suggest that you have your legal department review your COTS license agreements carefully so you know what costs you will be held liable once you purchase the product.

### 3.2.6.2   LANGUAGE TRADE STUDIES

Languages impact both productivity and the amount of code that will be generated. For example, you can write the same application in a fourth-generation language with much less code than with a third-generation language. An easy way to compare the relative productivity of using different programming languages is by looking at function point language expansion factors (i.e., the number of SLOC generated per function point in that language). For the case of C++ versus C, a ratio of 29/128 or about 0.23 exists per the table. This means that you could write the equivalent functionality of programs originally expressed in the C programming language with about a 77 percent decrease in effort under the assumption that you have equivalent skill and experience in the language. If this assumption were not true, you would have to estimate the cost of developing these skills and factor that into the study. For example, a spreadsheet representing the trades that you looked at might appear as in Table 3.12 for our case study.

Underlying the 77 percent savings is the assumption that your application and programmers will extensively use the powerful features of C++. In other words, just using a C subset of C++ will not result in a decrease in effort.

Let's look at how these numbers were derived and what they mean. First, the numbers for C++ represent the delta costs (i.e., those in addition to that which would have had to be spent anyway if the C programming language were used). In other words, training costs for C++ would be $50,000 more than that which would have been spent if the C language had been selected for use. Second, the

**Table 3.12    Case Study Spreadsheet 2**

| Factor | C | C++ |
|---|---|---|
| • Cost of compilers/tools (10 seats) | Norm | $8,000 |
| • Training costs | Norm | 50,000 |
| • Productivity | Norm | −187,500 |
| **Total** | Norm | −$129,500 |

gain in productivity caused by selecting of the C++ language was computed as follows:

$$\text{Cost reduction} = (\% \text{ of life cycle affected})(\text{productivity gain})$$
$$(\text{number of hours})(\text{cost/hour})$$
$$= (0.3)(0.5)(25{,}000)(\$50)$$
$$= \$187{,}500$$

We made the following very conservative assumptions to perform our analysis:

- The gains associated with the use of a programming languages were confined to the code and unit test portion of the life cycle.
- The relative productivity gain of C++ over C was only 50 percent (i.e., not the 70 percent the function point language expansion factors suggest).
- The cost of developing our application is 25,000 hours (somewhat between our COCOMO and WBS estimates).
- The cost per hour is $50 (i.e., does not include overhead and profit).

This trade study shows that it would be beneficial to move to the C++ programming language if we could afford the time needed to bring the staff up to speed on the effective use of the language and the methods it depends on to realize its potential.

### 3.2.6.3    PARADIGM TRADE STUDIES

As our last trade study, let's look at the differences in cost between developing our product incrementally versus a single build. As we noted in our treatment of risk, one of the most common approaches used to address aggressive schedule risk is incremental development. Here, we break the software development down into several deliverables each with partial functionality. Such deliveries can be generated in many ways. Two of the more popular of these are incremental delivery or incremental development. For incremental delivery, capability builds are developed, tested, and delivered as stand-alone entities. For this case, the cost of testing and packaging each build for delivery must be included in the estimate. For incremental development, the full testing can be delayed until the final delivery enters integration and test. Both approaches provide partial products. However, incremental development is normally cheaper because it cuts down the time and effort needed for test and packaging for delivery.

Let's look at the added time and effort needed for each incremental development approach using our TPS case study as our basis. The size of each increment will have to be estimated using functionality allocated to the build as its foundation. For simplicity, let's break the size as follows into two builds, one for systems software and the other for applications, as shown in Table 3.13.

You should have noticed that we have included Build 1 as part of our Build 2. This is necessary because the systems software will be used as the basis for generating Build 2. This software will be integrated and tested (and perhaps modified) as the functionality needed to implement our applications is developed as part of the second increment we develop using either the incremental development or delivery paradigm.

For both incremental paradigms, we will treat our two deliveries as two separate subprojects. Based upon the estimates presented at the start of this chapter, the effective size of first subproject would be 19,900 SLOC. We would estimate the size of Build 2 as follows:

$$\text{Effective size} = \text{Size} \, (0.4(\%DM) + 0.3(\%CM) + 0.3(\%IM))$$
$$= 19,900 \, (0.4(.20) + 0.3(.30) + 0.3(.30))$$
$$= 19,900(0.26) = 5,174 \; SLOC$$

$$\text{Size (Build 2)} = 5,174 + 800 + 23,100$$
$$= 29,074 \; SLOC$$

Where:

$$\%DM = \text{percentage design modified}$$
$$\%CM = \text{percent code modified}$$
$$\%IM = \text{percent integration modified}$$

**Table 3.13  Sizing Breakdown**

| Build No. | Module | Size (SLOC) |
|:---:|:---|:---|
| 1 | Systems software | 18,000 (new)<br>10,000 (reused equivalent = 1,900) |
| 2 | Applications software | Build 1 (19,900 SLOC) +<br>User applications (800 SLOC)<br>Fault diagnosis (24,000 SLOC) |

The difference between the two paradigms would be accounted for in the factors we use to compute the percent modified. Because incremental delivery entails more testing, the percentages assumed would undoubtedly be bigger. We would then use the COCOMO II model to compute the effort and duration for each of our two builds using the different size estimates to drive the output of our models. Our estimate for the total job would be the sum of the two build estimates. While the total estimate for incremental development would be higher than for a one-shot implementation, it would most likely result in an earlier Initial Operational Capability because the first build could be deployed as the second build was worked on in parallel.

These three trade studies serve as examples of how you would use a cost model to assess the cost/benefits of alternatives. As illustrated, you can conduct a simple parametric tradeoff by varying the parametric settings for either your scale factors or cost drivers. You can get more sophisticated and perform more elaborate analysis using one or more of the enclosed USC COCOMO II package's many capabilities. As we summarized in Figure 3.7 and elsewhere in the book, these capabilities include, but are not limited to, the following:

- *Resource estimation:* The base COCOMO II model generates effort and duration estimates under three scenarios: application composition, early design, and post-architecture. The underlying assumption is that your aim is to reduce the risk as you go through a spiral development process.
- *Equivalent size estimation:* The USC COCOMO II package converts function points to source lines of code using language expansion factors that appear in earlier chapters of this book. It also permits you to compute equivalent lines of code using the percentage-modified formulas that we covered earlier in this chapter.
- *Reuse impact assessment:* The COCOMO package now contains a new set of formulas for reuse which permit you to take effort needed for software understanding, assessment and assimilation, and unfamiliarity into account.
- *Reengineering or conversion estimation:* The COCOMO package contains a set of formulas that you can use to address reengineering and conversion ad-

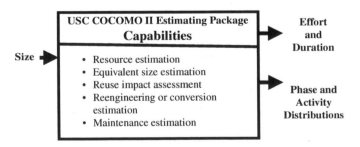

**Figure 3.7**    COCOMO II Estimating Package Capabilities

justments. These formulas use an automated translation productivity rate as their basis.

- *Maintenance estimation:* Finally, the package includes new mathematical formulas to estimate the effort required to maintain the package. These formulas use the code fragment subjected to change to compute the relative cost to update the software. Life-cycle costs equal the development costs plus whatever effort is needed to maintain the software across its projected life span. Maintenance addresses only the effort needed to add or change the base source code across the life of the project (i.e., no extra effort is estimated for deleting code per guidelines provided by the Software Engineering Institute).

You can even conduct cost-benefit analysis by running the model to compute both the investment and operating costs and the tangible and intangible benefits. We will perform such an analysis in the next paragraph as we assess life-cycle costs.

### 3.2.7 Assessing Life-Cycle Costs

The final thing you can use a cost model like COCOMO II to perform is life-cycle cost analysis. As already noted, life-cycle costs include, as a minimum, both the costs of development and maintenance. The USC COCOMO II package provides a maintenance model that can be used to estimate the costs associated with keeping a software product up to date after it is delivered and declared operational. The maintenance model for COCOMO II is new and improved. It assumes that the amount of code added or changed is more than 20 percent of the new code being developed. Else, we recommend that you use the reuse model to estimate the cost of the new version. Its basic formula is of the form:

$$PM_M = A(\text{Size}_M)^E \prod_{i=1}^{17} (EM_i)$$

Where:

$$\text{Size}_M = [(\text{BaseCodeSize})MCF]MAF$$

$$MAF = 1 + [SU/100)UNFM]$$

$$MCF = \frac{\text{SizeAdded} + \text{SizeModified}}{\text{BaseCode Size}}$$

The constants $A$ and $E$ have the same form as the COCOMO II development model. The effort multipliers, $EM_i$, are the same except for RELY, required reliability. Lower-reliability software will be more expensive rather than less expensive to maintain. In addition, the REUSE cost driver and SCED are ignored in the maintenance computation.

**Table 3.14   Case Study Spreadsheet 1 (Repeated)**

| Factor | COTS | New |
|---|---|---|
| • Cost of acquiring software | $100,000 (license) | $924,000 |
| • Integration & test costs | 100,000 | Included |
| • Run time license costs | 50,000 | Not applicable |
| • Maintenance costs | 500,000 | 92,400 |
| **Total** | **$300,000** | **$1,016,400** |

As the formula illustrates, the COCOMO II maintenance model estimates effort by looking at the percentage of the code that changes. The formula also suggests that you should modify your effort multipliers and scale factors to reflect your maintenance situation. For example, you might rate some of the personnel factors differently if the team assigned to maintain the software had dissimilar characteristics from the development team.

How would you perform a life-cycle analysis? Is it as simple as adding the development and annual maintenance costs across the life span of the software? Sometimes it is. However, in some cases a much more detailed analysis may be in order. Let's take the COTS software case that we discussed earlier in this chapter. The spreadsheet we used to compare costs was as follows in Table 3.14.

Let's use the spreadsheet that appears as Figure 3.8 to check to see if we bounded all the costs of using COTS versus developing the software anew over its life cycle. After a quick look, we can see that the analysis we conducted earlier was not really very comprehensive. We failed to take the following major costs into account (Table 3.15).

**Table 3.15   Previously Unaccounted Costs**

| Factor | COTS | New |
|---|---|---|
| • Glue code development (4 KSLOC @ $50) | $200,000 | Not applicable |
| • Integration & test costs—to test the interfaces between the glue code and COTS | 50,000 | Not applicable |
| • Education—to understand the COTS and its capabilities (includes programmer time) | 50,000 | Not applicable |
| • Documentation—to document the glue code and its interfaces with the COTS | 25,000 | Not applicable |
| • Risk reduction—assume 50 additional run-time licenses may be needed as a worse case | 50,000 | Not applicable |
| • Maintenance costs (5 year)—assume 10 percent annually for new and 25 percent annually for the glue software | 250,000 | 92,400 |
| • Acquisition costs | 100,000 | 924,000 |
| **Total** | **$725,000** | **$1,016,400** |

| Non-recurring Costs | Tangible Benefits |
|---|---|
| • Acquisition<br>  - Assets<br>  - Methods/tools<br>• Process adaptation<br>• Documentation<br>• Risk reduction<br>• Education & training<br>  - Development<br>  - Conduct<br>  - Beta test<br>• Other<br><br>Total | • Cost avoidance<br>  - Less time<br>  - Less effort<br>• Added capability<br>• Reduced cycle time<br>• Reduced cost of quality<br>• Cost savings<br>  - Less staff<br>  - Less equipment<br>  - Less overhead<br>• Other<br><br>Total |
| **Recurring Costs** | **Intangible Benefits** |
| • Administration<br>• Reengineering<br>• Maintenance<br>• Operations<br>• Continuing education<br>• Other<br><br>Total | • Better customer satisfaction<br>• Better fitness for use<br>• Reduced time to market<br>• Increased market penetration<br>• Improved image<br>• Other<br><br>Total |
| **Total Costs** | **Total Benefits** |

**Figure 3.8**   Cost/Benefit Analysis Worksheet

The cost differential between the two options is rapidly narrowing as we look into the future. The decision will now have to be made using risk and intangible factors. For example, you might opt to develop the application yourself if the vendor's health was suspect or if the application was one related to one of your core competencies. You might opt for COTS if you were focused on reducing your time to market or increasing market penetration. The more thorough your analysis, the better your decisions. This completes this example. In summary, it showed you the value of using models like COCOMO II to perform all sorts of trade studies and economic analysis.

## 3.3   AIRBORNE RADAR SYSTEM (ARS) OVERVIEW

This section provides several software cost estimates for a large, complex real-time embedded system that involves concurrent development of new hardware. The system is built using an evolutionary process, and this example will show all three submodels of COCOMO being used in tandem with iterative cycles of the spiral process. The product is a major upgrade to an existing system being used on military aircraft and will be constructed with substantial reuse and automatic translation. The ARS typifies the systems integration projects of many aerospace companies (and, increasingly, commercial and equipment manu-facturers).

The Applications Composition model will be used to estimate the initial prototyping that demonstrates a new user interface for improved radar process-ing capabilities using simulated radar input. This covers the major effort involved in the MBASE/RUP spiral cycles covering the Inception phase and culminating in the Life-Cycle Objectives (LCO) anchor point milestone. Note that the Applica-tions Composition model is not completely calibrated as of this writing, so these calculations only serve as an example (see Chapter 6 for this emerging extension). The Early Design model will be used for the Elaboration phase which will de-velop a working breadboard system with a subset of radar system capabilities and a fully defined software architecture. The Elaboration phase culminates in the Life-Cycle Architecture (LCA) milestone. Finally, the Post-Architecture model will be used for the Construction phase for actual flight usage culminating in the Initial Operational Capability (IOC).

This example demonstrates estimating a project with varying levels of de-tail, handling object-oriented development in the SLOC formulas, estimating reuse, and costing reengineering done via automatic language translation. The Post-Architecture exercise in this section will also introduce a simple and conve-nient method of recording cost driver ratings in an organization.

### 3.3.1   ARS Description

The Megaspace Corporation is developing the ARS. The ARS uses a central air-borne computer, a radar unit, other sensors and a display console all installed on-board a military jet. It is a hard real-time system with very stringent timing constraints. The overall complexity is very high because of multi-threading and multi-mode real-time processing. All the hardware is being developed from scratch. The central computer provides radar hardware commands, processes radar input, and manages radar and track data. The proprietary display console has a high-resolution color display and a full suite of input devices including a trackball, programmable touch panels and fixed function keys.

A high-level depiction of the system is shown in Figure 3.9. All system com-ponents are physically resident on the aircraft.

Table 3.16 lists the high-level software components in the ARS.

### 3.3.2   Prototype Demonstration (Inception Phase)

The U.S. Navy customer will witness the prototype demonstration, and there is only six weeks time to develop it. Megaspace has spent considerable effort con-ceiving the system upgrade, and it is vitally important that the demo shows ad-vancements to the Navy. A good deal of the functionality will be canned with simulated data, but the Radar Item Processing software will demonstrate some new algorithms. There will be no actual radar hardware and radar data will be

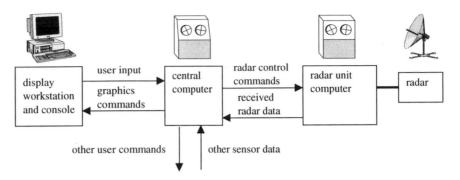

**Figure 3.9**   ARS Software Components

simulated, but there will be some stubs to receive and instrument simulated radar commands. There will be a small subset of display capabilities shown that will demonstrate the new algorithms. No Built-In Test software will be in the initial prototype. The prototype will be managed with a "cut and run" approach, whereby no major requirements changes will be incorporated (the requirements evolution and volatility will be essentially zero).

Since the prototype is largely graphic screens with little radar data processing, the Applications Composition model (see Chapter 5, Section 5.1) will be used. The prototype will be sized using application points. Many of the screens will be complex bit-mapped displays that are rated as difficult in the application-point procedure. Note there is only one report in the prototype system generated by Radar Item Processing—a time history of items tracked with the radar demonstrating a successful thread of the software. There is no Built-In Test software for the prototype.

After a couple of meetings with the system architects to assess the prototype functionality, the number and complexity of screens, reports and 3GL components were estimated as shown in Table 3.17. The number of elements could have also been derived using a more formal wideband Delphi approach.

Using the application point procedure, the following sizes shown in Table 3.18 were derived based on the elements in Table 3.17.

There is a pool of five senior developers that could be made available to work on the project, but they are also critical to ongoing projects. They would collectively and individually rate as "high" on the developer ICASE experience scale. Also, the ICASE toolset rates "high." Can the prototype be done in the required six weeks, and how many developers should be devoted to the project?

With a "high" productivity of 25 NAP/PM per the application point procedure in Section 5.1, the estimated prototype effort for 136.3 NAP would be:

$$PM = NAP/PROD = 136.3/25 = 5.45\ PM\ (\text{or } 23.6 \text{ person-weeks}).$$

This would require an average of (23.5 person-weeks/6 weeks) = 3.9 full-time personnel for the six-week period, or four of the five available developers.

**Table 3.16    ARS Software Components**

| Component | Functions | Implementation Notes |
|---|---|---|
| Radar Unit Control | Control of radar hardware, e.g., provide commands to change radar mode or scan particular area of sky | The hardware supports the same software commands as earlier generation hardware (backwards-compatible), thus there is some reuse (Ada) |
| Radar Item Processing | Radar-item data processing and radar-item identification, which informs the crew about what type of radar items are where | Some new object-oriented Ada development, updates for more sophisticated radar, some Fortran algorithms converted to Ada 95 |
| Radar Database | Data management of radar frequency and radar item data | New object-oriented Ada development |
| Display Manager | Management of interactive displays of radar and other sensor data; operates in the central embedded computer, and interfaces to the display console for lower level processing. The displays will be complex ones consisting of moving icons, adjustable-scale map displays, overlayed vector objects and bitmapped data, multiple video planes, etc. Sensor data from infrared and other devices will be displayed as real-time video. | Mostly new development, some COTS software (Ada and C). The development tools support a mixed-language environment. |
| Display Console | Operator input processing from the keyboard, trackball and other devices; graphics primitive processing resident in the display console computer that supports the high-level Display Manager (e.g. if the Display Manager sends a "draw rectangle" command, this software will actually draw the component lines and change the pixel states). | Custom hardware, some COTS software for image processing (C and microcode) |
| Built In Test | System performance monitoring, hardware fault detection and localization. This software is distributed in all processors and automatically tests for hardware faults. | New development (Ada for high-level control and assembler for access to lowlevel hardware) |

**Table 3.17  ARS Prototype Application Elements**

| Component | Number of Screens | | | Number of Reports | | | Number of 3 GL Components (weight = 10) | Total Application Points |
| --- | --- | --- | --- | --- | --- | --- | --- | --- |
| | *Simple Complexity (weight = 1)* | *Medium Complexity (weight = 2)* | *Difficult Complexity (weight = 3)* | *Simple Complexity (weight = 2)* | *Medium Complexity (weight = 5)* | *Difficult Complexity (weight = 8)* | | |
| Radar Unit Control | 0 | 1 | 3 | 0 | 0 | 0 | 0 | 11 |
| Radar Item Processing | 0 | 4 | 4 | 0 | 1 | 0 | 4 | 65 |
| Radar Database | 0 | 2 | 3 | 0 | 0 | 0 | 1 | 23 |
| Display Manager | 0 | 2 | 6 | 0 | 0 | 0 | 2 | 42 |
| Display Console | 1 | 2 | 4 | 0 | 0 | 0 | 0 | 17 |
| Built-In Test | 0 | 0 | 0 | 0 | 0 | 0 | 0 | 0 |

**Table 3.18   ARS Prototype Sizes**

| Component | Size (Application Points) | Estimated Reuse | New Application Points (NAP) |
|---|---|---|---|
| Radar Unit Control | 11 | 20 % | 8.8 |
| Radar Item Processing | 65 | 30 % | 45.5 |
| Radar Database | 23 | 0 % | 23 |
| Display Manager | 42 | 0 % | 42 |
| Display Console | 17 | 0 % | 17 |
| Built-In Test | 0 | 0 % | 0 |
| TOTAL | | | 136.3 |

### 3.3.3   Breadboard System (Elaboration Phase)

The breadboard system is planned to demonstrate a defined software architecture with advancements in newly developed hardware. It will be extensively tested operationally before committing to final development. There are still a good number of unknowns at this stage. Though the development platform is chosen, little is known about the final component sizes, the personnel available, the real-time performance of the new architecture, or the process to be used in the final development (there are several major process changes occurring as part of the software process improvement program). For these reasons, the coarse-grained Early Design model will be used.

At this relatively early project stage, the amount of functionality can be quantified easier than the lines of code. But since different designers handle the different components, the estimated sizes are a mixed bag of function points and SLOC. The unadjusted function points will be converted to SLOC for the COCOMO equations.

The breadboard development will also be used as a vehicle to collect cost-related data. The automated translation productivity will be measured for the FORTRAN to Ada reengineered portion in the Radar Item Processing software. Additionally, the object-oriented development in the Radar Item Processing and Radar Database will be used to get representative sizes on objects. This object data will be used later in full development to convert the remaining objects to be developed to lines of code for the Post-Architecture model.

Megaspace has also decided to implement Integrated Product Teams for the breadboard and full development. There is required reuse across a whole product line, the personnel are highly capable, but some of the staff is new to the domain. Tables 3.19 and 3.20 list the scale factor and cost driver ratings with associated rationale for the breadboard development.

**Table 3.19   ARS Breadboard System Early-Design Scale Factors**

| Scale Factor | Rating | Rationale |
|---|---|---|
| PREC | Nominal | Even though Megaspace has developed many radar systems, there is concurrent development of new hardware and innovative data processing. Data fusion from multiple sources will be done with a new fuzzy logic approach. |
| FLEX | Low | Development flexibility is low since there are stringent Navy requirements, but there is only a medium premium on early completion of the breadboard. |
| RESL | High | A subjective weighted average of the Architecture/Risk Resolution components in Table 2.13 is high. |
| TEAM | Nominal | There is considerable consistency between the stakeholder's objectives and their willingness to compromise with each other, but there has been just moderate effort in teambuilding and their experience together is moderate. |
| PMAT | Nominal | This division of Megaspace has achieved a Level 2 rating on the SEI-CMM process maturity scale. |

Table 3.21 shows the size calculations for the breadboard development. It implements the equivalent size calculations described in Chapter 2. Note that a component can be broken up based on sub-components, different languages, and/or grouped by different origins (e.g. new, reused, modified or COTS). The data in Table 3.21 is aggregated on a component basis. The granularity of the components will be dictated by the project nature. In general, finer breakdown is advantageous since it leads to better system understanding. The same methods of rolling up sizes apply in all cases. Note also that the reuse parameter heuristics in Table 2.8 have been followed (e.g., "reused code" implies $DM = 0$, $CM = 0$, and $SU/UNFM$ don't apply). Any software retained as is from the prototype is considered reused. Software changed from the prototype is considered "modified."

Some qualifications are necessary regarding the COTS data. Source code sizes for COTS are often unknowable since packages are insular, and source is not even provided in many cases. COTS size is also irrelevant in situations when its usage is essentially transparent. Often only a small part of the package is used as well. It is the interfaces that matter, and the development of glue code that requires effort. COTS must be handled in some fashion until the COCOTS model is fully available (see Chapter 5, Section 5.4).

In this application, there is access to the COTS source code. It has been integrated with the rest of the application and downloaded into the embedded processors. Thus there is complete visibility into the source code, including how to modify it.

**Table 3.20    ARS Breadboard System Early-Design Cost Drivers**

| Cost Driver | Rating | Rationale |
|---|---|---|
| RCPX | High | There is a strong emphasis on reliability and documentation, the product is very complex and the database size is moderate. These subattributes are combined to get an overall high rating. |
| RUSE | Very High | The organization intends to evolve a product line around this product. A great deal of early domain architecting effort has been invested to make the software highly reusable. |
| PDIF | High | The platform is a combination of off-the-shelf software, custom software, and custom made hardware. The time and storage constraints are at 70% and the platform volatility is somewhat volatile since the hardware is also under development. |
| PERS | High | Megaspace has retained a highly capable core of software engineers. The combined percentile for ACAP and PCAP is 70% and the annual personnel turnover is 11%. |
| PREX | Nominal | The retained staff is also high in domain experience, but they only have 9 months average experience in the language and toolsets, and the platform is new. |
| FCIL | Nominal | There are basic life-cycle tools and basic support of multisite development. |
| SCED | Nominal | The schedule is under no particular constraint. Cost minimization and product quality are higher priorities than cycle time. (The situation would be different if there was more industry competition.) |

Though the Early Design model can handle function points, the sizes in Table 3.21 are summarized in SLOC. The sizes of Radar Item Processing and Radar Database have been converted from function points as follows using the conversions in Table 2.4 for Ada 95.

Radar Item Processing:    $390\ FP * 49\ SLOC/FP = 19{,}110\ SLOC$

Radar Database:    $128\ FP * 49\ SLOC/FP = 6{,}272\ SLOC.$

In this and subsequent examples, requirements evolution and volatility (REVL) is assumed constant within a component regardless of whether it's new or adapted (although it doesn't always have to be the case). The last column in the table marked "Equivalent Size" adjusts for the adaptation parameters and adds on the specified percentage of requirements evolution and volatility. This is the size used in the COCOMO estimating equations.

Equivalent size calculations are not performed for automatically translated code. The overall effort is calculated with Equation 2.11, with a separate term for

**Table 3.21   ARS Breadboard System Size Calculations**

| Component | Size (SLOC) | Language | Type | REVL (%) | DM | CM | IM | AA | SU | UNFM | AAM | Equivalent Size (SLOC) |
|---|---|---|---|---|---|---|---|---|---|---|---|---|
| Radar Unit Control | 4500 | Ada 95 | New | 10 | — | — | — | — | — | — | — | 4950 |
| | 1238 | Ada 95 | Reused | 10 | 0 | 0 | 30 | 1 | — | — | 10 | 136 |
| Radar Item Processing | 19110 | Ada 95 | New | 20 | — | — | — | — | — | — | — | 22932 |
| | 25450 | Ada 95 | Translated | | — | — | — | — | — | — | — | 0 |
| Radar Database | 6272 | Ada 95 | New | 12 | — | — | — | — | — | — | 0 | 7025 |
| | 3222 | Ada 95 | Modified | 12 | 15 | 20 | 50 | 2 | 15 | .1 | 29.8 | 1076 |
| Display Manager | 12480 | Ada 95, C | New | 9 | — | — | — | — | — | — | — | 13603 |
| | 18960 | Ada 95, C | Reused | 9 | 0 | 0 | 25 | 2 | — | — | 9.5 | 1963 |
| | 24566 | C | COTS | 9 | 0 | 0 | 20 | 0 | — | — | 6 | 1607 |
| Display Console | 5400 | C, microcode | New | 7 | — | — | — | — | — | — | — | 5778 |
| | 2876 | C, microcode | COTS | 7 | 0 | 0 | 20 | 0 | — | — | 6 | 185 |
| Built In Test | 4200 | Ada 95, assembler | New | 15 | — | — | — | — | — | — | — | 4830 |
| TOTAL | | | | | | | | | | | | 64084 |

automatic translation. The effort for translating Fortran into Ada is done separately per Equation 2.6, where the translation effort is added to the standard COCOMO effort equation. At this stage, automatic translation productivity is not well-known, so 800 SLOC/PM will be used based on preliminary data from another program. Another assumption is that 90 percent of the Radar Item Processing 25,450 SLOC can be automatically translated, based on vendor information. The remaining 10 percent is developed anew, and shows up as part of the 19,100 new SLOC for the component. Using the 25,450 SLOC portion that will be converted to Ada, the automatic translation effort alone is:

$$PM_M = ASLOC\,(AT/100)/ATPROD$$
$$= 25,450\; ASLOC * (.9)/(800\; SLOC/\text{person-month})$$
$$= 28.6\; PM$$

Putting the equivalent size from Table 3.21 into the Early Design model effort formula (equation 2.11) gives:

$$PM = 2.94 \times Size^E \times \prod_{i=1}^{n} EM_i = 459.4 \text{ person-months.}$$

The overall effort is then 28.6 plus 459.4 = 488 person-months.

The overall schedule is calculated with equation 2.14, not including the separate automated translation effort which is assumed off the critical path:

$$TDEV = \left[ 3.67 \times (PM_{NS})^{(0.28 + 0.2 \times (E - 0.91))} \right] \times \frac{SCED\ \%}{100} = 25.6 \text{ months.}$$

Figure 3.10 shows the USC COCOMO output for this estimate using the Early Design model. In this case since the cost drivers apply to all components, the overall equivalent size for the system was input. It already takes into account the adaptation and REVL adjustments calculated in Table 3.21. A user does not need to produce a separate table like that in Table 3.21, since it was for demonstration only. Normally a cost estimation tool will do the size calculations.

### 3.3.4  Full Development—Top-Level Estimate

Several refinements to the system were required after test and evaluation of the breadboard system. The reengineered Radar Item Processing software required modifications to some real-time filtering modules, since the automatic translation didn't optimize for real-time performance. Additionally, the breadboard hardware performed slightly differently than anticipated, so the radar control software required some tweaking. A group of mostly experienced personnel has also been transferred to the project.

As previously mentioned, the breadboard experience was also used to refine some cost assumptions. The productivity of automatic translation measured in the breadboard will be used to estimate the translation effort in the full devel-

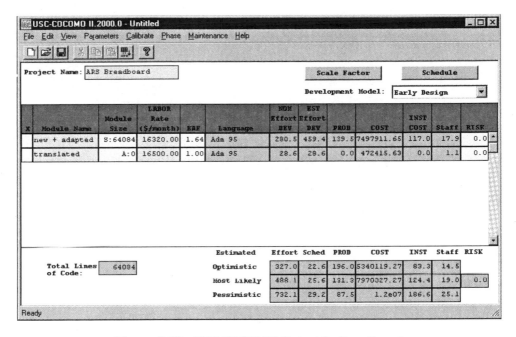

**Figure 3.10**   USC COCOMO Output for Breadboard

opment. Also, the subset of the object-oriented design developed in the bread-board was used to quantify the sizes of objects in lines of code. The remaining objects to be developed are converted to lines of code based on representative object samples measured in the breadboard. It is important to note that COCOMO II may eventually be formulated based on object-oriented size measures such as those in the Unified Modeling Language (UML), and those in object-oriented languages such as Ada 95, C++, and Java.

This last exercise for full development of the ARS will introduce the historical ratings profile which is used to assist in rating new projects. One of the difficulties of implementing COCOMO or other cost models is rating cost drivers in a consistent and objective fashion across an organization. To support consistent ratings of cost drivers among individuals and projects, a cost-driver ratings profile has been developed. The ratings profile as part of a defined cost-estimation process is consistent with SEI CMM guidelines, and is adjunct to other calibration data.

The cost-driver ratings profile is a graphical depiction of the objective rating criteria and historical ratings from past projects to be used as a reference baseline when performing estimates. It is used in conjunction with a COCOMO estimation tool, so that new or proposed projects can be easily gauged against past ones in an objective manner. Since an estimator needs to work closely with project engineers and architects to assess cost drivers, it is generally easier for project personnel who aren't COCOMO experts to perform relative assessments against known projects rather than starting with a blank slate.

A wideband Delphi technique [Boehm 1981] is used along with the ratings profile to reach consensus in the organization in order to determine the project's cost-driver ratings. There may often be separate profiles for different product lines.

Figure 3.11 shows the first two pages of an example Megaspace ratings profile (see the CD-ROM for an entire profile). The following project description is used in conjunction with the profile to estimate the effort and schedule for the final cycle of development. First we perform a top level estimate which assumes all components are rated the same.

The project is similar to the historical project BST-2 (another major upgrade to an existing system) except for the following differences:

- Most of the same staff will develop the system, except they now have two more years of experience relative to their BST-2 ratings. Despite the new hardware, assume that the platform appears very similar to the one used in BST-2.

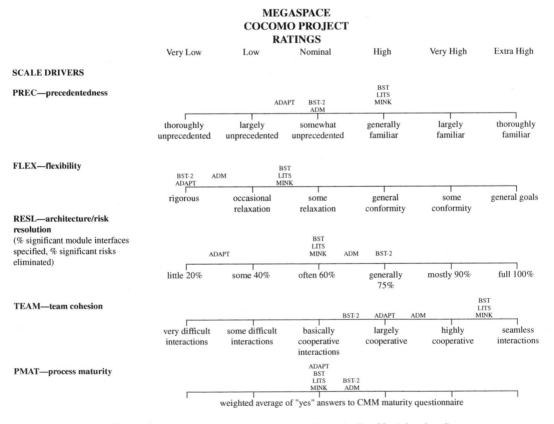

**Figure 3.11**   Megaspace Cost Driver Ratings Profile (abridged)

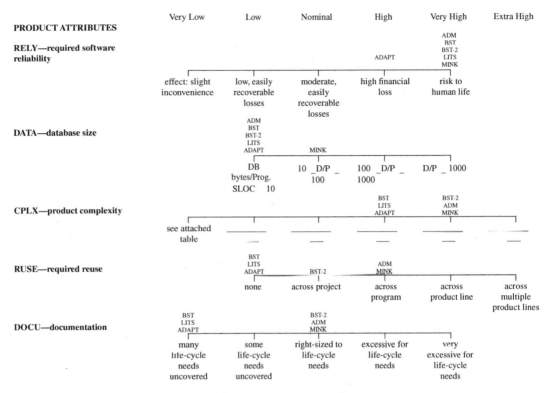

**Figure 3.11** *Continued*

- The spiral development approach has reduced the number of unspecified interfaces and remaining major risks to only 10 percent.
- A new operating system will be used for development. In the past year of its use, there have been five major changes to the OS.
- The project has also invested in an integrated software engineering environment that supports all life-cycle phases, and is mandated for use by the developers.
- The database size proportion will be very similar to the MINK project.
- Process improvement activities have resulted in an SEI CMM Level 3 rating.
- Same required reuseability as the breadboard development, i.e., it must be designed for reuse.

Using the above descriptions in conjunction with the BST-2 and MINK ratings, the scale and cost-driver ratings in Tables 3.22 and 3.23 are obtained.

For the Radar Unit Control component, the estimate of new code development is 3,215 SLOC of Ada, with 500 SLOC being modified from the breadboard

**Table 3.22    ARS Full Development Scale Drivers**

| Scale Driver | Rating | Rationale |
|---|---|---|
| PREC | Nominal | Same as BST-2 |
| FLEX | Very Low | Same as BST-2 |
| RESL | Very High | Unspecified interfaces and remaining major risks are 10%, (or 90% specified/eliminated) |
| TEAM | Nominal | Same as BST-2 (rounded to Nominal) |
| PMAT | High | SEI CMM Level 3 |

**Table 3.23    ARS Full-Development Cost Drivers (Top Level)**

| Cost Driver | Rating | Rationale |
|---|---|---|
| RELY | Very High | Same as BST-2 |
| DATA | Nominal | Same as MINK |
| CPLX | Very High | Same as BST-2 |
| RUSE | Very High | Must be reusable across the product line. |
| DOCU | Nominal | Same as BST-2 |
| TIME | Very High | Same as BST-2 |
| STOR | High | Same as BST-2 |
| PVOL | Nominal | A major OS change every 6 months. |
| ACAP | High | Same as BST-2 |
| PCAP | High | Same as BST-2 |
| PCON | High | Same as BST-2 |
| APEX | Very High | Eight years of average experience (off the chart) is still rated as Very High. |
| PLEX | Very High | Rounded off to Very High (5 years is closer to 6 than 3). |
| LTEX | Nominal | Even though the language experience is higher, it must be averaged with the brand new toolset. |
| TOOL | Very High | The highest capability and integration level of software toolsets. |
| SITE | Nominal | Same as BST-2 (rounded off to Nominal). |
| SCED | Very Low | The constrained schedule is 76% of the nominal schedule (i.e., the estimate when SCED is set to nominal). |

baseline. It is estimated that about 30 percent of the design will have to be modified with considerable test and evaluation of the modified components to assess them. It is thought that the code to be modified is fairly well-structured, but has little correlation between program and application views. There is a medium amount of documentation associated with the code.

The Radar Item Processing software can be subdivided into new, modified from the breadboard and automatically translated. In the modified portion of 11,500 SLOC, only 5 percent of the design needs to be changed, 14 percent of the code will be modified, and 100 percent retesting will be required. The breadboard development produced excellent documentation for the object-oriented Ada 95 portions. The design and code was made to be reused and requires no assessment. An estimated 13,715 SLOC will be developed new.

The Radar Database component will have 12,200 new SLOC, and the rest is reused.

The Display Manager software requires 15,400 new SLOC, and the rest will be reused from the breadboard.

The Display Console software is estimated as 13,200 new SLOC and very little modification from the breadboard. Only 1,800 SLOC will be modified by 20 percent for design and code.

Finally, the Built-In Test software needs 16,000 SLOC of new software, and the existing base is completely reused. It automatically diagnoses faults and identifies problems at the hardware replaceable unit level. It also supports fault tolerance since the system must be highly reliable.

One-half of the staff was present during the breadboard development, and the other half is new. The average familiarity with the existing software is somewhat familiar (assume this holds for all components). For all modified software, assume the same software understanding parameters hold as for Radar Unit Control.

Table 3.24 shows the size calculations based on these descriptions. Since there is more project detail known compared to the breadboard system, the component data is more detailed than the breadboard estimate. Note that the COTS code is treated as reused code. The equivalent size calculations are shown to illustrate the method, since most COCOMO tools automate the calculations based on input reuse parameters.

Unless stated otherwise, the Assessment and Assimilation increment is 0 for reused code, and 2 for modified code.

As in the breadboard system, equivalent size calculations are not performed for automatically translated code. For the ARS, automatic translation productivity was measured during the breadboard development as 1,150 SLOC/person-month. It was also found that only 75 percent of the original radar item processing code could be successfully translated by tools. The remaining portion to be converted to Ada is 58,320 SLOC. The automatic translation effort alone is:

**Table 3.24  ARS Full-Development System-Size Calculations**

| Component | Size | Language | Type | REVL (%) | DM | CM | IM | AA | SU | UNFM | AAM | Equivalent Size |
|---|---|---|---|---|---|---|---|---|---|---|---|---|
| Radar Unit Control | 3215 | Ada 95 | New | 2 | — | — | — | — | — | — | 0 | 3279 |
| | 500 | Ada 95 | Modified | 2 | 30 | 30 | 40 | 6 | 33 | .4 | 47.7 | 243 |
| | 5738 | Ada 95 | Reused | 2 | 0 | 0 | 40 | 0 | — | — | 12 | 702 |
| Radar Item Processing | 13715 | Ada 95 | New | 15 | — | — | — | — | — | — | 0 | 15772 |
| | 11500 | Ada 95 | Modified | 15 | 5 | 14 | 40 | 2 | 30 | .4 | 24.6 | 3249 |
| | 58320 | Ada 95 | Translated | 15 | — | — | — | — | — | — | 0 | 0 |
| Radar Database | 12200 | Ada 95 | New | 6 | — | — | — | — | — | — | 0 | 12932 |
| | 9494 | Ada 95 | Reused | 6 | — | — | 40 | 0 | — | — | 12 | 1208 |
| Display Manager | 15400 | Ada 95, C | New | 4 | — | — | — | — | — | — | 0 | 16016 |
| | 31440 | Ada 95, C | Reused | 4 | 0 | 0 | 40 | 0 | — | — | 12 | 3924 |
| | 24566 | C | COTS | 4 | 0 | 0 | 40 | 0 | — | — | 12 | 3066 |
| Display Console | 13200 | C | New | 4 | — | — | — | — | — | — | 0 | 13728 |
| | 1800 | C | Modified | 4 | 20 | 20 | 40 | 2 | 30 | .4 | 34.2 | 641 |
| | 2876 | C, microcode | COTS | 4 | 0 | 0 | 40 | 0 | — | — | 12 | 359 |
| Built-In Test | 16000 | Ada 95, assembler | New | 10 | — | — | — | — | — | — | 0 | 17600 |
| | 4200 | Ada 95, assembler | Reused | 10 | 0 | 0 | 40 | 0 | — | — | 12 | 554 |
| TOTAL | | | | | | | | | | | | 93274 |

$$PM_M = ASLOC\ (AT/100)/ATPROD$$
$$= 58{,}320\ ASLOC * (.75)/1{,}150\ SLOC/\text{person-month}$$
$$= 38.0\ \text{person-months.}$$

Note that schedule constraint effects are not applied to the automatic translation effort. The remaining effort for the rest of the system is estimated as:

$$PM = 2.94 \times Size^E \times \prod_{i=1}^{n} EM_i = 526.5\ \text{person-months.}$$

The overall effort is then 526.5 + 38 = 565 person-months.

The overall schedule is calculated with equation 2.14 (again excluding the automated translation effort):

$$TDEV = \left[ 3.67 \times (PM_{NS})^{(0.28 + 0.2 \times (E - 0.91)]} \right] \times \frac{SCED\ \%}{100} = 17.5\ \text{months.}$$

Even though the effort is larger than the breadboard development, the schedule time is less.

Figure 3.12 shows the USC COCOMO output screen for this case, and Figure 3.13 shows the cost-driver ratings. Since this was a top-level estimate, the system was treated as a single component with the total equivalent SLOC. Alternatively, component size information could have been input with each component having the same cost driver ratings.

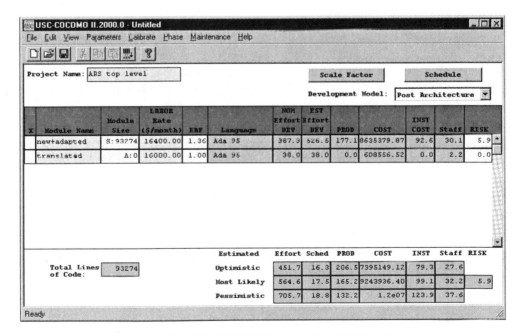

**Figure 3.12** USC COCOMO Output for ARS Top Level

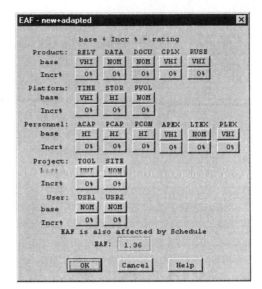

**Figure 3.13**  Cost Driver Ratings
for ARS Top-Level Estimate

### 3.3.5   Full Development—Detailed Component Estimate

The previous exercise demonstrated a top-level estimate, whereby all the components were treated in aggregate. This exercise will instead account for differences in the component cost-driver ratings. The scale drivers stay the same since they apply to the project as a whole.

Tables 3.25 through 3.30 show the detailed cost-driver ratings and rationale that differ from the top-level estimate. Most of the component cost drivers remain the same as the aggregate ones, so only the changed ones are listed for convenience.[1] Differences between components are primarily caused by different functional specifications, different teams, or varying development environments. For example, the Built-In Test TOOL rating is lower since standard tools don't cover the more complex and low-level hardware testing environment. The development and testing require more primitive operations.

As in the previous top-level estimate, automatic translation effort is calculated alone to be 38 person-months. Using the detailed component data, the remaining effort for the rest of the system is estimated as:

$$PM = 2.94 \times Size^E \times \prod_{i=1}^{n} EM_i = 718.4 \text{ person-months.}$$

The overall effort is then 718.4 + 38 = 756 person-months.

---

[1]Some estimation tools provide hierarchical inheritance of default cost-driver settings to minimize user inputs in such a situation.

**Table 3.25   Radar Unit Control Detailed Cost Drivers—Changes from Top-level**

| Cost Driver | Rating | Rationale |
|---|---|---|
| STOR | Very High | 85% utilization; the unique hardware constrains on-board memory additions |
| PLEX | Nominal | About 1 year of experience with the new hardware platform |

**Table 3.26   Radar Item Processing Detailed Cost Drivers—Changes from Top-level**

| Cost Driver | Rating | Rationale |
|---|---|---|
| CPLX | Extra High | Highly complex mathematics and radar processing algorithms with noisy data and realtime constraints |
| ACAP | Very High | 90th percentile; the very best analysts have been put on this critical component |
| PCON | Nominal | 12% per year estimated personnel attrition, since a couple team members are planned for transfer in the middle of the project |

**Table 3.27   Radar Database Detailed Cost Drivers—Changes from Top-level**

| Cost Driver | Rating | Rationale |
|---|---|---|
| DATA | Very High | 2000 database bytes per SLOC |
| CPLX | Nominal | The database implementation is straightforward with few real-time constraints |
| PLEX | Nominal | This team has about 1 year of average platform experience |

**Table 3.28   Display Manager Detailed Cost Drivers—Changes from Top-level**

| Cost Driver | Rating | Rationale |
|---|---|---|
| DATA | Low | Very small database |
| PCON | Nominal | Higher personnel attrition than rest of project; graphics programmers are relatively young and in high demand; estimated 12% attrition per year |

**Table 3.29    Display Console Detailed Cost Drivers—Changes from Top-level**

| Cost Driver | Rating | Rationale |
|---|---|---|
| DATA | Low | Very small database for the display console |
| CPLX | Extra High | Complex dynamic displays, micro-code control and hard real-time constraints |
| PVOL | High | Frequent hardware changes due to proprietary hardware developed in parallel with the software |
| PLEX | Low | Only 6 months experience on new hardware with revised graphics software version |
| LTEX | Nominal | Experienced C programmers are brand new to the toolset. |
| TOOL | Nominal | The software toolsets are not made for this hardware, so not all features can be used |

**Table 3.30    Built In Test Detailed Cost Drivers—Changes from Top-level**

| Cost Driver | Rating | Rationale |
|---|---|---|
| RUSE | High | Must be reusable across program. The nature of this function does not lend itself to very high reuse due to unique hardware environment. |
| TIME | Extra High | Using 95% of available CPU time in the central computer when Built In Test is running on top of other software. |
| TOOL | Nominal | This software is distributed in the two processors, and the tools are not made for the custom hardware environment. This software also requires low-level hardware monitoring. |

The overall schedule is calculated with equation 2.14:

$$TDEV = \left[ 3.67 \times (PM_{NS})^{(0.28 + 0.2 \times (E - 0.91))} \right] \times \frac{SCED\ \%}{100} = 19.3 \text{ months.}$$

Figure 3.14 shows the USC COCOMO output. The last column labeled "RISK" shows a top-level assessment of project risk based on cost driver ratings. The Expert COCOMO risk-assessment scheme is overviewed in Chapter 5 (Emerging Extensions), Section 5.7 and detailed in [Madachy 1997].

Refining an estimate in detail such as this serves to rethink assumptions and usually converges toward a better estimate. In this case, a more detailed look produces an estimate for 161 PM more effort and an extra month of schedule time compared to the top level estimate. The extra detail is also essential for large-

USC-COCOMO II.2000.0 - Untitled

File  Edit  View  Parameters  Calibrate  Phase  Maintenance  Help

Project Name: ARS detailed

Scale Factor          Schedule

Development Model: Post Architecture

| X | Module Name | Module Size | LABOR Rate ($/month) | EAF | Language | NOM Effort DEV | EST Effort DEV | PROD | COST | INST COST | Staff | RISK |
|---|---|---|---|---|---|---|---|---|---|---|---|---|
| | ruc new | S:3279 | 15400.00 | 1.78 | Ada 95 | 13.6 | 24.3 | 135.1 | 373692.42 | 114.0 | 1.3 | 6.7 |
| | ruc mod | A:243 | 15400.00 | 1.78 | Ada 95 | 1.0 | 1.8 | 135.1 | 27693.58 | 114.0 | 0.1 | 6.7 |
| | ruc reused | A:702 | 15400.00 | 1.78 | Ada 95 | 2.9 | 5.2 | 135.1 | 80003.68 | 114.0 | 0.3 | 6.7 |
| | rip new | S:15772 | 17000.00 | 1.64 | Ada 95 | 65.5 | 107.3 | 147.0 | 1824112.29 | 115.7 | 5.6 | 7.0 |
| | rip mod | A:3249 | 17000.00 | 1.64 | Ada 95 | 13.5 | 22.1 | 147.0 | 375763.43 | 115.7 | 1.1 | 7.0 |
| | rd new | S:12932 | 16800.00 | 1.53 | Ada 95 | 53.7 | 82.0 | 157.6 | 1378274.56 | 106.6 | 4.2 | 5.7 |
| | rd reused | A:1206 | 16800.00 | 1.53 | Ada 95 | 5.0 | 7.7 | 157.6 | 128533.80 | 106.6 | 0.4 | 5.7 |
| | dm new | S:16016 | 14900.00 | 1.36 | Ada 95 | 66.5 | 90.4 | 177.1 | 1347146.56 | 84.1 | 4.7 | 5.9 |
| | dm reused | A:3923 | 14900.00 | 1.36 | Ada 95 | 16.3 | 22.1 | 177.1 | 329973.52 | 84.1 | 1.1 | 5.9 |
| | dm cots | A:3065 | 14900.00 | 1.36 | C | 12.7 | 17.3 | 177.1 | 257804.96 | 84.1 | 0.9 | 5.9 |
| | dc new | S:13728 | 16500.00 | 3.00 | C | 57.0 | 171.2 | 80.2 | 2825293.05 | 205.8 | 8.9 | 10.4 |
| | dc mod | A:640 | 16500.00 | 3.00 | C | 2.7 | 8.0 | 80.2 | 131715.29 | 205.8 | 0.4 | 10.4 |
| | dc cots | A:358 | 16500.00 | 3.00 | C | 1.5 | 4.5 | 80.2 | 73678.24 | 205.8 | 0.2 | 10.4 |
| | bit new | S:17600 | 16200.00 | 2.05 | Ada 95 | 73.1 | 149.8 | 117.5 | 2426003.53 | 137.8 | 7.8 | 10.5 |
| | bit reused | A:554 | 16200.00 | 2.05 | Ada 95 | 2.3 | 4.7 | 117.5 | 76363.97 | 137.8 | 0.2 | 10.5 |
| | translated | A:0 | 16500.00 | 1.00 | Ada 95 | 28.0 | 30.0 | 0.0 | 627573.91 | 0.0 | 2.0 | 0.0 |

| Total Lines of Code: 93267 | | Effort | Sched | PROD | COST | INST | Staff | RISK |
|---|---|---|---|---|---|---|---|---|
| | Optimistic | 605.1 | 18.0 | 154.1 | 9826901.45 | 105.4 | 33.6 | |
| | Most Likely | 756.4 | 19.3 | 123.3 | 1.2e07 | 131.7 | 39.2 | 115.3 |
| | Pessimistic | 945.5 | 20.7 | 98.6 | 1.5e07 | 164.6 | 45.7 | |

Ready

**Figure 3.14**  USC COCOMO Output for ARS Detailed

project planning and control instruments such as Work Breakdown Structures and earned-value tracking systems.

### 3.3.6 Incremental Development Example

This section applies COCOMO II to incremental development, which is a commonly used lifecycle approach. The formulas for incremental COCOMO used in this example are described in Appendix B. This example separates the previous single-shot development shown in Section 3.3.5 into three time-phased increments, or individually delivered "builds" of software.

Incremental development reduces risk by providing reduced-scale increments of increasing functionality. It tends to create a flatter staffing profile compared to a single-shot waterfall approach, but increases schedule time somewhat.

The development process described here is also called an incremental waterfall, since requirements and preliminary design are conducted first for all increments before individual increments are developed. Implementation of separate increments is carefully scheduled in time, and normally there is some parallel work being done on more than one increment simultaneously.

The USC COCOMO tool used thus far is based on waterfall life-cycle activities (a single sequence of requirements, design, code/unit test, integration, and testing) with no explicit utilities for estimating multiple increments. In order to estimate incremental development with USC COCOMO, several runs would be made with manual adjustments to effort and schedule, and then the results would have to be combined. The commercial tool Costar provides a comprehensive implementation of incremental COCOMO consistent with the Appendix B definition, and will be used in this example.

When planning incremental builds, deciding which functions to deliver when depends on specific project factors. In this case of the radar system, the following constraints will guide the phasing of incremental functionality:

- A large portion of the Display software is wanted early for user interface and scenario evaluation, and the remainder will be split among the later two builds. Nearly the entire set of graphic primitives is needed first to enable the sophisticated displays, and for general performance testing of the graphics engine and human-machine interface.
- There is an urgent need for a subset of the Radar Item Processing and Radar Database software dedicated to specific vehicles involved in a current military situation, so it's critical that this software is delivered in the first increment. To enable quickest delivery of this capability, all other radar items will be deferred until later builds.
- Most of the Radar Unit Control functionality will be present in the first increment, since the interface and basic operating parameters are well-known from previous experience. However, the radar hardware is new and there are some new capabilities planned for the latter two increments.
- The Built-In Test software requires the final radar item hardware for most of its operations, so only a shell process will exist until the final build when the hardware will be ready.

Given these constraints, the following portions of software are planned per increment:

Increment 1
    50 percent of Display Manager
    80 percent of Display Console
    25 percent of Radar Item Processing and Radar Database
     5 percent of Built In Test
    70 percent of Radar Unit Control

Increment 2
  25 percent of Display Manager
  15 percent of Display Console
  45 percent of Radar Item Processing and Radar Database
  10 percent of Built In Test
  15 percent of Radar Unit Control

Increment 3
  25 percent of Display Manager
   5 percent of Display Console
  30 percent of Radar Item Processing and Radar Database
  85 percent of Built In Test
  15 percent of Radar Unit Control

**Increment Volatility.** A nominal amount of requirements evolution and volatility is expected. Specifications for the new radar items are volatile since intelligence information is still being gathered, so 30 percent requirements evolution and volatility is expected for Increment 1 in the Radar Item Processing and Radar Database areas. The requirements evolution and volatility in these areas is estimated to be only 20 percent and 15 percent for the last increments. Experience with Increment 1 displays will likely cause a little volatility during the latter increments, so 10 percent will be assumed for the latter increments for both Display Manager and Display Console. Only 10 percent requirements evolution and volatility of the first increment of Radar Unit Control is expected, but 20 percent for the last two since those represent untried capabilities. Most of the changes to Built-In Test will occur after field testing, and do not show up in this estimate.

The personnel experience factors will improve slightly between increments to represent the staff experience gains over the project duration (it's expected that most people will stay on the project, and there will be little attrition). A few of the product factors will also vary between increments for a given component, to describe the portion of software being worked at different times.

The chosen incremental phasing model determines the beginning of each increment relative to predecessor increments. In this example, the starting points for increments 2 and 3 are the Preliminary Design Walkthrough (PDW) milestones of the previous increments.

Summary Costar reports are shown in the following figures. Figure 3.15 shows the hierarchical structure of the software components with their respective equivalent sizes. Note that the three builds serve as hierarchy branches containing their software components as leaves. One difference with size tables shown earlier in this section and Figure 3.15 is that a component in Costar has both new and adapted portions; thus new and modified (or new and reused) parts of a component are listed as a single component using the Costar tool.

Figure 3.16 shows increment time-phasing assumptions, including the start point of each increment and any phasing delays. Note the convention that re-

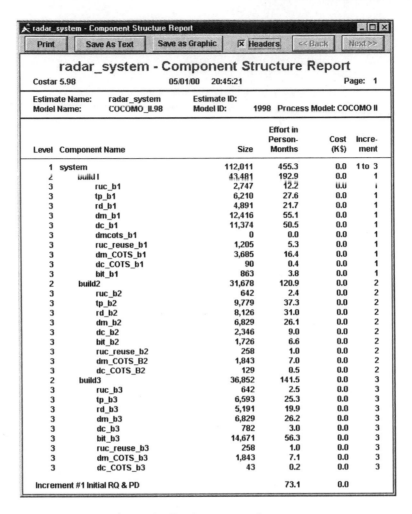

**Figure 3.15**   Component Structure

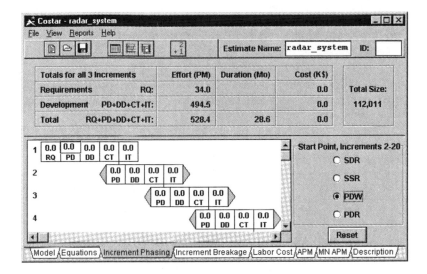

**Figure 3.16** Increment Phasing

quirements work is done once for all increments, and that development of the individual increments includes preliminary design through testing. Figure 3.17 shows increment summary information. There are numerous other screens and detailed graphical or tabular reports available in Costar.

**radar_system - Increment Summary Report**

Costar 5.98    05/01/00    20:41:47    Page: 1

| Estimate Name: | radar_system | Estimate ID: | |
|---|---|---|---|
| Model Name: | COCOMO_II.98 | Model ID: | 1990 Process Model: COCOMO II |

Starting Point for each Increment:    PDW

| Incr | Size | Break -age | Effort in Person-Months | Cost (K$) | Mile- stone | Start Month | Months | Stop Month |
|---|---|---|---|---|---|---|---|---|
| 1 | 43,481 | -- | 266.1 | 0.0 | -- | 0.0 | 16.9 | 16.9 |
| 2 | 31,678 | 0% | 120.9 | 0.0 | UTC | 13.4 | 9.0 | 22.4 |
| 3 | 36,852 | 0% | 141.5 | 0.0 | UTC | 19.2 | 9.4 | 28.6 |

**Figure 3.17** Increment Summary

# 4

# Calibration[†]

## 4.1  BAYESIAN CALIBRATION AND COCOMO II MODELING METHODOLOGY

Suppose you have two software cost estimation models. Model D (data-determined) has had all its cost-driver values calibrated to the best data you have available. However, because software project data inevitably is collected with imprecise definitions of what is included in the product, in the process, and in the workforce, some of the cost driver values calibrated to the noisy data do not square with your experts' experience.

This has led to Model E (expert-determined). It uses the same form and cost drivers as Model D, but its cost-driver values have been determined by expert consensus. By definition, Model E's values cannot provide a better fit to your existing project data than the best-fit values of Model D. Some of your experts

---

[†]The work that formed the basis for this chapter first appeared in the paper "From Multiple Regression to Bayesian Analysis for COCOMO II," co-authored by Sunita Chulani, Barry Boehm, and Bert Steece, and which was presented at the combined 21st Annual Conference of the International Society of Parametric Analysts (ISPA)/9th Annual Conference of the Society of Cost Estimating and Analysis (SCEA) held in June 1999 in San Antonio, Texas. The work was recognized at this gathering with two awards: best paper in the software track as well as best paper overall in the conference, for which the authors are most appreciative.

clearly believe that Model E captures some software phenomena better than Model D, and may be a better estimator for future projects. But others don't.

Now, suppose you have a new project to estimate. Model D estimates it will take 122 person-months (PM) to complete; Model E estimates 236 PM. Which value should you choose? If you want to average the estimates, do you just go halfway, at 179 PM? How do you justify your estimate to your management, your venture capitalist, or to the source selection authority for your competitive proposal?

### 4.1.1   Bayesian Calibration

What you would like is a technique for creating a Model B (Balanced), that favors the experts for cost drivers where they are in strong agreement and the data fit is weak, and favors the data fit for cost drivers where it is strong and the experts disagree. You would also like a technique that has a strong theoretical foundation to justify its results.

This technique is provided by the Bayesian approach to determining model parameters [Box-Tiao 1973; Gelman et al. 1995]. In the COCOMO II version of the Bayesian approach, the Model E parameter values and their variances are taken as the *a priori* knowledge about the parameter values. The Model D parameter values and their variances are then taken as new information which can be used to determine an *a posteriori* update of the parameter values. The Bayesian approach basically produces a weighted average of the Model D and E values, which gives higher weights to parameter values with smaller variances. The detailed approach and formulas are provided in this chapter.

We encountered the Model E–Model D problem when calibrating the 1997 version of COCOMO II to eighty-three project data points. Because of data imprecision and lack of dispersion of rating values, one of the cost-driver parameters (for Develop for Reusability) emerged from the Model D analysis with a negative sign (indicating a trend opposite to expert judgment) and a large variance. Model D's estimates for the eighty-three 1997 data points came within 30 percent of the actuals 64 percent of the time [PRED(.30) = 64%]. But when it was used on the calibration year 2000 sample of 161 data points, it achieved only a PRED(.30) of 44 percent.

When we applied the Bayesian approach to the Model E and 1997 Model D parameter values and their variances, the Develop for Reusability parameter emerged with a positive sign. The resulting Bayesian model achieved only a PRED(.30) of 58 percent on the 1997 data, but it achieved a much stronger PRED (.30) of 64 percent on the 2000 sample of 161 data points.

Using the Bayesian approach to combine Model E with a 2000 Model D calibrated to the full 2000 set of 161 data points produced even stronger results: a PRED(.30) of 75 percent for the general calibration and a PRED(.30) of 80 percent when each organization's data was separately calibrated to its own coefficient value. Thus, we believe that the Bayesian calibration approach has provided a robust estimation model (now called COCOMO II.2000) with a sound underlying rationale for its results. Again, further specifics are provided in this chapter and also in further detail in [Chulani 1999 and Chulani et al. 1999].

### 4.1.2    COCOMO II Modeling Methodology

Before one can poll experts and collect data on the parameters of an estimation model, one needs to carefully define the parameters. Also, one needs to have a good idea of how the parameters are going to be used to produce effective estimates.

This means that one needs to do a lot of early homework to determine an appropriate functional form for the estimation model, and to determine which parameters are most likely to significantly influence the quantity being estimated. One needs to ensure that the parameters are sufficiently well defined to obtain consistent values for parameter estimates and project data.

We have developed a seven-step modeling methodology to minimize the risk that we consume a lot of people's time and effort supplying data that produces poor estimates. We began by using it for COCOMO II and have continued to use it for COCOTS, COQUALMO, COPSEMO, and CORADMO.

#### 4.1.2.1    MODELING STEPS

The seven steps are summarized in Figure 4.1.

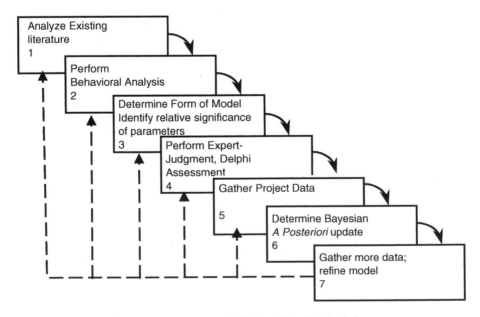

**Figure 4.1**    COCOMO II Modeling Methodology

For COCOMO II, we performed Step 1 by reviewing the software cost modeling literature for insights on improved functional forms, potentially significant parameters, and parameter definition issues (e.g., size). This led to the identification of potential new parameters such as Process Maturity and Multisite Development, the continuation of a number of parameters from COCOMO 81, and the dropping of such COCOMO 81 parameters as Turnaround Time (no longer relevant because of the widespread use of interactive workstations) and Modern Programming Practices (subsumed by Process Maturity). It also led to the reformulation of some of the models such as the linear software reuse model.

Step 2 in Figure 4.1 involves a behavioral analysis to determine what the difference between a low- and high-parameter rating means to the performance of project tasks and the resulting project effort and schedule. These analyses help determine the relative significance of each potential model parameter in terms of its effect on project effort and schedule (COCOMO 81 also used such behavioral analyses; see the "Project Activity Differences" tables in Chapters 24 to 27 of [Boehm 1981]). This can lead to dropping some parameters and combining others, e.g., combining Language Experience and Tool Experience into a single parameter (Step 3).

The results of these analyses are presented in a COCOMO II Affiliates' workshop, frequently leading to some further changes. The final set of parameters are provided with carefully defined rating scales, which undergo a dry run before being used to collect data and perform expert, Delphi parameter-value assessments (Step 4).

We use a Wideband Delphi process [Helmer 1966; Boehm 1981, Chapter 22], which stimulates consistency of interpretations and increased consensus among the experts. But it inevitably ends with some variance around the experts' mean parameter values, indicating the degree to which the experts disagree on the parameter's effect on the quantity being estimated. These parameter means and variances can be used as the *a priori* Model E, which can then be updated with the data-determined Model D values and variances to produce the *a posteriori* Bayesian Model B values (Steps 5 and 6).

Of course, even with all of this cross-checking between experts and data, new insights emerge which require refinement of the model (Step 7). For example, in trying to fit the model to a large maintenance organization's data, we found that our original attempt to unify the COCOMO II maintenance and reuse models was unrealistic, and that we needed to add another parameter to the separate reuse and maintenance models to reflect the relative familiarity of the personnel with the software they were modifying.

### 4.1.2.2  OPERATIONAL IMPLICATIONS

That we remain convinced of the need to treat COCOMO II as an evolving model is good because it will keep COCOMO II up with the times. But it has the complicating effect that each time COCOMO II is revised, its new estimates will not match the old ones.

This may cause you complications in working out with your manager or customer what to do about your negotiated budgets and schedules based on the older version of COCOMO II. The best we have found to help you in this situation is the following:

- *Plan for new COCOMO II releases every two years*, so that nobody is surprised when a new version becomes available;
- *Continue to support and publish the parameter values for all the previous releases*, so that you can continue to use a previous version if that best fits your situation, or so that you can assess the differences in estimates as applied to your project.

## 4.2    TOPICS ADDRESSED

Section 4.3 covers the COCOMO II data collection approach and describes the Rosetta Stone that converts COCOMO 81 project files to COCOMO II.2000 project files. Section 4.4 discusses the statistical modeling methodology used in this new calibration effort and elaborates on the problems caused by our use of observational, as opposed to experimental, data. Section 4.5 describes data and the calibration approaches used in COCOMO II. Section 4.6 presents several ways that COCOMO II can be locally tailored to a particular environment to improve prediction accuracy. Section 4.7 summarizes the COCOMO II.2000 data. Section 4.8 presents our conclusions.

## 4.3    COCOMO II DATA COLLECTION APPROACH

### 4.3.1    Obtaining Consistent Data

Model calibration results become suspect if they are based on data that were collected using incompatible definitions and assumptions. We have described COCOMO II's definitions and assumptions in detail in Chapter 2, and have incorporated these in our data collection efforts. The COCOMO II data collection forms in Appendix C include questions about these definitions and assumptions. We have filtered over 2000 candidate project data points to get the current set of 161 data points in the COCOMO II database. For each of these 161 data points, we have performed follow up interviews and many site visits with the relevant project personnel to ensure that the data reflect COCOMO II-consistent definitions and assumptions

### 4.3.2    The Rosetta Stone

We have developed a system to update COCOMO 81 so that it can be used with the COCOMO II model. We call the system the Rosetta Stone [Reifer et al. 1999] because it is not unlike the black slab found by French troops in 1799 in Egypt containing three scripts (Greek, demotic and hieroglyphics) that enabled archae-ologists to construct translations among the three languages. The Rosetta Stone permits users to translate project files prepared using the original COCOMO 81 model to a form compatible with COCOMO II.

Why is the creation of the Rosetta Stone important? While many of our users wanted to take advantage of the many enhanced capabilities of COCOMO II, they needed to maintain their historical databases created for COCOMO 81. Since the new version of the model has a different structure, different parameters and parametric ratings, the conversion of the files was not a straightfoward task.

### 4.3.2.1   THE COCOMO II ESTIMATING MODEL

To understand the Rosetta Stone, one must clearly comprehend the differ-ences between COCOMO 81 and COCOMO II and why the differences are im-portant. Model differences are summarized in Table 4.1. These changes are important because they reflect how the state of software engineering technology has evolved over the past two decades. For example, programmers submitted batch jobs when the COCOMO 81 model was first published. Turnaround time clearly affected their productivity. Therefore, a model parameter TURN reflected the average wait the programmers experienced before receiving their job back. Such a parameter is no longer important because most programmers have instant access to computational facilities through their workstation. Therefore, the para-meter has been removed in the COCOMO II model.

The following summary of Table 4.1 highlights the major differences be-tween COCOMO 81 and COCOMO II (see Table 2.58 for a full summary of the changes made to enhance COCOMO 81):

- COCOMO II addresses the following three phases of the spiral life cycle: Applications Development, Early Design and Post-Architecture.
- The estimating equation exponent (the three different software develop-ment modes in COCOMO 81) is determined by five Scale Factors.
- The following cost drivers were added to COCOMO II: DOCU, RUSE, PVOL, PLEX, LTEX, PCON, and SITE.
- The following cost drivers were deleted from the original COCOMO: VIRT, TURN, VEXP, LEXP, and MODP.
- The ratings for those cost drivers retained in COCOMO II were altered con-siderably to reflect more up-to-date software practices.

### 4.3.2.2   THE ROSETTA STONE

As shown in Table 4.1, users need to convert factors in the COCOMO equa-tions (i.e., the exponent, the size estimate, and the ratings for the cost drivers) from the original to the new version of the model.

We suggest that users employ the following steps to make the conversion so original COCOMO 81 project files can be used with the COCOMO II model:

**Table 4.1   Model Comparisons**

|  | COCOMO 81 | COCOMO II |
|---|---|---|
| Model structure | Single model which assumes you start with requirements allocated to software | Three models which assume you progress through a spiral type development to solidify your requirements, solidify the architecture and reduce risk |
| Mathematical form of effort equation | $Effort - A*\Pi(c_i)* (Size)^{Exponent}$ | $Effort = A*\Pi(c_i)* (Size)^{Exponent}$ |
| Exponent | Exponent = fixed constant selected as a function of mode<br>–Organic = 1.05<br>–Semidetached = 1.12<br>–Embedded = 1.20 | Exponent = variable established based upon rating of five scale factors<br>–**PREC**, Precedentedness<br>–**FLEX**, Development Flexibility<br>–**RESL**, Architecture/Risk Resolution<br>–**TEAM**, Team Cohesion<br>–**PMAT**, Process Maturity |
| Size | Source lines of code (with extensions for function points) | Application points, function points or source lines of code |
| Cost Drivers ($c_i$) | Fifteen drivers each of which must be rated:<br>–**RELY**, Reliability<br>–**DATA**, Data Base Size<br>–**CPLX**, Complexity<br>–**TIME**, Execution Time Constraint<br>–**STOR**, Main Storage Constraint<br>–**VIRT**, Virtual Machine Volatility<br>–**TURN**, Turnaround Time<br>–**ACAP**, Analyst Capability<br>–**PCAP**, Programmer Capability<br>–**AEXP**, Applications Experience<br>–**VEXP**, Virt. Machine Experience<br>–**LEXP**, Language Experience<br>–**TOOL**, Use of Software Tools<br>–**MODP**, Use of Modern Programming Techniques | Seventeen drivers each of which must be rated<br>–**RELY**, Required Reliability<br>–**DATA**, Testing Database Size<br>–**CPLX**, Product Complexity<br>–**RUSE**, Develop for Reusability<br>–**DOCU**, Documentation to Meet Life Cycle Needs<br>–**TIME**, Execution Time Constraint<br>–**STOR**, Main Storage Constraint<br>–**PVOL**, Platform Volatility<br>–**ACAP**, Analyst Capability<br>–**PCAP**, Programmer Capability<br>–**APEX**, Applications Experience<br>–**PCON**, Personnel Continuity<br>–**PLEX**, Platform Experience<br>–**LTEX**, Language & Tool Experience<br>–**TOOL**, Use of Software Tools<br>–**SITE**, Multisite Development<br>–**SCED**, Required Schedule |
| Other model differences | Model based upon:<br>–Linear reuse formula<br>–Assumption of reasonably stable requirements | Has many other enhancements including:<br>–Nonlinear reuse formula<br>–Reuse model which looks at effort needed to understand and assimilate<br>–Ratings which are used to address requirements volatility |

**4.3.2.2.1 Update Size.** The original COCOMO cost-estimating model used deliverable source lines of code (DSI) as its measure of the size of the software job. DSI were defined in terms of non-comment physical card images. COCOMO II uses the following three different measures to bound the volume of work associated with a software job: source lines of code (SLOC's), function points and application points. SLOC's are counted using logical language statements per Software Engineering Institute guidelines (e.g., IF-THEN-ELSE, ELSE IF is considered a single statement, not two statements) [Park 1992]. Table 4.2 provides guidelines for converting size in DSI to SLOC's so that they can be used with the COCOMO II model. It is important that you use counts for the actual size for the file instead of the original estimate. Such practices allow you to correlate your actuals (e.g., the actual application size with the effort required to do the work associated with developing the software)

The size reduction in COCOMO II is attributable to the need to convert physical card images to source line of code counts. As noted earlier, the pair IF-THEN-ELSE and END IF are counted *as two card images* in COCOMO 81 and as a single source instruction in COCOMO II. While the guidelines offered in Table 4.2 are based on statistical averages, we encourage you to use your actuals if you have them at your disposal.

**4.3.2.2.2 Convert Exponent.** Convert the original COCOMO 81 modes to Scale Factor settings using the Rosetta Stone values in Table 4.3. Then, adjust the ratings to reflect the actual situation. For example, the Rosetta Stone rating for PREC and FLEX represent the normal interpretation of the precedentedness and flexibility factors in the COCOMO 81 mode definition table [Boehm 1981; Table 4.3]. However, an Embedded project's actual precedentedness, for example, may have been even lower, and an adjustment to a Very Low rating may be in order.

A special case is the Process Maturity (PMAT) scale factor, which replaces the COCOMO 81 Modern Programming Practices (MODP) multiplicative cost driver. As seen in Table 4.4, MODP ratings of Very Low or Low translate into a

**Table 4.2    Converting Size Estimates**

| COCOMO 81 | COCOMO II |
|---|---|
| DSI | SLOC |
| –2nd generation languages | –reduce DSI by 35% |
| –3rd generation languages | –reduce DSI by 25% |
| –4th generation languages | –reduce DSI by 40% |
| –object-oriented languages | –reduce DSI by 30% |
| Function points | Use the expansion factors developed by Capers Jones [refer to http://www.spr.com for the latest set] to determine equivalent SLOC's |
| Feature points | Use the expansion factors developed by Capers Jones [refer to http://www.spr.com for the latest set] to determine equivalent SLOC's |

**Table 4.3    Mode/Scale Factor Conversion Ratings**

| Mode/scale factors | Organic | SEMIDETACHED | EMBEDDED |
|---|---|---|---|
| Precedentedness (PREC) | XH | H | L |
| Development flexibility (FLEX) | XH | H | L |
| Architecture/risk resolution (RESL) | XH | H | L |
| Team cohesion (TEAM) | XH | VH | N |
| Process maturity (PMAT) | $f$(MODP) | $f$(MODP) | $f$(MODP) |

**Table 4.4    Cost Drivers Conversions**

| COCOMO 81 DRIVERS | COCOMO II DRIVERS | CONVERSION FACTORS |
|---|---|---|
| RELY | RELY | None, rate the same or the actual |
| DATA | DATA | None, rate the same or the actual |
| CPLX | CPLX | None, rate the same or the actual |
| TIME | TIME | None, rate the same or the actual |
| STOR | STOR | None, rate the same or the actual |
| VIRT | PVOL | None, rate the same or the actual |
| TURN | | Use values in Table 4.5 |
| ACAP | ACAP | None, rate the same or the actual |
| PCAP | PCAP | None, rate the same or the actual |
| AEXP | APEX | Use next-highest rating. 1-year AEXP was rated L; for COCOMO II APEX 1 year is rated N. VH stays VH. |
| VEXP | PLEX | None, rate the same or the actual |
| LEXP | LTEX | None, rate the same or the actual |
| TOOL | TOOL | Use values in Table 4.5 |
| MODP | Adjust PMAT settings | If MODP is rated *VL* or *L*, set *PMAT* to *VL* <br> *N*, set PMAT to *L* <br> *H* or *VH*, set *PMAT* to *N* |
| SCED | SCED | None, rate the same or the actual |
| | RUSE | Set to *N*, or actual if available |
| | DOCU | If Mode = Organic, set to *L* <br> = Semidetached, set to *N* <br> = Embedded, set to *H* |
| | PCON | Set to *N*, or actual if available |
| | SITE | Set to *H*, or actual if available |

PMAT rating of Very Low, or a low Level 1 on the SEI CMM scale. A MODP rating of Nominal translates into a PMAT rating of Low, or a high Level 1. A MODP rating of High or Very High translates into a PMAT rating of Nominal or CMM Level 2. As with the other factors, if you know that the project's actual rating was different from the one provided by the Rosetta Stone, use the actual value.

The movement from modes to scale factors represents a major change in the model. To determine the economies/diseconomies of scale, five factors have been introduced. Because each of these factors can influence the power to which size is raised in the COCOMO II equation, they can profoundly impact cost and productivity. For example, increasing the rating from High to Very High in these parameters can introduce as much as an 11 percent swing in the resulting resource estimate for a million-SLOC product. Most of these factors are modern in their derivation. For example, the concept of process maturity wasn't even in its formative stages when the original COCOMO 81 model was published. In addition, the final three factors, RESL, TEAM and PMAT, show how an organization (and its customer working as a team) can mitigate the impact of diseconomy of scale. Finally, the first two, PREC and FLEX, correspond to the less controllable factors contributing to COCOMO 81 modes or interactions.

**4.3.2.2.3   Rate Cost Drivers.**   Because effort is also quite sensitive to cost drivers, proper conversion of these drivers is critical. For example, as with the scale factors we expect using experienced staff will make software development less expensive. Otherwise, why use expensive labor? Because the new version of the model uses altered drivers, the accuracy of the Rosetta Stone conversion guidelines outlined in Table 4.4 are quite important. Chapter 2 of this book describes the cost drivers in detail. Again, the ratings need to be adjusted to reflect what actually happened on the project. For example, while the original estimate may have assumed a very high level of analyst capability, perhaps we now know, in retrospect, that the caliber of analysts actually assigned should have been rated nominal. In instances like this, you should take advantage of your actual knowledge of what occurred on the project in order to make your estimates more reflective of what actually happened during the development process. Using such knowledge can significantly improve the credibility and accuracy of your predictions.

Since 1981, technology changes have significantly affected the TURN and TOOL rating scales. Because in today's computing environment virtually everyone uses interactive workstations to develop software, we have eliminated TURN from COCOMO II. Table 4.5 provides alternative multipliers for other COCOMO 81 TURN ratings.

The tool suites available in the 1990s far exceed those assumed by the COCOMO 81 Very High TOOL rating and virtually no projects operate at the COCOMO 81 Very Low or Low TOOL levels. COCOMO II has shifted the TOOL rating scale two levels higher so that a COCOMO 81 Nominal TOOL rating corresponds to a Very Low COCOMO II TOOL rating. Table 4.5 also provides a set of

**Table 4.5    TURN and TOOL Adjustments**

| COCOMO II MULTIPLIER ADJUSTMENT / COCOMO 81 RATING | VL | L | N | H | VH |
|---|---|---|---|---|---|
| TURN | | 1.00 | 1.15 | 1.23 | 1.32 |
| TOOL | VL*1.24 | VL*1.10 | VL | L | N |

COCOMO II multiplier adjustments corresponding to COCOMO 81 project ratings.

Some implementations of COCOMO II, such as the USC COCOMO II package, provide slots for extra user-defined cost drivers. The values in Table 4.5 can be put into such slots. If you do this for TOOL, use the ratings indicated and the adjustments (1.24, 1.10, 1.0, 1.0. 1.0).

**4.3.2.2.4    Experimental Accuracy.**  To assess the accuracy of the translations, we used the Rosetta Stone to convert eighty-nine projects representing clustered subsets of the database used for model calibration. These clusters were obtained by classifying the data based on specific domains. We updated our estimates using actuals whenever available. We then used the auto-calibration feature of the USC COCOMO II package to develop a constant for the effort equation (i.e., the $A$ in the equation: Effort $= A(Size)^P$). Finally, we compared our estimates to actuals and computed the relative error as a function of the following cases:

- Using the Rosetta Stone with no adjustments,
- Using the Rosetta Stone with knowledge base adjustments (i.e., updating the estimate files with actuals when available), and
- Using the Rosetta Stone with knowledge base adjustments and domain clustering (i.e., segmenting the data based upon organization or application area).

The results of these analyses, summarized in Table 4.6, show that we can achieve an acceptable degree of estimating accuracy using the Rosetta Stone to convert COCOMO 81 project files to run with the COCOMO II software cost model.

**4.3.2.2.5    Summary of Rosetta Stone and Its Usage Profile.**  The Rosetta Stone provides its users with both a process and tool for converting their original COCOMO 81 project files to COCOMO II project files. Remember that the Rosetta Stone provides a starting point for such efforts but does not replace the need to understand either the scope of the estimate or the changes that occurred as the project unfolded. Rather, the Rosetta Stone takes these considerations into account as you update its knowledge base with actuals.

**Table 4.6   Estimate Accuracy Analysis Results**

| Cases | Accuracy |
|---|---|
| Using the COCOMO II model as calibrated | Estimates within 25% of actuals, 68% of the time |
| Using the COCOMO II model as calibrated using developer or domain clustering | Estimates within 25% of actuals, 76% of the time |
| Using Rosetta Stone with no adjustments | Estimates within 25% of actuals, 60% of the time |
| Using the Rosetta Stone with knowledge base adjustments | Estimates within 25% of actuals, 68% of the time |
| Using the Rosetta Stone with knowledge base adjustments and domain clustering | Estimates within 25% of actuals, 74% of the time |

The eighty-nine-project database discussed above demonstrates the value of the Rosetta Stone. As expected, the accuracy increased as we adjusted the estimates using actuals and looked at results based upon domain segmentations. We are encouraged by the results and plan to continue our efforts to provide structure and support for such conversion efforts.

## 4.4   MODEL BUILDING

This section is divided into two parts: a description of the statistical model-building process and a discussion of several issues you should be aware of in observational data.

### 4.4.1   Statistical Model-Building Process

Knowledge of the software development process begins with the process of abstraction. For example, the COCOMO model represents a mathematical system for describing the development process. Using economic theory and behavioral analysis (Steps 1 and 2 in Figure 4.1), COCOMO postulates a set of assertions from which consequences are derived (Step 3 in Figure 4.1). Thus, COCOMO attempts to capture the essential features of the software development process. Statistical estimation of the parameters of the COCOMO model and the resulting predictive equation address the question of how well COCOMO captures these essential features. Stated differently, does the model adequately predict effort and do the effects of the various factors as measured by the estimated parameters seem intuitively reasonable?

The process of developing a statistical model for software development requires an iterative data analytic process like that described by Figure 4.2. The process is iterative in nature in that the various steps should be repeated until we judge the model to be adequate. This corresponds with the feedback cycles in Steps 5, 6, and 7 in Figure 4.1.

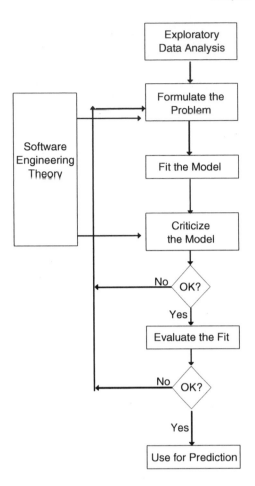

**Figure 4.2**  Statistical Model-
Building Process

The initial step in Figure 4.1 requires that the functional form of the model be specified including identifying relevant predictor variables. We then recommend that the quality of the data be thoroughly scrutinized (i.e., audited) using the methods of exploratory data analysis (EDA). Have particular observations been inappropriately recorded? Remember that a single extraordinary observation can unduly influence our estimated model. Are there inhomogeneities in the data? These may take the form of anomalous observations, nonconstant variance, or subgroup behavior. Should the response and/or predictor variables be transformed?

After auditing our data, we estimate the model. We now play the role of model critics. Are particular observations not explained well by the model (i.e., outliers)? Is this a data or model problem? Are estimated parameters unduly influenced by a single observation? The conclusions from a robust data set remain essentially the same under reasonable variation in the data. In other words, if an analysis depends heavily on the behavior of a few cases, the stability of the model is called into question. Do the estimated parameters have correct signs and magnitude? If not, why not?

The next step addresses these problems by modifying the model and/or the information set (i.e., data). For example, remedies for outliers and unduly influential observations include deleting observations and correcting misrecorded values. Incorrect signs generally occur because of collinear relationships or because of a lack of dispersion away from predictor variables. Bayesian methodology resolves this particular problem by introducing expert judgment (i.e. prior opinion) into the estimation process. Model respecification, such as combining variables, also may resolve collinearity among predictor variables.

Does the model provide useful predictions? Since the fitted model will "bend" to accommodate the data, summary statistics such as the coefficient of determination, $R^2$, and the sum-of-squares errors do not measure the ability of the model to predict. Therefore, proper assessment of a model's ability to predict requires an independent set of data. To obtain such data we recommend data splitting (e.g., cross-validation) [Snee 1977]. Data splitting simply divides the data into two distinct sets: One set is used to estimate the model while the other set provides an independent source of data for determining how well the fitted model predicts.

### 4.4.2   Analysis of Observational Data

Observational, as opposed to experimental, data present numerous challenges to the analyst. Because standards and processes are modified across time or across organizations, such data are rarely consistent and comparable. Key variables are either restricted to a narrow range because of tightly controlled operating procedures or, at the other extreme, misrecorded or ignored because existing procedures did not recognize their importance. As a result, we frequently encounter the following problems: inadequate sampling of the predictor region, highly correlated (i.e., collinearity) predictor variables, outliers, and measurement errors associated with the predictor variables.

#### 4.4.2.1   COLLINEARITY

Collinearities among the predictor variables can cause coefficient estimates to have incorrect signs and large variances and covariances. How do we know if collinearity is a problem? One easy-to-interpret measure is the variance inflation factor (VIF). To understand this measure, we begin by noting that the variance of the *jth* regression coefficient $b_j$ can be expressed as

$$V(b_j) = \frac{s^2}{(1 - R_j^2) \sum_{i=1}^{n} (X_{ij} - \overline{X}_j)^2} \qquad \text{Eq. 4.1}$$

where $s^2$ is the mean-square error (i.e., estimated variance of the regression process), $R_j$ is the multiple correlation between $X_j$ and the other predictor variables. The variance inflation factor is defined as

$$VIF_j = \frac{1}{(1 - R_j^2)}$$                                      Eq. 4.2

We note that the variance of each regression coefficient is inversely proportional to $R_j$ and directly proportional to the variance inflation factor. If predictor variables are *not* correlated with each other (as we might observe in a designed experiment), then the VIFs for the coefficients would be one. On the other hand, if $R_j = 0.95$, then the variance of the *jth* coefficient would be inflated by a factor of ten. Experience indicates that VIFs larger than ten indicate coefficients that are poorly estimated because of collinearity.

The correlation among the predictors may be caused in one of two ways:

• Correlation is inherent in the model
• Correlation results from inadequate sampling of the predictor region

When the collinearities are inherent in the model, then eliminating one or more predictors may be appropriate. Consider, for example, the case where two predictors will always be approximately proportional to one another. Since adding both predictors does not result in more information, eliminating one of the two predictors avoids the problem of explaining an unusual estimate such as an incorrect sign.

When collinearities arise because of inadequate sampling of the predictor region, two possible remedies exist. One obvious, but not necessarily implementable, solution is to collect additional data. A second approach introduces additional information in the form of expert opinion (e.g., Bayesian regression) or dummy data (e.g., ridge regression).

### 4.4.2.2   INADEQUATE SAMPLING OF PREDICTOR REGION

Inadequate sampling of the predictor region may cause two problems: lack of dispersion and collinearity. Consider the consequences associated with lack of dispersion. Examination of Equation 4.1 above shows that the variance of the *jth* coefficient is inversely proportional to the dispersion of the *jth* predictor as measured by $\sum_{i=1}^{n} (X_{ij} - \bar{X}_j)^2$. Thus, if the predictor variable is observed over a narrow range of values, even though *no* collinearity exists, then variance of its coefficient will be large.

Figure 4.3 illustrates an adequate sampling plan for this region while Figure 4.4 displays an inadequate sampling plan. Hocking and Pendleton [Hocking-Pendleton 1983] describe this inadequate sampling of the region as the picket fence problem as shown in Figure 4.5.

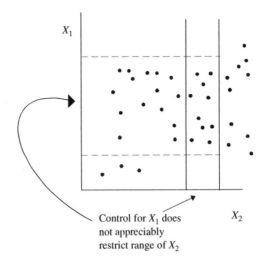

**Figure 4.3** Adequate Sampling Plan: $X_1$ and $X_2$ are not highly correlated.

Control for $X_1$ does not appreciably restrict range of $X_2$

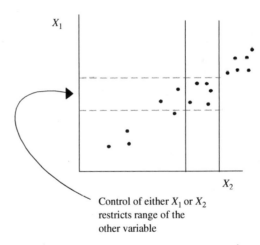

**Figure 4.4** Inadequate Sampling Plan: $X_1$ and $X_2$ are highly correlated.

Control of either $X_1$ or $X_2$ restricts range of the other variable

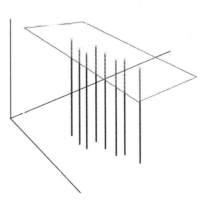

**Figure 4.5** Picket Fence View

This figure illustrates that inadequate sampling has caused the fitted plane to lack proper support and, hence, the plane is unstable. Recall that points on this fitted plane represent the predicted responses for various values of the predictors. Because this plane is unstable, predicted responses for values away from the picket fence will be problematic. Stated differently, while the value of each individual predictor may be within the range of the observed data, the joint value may be a point of extrapolation in two-dimensional space.

### 4.4.2.3   OUTLIERS AND INFLUENTIAL OBSERVATIONS

Outliers are observations that differ from the main body of the data. Outliers in response space refer to $y$-values or residuals that are either too small or too large. In other words, the response lies well above the fitted regression plane. The difficulty with such points is that the fitted surface has been shifted to accommodate the observation. That is, least-squares attempts to accommodate the discordant observation at the expense of the overall fit.

Outliers in predictor space refer to a set of values for the predictor variables that are extreme relative to the other observed values of the predictors. The difficulty with such points is that they have the potential to significantly influence the fitted model because least squares will result in a small residual. The amount of influence exerted by such an outlier depends on the value of the associated response.

Influential observations refer to observations whose inclusion substantially alters the estimates.

## 4.5   COCOMO II CALIBRATION

In Section 4.4, we discussed the statistical model building process. In this section, we focus on the calibration of the first two successive publicly available calibrations of the Post Architecture COCOMO II model.

### 4.5.1   COCOMO II.1997

A variation of the popular multiple regression was used to calibrate COCOMO II.1997 employing a dataset of 83 data points. Multiple Regression expresses the response (e.g., person-months) as a linear function of $k$ predictors (e.g., Source Lines of Code, Product Complexity, etc.). This linear function is estimated from the data using the ordinary-least-squares approach discussed in numerous books such as [Judge et al. 1993, Weisberg 1985]. A multiple regression model can be written as

$$y_i = \beta_0 + \beta_1 x_{i1} + \ldots + \beta_k x_{ik} + \varepsilon_i \qquad \text{Eq. 4.3}$$

where $x_{i1} \ldots x_{ik}$ are the values of the predictor (or regressor) variables for observation $i$, $\beta_0 \ldots \beta_k$ are the coefficients to be estimated, $\epsilon_i$ is the usual error term, and $y_i$ is the response variable for the $i$th observation.

Our original COCOMO II model has the following mathematical form:

$$Effort = A \times [Size]^{\beta_1 + \sum_{j=1}^{5} \beta_{j+1} SF_j} \times \prod_{j=1}^{17} \beta_{j+6} EM_j \omega \qquad \text{Eq. 4.4}$$

where,

> $A$ = Multiplicative Constant
>
> $Size$ = Size of the software project measured in terms of KSLOC (thousands of Source Lines of Code) [Park 1992] or Function Points [IFPUG 1994] and programming language.
>
> $SF$ = Scale Factor
>
> $EM$ = Effort Multiplier [refer to Chapter 2 for further explanation of COCOMO II terms]
>
> $\omega$ = the log-normally distributed error term and $\ln(\omega) = \varepsilon$

Please note that the original COCOMO II model had an exponent of 1.01 plus the sum of the scale factors. This was done to force the composite exponent to be greater than 1 to maintain the original belief that software exhibits diseconomies of scale. Later, in Section 4.5, in the calibration of COCOMO II.2000, the 1.01 value is replaced by 0.91. This doesn't necessarily indicate economies of scale, since the exponent is still the sum of 0.91 and the five scale factors and may very well be greater than 1. However, COCOMO II.2000 now permits economies of scale if all the five scale factors are rated close to Extra High.

We can linearize the COCOMO II equation by taking logarithms on both sides of the equation as shown:

$$\ln(Effort) = \beta_0 + \beta_1 \ln[Size] + \beta_2 SF_1 \ln[Size] + \ldots + \beta_6 SF_5 \ln[Size]$$
$$+ \beta_7 \ln[EM_1] + \ldots + \beta_{23} \ln[EM_{17}] + \varepsilon \qquad \text{Eq. 4.5}$$

Using Equation 4.5 and the 1997 COCOMO II dataset consisting of 83 completed projects, we employed the multiple regression approach [Chulani et al. 1997]. Because some of the predictor variables had high correlations we formed new aggregate predictor variables. These included Analyst Capability and Programmer Capability which were aggregated into Personnel Capability, PERS, and Time Constraints and Storage Constraints which were aggregated into Resource Constraints, RCON. We used a threshold value of 0.65 for high correlation among predictor variables.

Table 4.7 shows the highly correlated parameters that were aggregated for the 1997 calibration of COCOMO II.

The regression estimated the $\beta$ coefficients associated with the scale factors and effort multipliers as shown in Table 4.8 using Arc (Cook-Weisberg 1994).

As the results indicate, some of the regression estimates had counter intuitive values, i.e., negative coefficients (shown in bold).

**Table 4.7    COCOMO II.1997 Highly Correlated Parameters**

|          | TIME    | STOR    | ACAP    | PCAP    | New Parameter |
|----------|---------|---------|---------|---------|---------------|
| **TIME** | 1.0000  |         |         |         | **RCON**      |
| **STOR** | **0.6860** | 1.0000 |       |         |               |
| **ACAP** | −0.2855 | −0.0769 | 1.0000  |         | **PERS**      |
| **PCAP** | −0.2015 | −0.0027 | **0.7339** | 1.0000 |             |

Legend:   TIME (Timing Constraints)                 ACAP (Analyst Capability)
          STOR (Storage Constraints)               PCAP (Programmer Capability)
          **RCON (Resource Constraints)**          **PERS (Personnel Capability)**

As an example, consider the Develop for Reusability (RUSE) effort multiplier. This multiplicative parameter captures the additional effort required to develop components intended for reuse on current or future projects. As shown in Table 4.9a, if the RUSE rating is Extra High (XH), i.e., developing for reusability across multiple product lines, it will cause an increase in effort by a factor of 1.56. On the other hand, if the RUSE rating is Low (L), i.e., developing with no consideration of future reuse, it will cause effort to decrease by a factor of 0.89. This rationale is consistent with the results of twelve published studies of the relative cost of developing for reusability compiled in [Poulin 1997] and was based on the expert judgment of the researchers of the COCOMO II team and previous experience with a RUSE factor in Ada COCOMO. But, the regression results produced a negative coefficient for the $\beta$ coefficient associated with RUSE. This negative coefficient results in the counter intuitive rating scale shown in Table 4.9b, i.e., an Extra High rating for RUSE causes a decrease in effort and a Low rating causes an increase in effort. Note the opposite trends followed in Tables 4.9a and 4.9b.

A possible explanation for this contradiction discussed in a study by [Mullet 1976] on "Why regression coefficients have the wrong sign" may be the lack of dispersion in the responses associated with RUSE. A possible reason for this lack of dispersion is that RUSE is a relatively new cost factor, and our follow-up indicated that the respondents did not have enough information to report its rating accurately during the data collection process. Also, the respondents may have been confused with the definition of RUSE, i.e., are we reusing from the past or are we developing for future reuse? Additionally, many of the "I don't know" and "It does not apply" responses had to be coded as 1.0 (since this is the only way to code no impact on effort). Note (see Figure 4.6) that with slightly more than fifty of the eighty-three data points for RUSE being set at Nominal and with no observations at Extra High, the data for RUSE does not exhibit enough dispersion along the entire range of possible values for RUSE. While this is the familiar errors-in-variables problem, our data doesn't allow us to resolve this difficulty.

**Table 4.8   Regression Run Using 1997 Dataset**

Data set = COCOMOII.1997
Response = log[PM] – 1.01*log[SIZE]
**Coefficient Estimates**

| Label | Estimate | Std. Error | t-value |
|---|---|---|---|
| Constant  A | 0.701883 | 0.231930 | 3.026 |
| PMAT*log[SIZE] | 0.000884288 | 0.0130658 | 0.068 |
| **PREC*log[SIZE]** | **–0.00901971** | **0.0145235** | **–0.621** |
| TEAM*log[SIZE] | 0.00866128 | 0.0170206 | 0.509 |
| FLEX*log[SIZE] | 0.0314220 | 0.0151538 | 2.074 |
| **RESL*log[SIZE]** | **–0.00558590** | **0.019035** | **-0.293** |
| log[PERS] | 0.987472 | 0.230583 | 4.282 |
| log[RELY] | 0.798808 | 0.528549 | 1.511 |
| log[CPLX] | 1.13191 | 0.434550 | 2.605 |
| log[RCON] | 1.36588 | 0.273141 | 5.001 |
| log[PLEX] | 0.696906 | 0.527474 | 1.321 |
| **log[LTEX]** | **–0.0421480** | **0.672890** | **–0.063** |
| log[DATA] | 2.52796 | 0.723645 | 3.493 |
| **log[RUSE]** | **–0.444102** | **0.486480** | **–0.913** |
| **log[DOCU]** | **–1.32818** | **0.664557** | **–1.999** |
| log[PVOL] | 0.858302 | 0.532544 | 1.612 |
| log[APEX] | 0.560542 | 0.609259 | 0.920 |
| log[PCON] | 0.488392 | 0.322021 | 1.517 |
| log[TOOL] | 2.49512 | 1.11222 | 2.243 |
| log[SITE] | 1.39701 | 0.831993 | 1.679 |
| log[SCED] | 2.84074 | 0.774020 | 3.670 |

Thus, the authors were forced to assume that the random variation in the responses for RUSE is small compared to the range of RUSE. The reader should note that all other cost models that use the multiple regression approach rarely explicitly state this assumption, even though it is implicitly assumed.

Other reasons for the counter intuitive results include the violation of some of the restrictions imposed by multiple regression [Briand et al. 1992; Chulani 1999]:

(i) The number of data points should be large relative to the number of model parameters (i.e. there are many degrees of freedom). Unfortunately, collecting data has and continues to be one of the biggest challenges in the software estimation field, primarily because of immature collection/reporting processes

**Table 4.9a    RUSE—Expert-determined *a priori* rating scale, consistent with twelve published studies**

| Develop for Reusability (RUSE) | Low (L) | Nominal (N) | High (H) | Very High (VH) | Extra High (XH) |
|---|---|---|---|---|---|
| Definition | None | Across project | Across program | Across product line | Across multiple product lines |
| 1997 *A priori* Values | 0.89 | 1.00 | 1.16 | 1.34 | 1.56 |

**Table 4.9b    RUSE—Data-determined rating scale, contradicting twelve published studies**

| Develop for Reusability (RUSE) | Low (L) | Nominal (N) | High (H) | Very High (VH) | Extra High (XH) |
|---|---|---|---|---|---|
| Definition | None | Across project | Across program | Across product line | Across multiple product lines |
| 1997 Data-Determined Values | 1.05 | 1.00 | 0.94 | 0.88 | 0.82 |

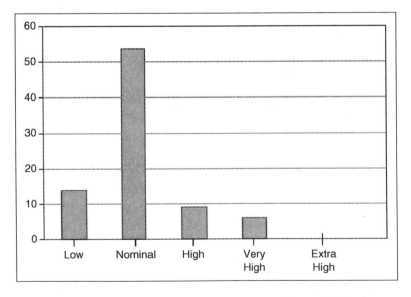

**Figure 4.6**  Distribution of RUSE (Develop for Reusability)

which include lack of common definitions and tools and management reluctance to release cost-related data.

(ii) There should be no extreme cases (i.e., outliers). Extreme cases can distort parameter estimates, and such cases frequently occur in software engineering data due to the lack of precision in the data collection/reporting process.

(iii) The predictor variables (cost drivers and scale factors) should not be highly correlated. Unfortunately, because cost data is historically, rather than experimentally collected, correlations among the predictor variables are unavoidable.

The above restrictions are violated to some extent by the COCOMO II dataset. The COCOMO II calibration approach determines the coefficients for the five scale factors and the seventeen effort multipliers (merged into fifteen because of high correlation as discussed above). Considering the rule of thumb—that every parameter being calibrated should have at least five data points—requires that the COCOMO II dataset have data on at least 110, i.e., (5 scale factors + 17 effort multipliers) ∗ 5; (or 100, i.e., (5 scale factors + 15 effort multipliers) ∗ 5, if we consider that parameters are merged) completed projects. We note that the COCOMO II.1997 dataset has just eighty-three data points.

The second point above indicates that because of the imprecision in the data collection process, outliers can occur, causing problems in the calibration. For example, if a particular organization had extraordinary documentation requirements imposed by the management or the customer, then even a very small project expends a lot of effort producing the excessive documentation demanded by the life cycle. If the data collected simply used the highest DOCU rating provided in the model, then the huge amount of effort caused by the stringent documentation needs would be underrepresented, and the project would have the potential of being an outlier. Outliers in software engineering data, as indicated above, are mostly caused by inaccuracy in the data collection process.

The third restriction imposed requires that no parameters be highly correlated. As described above, in the COCOMO II.1997 calibration, a few parameters were aggregated to alleviate this problem.

To resolve some of the counter-intuitive results produced by the regression analysis (e.g., the negative coefficient for RUSE as explained above), we used a weighted average of the expert-judgment results and the regression results, with only 10 percent of the weight going to the regression results for all the parameters. We selected the 10 percent weighting factor because models with 40 percent and 25 percent weighting factors produced fewer accurate predictions. This pragmatic calibrating procedure moved the model parameters in the direction suggested by the sample data but retained the rationale contained within the *a priori* values. An example of the 10 percent application using the RUSE effort multiplier is given in Figure 4.7. As shown in the graph, the trends followed by the *a priori* and the data-determined curves are opposite. The data-determined curve has a negative slope and, as shown in Figure 4.7, violates expert opinion.

Table 4.10 provides the COCOMO II.1997 parameter values.

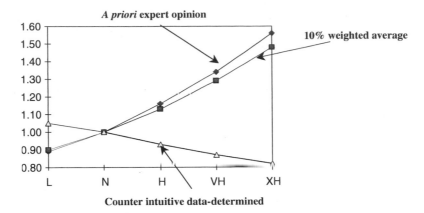

**Figure 4.7**  Example of the 10 percent weighted average approach: RUSE Rating Scale

The resulting calibration of the COCOMO II model, using the 1997 dataset of eighty-three projects, produced estimates for effort that are within 30 percent of the actuals 52 percent of the time. The prediction accuracy improved to 64 percent when the data were stratified into sets based on the eighteen unique sources of the data [see Kemerer 1987; Kitchenham-Taylor 1984; Jeffery-Low 1990 for further confirmation of local calibration improving accuracy]. The constant, *A*, of the COCOMO II equation was recalibrated for each of these sets, i.e., a different intercept was computed for each set. The constant value ranged from 1.23 to 3.72 for the eighteen sets and yielded the prediction accuracies as shown in Table 4.11.

While the 10 percent weighted average procedure produced a workable initial model, it was not giving sufficient weight to those data-determined values with strong statistical significance (high *t*-values) in Table 4.8 (e.g., PERS, RCON, DATA, SCED). Thus, we wanted to develop a more formal and balanced methodology for combining expert judgment and sample information. Bayesian analysis with an informative prior provides such a framework and was used for the CO-COMO II.2000 calibration.

### 4.5.2   COCOMO II.2000

#### 4.5.2.1   BASIC FRAMEWORK—TERMINOLOGY AND THEORY

The Bayesian approach provides a formal process by which *a priori* expert judgment can be combined with sampling information (data) to produce a robust *a posteriori* model. Using Bayes's theorem, we can combine our two information sources as follows:

$$f(\beta|y) = \frac{f(y|\beta)\,f(\beta)}{f(y)}$$

Eq. 4.6

**Table 4.10    COCOMO II.1997 Values**

| Driver | Symbol | VL | L | N | H | VH | XH |
|--------|--------|------|------|------|------|------|------|
| **PREC** | $SF_1$ | 0.0405 | 0.0324 | 0.0243 | 0.0162 | 0.0081 | 0.00 |
| **FLEX** | $SF_2$ | 0.0607 | 0.0486 | 0.0364 | 0.0243 | 0.0121 | 0.00 |
| **RESL** | $SF_3$ | 0.0422 | 0.0338 | 0.0253 | 0.0169 | 0.0084 | 0.00 |
| **TEAM** | $SF_4$ | 0.0494 | 0.0395 | 0.0297 | 0.0198 | 0.0099 | 0.00 |
| **PMAT** | $SF_5$ | 0.0454 | 0.0364 | 0.0273 | 0.0182 | 0.0091 | 0.00 |
| **RELY** | $EM_1$ | 0.75 | 0.88 | 1.00 | 1.15 | 1.39 | |
| **DATA** | $EM_2$ | | 0.93 | 1.00 | 1.09 | 1.19 | |
| **RUSE** | $EM_3$ | | 0.91 | 1.00 | 1.14 | 1.29 | 1.49 |
| **DOCU** | $EM_4$ | 0.89 | 0.95 | 1.00 | 1.06 | 1.13 | |
| **CPLX** | $EM_5$ | 0.75 | 0.88 | 1.00 | 1.15 | 1.30 | 1.66 |
| **TIME** | $EM_6$ | | | 1.00 | 1.11 | 1.31 | 1.67 |
| **STOR** | $EM_7$ | | | 1.00 | 1.06 | 1.21 | 1.57 |
| **PVOL** | $EM_8$ | | 0.87 | 1.00 | 1.15 | 1.30 | |
| **ACAP** | $EM_9$ | 1.50 | 1.22 | 1.00 | 0.83 | 0.67 | |
| **PCAP** | $EM_{10}$ | 1.37 | 1.16 | 1.00 | 0.87 | 0.74 | |
| **PCON** | $EM_{11}$ | 1.24 | 1.10 | 1.00 | 0.92 | 0.84 | |
| **APEX** | $EM_{12}$ | 1.22 | 1.10 | 1.00 | 0.89 | 0.81 | |
| **PLEX** | $EM_{13}$ | 1.25 | 1.12 | 1.00 | 0.88 | 0.81 | |
| **LTEX** | $EM_{14}$ | 1.22 | 1.10 | 1.00 | 0.91 | 0.84 | |
| **TOOL** | $EM_{15}$ | 1.24 | 1.12 | 1.00 | 0.86 | 0.72 | |
| **SITE** | $EM_{16}$ | 1.25 | 1.10 | 1.00 | 0.92 | 0.84 | 0.78 |
| **SCED** | $EM_{17}$ | 1.29 | 1.10 | 1.00 | 1.00 | 1.00 | |

For Effort Calculations:
Multiplicative constant $A = 2.45$;
Exponential constant $B = 1.01$

For Schedule Calculations:
Multiplicative constant $C = 2.66$;
Exponential constant $D = 0.33$

**Table 4.11    Prediction Accuracy of COCOMO II.1997**

| COCOMO II.1997 | Before Stratification by Organization | After Stratification by Organization |
|----------------|---------------------------------------|--------------------------------------|
| PRED(.20) | 46% | 49% |
| PRED(.25) | 49% | 55% |
| PRED(.30) | 52% | 64% |

where $\beta$ is the vector of parameters in which we are interested, and $y$ is the vector of sample observations from the joint density function $f(\beta|y)$. In Equation 4.6, $f(\beta|y)$, the posterior distribution for $\beta$, summarizes all the information we have about $\beta$; and $f(\beta)$ represents a summary of the prior information obtained from experts. $l(\beta|y)$ represents the sample information and is commonly known as the likelihood function for

$$f(\beta|y) \propto l(\beta|y)f(\beta) \qquad \text{Eq. 4.7}$$

Equation 4.7 means:

$$\textit{Posterior} \propto \textit{Sample} \times \textit{Prior}$$

In the Bayesian analysis context, the "prior" probabilities are the simple "unconditional" probabilities to the sample information, while the "posterior" probabilities are the "conditional" probabilities given sample and prior information.

The Bayesian approach makes use of prior information that is not part of the sample data by providing an optimal combination of the two sources of information. As described in many books on Bayesian analysis [Leamer 1978; Box-Tiao, 1973], the posterior mean, $b^{**}$, and variance, $Var(b^{**})$, are defined as:

$$b^{**} = \left[\frac{1}{s^2}X'X + H^*\right]^{-1} \times \left[\frac{1}{s^2}X'Xb + H^*b^*\right] \qquad \text{Eq. 4.8a}$$

*and*

$$Var(b^{**}) = \left[\frac{1}{s^2}X'X + H^*\right]^{-1} \qquad \text{Eq. 4.8b}$$

where $X$ is the matrix of predictor variables, $s^2$ is the variance of the residual for the sample data; and $H^*$ and $b^*$ are the precision (inverse of variance) and mean of the prior information, respectively.

From Equations 4.8a and 4.8b, it is clear that in order to determine the Bayesian posterior mean and variance, we need to determine the mean and precision of the prior information and the sampling information. The next two subsections describe the approach taken to determine the prior and sampling information, followed by a subsection on the Bayesian *a posteriori* model.

**4.5.2.1.1   Prior Information.**   To determine the prior information for the coefficients (i.e., $b^*$ and $H^*$) for our example model, COCOMO II, we conducted a Delphi exercise [Helmer 1966; Boehm 1981; Shepperd-Schofield 1997]. Eight experts from the field of software estimation were asked to independently provide their estimate of the numeric values associated with each COCOMO II cost driver. Roughly half of these participating experts served as lead cost experts for large software development organizations, and a few of them are originators of other proprietary cost models. All of the participants had at least ten years of industrial software cost estimation experience. Based on the credibility of the participants, the authors felt very comfortable using the results of the Delphi rounds as the prior information for the purposes of calibrating COCOMO II.2000. The reader is urged to refer to [Vicinanza et al. 1991] where a study showed that estimates made by experts were more accurate than model-determined estimates. However, in [Johnson 1988] evidence showing the inefficiencies of expert judgment in other domains is highlighted.

Once the first round of the Delphi was completed, we summarized the results in terms of the means and the ranges of the responses. These summarized results were quite raw with significant variances caused by misunderstanding of the parameter definitions. In an attempt to improve the accuracy of these results and to attain better consensus among the experts, the authors distributed the results back to the participants. A better explanation of the behavior of the scale factors was provided since there was highest variance in the scale factor responses. Each of the participants got a second opportunity to independently refine his/her response based on the responses of the rest of the participants in round 1. The authors felt that for the seventeen effort multipliers the summarized results of round 2 were representative of the real world phenomena and decided to use these as the *a priori* information. But, for the five scale factors, the authors conducted a third round and made sure that the participants had a very good understanding of the exponential behavior of these parameters. The results of the third and final round were used as *a priori* information for the five scale factors. Please note if the prior variance for any parameter is zero (in our case, if all experts responded with the same value) then the Bayesian approach will completely rely on expert opinion. However, this did not happen here, since not surprisingly in the software field, disagreement and variability existed among the expert's opinions.

Table 4.12 provides the *a priori* set of values for the RUSE parameter, i.e. the Develop for Reusability parameter. As discussed earlier, this multiplicative parameter captures the additional effort required to develop components intended for reuse on current or future projects. As shown in Table 4.12, if the RUSE rating is

**Table 4.12   COCOMO II.2000 "A-Priori" Rating Scale for Develop for Reusability (RUSE)**

| Develop for Reusability (RUSE) | Productivity Range | Low (L) | Nominal (N) | High (H) | Very High (VH) | Extra High (XH) |
|---|---|---|---|---|---|---|
| Definition | Least Productive Rating/Most Productive Rating | None | Across project | Across program | Across product line | Across multiple product lines |
| COCOMO II.2000 *A priori* Values | Mean = 1.73 Variance = 0.05 | 0.89 | 1.0 | 1.15 | 1.33 | 1.54 |

Extra High (XH), i.e., developing for Reusability across multiple product lines, it will cause an increase in effort by a factor of 1.54. On the other hand, if the RUSE rating is Low (L), i.e., developing with no consideration of future reuse, it will cause effort to decrease by a factor of 0.89. The resulting range of productivity for RUSE is 1.73 (= 1.54/0.89) and the variance computed from the second Delphi round is 0.05. Comparing the results of Table 4.12 with the expert-determined, *a priori* rating scale for the 1997 calibration illustrated in Table 4.9a validates the strong consensus of the experts in the Productivity Range of RUSE of ~1.7.

**4.5.2.1.2  Sample Information**   The sampling information is the result of a data collection activity initiated in September 1994, soon after the initial publication of the COCOMO II description [Boehm et al. 1995]. Affiliates of the Center for Software Engineering at the University of Southern California provided most of the data. These organizations represent the Commercial, Aerospace, and FFRDC (Federally Funded Research and Development Center) sectors of software development.

Data of completed software projects are recorded on a data collection form that asks between thirty-three and fifty-nine questions depending on the degree of source code reuse and the level of detail used in assessing Process Maturity (see Appendix C for data collection questionnaire). A question asked very frequently is the definition of software size, i.e., what defines a line of source code or a Function Point (FP)? Chapter 2 defines a logical line of code using the framework described in [Park 1992], and [IFPUG 1994] gives details on the counting rules of FPs. In spite of the definitions, the data collected to date exhibit local variations caused by differing interpretations of the counting rules. Another parameter that has different definitions within different organizations is effort, i.e. what is a person-month (PM)? In COCOMO II, we define a PM as 152 person hours. But, this varies from organization to organization. This information is usually derived from time cards maintained by employees. But, uncompensated overtime hours are often problematic to collect and hence do not get accounted for in the PM count. Organizations also differ on whose effort is directly charged to the project. COCOMO II includes CM, QA, and project management personnel, and excludes higher management, secretaries, and computer operators—but your organization may differ. This leads to variations in the data reported and the authors asked as many clarifying questions as possible while collecting the data. Variations also occur in the understanding of the subjective rating scale of the scale factors and effort multipliers [Cuelenaere et al. 1987, developed a system to alleviate this problem and to help users apply cost driver definitions consistently for the PRICE S model; Figure 3.11 shows a similar system for COCOMO II]. For example, a very high rating for analyst capability in one organization could be equivalent to a nominal rating in another organization. All these variations suggest that any organization using a parametric cost model should locally calibrate the model to produce better estimates. Please refer to the local calibration results discussed in Table 4.11.

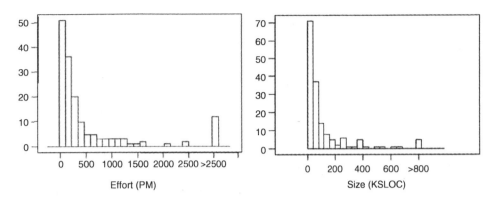

**Figure 4.8**   Distribution of Effort and Size: 2000 dataset of 161 observations

The sampling information includes data on the response variable effort in PM, where 1 PM = 152 hours and predictor variables such as actual size of the software in KSLOC (thousands of Source Lines of Code adjusted for requirements evolution and volatility, REVL). The database has grown from 83 data points in 1997 to 161 data points in 2000. The distributions of effort and size for the 2000 database of 161 data points are shown in Figure 4.8.

As can be noted, both histograms are positively skewed with the bulk of the projects in the database with effort less than 500 PM and size less than 150 KSLOC. Since the multiple regression approach based on least squares estimation assumes that the response variable is normally distributed, the positively skewed histogram for effort indicates the need for a transformation. We also want the relationships between the response variable and the predictor variables to be linear. The histograms for size in Figures 4.8 and 4.9 and the scatter plot in Figure 4.10 show that a log transformation is appropriate for size. Furthermore, the log transformations on effort and size are consistent with Equations 4.4 and 4.5 above.

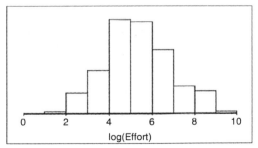
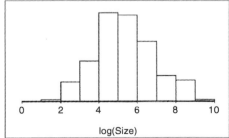

**Figure 4.9**   Distribution of log transformed Effort and Size: 2000 dataset of 161 observations

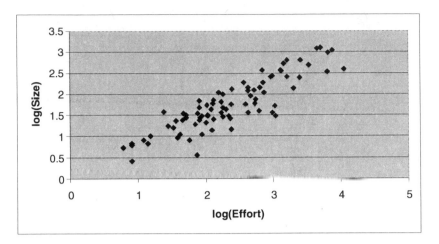

**Figure 4.10**   Correlation between log[Effort] and log[Size]

The regression analysis done in Arc on the log transformed COCOMO II parameters using a dataset of 161 data points yields the results shown in Table 4.13.

The above results provide the estimates for the β coefficients associated with each of the predictor variables (see Eq. 4.5). The $t$-value (ratio between the estimate and corresponding standard error, where standard error is the square root of the variance) may be interpreted as the signal-to-noise ratio associated with the corresponding predictor variables. Hence, the higher the $t$-value, the stronger the signal (i.e., statistical significance) being sent by the predictor variable. For example, the high $t$-value for CPLX of 4.448 indicates that CPLX is statistically very significant. These coefficients can be used to adjust the *a priori* Productivity Ranges (PRs) to determine the data-determined PRs for each of the 22 parameters. For example, the data-determined PR for $RUSE = (1.73)^{-0.34} = 0.83$ where 1.73 is the *a priori* PR as shown in Table 4.14.

While the regression provides intuitively reasonable estimates for most of the predictor variables, the negative coefficient estimate for RUSE (as discussed earlier) and the magnitudes for the coefficients on APEX (Applications Experience), LTEX (Language and Tool Experience), FLEX (Development Flexibility), and TEAM (Team Cohesion), violate our prior opinion about the impact of these parameters on Effort (i.e., PM). The quality of the data probably explains some of the conflicts between the prior information and sample data. However, when compared to the results reported in the COCOMO II.1997, these regression results (using 161 data points) produced better estimates. Only RUSE has a negative coefficient associated with it compared to PREC, RESL, LTEX, DOCU and RUSE in the regression results using only 83 data points. Thus, adding more data points (which results in an increase in the degrees of freedom) reduced the problems of counter intuitive results.

**Table 4.13  Regression Run Using 2000 Dataset**

Data set = COCOMO II.2000
Response = log[PM]
Coefficient Estimates

| Label | Estimate | Std. Error | t-value |
|---|---|---|---|
| Constant A | 0.961552 | 0.103346 | 9.304 |
| log[SIZE] | 0.921827 | 0.0460578 | 20.015 |
| PMAT*log[SIZE] | 0.684836 | 0.481078 | 1.424 |
| PREC*log[SIZE] | 1.10203 | 0.373961 | 2.947 |
| TEAM*log[SIZE] | 0.323318 | 0.497475 | 0.650 |
| FLEX*log[SIZE] | 0.354658 | 0.686944 | 0.516 |
| RESL*log[SIZE] | 1.32890 | 0.637678 | 2.084 |
| log[PCAP] | 1.20332 | 0.307956 | 3.907 |
| log[RELY] | 0.641228 | 0.246435 | 2.602 |
| log[CPLX] | 1.03515 | 0.232735 | 4.448 |
| log[TIME] | 1.58101 | 0.385646 | 4.100 |
| log[STOR] | 0.784218 | 0.352459 | 2.225 |
| log[ACAP] | 0.926205 | 0.272413 | 3.400 |
| log[PLEX] | 0.755345 | 0.356509 | 2.119 |
| log[LTEX] | 0.171569 | 0.416269 | 0.412 |
| log[DATA] | 0.783232 | 0.218376 | 3.587 |
| **log[RUSE]** | **−0.339964** | **0.286225** | **−1.188** |
| log[DOCU] | 2.05772 | 0.622163 | 3.307 |
| log[PVOL] | 0.867162 | 0.227311 | 3.815 |
| log[APEX] | 0.137859 | 0.330482 | 0.417 |
| log[PCON] | 0.488392 | 0.322021 | 1.517 |
| log[TOOL] | 0.551063 | 0.221514 | 2.488 |
| log[SITE] | 0.674702 | 0.498431 | 1.354 |
| log[SCED] | 1.11858 | 0.275329 | 4.063 |

**4.5.2.1.3  Combining Prior and Sampling Information: Posterior Bayesian Update.**  As a means of resolving the above conflicts, we will now use the Bayesian paradigm as a means of formally combining prior expert judgment with our sample data.

Equation 4.8 reveals that if the precision of the *a priori* information ($H^*$) is bigger (or the variance of the *a priori* information is smaller) than the precision (or the variance) of the sampling information ($1/s^2 X'X$), the posterior values will be closer to the *a priori* values. This situation can arise when the data is noisy. For example, consider the cost factor RUSE ( Develop for Reusability). Because the information for this factor is noisy, the degree-of-belief in the prior information exceeds the degree-of-belief in the sample data as depicted in Figure 4.11. As a consequence, a stronger weight is assigned to the prior information causing the posterior mean to be closer to the prior mean. On the other hand (not illustrated), if the precision of the sampling information $(1/s^2 X'X)$ is larger than the precision of the prior information $(H^*)$, then a higher weight is assigned to the sampling information causing the posterior mean to be closer to the mean of the sampling data. The resulting posterior precision will always be higher than the *a priori* precision or the sample data precision. Note that if the prior variance of any parameter is zero, then the parameter will be completely determined by the prior information. Although, this is a restriction imposed by the Bayesian approach, it is generally of little concern as the situation of complete consensus very rarely arises in the software engineering domain.

The complete Bayesian analysis on COCOMO II yields the Productivity Ranges (ratio between the least productive parameter rating, i.e., the highest rating, and the most productive parameter rating, i.e., the lowest rating) illustrated in Figure 4.12. Figure 4.12 gives an overall perspective of the relative Software Productivity Ranges (PRs) provided by the COCOMO II.2000 parameters. The PRs provide insight into identifying the high payoff areas to focus on in a software productivity improvement activity. For example, CPLX (Product Complexity) is the highest payoff parameter and FLEX (Development Flexibility) is the lowest payoff parameter. The variance associated with each parameter is indicated along each bar. This indicates that even though the two parameters, Multisite Development (SITE) and Documentation Match to Life-Cycle Needs (DOCU), have the same PR, the PR of SITE (variance of 0.007) is predicted with more than five times the certainty than the PR of DOCU (variance of 0.037).

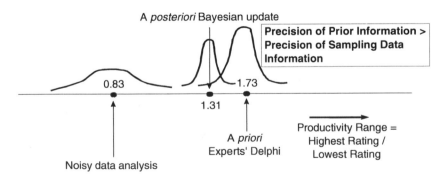

**Figure 4.11**  *A Posteriori* Bayesian Update in the Presence of Noisy Data (Develop for Reusability, RUSE)

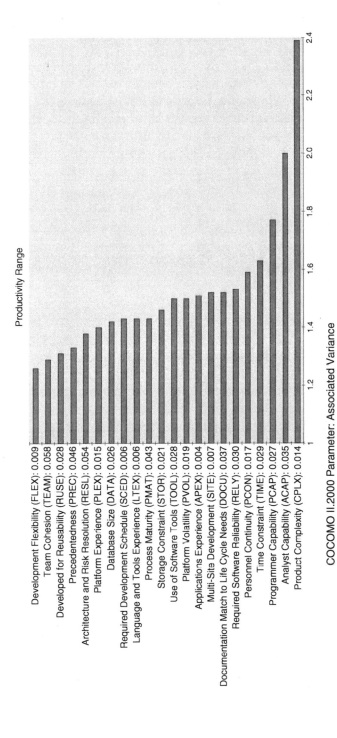

Productivity Range

COCOMO II.2000 Parameter: Associated Variance

**Figure 4.12** Bayesian *A Posteriori* Productivity Ranges for COCOMO II.2000

171

The resulting COCOMO II.2000 model (parameter values are shown in Table 4.14) calibrated to 161 data points produces estimates for effort that are within 30 percent of the actuals 75 percent of the time. The Bayesian estimate for log[Size]'s coefficient evaluates to 0.91. This is the same as the value for B in the Post-Architecture equation. As discussed below Equation 4.4, the new value of 0.91 permits economies of scale for projects when all five scale factor rating close to Extra High. The Bayesian estimate for Constant A's coefficient evaluates to 1.078. Taking antilogs we get the value for A in the Post-Architecture equation as 2.94. If the model's multiplicative coefficient, A, is calibrated to each of the eigh-

**Table 4.14    COCOMO II.2000 Values**

| Driver | Symbol | VL | L | N | H | VH | XH |
|--------|--------|------|------|------|------|------|------|
| PREC | $SF_1$ | 6.20 | 4.96 | 3.72 | 2.48 | 1.24 | 0.00 |
| FLEX | $SF_2$ | 5.07 | 4.05 | 3.04 | 2.03 | 1.01 | 0.00 |
| RESL | $SF_3$ | 7.07 | 5.65 | 4.24 | 2.83 | 1.41 | 0.00 |
| TEAM | $SF_4$ | 5.48 | 4.38 | 3.29 | 2.19 | 1.10 | 0.00 |
| PMAT | $SF_5$ | 7.80 | 6.24 | 4.68 | 3.12 | 1.56 | 0.00 |
| RELY | $EM_1$ | 0.82 | 0.92 | 1.00 | 1.10 | 1.26 | |
| DATA | $EM_2$ | | 0.90 | 1.00 | 1.14 | 1.28 | |
| CPLX | $EM_3$ | 0.73 | 0.87 | 1.00 | 1.17 | 1.34 | 1.74 |
| RUSE | $EM_4$ | | 0.95 | 1.00 | 1.07 | 1.15 | 1.24 |
| DOCU | $EM_5$ | 0.81 | 0.91 | 1.00 | 1.11 | 1.23 | |
| TIME | $EM_6$ | | | 1.00 | 1.11 | 1.29 | 1.63 |
| STOR | $EM_7$ | | | 1.00 | 1.05 | 1.17 | 1.46 |
| PVOL | $EM_8$ | | 0.87 | 1.00 | 1.15 | 1.30 | |
| ACAP | $EM_9$ | 1.42 | 1.19 | 1.00 | 0.85 | 0.71 | |
| PCAP | $EM_{10}$ | 1.34 | 1.15 | 1.00 | 0.88 | 0.76 | |
| PCON | $EM_{11}$ | 1.29 | 1.12 | 1.00 | 0.90 | 0.81 | |
| APEX | $EM_{12}$ | 1.22 | 1.10 | 1.00 | 0.88 | 0.81 | |
| PLEX | $EM_{13}$ | 1.19 | 1.09 | 1.00 | 0.91 | 0.85 | |
| LTEX | $EM_{14}$ | 1.20 | 1.09 | 1.00 | 0.91 | 0.84 | |
| TOOL | $EM_{15}$ | 1.17 | 1.09 | 1.00 | 0.90 | 0.78 | |
| SITE | $EM_{16}$ | 1.22 | 1.09 | 1.00 | 0.93 | 0.86 | 0.80 |
| SCED | $EM_{17}$ | 1.43 | 1.14 | 1.00 | 1.00 | 1.00 | |

For Effort Calculations:
Multiplicative constant $A = 2.94$;
Exponential constant $B = 0.91$

For Schedule Calculations:
Multiplicative constant $C = 3.67$;
Exponential constant $D = 0.28$

teen major sources of project data, the resulting model (with the coefficient ranging from 1.5 to 4.1) produces estimates within 30 percent of the actuals 80 percent
of the time (please refer to Table 4.15). It is therefore recommended that organizations using the model calibrate it using their own data to increase model accuracy
and produce a local optimum estimate for similar type projects as discussed in
the next section, Section 4.6.

### 4.5.2.2   CROSS-VALIDATION OF THE BAYESIAN CALIBRATED MODEL

The COCOMO II.2000 Bayesian calibration discussed above uses the complete dataset of 161 data points. Thus, the prediction accuracies of COCOMO
II.2000 (depicted in Table 4.15) are based on the same dataset of 161 data points.
That is, the calibration and validation datasets are the same. A natural question
that arises in this context is how well will the model predict new software development projects? To address this issue, we randomly selected 121 observations
for our calibration dataset with the remaining 40 becoming assigned to the validation dataset (i.e., " new" data). We repeated this process 15 times creating
15 calibration and 15 validation datasets, each of size 121 and 40, respectively.

We then developed a prediction equation for each of the 15 calibration
datasets. We used the resulting *a posteriori* models to predict the development effort of the 40 "new" projects in the validation datasets. This validation approach,
known as out-of-sample validation, provides a true measure of the model's predictive abilities. This out-of-sample test yielded an average PRED(.30) of 69 percent; indicating that on average, the out-of-sample validation results produced
estimates within 30 percent of the actuals 69 percent of the time. Hence, we conclude that our Bayesian model has reasonably good predictive qualities.

### 4.5.2.3   FURTHER VALIDATION OF THE BAYESIAN APPROACH

In this section, three models *A*, *B*, and *C*, are generated using only the 83
data points available in 1997. Then, each of these models is validated against the
161 data points to see how well they perform when new data become available.

**Table 4.15   Prediction Accuracies of Bayesian *A Posteriori* COCOMOII.2000
Before and After Stratification**

| Prediction Accuracy | Bayesian *A Posteriori* COCOMO II.2000 | |
|---|---|---|
| | **Before** | **After** |
| PRED(.20) | 63% | 70% |
| PRED(.25) | 68% | 76% |
| PRED(.30) | 75% | 80% |

Model A: This is a pure-regression based model calibrated using 83 data points.

Model B: This is the published COCOMO II.1997 model that uses the 10% weighted-average approach discussed earlier on 83 data points.

Model C: This is a Bayesian model calibrated using 83 data points (Please note that this is not the same as the Bayesian COCOMO II.2000 model which is calibrated using 161 data points; although the approach used, *i.e.* the Bayesian approach is identical).

Each of these models is then used to determine prediction accuracy on the 1997 dataset of 83 data points (the same dataset used to calibrate the model) and on the 2000 dataset of 161 data points. These accuracies are shown in Table 4.16, and a discussion based on these results follows the table.

From Table 4.16, it is clear that model *A* yields the highest accuracies on the 83 data points. This is true because ordinary least squares makes specific accommodations for the 83 data points and as a consequence no model other than the pure-regression-based model will give better prediction accuracies for these 83 data points. But as discussed in the section on the COCOMO II.1997 calibration, believing the data completely to determine our estimation model for the future purely on the results of analyzing the 1997 dataset of 83 data points results in a model that produces counter-intuitive results. Further, when model A is used on the newer 2000 dataset of 161 data points, the prediction accuracies are relatively poor: only 44 percent of the projects are estimated within 30 percent of the actuals.

Model B performs better on the 2000 dataset of 161 data points and produces estimates that are within 30 percent of the actuals 63 percent of the time. But, the Bayesian model (model C) outperforms models *A* and *B* giving the high-

**Table 4.16    Prediction Accuracies Using the Pure-Regression, the 10% Weighted-Average Multiple-Regression and the Bayesian Based Models Calibrated Using the 1997 Dataset of 83 data points and Validated Against 83 and 161 datapoints**

| | Calibrated Using 83 data points | | | | | |
|---|---|---|---|---|---|---|
| Prediction Accuracy | *Pure-Regression Based Model (Model A)* | | *COCOMO II.1997—10% Weighted-Average Based Model (Model B)* | | *Bayesian Approach Based Model (Model C)* | |
| | **Number of data points used to validated** | | | | | |
| | 83 | 161 | 83 | 161 | 83 | 161 |
| PRED(.20) | 49% | 31% | 46% | 54% | 41% | 54% |
| PRED(.25) | 63% | 39% | 49% | 59% | 53% | 62% |
| PRED(.30) | 64% | 44% | 52% | 63% | 58% | 66% |

est prediction accuracy on our validation dataset of 161 data points. It produces estimates that are within 30 percent of the actuals 66 percent of the time. Based on these results, we can expect that the Bayesian-calibrated COCOMO II.2000 model will produce the highest accuracies in estimating newly gathered data. In fact, as shown in Table 4.16, the Bayesian-calibrated COCOMO II.2000 performs better than the 10 percent weighted-average model, when both are calibrated using 161 data points and validated on the same dataset of 161 data points.

## 4.6    TAILORING COCOMO II TO A PARTICULAR ORGANIZATION

The generic model presented in this chapter can be used to estimate software development efforts for a variety of different project types. However, the COCOMO model can be tailored to a particular organizational environment. Results presented below show that locally calibrating COCOMO II to an organization typically results in better estimates. The major opportunities for tailoring and locally calibrating to a particular organization include

- Calibrating the model to existing project data
- Consolidating or eliminating redundant parameters
- Adding significant cost drivers that are not explicit in the model

Below, we consider each of these opportunities in further detail.

### 4.6.1    Calibrating the Model to Existing Project Data

Using data on completed projects, we can choose to either calibrate the multiplicative constant, $A$, or to calibrate both $A$ and the baseline exponent B. We recommend having at least 5 data points for locally calibrating the multiplicative constant, $A$, and at least 10 data points for calibrating both the multiplicative constant, $A$, and the baseline exponent, $B$. Local calibration usually improves prediction accuracies because

- The rating scale for COCOMO II is subjective leading to inconsistencies across different organizations. For example, the ratings of personnel factors such as ACAP (Analyst Capability), PCAP (Programmer Capability), PLEX (Platform Experience), etc. are particularly susceptible to this unwanted variation.
- The life-cycle activities covered by COCOMO II may be slightly different from the life-cycle activities being covered by the particular organization. The simplest way to account for this is to calibrate the multiplicative constant.
- The definitions used by COCOMO II may differ slightly from those being used by a particular organization. For example, while COCOMO II defines

1 PM as 152 person-hours, this definition may exhibit considerable variation across organizations. Here again, the simplest way to account for the differences is to locally calibrate the multiplicative constant.

Local calibration of the multiplicative constant, A, can be done by using the linear regression approach. As shown in the log-transformed COCOMO II effort equation below, $A = e^{\beta 0}$, and the exponential constant, $B = \beta_1$. For COCOMO II.2000, $A = 2.94$ and $B = 0.91$.

$$\ln(\mathit{Effort}) = \beta_0 + \beta_1 \times \ln(\mathit{Size}) + \beta_2 \times SF_1 \times \ln(\mathit{Size})$$
$$+ \ldots + \beta_6 \times SF_5 \times \ln(\mathit{Size}) + \beta_7 \times \ln(EM_1) + \beta_8 \times \ln(EM_2) \quad \text{Eq. 4.9}$$
$$+ \ldots + \beta_{22} \times \ln(EM_{16}) + \beta_{23} \times \ln(EM_{17})$$

To compute a locally calibrated A using COCOMO II.2000, our new regression equation is:

$$\ln(\mathit{Effort}) - [0.91 \times \ln(\mathit{Size}) + \beta_2 \times SF_1 \times \ln(\mathit{Size})$$
$$+ \ldots + \beta_6 \times SF_5 \times \ln(\mathit{Size}) + \beta_7 \times \ln(EM_1) + \beta_8 \times \ln(EM_2) \quad \text{Eq. 4.10}$$
$$+ \ldots + \beta_{22} \times \ln(EM_{16}) + \beta_{23} \times \ln(EM_{17})] = \beta_0$$

where the left-hand side of the equation is the response variable and the exponential value of $\beta_0$ is the new locally calibrated A.

Consider the following example where a particular organization has data on eight completed projects whose sizes $kSLOC_i$, actual development efforts $PM_i$, product of the effort adjustment factors $\Pi EM_i$, sum of the scale factors $\Sigma SF_i$, are those given in Table 4.17. The right-most column in Table 4.17, $Effort_i$ is the effort estimated by the generic COCOMO II.2000 discussed in Section 4.5, i.e., using $A = 2.94$.

**Table 4.17   Calibrating the Multiplicative Constant to Project Data**

| Project Number (*i*) | $PM_i$ | $kSLOC_i$ | $\Pi EM_i$ | $\Sigma SF_i$ | $Effort_i$ |
|---|---|---|---|---|---|
| 1 | 1854.55 | 134.47 | 1.89 | 29.28 | 2014.04 |
| 2 | 258.51 | 132 | 0.49 | 16.72 | 278.777 |
| 3 | 201.00 | 44.03 | 1.06 | 22.48 | 227.996 |
| 4 | 58.87 | 3.57 | 5.05 | 18.19 | 59.56684 |
| 5 | 9661.02 | 380.8 | 3.05 | 26.77 | 9819.961 |
| 6 | 7021.28 | 980 | 0.92 | 25.21 | 8092.762 |
| 7 | 91.67 | 11.186 | 2.45 | 23.5 | 114.2832 |
| 8 | 689.66 | 61.56 | 2.38 | 26.48 | 886.2177 |

From Equation 4.10, and by using a regression tool, we can compute $\beta_0$ as shown below in Table 4.18.

From the above regression run in Table 4.18, we see that the value of $A = exp(\beta_0) = exp(0.962733)$ which is approximately 2.6188.

Finally, $A$ may be computed using the local calibration feature of USC COCOMO II.2000.0 (or commercial implementations of COCOMO II such as Costar [http://www.SoftstarSystems.com]) as shown in Figure 4.13.

Using the new calibrated constant, $A$, in our effort computations, we see that the accuracy of the COCOMO II model improves. As shown in Table 4.19, only six of the eight projects are estimated within 20 percent of the actuals using the generic version COCOMO II.2000. If we use the locally calibrated value for the multiplicative constant, $A$ (i.e., 2.62 instead of 2.94), all eight projects are estimated within 20 percent (actually within 15 percent) of the actuals.

The Bayesian *a posteriori* COCOMO II.2000 model calibrated to 161 data points produces estimates within 30 percent of the actuals 75 percent of the time for effort. The prediction accuracy improved to 80 percent when the data was stratified into sets based on the eighteen unique sources of the data [see Kemerer 1987; Kitchenham-Taylor, 1984; Jeffery-Low 1990 for further confirmation that local calibration improves accuracy]. The constant, $A$, of the COCOMO II equa-

**Table 4.18   Regression Run: Calibrating Multiplicative Constant to Project Data**

Data set = Local Calibration A, Name of Model = L1

Normal Regression Model

Mean function = Identity

Response = $\ln[Effort]-(0.91 \times \ln[Size]+\beta_1 \times SF_1 \times \ln[Size] +\beta_2 \times SF_2 \times \ln[Size]+...+ +\beta_5 \times SF_5 \times \ln[Size]+\beta_6 \times \ln[EM_1]+\beta_7 \times \ln[EM_2]+...+ \beta_{22} \times \ln[EM_{22}])$

Predictors = $\beta_0$

With no intercept.

Coefficient Estimates

| Label | Estimate | Std. Error | t-value |
|---|---|---|---|
| $\beta_0$ | 0.962733 | 0.0308810 | 31.176 |
| Sigma hat | | 0.0873447 | |
| Number of cases | | 8 | |
| Degrees of freedom | | 7 | |

Summary Analysis of Variance Table

| Source | df | SS | MS | F |
|---|---|---|---|---|
| Regression | 1 | 7.41483 | 7.41483 | 971.91 |
| Residual | 7 | 0.0534037 | 0.0076291 | |
| Pure Error | 7 | 0.0534037 | 0.0076291 | |

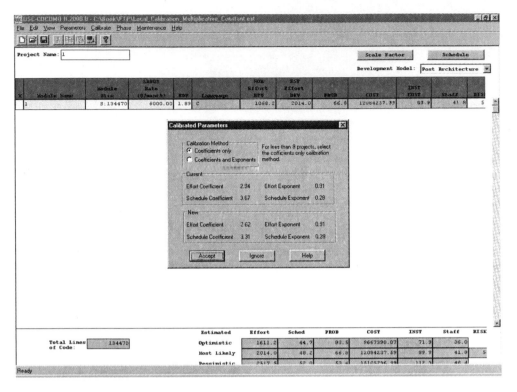

**Figure 4.13** Calibrating the Multiplicative Constant to Project Data Using USC COCOMO II.2000.0

**Table 4.19   Improvement in Accuracy of COCOMO II.2000 Using Locally Calibrated Multiplicative Constant, A**

| Project Number (*I*) | $PM_i$ | *Effort<sub>i</sub>* Using COCOMO II.2000 | Error Using COCOMO II.2000 | *Effort<sub>i</sub>* Using Local *A* | Error Using Local *A* |
|---|---|---|---|---|---|
| 1 | 1854.55 | 2014.04 | 0.09 | 1794.00 | 0.03 |
| 2 | 258.51 | 278.777 | 0.08 | 248.32 | 0.04 |
| 3 | 201.00 | 227.996 | 0.13 | 203.09 | 0.01 |
| 4 | 58.87 | 59.56684 | 0.01 | 53.06 | 0.10 |
| 5 | 9661.02 | 9819.961 | 0.02 | 8747.11 | 0.09 |
| 6 | 7021.28 | 8092.762 | 0.15 | 7208.61 | 0.03 |
| 7 | 91.67 | 114.2832 | 0.25 | 101.80 | 0.11 |
| 8 | 689.66 | 886.2177 | 0.29 | 789.40 | 0.14 |

**Table 4.20   Prediction Accuracy of COCOMO II.2000**

| COCOMO II.2000 | Before Stratification by Organization | After Stratification by Organization |
|---|---|---|
| PRED(.20) | 63% | 70% |
| PRED(.25) | 68% | 76% |
| PRED(.30) | 75% | 80% |

tion was recalibrated for each of these sets, i.e., a different intercept was computed for each set. The constant value ranged from 1.5 to 4.1 for the eighteen sets and yielded the prediction accuracies shown in Table 4.20.

We therefore recommend that organizations using the model calibrate it using their own data to increase model accuracy and produce a local optimum estimate for similar type projects.

Similarly, Table 4.21 also shows improvement in schedule prediction accuracy when we stratify the data by organization and recalibrate the multiplicative constant.

A similar regression approach can be used to simultaneously calibrate both the multiplicative constant, $A$, and the exponential constant, $B$. The linear regression equation is as shown below:

$$\ln(\textit{Effort}) - [\beta_2 \times SF_1 \times \ln(\textit{Size}) + \ldots + \beta_6 \times SF_5 \times \ln(\textit{Size})$$
$$+ \beta_7 \times \ln(EM_1) + \beta_8 \times \ln(EM_2) + \ldots + \beta_{22} \times \ln(EM_{16}) \qquad \text{Eq. 4.11}$$
$$+ \beta_{23} \times \ln(EM_{17})] = \beta_0 + \beta_1 \times \ln(\textit{Size})$$

where $A = e^{\beta_0}$ and $B = \beta_1$

The regression tool results, using the data of Table 4.17, are shown below in Table 4.22.

The value of $A$ is approximately $e^{0.953} = 2.59$, and the value of $B$ is 0.912.

$A$ and $B$ may also be computed using the local calibration feature of USC COCOMO II.2000.0 (or commercial implementations of COCOMO II such as Costar) as shown in Figure 4.14.

**Table 4.21   Schedule Prediction Accuracy of COCOMO II.2000**

| COCOMO II.2000 | Before Stratification by Organization | After Stratification by Organization |
|---|---|---|
| PRED (.20) | 50% | 50% |
| PRED (.25) | 55% | 67% |
| PRED (.30) | 64% | 75% |

**Table 4.22   Regression Run: Calibrating Multiplicative and Exponential Constants to Project Data**

| Data set = Local_Calibration_A_and_B, Name of Model = L2 | | | |
|---|---|---|---|
| Normal Regression Model | | | |
| Mean function = Identity | | | |
| Response = ln[*Effort*]−($\beta_1$*SF$_1$* ln[*Size*] +$\beta_2$*SF$_2$* ln[*Size*]+...+ +$\beta_5$*SF$_5$* ln[*Size*]+$\beta_6$*ln[*EM$_1$*]+$\beta_7$*ln[*EM$_2$*]+...+ $\beta_{22}$*ln[*EM$_{22}$*]) | | | |
| Predictors = ($\beta_0$*$\beta_1$* ln[Size]) | | | |
| Coefficient Estimates | | | |
| Label | Estimate | Std. Error | t-value |
| $\beta_0$ | 0.953288 | 0.0902335 | 10.565 |
| $\beta_1$ | 0.912210 | 0.0196111 | 46.515 |
| R Squared | 0.997235 | | |
| Sigma hat | 0. 0942695 | | |
| Number of cases | 8 | | |
| Degrees of freedom | 6 | | |
| Summary Analysis of Variance Table | | | |

| Source | df | SS | MS | F |
|---|---|---|---|---|
| Regression | 1 | 19.2277 | 19.2277 | 2163.63 |
| Residual | 6 | 0.0533205 | 0.00888675 | |

Using both of the new calibrated constants, *A* and *B,* in our effort computations, we observe that the accuracy of the COCOMO II model further improves for project 7 but worsens a little bit for project 4, as shown in Table 4.23. Because the locally calibrated value of *B* is approximately the same as the estimate provided by COCOMO II.2000, accuracy is not significantly improved by locally calibrating both parameters. However, for different data, local calibration of *A* and *B* can improve predictive performance. The local calibration of *A* and *B* is more beneficial when there is data on many projects versus just 8.

*Note:* The local calibration equations described in Chapter 29 of *Software Engineering Economics* [Boehm 1981] for local calibration will yield results that differ from those obtained by the above local calibration equations. The reason for this difference is that Boehm assumes an additive error structure when deriving his local calibration equations. We, on the other hand, use the multiplicative error structure given in Equation 4.4. In other words, we are minimizing the sum-of-squared residuals in log space. As shown in Figures 4.8 and 4.9, log transformations remove asymmetry and thus reduce the undue influence of those projects in the tail of the distribution (i.e., extremely large projects)

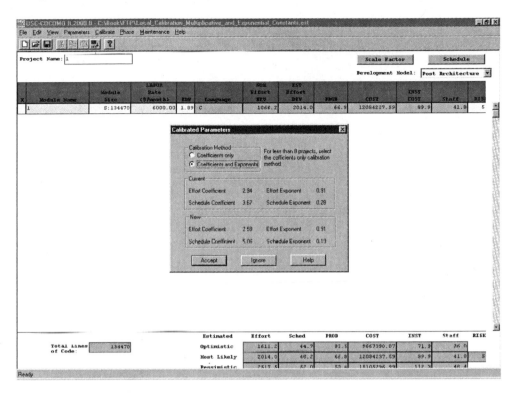

**Figure 4.14** Calibrating the Multiplicative and Exponential Constants to Project Data Using USC COCOMO II. 2000.0

### 4.6.2 Consolidating or Eliminating Redundant Parameters

There are numerous situations where an organization may wish to consolidate two or more parameters. For example, in some organizations, the analysts and the programmers are the same people. In these situations, the ratings for the personnel factors, ACAP and PCAP should be virtually the same; hence these two factors should be merged into a single factor. Another set of parameters that can be consolidated in many situations is TIME and STOR. Table 4.24 shows an example of consolidating ACAP and PCAP into PERS (Personnel Capability).

In situations where all the projects in the organization have the same factor rating, that factor should be eliminated from the model and accounted for by calibrating the constants. For example, DATA can be eliminated if the organization always develops real-time control systems with very small (low-rated) databases.

**Table 4.23  Improvement in Accuracy of COCOMO II.2000 Using Locally Calibrated Constants, A and B**

| Project Number ($i$) | $PM_i$ | $Effort_i$ Using COCOMO II.2000 | Error Using COCOMO II.2000 | $Effort_i$ Using Local A | Error Using Local A | $Effort_i$ Using Local A and B | Error Using Local A |
|---|---|---|---|---|---|---|---|
| 1 | 1854.55 | 2014.04 | 0.09 | 1794.00 | 0.03 | 1791.75 | 0.03 |
| 2 | 258.51 | 278.777 | 0.08 | 248.32 | 0.04 | 248.00 | 0.04 |
| 3 | 201.00 | 227.996 | 0.13 | 203.09 | 0.01 | 202.38 | 0.01 |
| 4 | 58.87 | 59.56684 | 0.01 | 53.06 | 0.10 | 52.61 | 0.11 |
| 5 | 9661.02 | 9819.961 | 0.02 | 8747.11 | 0.09 | 8754.34 | 0.09 |
| 6 | 7021.28 | 8092.762 | 0.15 | 7208.61 | 0.03 | 7228.22 | 0.03 |
| 7 | 91.67 | 114.2832 | 0.25 | 101.80 | 0.11 | 101.17 | 0.10 |
| 8 | 689.66 | 886.2177 | 0.29 | 789.40 | 0.14 | 787.18 | 0.14 |

**Table 4.24   Consolidating Analyst Capability and Programmer Capability**

| Capability Scale | ACAP | PCAP | PERS = ACAP * PCAP |
|:---:|:---:|:---:|:---:|
| VL | 1.42 | 1.34 | 1.90 |
| L | 1.19 | 1.15 | 1.37 |
| N | 1.0 | 1.0 | 1.0 |
| H | 0.85 | 0.88 | 0.75 |
| VH | 0.71 | 0.76 | 0.54 |

### 4.6.3   Adding Significant Cost Drivers That are not Explicit in the Model

In some situations, the COCOMO II model might lack an important cost driver. For example, an organization may have projects with different security constraints. In this situation, it might be necessary to add a new cost driver, called SCON (for Security Constraints) to the model. The organization would then have to develop a suitable rating scale for SCON and locally calibrate the parameter using data from completed projects or rely on expert opinion. USC COCOMO II.2000 and some commercial implementations such as Costar provide this feature for you to easily add new cost drivers to the model.

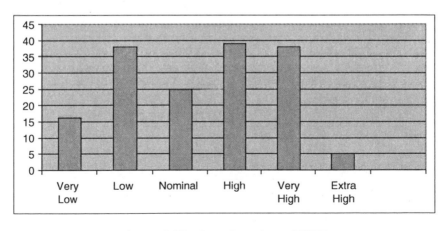

**Figure 4.15**   Precedentedness (PREC)

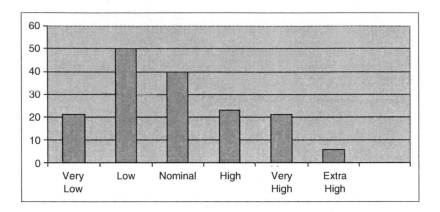

**Figure 4.16**    Development Flexibility (FLEX)

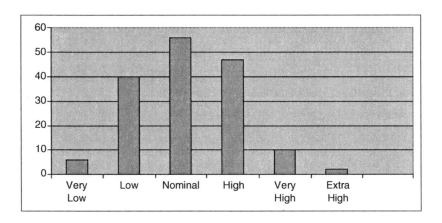

**Figure 4.17**    Architecture/Risk Resolution (RESL)

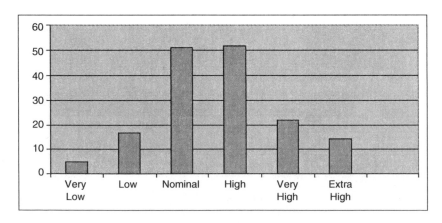

**Figure 4.18**    Team Cohesion (TEAM)

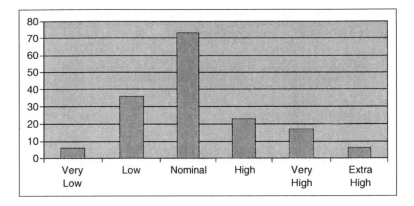

**Figure 4.19** Process Maturity (PMAT)

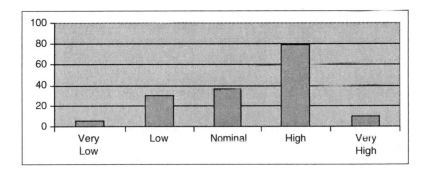

**Figure 4.20** Required Software Reliability (RELY)

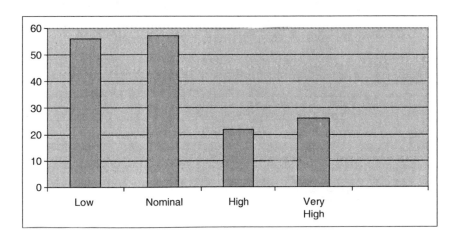

**Figure 4.21** Databasesize (DATA)

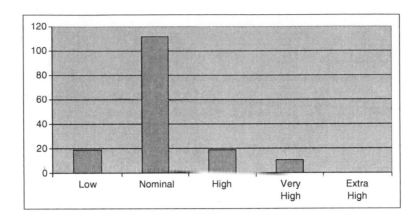

**Figure 4.22**   Developed for Reusability (RUSE)

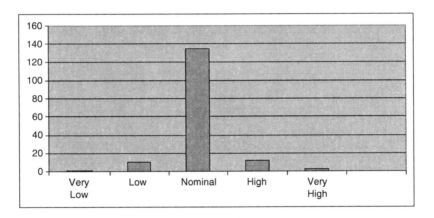

**Figure 4.23**   Documentation Match to Life-Cycle Needs (DOCU)

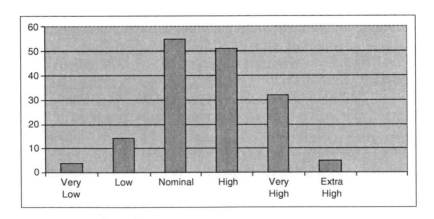

**Figure 4.24**   Product Complexity (CPLX)

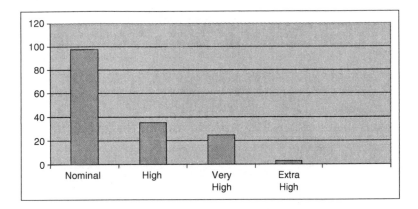

**Figure 4.25**   Execution Time Constraint (TIME)

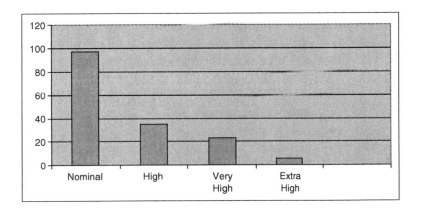

**Figure 4.26**   Main Storage Constraint (STOR)

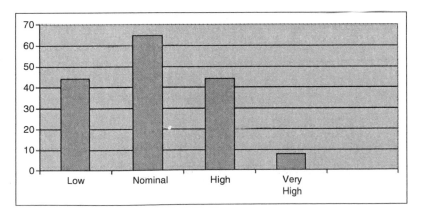

**Figure 4.27**   Platform Volatility (PVOL)

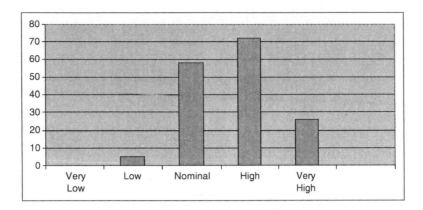

**Figure 4.28**    Analyst Capability (ACAP)

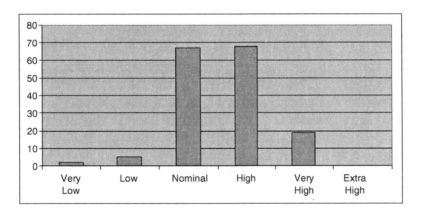

**Figure 4.29**    Programmer Capability (PCAP)

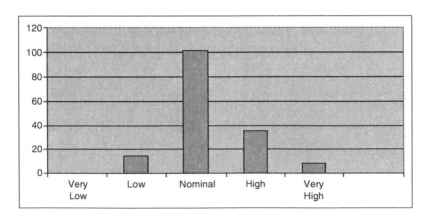

**Figure 4.30**    Personnel Continuity (PCON)

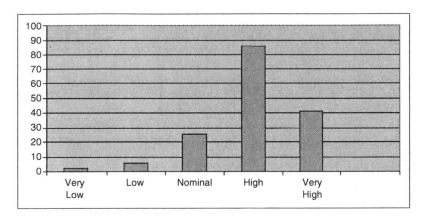

**Figure 4.31**   Applications Experience (APEX)

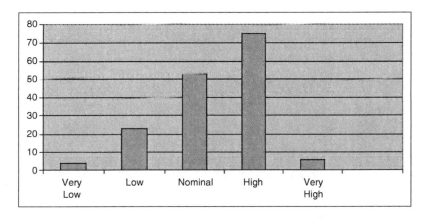

**Figure 4.32**   Platform Experience (PLEX)

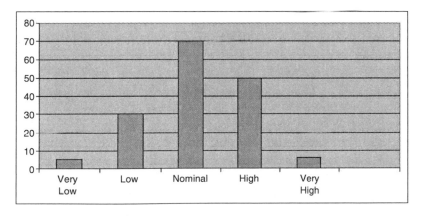

**Figure 4.33**   Language and Tool Experience (LTEX)

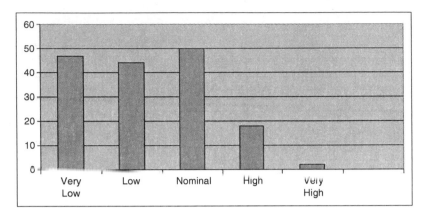

**Figure 4.34**   Use of Software Tools (TOOL)

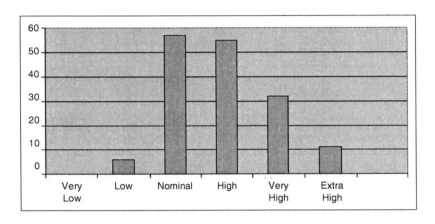

**Figure 4.35**   Multisite Development (SITE)

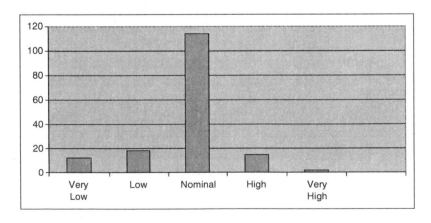

**Figure 4.36**   Required Development Schedule (SCED)

## 4.7   SUMMARY OF COCOMO II DATA

This section provides the summary of the data used for the Bayesian calibration of COCOMO II.2000. It illustrates the distribution of the 161 datapoints that compose the COCOMO II.200 dataset in terms of histograms for each of the five scale factors and seventeen effort multipliers of the COCOMO II Post Architecture model as shown in Figures 4.15 to 4.36. This section has been adapted from Appendix C of [Chulani 1999].

## 4.8   CONCLUSIONS

This chapter presents the Rosetta Stone and shows how it may be used to convert COCOMO 81 data files to COCOMO II data files. We then discuss statistical modeling approaches used to calibrate COCOMO II. Calibration methods for both versions of COCOMO II (1997 and 2000) publicly available as of this writing are discussed as well as methods for locally calibrating the model so that it more accurately reflects a particular environment.

Our model validations show that COCOMO II.2000 yields estimates within 30 percent of the actuals 75 percent of the time for effort and within 30 percent of the actuals 64 percent of the time for schedule. If the multiplicative constant is calibrated, the prediction accuracy improves to within 30 percent of the actuals 80 percent of the time for effort and within 30 percent of the actuals 75 percent of the time for schedule.

# 5

# Emerging Extensions

## 5.1 APPLICATIONS COMPOSITION: THE APPLICATION POINT MODEL

As discussed under future trends in Chapter 1, a rapidly increasing number of projects are being developed using Applications Composition methods. These methods rely on having an Integrated Computer-Aided Software Engineering (ICASE) environment to expedite product development. ICASE environments generally include the following capabilities:

1. An applications framework (e.g., client-server or peer-to-peer message-passing) with middleware to integrate and manage the execution of the applications components.
2. A set of common utilities, such as a graphic user interface (GUI) builder, a database management system, and a networking support package.
3. Frequently, a domain architecture and set of reusable domain components, and a repository for managing and accessing the components and other reusable assets.
4. Development tools for design, construction, integration, and test.

Not all applications can be developed this way. But for applications which fit the ICASE capabilities, products traditionally requiring ten to twenty people for one to two years can be developed by two to six people in two to six months.

Applications composition products clearly cannot be sized in source lines of code (SLOC). Capabilities such as GUI builders and visual programming systems make the concept of SLOC largely irrelevant. To a lesser degree, sizing metrics such as function points (FP) are too low-level to match the degree of generality and variability often used to scope an applications composition project in its early stages. Often, the product goes through several GUI iterations and is well along toward completion before such quantities as the number of inputs or queries can be estimated well.

In searching for an appropriate sizing metric for applications composition, we found a highly attractive metric called Object Points, developed by Banker, Kauffman, and Kumar for estimation of ICASE-based financial applications. They used the number of screens, reports, and third-generation language (3GL) modules for their basic sizing primitives. They followed the function point convention of weighting these by complexity and adding them together to obtain an overall size metric, which they then adjusted for reuse.

### 5.1.1    Object Point Data and Experiments

In [Banker et al. 1991], they analyzed nineteen applications composition projects developed over two years with an ICASE environment in a banking organization. They found that Object Points correlated with reuse-adjusted effort about as well as Function Points (the R-squared values were 0.73 for OP's and 0.75 for FP's). They also found that productivity went up significantly between year 1 and year 2, as indicated by the NOP/PM (New Object Points per person-month) data in Table 5.1. In performing a further regression analysis across the year-1 and year-2 projects, they found that OP's accounted for the productivity gain more accurately than did FP's. Note also that the project efforts tend to be relatively small; none is higher than 72 person-months (PM). New OP's (NOP) are total OP's adjusted for reuse.

A subsequent statistically designed experiment [Kauffman-Kumar 1993] involved four experienced project managers using Object Points and Function Points to estimate the effort required on two completed projects (3.5 and 6 actual PM), based on project descriptions of the type available at the beginning of such projects. The experiment found that Object Points and Function Points produced comparably accurate results (slightly more accurate with Object Points, but not statistically significant). From a usage standpoint, the average time to produce an Object Point estimate was about 47 percent of the corresponding average time for Function Point estimates. Also, the managers considered the Object Point method easier to use (both of these results were statistically significant).

### 5.1.2    Application Point Estimation Procedure

In reviewing these studies, we felt that their OP's were a better match than FP's for estimating Applications Composition project effort. We adopted their OP counting rules, but made two changes to their approach:

**Table 5.1    Object Point (OP) Data [Banker et al. 1991]**

| Project No. | Year | Total OP's | New OP's (NOP) | Person Months(PM) | NOP/PM |
|---|---|---|---|---|---|
| 1 | 1 | 1768 | 410 | 59 | 7 |
| 2 | 1 | 144 | 144 | 41 | 4 |
| 3 | 1 | 499 | 271 | 27 | 10 |
| 4 | 1 | 600 | 211 | 29 | 7 |
| 5 | 1 | 271 | 165 | 72 | 2 |
| 6 | 1 | 523 | 258 | 16 | 16 |
| 7 | 1 | 231 | 111 | 26 | 4 |
| 8 | 1 | 87 | 81 | 8 | 10 |
| 9 | 1 | 123 | 118 | 24 | 5 |
| 10 | 1 | 376 | 259 | 48 | 5 |
| 11 | 1 | 124 | 56 | 8 | 7 |
| 12 | 1 | 276 | 126 | 13 | 10 |
| 13 | 2 | 2258 | 601 | 38 | 16 |
| 14 | 2 | 1262 | 438 | 21 | 21 |
| 15 | 2 | 2023 | 591 | 26 | 23 |
| 16 | 2 | 163 | 127 | 5 | 25 |
| 17 | 2 | 2698 | 623 | 36 | 17 |
| 18 | 2 | 3657 | 589 | 13 | 45 |
| 19 | 2 | 1915 | 628 | 23 | 27 |

1. We added rating scales for determining a project's productivity rate in NOP/PM, in terms of the ICASE system's maturity and capability, and the developers' experience and capability in using the ICASE environment. As the year 1 projects in Table 5.1 had an average productivity of 7 NOP/PM (and an average maturity and experience of 6 months: the ICASE tool was under construction and the developers were new to its use), while the year 2 projects had an average productivity of 25 NOP/PM and an average maturity and experience of 18 months, we used these as the Low and High levels in rating scale for determining the productivity rate.

2. We changed the name from Object Points to Application Points, to avoid confusion with a number of sizing metrics for more conventional object-oriented applications using such features as class affiliation, inheritance, encapsulation, and message passing [Chidamber-Kemerer 1994; Henderson-Sellers 1996].

Figure 5.1 presents the baseline COCOMO II Application Point procedure for estimating the effort involved in Application Composition and prototyping projects. It is a synthesis of the procedure in Appendix B.3 of [Kauffman-Kumar 1993] and the productivity data from the nineteen project data points in [Banker et al. 1991]. Definitions of terms in Figure 5.1 are as follows:

- NOP: New Object Points (Object Point count adjusted for reuse).
- srvr: number of server (mainframe or equivalent) data tables used in conjunction with the SCREEN or REPORT.

---

Step 1: Assess Application Counts: estimate the number of screens, reports, and 3GL components that will comprise this application. Assume the standard definitions of these elements in your ICASE environment.

Step 2: Classify each element instance into simple, medium and difficult complexity levels depending on values of characteristic dimensions. Use the following scheme:

| For Screens | | | | For Reports | | | |
|---|---|---|---|---|---|---|---|
| | # and source of data tables | | | | #and source of data tables | | |
| Number of Views contained | Total<4 (<2 srvr <3clnt) | Total<8 (2/3 srvr 3-5 clnt) | Total 8+ (>3 srvr >5 clnt) | Number of Sections contained | Total<4 (<2 srvr <3 clnt) | Total<8 (2/3 srvr 3-5 clnt) | Total 8+ (>3 srvr >5 clnt) |
| <3 | simple | simple | medium | 0–1 | simple | simple | medium |
| 3–7 | simple | medium | difficult | 2 or 3 | simple | medium | difficult |
| ≥8 | medium | difficult | difficult | 4+ | medium | difficult | difficult |

Step 3: Weigh the number in each cell using the following scheme. The weights reflect the relative effort required to implement an instance of that complexity level:

| Element Type | Complexity-Weight | | |
|---|---|---|---|
| | Simple | Medium | Difficult |
| Screen | 1 | 2 | 3 |
| Report | 2 | 5 | 8 |
| 3GL Component | | | 10 |

Step 4: Determine Application Points: add all the weighted element instances to get one number, the Application Point count.

Step 5: Estimate percentage of reuse you expect to be achieved in this project. Compute the New Application Points to be developed, NAP=(Application Points) (100-%reuse)/100.

Step 6: Determine a productivity rate, PROD=NAP/person-month, from the following scheme.

| Developers' experience and capability | Very Low | Low | Nominal | High | Very High |
|---|---|---|---|---|---|
| ICASE maturity and capability | Very Low | Low | Nominal | High | Very High |
| PROD | 4 | 7 | 13 | 25 | 50 |

Step 7: Compute the estimated person-months: PM=NAP/PROD.

**Figure 5.1**   Baseline Application Point Estimation Procedure

- clnt: number of client (personal workstation) data tables used in conjunction with the SCREEN or REPORT.
- %reuse: the percentage of screens, reports, and 3GL modules reused from previous applications, prorated by degree of reuse.

Analogous definitions of Total Screen Views and Total Report Sections can be applied to a non client-server application.

The Application Point procedure can be applied fairly straightforwardly by hand. Thus, for example, if your application has ten medium-complexity screens, eight medium-complexity reports, and six 3GL modules, your total application-point size is:

$$2*10 + 5*8 + 10*6 = 20 + 40 + 60 = 120 \ AP$$

If you expect 25 percent reuse, your new application-point size is:

$$(120 \ AP)(.75) = 90 \ NAP$$

If you have a relatively mature and capable (high-rated) ICASE environment and a relatively immature and less capable (low-rated) team in ICASE usage, your average rating is nominal, and your expected productivity rate will 13 $NAP/PM$. Your estimated project effort is thus:

$$90 \ NAP/13 \ NAP/PM \cong 7 \ PM$$

### 5.1.3    Application Point Estimation Accuracy and Maturity

Table 5.2 summarizes the accuracy of the Application Point procedure in estimating the effort for the nineteen projects in Table 5.1.

Even on the calibration data, the percentage of estimates within 30 percent of the actuals [Pred (.30)] is less than 50 percent for the full sample. However, the percentage of estimates within a factor of 2 of the actuals [Pred (X2)] is 89 percent for the full sample. Thus, it appears reasonable to associate a factor of 2 with the optimistic and pessimistic range limits for an Application Point estimate.

We have not been able to collect much further data on applications composition projects. Thus, at this time, we prefer to present Application Points as an emerging extension of COCOMO II. It is relatively easy to apply by hand and is

**Table 5.2    Application Point Estimation Accuracy on Calibration Data**

|            | Year 1 Projects | Year 2 Projects | All Projects |
|------------|-----------------|-----------------|--------------|
| **Pred (.30)** | 42%         | 57%             | 47%          |
| **Pred (X2)**  | 83%         | 100%            | 89%          |

worth using experimentally on applications composition projects, even though there is considerable more work to be done on detailed counting rules and cost drivers, relative to Figure 5.1. Also, there are other possible approaches being experimentally applied such as Enhanced Object Points [Stensrud 1998] and Unified Modeling Language use cases. Our experience so far with use cases is that they still have a very wide range of interpretation, which makes it difficult for them to be used confidently as a sizing metric outside a relatively uniform group of applications and practitioners.

## 5.2  COPSEMO: PHASE SCHEDULE AND EFFORT ESTIMATION

The COnstructive Phased Schedule and Effort MOdel (COPSEMO) was initially developed as a base for the COnstructive RAD MOdel (CORADMO), described in a later section of this chapter. CORADMO required a distribution of schedule and effort over the life-cycle phases as described in Chapter 1. COPSEMO was also needed to compensate for the inadequacy of the waterfall process model that was used in COCOMO 81 for both system-level evolution and smaller, shorter development projects. While actually developed as part of the early CORADMO models, COPSEMO is now recognized as a separate, independent model that will be used as the basis for other COCOMO II model extensions.

The need to accommodate smaller, shorter projects seen in the 1990s manifested itself in the growing application of COCOMO to business and information system that evolve at the system level, often with independently managed projects for each area of evolution. Also, the advent of the SEI's CMM and its application to all projects within an organization following the SEI's process improvement paradigms, increased the visibility of the numerous small development projects in government contractors such as Independent Research and Development (IRAD) or Contracted Research and Development (CRAD). These smaller, shorter duration projects require a new mathematical formula to calculate the duration of the project; COCOMO II's duration calculations often would be wildly unreasonable for projects with under-two person years of effort.

The more modern life-cycle models like MBASE/RUP (Model-Based [System] Architecting and Software Engineering and Rational Unified Process), as described in Appendix A, have differently defined phases outside of COCOMO's original main focus which is used to calculate effort, schedule, and staffing. COCOMO's main focus is product design, programming, and integration and test in the waterfall lifecycle model, also called Elaboration and Construction in the MBASE/RUP life-cycle model. Phases outside COCOMO's original focus, Plans and Requirements and Operations and Maintenance in the waterfall life-cycle model, are called Inception and Transition in the MBASE/RUP life-cycle model.

CORADMO has drivers that impact the Inception phase schedule and effort. Thus it became necessary to distribute or project the COCOMO II calculated effort and schedule over the MBASE/RUP phases. As mentioned in Chapter 1, there are no convenient algorithms for either the distribution of the COCOMO II effort and schedule over Elaboration and Construction, nor do they exist for the projection of COCOMO II calculated effort and schedule over Inception or Transition. As a result, the current implementations of COPSEMO simply allow the users to specify to the percentage allocations for both effort and schedule for the four phases.

Sections 5.2.1 through 5.2.4 describe and illustrate the various aspects of COPSEMO: further explanation of the phase end points defined in Appendix A; an alternative cost schedule relationship for schedule-intensive small projects; an overview of the model algorithms; and a description of the spreadsheet implementation with examples of use. Section 5.2.5 describes an alternative approach for exploring effort and schedule phase distributions: a system dynamic's model of the software development process.

## 5.2.1    Background

Significant variations in development life cycles have arisen over the twenty years since COCOMO was originally conceived. One of the more recent models for life cycles is the MBASE model which shares significant features with the Rational Unified Process's model. At the same time, COCOMO is being asked to provide estimates for smaller and smaller projects, in both staff and duration, including those using Rapid Application Development (RAD) techniques. COCOMO was originally conceived for large projects. However, the COCOMO II model is calibrated for projects down to 2000 lines of code. But, for that 2000 SLOC project, the model estimates a 6.3 PM effort (assuming all nominal ratings for the drivers) over 6.6 months with a staff of 1, which is clearly unreasonable for modern life-cycle model projects.

### 5.2.1.1    DEVELOPMENT LIFE CYCLES

COPSEMO uses the MBASE and Rational Unified Process Milestones described in Chapter 1. There are three milestones which separate the effort and schedule phases of COPSEMO: Life Cycle Objectives review (LCO), Life Cycle Architecture review (LCA), and Initial Operational Capability (IOC). Two more milestones serve as end points at the beginning and end of the effort and schedule phases, respectively: Project Start (PS) and Product Release (PR).

One way of looking at these milestones is architecture centric and focused on the software development aspects of the system and project. While there are many aspects that must be considered at each of the milestones, the architecture-centric approach is the focus of the following discussion.

In this light, PS is the point where resources are explicitly allocated to a development effort and tracked from then on. LCO is the point at which a possible architecture for the project is picked. It may not necessarily be the architecture that is eventually used, but one that can satisfy the requirements, and is judged buildable. LCA is the point when the architecture actually to be used is finalized. Again, this may not be the architecture picked at LCO, but will be the one used to construct the system. IOC is the point when the software system development is finished and the system is ready for deployment and final testing. Finally, at PR the system is fully operational, and ready for a fully supported release.

Between these five milestones are four phases: Inception, Elaboration, Construction, and Transition. Inception goes from PS to LCO, or, from initiation of the project to selecting a viable architecture. Inception is the phase where "Requirements Capture" starts as can be seen in Figure 5.2, adapted from Rational Corporation [Krutchen 1999]. Requirements Capture is an activity similar to COCOMO's "Requirements" activity; it is when the project's needs and objectives are decided and used to drive the selection of an architecture. Notice, however, that this activity does not only lie in the Inception phase but also continues over into the next phase, Elaboration. The supporting activity of Management in this phase corresponds mainly to the "Plans" portion of the "Plans and Requirements" phase of the Waterfall life-cycle model although there is often a portion devoted to requirements negotiation with the clients or customer.

Elaboration goes from LCO to LCA, or, from picking a possible architecture to deciding on the right one. The bulk of this phase is devoted to the activity "Analysis & Design." Essentially, the architecture picked at LCO is investigated, in the light of evolving requirements and understanding of the problem, to see if

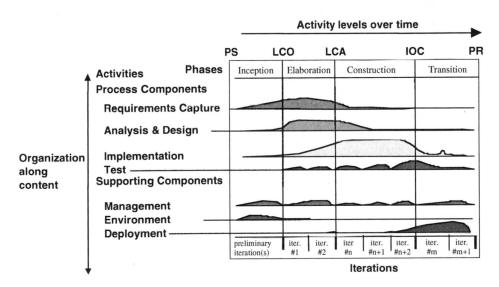

**Figure 5.2**   Activity Levels

it really is the one to be carried through into Construction, or whether an alternate architecture identified at LCO or a new one is the correct one. The architecture is "designed" to satisfy the requirements and "analyzed" to see if it does. Of course, to give the analysis context, the success criterion for the project may have to be evolved and reevaluated. Therefore the Requirements Capture activity is shown to continue into Elaboration. Notice also that the activity "Implementation" is started in the Elaboration phase: to analyze the architecture it may be necessary to develop some preliminary implementation of the architecture to see how it works and if it satisfies all the identified needs. Alternatively, even if there is no change in architecture, prototype development (whether throw-away or retained) may go on during Elaboration to help identify risks and increase understanding of the requirements. These two types of development activities are also why the activity "Test" is shown to occur during this phase.

The next phase, Construction, is from LCA to IOC, or from deciding on the final architecture to having an executable system. In other words, Construction is programming and/or constructing the system following the architecture. Most of the Implementation effort is here because implementing the architecture builds the system. Some Requirements Capture is still done, as the architecture and its implementation may need to be modified as the system is being built. After reevaluating the needs and objectives, the developers should see if they are met, i.e., by Analysis & Design and Test. This Analysis & Design is done in Construction the same way it was done in Elaboration. The same risk-driven methodology that was used to see if the right architecture was picked, is used to see how the architecture may need to be modified. Since the modifications should be minimal, there is less Requirements Capture and Analysis & Design. However, testing is even greater in this phase, as there is much more to be tested as the software system evolves during development. If the LCA milestone compliance is done properly, the need for modifications should taper off with time, as shown in the diagram.

The last phase, Transition, goes from IOC to PR, or, from having an executable system to having it operational and ready for a fully supported release. This involves finalizing the appropriate documentation for the system, getting the necessary licenses, testing it for operational readiness, etc., so that it can be made operational in its target environment. This may require more work on the system, since real-world application of the system may reveal problems with the design, so there is some final Implementation in this phase. There is also the final system testing to assure that it is working properly once it is operational. Note how "Deployment" under "Supporting Components" is gradually increasing as Test and Implementation decreases: First one would deploy some of the product slowly, then test and fix errors, and increase deployment as one became more confident in the system. Ideally, once the system is fully operational and ready for officially supported release, there should be no need for further Implementation and Test.

### 5.2.1.2 SCHEDULE AS A FUNCTION OF EFFORT FOR SMALL PROJECTS

**5.2.1.2.1 TDEV.** COCOMO II provides a simple schedule estimation capability based on the effort as seen in Chapter 2. The underlying equation for effort in COCOMO II is

$$PM_{NS} = A \times (Size)^E \times \prod_{i=1}^{n} EM_i \qquad \text{Eq. 5.1}$$

Where

$PM_{NS}$ is COCOMO II's effort with nominal schedule as in Chapter 2, Eq. 2;

$A$ is a calibration constant;

$E$, the scale (or exponential) factor, accounts for the relative economies or diseconomies of scale encountered for software projects of different sizes [Banker et al 1994] as in Chapter 2, Eq. 2.1, and shown below in Eq. 5.2;

$n$ is 16 for the number of COCOMO II effort multipliers $EM_i$ excluding SCED;

and

$$E = B + 0.01 \times \sum_{j=1}^{5} SF_j \qquad \text{Eq. 5.2}$$

Where

$B$ is another calibration constant; and

$SF_j$ are the five COCOMO II scale factors.

Finally COCOMO II's simple schedule estimate, $TDEV$, is given by

$$TDEV_{COCOMO} = TDEV_{NS} \times \frac{SCED\%}{100} \qquad \text{Eq. 5.3}$$

Where

$TDEV_{COCOMO}$ is II's estimated calendar time in months from the determination of a product's initial requirements baseline to the completion of a software acceptance activity certifying that the product satisfies its requirements, as in Chapter 2; $TDEV_{NS}$, given below, is the COCOMO II estimated PM *excluding* the SCED effort multiplier; and $SCED\%$ is the corresponding compression or expansion percentage related to the SCED effort multiplier, as discussed in Chapter 2.

$$TDEV_{NS} = C \times (PM_{NS})^F \qquad \text{Eq. 5.4}$$

$$F = D + 0.2 \times \left( 0.01 \times \sum_{j=1}^{5} SF_j \right) = D + 0.2 \times (E - B) \qquad \text{Eq. 5.5}$$

Where

$C$ and $D$ are calibration constants with values of 3.67 and 0.28, respectively, for COCOMO II 2000;

$E$ was calculated by Eqn. 5.2;

and

> $B$ is a calibration constant with the value of 0.91 for COCOMO II 2000.
>
> $F$ evaluates to about 1/3 for all COCOMO II 2000 scale factors at the nominal rating level: $F = 0.28 + 0.2(0.01 \times 19) = 0.28 + .04$.

**5.2.1.2.2   Observation: Staffing to Schedule Relationship in Low Effort Projects.**   While COCOMO's TDEV is proportional to approximately the cube root of the effort in PM, for nominal values of all drivers, this value is unrealistic for small, short duration projects of less than 16 PM. Using COCOMO II's TDEV, a project with 4700 SLOC and all nominal drivers is estimated to take 16.1 PM over 8.9 calendar months with a staff of 1.8 persons. Reasonable engineering project management judgement would put four people on such a project for four calendar months. 4700 SLOC is well above the minimum 2000 SLOC for which COCOMO II is calibrated.

A different simple schedule estimation method is needed for COPSEMO and especially for CORADMO, the reason COPSEMO was developed. A reasonable first approximation would seem to be a simple square root of the person months of effort to estimate both people and calendar months.

**5.2.1.2.3   Observation: Simple, Smooth Effort to Schedule Curve Not Possible.**   Unfortunately, the cube-root like COCOMO II TDEV function and the simpler square root function do not intersect as can be seen in Figure 5.3. The solution to this discontinuity was to lay in a straight line between the square root function and the COCOMO II function. The reasonable lower bound, 16 person months and 4 months, was selected based on a reasonable slope change; the upper bound was selected by incrementally increasing the calendar months until

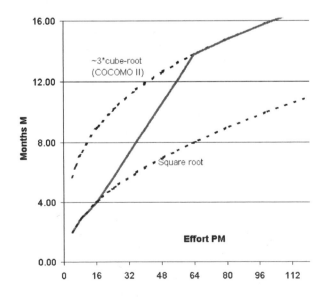

**Figure 5.3**   COCOMO II Schedule Estimate vs. COPSEMO Schedule Estimate

a COCOMO II produced a reasonable TDEV and staff estimate. Again using COCOMO II's TDEV, a project with 16500 SLOC program with all nominal drivers is estimated to take 64.2 PM over 13.8 calendar months with a staff of 4.7 persons. This seems quite reasonable, and so PM = 64 was selected as the upper bound.

### 5.2.1.3 DISTRIBUTION OF EFFORT AND SCHEDULE TO PHASES

There are no obvious or convenient algorithms for either the distribution of the COCOMO II effort and schedule over Elaboration and Construction, nor do they exist for the projection of COCOMO II calculated effort and schedule over Inception or Transition, as mentioned in Chapter 1. However, Chapter 1 did give reasonable initial values and ranges for those percentages.

The current implementations of COPSEMO simply allow the users to specify to the percentage allocations for both effort and schedule for the four phases, subject to the restriction imposed from using the COCOMO II's calculated effort and schedule as the total effort and total schedule over Elaboration and Construction phases. Thus, only three percentages need to be supplied to COPSEMO for each of effort and schedule.

## 5.2.2 Model Overview

### 5.2.2.1 INPUTS FROM COCOMO II

In order to do the redistribution of schedule and effort, COPSEMO needs values from COCOMO II: Effort, Schedule, SCED (Effort Multiplier) driver value, and SCED%. The later two are needed so COPSEMO can backout the SCED% from the TDEV schedule calculation and SCED from the effort calculation.

### 5.2.2.2 CALCULATION OF SCHEDULE (M) BASED ON EFFORT (PM)

While all the calculations of COCOMO II for effort and schedule could be repeated, the actual model and implementation simply recalculates a new COPSEMO base-line for effort and schedule. Combining Eq. 5.1 with Eq. 5.4, one gets

$$PM_{COCOMO} = A \times \left( \prod_{i=1}^{16} EM_i \right) \times Size^E \times EM_{SCED} \qquad \text{Eq. 5.6}$$

Where

$E$, the scale factor, is as before (and is not impacted);

$EM_i$ represents one of the sixteen (16) post-architecture EMs;

and

$EM_{SCED}$ is the Post Architecture schedule multiplier, SCED.

The COPSEMO baseline thus becomes

$$PM_{COPSEMO} = PM_{COCOMO} \times EM_{SCED} \qquad \text{Eq. 5.7}$$

Similarly, COPSEMO's TDEV when the effort is greater than 64 PM, is given by

$$TDEV_{COPSEMO(PM>64)} = TDEV_{COCOMO} \div \frac{SCED\%}{100} \qquad \text{Eq. 5.8}$$

Where

$TDEV_{COCOMO}$ is from Eq. 5.3; and

SCED% is the corresponding compression or expansion percentage related to the SCED effort multiplier, as discussed in Chapter 2.

### 5.2.2.3   SOLVING THE LINEAR EQUATIONS

In order to solve for the straight line to connect the square root based effort calculation with COCOMO II's value, only one new value must be calculated: Mof64, which represents the schedule at 64 PM for the given driver ratings, all the rest of the values are constants ( since for efforts less than or equal to 16 PM a simple square root is followed). The $(x,y)$ points that the line must go through are thus (16,4) and $(PM_{COPSEMO}, Mof64)$, and as a straight line it should be compatible with the linear equation $Y = SLOPE \bullet X + INTERCEPT$, where $Y$ is $TDEV_{COPSEMO}$ and $X$ is $PM_{COPSEMO}$.

Inserting the known values, one gets: $4 = SLOPE \sum 16 + INTERCEPT$ and $Mof64 = SLOPE \bullet PM_{COPSEMO} + INTERCEPT$.

Solving for INTERCEPT and SLOPE, one gets:

$$SLOPE = (Mof64 - 4)/48 \qquad \text{Eq. 5.9}$$

and

$$INTERCEPT = 4 - (Mof64 - 4)/48 \times 16 \qquad \text{Eq. 5.10}$$

yielding

$$TDEV_{COPSEMO(16<\,=PM<64)} =$$
$$(Mof64 - 4)/48 \cdot 16 + (4 - (Mof64 - 4)/48 \times 16) \qquad \text{Eq. 5.11}$$

And finally,

$$TDEV_{COPSEMO(PM<16)} = Sqrt(PM_{COPSEMO}) \qquad \text{Eq. 5.12}$$

### 5.2.2.4   RESULTING GRAPH

The resulting curve for schedule $(M)$ versus effort $(PM)$ for COPSEMO is shown in Figure 5.4. Since $PM$ and $M$ are dependent on drivers and sign, the figure shows the specific values for a 32 KSLOC estimation with all nominal drivers.

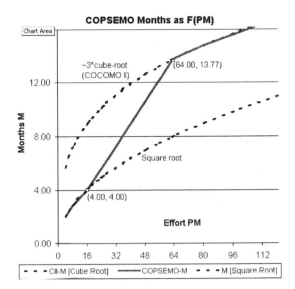

**Figure 5.4** COCOMO II Schedule Estimate vs. COPSEMO Schedule Estimate

### 5.2.2.5 DISTRIBUTION OF EFFORT AND SCHEDULE TO PHASES

The distribution of Effort ($E$) and Schedule ($S$) is done with simple percentage distributions, such that

$$E_{phase} = E\%_{phase} \cdot PM_{COPSEMO} \qquad \text{Eq. 5.13}$$

and

$$S_{phase} = S\%_{phase} \cdot TDEV_{COPSEMO} \qquad \text{Eq. 5.14}$$

with $TDEV_{COPSEMO}$ taking one of the three forms depending on the value of $PM_{COPSEMO}$, and the constraints that $E\%_{Elaboration} + E\%_{Construction} = 100$ and $S\%_{Elaboration} + S\%_{Construction} = 100$.

### 5.2.2.6 DRIVERS FOR COPSEMO

At the present time there are no drivers impacting the distributions of Effort and Schedule identified above.

### 5.2.2.7 COPSEMO OUTPUTS

Since there are no adjustments for drivers at this time, the outputs of the model are nothing more than $E_{phase}$ and $S_{phase}$ values identified above.

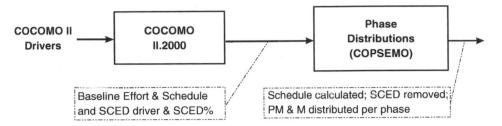

**Figure 5.5**   COPSEMO Logical Model

### 5.2.3   Model Implementation

A logical model for implementation is shown in Figure 5.5.

A physical model for implementation using spreadsheets is shown in Figure 5.6.

The physical model has been implemented and is available at the USC CSE website and on the CD-ROM accompanying this book. The form of the output of the implementation model is tables showing the distributions and a plot of the staffing ($P$) over the schedule ($M$), where $P$ is calculated by dividing $E_{phase}$ by $S_{phase}$.

The spreadsheet with the default distributions for an all nominal 5KSLOC estimate is shown in Figure 5.7.

### 5.2.4   Examples of Use

Figures 5.8 through 5.11 show the COPSEMO results ($2^{nd}$ printed page which represents a summary of the tools results) for COCOMO II.2000 estimates for different sizes of programs, with all nominal drives, of 2,000, 5,000, 12,000, and 25,000 SLOC, respectively.

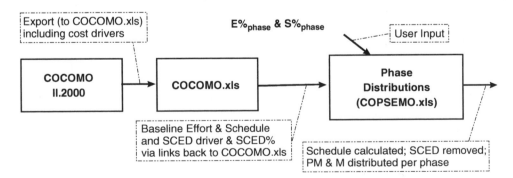

**Figure 5.6**   COPSEMO Physical Model

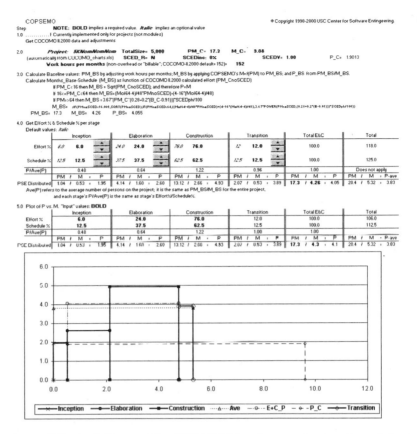

**Figure 5.7** Both Pages of the COPSEMO Implementation in a Spreadsheet

As can be seen from the figures above, the combination of both the COPSEMO M(PM) function and the distribution of effort and schedule to the phases produces very different staffing profiles than COCOMO II.2000's calculated values (the P_C profile which is supposed to cover only the elaboration and construction phases) as long as the COCOMO II calculated effort is less than 64 person-months.

## 5.2.5 Dynamic COCOMO

### 5.2.5.1 INTRODUCTION AND BACKGROUND

Dynamic COCOMO is an extension based on cost parameters varying over time versus traditional static assumptions. It is a family of simulation models using system dynamics that implement COCOMO with varying degrees of dynamic assumptions, including information feedback loops. A simple example is

COPSEMO

Step

**NOTE:** **BOLD** implies a required value. *Italic* implies an optional value

1.0 ............ Currently implemented only for projects (not modules)

Get COCOMO II.2000 data and adjustments

5.0 Plot of P vs. M. "Input" values: **BOLD**

| | Inception | Elaboration | Construction | Transition | Total E&C | Total |
|---|---|---|---|---|---|---|
| Effort % | **6.0** | **24.0** | **76.0** | 12.0 | 100.0 | 106.0 |
| Schedule % | **12.5** | **37.5** | **62.5** | 12.5 | 100.0 | 112.5 |
| P/Ave(P) | 0.48 | 0.64 | 1.22 | 1.00 | 1.00 | |
| | PM / M : P | PM / M : P | PM / M : P | PM / M : P | PM / M : P | PM / M : P-ave |
| PSE Distributed | 0.38 / 0.31 = 1.20 | 1.51 / 0.94 = 1.61 | 4.79 / 1.57 = 3.05 | 0.76 / 0.31 = 2.41 | **6.3** / **2.5** = 2.5 | 7.4 / 3.14 = 2.37 |

**Figure 5.8**  Second Page of the COPSEMO Implementation for 2000 SLOC

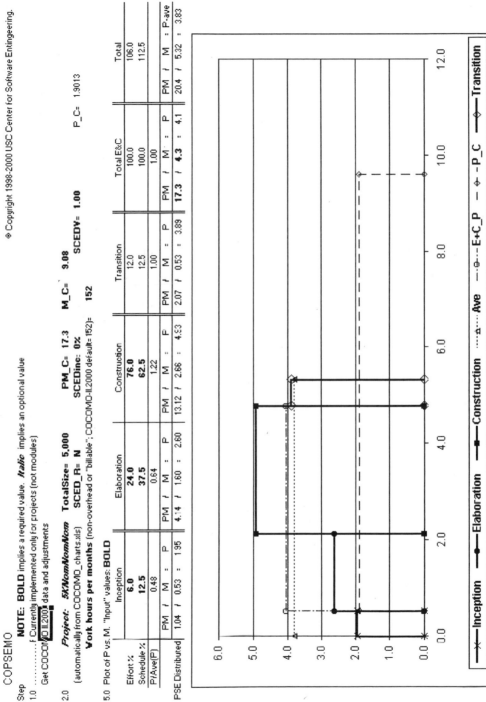

**Figure 5.9** Second Page of the COPSEMO Implementation for 5000 SLOC

COPSEMO

Step
1.0 .......... Currently implemented only for projects (not modules)
Get COCOMO II.2000 data and adjustments

NOTE: **BOLD** implies a required value. *Italic* implies an optional value

2.0  Project: *12XNcomNcomNcom* TotalSize= **12,000**   PM_C= 45.2   M_C= 12.33
(automatically from COCOMO_charts.xls)  SCED_R= **N**   SCEDinc: 0%   SCEDv= 1.00   P_C= 3.666
**Work hours per months** (non-overhead or "billable"; COCOMO-II.2000 default=152)= **152**

5.0 Plot of P vs. M. "Input" values: **BOLD**

| | Inception | Elaboration | Construction | Transition | Total E&C | Total |
|---|---|---|---|---|---|---|
| Effort % | **6.0** | **24.0** | **76.0** | **12.0** | 0.0 | 106.0 |
| Schedule % | **12.5** | **37.5** | **62.5** | **12.5** | 0.0 | 112.5 |
| P/Ave(P) | 0.48 | 0.64 | 1.22 | 1.00 | .00 | |
| | PM / M = P | PM / M = P | PM / M = P | PM / M = P | PM / M = P | PM / M = P-ave |
| PSE Distributed | 2.71 / 1.24 = 2.18 | 10.85 / 3.73 = 2.91 | 34.35 / 6.21 = 5.53 | 5.42 / 1.24 = 4.36 | **45.2 / 9.9 = 4.5** | 53.3 / 12.43 = 4.29 |

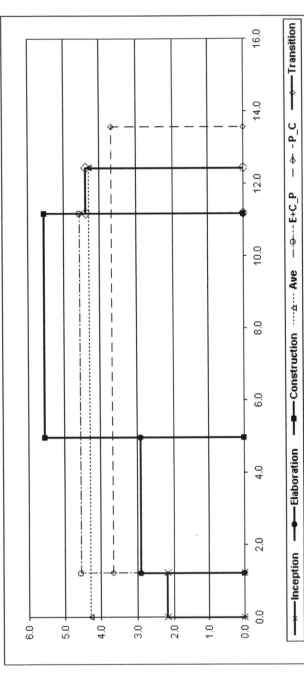

**Figure 5.10**  Second Page of the COPSEMO Implementation for 1200 SLOC

COPSEMO

Step

**NOTE:** **BOLD** implies a required value. *Italic* implies an optional value.

1.0 ............ Currently implemented only for projects (not modules)

Get COCOMO II.2000 data and adjustments

2.0 *Project:* *25KNomNomNom* TotalSize= **25,000**  PM_C= **101.3**  M_C= **15.93**

(automatically from COCOMO_charts.xls)  SCED_R= **N**  SCEDinc: **0%**  SCEDV= **1.00**  P_C= 6.358

**Work hours per months** (non-overhead or "billable"; COCOMO-II.2000 default= 152)= **152**

5.0 Plot of P vs. M. "Input" values: **BOLD**

| | Inception | Elaboration | Construction | Transition | Total E&C | Total |
|---|---|---|---|---|---|---|
| Effort % | **6.0** | **24.0** | **76.0** | **12.0** | 100.0 | 106.0 |
| Schedule % | **12.5** | **37.5** | **62.5** | **12.5** | 100.0 | 112.5 |
| P/Ave(P) | 0.48 | 0.64 | 1.22 | 1.00 | 1.00 | |
| | PM / M = P | PM / M = P | PM / M = P | PM / M = P | PM : M = P | PM : M = P-ave |
| PSE Distributed | 6.08 / 1.99 = 3.05 | 24.31 / 5.98 = 4.07 | 77.30 / 9.96 = 7.73 | 12.16 / 1.99 = 6.10 | **101.3** / **15.9** = 6.4 | 119.5 / 19.92 = 6.00 |

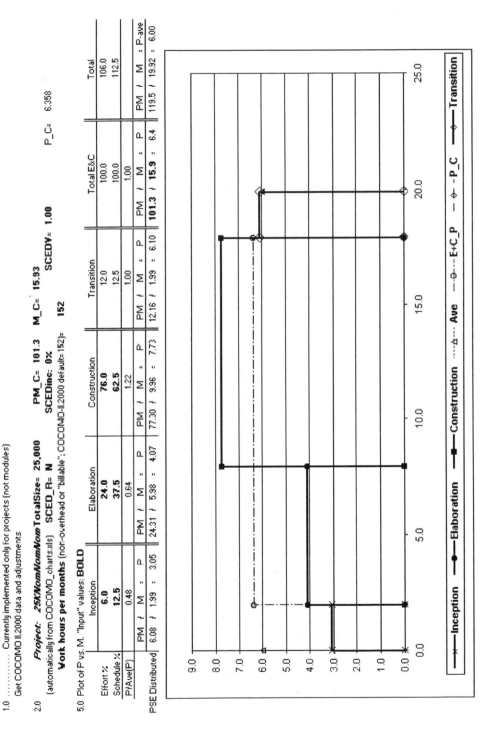

**Figure 5.11**  Second Page of the COPSEMO Implementation for 25,000 SLOC

replacing the personnel experience factors with time-based representations to reflect increasing productivity caused by learning. Learning formulations could be table functions or feedback loops based on the volume of software output.

Static models assume that project factors are invariant over the duration of a project and that time plays no role. Dynamic models are used when the behavior of the system changes over time and is of particular interest or significance. Rates in the process such as productivity are known to change over time as opposed to staying constant. These changes are significant and need to be addressed.

System dynamics and static models such as COCOMO rest on different assumptions, but the two perspectives can contribute to each other in a symbiotic and synergistic fashion. Calibrations can go both ways, and one model type can pick up where the other leaves off. As a static model, COCOMO represents a time-aggregation of all major process/project effects. Dynamic effects are modeled as constant parameters. For example, though the analyst or programming capabilities may wax and wane as a team throughout a project, the associated effort multipliers are constant in COCOMO.

COCOMO is largely used as a static model, but there is actually a continuum between static and dynamic versions of COCOMO. There are variations possible to introduce time into the calculations. At a high level, some parameters are a function of project phase—a coarse time division. For example, the original Detailed COCOMO [Boehm 1981] has phase-dependent effort multipliers. Figure 5.12 depicts the continuum between static implementations of COCOMO and the dynamic version.

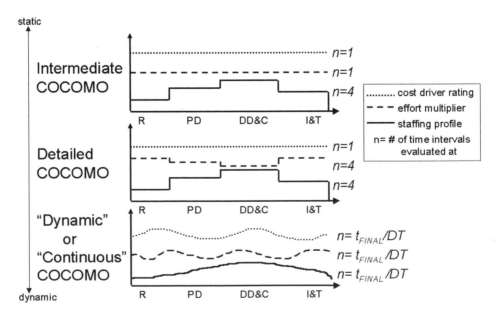

**Figure 5.12**  Hierarchy of COCOMO Dynamism

### 5.2.5.2 SAMPLE IMPLEMENTATIONS

In [Madachy 1996], a system dynamics model of an inspection-based life-cycle process was used to go beyond COCOMO for evaluating dynamic project effects of inspections. Using the inspection model as a backdrop, [Madachy 1995] shows how a static model can be used to calibrate portions of a dynamic model via scalable staffing profiles, and the dynamic model can then incorporate more realistic assumptions of time-varying phenomena that are treated as static in CO-COMO. The dynamic model was also used to derive phase-sensitive effort multipliers for COCOMO through simulation experiments.

Phase effort and schedule from COCOMO was used to nominally calibrate the dynamic model, and the dynamic model furthers COCOMO by accounting for dynamic error generation. One salient feature of using system dynamics for software processes is that defects can be represented as levels, thus providing an inherent cost/quality tradeoff feature that is lacking in most cost models such as COCOMO. The test effort was thus modeled with two components: a fixed portion for test planning and execution, and a variable component for error detection and correction as a function of error levels.

Common factors for schedule constraint and experience were used, with the dynamic model improving on static assumptions. For example, a learning curve was implemented to simulate increasing productivity in the experience cost drivers. To derive phase-sensitive effort multipliers for a proposed cost driver *Use of Inspections*, simulation model parameters were mapped into cost-driver ratings and simulation runs performed that isolated the effect of inspections.

As another example, Figure 5.13 is a sample interface to a dynamic implementation of the COCOMO II Early Design model. The model is used in a "flight simulation" mode whereby the user can interact with it while the simulation is running. Cost drivers can be varied as well as the input size and schedule constraint. The model is driven with a modified Rayleigh staffing curve calibrated to COCOMO II and can take midstream changes to its inputs. The example demonstrates size increasing at about day 130, which could be the effect of newly added requirements.

### 5.2.5.3 FUTURE DIRECTIONS AND FURTHER REFERENCES

Future directions include several variants of Dynamic COCOMO. Modeling Rapid Application Development (RAD) processes are one such area. Another will be to incorporate alternative cost/quality tradeoffs in COCOMO, such as that demonstrated in [Madachy 1996]. For example, dynamic modeling could be combined with COQUALMO. See [Chulani 1997a] and Section 5.5 for an extension that models defect introduction and elimination rates based on cost drivers. These rates can be used for dynamic defect modeling. More examples and theory behind Dynamic COCOMO will be published in [Madachy-Boehm 2001], and some of the material will be available on the Internet at *http://sunset.usc.edu/ COCOMOII/spd*.

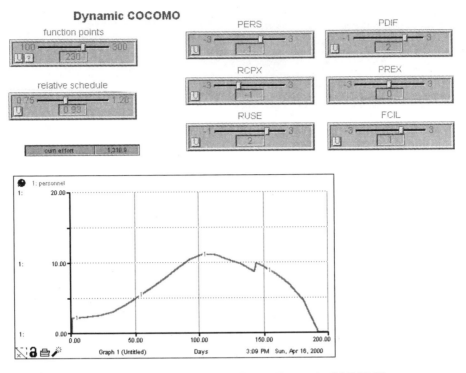

**Figure 5.13**    Sample Interface to Dynamic COCOMO

## 5.3.    CORADMO: RAPID APPLICATION DEVELOPMENT ESTIMATION

When COCOMO II was introduced in 1981, it was a fairly adequate model for large products, but used a waterfall process model that did not address any Rapid Application Development (RAD) strategies. Also, when calculations were done on small projects the results were unreasonable. The COnstructive RAD schedule estimation MOdel (CORADMO) and its companion model COnstructive Phased Schedule & Effort MOdel (COPSEMO) were developed to overcome shortcomings in the classic COCOMO model. These deficiencies are in several areas: a waterfall predisposition, no drivers reflecting modern schedule reduction efforts, and small-effort projects. CORADMO is based on the concept of RAD as a set of strategies for accelerating application development. RAD in this sense is the use of any of a number of techniques or methods to reduce software development cycle time. The initial version of CORADMO presented here is undergoing revision based on a recent USC-CSE Affiliates' workshop (see Section 5.3.9).

### 5.3.1  Background and Rationale

The COCOMO II schedule, as presently implemented in COCOMO II.2000 does not reflect any of the currently accepted alternatives such as iterative, spiral or evolutionary development. Obviously, COCOMO II does not address any of the Rapid Application Development (RAD) strategies that are being employed to reduce schedule and sometimes effort as well. Many of these techniques were identified in the 1997 USC-CSE Rapid Application Development Focused Workshop [USC-CSE 1997b].

#### 5.3.1.1  TYPES OF RAD

A column [Boehm 1999] by Dr. Barry Boehm defined several RAD forms: Generator RAD (GRAD), Composition RAD (CRAD), Full-System RAD (FRAD) and Dumb RAD (DRAD). DRAD is the most frequently used form on ambitious systems and is not recommended in any situation.

Generator RAD involves the use of very high level languages such as spreadsheets, business fourth generation languages such as IDEAL or Focus, or other domain-specific languages for such domains as finance, industrial process control, or equipment testing. Composition RAD (CRAD) involves the use of small "tiger teams" to rapidly assemble small to medium-large systems based on large components (networking packages, GUI builders, database management systems, distributed middleware) and applications-domain class libraries. Full-scale RAD (FRAD) represents a number of effective techniques for reducing cycle time for larger systems that are not well suited to GRAD and CRAD. FRAD is discussed in more detail in the column cited above. Dumb RAD (DRAD) is most frequently encountered when a decision-maker sets an arbitrarily short deadline for the completion of a software project, without having done any analysis of its feasibility.

CORADMO applies to GRAD, CRAD, and FRAD, but NOT to DRAD.

#### 5.3.1.2  NEW DRIVERS

In CSE's 1997 Focussed Workshop #9 on RAD [USC-CSE 1997b], a RAD Opportunity Tree of strategies, extended in Figure 5.14, was presented. The strategies included some techniques that were already covered by the drivers of COCOMO II as well as several that were not. An analysis of these new drivers produced a set of five drivers that reflect identifiable behavioral characteristics. These drivers were

1. Reuse and Very High-level Languages (RVHL)
2. Development Process Reengineering (DPRS)
3. Collaboration Efficiency (CLAB)

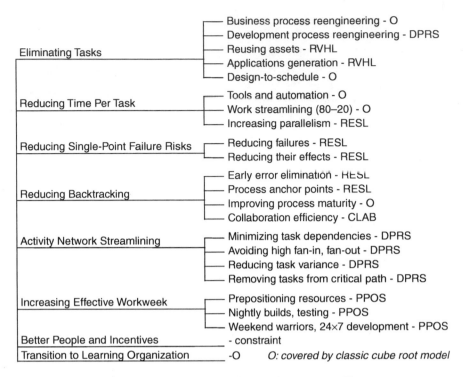

**Figure 5.14**   Annotated RAD Opportunity Tree

**4.** Architecture, Risk Resolution (RESL)

**5.** Pre-positioning Assets (PPOS)

These new drivers and some constraints are reflected in the annotated "RAD Opportunity Tree" shown below.

In Figure 5.14, the Opportunities labeled with O are covered by the regular COCOMO II model. The benefit and legitimate application of the RAD techniques and drivers is valid ONLY if the development activity is planned, actively managed, and supported. For example, PPOS must be supported by investment. "Better People" is an example of a constraint, especially on the RESL benefits.

### 5.3.2   Relation To COCOMO II

CORADMO applies primarily to the early phases of the Anchor Point based lifecycle models, like Inception and Elaboration, and only to a lesser extent to Construction. CORADMO relies on COPSEMO for the initial distribution of schedule and effort before its driver's impacts are applied.

CORADMO is implementable as an add-on because its multipliers allow a re-distribution of both effort and schedule over all three phases of the lifecycle.

CORADMO also uses some of the same driver names and ratings that are part of COCOMO II. Architecture and Risk Resolution (RESL) is used directly and without change. Also used indirectly, as part of CLAB, are Team Cohesion (TEAM), Multisite Development (SITE), and Personnel experience (PREX, the Early Design driver). PREX can be assessed based on its Post-Architecture constituents, Application Experience (APEX), Platform Experience (PLEX) and Language and Tool Experience (LTEX). The personnel capability ratings, as assessed by Personnel Capability (PERS) or summarized from the PA drivers Analyst Capability (ACAP), Programmer Capability (PCAP) and Personnel Continuity (PCON), should act as a constraint on the overall CORADMO driver ratings.

### 5.3.3   Model Overview

#### 5.3.3.1   LOGICAL IMPLEMENTATION

COPSEMO's logical model for implementation, reshown in Figure 5.15 provides a base for CORADMO's logical model for implementation as shown in Figure 5.16.

#### 5.3.3.2   DRIVERS AND CONSTRAINTS

The five drivers identified for CORADMO are:

1. Reuse and Very High-level Languages (RVHL)
2. Development Process Reengineering (DPRS)
3. Collaboration Efficiency (CLAB)
4. Architecture, Risk Resolution (RESL)
5. Pre-positioning Assets (PPOS)

Each driver is assigned a rating similar to those in COCOMO II, ranging from Very Low (VL) to Very High (VH) or Extra High (EH). Each driver represents multiplicative factor that adjusts both effort and schedule for each of the

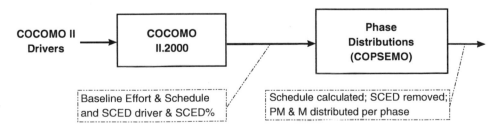

**Figure 5.15**   COPSEMO Logical Model

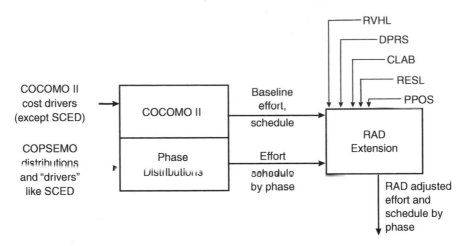

**Figure 5.16**   RAD Extension Logical Model

three phases. The five driver ratings represent a total of thirty multiplicative values. Thus, selection of the driver rating level impacts six values in the mathematical version of the model shown below.

Many of the drivers have the same effect on effort and schedule (i.e. personnel is held constant). Each of the driver levels imply the set of values of the multipliers for each of the phases. The association of driver-rating levels with the set of numerical values is shown below.

As mentioned before, in order for the RAD model to apply, the activities implied by the drivers must be planned, actively managed, and supported. Thus, investment is one of the constraints. People capability and experience is an example of another constraint, especially on the RESL benefits. At the current time, these constraints are not implemented in the logical model or physical implementation of CORADMO.

### 5.3.3.3   EQUATIONS

The mathematical form of the CORADOMO model is a simple application of the product of the Schedule Multipliers (*SMult*) or Effort Multipliers (*EMult*) to the COPSEMO determined Schedule (SCOPSEMO) or Effort (ECOPSEMO) for the phase, respectively. This results in the new Schedule (*S*) or Effort (*E*) per phase that is the primary result of the model:

$$M_{phase} = \prod_{driver=1}^{5} SMult_{driver,phase} \times S_{phase} \qquad \text{Eq. 5.15}$$

and

$$PM_{phase} = \prod_{driver=1}^{5} EMult_{driver,phase} \times E_{phase} \qquad \text{Eq. 5.16}$$

The total schedule and effort thus becomes

$$M_{CORADMO} = \sum_{phase=inception}^{cos\,ntrtuction} M_{phase} \qquad \text{Eqn. 5.17}$$

and

$$PM_{CORADMO} = \sum_{phase=inception}^{cos\,ntrtuction} PM_{phase} \qquad \text{Eqn. 5.18}$$

### 5.3.4  Model Details

The following sections explain the drivers, their ratings and their values.

#### 5.3.4.1  REUSE AND VHLLS (RVHL)

RVHL expresses the degree to which re-use of artifacts other than code and/or very high level languages are utilized. Normal 3GL module reuse requires no CORADMO adjustment since it is handled by COCOMO II.2000. This driver reflects schedule compression in Inception and Elaboration stages due to faster prototyping or option exploration. The degree of impact depends on the level of capability and experience in doing this (similar to Rapid Prototyping experience), and the impact is the same on both effort and schedule (essentially the staff level is held constant).

The rating for this driver depends on the amount of Rapid Prototyping Experience the development team has had in the domain of the project being evaluated. Since the rating applies to the team, it must include the experience of the managers and team leaders and their experience takes precedence over the average of the rest of the team working in the Inception and Elaboration phases (see Table 5.3).

As can be seen in the numerical ratings in Table 5.4, there are different schedule and effort impacts in different phases. There is no impact in Construc-

**Table 5.3  RVHL Rating Scale**

| Very Low | Low | Nominal | High | Very High |
|---|---|---|---|---|
| none | On average, personnel have experience on less than one recent project using Rapid Prototyping | Most personnel have worked on more than one project using Rapid Prototyping | On average, personnel have worked on more than two projects using Rapid Prototyping | All personnel have worked on at least three projects using Rapid Prototyping |

**Table 5.4   RVHL Multiplier Values**

| Schedule and Effort Multipliers | Rapid Prototyping Experience Level | | | | |
|---|---|---|---|---|---|
| | VL | L | N | H | VH |
| Inception | 1.04 | 1.0 | .98 | .94 | .90 |
| Elaboration | 1.02 | 1.0 | .99 | .97 | .95 |
| Construction | 1.0 | 1.0 | 1.0 | 1.0 | 1.0 |

tion beyond COCOMO II 3GL reuse which should have already been accounted for (see reuse model in Chapter 2). The impacts in Inception and Elaboration are from more rapid prototyping and option exploration. The same multiplier values apply to both effort and schedule.

### 5.3.4.2   DEVELOPMENT PROCESS REENGINEERING AND STREAMLINING (DPRS)

The degree to which the project and organization allow and encourage streamlined or reengineered development process: the current level of bureaucracy is a clear indicator. The following Table 5.5, can be used to make a subjective average to determine the level of bureaucracy.

The DPRS rating scale is shown in Table 5.6.

The DPRS multiplier values for each rating are shown in Table 5.7.

The same multiplier values apply to both schedule and effort. Thus, the resulting compression or expansion because of this driver does not alter staff level ($P$).

**Table 5.5   Subjective Determinants of Bureaucracy**

| | VL | L | N | H | VH |
|---|---|---|---|---|---|
| Number of approvals required per task | Excessive | Occasionally reduced | Mature | Actively Reduced | Actively Minimized |
| Time taken per approval | Excessive | Occasionally reduced | Mature | Actively Reduced | Actively Minimized |
| Reduced task dependencies, critical path tasks | None | Little | Mature Tech. Adopted | Advanced Tech. Adopted | Pioneering |
| Follow-up to expedite task completion | None | Little | Encouraged | Emphasized | Strongly Emphasized |
| Process measurement & streamlining | None | Little | Mature Tech. Adopted | Advanced Tech. Adopted | Pioneering |

**Table 5.6    DPRS Rating Scale**

| Very Low | Low | Nominal | High | Very High |
|---|---|---|---|---|
| Heavily Bureaucratic | Bureaucratic | Basic good business practices | Partly streamlined | Fully streamlined |

### 5.3.4.3   COLLABORATION EFFICIENCY (CLAB)

Teams and team members who can collaborate effectively can reduce both effort and schedule; those that don't collaborate effectively have increased schedule and effort (because of wasted time/effort). Collaboration efficiency is impacted by traditional COCOMO II 2000 TEAM and SITE ratings. Collaboration efficiency is also impacted by COCOMO II 2000 TOOL rating, but only for tools that support or enable collaboration. However, the tool technology impact is lessened in the case of a co-located team with high experience ratings (PREX from the COCOMO II 2000 Early Design ratings, or the combination of application, platform, language, and tool experience taken from the COCOMO II 2000 Post-Architecture ratings). This is shown in Table 5.8.

Each of these contributing COCOMO II drivers (TEAM, SITE, and PREX) is summarized below; where appropriate their consistent parts are discussed, leading to the ability to come up with one rating value for CLAB.

The Team Cohesion (TEAM) cost driver accounts for the sources of project turbulence and extra effort caused by difficulties in synchronizing the project's stakeholders: users, customers, developers, maintainers, interfacers, and others, as shown in Table 5.9.

Given the increasing frequency of multisite developments, and indications that multisite development effects are significant, the Multisite Development cost driver, SITE, was added to COCOMO II in 1997. Determining its cost-driver rating involves the assessment and combining of two factors: site collocation (from fully collocated to international distribution) and communication support (from surface mail and some phone access to full interactive multimedia). CORADMO

**Table 5.7    DPRS Multiplier Values for Each Rating**

| Schedule and Effort Multipliers | Inception | Elaboration | Construction |
|---|---|---|---|
| VL—Heavily Bureaucratic | 1.20 | 1.15 | 1.15 |
| L—Bureaucratic | 1.08 | 1.06 | 1.06 |
| N—Basic good business practices | 1.0 | 1.0 | 1.0 |
| H—Partly streamlined | .96 | .98 | .98 |
| VH—Fully streamlined | .90 | .95 | .95 |

**Table 5.8   CLAB Contributing Components**

|        | VL | L | N | H | VH | EH |
|--------|----|---|---|---|----|----|
| TEAM   | <=== <=== <=== COCOMO II Scale Factor Ratings ===> ===> ===> | | | | | |
| SITE   | <== COCOMO II Post-Arch. Ratings ==> | | | | plus negotiation/tradeoff tools<br>basic                                    advanced | |
| PREX   | (EL & VL) <=== <=== <=== COCOMO II Early Design Ratings ===> ===> ===> | | | | | |

recommends 70 percent and 30 percent weightings for Collocation and Communications, respectively, when making your subjective average of these two components of SITE, as shown in Table 5.10.

As mentioned earlier, there are two alternative assessments for PREX, either directly from the COCOMO II 2000 Early Design ratings, or the combination of application, platform, language and tool experience taken from the COCOMO II 2000 Post-Architecture ratings.

When taken directly from the Early Design model, PREX has the ratings definition shown in Table 5.11.

Alternatively, PREX can be assessed based on the combination of its Post-Architecture (PA) components, Application Experience (APEX), Platform Experience (PLEX) and Language and Tool Experience (LTEX).

The rating Applications Experience (APEX) is dependent on the level of applications experience of the project team developing the software system or subsystem. The ratings are defined in terms of the project team's equivalent level of experience with this type of application, as shown in Table 5.12.

The Post-Architecture model broadens the productivity influence of Platform Experience (PLEX), recognizing the importance of understanding the use of more powerful platforms, including more GUI, database, networking, and distributed middleware capabilities, as shown in Table 5.13.

Language and Tool Experience (LTEX) is a measure of the level of programming language and software tool experience of the project team developing the software system or subsystem, as shown in Table 5.14.

**Table 5.9   TEAM Rating Scale**

| TEAM for<br>CORADMO | Very Low | Low | Nominal | High | Very High | Extra High |
|---------------------|----------|-----|---------|------|-----------|------------|
|                     | Very difficult interactions | Some difficult interactions | Basically cooperative interactions | Largely cooperative | Highly cooperative | Seamless interactions |

**Table 5.10  SITE Rating Scale**

|  | Very Low | Low | Nominal | High | Very High | Extra High |
|---|---|---|---|---|---|---|
| SITE: Collocation | Inter-national | Multi-city and Multi-company | Multi-city or Multi-company | Same city or metro area | Same building or complex | Fully collocated |
| SITE: Communications | Some phone, mail | Individual phone, FAX | Narrowband email | Wideband electronic communication | Wideband elect. comm., occasional video conference | Interactive multimedia |
| **SITE for CORADMO** | **Very Low** | **Low** | **Nominal** | **High** | **Very High** | **Extra High** |

**Table 5.11   PREX Rating Scale**

| PREX | Extra Low | Very Low | Low | Nominal | High | Very High | Extra High |
|---|---|---|---|---|---|---|---|
| Applications, platform, language, and tool experience | ≤ 3 months | 5 months | 9 months | 1 year | 2 years | 4 years | 6 years |

**Table 5.12   APEX Rating Scale**

| APEX | Very Low | Low | Nominal | High | Very High |
|---|---|---|---|---|---|
| | ≤ 2 months | 6 months | 1 year | 3 years | ≥6 years |

**Table 5.13   PLEX Rating Scale**

| PLEX | Very Low | Low | Nominal | High | Very High |
|---|---|---|---|---|---|
| | ≤ 2 months | 6 months | 1 year | 3 years | ≥6 years |

**Table 5.14   LTEX Rating Scale**

| LTEX | Very Low | Low | Nominal | High | Very High |
|---|---|---|---|---|---|
| | ≤ 2 months | 6 months | 1 year | 3 years | ≥6 years |

The Early Design cost driver, Personnel Experience (PREX), combines the three Post-Architecture cost drivers: application experience (APEX), platform experience (PLEX), and language and tool experience (LTEX). While these three Post-Architecture ratings normally apply to a module, for CORADMO they are applied across the entire project. Their individual rating information is given above.

The approach for mapping the Post-Architecture cost drivers and rating scales onto their Early Design model counterparts involves the use and combination of numerical equivalents of the rating levels. Specifically, a Very Low Post-Architecture cost driver rating corresponds to a numerical rating of 1, Low is 2,

**Table 5.15 PREX Rating Scale**

| PREX | Extra Low | Very Low | Low | Nominal | High | Very High | Extra High |
|---|---|---|---|---|---|---|---|
| Sum of APEX, PLEX and LTEX ratings | 3, 4 | 5, 6 | 7, 8 | 9 | 10, 11 | 12, 13 | 14, 15 |
| Applications, Platform, Language and Tool Experience | ≤ 3 mo. | 5 months | 9 months | 1 year | 2 years | 4 years | ≥ 6 years |

Nominal is 3, High is 4, Very High is 5, and Extra High is 6. For the combined Early Design cost drivers, the numerical values of the contributing Post-Architecture cost drivers are summed, and the resulting totals are allocated to an expanded Early Design model rating scale going from Extra Low to Extra High. The Early Design model rating scales always have a Nominal total equal to the sum of the Nominal ratings of its contributing Post-Architecture elements.

Table 5.15, below, assigns PREX ratings across this range, and associates appropriate effort multipliers and rating scales to each of the rating levels.

Finally, to determine the CORADMO's CLAB rating, use the subjective/fuzzy average of TEAM and SITE ratings from COCOMO II's Post-Architecture definitions and the PREX ratings using COCOMO II's Early Design definitions, as shown in Table 5.16.

The CLAB multiplier values for each rating are shown in Table 5.17. The CLAB multiplier has the same effect on effort and schedule, and so staffing level does not change based on collaboration efficiency.

**Table 5.16 CLAB Rating Scale**

| | Very Low | Low | Nominal | High | Very High | Extra High |
|---|---|---|---|---|---|---|
| **SITE** | <== COCOMO II Post-Arch. Ratings ==> | | | | High plus negotiation/tradeoff tools | |
| | | | | | basic | advanced |
| **TEAM** | <=== <=== <=== COCOMO II Scale Factor Ratings ===> ===> ===> | | | | | |
| **PREX** | (EL & VL) <=== <=== <=== COCOMO II Early Design Ratings ===> ===> ===> | | | | | |
| **Fuzzy Average** | | | | | | |
| **CLAB** | Very Low | Low | Nominal | High | Very High | Extra High |
| | <== Use the most appropriate rating level based on fuzzy average ==> | | | | | |

**Table 5.17   CLAB multiplier Values for Each Rating**

| Schedule & Effort Multipliers | VL | L | N | H | VH | EH |
|---|---|---|---|---|---|---|
| Inception | 1.21 | 1.10 | 1.00 | 0.93 | 0.86 | 0.80 |
| Elaboration | 1.15 | 1.07 | 1.00 | 0.95 | 0.90 | 0.86 |
| Construction | 1.10 | 1.05 | 1.00 | 0.98 | 0.95 | 0.93 |

### 5.3.4.4   ARCHITECTURE / RISK RESOLUTION (RESL)

This rating is exactly the same as the COCOMO II RESL rating. The architecture portion of RESL enables parallel construction, thus reducing schedule during the Construction phase assuming that staff level increases during Construction while applying the same effort. Good risk resolution in a schedule-driven development effort applying RAD strategies increases the probability of the strategy's success.

The potential impacts of RESL are shown in three situations in Figure 5.17. Even with good RESL but no active planning for and increases in staffing, there will be no impact as shown in (a). With good RESL and increased staffing, case

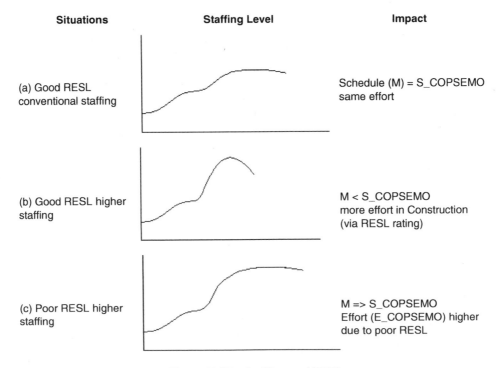

| Situations | Staffing Level | Impact |
|---|---|---|
| (a) Good RESL conventional staffing | | Schedule (M) = S_COPSEMO same effort |
| (b) Good RESL higher staffing | | M < S_COPSEMO more effort in Construction (via RESL rating) |
| (c) Poor RESL higher staffing | | M => S_COPSEMO Effort (E_COPSEMO) higher due to poor RESL |

**Figure 5.17**   Staffing and RESL

(b), a shortening of schedule can be expected. Finally, (c) shows what happens with poor RESL and increased staffing—at best no impact on schedule, but with wasted effort, or at the worse both wasted effort and an increase in schedule.

The assessment of the Architecture and Risk Resolution (RESL) ratings in CORADMO is exactly the same as the COCOMO II RESL rating. Those level ratings are simply used to select CORADMO schedule and effort driver values.

One assessment method for RESL is based on the percentage of significant module interfaces specified, and the percentage of significant risks eliminated, as shown in Table 5.18.

Alternatively, RESL can be assessed by looking at it's origins where it combines two scale factor concepts, "Design Thoroughness by Product Design Review (PDR)" and "Risk Elimination by PDR" [Boehm-Royce 1989; Figures 4 and 5]. Table 5.19 consolidates the concepts to form a comprehensive definition for the RESL rating levels. The RESL rating is the subjective weighted average of the listed characteristics.

The RESL multiplier values for each rating are shown in Table 5.20.

### 5.3.4.5 PRE-POSITIONING ASSETS (PPOS)

This driver assesses the degree to which assets are pre-tailored to a project and furnished to the project for use on demand. This clearly is impacted by people skills and planned and reinforced team building. The assets that are being pre-positioned, besides personnel capabilities, include processes and tools, and architecture and components.

In order to take advantage of PPOS, the organization must either be taking a product-line approach or have made a 3 to 10 percent pre-Inception effort investment!

The PPOS multiplier values for each rating in Table 5.21 are shown in Table 5.22. This is the one driver that has impact on all of the multipliers. Since Effort, Schedule, and Staffing must abide by the simple formula that Effort/Schedule = Staffing (or $PM/M = P$), and since the pre-positioning implies applying additional, specialized (even though possibly multipurposed) staff and effort for the assets, a corresponding reduction in schedule ensues.

### 5.3.4.6 PEOPLE FACTORS

Staff capability should be applied as a constraint. While experience is reflected as a factor in CLAB, capability has not been explicitly addressed. Utilizing PERS, the Early Design Personnel Capability Rating, as a constraint would mean limiting ALL of the RAD driver ratings to the PERS rating level. PERS covers the

**Table 5.18  RESL Rating Scale Based on Percentage of Risks Mitigated**

| RESL | Very Low | Low | Nominal | High | Very High | Extra High |
|---|---|---|---|---|---|---|
| | little (20%) | some (40%) | often (60%) | generally (75%) | mostly (90%) | full (100%) |

**Table 5.19   RESL Rating Scale Based on Design Thoroughness/risk Elimination by PDR**

| Characteristic | Very Low | Low | Nominal | High | Very High | Extra High |
|---|---|---|---|---|---|---|
| Risk Management Plan identifies all critical risk items, establishes milestones for resolving them by PDR. | Never | Seldomly | Occasionally | Generally | Mostly | Fully |
| Schedule, budget, and internal milestones through PDR compatible with Risk Management Plan | None | Little | Some | Half | Most | All |
| Percent of development schedule devoted to establishing architecture, given general product objectives | 5 | 10 | 17 | 25 | 33 | 40 |
| Percent of required top software architects available to project | 20 | 40 | 60 | 80 | 100 | 120 |
| Tool support available for resolving risk items, developing and verifying architectural specs | None | Little | Some | Good | Strong | Full |
| Level of uncertainty in Key architecture drivers: mission, user interface, COTS, hardware, technology, performance. | Extreme | Significant | Considerable | Some | Little | Very Little |
| Number and criticality of risk items | > 10 Critical | 5–10 Critical | 2–4 Critical | 1 Critical | > 5 Non-Critical | < 5 Non-Critical |
| **RESL for CORADMO** | **Very Low** | **Low** | **Nominal** | **High** | **Very High** | **Extra High** |
| | < == Use COCOMO II's RESL Rating Level == > | | | | | |

**Table 5.20   RESL Multiplier Values for Each Rating**

| Schedule Multipliers (Effort Unchanged) | VL | L | N | H | VH | EH |
|---|---|---|---|---|---|---|
| Inception | 1.0 | 1.0 | 1.0 | 1.0 | 1.0 | 1.0 |
| Elaboration | 1.0 | 1.0 | 1.0 | 1.0 | 1.0 | 1.0 |
| Construction | 1.0 | 1.0 | 1.0 | .91 | .83 | .75 |

**Table 5.21    PPOS Rating Scale**

|        | Nominal | High | Very High | Extra High |
|--------|---------|------|-----------|------------|
| **PPOS** | Basic project legacy, no tailoring | Some prepositioning & tailoring | Key items prepositioned & tailored | All items prepositioned & tailored |

**Table 5.22    PPOS Multiplier Values for Each Rating**

| PM/M = P Multipliers | N | H | VH | EH |
|----------------------|---|---|----|----|
| **Rating** | Basic project legacy, no tailoring | Some prepositioning & tailoring | Key items prepositioned & tailored | All items prepositioned & tailored |
| **Inception** | 1.0/1.0 = 1.0 | 1.03/.93 = 1.11 | 1.06/.86 = 1.23 | 1.1/.80 = 1.37 |
| **Elaboration** | 1.0/1.0 = 1.0 | 1.03/.93 = 1.11 | 1.06/.86 = 1.23 | 1.1/.80 = 1.37 |
| **Construction** | 1.0/1.0 = 1.0 | 1.03/.93 = 1.11 | 1.06/.86 = 1.23 | 1.1/.80 = 1.37 |

primary range of people's capabilities, from the fifteenth percentile at the low end to the ninetieth percentile on the high end. It is too difficult to calibrate models outside the 15 to 90 percent range because of the wide range of effects, lack of data points, and the difficulty in creating an organization-independent rating scale. A similar logic for RAD can be applied—large schedule compressions achievable with outstanding people. However, such extreme impacts can only be assessed outside the model.

The Early Design cost driver Personnel Capability (PERS) combines three Post-Architecture cost drivers: Analyst Capability (ACAP), Programmer Capability (PCAP), and Personnel Continuity (PCON).

The Analyst Capability (ACAP) rating scale is shown in Table 5.23. Analysts are personnel that work on requirements, high level design and detailed design.

The Programmer Capability (PCAP) rating scale is shown in Table 5.24. The evaluation should be based on the capability of the programmers as a team rather than as individuals. Major factors which should be considered in the rating are ability, efficiency, and thoroughness, and the ability to communicate and cooperate.

**Table 5.23    PERS Rating Scale**

| (ACAP) | Very Low | Low | Nominal | High | Very High |
|--------|----------|-----|---------|------|-----------|
|        | 15th percentile | 35th percentile | 55th percentile | 75th percentile | 90th percentile |

**Table 5.24   PCAP Rating Scale**

| PCAP | Very Low | Low | Nominal | High | Very High |
|------|----------|-----|---------|------|-----------|
|  | 15th percentile | 35th percentile | 55th percentile | 75th percentile | 90th percentile |

**Table 5.25   PCON Rating Scale**

| PCON | Very Low | Low | Nominal | High | Very High |
|------|----------|-----|---------|------|-----------|
|  | 48%/year | 24%/year | 12%/year | 6%/year | 3%/year |

The Personnel Continuity (PCON) rating values are shown in Table 5.25. The rating scale for PCON is in terms of the project's annual personnel turnover.

These three factors are combined for CORADMO but in a way different from that of COCOMO II Early Design. Since PERS is used as a constraint, and the three factors are orthogonal, the appropriate value for PERS for CORADMO is the minimum of the three ratings, shown in Table 5.26.

Since PERS for CORADMO is to be applied as a general constraint, all other driver rating levels should then be limited (capped) to this value of PERS.

### 5.3.5   Scope And Life-cycle Addressed

The scope of the present CORADMO model excludes both commercial-off-the-shelf (COTS) impacts (COCOTS) and the quality extensions (COQUALMO). CORADMO does include and use the COPSEMO model. The only drivers for CORADMO are those from the RAD Strategies Opportunity Tree discussed earlier. CORADMO can easily handle low effort projects under 12 PM, in fact projects as low as 6 PM seem reasonable.

While CORADMO is currently life-cycle model independent, since it works with data between anchor points, it expresses the phases using the MBASE/RUP life cycle. Only the first three phases, Inception, Elaboration, and Construction are affected by CORADMO.

**Table 5.26   PERS Rating Scale for CORADMO**

| PERS for CORADMO | Very Low | Low | Nominal | High | Very High |
|------------------|----------|-----|---------|------|-----------|
|  | < == Use minimum of ACAP, PCAP and PCON == > | | | | |

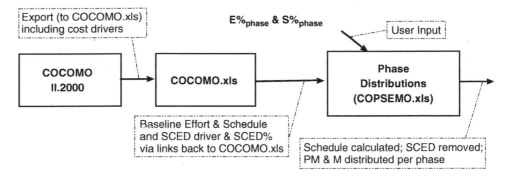

**Figure 5.18**   COPSEMO Physical Model

### 5.3.6   Spreadsheet Model Implementation

#### 5.3.6.1   PHYSICAL MODEL

A physical model for the COPSEMO implementation using spreadsheets is shown in Figure 5.18. It provides the basis for the CORADMO implementation using spreadsheets, as shown in Figure 5.19 by physical inclusion into the same spreadsheet.

#### 5.3.6.2   SPREADSHEET

The current spreadsheet implementation does *not* automatically apply PERS as an overall constraint, nor PREX as a constraint on RVHL.

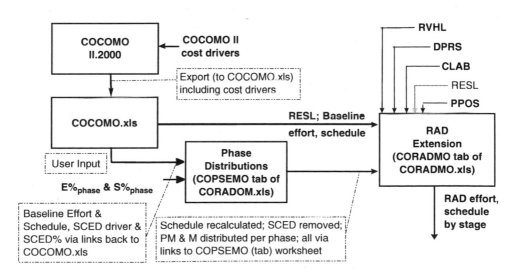

**Figure 5.19**   CORADMO Physical Model

Figure 5.20 and Figure 5.21 show the full implementation of CORADMO based on COPSEMO, including the plot of Effort over Schedule, for a 5000 SLOC development project with all COCOMO II and CORADMO driver and scale factor ratings at nominal and high, respectively. The COPSEMO worksheet is integral to the CORADMO spreadsheet. The CORADMO model extension is actually implemented on a second worksheet in the CORADMO spreadsheet. Figure 5.20, which is based on the same estimation as shown in Figure 5.9, shows the minimal impact of all nominal drivers.

CORADMO goes step-wise through the following process as shown on Figure 5.21:

1. Get COCOMO II values via COPSEMO.xls or direct input

   Required values:

   $PM\_C = 15.0$
   $M\_C = 10.90$
   $SCED\_R = H$
   $SCEDinc:$ 0%
   $SCEDV = 1.00$
   $P\_C = 1.372$
   $RESL\_R: H$

   Pick up optional values from COPSEMO worksheet by default:

   *Project:* 5K Hi Hi Hi
   $TotalSize = 5,000$

   Show values of imported scale factor ratings:

   $PREC\_R: H$
   $FLEX\_R: H$
   $RESL\_R: H$
   $TEAM\_R: H$
   $PMAT\_R: H$

2. Get the COPSEMO distribution percentages of Schedule, Effort, and Staffing, again from the COPSEMO worksheet, and compute the resulting Schedule, Effort, and Staffing. This row is labeled *PSE Distributed.*

3. Set the CORADMO drivers via drop-down list boxes, all to $H$ in this case. Show the product, P, of all the drivers (RVHL, DPRS, CLAB, RESL, and PPOS) by Phase and estimated value to be impacted ($PM$, $M$, and $P$). As can be seen in Figure 5.20, even a nominal RVHL impacts the schedule and effort in the early phases.

4. Apply products to the corresponding COPSEMO calculated (and distributed) effort ($PM$), schedule ($M$), and staffing ($P$) per stage, resulting in the "RAD Eff&Schd" row. The COPSEMO calculated row is labeled *PSE Distributed.*

5. Do a plot of effort ($P$) over time ($M$), as shown on the bottom of the spreadsheet (Figure 5.21).

CORADMO      . Currently implemented only for projects (not modules)                    ® Copyright 1998-2000 USC Center for Software Entingeering.

Step          **BOLD: required values carried forward from COPSEMO;**    *Ralic: optional values carried forward from COPSEMO*

1.0  Get COCOMO II.2000 data and adjustments from COPSEMO

| | | | | |
|---|---|---|---|---|
| *Project: 5KNomNomNom* | TotalSize= **5,000** | **PM_C= 17.3** | **M_C=** `9.08` | P_C=  1.901 |
| Including Schedule parameters | SCED_R= **N** | SCEDinc: **0%** | SCEDV= **1.00** | |
| Including Scale Factor Ratings | PREC_R: **N** | FLEX_R: **N** | RESL_R: **N** | TEAM_R: **N**     PMAT_R: **N** |

2.0  Get COPSEMO Distribution information: Values specified or Calculated in COPSEMO. Baseline/Input vales: **BOLD**

Eff% & Sched % per stage (per CoPSEMo)

| | Inception | | | Elaboration | | | Construction | | | Total E&C | | | Total | | |
|---|---|---|---|---|---|---|---|---|---|---|---|---|---|---|---|
| Effort % | **6.0** | | | **24.0** | | | **76.0** | | | 100.0 | | | 118.0 | | |
| Schedule % | **12.5** | | | **37.5** | | | **62.5** | | | 100.0 | | | 125.0 | | |
| P/Ave(P) | 0.48 | | | 0.64 | | | 1.22 | | | 1.00 | | | Does not apply | | |
| | PM | / M | = P | PM | / M | = P | PM | / M | = P | PM | / M | = P | PM | / M | = P-ave |
| PSE Distributed | 1.04 | / 0.53 | = 1.95 | 4.14 | / 1.60 | = 2.60 | 13.12 | / 2.66 | = 4.93 | **17.3** | / **4.26** | = 4.05 | 20.4 | / 5.32 | = 3.83 |

3.0  Get the Schedule Multipliers values.

RVHL [N ▼]   DPRS [N ▼]   CLAB [N ▼]   RESL [N ▼]   PPOS [N ▼]

| | | Inception | | | Elaboration | | | Construction | | |
|---|---|---|---|---|---|---|---|---|---|---|
| | | PM | / M | = P | PM | / M | = P | PM | / M | = P |
| N | RVHL | 0.980 | 0.980 | 1.000 | 0.990 | 0.990 | 1.000 | 1.000 | 1.000 | 1.000 |
| N | DPRS | 1.000 | 1.000 | 1.000 | 1.000 | 1.000 | 1.000 | 1.000 | 1.000 | 1.000 |
| N | CLAB | 1.000 | 1.000 | 1.000 | 1.000 | 1.000 | 1.000 | 1.000 | 1.000 | 1.000 |
| N | RESL | 1.000 | 1.000 | 1.000 | 1.000 | 1.000 | 1.000 | 1.000 | 1.000 | 1.000 |
| N | PPOS | 1.000 | 1.000 | 1.000 | 1.000 | 1.000 | 1.000 | 1.000 | 1.000 | 1.000 |
| | Π | 0.980 | 0.980 | 1.000 | 0.990 | 0.990 | 1.000 | 1.000 | 1.000 | 1.000 |

4.0  Apply the product of user selected Schedule and Effort Multipliers to each PM, M and P in each stage.

Input vales: **BOLD**

| | Inception | | | Elaboration | | | Construction | | | Total E&C | | | Total | | |
|---|---|---|---|---|---|---|---|---|---|---|---|---|---|---|---|
| | PM | / M | = P | PM | / M | = P | PM | / M | = P | PM | / M | = P | PM | / M | = P-ave |
| PSE Distributed | 1.04 | / 0.53 | - 1.95 | 4.14 | / 1.60 | = 2.60 | 13.12 | / 2.66 | = 4.93 | **17.3** | / **4.3** | = 4.1 | 18.3 | / 4.8 | = 3.0 |
| Π | 0.98 | 0.98 | 1.00 | 0.99 | 0.99 | 1.00 | 1.00 | 1.00 | 1.00 | | | | | | |
| RAD Eff&Schd | 1.01 | / 0.52 | = 1.95 | 4.10 | / 1.58 | = 2.60 | 13.12 | / 2.66 | = 4.93 | 17.2 | / 4.2 | = 4.1 | 18.2 | / 4.8 | = 3.8 |

Ave(P) refers to the average number of persons on the project: in the absence of Schedule Multiplier effects.
it is the same as PM_BS/M_BS for the entire project, and each stage's P/Ave(P) is the same as stage's Effort%/Schedule%.

5.0  Plot of P vs M. Input values in **BOLD**

RVHL= **N**        DPRS= **N**           CLAB= **N**        RESL= **N**        PPOS= **N**

| | Inception | | | Elaboration | | | Construction | | | Total E&C | | | Total | | |
|---|---|---|---|---|---|---|---|---|---|---|---|---|---|---|---|
| Effort % | **6.0** | | | **24.0** | | | **76.0** | | | 100.0 | | | 106.0 | | |
| Schedule | **12.5** | | | **37.5** | | | **62.5** | | | 100.0 | | | 112.5 | | |
| P/Ave(P) | 0.48 | | | 0.64 | | | 1.22 | | | 1.00 | | | | | |
| | PM | / M | = P | PM | / M | = P | PM | / M | = P | PM | / M | = P | PM | / M | = P-ave |
| PSE Distributed | 1.04 | / 0.53 | = 1.95 | 4.14 | / 1.60 | = 2.60 | 13.12 | / 2.66 | = 4.93 | **17.3** | / **4.3** | = 4.1 | 18.3 | / 4.8 | = 3.8 |
| Π | 0.98 | 0.98 | 1.00 | 0.99 | 0.99 | 1.00 | 1.00 | 1.00 | 1.00 | | | | | | |
| RAD Eff&Schd | 1.01 | / 0.52 | = 1.95 | 4.10 | / 1.58 | = 2.60 | 13.12 | / 2.66 | = 4.93 | 17.2 | / 4.2 | = 4.1 | 18.2 | / 4.8 | = 3.8 |

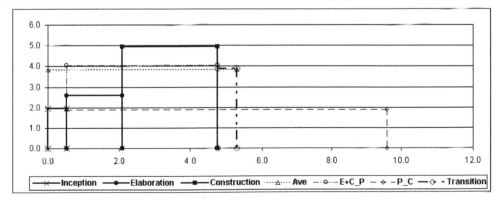

**Figure 5.20**   5000 SLOC All Nominal CORADMO Spreadsheet (Worksheet) Implementation

CORADMO          . Currently implemented only for projects (not modules)          ® Copyright 1998-2000 USC Center for Software Entingeering.

Step          **BOLD: required values carried forward from COPSEMO;**      *Italic: optional values carried forward from COPSEMO*

1.0  Get COCOMO II.2000 data and adjustments from COPSEMO

*Project: 5KHiHiHiHi*          TotalSize= 5,000          PM_C= 15.0          M_C=' 10.90|          P_C= 1.372

Including Schedule parameters          SCED_R= H          SCEDinc: 0%          SCEDV= 1.00

Including Scale Factor Ratings          PREC_R: H          FLEX_R: H          RESL_R: H          TEAM_R: H          PMAT_R: H

2.0  Get COPSEMO Distribution information: Values specified or Calculated in COPSEMO. Baseline/Input vales: **BOLD**

Eff% & Sched % per stage (per CoPSEMo)

|  | Inception | | | Elaboration | | | Construction | | | Total E&C | | | Total | | |
|---|---|---|---|---|---|---|---|---|---|---|---|---|---|---|---|
| Effort % | **6.0** | | | **24.0** | | | **76.0** | | | 100.0 | | | 118.0 | | |
| Schedule % | **12.5** | | | **37.5** | | | **62.5** | | | 100.0 | | | 125.0 | | |
| P/Ave(P) | 0.48 | | | 0.64 | | | 1.22 | | | 1.00 | | | Does not apply | | |
|  | PM | / | M | = | P | PM | / | M | = | P | PM | / | M | = | P | PM | / | M | = | P | PM | / | M | = | P-ave |
| PSE Distributed | 0.90 | / | 0.48 | = | 1.08 | 3.59 | / | 1.45 | = | 2.47 | 11.36 | / | 2.42 | = | 4.70 | **15.0** | / | 3.87 | = | 3.87 | 17.6 | / | 4.83 | = | 3.65 |

3.0  Get the Schedule Multipliers values.

RVHL [ H ▼ ]    DPRS [ H ▼ ]    CLAB [ H ▼ ]    RESL [ H ▼ ]    PPOS [ H ▼ ]

|  |  | Inception | | | Elaboration | | | Construction | | |
|---|---|---|---|---|---|---|---|---|---|---|
|  |  | PM | / | M | = | P | PM | / | M | = | P | PM | / | M | = | P |
| H | RVHL | 0.940 | 0.940 | 1.000 | 0.970 | 0.970 | 1.000 | 1.000 | 1.000 | 1.000 |
| H | DPRS | 0.960 | 0.960 | 1.000 | 0.980 | 0.980 | 1.000 | 0.980 | 0.980 | 1.000 |
| H | CLAB | 0.930 | 0.930 | 1.000 | 0.950 | 0.950 | 1.000 | 0.980 | 0.980 | 1.000 |
| H | RESL | 1.000 | 1.000 | 1.000 | 1.000 | 1.000 | 1.000 | 1.000 | 0.910 | 1.099 |
| H | PPOS | 1.030 | 0.930 | 1.108 | 1.030 | 0.930 | 1.108 | 1.030 | 0.930 | 1.108 |
|  | Π | 0.864 | 0.780 | 1.108 | 0.930 | 0.840 | 1.108 | 0.989 | 0.813 | 1.217 |

4.0  Apply the product of user selected Schedule and Effort Multipliers to each PM, M and P in each stage.

Input vales: **BOLD**

|  | Inception | | | | | Elaboration | | | | | Construction | | | | | Total E&C | | | | | Total | | | | |
|---|---|---|---|---|---|---|---|---|---|---|---|---|---|---|---|---|---|---|---|---|---|---|---|---|---|
|  | PM | / | M | = | P | PM | / | M | = | P | PM | / | M | = | P | PM | / | M | = | P | PM | / | M | = | P-ave |
| PSE Distributed | 0.90 | / | 0.48 | = | 1.86 | 3.59 | / | 1.45 | = | 2.47 | 11.36 | / | 2.42 | = | 4.70 | **15.0** | / | 3.9 | = | 3.9 | 15.8 | / | 4.3 | = | 3.6 |
| Π | 0.86 | | 0.78 | | 1.11 | 0.93 | | 0.84 | | 1.11 | 0.99 | | 0.81 | | 1.22 | | | | | | | | | | | |
| RAD Eff&Schd | 0.78 | / | 0.38 | = | 2.06 | 3.34 | / | 1.22 | = | 2.74 | 11.24 | / | 1.96 | = | 5.72 | 14.6 | / | 3.2 | = | 4.6 | 15.4 | / | 3.6 | = | 4.3 |

Ave(P) refers to the average number of persons on the project;  in the absence of Schedule Multiplier effects,
it is the same as PM_PC/M_PC for the entire project, and each stage's P/Ave(P) is the same as stage's Effort%/Schedule%

5.0  Plot of P vs M.  Input values in **BOLD**

RVHL= **H**        DPRS= **H**        CLAB= **H**        RESL= **H**        PPOS= **H**

|  | Inception | | | | | Elaboration | | | | | Construction | | | | | Total E&C | | | | | Total | | | | |
|---|---|---|---|---|---|---|---|---|---|---|---|---|---|---|---|---|---|---|---|---|---|---|---|---|---|
| Effort % | **6.0** | | | | | **24.0** | | | | | **76.0** | | | | | 100.0 | | | | | 106.0 | | | | |
| Schedule | **12.5** | | | | | **37.5** | | | | | **62.5** | | | | | 100.0 | | | | | 112.5 | | | | |
| P/Ave(P) | 0.48 | | | | | 0.64 | | | | | 1.22 | | | | | 1.00 | | | | | | | | | |
|  | PM | / | M | = | P | PM | / | M | = | P | PM | / | M | = | P | PM | / | M | = | P | PM | / | M | = | P-ave |
| PSE Distributed | 0.90 | / | 0.48 | = | 1.86 | 3.59 | / | 1.45 | = | 2.47 | 11.36 | / | 2.42 | = | 4.70 | **15.0** | / | 3.9 | = | 3.9 | 15.8 | / | 4.3 | = | 3.6 |
| Π | 0.86 | | 0.78 | | 1.11 | 0.93 | | 0.84 | | 1.11 | 0.99 | | 0.81 | | 1.22 | | | | | | | | | | | |
| RAD Eff&Schd | 0.78 | / | 0.38 | = | 2.06 | 3.34 | / | 1.22 | = | 2.74 | 11.24 | / | 1.96 | = | 5.72 | 14.6 | / | 3.2 | = | 4.6 | 15.4 | / | 3.6 | = | 4.3 |

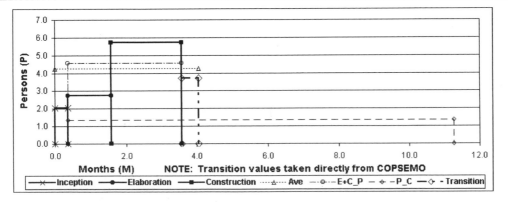

**Figure 5.21**    5000 SLOC All High CORADMO Spreadsheet (Worksheet) Implementation

The impact of the RAD drivers, as shown in Figure 5.21, is considerable. While COCOMO II.2000 estimated 15.0 PM over 10.90 months at a staffing level of 1.372 persons, CORADMO's values over the same phases were 14.6 PM over 3.2 months at a weighted average staffing level of 3.9 persons. The impacts in the construction phase are even more dramatic, reducing its duration to 1.96 months from 2.42 months for COPSEMO, an almost 25% improvement.

The second page of CORADMO spreadsheet (Figure 5.21), repeats the most important values from the first page and adds the courtesy plot.

### 5.3.7  Examples of Use

The following tables show Application Development examples using the best possible schedule compression ratings.

Table 5.27a shows the multiplier ratings for maximum schedule compression.

Table 5.27b shows the results from CORADMO when the ratings are applied to a 32 KSLOC Project with a COCOMO II projected effort of 120 PM and a schedule of twelve months.

**Table 5.27a  Multiplier Ratings (Best Schedule Compression)**

| Multipliers | Inception<br>PM / M   = P | Elaboration<br>PM / M   = P | Construction<br>PM / M   = P |
|---|---|---|---|
| RVHL | 0.90 / 0.90 = 1.00 | 0.95 / 0.95 = 1.00 | 1.00 / 1.00 = 1.00 |
| DPRS | 0.90 / 0.90 = 1.00 | 0.95 / 0.95 = 1.00 | 0.95 / 0.95 = 1.00 |
| CLAB | 0.80 / 0.80 = 1.00 | 0.86 / 0.86 = 1.00 | 0.93 / 0.93 = 1.00 |
| RESL | 1.00 / 1.00 = 1.00 | 1.00 / 1.00 = 1.00 | 1.00 / 0.75 = 1.33 |
| PPOS | 1.10 / 0.80 = 1.38 | 1.10 / 0.80 = 1.38 | 1.10 / 0.80 = 1.38 |
| $\Pi$ | 0.71 / 0.52 = 1.38 | 0.85 / 0.62 = 1.38 | 0.97 / 0.53 = 1.83 |

**Table 5.27b  Results for a 32-KSLOC Project (Effort: 120 PM/Schedule: 12.0 Months)**

| | Inception<br>PM / M = P | Elaboration<br>PM / M = P | Construction<br>PM / M = P | Total for E&C<br>PM / M = P |
|---|---|---|---|---|
| Baseline | 16.8 / 9.80 = 1.7 | 33.6 / 4.80 = 7.0 | 86.4 / 7.20 = 12.0 | 120.0 / 12.0 = 10.0 |
| $\Pi$ | 0.71 / 0.52 = 1.38 | 0.85 / 0.62 = 1.38 | 0.97 / 0.53 = 1.83 | |
| RAD | 12.0 / 5.10 = 2.4 | 28.7 / 3.00 = 9.6 | 84.0 / 3.80 = 22.0 | 112.7 / 6.80 − 16.64 |

Total for I&E&C  124.63 /  6.80 = 18.34

**Table 5.27c   Results for a 512-KSLOC Project (Effort: 2580 PM/Schedule: 34.3 Months)**

|  | *Inception* | *Elaboration* | *Construction* | *Total for E&C* |
|---|---|---|---|---|
|  | PM / M = P | PM / M = P | PM / M = P | PM / M = P |
| Baseline | 361.0 / 13.7 = 26.4 | 722.0 / 13.7 = 52.7 | 1868.0 / 20.6 = 90.7 | 2580.0 / 34.3 = 75.2 |
| $\Pi$ | 0.71 / 0.52 = 1.38 | 0.85 / 0.62 = 1.38 | 0.97 / 0.53 = 1.83 |  |
| RAD | 257.3 / 7.10 = 36.2 | 616.4 / 8.50 = 72.5 | 1815.4 / 10.9 = 166.2 | 2689.2 / 26.5 = 101.4 |

Total for I&E&C    2932.0 / 28.2 = 104.0

Table 5.27c shows the results from CORADMO when the ratings are applied to a 512 KSLOC Project with a COCOMO II projected effort of 2580 PM and a schedule of 34.3 months.

### 5.3.8   Conclusions

CORADMO is the constructive RAD model extension to COCOMO II, where RAD (Rapid Application Development) is an application of any of a number of techniques or strategies to reduce software development cycle time. It represents another step in the evolution of COCOMO II, representing a more extensive schedule estimation model. Combined with its preprocessor model COPSEMO, it overcomes some of the problems of different classes of process models, and reusable software and software artifacts.

The CORADMO parametric model, although not yet calibrated, has been implemented in a spreadsheet extension to COCOMO II. Data gathering forms have been developed and are shown in Appendix C. Printable copies of driver rating evaluation worksheets, that are condensed versions of material in this section of the book, are included on the accompanying CD.

### 5.3.9   Future Work

In a recent USC-CSE Affiliates' workshop, we identified several additional CO-COMO II cost drivers whose additional effect on schedule may be significant. These include personnel experience, capability, and continuity factors, as well as requirements volatility.

The workshop also determined that RAD effects on small and large projects will differ. We are currently revising the existing CORADMO model to reflect these considerations and are preparing to gather data to evaluate it.

As experience data is gathered from users of CORADMO, the CORADMO model will be calibrated to actual values. Questionnaires to assist in CORADMO data gathering are included on this book's accompanying CD.

At this time, the drivers represent engineering judgment derived from an ad hoc wideband delphi [Boehm 1981]. A more extensive, structured wideband delphi will be held, and that data combined with the actual results (drivers and effort, schedule, and staffing) reported from the field in the same Bayesian calibration approach that was used on COCOMO II (see Chapter 4).

The parametric model will need to be extended to cover an expected multi-iteration COPSEMO model. This may result in new drivers for CORADMO, or perhaps all the information is derivable from the COCOMO II and COPSEMO parametric models.

The CORADMO model also needs to be extended to cover COTS, either by working with the COCOTS model and its implementation, or by incorporation of its drivers directly into CORADMO. The applicability and utility of the CORADMO approach to the quality model extension of COCOMO II, COQUALMO, needs to be investigated.

Finally, but perhaps firstly, the spreadsheet implementation of CORADMO needs to fully reflect people factors as constraints. As calibration is performed, the spreadsheet must reflect its results. The spreadsheet also needs to incorporate any model evolutions. As usual, such evolutions will first be made available to CSE Affiliates. See information on affiliation in Appendix D, or on the accompanying CD.

## 5.4   COCOTS: COTS INTEGRATION ESTIMATION

### 5.4.1   Background and Rationale

The next extension to the COCOMO model we will discuss in this chapter is COCOTS, which is the acronym for the *COnstructive COTS* integration cost model. COTS in turn is short for *commercial-off-the-shelf*, and refers to those pre-built, commercially available software components that are becoming evermore important in the creation of new software systems.

The rationale for building systems with COTS components is that they will require less development time by taking advantage of existing, market-proven, vendor-supported products, thereby reducing overall system development costs. But there are two defining characteristics of COTS software, and they drive the whole COTS usage process:

1) the COTS product source code is not available to the application developer, and

2) the future evolution of the COTS product is not under the control of the application developer.

Because of these characteristics, there is a trade-off in using the COTS approach in that new software development time can indeed be reduced, but generally at the cost of an increase in software component integration work. The long-term cost implications of adopting the COTS approach are even more profound, because you are in fact adopting a new way of doing business from the moment you start considering COTS components for your new system to the day you finally retire that system. This is because COTS software is not static, it continually evolves in response to the market, and you as the system developer must adopt methodologies that cost effectively manage the use of those evolving components.

The fact is that using COTS software brings with it a host of unique risks quite different from those associated with software developed in-house.

Included among those risks or factors which should be examined when determining the true cost of integrating a COTS software component into a larger system are the following:

- The traditional costs associated with new software development such as the cost of requirements definition, design, code, test, and software maintenance.
- Additionally, the cost of licensing and redistribution rights, royalties, effort needed to understand the COTS software, pre-integration assessment and evaluation, post-integration certification of compliance with mission critical or safety critical requirements, indemnification against faults or damage caused by vendor supplied components, and costs incurred because of incompatibilities with other needed software and/or hardware.

Because of these unique risks, using COTS components in the development of new systems is not the universal solution to reducing cost and schedule while maintaining desired quality and functionality. However, if these risks can be managed, using COTS components can frequently be the right solution, offering the most cost-effective, shortest schedule approach to assembling major software systems.

COTS components are the right solution when they lie at the intersection of the three determinants of feasibility—technical, economic, and strategic constraints (see Figure 5.22)—and do so in a way demonstrably better than if a new system were to be constructed entirely out of original software. The key to success in using COTS components is being able to identify whether they fit the current procurement situation—technically, economically, and strategically. Technically, they have to be able to supply the desired functionality at the required level of reliability. Economically, they have to be able to be incorporated and maintained in the new system within the available budget and schedule. Strategically, they have to meet the needs of the system operating environment— which includes technical, political, and legal considerations—now, and as that environment is expected to evolve in the future.

Technical and strategic feasibility is determined during the candidate assessment phase of procuring COTS products, which occurs at the start of a COTS integration activity. How to determine the viability of a COTS product in either

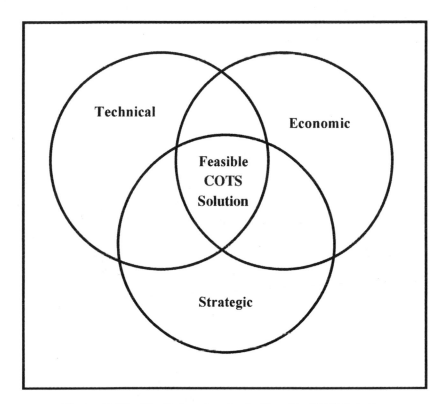

**Figure 5.22**   The Determinants of a Feasible COTS Solution

of these two dimensions is not a trivial question, and can be partially addressed by using the COCOTS Assessment submodel. However, it is the third dimension of determining economic feasibility which is the main intended use of COCOTS.

To answer the question of economic feasibility, cost-estimation models exist which capture the traditional costs associated with new software development noted above, COCOMO itself being among the most prominent of these models. To date, however, very few estimation models have been developed which try to capture those other costs unique to using COTS components in a software system development. The number of COTS integration cost models available in the public domain is even fewer. Hence the effort was undertaken to extend COCOMO II to cover the case in which software systems are built using COTS components.

### 5.4.2   Relation to COCOMO II

COCOMO II as currently formulated creates effort and schedule estimates for software systems built using a variety of techniques or approaches. The first and primary approach modeled by COCOMO is of course the use of system components that are built from scratch, that is, *new* code. But COCOMO II also allows you to model the case in which system components are built out of preexisting source code that is modified or adapted to your current purpose, i.e., *reused* code. The key word in the preceding sentence is *source*. Even though you're not building the reuse component from scratch, you still have access to the component's source code and can rewrite or modify it specifically to suit your needs.

What COCOMO II currently does not model is that case in which you do not have access to a preexisting component's source code. You have to take the component as is, working only with its executable file, and at most are able to build a software shell *around* the component to adapt its functionality to your needs.

This is where COCOTS comes in. COCOTS is being designed specifically to model the unique conditions and practices obtaining when you incorporate these kinds of components into your new system.

One final note before we continue: The model that is described below is still in its formulation stage. At the moment, it is presented as something wholly separate from COCOMO II, but in its mature incarnation it is anticipated that COCOTS will be folded directly into some future release of the USC COCOMO II tool that is available on the CD-ROM accompanying this book, providing a unified estimating tool with the capability of modeling all modes of software system development: new code, reuse code, and COTS component usage.

### 5.4.3   Model Overview

COCOTS is an amalgam of four related submodels, each addressing individually what we have identified as the four primary sources of COTS software integration costs. (This is another key point. COCOTS at the stage of development being described herein deals only with initial *integration* efforts. The long-term operation and maintenance effort is to be modeled in a future release of COCOTS.)

Initial integration costs are attributed to the effort needed to perform (1) candidate COTS component assessment, (2) COTS component tailoring, (3) the development and testing of any integration or "glue" code needed to plug a COTS component into a larger system, and (4) increased system level programming due to volatility in incorporated COTS components.

(A fifth cost source was actually identified early in our research. This was the cost related to the increased IV&V effort usually required when using COTS components. But attempts have been made to capture these costs within the glue code and tailoring submodels directly rather than specify a fifth independent submodel.)

*Assessment* is the process by which COTS components are selected for use in the larger system being developed. *Tailoring* refers to those activities that would have to be performed to prepare a particular COTS program for use, regardless of the system into which it is being incorporated, or even if operating as a stand-alone item. These are things such as initializing parameter values, specifying I/O screens or report formats, setting up security protocols, etc. *Glue code* development and testing refers to the new code external to the COTS component itself that must be written in order to plug the component into the larger system. This code by nature is unique to the particular context in which the COTS component is being used, and must not be confused with tailoring activity as defined above. *Volatility* in this context refers to the frequency with which new versions or updates of the COTS software being used in a larger system are released by the vendors over the course of the system's development and subsequent deployment.

### 5.4.4 Scope and Life Cycle Presently Addressed

At the moment, COCOTS addresses only the cost of software COTS components. The cost associated with hardware COTS elements used in a system will be addressed in future refinements of the model. A further consequence of this current limitation is that firmware components are also presently excluded. That is, the cost of using any COTS software that must run on a particular piece of COTS hardware is not captured independently in the current version of the model.

Also, the current incarnation of the model estimates needed effort only. Schedule estimation will most reasonably be addressed as COCOTS is folded directly into the USC COCOMO II tool.

As for life cycle, as was noted above, the current version of COCOTS addresses only development costs associated with using COTS components. Long-term operation and maintenance costs associated with using COTS components again are intended to be captured in future model versions.

In terms of a waterfall development process, the specific project phases currently covered by the model are these:

- Requirements Definition
- Preliminary Code Design
- Detailed Code Design and Unit Test
- Integration and Test

The inclusion of the Requirements Definition phase at the top of this list is significant. This phase traditionally has *not* been covered by COCOMO estimates. The fact that assessment and requirements definition must be done in tandem when using COTS components if you are to realize the full benefit of adopting the COTS approach to system development necessitates the inclusion of the Requirements Definition phase in COCOTS estimates.

In terms of a spiral development process, COCOTS covers the following MBASE/RUP milestones discussed in Chapter 1:

- Inception
  → Life-cycle Objectives
- Elaboration
  → Life-cycle Architecture
- Construction
  → Initial Operational Capability

242        Chapter 5   Emerging Extensions

### 5.4.5  Cost Sources

In terms of level of effort involved, we have determined that the "big three" cost sinks tend to be Tailoring, Glue Code development, and managing the System Volatility. Added System Verification & Validation and COTS product Assessment are significant but tend to have less impact. (Keep in mind that the last item, System V & V, is captured across and within the Tailoring, Glue Code, and Volatility submodels.)

Figures 5.23 and 5.24 illustrate how the modeling of these costs in COCOTS is related to costs modeled by COCOMO II. Figure 5.23 represents the total effort to build a software system entirely of new code as estimated by COCOMO II. Figure 5.24 represents the total effort to build a software system out of a mix of new code and COTS components as estimated by a combination of COCOMO II and COCOTS. The central blocks in the two figures indicate COCOMO II estimates. The additional peripheral blocks in Figure 5.24 indicate COCOTS estimates. The relative size of the peripheral and central blocks in this figure is a function of the number of COTS components relative to the amount of new code in the system, and of the nature of the COTS component integration efforts themselves. The more complex the tailoring and/or glue code writing efforts, the larger these blocks will be relative to the assessment block. Also, note that addressing the system wide volatility due to volatility in the COTS components is an effort that will

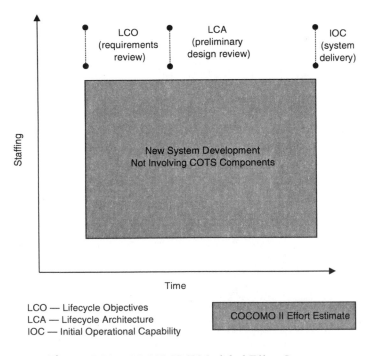

**Figure 5.23**  COCOMO II Modeled Effort Sources

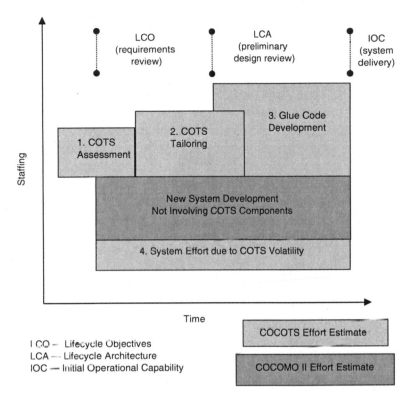

**Figure 5.24**   COCOTS Modeled Effort Sources

span throughout the entire system development cycle, as indicated by the large peripheral block running along the bottom of Figure 5.24.

### 5.4.6   The Four Submodels

As has been indicated, the heart of COCOTS is its four separate submodels, each one designed to capture a different element of the total cost of using COTS software components in building new software systems—keeping in mind that the fifth cost element of additional System V & V noted above is to be captured within the Tailoring, Glue Code, and Volatility submodels.

It should also be noted, however, that while the Assessment submodel lends itself easily to use very early in the project planning stages, the Tailoring, Glue Code, and Volatility submodels by the very nature of the costs they are trying to address are more problematic if used before the specific COTS products that will actually be integrated into a new system have been identified. The reason is that the costs covered by these models are extremely dependent on the unique characteristics of any given set of COTS products and their vendors.

### 5.4.7  Assessment

Assessment is the activity whereby COTS software products are vetted and se-lected as viable components for integration into a larger system. In general terms, viable COTS candidates are determined based on the following:

- Functional Requirements—capability offered
- Performance Requirements—timing and sizing constraints
- Nonfunctional Requirements—cost/training/installation/maintenance/re-liability

The key thing to remember is that COTS assessment and requirements defi-nition must be done in concert. Final system requirements must be shaped based upon the capabilities of COTS products on the market if one is to reap the full benefit of taking the COTS approach to system development.

In the specific terms of our model, assessment is done in two passes. When selecting candidate COTS components, there is usually a "quick and dirty" first effort intended to very rapidly cull products patently unsuitable in the current context. The remaining products are then examined more carefully to determine the final set of COTS components to be included in the system being developed. (We use the terms initial filtering and final selection, both under the banner of "assessment." Others use a slightly different terminology, referring to what we call initial filtering as "assessment," and to what we call final selection as "evalu-ation." No matter what words one uses, however, the concept of a need for a two-pass approach is the same.)

Figure 5.25 shows the basic formulation of the assessment submodel, illus-trating the two-pass approach. The intent is that the specific parameter values re-

---

*Initial Filtering Effort (IFE)=*

   *Σ [(#COTS candidates in class)(average initial filtering effort for class)] over all classes*

*Detailed Assessment Effort (DAE) =*

   *Σ [(#COTS candidates in class)(average detailed assessment effort for class)] over all classes, by project domain*

*where*

   *the average detailed assessment effort for a given class is qualified by the attributes usually assessed for that class*

*Final Project Assessment Effort = IFE + DAE*

---

**Figure 5.25**   The Assessment Submodel

quired for these formulas will eventually be specified by project domain. (How quickly that happens in the evolution of this model is a function of how long it takes to gather enough model calibration data points to allow the formal specification of unique domains.)

The initial filtering formula presumes a parameterized value for a rough average filtering effort can be determined for a given domain. The total initial filtering effort for a project then becomes a simple function of the number of candidate COTS products that are being filtered for that project and the average filtering effort per candidate specified for that project's domain.

The final selection formula is more complex. It posits that final selection of COTS products will be based on an assessment of each product in light of certain product attributes. Table 5.28 illustrates our current set of proposed most typical assessment attributes based upon software attributes found in IEEE Standards.

**Table 5.28    COTS assessment attributes**

| **Correctness** | **Understandability** | **Portability** |
|---|---|---|
| accuracy | documentation quality | portability |
| correctness | simplicity | **Functionality** |
| **Availability/Robustness** | testability | functionality |
| availability | **Ease of Use** | **Price** |
| fail safe | usability/human factors | initial purchase or lease |
| fail soft | **Version Compatibility** | recurring costs |
| fault tolerance | downward compatibility | **Maturity** |
| input error tolerance | upward compatibility | product maturity |
| redundancy | **Intercomponent Compatibility** | vendor maturity |
| reliability | with other components | **Vendor Support** |
| robustness | interoperability | response time for critical problem |
| safety | **Flexibility** | support |
| **Security** | extendibility | warranty |
| access related | flexibility | **Training** |
| sabotage related | **Installation/Upgrade Ease** | user training |
| **Product Performance** | installation ease | **Vendor Concessions** |
| execution performance | upgrade/refresh ease | will escrow code |
| information/data capacity | | will make modifications |
| precision | | |
| memory performance | | |
| response time | | |
| throughput | | |

Depending upon the project domain, more effort will be expended assessing a COTS product in terms of some attributes as opposed to others. For example, within one domain, price and ease of use may be critical, whereas in a different domain, security and portability may be paramount. Thus it follows that in the first domain, more effort will be expended assessing candidate COTS products according to their purchase price and their user friendliness, while less effort (if any) will be expended assessing those same products according to the security features and portability they offer. In the second domain, the relative effort expended assessing each candidate product in terms of these four attributes should be just the reverse. Based on this idea, the final selection filtering formula then presumes parameterized values for a rough average assessment effort per attribute can be determined for a given domain. This is carried even further within the formula by refining the parameterization of each attribute according to a standardized rating of its relative importance on a scale from extra low to extra high, again by domain. The total final selection effort for a project then becomes a function of the number of candidate COTS products that are being finally assessed for that project and the average assessment effort per rated attribute per candidate as specified for that project's domain and summed over all attributes.

Whether or not you actually know the number of candidate COTS products that are to go through the more detailed final selection assessment needed for this formula is a function of when you are doing your estimate. If your estimation of the final assessment effort is being performed literally after the initial filtering has been performed, then this is a non-issue since the number of products to go through final assessment will be a known quantity. If, however, you are doing your final assessment effort estimation while the project is still in the planning stages, you will have to use some rule of thumb to estimate a typical percentage of COTS products that make it through initial filtering to final selection. As part of our modeling effort, we attempt to provide a useful initial rule of thumb percentage for this quantity, but experience with these kinds of models has shown that the more quickly you start using such a rule of thumb determined from your own organization's past experience, the more accurate your overall estimate assessment effort will be.

(If your assessment efforts are in fact being done very early in the planning process, a similar rule of thumb might be required for estimating a typical number of candidate COTS products that will go through the initial filtering effort as well. This would seem to be such a project dependent or at least organization dependent quantity, however, that it seems unlikely that we will be able to provide a useful initial generic quantity for you along these lines. We recommend that if you do indeed find yourself having to estimate this quantity, your best approach is to interview engineers in your organization who have experience assessing COTS products for the kinds of functionality that are being proposed in your current project and who are up to date on the COTS products currently on the market that claim to provide that functionality. These individuals are the ones most likely able to provide at least a ballpark estimate of how many COTS products might potentially go through initial filtering on the project for which you are currently doing estimates.)

The total effort expended doing COTS product assessment for the current project is the sum of the initial filtering effort plus the final selection effort.

### 5.4.8 Tailoring

Tailoring is the activity whereby COTS software products are configured for use in a specific context. These are the normal things that would have to be done to a product no matter what system into which it is being integrated. These are things like parameter initialization, input/GUI screen and output report layout, security protocols set-up, etc. Specifically excluded from this definition is anything that could be considered a unique or atypical modification or expansion of the functionality of the COTS product as delivered by the vendor. (These activities would be covered under the Glue Code model.)

The basic approach taken to capturing this effort in our model is illustrated in Figure 5.26. The formulation of the tailoring submodel presumes that the difficulty or complexity of the tailoring work that is going to be required to get a given COTS product integrated into a system can be anticipated and even characterized by standardized rating criteria. The submodel then presumes that a parameterized value for a rough average tailoring effort per complexity rating can be determined for a given domain. The total tailoring effort for a project then becomes a function of the number of COTS products whose needed tailoring is estimated to be at a given rated level of complexity and the average tailoring effort at the given complexity rating per candidate, again as specified by the project's domain and summed over all tailoring complexity rating levels.

We have defined five overall tailoring effort complexity levels or ratings, ranging from very low to very high. To arrive, however, at a particular complexity rating for a given tailoring job requires examining individual tailoring activities which affect the aggregate complexity of the job. Table 5.29 illustrates this concept. The first five cells in the first column under the heading "Tailoring Activities & Aids" identify the major activities that fall under our definition of COTS Tailoring, while the last cell refers to automated tools which may mitigate the difficulty of doing a given COTS tailoring job. Moving to the right across the other columns in the table you will find specific criteria for rating the complexity

---

*Project Tailoring Effort  =*

$\Sigma$ *[(#COTS tailored in class)(average tailoring effort for class and complexity)] over all classes, by project domain*

*where*
   *the average tailoring effort for a given class is qualified by the complexity of the overall tailoring task usually associated with that class, rated over five levels from Very Low to Very High*

---

**Figure 5.26**  The Tailoring Submodel

**Table 5.29   Dimensions of Tailoring Difficulty**

| Tailoring Activities & Aids | Individual Activity & Tool Aid Complexity Ratings | | | | | |
|---|---|---|---|---|---|---|
| | Very Low | Low | Nominal | High | Very High | Point Value |
| Parameter Spec. | 1 | 2 | 3 | 4 | 5 | |
| Script Writing | 1 | 2 | 3 | 4 | 5 | |
| I/O Report Layout | 1 | 2 | 3 | 4 | 5 | |
| GUI Screen Spec. | 1 | 2 | 3 | 4 | 5 | |
| Security /Access Protocol Initialization & Set-up | 1 | 2 | 3 | 4 | 5 | |
| Availability of COTS Tailoring Tools | 1 | 2 | 3 | 4 | 5 | |
| | | | | | Total Points: | |

of the individual activities represented by each row, or the utility of the any available tailoring tools in the case of the last row. The last column at the far right of the table provides space for recording the point values associated with the rating given to each individual item identified in the first column on the far left. These individual point values are then summed to provide the total point score indicated in the extreme lower right-corner of the table. This total score is then used to characterize the overall complexity of the COTS tailoring effort required for COTS components in the current project by using Table 5.30 titled "Final Tailoring Activity Complexity Rating Scale." You determine where the point total falls on the scale shown in that table and from that identify the COTS tailoring effort complexity rating associated with that point total for all COTS components being used in the current project.

**Table 5.30   Final Tailoring Activity Complexity Rating Scale**

| 5 to 7 points | 8 to 12 points | 13 to 17 points | 18 to 22 points | 23 to 25 points |
|---|---|---|---|---|
| Very Low | Low | Nominal | High | Very High |

### 5.4.9   Glue Code

Glue code (sometimes called "glueware" or "binding" code) is the new code needed to get a COTS product integrated into a larger system. It can be code needed to connect a COTS component either to higher level system code, or to other COTS or NDI (Non-Developed Item) components also being used in the system. Reaching consensus on just what exactly constitutes glue code has not always been easy. For the purposes of our model, we finally decided on the following three part definition: glue code is software developed in-house and composed of: 1) code needed to facilitate data or information exchange between the COTS component and the system or some other COTS/NDI component into which it is being integrated or to which it is being connected, 2) code needed to connect or "hook" the COTS component into the system or some other COTS/NDI component but does not necessarily enable data exchange between the COTS component and those other elements, and 3) code needed to provide required functionality missing in the COTS component and which depends upon or must interact with the COTS component (see Figure 5.27).

The first two parts of our definition are straightforward and have not caused any controversy. The last part of our definition, however, regarding new functionality still causes some debate. It arose out of the fact that often functionality that was originally expected to be provided by a COTS component itself is

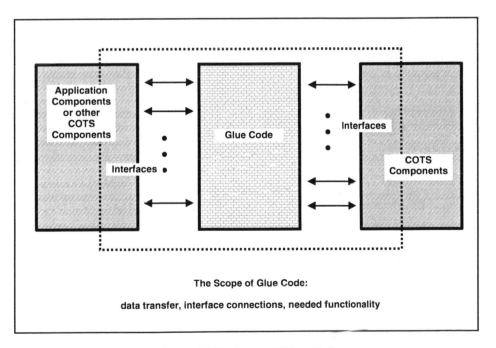

**The Scope of Glue Code:**

**data transfer, interface connections, needed functionality**

**Figure 5.27**   Scope of Glue Code

found to be unavailable in the COTS component. Sometimes this deficiency is known before a COTS component is actually selected for integration, but for other reasons is selected anyway. In this case, it is known ahead of time that this needed functionality is going to have to be created. Often, however (unfortunately, probably too often and this may speak to weaknesses in the state of the art of COTS assessment processes), deficiencies in COTS functionality are not discovered until the COTS integration activity is well under way. The choice then is to either go back and select a different COTS product, or as is more typical, to go ahead and create the required functionality with original code—and more often than not the person responsible for creating that original code is the individual tasked to integrate the COTS component in the first place. So from a practical point of view, creating that new functionality just becomes part and parcel to integrating the COTS component itself. Thus counting that effort as part of the overall effort to write the glue code seems reasonable to us. The real issue, however, is to avoid double counting of code writing effort. If you know before COTS integration has begun that some functionality will have to be created, whether you choose to treat its creation as part of the glue code, or as simply more lines of new code that must be written for the overall system and thus capturable under a cost model like COCOMO, as long as you are consistent, then you should be okay.

(The last sentence in the preceding paragraph actually goes to the heart of another sometimes controversial subject, and which in truth qualifies the claim above that "as long as you are consistent, then you should be okay." The controversy is whether or not the programming effort required to create "glue" code is in fact qualitatively different from that required to create any other kind of original code. After all, as some people say, "code is code is code, right?" The answer is, *maybe*, in some people's minds, but the majority of software professionals we have interviewed during the course of our research do not hold this view. If "code is code is code," then the COCOMO II cost drivers should work just fine when trying to estimate the effort required to create glue code. But the experience of these professionals has been that this is not the case. Their explanation as to why this is true is that the structure and design of glue code is highly constrained by both the design of the COTS component itself, and the behavior of its vendor, factors that do not apply to "conventional" new code. Thus they feel that a set of cost drivers different from those in COCOMO II do often obtain. This provides the rationale for the set of COTS Glue Code Cost Drivers presented below.)

The basic approach taken to modeling COTS glue code writing effort is shown in Figure 5.28. The formulation of the Glue Code submodel uses the same general form as does COCOMO. The model presumes that the total amount of glue code to be written for a project can be predicted and quantified (in either source lines of code or function points), including the amount of reworking of that code that will likely occur because of changes in requirements or new releases of COTS components by the vendors during the integration period; also presumed to be predictable are the broad conditions that will obtain while that

---

*Glue Code Effort =*

   *A• [(size)(1+CREVOL)]* $^B$*•∏(effort multipliers)*

*where*
- *A = linear scaling constant*
- *Size = of the glue code in source-lines of code or function points*
- *CREVOL = percentage rework of the glue code due to requirements change or volatility in the COTS products*
- *B = an architectural nonlinear scaling factor*
- *Effort multipliers = 13 multiplicative effort adjustment factors with ratings from very low to very high*

---

**Figure 5.28**   The Glue Code Submodel

glue code is being written—in terms of personnel, product, system, and architectural issues—and that these too can be characterized by standardized rating criteria. The model then presumes that a parameterized value for a linear scaling constant (in either units of person-months per source lines of code or person-months per function points) can be determined for a given domain (this is the constant *A* in the formula in Figure 5.28). Other parameterized values are also presumed to be determinable by domain: a nonlinear scale factor that accounts for diseconomies of scale that can occur depending on how well or poorly the architecting of the overall system into which the COTS component is being integrated was conducted; and some thirteen effort cost drivers that linearly inflate or deflate the estimated size of the glue code writing effort based upon a rating from very low to very high of specific project conditions.

The total glue code writing effort for a project then becomes a function of the amount (or size) of glue code to be written, its estimated percentage rework (CREVOL), the linear constant *A*, the rated nonlinear architectural scale factor, and the individual rated effort cost drivers.

The Table 5.31 summarizes the thirteen linear cost drivers and one nonlinear scale factor that currently appear in the model.

Each of these drivers has detailed definitions and rating criteria, and the interested reader is referred to the URL given at the end of this section which identifies the location of the COCOTS home page on the web.

### 5.4.10   System Volatility

System Volatility effort refers to that extra effort which occurs during the development of the larger application as a result of the use of COTS components in that system development. Specifically, it is the effort that results from the impact on the larger system of the effects of swapping COTS components out of the sys-

**Table 5.31   COTS Glue Code Cost Drivers**

**Personnel Drivers**
1) ACIEP—COTS Integrator Experience with Product
2) ACIPC—COTS Integrator Personnel Capability
3) AXCIP—Integrator Experience with COTS Integration Processes
4) APCON—Integrator Personnel Continuity

**COTS Component Drivers**
5) ACPMT—COTS Product Maturity
6) ACSEW—COTS Supplier Product Extension Willingness
7) APCPX—COTS Product Interface Complexity
8) ACPPS—COTS Supplier Product Support
9) ACPTD—COTS Supplier Provided Training and Documentation

**Application/System Drivers**
10) ACREL—Constraints on Application System/Subsystem Reliability
11) AACPX—Application Interface Complexity
12) ACPER—Constraints on COTS Technical Performance
13) ASPRT—Application System Portability

**Nonlinear Scale Factor**
AAREN—Application Architectural Engineering

tem with newer versions of those components that have been released by the COTS vendors. Over a long initial development, these impacts can be significant. Once the project has moved into the long-term maintenance phase, these impacts *will* be significant, and may in fact dominate your system maintenance processes, depending upon the number and nature of the COTS components you have used in your system.

The Volatility submodel tries to capture these effects by again borrowing from COCOMO the concept of *rework*. In COCOMO, rework is defined to be the effort expended to revisit "completed" code, not because of errors in the initial programming, but rather because of changes in system requirements (see the discussion of REVL in Chapter 2, Section 2.2.5). In the Glue Code submodel, we added the additional qualifier of work that must be redone in the glue code not just because of requirements change, but also as a result of integrating upgraded versions of a COTS component (CREVOL).

The Volatility submodel adds two more kinds of rework: that in the larger *application* code caused by integrating updated COTS software versions, SCREVOL, and that in the application code *independent* of COTS product effects. (This latter rework is actually the same rework as captured by the REVL term within COCOMO itself.)

Figure 5.29 illustrates the formulation of the Volatility submodel. The application effort term appearing in these equations is that effort that would be mod-

---

**System Volatility Effort =**

(application effort) • {[1+(SCREVOL/1+REVL)] E –1}
• (COTS effort multipliers)

**where**

• **Application effort = new coding effort separate from COTS integration effects**
• **SCREVOL = percentage rework in the system due to COTS volatility and COTS requirements change**
• **REVL = percentage rework in the system independent of COTS effects due to requirements change**

---

**Figure 5.29**   The Volatility submodel

eled directly by COCOMO II. The effort cost drivers, however, are those that appear in the COCOTS Glue Code submodel. Finally, the scale factor term appearing in the detailed equation uses the same COCOMO II scale factors described in Chapter 2.

### 5.4.11   Total COTS Integration Effort

At the moment, the total COTS integration effort provided by COCOTS is being treated as the linear sum of the efforts determined by the individual submodels. This will likely change as our experience with the model grows.

$$\text{Total Effort} = \text{Assessment Effort} + \text{Tailoring Effort} + \text{Glue Code Effort} + \text{Volatility Effort}$$

where

$$\text{Assessment Effort} = \text{Filtering Effort} + \text{Detailed Assessment Effort}$$

### 5.4.12   Conclusion

As indicated at the start of this section, COCOTS as of this writing is still very much a work in process. It is the hope of the COCOTS researchers that by the next edition of this text COCOTS will have achieved a level of maturity that will allow it to assume a solid role in the capability offered by the USC COCOMO II tool.

Further information on the current status of the model and on COTS integration processes in general can be found on the COCOTS web page: http://sunset.usc.edu/research/COCOTS/html

## 5.5   COQUALMO: QUALITY ESTIMATION

This section describes COQUALMO, the expert-determined Defect Introduction and Defect Removal submodels that compose the quality model extension to COCOMO II.

### 5.5.1 Introduction

Cost, schedule, and quality are highly correlated factors in software development. They basically form three sides of the same triangle. Beyond a certain point (the "Quality is Free" point), it is difficult to increase the quality without increasing either the cost or schedule or both for the software under development. Similarly, development schedule cannot be drastically compressed without hampering the quality of the software product and/or increasing the cost of development. Software estimation models can (and should) play an important role in facilitating the balance of cost/schedule and quality.

Recognizing this important association, an attempt is being made to develop a quality model extension to COCOMO II, namely COQUALMO. An initial description of this model focusing on defect introduction was provided in [Chulani 1997a]. The model has evolved considerably since then and is now very well defined and calibrated to Delphi-gathered expert opinion. The data collection activity is underway and the aim is to have a statistically calibrated model by the onset of the next millennium.

This section presents the two submodels, i.e., the Defect Introduction and the Defect Removal submodels, of COQUALMO. It also illustrates the integration of COQUALMO with COCOMO II to facilitate cost/schedule/quality trade-offs.

*Topics Addressed*   The background model that forms the basis of the Cost/Quality model is described in Section 5.5.2. Sections 5.5.3 and 5.5.4 present the Defect Introduction and the Defect Removal submodels that are introduced in Section 5.5.2 as the submodels of the composite quality model. Section 5.5.5 presents COQUALMO integrated with COCOMO II. And, finally Section 5.5.6 concludes with the ongoing research and future plans for using the Bayesian approach for calibrating and validating the model to completed software projects.

### 5.5.2.   Background Model

The Quality model is an extension of the existing COCOMO II [Boehm et al. 1995; USC-CSE 1997a] model. It is based on "The Software Defect Introduction and Removal Model" described by Barry Boehm in [Boehm 1981] which is analogous to the "tank and pipe" model introduced by Capers Jones [Jones 1975] and illustrated in Figure 5.30.

Figure 5.30 shows that defects conceptually flow into a holding tank through various defect source pipes. These defect source pipes are modeled in

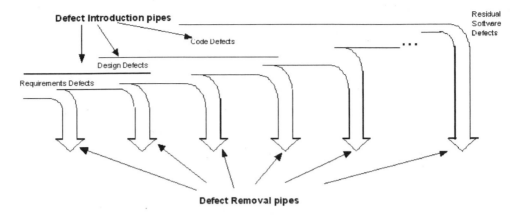

**Figure 5.30** The Software Defect Introduction and Removal Model

COQUALMO as the Software Defect Introduction Model. The figure also depicts that defects are drained off through various defect elimination pipes, which in the context of COQUALMO are modeled as the Software Defect Removal Model. Each of these two submodels is discussed in further detail in the next two sections.

### 5.5.3. The Software Defect Introduction (DI) Model

Defects can be introduced in several activities of the software development life cycle. For the purpose of COQUALMO, defects are classified based on their origin as *Requirements Defects* (e.g., leaving out a required Cancel option in an Input screen), *Design Defects* (e.g., error in the algorithm), *Coding Defects* (e.g., looping nine instead of ten times). Figure 5.31 provides an overview of the DI model.

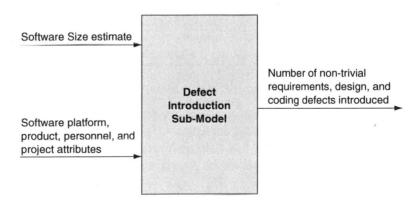

**Figure 5.31** The Defect Introduction Submodel of COQUALMO

**Table 5.32   Defect Introduction Drivers**

| Category | Post-Architecture Model |
| --- | --- |
| Platform | Required Software Reliability (RELY)<br>Data Base Size (DATA)<br>Required Reusability (RUSE)<br>Documentation Match to Life-Cycle Needs (DOCU)<br>Product Complexity (CPLX) |
| Product | Execution Time Constraint (TIME)<br>Main Storage Constraint (STOR)<br>Platform Volatility (PVOL) |
| Personnel | Analyst Capability (ACAP)<br>Programmer Capability (PCAP)<br>Applications Experience (AEXP)<br>Platform Experience (PEXP)<br>Language and Tool Experience (LTEX)<br>Personnel Continuity (PCON) |
| Project | Use of Software Tools (TOOL)<br>Multisite Development (SITE)<br>Required Development Schedule (SCED)<br>Precedentedness (PREC)<br>Architecture/Risk Resolution (RESL)<br>Team Cohesion (TEAM)<br>Process Maturity (PMAT) |

The DI model's inputs include Source Lines of Code and/or Function Points as the sizing parameter, adjusted for both reuse and breakage and a set of twenty-one multiplicative DI-drivers divided into four categories—platform, product, personnel, and project—as summarized in Table 5.32. These twenty-one DI-drivers are a subset of the twenty-two cost parameters required as input for COCOMO II. The decision to use these drivers was taken after we did an extensive literature search and did some behavioral analyses on factors affecting defect introduction. An example DI-driver and the behavioral analysis done is shown in Table 5.33 (the numbers in this table will be discussed later in this section). The choice of using COCOMO II drivers not only makes it relatively straightforward to integrate COQUALMO with COCOMO II but also simplifies the data collection activity which has already been set up for COCOMO II.

The DI model's output is the predicted number of nontrivial requirements, design and coding defects introduced in the development life cycle; where nontrivial defects[1] include:

---

[1] Adapted from IEEE Std 1044.1-1995

**Table 5.33  Programmer Capability (PCAP) Differences in Defect Introduction**

| PCAP level | Requirements | Design | Code |
|---|---|---|---|
| VH | N/A | Fewer Design defects due to easy interaction with analysts Fewer defects introduced in fixing defects | Fewer Coding defects due to fewer detailed design reworks, conceptual misunderstandings, coding mistakes |
| | 1.0 | 0.85 | 0.76 |
| Nominal | 1.0 | | |
| VL | N/A | More Design defects due to less easy interaction with analysts More defects introduced in fixing defects | More Coding defects due to more detailed design reworks, conceptual misunderstandings, coding mistakes |
| | 1.0 | 1.17 | 1.32 |
| Initial Defect Introduction Range | 1.0 | 1.23 | 1.77 |
| Range—Round 1 | 1–1.2 | 1–1.75 | 1.3–2.2 |
| Median—Round 1 | 1 | 1.4 | 1.75 |
| Range—Round 2 | 1–1.1 | 1.1–1.75 | 1.5–2.2 |
| Final Defect Introduction Range (Median-Round 2) | 1.0 | 1.38 | 1.75 |

| PCAP | Very Low | Low | Nominal | High | Very High |
|---|---|---|---|---|---|
| | 15th percentile | 35th percentile | 55th percentile | 75th percentile | 90th percentile |

- *Critical* (causes a system crash or unrecoverable data loss or jeopardizes personnel)
- *High* (causes impairment of critical system functions and no workaround solution exists)
- *Medium* (causes impairment of critical system function, though a workaround solution does exist).

$$\textit{The total number of defects introduced} = \sum_{j-1}^{3} A_j * (Size)^{B_j} * \prod_{i=1}^{21} (DI - driver)_{ij} \qquad \text{Eq. 5.19}$$

where:

$j$ identifies the three artifact types (requirements, design, and coding)

$A_j$ is the baseline DI Rate Adjustment Factor for artifact type $j$

*Size* is the size of the software project measured in terms of kSLOC (thousands of Source Lines of Code [Park 1992], Function Points [IFPUG 1994] or any other unit of size

*B* is initially set to 1 and accounts for economies/diseconomies of scale. It is unclear if Defect Introduction Rates will exhibit economies or diseconomies of scale as indicated in [Banker et al. 1994] and [Gulledge-Hutzler 1993]. The question is if Size doubles, then will the Defect Introduction Rate increase by more than twice the original rate? This indicates diseconomies of scale implying $B > 1$. Or will Defect Introduction Rate increase by a factor less than twice the original rate, indicating economies of scale, giving $B < 1$?

(*DI* - driver)$_{ij}$ is the Defect Introduction driver for the *j*th artifact and the *i*th factor.

For each *j*th artifact, defining a new parameter, $QAF_j$ such that

$$QAF_j = \prod_{i=1}^{21} DI - driver_{ij} \qquad \text{Eq. 5.20}$$

simplifies Equation 5.13 to:

$$\textit{The total number of defects introduced} = \sum_{j=1}^{3} A_j * (Size)^{B_j} * QAF_j \qquad \text{Eq. 5.21}$$

where for each of the three artifacts we have:

$$\textit{Requirements Defects Introduced } (DI_{Est;\,req}) = A_{req} * (Size)^{B_{req}} * QAF_{req}$$
$$\textit{Design Defects Introduced } (DI_{Est;\,des}) = A_{des} * (Size)^{B_{des}} * QAF_{des}$$
$$\textit{Coding Defects Introduced } (DI_{Est\,cod}) = A_{cod} * (Size)^{B_{cod}} * QAF_{cod}$$

For the empirical formulation of the Defect Introduction Model, as with CO-COMO II, it was essential to assign numerical values to each of the ratings of the DI drivers. Based on expert-judgment an initial set of values was proposed for the model as shown in Table 5.33. If the DI driver > 1 then it has a detrimental effect on the number of defects introduced and overall software quality; and if the DI driver < 1 then fewer number of defects are introduced, improving the quality of the software being developed. This is analogous to the effect the COCOMO II multiplicative cost drivers have on effort. So, for example, for a project with programmers having Very High Capability ratings (Programmers of the 90th percentile level), only 76 percent of the nominal number of defects will be introduced during the coding activity. Whereas, if the project had programmers with Very Low Capability ratings (Programmers of the 15th percentile level), then 132 percent of the nominal number of coding defects will be introduced. This would cause the Defect Introduction Range to be 1.32/0.76 = 1.77, where the Defect Introduction Range is defined as the ratio between the largest DI driver and the smallest DI driver.

To get further group consensus, a two-round Delphi involving nine experts in the field of software quality was conducted. The nine participants selected for the Delphi process were representatives of Commercial, Aerospace, Government, and FFRDC and Consortia organizations. Each of the participants had notable expertise in the area of software metrics and quality management and a few of them had developed their own proprietary cost/schedule/quality estimation models. Readers not familiar with the Delphi technique can refer to Chapter 22 of [Boehm 1981] for an overview of common methods used for software estimation or [Helmer 1966]. The rates determined by the COCOMO team were used as initial values and each of the participants independently provided their own assessments. The quantitative relationships and their potential range of variability for each of the twenty-one DI-drivers were summarized and sent back to each of the nine Delphi participants for a second assessment. The participants then had the opportunity to update their rates based on the summarized results of Round 1. It was observed that the range in Round 2 was typically narrower than the range in Round 1, i.e., Round 2 resulted in better agreement among the experts.

The Delphi approach used is summarized below:

### Round 1—Steps

1. Provided Participants with Round 1 Delphi Questionnaire with a proposed set of values for the Defect Introduction Ranges.
2. Received nine completed Round 1 Delphi Questionnaires.
3. Ensured validity of responses by correspondence with the participants.
4. Did simple analysis based on ranges and medians of the responses.

### Round 2—Steps

1. Provided participants with Round 2 Delphi Questionnaire—based on analysis of Round 1.
2. Repeated steps 2, 3, 4 (above).
3. Converged to Final Delphi Results which resulted in the definition of the initial model.

Figure 5.32 provides a graphical view of the relative Defect Introduction Ranges for Coding Defects provided by all twenty-one Defect Drivers. For example, if all other parameters are held constant, a Very Low (VL) rating for Process Maturity (PMAT) will result in a software project with 2.5 times the number of Coding Defects introduced as compared to an Extra High (XH) rating. The figure also illustrates that the experts' opinion suggested that PMAT has the highest impact and RUSE has the lowest impact on the introduction of coding defects.

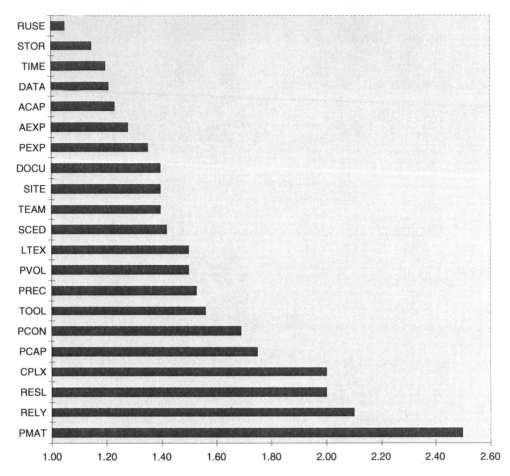

**Figure 5.32**   Coding Defect Introduction Ranges

A detailed description of each of the other twenty-one DIR drivers and its impact on defect introduction for each type of defect artifact can be found in [Chulani 1997b].

Some initial data analysis (data gathered from USC's COCOMO II affiliates) was used to update the 1970s' baseline Defect Introduction Rates (DIRs) [presented in Boehm et al. 1995] of five requirements defects, twenty-five design defects and fifteen coding defects. Table 5.34 illustrates the details.

The updated 1990s' nominal DIRs (i.e., the number of defects per kSLOC without the impact of the Quality Adjustment Factor) are approximately ten requirements defects, twenty design defects and thirty coding defects, i.e., $DIR_{req;nom} = 10$, $DIR_{des;nom} = 20$, $DIR_{cod;nom} = 30$. For readers familiar with COCOMO, this is analogous to the nominal effort without the impact of the Effort Adjust-

**Table 5.34   Initial Data Analysis on the Defect Introduction Model**

| Type of Artifact | 1970's Baseline DIRs | Quality Adjustment Factor (QAF$_j$) | Predicted DIR | Actual DIR; 1990's project | Baseline DIR Adjustment Factor (A$_j$) | 1990's Baseline DIRs |
|---|---|---|---|---|---|---|
| Reqts | 5 | 0.5 | 2.5 | 4.5 | 1.8 | 9 |
| Design | 25 | 0.44 | 11 | 8.4 | 0.77 | 19 |
| Code | 15 | 0.5 | 7.5 | 16.6 | 2.21 | 33 |

ment Factor. Note that for each artifact $j$, the exponent $B_j = 1$, for the initial data analysis. When more data is available this factor will also be calibrated and may result in values other than 1. But for now, because of lack of enough datapoints and lack of expert opinion on this factor, it has been set to 1.

### 5.5.4.  The Software Defect Removel Model

The aim of the Defect Removal (DR) model is to estimate the number of defects removed by several defect-removal activities depicted as defect-removal pipes in Figure 5.30. The DR model is a post-processor to the DI model and is formulated by classifying defect-removal activities into three relatively orthogonal profiles namely Automated Analysis, People Reviews and Execution Testing and Tools (see Figure 5.33).

Each of these three defect-removal profiles removes a fraction of the requirements, design, and coding defects introduced in the DI pipes of Figure 5.30 described as the DI model in Section 5.5.3. Each profile has six levels of increasing defect-removal capability, namely Very Low, Low, Nominal, High, Very High,

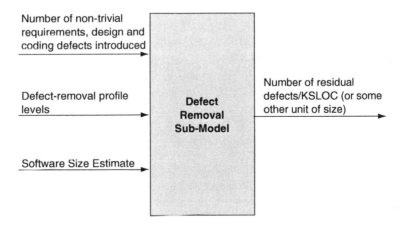

**Figure 5.33**   The Defect Removal Submodel of COQUALMO

and Extra High, with Very Low being the least effective and Extra High being the most effective in defect removal. Table 5.35 describes the three profiles and the six levels for each of these profiles.

The Automated Analysis profile includes code analyzers, syntax and semantics analyzers, type checkers, requirements and design consistency and traceability checkers, model checkers, formal verification and validation etc.

The People Reviews profile covers the spectrum of all peer group discussion activities. The Very Low level is when no people reviews take place and the Extra High level is the other end of the spectrum when extensive amount of preparation with formal review roles assigned to the participants and extensive User/Customer involvement. A formal change control process is incorporated with procedures for fixes. Extensive review checklists are prepared with thorough root cause analysis. A continuous review process improvement is also incorporated with statistical process control.

The Execution Testing and Tools profile, as the name suggests, covers all tools used for testing with the Very Low level being when no testing takes place. Not a whole lot of software development is done this way. The Nominal level involves the use of a basic testing process with unit testing, integration testing and system testing with test criteria based on simple checklists and with a simple problem tracking support system in place and basic test data management. The Extra High level involves the use of highly advanced tools for test oracles with the integration of automated analysis and test tools and distributed monitoring and analysis. Sophisticated model-based test process management is also employed at this level.

To determine the Defect Removal Fractions (DRFs) associated with each of the six levels (i.e., Very Low, Low, Nominal, High, Very High, Extra High) of the three profiles (i.e., automated analysis, people reviews, execution testing and tools) for each of the three types of defect artifacts (i.e., requirements defects, design defects, and code defects), we conducted a two-round Delphi. Unlike the Delphi conducted for the DI model where initial values were provided, we did not provide initial values for the DRFs of the DR model. This decision was made when the participants wanted to see how divergent the results would be if no initial values were provided.[2] Fortunately though (as shown in Table 5.36), the results didn't diverge a lot and the outcome of the 2-round Delphi was a robust expert-determined DR model.

The results of the Round 2 Delphi were used as the DRFs to formulate the initial version of the DR model as shown in Equation 5.22.

---

[2]The Delphi was done at a workshop focused on COQUALMO held in conjunction with the 13th International Forum on COCOMO and Software Cost Modeling. The ten workshop participants included practitioners in the field of software estimation and modeling and quality assurance and most of them had participated in the Delphi rounds of the DI model. We are very grateful to the participants who not only attended the workshop but also spent a significant amount of their time providing follow-up and useful feedback to resolve pending issues even after the workshop was over.

**Table 5.35   The Defect Removal Profiles**

| Rating | Automated Analysis | Peer Reviews | Execution Testing and Tools |
|---|---|---|---|
| Very Low | Simple compiler syntax checking. | No peer review. | No testing. |
| Low | Basic compiler capabilities for static module-level code analysis, syntax, type-checking. | Ad-hoc informal walk-throughs<br>Minimal preparation, no follow-up | Ad-hoc testing and debugging.<br>Basic text-based debugger. |
| Nominal | Some compiler extensions for static module and inter-module level code analysis, syntax, type-checking.<br>Basic requirements and design consistency, trace-ability checking. | Well-defined sequence of preparation, review, min-imal follow-up.<br>Informal review roles and procedures. | Basic unit test, integration test, system test process.<br>Basic test data manage-ment, problem tracking support.<br>Tests criteria based on checklists. |
| High | Intermediate-level module and inter-module code syntax and semantic analysis.<br>Simple requirements/design view consistency checking. | Formal review roles with all participants well-trained and procedures applied to all products using basic checklists, follow up. | Well-defined test sequence tailored to organization (acceptance/alpha/beta/flight/etc.) test.<br>Basic test coverage tools, test support system.<br>Basic test process manage-ment. |
| Very High | More elaborate require-ments/design view con-sistency checking.<br>Basic distributed-proces-sing and temporal analy-sis, model checking, symbolic execution. | Formal review roles with all participants well-trained and procedures applied to all product artifacts & changes (formal change control boards).<br>Basic review checklists, root cause analysis.<br>Formal follow-up.<br>Use of historical data on inspection rate, prepara-tion rate, fault density. | More advanced test tools, test data preparation, basic test oracle support, distributed monitoring and analysis, assertion checking.<br>Metrics-based test process management. |
| Extra High | Formalized* specification and verification.<br>Advanced distributed processing and temporal analysis, model checking, symbolic execution.<br><br>*Consistency-checkable pre-conditions and post-conditions, but not math-ematical theorems. | Formal review roles and procedures for fixes, change control.<br>Extensive review check-lists, root cause analysis.<br>Continuous review pro-cess improvement.<br>User/Customer involve-ment, Statistical Process Control. | Highly advanced tools for test oracles, distributed monitoring and analysis, assertion checking<br>Integration of automated analysis and test tools.<br>Model-based test process management. |

**Table 5.36    Results of Two-Round Delphi Exercise for Defect-Removal Fractions**

### Automated Analysis

|  |  | Round 1 | | | Round 2 | | |
|---|---|---|---|---|---|---|---|
|  |  | Median | Range (min \| max) | | Median | Range (min \| max) | |
| Very Low | Requirements defects | 0.00 | 0.00 | 0.00 | 0.00 | 0.00 | 0.00 |
|  | Design defects | 0.00 | 0.00 | 0.00 | 0.00 | 0.00 | 0.00 |
|  | Code defects | 0.00 | 0.00 | 0.05 | 0.00 | 0.00 | 0.05 |
| Low | Requirements defects | 0.00 | 0.00 | 0.15 | 0.00 | 0.00 | 0.15 |
|  | Design defects | 0.00 | 0.00 | 0.20 | 0.00 | 0.00 | 0.20 |
|  | Code defects | 0.10 | 0.00 | 0.25 | 0.10 | 0.00 | 0.25 |
| Nominal | Requirements defects | 0.10 | 0.00 | 0.40 | 0.10 | 0.00 | 0.40 |
|  | Design defects | 0.15 | 0.00 | 0.45 | 0.13 | 0.00 | 0.45 |
|  | Code defects | 0.20 | 0.05 | 0.45 | 0.20 | 0.05 | 0.45 |
| High | Requirements defects | 0.25 | 0.10 | 0.60 | 0.27 | 0.10 | 0.60 |
|  | Design defects | 0.33 | 0.10 | 0.65 | 0.28 | 0.10 | 0.65 |
|  | Code defects | 0.30 | 0.10 | 0.60 | 0.30 | 0.10 | 0.60 |
| Very High | Requirements defects | 0.33 | 0.10 | 0.85 | 0.34 | 0.15 | 0.85 |
|  | Design defects | 0.50 | 0.15 | 0.85 | 0.44 | 0.15 | 0.85 |
|  | Code defects | 0.48 | 0.15 | 0.75 | 0.48 | 0.15 | 0.75 |
| Extra High | Requirements defects | 0.40 | 0.20 | 0.90 | 0.40 | 0.20 | 0.90 |
|  | Design defects | 0.58 | 0.20 | 0.90 | 0.50 | 0.20 | 0.90 |
|  | Code defects | 0.55 | 0.15 | 0.85 | 0.55 | 0.20 | 0.85 |

### People Reviews

|  |  | Round 1 | | | Round 2 | | |
|---|---|---|---|---|---|---|---|
|  |  | Median | Range (min \| max) | | Median | Range (min \| max) | |
| Very Low | Requirements defects | 0.00 | 0.00 | 0.10 | 0.00 | 0.00 | 0.00 |
|  | Design defects | 0.00 | 0.00 | 0.20 | 0.00 | 0.00 | 0.00 |
|  | Code defects | 0.00 | 0.00 | 0.20 | 0.00 | 0.00 | 0.00 |
| Low | Requirements defects | 0.25 | 0.05 | 0.30 | 0.25 | 0.05 | 0.30 |
|  | Design defects | 0.30 | 0.05 | 0.40 | 0.28 | 0.05 | 0.40 |
|  | Code defects | 0.30 | 0.05 | 0.40 | 0.30 | 0.05 | 0.40 |
| Nominal | Requirements defects | 0.40 | 0.05 | 0.65 | 0.40 | 0.05 | 0.65 |
|  | Design defects | 0.40 | 0.10 | 0.70 | 0.40 | 0.10 | 0.70 |
|  | Code defects | 0.48 | 0.05 | 0.70 | 0.48 | 0.05 | 0.70 |
| High | Requirements defects | 0.50 | 0.05 | 0.75 | 0.50 | 0.10 | 0.75 |
|  | Design defects | 0.54 | 0.15 | 0.75 | 0.54 | 0.30 | 0.75 |
|  | Code defects | 0.60 | 0.40 | 0.80 | 0.60 | 0.40 | 0.80 |

|        |                     | Round 1 | | | Round 2 | | |
|--------|---------------------|--------|----------------|------|--------|----------------|------|
|        |                     | Median | Range (min \| max) | | Median | Range (min \| max) | |
| Very   | Requirements defects | 0.54 | 0.05 | 0.85 | 0.58 | 0.20 | 0.85 |
| High   | Design defects       | 0.68 | 0.30 | 0.85 | 0.70 | 0.40 | 0.85 |
|        | Code defects         | 0.73 | 0.48 | 0.90 | 0.73 | 0.48 | 0.90 |
| Extra  | Requirements defects | 0.63 | 0.05 | 0.95 | 0.70 | 0.30 | 0.95 |
| High   | Design defects       | 0.75 | 0.35 | 0.95 | 0.78 | 0.48 | 0.95 |
|        | Code defects         | 0.83 | 0.56 | 0.95 | 0.83 | 0.56 | 0.95 |

### Execution Testing and Tools

|         |                     | Round 1 | | | Round 2 | | |
|---------|---------------------|--------|----------------|------|--------|----------------|------|
|         |                     | Median | Range (min \| max) | | Median | Range (min \| max) | |
| Very    | Requirements defects | 0.00 | 0.00 | 0.30 | 0.00 | 0.00 | 0.00 |
| Low     | Design defects       | 0.00 | 0.00 | 0.40 | 0.00 | 0.00 | 0.00 |
|         | Code defects         | 0.00 | 0.00 | 0.60 | 0.00 | 0.00 | 0.00 |
| Low     | Requirements defects | 0.23 | 0.00 | 0.50 | 0.23 | 0.00 | 0.50 |
|         | Design defects       | 0.28 | 0.00 | 0.60 | 0.23 | 0.00 | 0.60 |
|         | Code defects         | 0.40 | 0.20 | 0.70 | 0.38 | 0.20 | 0.70 |
| Nominal | Requirements defects | 0.40 | 0.10 | 0.75 | 0.40 | 0.10 | 0.75 |
|         | Design defects       | 0.45 | 0.15 | 0.80 | 0.43 | 0.15 | 0.80 |
|         | Code defects         | 0.60 | 0.30 | 0.90 | 0.58 | 0.30 | 0.90 |
| High    | Requirements defects | 0.50 | 0.10 | 0.90 | 0.50 | 0.10 | 0.90 |
|         | Design defects       | 0.55 | 0.15 | 0.93 | 0.54 | 0.15 | 0.93 |
|         | Code defects         | 0.73 | 0.35 | 0.96 | 0.69 | 0.35 | 0.96 |
| Very    | Requirements defects | 0.60 | 0.10 | 0.97 | 0.57 | 0.10 | 0.97 |
| High    | Design defects       | 0.68 | 0.15 | 0.98 | 0.65 | 0.15 | 0.98 |
|         | Code defects         | 0.83 | 0.45 | 0.99 | 0.78 | 0.45 | 0.99 |
| Extra   | Requirements defects | 0.70 | 0.10 | 0.99 | 0.60 | 0.10 | 0.99 |
| High    | Design defects       | 0.78 | 0.20 | 0.992 | 0.70 | 0.15 | 0.992 |
|         | Code defects         | 0.90 | 0.50 | 0.995 | 0.88 | 0.50 | 0.995 |

For artifact, $j$,

$$D\,Res_{Est,j} = C_j \times DI_{Est,j} \times \prod_i (1 - DRF_{ij}) \qquad \text{Eq. 5.22}$$

where:

$DRes_{Est,j}$ = Estimated number of residual defects for $j$th artifact

$C_j$ = Baseline DR constant for the $j$th artifact

$DI_{Est,j}$ = Estimated number of defects introduced for artifact type $j$

$i = 1$ to 3 for each DR profile, namely automated analysis, people reviews, execution testing and tools

$DRF_{ij}$ = Defect Removal Fraction for defect removal profile $i$ and artifact type $j$

Using the nominal DIRs (see last paragraph of previous section and Table 5.34) and the DRFs of the second round of the Delphi, the residual defect density was computed when each of the three profiles were at Very Low, Low, Nominal, High, Very High, and Extra High levels (Table 5.37).

For example, the Very Low level values for each of the three profiles yield a residual defect density of 60 defects/kSLOC and the Extra High values yield a residual defect density of 1.57 defects/kSLOC (see Table 5.37).

**Table 5.37   Defect Density Results from Initial Defect Removal Fraction Values**

| | Automated Analysis DRF | People Reviews DRF | Execution Testing and Tools DRF | Product $(1-DRF_{ij})$ | DI/ kSLOC | DRes/ kSLOC |
|---|---|---|---|---|---|---|
| Very | 0.00 | 0.00 | 0.00 | 1.00 | 10 | 10 |
| Low | 0.00 | 0.00 | 0.00 | 1.00 | 20 | 20 |
| | 0.00 | 0.00 | 0.00 | 1.00 | 30 | 30 |
| | | | | | Total: | 60 |
| Low | 0.00 | 0.25 | 0.23 | 0.58 | 10 | 5.8 |
| | 0.00 | 0.28 | 0.23 | 0.55 | 20 | 11 |
| | 0.10 | 0.30 | 0.38 | 0.39 | 30 | 11.7 |
| | | | | | Total: | 28.5 |
| Nominal | 0.10 | 0.40 | 0.40 | 0.32 | 10 | 3.2 |
| | 0.13 | 0.40 | 0.43 | 0.3 | 20 | 6 |
| | 0.20 | 0.48 | 0.58 | 0.17 | 30 | 5.1 |
| | | | | | Total: | 14.3 |
| High | 0.27 | 0.50 | 0.50 | 0.18 | 10 | 1.8 |
| | 0.28 | 0.54 | 0.54 | 0.15 | 20 | 3 |
| | 0.30 | 0.60 | 0.69 | 0.09 | 30 | 2.7 |
| | | | | | Total: | 7.5 |
| Very | 0.34 | 0.58 | 0.57 | 0.14 | 10 | 1.4 |
| High | 0.44 | 0.70 | 0.65 | 0.06 | 20 | 1.2 |
| | 0.48 | 0.73 | 0.78 | 0.03 | 30 | 0.9 |
| | | | | | Total: | 3.5 |
| Extra | 0.40 | 0.70 | 0.60 | 0.07 | 10 | 0.7 |
| High | 0.50 | 0.78 | 0.70 | 0.03 | 20 | 0.6 |
| | 0.55 | 0.83 | 0.88 | 0.009 | 30 | 0.27 |
| | | | | | Total: | 1.57 |

Thus, using the quality model described in this section, one can conclude that for a project with nominal characteristics (or average ratings) the residual defect density is approximately 14 defects/kSLOC.

### 5.5.5    COQUALMO Integrated with COCOMO II

The Defect Introduction and Defect Removal Submodels described above can be integrated to the existing COCOMO II cost, effort, and schedule estimation model as shown in Figure 5.34. The dotted lines in Figure 5.34 are the inputs and outputs of COCOMO II. In addition to the sizing estimate and the platform, project, product and personnel attributes, COQUALMO requires the defect-removal profile levels as input to predict the number of nontrivial residual requirements, design, and code defects.

### 5.5.6.    Conclusions and Ongoing Research

As discussed in Section 5.5.2, COQUALMO is based on the tank-and-pipe model where defects are introduced through several defect source pipes described as the Defect Introduction model and removed through several defect elimination pipes modeled as the Defect Removal model. This section discussed the Delphi approach used to calibrate the initial version of the model to expert-opinion. The expert-calibrated COQUALMO when used on a project with nominal characteristics (or average ratings) predicts that approximately 14 defects per kSLOC are remaining. When more data on actual completed projects is available we plan to calibrate the model using the Bayesian approach. This statistical approach has been successfully used to calibrate COCOMO II to 161 projects. The Bayesian ap-

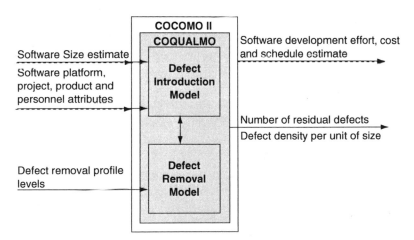

**Figure   5.34**  The  Cost/Schedule/Quality  Model:  COQUALMO  Integrated  with COCOMO II

proach can be used on COQUALMO to merge expert-opinion and project data, based on the variance of the two sources of information to determine a more robust posterior model. In the meanwhile, the model described in this section can be used as is or can be locally calibrated to a particular organization to predict the cost, schedule and residual defect density of the software under development. Extensive sensitivity analyses to understand the interactions between these parameters to do tradeoffs, risk analysis and return on investment can also be done.

## 5.6   COPROMO: PRODUCTIVITY ESTIMATION

The Constructive Process-Improvement Model (COPROMO) focuses on estimating the cost-effectiveness of allocations of investment resources, like new technologies or processes, to improve productivity.

COPROMO is a strategic planning decision assistant model for software engineering senior management. It is supported by a technology impact evaluation tool and an assessment approach. The model is based on the use of COCOMO II[3] and CORADMO[4] as productivity-estimating mechanisms. The implementation approach uses a representative application from a domain of concern to the senior management, and the identification of technology drivers and time frames. One version of the tool, COPROMO 0.3, has been implemented and used in the evaluation of the Knowledge Based Software Assistant [Boehm et al. 1999a].

COPROMO has a demonstrated approach, an adaptable implementation of an evaluation tool and supporting constructive models: COCOMO II.2000, an industry-accepted parametric cost-estimation model; COPSEMO, the effort and schedule distribution model; and CORADMO, the RAD techniques-oriented extended schedule and effort estimation model. CORADMO estimates the schedule in months ($M$), personnel staffing ($P$), and adjusted effort in person-months ($PM$) based on the distribution of effort and schedule of the various stages done by COPSEMO, and the impacts of selected RAD-related schedule driver ratings on the $M$, $P$, and $PM$ of each stage. Finally, the COPROMO contribution is showing estimated project development productivity improvement through impact evaluation.

### 5.6.1   Background and Rationale

COPROMO is a different kind of "extension" than those in the previous sections. It is a systematic, structured application of multiple models coupled with methods for indicating driver values.

---

[3]Constructive Cost Model, version II, 2000 calibration.
[4]Constructive RAD-schedule Model, a currently uncalibrated extension to COCOMO II.

As a strategic-planning tool, COPROMO calculates the impact of proposed technology or process improvement investments. It uses industry-accepted parametric models to evaluate the impact on a development project. In order to show impact, a baseline development project must be selected.

The current COPROMO 0.3 approach or method is to identify an application, time frames and specific technologies that are expected to impact productivity for the archetypal application over the time frames selected. The representative application should be one that is representative of the domain of concern of the senior management. The time frames should be long enough to have the selected technology mature and come into use, spanning at least eight to fifteen years. The specific technologies should be identifiable and have relatively clearly scoped, even if still evolving, definition and content. One of the technologies should always be the commercial- and milieu-specific (e.g., DoD) technologies that will evolve independently of the specific technologies.

The valuation model's parametric drivers include COCOMO II's effort scale factors and multipliers, which cover process, product, platform, personnel and project, and CORADMO's drivers that modify estimated schedule and effort multipliers. Each of the drivers' values are then gathered for the current baseline and assessed into the future using engineering judgement based on the assumed impacts of the selected, specific technologies.

All of the information on the drivers, their evolution over time and their rationale(s), are then entered into a spreadsheet tool. The tool, called COPROMO 0.3, consists of multiple, parallel COCOMO II and CORADMO parametric model calculations. The tool graphically displays each of the drivers' values over time to allow reasoning and discourse about their values and evolution over time. The tool also provides fields for the capture of the rationales for each of the drivers' values and evolution on the same page as the tabular and graphic display of values. Finally, the tool displays a comprehensive set of graphs showing the impact of the selected technologies over time for the issues of concern: effort, schedule and corresponding staffing level.

### 5.6.2  Relation to COCOMO II

As mentioned above, COPROMO applies the COCOMO II, COPSEMO and CORADMO models. The full parametric model of COCOMO II is used in its entirety. COPSEMO's new "schedule ($M$) as a function of effort ($PM$ or person-months)" equation and the default distribution of effort and schedule to phases are its primary contribution. The entire CORADMO model, to the extent it was specified in 1999, is used by COPROMO. It has no additional drivers or calculations.

Because of the impracticality of invoking and controlling multiple instances of COCOMO II, COPSEMO, and CORADMO tools, COPROMO does not use any of them. Instead, it implements the core parts of the models in spreadsheets. Its only additional capabilities are the numeric entry of driver values spread over time; the display of those values; and the graphs of the results.

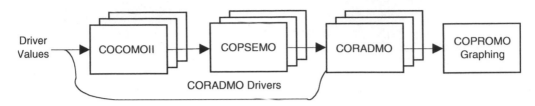

**Figure 5.35**   A Logical Model of COPROMO

### 5.6.3   Model Overview

The COPROMO logical model is essentially multiple parallel invocations of the COCOMO II, COPSEMO and CORADMO models, as is shown in Figure 5.35.

Activities in the application of COPROMO include identifying the domain of interest, an application archetype, initial driver values, time frames, and specific technologies. These activities are shown in a UML activity model in Figure 5.36.

The technologies should be specific and identifiable, and have relatively clearly defined, even if still evolving, content. One of the technologies should be the commercial- and milieu-specific (e.g., DoD) technologies that will evolve independently of the specific technologies.

### 5.6.4   Scope and Life Cycle Presently Addressed

At present, the COPROMO Model covers the same scope as CORADMO. The CORADMO model presently excludes both COTS impacts (COCOTS) and the quality extensions (COQUALMO). CORADMO does include and use the

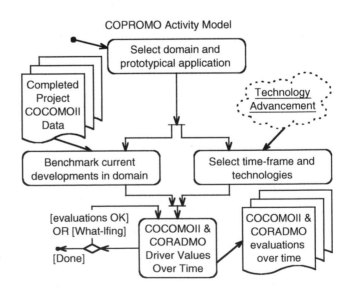

**Figure 5.36**   COPROMO Activity Model

COPSEMO model for effort and schedule redistribution. However, the percentage allocations per phase are fixed (not allowed to vary over time or technology).

COPROMO currently has the same restriction on life-cycle anchor points as CORADMO. While CORADMO is currently life-cycle model independent, since it works with data between anchor points, it expresses the phases using the MBASE/RUP life-cycle terminology. Only the first three phases—Inception, Elaboration, and Construction—are affected by CORADMO. These are the same three phases that COPROMO reports on.

At present there is only a single COPROMO point solution. It was developed to evaluate the life-cycle implication of the Knowledge Based Software Assistant (KBSA), an air-force-sponsored software engineering/development research program.

### 5.6.5  Model Details

The activities, and logical structuring of COPROMO's constituent models are detailed below. COPROMO is as much method or technique as it is parametric model.

The activities shown in Figure 5.37 represent the steps necessary to do a COPROMO 0.3 estimation; many steps can happen in parallel. Preparing the future ratings can only happen after both of its predecessor steps have been com-

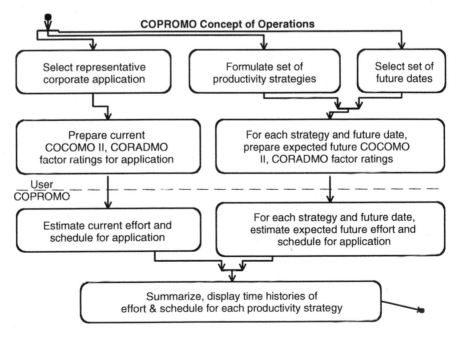

**Figure 5.37**  COPROMO Activities Based on a Concept of Operations

pleted. Finally, the primary result, the summary over time histories, can only happen after both of its two predecessor steps have been completed.

Selecting the representative application should be based on the organization for which the future productivity is desired. It should be at the core of the business on which that organization focuses. It should be both typical and average for the sizes in both that domain and for the organization. The corresponding size range of the software produced by the organization being evaluated should not be more than plus or minus 50 percent of this average, so it can be considered truly representative.

The productivity improvement strategies can include tools, techniques, or process improvements. They should be relatively clearly defined and understood. One "strategy" should encompass the expected commercial and milieu advances that will happen independently of any specially selected strategies.

The time frames for the future dates should be long enough to have technologies evolve and mature. If new technologies are involved in the estimation, the time frames would typically be eight and fifteen years. Other considerations depend on the life cycle of the strategies, e.g., two to three years for a CMM-level process level increase; for this case, the time frames might be three and seven years.

Identifying the current COCOMO II and CORADMO driver ratings is essentially a benchmarking activity using recently completed projects. A COCOMO II estimate should be performed for each of the completed projects, and a COCOMO II local calibration using all these projects would be wise too. An analysis of the ratings should be oriented towards selecting representative (or average) values which then become the baseline for the estimation.

To select the expected future COCOMO II driver ratings, a wide-band delphi [Boehm 1981] is suggested. Initially, such phrases as "some," "moderate," "solid," "significant," and "major" might be used to describe the gains. This might be followed by agreements in the magnitude or percentage of increase or decrease corresponding to each of the drivers' values. Clearly, both the COCOMO II scale factors and effort multipliers must be specified. Also, the impacts on the SIZE of the product due to the strategies should be assessed. Since some of the strategies may be complementary or interfering, these situations should be taken into account too. Finally, both the drivers' values over time and their rationales should be recorded, preferably in the COPROMO 0.3 tool.

Similar selection activities should be undertaken for the expected COPSEMO distribution percentages and for the CORADMO drivers. At the present time, the COPSEMO distribution percentages are not variable over time, but clearly the CORADMO drivers, rightfully, are. Again, both the driver values over time and their rationales should be recorded, preferably in the COPROMO 0.3 tool.

After all the drivers and rationales have been entered into COPROMO 0.3, the spreadsheet summarizes the results of the parallel runs of COCOMO II and CORADMO. Summary charts of the time history of the drivers and the impact on effort and schedule are shown by the tool.

Figure 5.38 shows the multiple COCOMO II (1) and CORADMO inputs (4). For COCOMO II, there are 24 parameters for each of the set of combinations of productivity improvement strategies at each of the dates selected.

The twenty-four COCOMO II parameters include the five scale factors, the 17 effort multipliers, the schedule parameter, and size. In the example shown later, there are 13 combinations of strategies and dates, leading to a total of 312 parameters. For CORADMO, there are four new schedule drivers, with the fifth driver (RESL) having the same rating as it does in COCOMO II. Although the CORADMO tool does not support it, each of the five drivers can have different value levels for the different phases as they do in COPROMO. Table 5.38 indicates there are 10 different CORADMO drivers to be set. Again for the example shown later, there are 13 combinations of strategies and dates, leading to a total of 130 parameters representing the CORADMO driver ratings. There are an additional four more parameters for the COPSEMO effort and schedule distribution, however in COPROMO 0.3 these are held fixed over the combinations of strategies and dates.

For each of the thirteen combinations of productivity improvement strategies at each of the dates selected, there is a complete calculation of the

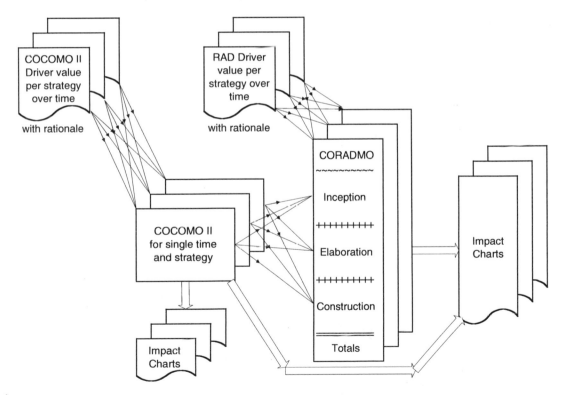

**Figure 5.38**  Evaluator Logical Structure

**Table 5.38  CORADMO Drivers**

| CORADMO driver | Multipliers per set of strategies | | Phases per set of strategies | | Multipliers and Phases per set of strategies |
|---|---|---|---|---|---|
| | Number | Reason | Number | Reason | |
| RVHL | 1 | Schedule value = Effort value | 2 | Inception & Elaboration phases (No Construction impact) | 2 |
| DPRS | 1 | Schedule value = Effort value | 2 | Inception & Elaboration (Construction) | 2 |
| CLAB | 1 | Schedule value = Effort value | 3 | Inception, Elaboration & Construction | 3 |
| RESL | 1 | Schedule value = Effort value | 1 | Only Construction | 1 |
| PPOS | 2 | Separate Schedule & Effort values | 1 | Inception = Elaboration = Construction | 2 |
| | | | | Total | 10 |

COCOMO II effort and schedule (two), and CORADMO effort, schedule and staffing (five) results. The results of these calculations are used to produce the COCOMO II and COCOMO II plus CORADMO impact charts (three and six, respectively) of effort and schedule for review and analysis.

### 5.6.6 Spreadsheet Model Overview

The COPROMO 0.3 tool is a multi-worksheet Excel workbook that shows the impacts of the COCOMO II and CORADMO drivers projected over time and technology-type on a selected domain's typically sized application. The first worksheet includes a description of all the other sheets and the COCOMO II.2000 calibration values and ranges for reference. The other worksheets are for the COCOMO II and CORADMO driver inputs, calculation of the models' outputs, and graphical displays of the impacts.

The COPROMO 0.3 workbook also has several protected sheets which are used for the detailed layout of the drivers to facilitate the graphs shown in the "Drivers" sections. There are also protected sheets for the default values (i.e., the USC Center for Software Engineering assessed values) of the COCOMO II and CORADMO drivers.

### 5.6.7 Example of Use

While most of the elements of the COPROMO 0.3 tool have been discussed, the following will help put the detailed description of the COPROMO 0.3 tool into perspective.

#### 5.6.7.1 EXAMPLE—AFRL RESEARCH CONTRACT OBJECTIVES AND APPROACH

The *objective* of a 1998 CSE research contract with the U.S. Air Force Rome Laboratories (AFRL) was to develop and validate technical approaches for evaluating the effects of Knowledge Based Software Assistant (KBSA) process concepts and technology on software development effort and schedule, and to use these approaches to perform comparative evaluations of KBSA and other sources of software technology.

The research *approach* involved three tasks and our responses that provide background or are directly relevant to COPROMO 0.3.

*Task 1. Characterize KBSA and other sources of software technology in the context of recent and emerging software trends.*

We provided a summary of KBSA technology, concentrating on the KBSA Advanced Development Model developed by Andersen Consulting. We also summarized two other comparable sources of software technology: the commercial and DoD development marketplaces, and the DARPA/AFRL Evolutionary Design of Complex Software (EDCS) program.

*Task 2. Develop models and an evaluation framework for assessing the effects of KBSA and other sources of software technology on software development effort and schedule.*

The recently developed and calibrated COCOMO II model provided an approach for evaluation based on the effects of alternative software technologies on the model's effort-driver parameters. The model's calibration to over 100 1990s' software projects also provided a 1990s' baseline from which to evaluate the technologies' effects.

For assessing schedule effects, two other models, CORADMO and COPSEMO, were used to evaluate the effects of rapid application development (RAD). The evaluation framework included a domain focus: DoD embedded systems; and a particular evaluation example: a representative embedded, high-assurance, real-time (EHART) missile software project. A spreadsheet version of the evaluation model, a precursor to COPROMO 0.3, was developed. This spreadsheet was designed to enable technology decision-makers to perform trade-off and sensitivity analyses of alternative software technology investment strategies.

*Task 3. Use the models to evaluate KBSA, EDCS, and commercial technology with respect to the baseline.*

The primary result of the research compared the technologies' relative effects on development effort, using relatively conservative assumptions. It showed that commercial and general DoD related technology are likely to reduce development effort of the EHART 1998 baseline project by a factor of 2.5 in 8 years (2006) and another factor of 3 in 15 years (2013). Relative to commercial technology, a fully-supported mix of KBSA and EDCS technologies could reduce development effort by another factor of 3 in 8 years and another factor of 6 in 15 years.

### 5.6.7.2.  EXAMPLE'S VALUES USED

Each of the major factors for the COPROMO 0.3 evaluation of the KBSA and other technologies are described in this section.

Since the Knowledge Based Software Assistant was developed under a U.S. Air Force contract, an embedded, high-assurance real-time (EHART) application was selected as the representative "corporate application." Such applications are critical to DoD weapons. Also, the commercial technology investment that is directly in this domain is relatively low. A typical size of 100K SLOC was selected.

As a baseline, a subset of 106 of the 161 1990s projects for which there is calibration data was selected. These 106 projects reflected current practice in the domains related to an EHART application (projects normalized for 100 KSLOC applications). The range and average for the COCOMO II drivers is shown in Figure 5.39. The average values used as the baseline are shown in Table 5.39 and Table 5.40.

These are considered to be conservative ratings since those with well collected data, data necessary for inclusion in the COCOMO II calibration set, are generally more advanced. This is also tempered by the fact that the average year of completion of the calibration data was 1994.

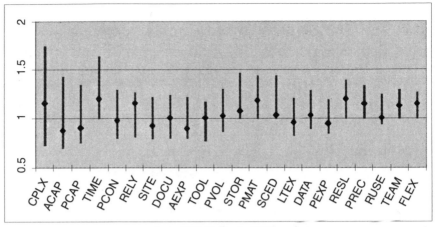

◆ Average Multiplier for 1990s projects

**Figure 5.39** Productivity Multipliers

The selected dates for the example were 2006 and 2013. These relatively long time frames of eight and fifteen years were selected because of the recognition of how long it takes technologies like KBSA to be fielded and generally adopted.

The primary focus of the Productivity Improvement estimation was potential impact of the overall KBSA technology, not just the current version of the tool. The overall technology had two major components: application generation and knowledge based project development decision support. The application generation portion included the domain engineering knowledge base. The decision support capability is typical of emerging Software Engineering Decision Assistants concepts. A related software technology development activity was going on in the Evolutionary Development of Complex Systems (EDCS), and this technology was also factored in to the Productivity Improvement estimates.

The following named sets of combined technologies were selected for inclusion in the estimate:

- CD: for the combination of Commercial technology and DoD general practice
- KG: for KBSA applications generations technologies combined with CD
- KD: KBSA project decision support technologies combined with CD

**Table 5.39  Baseline Scale Factor Values**

| SF | PREC | FLEX | RESL | TEAM | PMAT |
|------|------|------|------|------|------|
| Mean | 3.06 | 3.15 | 3.97 | 2.7 | 3.72 |

**Table 5.40    Baseline Effort Multiplier Values**

| EAF | RELY | DATA | CPLX | RUSE | DOCU | TIME | STOR | PVOL | ACAP |
|------|------|------|------|------|------|------|------|------|------|
| Mean | 1.06 | 1.04 | 1.16 | 1.01 | 1.01 | 1.08 | 1.03 | 1.03 | 0.88 |

| EAF | PCAP | PCON | APEX | PLEX | LTEX | TOOL | SITE | SCED |
|------|------|------|------|------|------|------|------|------|
| Mean | 0.91 | 0.98 | 0.9 | 0.95 | 0.97 | 1.01 | 0.93 | 1.04 |

- K: for the combination of both KG and KD, because there were synergies, and CD
- E: for the EDCS technologies combined with CD
- EK: both EDCS and KBSA (the full K), which also thus included CD

The driver value selection and rationales that were developed were based initially on Dr. Barry Boehm's expert engineering judgment. Modifications were made in the driver-value selections based on feedback from two knowledgeable

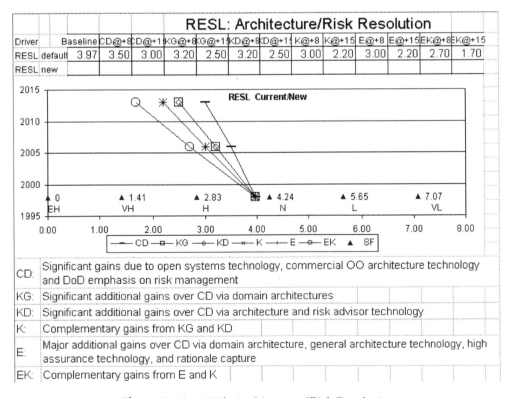

**Figure 5.40**    RESL: Architecture/Risk Resolution

and respected individuals. After the driver values had settled, the rationales were updated to reflect the consensus on the values.

### 5.6.7.3   EXAMPLES OF COCOMO DRIVER-RATINGS SELECTIONS AND RATIONALES

Figures 5.40 and 5.41 are examples of the driver-ratings and rationales (for RESL and TOOL, respectively) as supported by the COPROMO 0.3 tool.

SIZE (KSLOC) is the primary determinant of software effort in COCOMO II (and other software cost estimation models). For COCOMO II, effective size is a function of KSLOC or FP, REVL, ADSI, DM, CM, IM, SU, AA, and UNFM. The baseline value was the 100 KSLOC embedded, high assurance, real-time (EHART) software application.

The driver ratings for SIZE are shown in Figure 5.42, and the rationales for the size values over time and technologies are shown in Table 5.41.

### 5.6.7.4   EXAMPLES OF CORADMO DRIVER-RATINGS SELECTIONS AND RATIONALES

Figures 5.42 and 5.43 show the CORADMO RVHL driver ratings and rationales as supported by the COPROMO 0.3 tool. As mentioned earlier, not all the drivers for all the phases are relevant (see note at bottom of Figure 5.44).

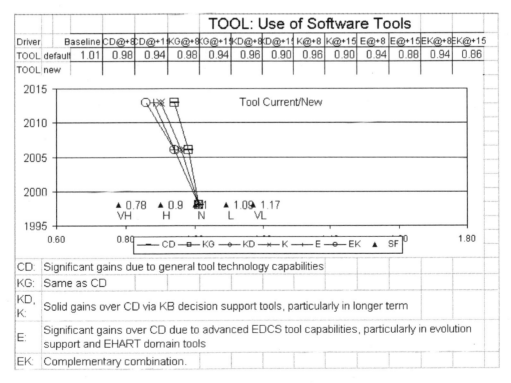

**Figure 5.41**   TOOL: Use of Software Tools

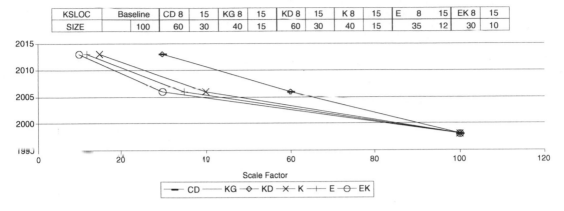

| KSLOC | Baseline |  | CD 8 | 15 | KG 8 | 15 | KD 8 | 15 | K 8 | 15 | E | 8 | 15 | EK 8 | 15 |
|---|---|---|---|---|---|---|---|---|---|---|---|---|---|---|---|
| SIZE |  | 100 | 60 | 30 | 40 | 15 | 60 | 30 | 40 | 15 |  | 35 | 12 | 30 | 10 |

**Figure 5.42**    SIZE: KSLOC

### 5.6.7.5    EXAMPLES OF COPROMO CHARTS

Figures 5.45 and 5.46 show some of the charts generated by the COPROMO 0.3 tool.

### 5.6.7.6    COPROMO APPLIED TO KBSA: CONCLUSIONS

Results are conservative, particularly for EDCS, as maintenance savings would be greater than development savings, due to reductions in amount of software understanding, redesign, recode, and retest effort. This is especially true as

**Table 5.41    Rationales for the SIZE Factor Value Over Time and Technologies**

| | |
|---|---|
| CD | "Commercial technology will provide better reuse infrastructure (e.g., ORBs) and some of the componentry technology need for EHART applications. Better requirements technology will reduce breakage somewhat. The overall effects for EHART applications will be less than the effects for mainstream commercial applications since much of the commercial technology will not fit EHART applications.<br>Significant gains will come from existing DoD initiatives such as the SEI Product Line Systems program. |
| KD | Same as CD |
| KG & K | Significant gains over CD due to EHART domain-specific architectures, reuse, and application generators |
| E | Similar domain-specific gains, plus additional reduced breakage due to requirements and rationale capture technology, and reduced software understanding penalties due to software understanding technology |
| EK | Gains over E due to stronger KB application generator technology |

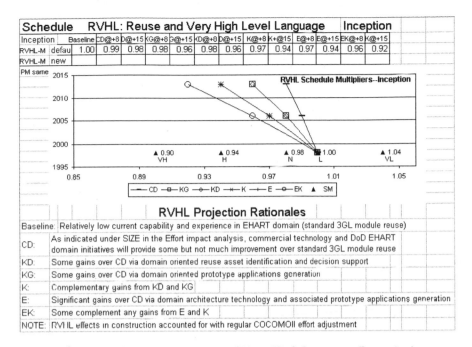

## Schedule  RVHL: Reuse and Very High Level Language  Inception

| Inception | Baseline | CD@+8 | D@+15 | KG@+8 | G@+15 | KD@+8 | D@+15 | K@+8 | K+@15 | E@+8 | E@+15 | EK@+8 | K@+15 |
|---|---|---|---|---|---|---|---|---|---|---|---|---|---|
| RVHL-M default | 1.00 | 0.99 | 0.98 | 0.98 | 0.96 | 0.98 | 0.96 | 0.97 | 0.94 | 0.97 | 0.94 | 0.96 | 0.92 |
| RVHL-M new | | | | | | | | | | | | | |
| PM same | | | | | | | | | | | | | |

### RVHL Projection Rationales

| | |
|---|---|
| Baseline: | Relatively low current capability and experience in EHART domain (standard 3GL module reuse) |
| CD: | As indicated under SIZE in the Effort impact analysis, commercial technology and DoD EHART domain initiatives will provide some but not much improvement over standard 3GL module reuse |
| KD: | Some gains over CD via domain oriented reuse asset identification and decision support |
| KG: | Some gains over CD via domain oriented prototype applications generation |
| K: | Complementary gains from KD and KG |
| E: | Significant gains over CD via domain architecture technology and associated prototype applications generation |
| EK: | Some complement any gains from E and K |
| NOTE: | RVHL effects in construction accounted for with regular COCOMOII effort adjustment |

**Figure 5.43**   RVHL: Resuse and Very High Language (Inception)

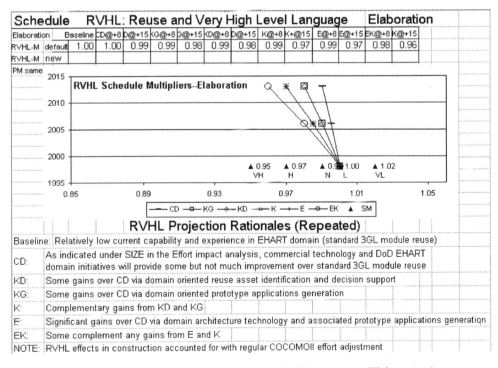

## Schedule  RVHL: Reuse and Very High Level Language  Elaboration

| Elaboration | Baseline | CD@+8 | D@+15 | KG@+8 | G@+15 | KD@+8 | D@+15 | K@+8 | K+@15 | E@+8 | E@+15 | EK@+8 | K@+15 |
|---|---|---|---|---|---|---|---|---|---|---|---|---|---|
| RVHL-M default | 1.00 | 1.00 | 0.99 | 0.99 | 0.98 | 0.99 | 0.98 | 0.99 | 0.97 | 0.99 | 0.97 | 0.98 | 0.96 |
| RVHL-M new | | | | | | | | | | | | | |
| PM same | | | | | | | | | | | | | |

### RVHL Projection Rationales (Repeated)

| | |
|---|---|
| Baseline: | Relatively low current capability and experience in EHART domain (standard 3GL module reuse) |
| CD: | As indicated under SIZE in the Effort impact analysis, commercial technology and DoD EHART domain initiatives will provide some but not much improvement over standard 3GL module reuse |
| KD: | Some gains over CD via domain oriented reuse asset identification and decision support |
| KG: | Some gains over CD via domain oriented prototype applications generation |
| K: | Complementary gains from KD and KG |
| E: | Significant gains over CD via domain architecture technology and associated prototype applications generation |
| EK: | Some complement any gains from E and K |
| NOTE: | RVHL effects in construction accounted for with regular COCOMOII effort adjustment |

**Figure 5.44**   RVHL: Resuse and Very High Language (Elaboration)

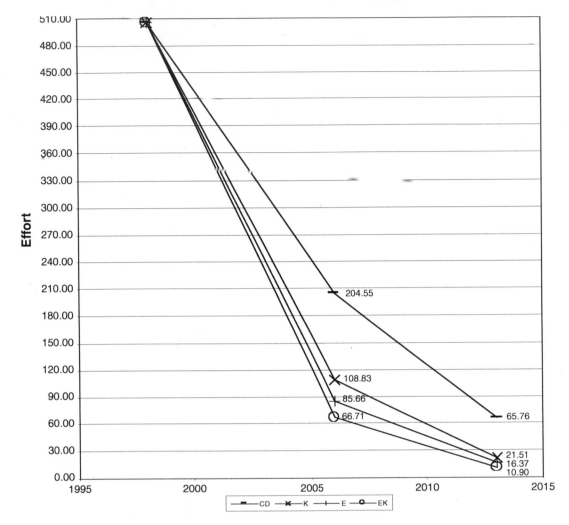

**Figure 5.45**   Impact of Technologies on Software Effort or Cost

when incremental development and delivery techniques are applied to analysis and development, and considering the new verification technologies.

### 5.6.8   COPROMO 0.3 Documentation

More information on the COPROMO 0.3 tool can be found in the "CO-PROMO 0.3-Users-Manual" included on the CD that accompanies this book. Also on the CD are the full COPROMO 0.3 tool and a report with a detailed discussion of the sensitivity analysis for the KBSA Evaluation.

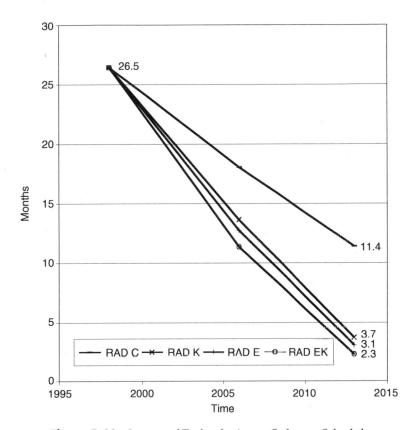

**Figure 5.46** Impact of Technologies on Software Schedule

## 5.6.9 Conclusions and Future Work

We are looking for people who will use COPROMO 0.3 and experiment with it. We are also looking for early adopters to work with us to generate more examples and experience. While COPROMO 0.3 is a point solution applied to the KBSA Life-cycle Evaluation, the processes and concepts are clear and have been successfully applied. Different baselines and representative applications can be handled with the current tool. However, as a point solution, COPROMO 0.3 requires custom tailoring for different sets of productivity strategies and future dates. We are on the look-out for future applications where we can directly leverage our experience and tool. Such future applications will require direct involvement with the organization applying variants of our tool.

One of the most interesting and useful extensions will be the inclusion of the COCOTS model. This would allow predicting the productivity impact of the use of COTS. As the COCOTS model becomes implemented in a tool or tools, it becomes possible to establish baselines, which is one of the pre-requisites for COPROMO.

The impacts of process improvement, and process model change or product model change (e.g., from one of a kind to part of a product line) will often change the proportion of effort and schedule allocated to phases. Such an extension appears relatively easy to apply since the same techniques used for driver value change over time and technology can be applied to the COPSEMO model.

Investment cost tracking would enable the tool to project ROI. Clearly, this can only happen in organizations that are so advanced that they can accurately assess the costs of prior investments in productivity improvement technologies. Given such data, it is clearly possible to apply the COPROMO techniques to project both investment costs and ROI.

It is expected that there will be advances in COPSEMO and CORADMO models. Incorporation of these advances into COPROMO will lead to an improved tool.

The COQUALMO model is expected to eventually be implemented in a tool and calibrated based on real data. Incorporation of this calibrated model, including the tracking of quality improvement impacts on effort, should produce a model that includes quality (defect reduction) in the projected cost and effort calculations.

Given sufficient interest and need, the COPROMO tool framework could be enhanced to automatically generate custom COPROMO tools given identification of future dates and named sets of productivity strategies. Such future custom tools would retain the openness and fidelity to the COCOMO II, COPSEMO and CORADMO models, but would be much more useful to many organizations.

Evolutions of the model and tool(s) are first made available to CSE and COCOMO II Affiliates. See information on affiliation in Appendix D, or the accompanying CD.

## 5.7   EXPERT COCOMO: RISK ASSESSMENT

### 5.7.1   Introduction and Background

Expert COCOMO is an extension that aids in project planning by identifying, categorizing, quantifying, and prioritizing project risks. It also detects cost estimate input anomalies and provides risk control advice in addition to conventional COCOMO cost and schedule calculation. The technique is an automated heuristic method for conducting software project risk assessment in union with cost estimation. The heuristics are rules that analyze risk items based on cost factor information, and essentially decompose cost driver effects into constituent risk escalating situations.

Good software risk management requires human judgement, and is often difficult to implement because of the scarcity of seasoned experts and the unique characteristics of individual projects. However, risk management can be improved by leveraging on existing knowledge and expertise. Expert COCOMO is a knowledge-based method employed during cost estimation to detect patterns of project risk based on cost driver information.

Particularly in an era of rapid development and hasty project decisions, a project estimator may overlook project definition discrepancies and fail to identify critical project risks. Approaches for identifying risks are usually separate from cost estimation, thus a technique that identifies risk in conjunction with cost estimation is an improvement.

At project inception for example, a manager who is inexperienced and/or lacking sufficient time to do a thorough analysis may have a vague idea that the project is risky. But he/she will not know exactly which risks to mitigate and how. With automated assistance, the identified risks derived from cost inputs are used to create mitigation plans based on the relative risk severities and provided advice.

Each individual risk item that is automatically identified may be evident to an experienced software manager, but particularly under time pressure the risks may not be considered. An automated tool helps calibrate and rank collections of risk items, which many managers wouldn't do otherwise. Incorporation of expert system rules can place considerable added knowledge at the disposal of the project planner or manager to help avoid high-risk situations and cost overruns.

### 5.7.2  Risk Description

The risks assessed by Expert COCOMO are those of not delivering a satisfactory software product within the available budget and schedule. A risk situation can be described as a combination of extreme cost driver values indicating increased effort with a potential for more problems, whereas an input anomaly is a violation of COCOMO consistency constraints. Risk items are identified, quantified, prioritized, and classified depending on the cost drivers involved and their ratings. Interactions of cost attributes which are essentially orthogonal to each other are not identified as risk situations.

One risk example is a project condition whereby the schedule is tight and the staff applications experience is low. Cost and/or schedule goals may not be met since time will have to be spent understanding the application domain, and this extra time may not have been planned for. An associated rule would be:

*IF ((required development schedule < nominal) and*
*(applications experience < nominal))*
*THEN there is a project risk.*

In the next level of detail, different rating combinations are evaluated to determine the level of risk. Follow-on advice rules can provide suggestions for relaxing the schedule or improving the staffing situation.

A typical risk situation can be visualized in a two-dimensional plane as shown in Figure 5.47, where each axis is defined as a cost attribute rating range. As seen in the figure, the continuous representation is broken into distinct units represented as a table. A risk condition corresponds to an individual cell containing an identified risk level. The rules use cost driver ratings to index directly into these tables of risk levels. The tables constitute the knowledge base for risk situations defined as interactions of cost attributes.

### 5.7.3   Risk Taxonomy and Rule Base

A risk taxonomy was developed in order to categorize the risks. The risk categories, which are generally aligned with the cost attribute categories in CO-COMO, include schedule, product, platform, personnel, process, reuse, and cost estimation risks.

Currently, ninety-four rules have been identified which deal with project risk, fifteen are input anomalies and a handful have been generated to provide advice. There are nearly six-hundred risk conditions, or discrete combinations of input parameters that are covered by the rule base. A natural extension of the assessment technique is to generate specific advice for each project risk condition, and this effort is currently underway.

Figure 5.48 shows the rule taxonomy and corresponding risk taxonomy. Not shown are the cost factors and rules for input anomalies (cost estimation risk)

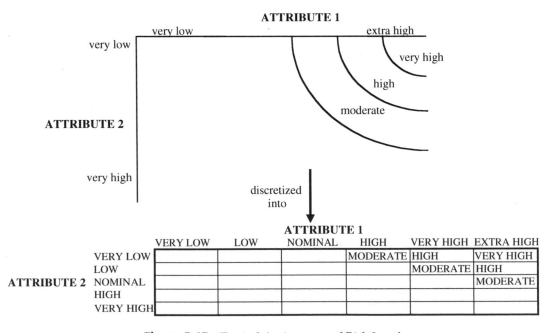

**Figure 5.47**   Typical Assignment of Risk Levels

**Overall Project Risk**

| Schedule risk SCED | Product risk RELY | Platform risk TIME | Personnel risk ACAP | Process risk TOOL | Reuse risk RUSE |
|---|---|---|---|---|---|
| sced_cplx | rely_accp | sced_time | acap_risk | sced_tool | ruse_rely |
| sced_rely | rely_pcap | time_pcap | cplx_acap | tool_acap | ruse_aexp |
| sced_time | rely_pmat | time_acap | *cplx_acap_pcap* | tool_pcap | ruse_itex |
| sced_pvol | sced_rely | cplx_time_sced | pmat_acap | aplx_tool | ruse_acap |
| sced_tool | *rely_data_sced* | *time_stor_sced* | rely_acap | time_tool | ruse_time |
| sced_acap | rely_star_sced | *time_pvol_sced* | *rely_acap_pcap* | tool_pmat | ruse_stor |
| sced_aexp | rely_aoap_pcap | ruse_time | ruse_acap | pcon_tool | ruse_docu |
| sced_pcap | prec_rely | time_tool | sced_acap | *site_tool* | prec_ruse |
| sced_vexp | resl_rely | prec_time | stor_acap | *resl_tool* | resl_ruse |
| sced_itex | ruse_rely | flex_time | time_acap | **SITE** | |
| sced_pmat | **DATA** | resl_time | tool_acap | site_docu | |
| sced_docu | *rely_data_sced* | **STOR** | *pcon_acap* | *site_tool* | |
| sced_pcon | **SIZE** | stor_acap | prec_acap | pcon_site | |
| sced_site | size_pccp | stor_pcap | resl_acap | sced_site | |
| sced_prec | **CPLX** | ruse_stor | **AEXP** | *prec_site* | |
| sced_flex | cplx_acap | cplx_stor_sced | *itex_aexp_sced* | *team_site* | |
| sced_resl | cplx_acap_pcap | *time_stor_sced* | ruse_aexp | **PREC** | |
| sced_team | cplx_pcap | prec_stor | sced_aexp | *prec_flex* | |

**Figure 5.48**   Partial Rule Taxonomy

and advice. Involved cost drivers are shown in boldface, while specific rules are named as concatenations of the cost factors.

### 5.7.4  Risk Quantification

Risk impact, or risk exposure is defined as the probability of loss multiplied by the cost of the loss. A quantitative risk weighting scheme was developed that accounts for the nonlinearity of the assigned risk levels and cost multiplier data to compute overall risks for each category and the entire project according to

$$Project\ Risk = \sum_{j=1}^{\#categories} \sum_{i=1}^{\#category\ risks} (Risk\ Level_{i,j} * Effort\ MultiplierProduct_{i,j})$$

where

$$Risk\ Level = 1 \quad \rightarrow moderate\ risk$$
$$2 \quad \rightarrow high\ risk$$
$$3 \quad \rightarrow very\ high\ risk$$

and

$$Effort\ Multiplier\ Product =$$
$$(driver\ \#1\ effort\ multiplier)*(driver\ \#2\ effort\ multiplier) \ldots$$
$$*(driver\ \#n\ effort\ multiplier).$$

If the risk involves a schedule constraint (SCED), then the risk weighting is proportional to the increase in staff level (relative effort/relative schedule), as follows:

$$Effort\ Multiplier\ Product =$$
$$(SCED\ effort\ multiplier)/(relative\ schedule)$$
$$*(driver\ \#2\ effort\ multiplier) \ldots *(driver\ \#n\ effort\ multiplier).$$

Following the definition that Risk Exposure = (risk probability) * (risk loss), the risk level corresponds to the nonlinear relative probability of the risk occurring and the effort multiplier product represents the cost consequence of the risk. The product involves those effort multipliers involved in the risk situation.

The risk levels were normalized to provide meaningful relative risk indications as follows: 0–5 low risk, 5–15 medium risk, 15–50 high risk, and 50–100 very high risk. A value of 100 denotes that each cost factor is rated at its most expensive (an unlikely project to be undertaken). The different risk categories are also normalized relative to their maximum values.

### 5.7.5   Input Anomalies

An input anomaly is basically an incompatible set of inputs. An example of an input anomaly would be:

$$IF\ ((size > 500\ KSLOC)\ and\ (precedentedness = very\ low)$$
$$and\ (product\ complexity = very\ low))$$
$$THEN\ there\ is\ an\ input\ anomaly.$$

This is because a large application that has never been developed before more than likely necessitates a complex solution. The size alone is highly likely to induce complexity.

### 5.7.6   Implementation

The Internet implementation of the tool is at *http://sunset.usc.edu/research/ COCOMOII/expert_cocomo/expert_cocomo.html.* A link to it is also provided on the enclosed CD-ROM. Figure 5.49 is a partial input screen showing the rated attributes for the project. This data also constitutes the input for a cost estimate. Explanatory help is suppressed; a description of the model, input definitions and rating guidelines are also provided via hypertext links. In this example, the project has a tightly constrained schedule as well as some stringent product attributes and less than ideal personnel attributes. With this input data, the expert system identifies specific risk situations and quantifies them per the aforementioned formulas.

The individual risks are ranked, and the different risk summaries are presented in a set of tables. A partial example output is seen in Figure 5.50 showing the overall project risk, risks for subcategories, and a prioritized list of risk situa-

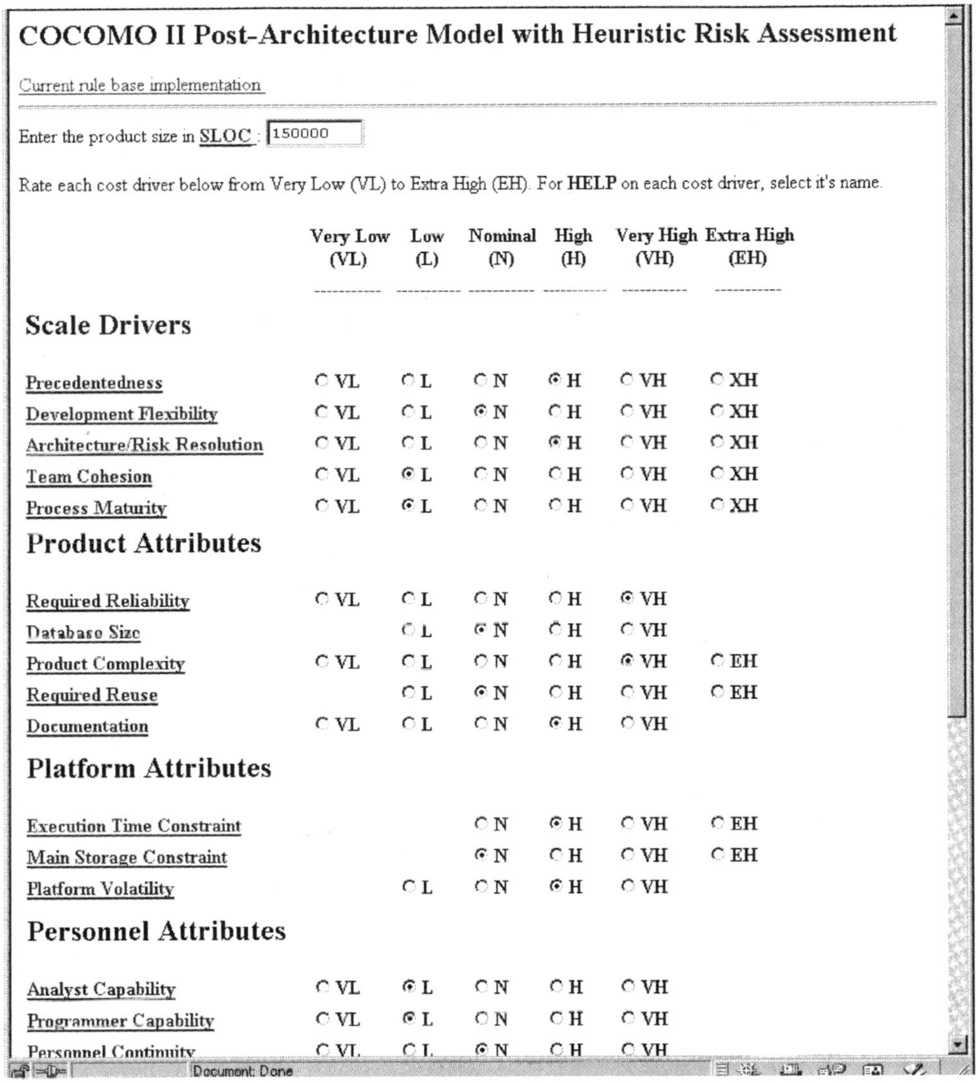

---

## COCOMO II Post-Architecture Model with Heuristic Risk Assessment

Current rule base implementation

Enter the product size in SLOC : `150000`

Rate each cost driver below from Very Low (VL) to Extra High (EH). For **HELP** on each cost driver, select it's name.

| | Very Low (VL) | Low (L) | Nominal (N) | High (H) | Very High (VH) | Extra High (EH) |
|---|---|---|---|---|---|---|

### Scale Drivers

| | VL | L | N | H | VH | XH |
|---|---|---|---|---|---|---|
| Precedentedness | ○ VL | ○ L | ○ N | ⦿ H | ○ VH | ○ XH |
| Development Flexibility | ○ VL | ○ L | ⦿ N | ○ H | ○ VH | ○ XH |
| Architecture/Risk Resolution | ○ VL | ○ L | ○ N | ⦿ H | ○ VH | ○ XH |
| Team Cohesion | ○ VL | ⦿ L | ○ N | ○ H | ○ VH | ○ XH |
| Process Maturity | ○ VL | ⦿ L | ○ N | ○ H | ○ VH | ○ XH |

### Product Attributes

| | VL | L | N | H | VH | EH |
|---|---|---|---|---|---|---|
| Required Reliability | ○ VL | ○ L | ○ N | ○ H | ⦿ VH | |
| Database Size | | ○ L | ⦿ N | ○ H | ○ VH | |
| Product Complexity | ○ VL | ○ L | ○ N | ○ H | ⦿ VH | ○ EH |
| Required Reuse | | ○ L | ⦿ N | ○ H | ○ VH | ○ EH |
| Documentation | ○ VL | ○ L | ○ N | ⦿ H | ○ VH | |

### Platform Attributes

| | VL | L | N | H | VH | EH |
|---|---|---|---|---|---|---|
| Execution Time Constraint | | | ○ N | ⦿ H | ○ VH | ○ EH |
| Main Storage Constraint | | | ⦿ N | ○ H | ○ VH | ○ EH |
| Platform Volatility | | ○ L | ○ N | ⦿ H | ○ VH | |

### Personnel Attributes

| | VL | L | N | H | VH |
|---|---|---|---|---|---|
| Analyst Capability | ○ VL | ⦿ L | ○ N | ○ H | ○ VH |
| Programmer Capability | ○ VL | ⦿ L | ○ N | ○ H | ○ VH |
| Personnel Continuity | ○ VL | ○ L | ⦿ N | ○ H | ○ VH |

Document: Done

**Figure 5.49**   Partial Sample Input Screen

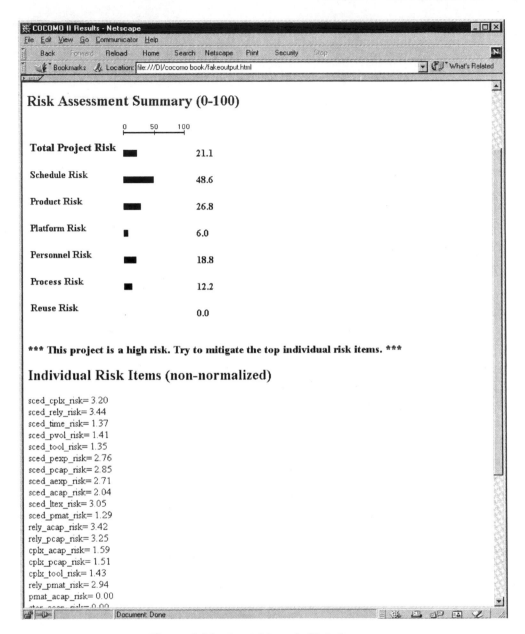

**Figure 5.50**  Partial Sample Risk Outputs

tions (not shown are the cost and schedule estimates). It is seen that the leading subcategories of risk are schedule, product, and personnel. Other outputs include prioritized risk items in each category and a list of advice to help manage the risks. The highest risks in this example deal with schedule and reliability, and appropriate advice would be provided to the user.

The Expert COCOMO method only solves part of the puzzle for project planning. Though no tool can totally replace humans in the loop for risk management, this technique goes a long way to minimize effort by killing two birds with one stone (i.e., cost estimation and risk management), and to help prevent risks from falling through the cracks.

### 5.7.7  Current Status and Further References

USC COCOMO currently has the risk assessment implemented at a high level without the risk condition weightings or risk normalization. It will be refined in a later version to include the detailed weightings and risk categories. Until then, use the online Expert COCOMO tool for the most complete implementation.

See the IEEE article [Madachy 1997] for general background and more details on the risk taxonomy, tool implementation, validation, conclusions, and future work. We are also contemplating similar risk assessment aids to assess risky combinations of cost/schedule driver inputs to COCOTS and CORADMO.

# 6

# Future Trends

## 6.1    TRENDS IN SOFTWARE PRODUCTIVITY AND ESTIMATING ACCURACY

In principle, your organization should be able to continuously measure, recalibrate, and refine models such as COCOMO II to converge uniformly toward perfection in understanding your software applications and in accurately estimating their costs and schedules.

In practice, your convergence toward perfection in estimation is not likely to be uniform. Two major phenomena are likely to interrupt your progress in estimation accuracy:

1. As you increase your understanding of the nature of your applications domain, you will also be able to improve your software productivity and quality by using larger solution components and more powerful applications definition languages. Changing to these construction methods will require you to revise your estimation techniques, and will cause your estimation error to increase.

2. The overall pace of change via new technologies and paradigm shifts in the nature of software products, processes, organizations, and people will cause both the inputs to and the outputs of software estimation models to change. Again, these changes are likely to improve your software productivity and quality, but to cause your estimation error to increase.

Sections 6.2 and 6.3 will discuss these two trends. Section 6.4 will describe how the COCOMO II project is addressing the estimation challenges presented by those trends. Section 6.5 will discuss how your organization can use the COCOMO II framework to best capitalize on these trends at both project level and the organizational level.

## 6.2   EFFECTS OF INCREASING DOMAIN UNDERSTANDING

Suppose you are entering a new applications domain, e.g., control of distributed, heterogeneous, real-time automated agents for robotics devices. Your initial software productivity in this domain is likely to be low, largely due to the effects of such COCOMO II variables as Precendentedness, Architecture and Risk Resolution, Complexity, and Applications Experience. In particular, your understanding of the architecture for such systems and your ability to reuse components will be low. And your unfamiliarity with the domain will cause your cost and schedule estimation errors to be relatively high.

As you increase your understanding of how to build such systems and their components, both your productivity and your estimation accuracy will improve. However, at some point, you will understand enough about the domain to begin developing a product line architecture and reusable components to be used in future products. At this point (point A in Figure 6.1), your productivity will go up faster, as you will be reusing rather than developing more and more of the software (in COCOMO II terms, your equivalent Source Lines of Code will decrease for the same type of project). However, at point A, your estimation error will go

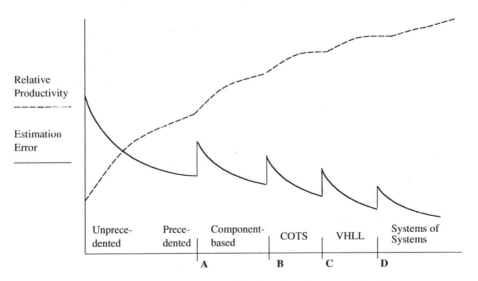

**Figure 6.1**   Productivity and Estimation Accuracy Trends

up, as your previous cost driver ratings will be less relevant, and you will be just beginning on the learning curve in rating your reuse parameters. You will also find that reuse and product line management cause significant changes in your processes [Boehm et al. 1998; Reifer 1997a].

As you improve your understanding of how to increase productivity and reduce estimation error in using component-based development, you will often find that other organizations in the domain are doing so as well. Soon, some of the more general components will be either shared across organizations or offered as commercial-off-the-shelf (COTS) products. With their development and maintenance costs amortized over more and more user organizations, they become cheaper to employ than some of your own reusable components. Again, using these COTS products or shared components will increase your productivity rate (point B in Figure 6.1). But initially, you will find it harder to predict the cost and schedule of integrating heterogeneous COTS components with your components and with each other, and your estimation error at point B will go up also.

### VHLL's AND SYSTEMS OF SYSTEMS

This scenario will generally repeat itself at points C and D in Figure 6.1. At point C, you and/or others will know enough about how to compose the domain components to be able to automate their composition, and to provide a domain-specific Very High Level Language (VHLL) with user-oriented terminology to specify the particular application desired. Again, productivity rates will increase (in COCOMO II terms, via the need for much fewer source lines of code), but estimation errors will initially go up also.

At point D, you will find that there is a demand to closely integrate your VHLL-driven robotic devices for, say, subassembly manufacturing, with other VHLL's and application generators for, say, factory control and electronic commerce, into a Total Factory system of systems. Integrating the systems will certainly be more productive than building a whole new Total Factory system, but your error in estimating cost and schedule will be higher than for an individual system. This is because of the uncertainties you will have in estimating the effort required to reconcile the unpredictable incompatibilities in interfaces, priorities, assumptions, and usage conventions among the subassembly manufacturing, factory control, and electronic commerce VHLL's and systems [Maier 1998].

## 6.3   EFFECTS OF INNOVATION AND CHANGE

Other sources of innovation and change may cause changes in the nature of your software projects' product, process, organization, and people. These may improve your organization's overall productivity, but their effect on your projects' practice may again increase your estimation error.

In the area of product technology, such changes have included changes from batch-processing to interactive systems, and from single mainframes to distributed and networked systems. Other product technologies such as graphic user interface (GUI) builders will also increase productivity, but increase estimation error because of new challenges in determining what to count as product size.

In the area of process technology, the charge from waterfall to evolutionary or spiral development requires rethinking of the project's endpoints and phases. Incremental development, rapid application development (RAD), cost-as-independent-variable (CAIV), or schedule-as-independent-variable (SAIV) all cause further rethinking of process strategies, endpoints, and phases. With CAIV or SAIV, for example, you may specify and design more product than you deliver when you run out of budget or schedule. Collaborative processes (Joint Application Development, Integrated Product Team, etc.) require involvement of users, operators, and others in product definition; should their effort be included in the estimate? To what extent will virtual-reality distributed collaboration technology improve software costs and schedules?

In the area of organizations and people, changes in organizational objectives affect products, processes, and estimation accuracy. One example is the increasing emphasis on reducing schedule (time to market) in order to remain competitive, rather than minimizing cost. Another example is the effect of increasing emphasis on software quality as a competitive discriminator.

The effects of having tens of millions of computer-literate people will also change the nature of software products and processes. Also, the increasingly critical nature of software to an organization's competitive success creates stronger needs for integrating software estimates into business-case and financial performance models. And trends toward human economics will affect both software products' required functions and user interfaces.

### ESTIMATION ACCURACY: THE BOTTOM LINE

If only our software engineering domain understanding, product and process technology, and organization and people factors stayed constant, we could get uniformly better and better at estimating. But they don't stay constant, and their changes are generally good for people and organizations. So the need to continually rethink and reengineer our software estimation models is a necessary price to pay for the ability to incorporate software engineering improvements.

## 6.4  COPING WITH CHANGE: COCOMO II

We are trying to ensure that COCOMO II will be adaptive to change by attempting to anticipate future trends in software engineering practice, as in the three-layer model shown in Figure 1.1. The resulting three-stage set of COCOMO II models (Application Composition, Early Design, Post-Architecture) anticipates some dimensions of future change. Other dimensions are addressed by the new or extended cost drivers such as Process Maturity, Architecture and Risk Resolution, Team Cohesion, Multisite Development, Use of Tools, and the various reuse parameters.

We are also attempting to anticipate future trends via our overall Model-Based (System) Architecting and Software Engineering (MBASE) project. The key objective in MBASE is to avoid harmful model clashes by integrating a project's product, process, property, and success models [Boehm-Port 1999a]. The COCOMO II suite of models is our main effort in the property model area. Concurrently, we are integrating complementary research into product models (domain, requirements, and architecture models); process models (WinWin spiral model, process anchor points); and success models (stakeholder win-win, business-case analysis, IKIWISI—I'll know it when I see it—prototyping).

We have been trying to understand and anticipate trends in software engineering product, process, property, and success models via workshops with our Affiliates, via model research, and via model experimentation with our annual series of digital library applications projects using MBASE [Boehm et al. 1998]. For example, our initial formulation of COCOTS was based on an Affiliates' workshop on COTS integration, and on our efforts to incorporate COTS assessment and integration into MBASE extensions of spiral process models and object-oriented product models. Our major refinement of COCOTS into a family of four models was based on analysis of COTS integration experience data from the MBASE digital library projects.

Similarly, our formulation of CORADMO has been based on an Affiliates' RAD (rapid application development) workshop, and on integrating RAD process models such as schedule-as-independent-variable (SAIV) into MBASE. This was done via RAD experimentation using the digital library projects. These projects are good RAD examples, as our semester constraints require them to be fully architected in eleven weeks, and fully developed and transitioned in another twelve weeks.

Thus, the emerging extensions of COCOMO II discussed in Chapter 5 (COCOTS, COQUALMO, COPSEMO, CORADMO, COPROMO, Applications Composition) represent hypotheses of how to model the cost, schedule, and quality effects of current and future trends in software engineering practice. As we gather further data, we will be able to test and refine these models, and to identify further models or extensions likely to be important for future software engineering practice.

## 6.5   COPING WITH CHANGE: COCOMO II AND YOUR ORGANIZATION

COCOMO II can be a useful tool for your organization to use in adapting to future change, both at the project level and at the organizational level.

### 6.5.1    Coping with Change During Project Definition

Figure 6.2 shows how COCOMO II can be used to help address issues of change at the project definition level. Via the COCOMO II parameters, you can enter your organization's customary values, and then indicate which ones will be undergoing change. COCOMO II will then estimate how these changes will affect the project's expected cost and schedule, and will provide you and your stakeholders with a framework for rescoping the project if estimated cost and schedule are unsatisfactory.

### 6.5.2    Coping with Change During Project Execution

Frequently, changes in project objectives, priorities, available componentry, or personnel will occur during project execution. If these are anticipated, COCOMO II can support a variant of the project definition process above to converge on a stakeholder-satisfactory rescoping of the project.

A more serious case occurs when the changes are unanticipated and largely unnoticed. This can frequently happen via personnel changes; COTS product, reusable component, or tool shortfalls; requirements creep; or platform discontinuities. For such cases, the COCOMO II phase and activity distributions can be used to develop a quantitative milestone plan or an earned-value system [Boehm 1981; Chapter 32] for the project. These enable deviations from the plan to be detected, and appropriate corrective actions taken (Figure 6.3). These again may involve the use of COCOMO II in project rescoping.

### 6.5.3    Coping with Required COCOMO II Model Changes

At times, unanticipated project changes are indications that your COCOMO II model needs to be recalibrated or extended. The more management data you collect on actual project costs and schedules, the better you will be able to do this (see Figure 6.4).

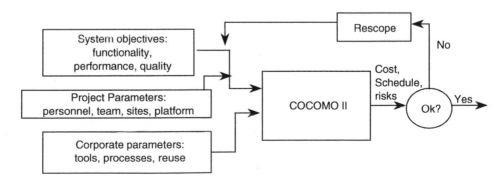

**Figure 6.2**    Using COCOMO II to Cope with Change: I

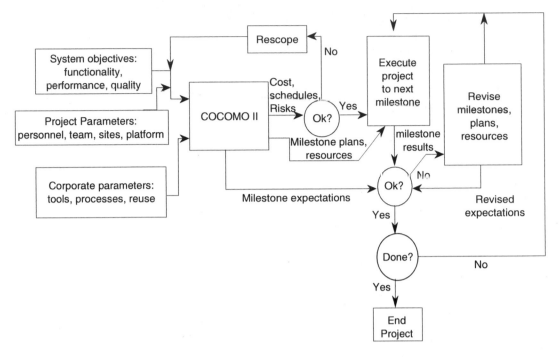

**Figure 6.3**    Using COCOMO II to Cope with Change: II

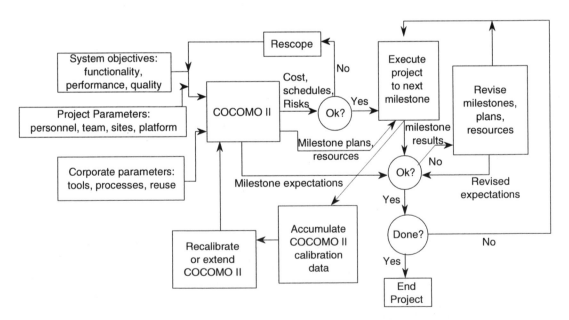

**Figure 6.4**    Using COCOMO II to Cope with Change: III

Recalibration might be appropriate, for example, if your organization is acquired by or merged into an organization with different definitions of project endpoints, or with different definitions of which types of employees are directly-changed to the project vs. being changed to overhead. As described in Chapter 4, techniques are available to recalibrate COCOMO II's base coefficients and exponents for cost and schedule estimation. Some COCOMO II tools such as USC COCOMO II and COSTAR provide such calibration features.

Extending the model will be appropriate if some factor assumed to be constant or insignificant turns out to be a significant cost driver. For example, the COCOMO 81 TOOL Factor was not in the original 1978 TRW version of COCOMO, as previous TRW projects had operated with a relatively uniform set of mainframe tools. The TOOL Factor was added after TRW had completed some microprocessor software projects with unexpectedly high costs. After investigation, the scanty microprocessor tool support was the primary factor that accounted for the extra project effort and cost. Subsequent data from other organizations confirmed the validity of the TOOL variable as a significant COCOMO 81 cost driver.

Similarly, several variables were added to COCOMO 81 to produce COCOMO II, in response to Affiliate indications of need and our confirmation via behavioral analysis.

### 6.5.4   Proactive Organizational Change Management

Your organization will be much better off once it evolves away from reacting to change, and toward proactive anticipation and management of change. This is what Level 5 of the SEI-CMM is all about, particularly the key process areas of Technical Change Management and Process Change Management.

The COCOMO II model and parameters can help you to evaluate candidate change management strategies. For example, investing in sufficient software tool acquisition and training to bring your projects' TOOL rating from Nominal to High will replace a 1.0 effort multiplier by an 0.90, for a 10 percent productivity gain. Similar investments in improving Process Maturity, Architecture and Risk Resolution, Team Cohesion, Multisite Development, reuse, or any of the personnel factors can also have significant benefits that can be investigated via COCOMO II (see Figure 6.5). The cost, schedule, and quality drivers of COCOTS, CORADMO, and COQUALMO can be used similarly.

An integrated capability for using COCOMO II and CORADMO for evaluating the payoff of cost and schedule improvement strategies is provided by the COPROMO extension described in Chapter 5. It enables you to start from a current baseline of cost and schedule drivers from either your own organization's data or the COCOMO II database; and to express candidate cost and schedule improvement strategies in terms of achievable time-phased improvements in cost and schedule drivers. COPROMO will then generate the resulting estimates and provide time histories of cost and schedule improvements for each of the candidate strategies.

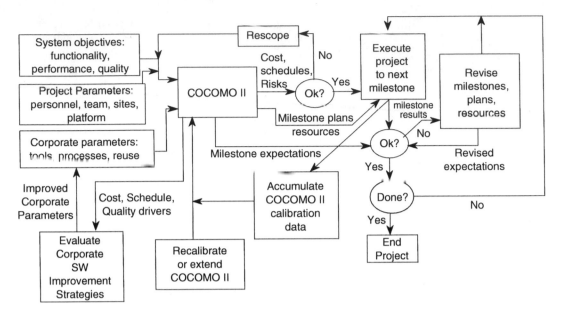

**Figure 6.5**   Using COCOMO II to Cope with Change: IV

Put together, the four COCOMO II feedback cycles in Figure 6.5 can enable your organization to determine and evolve project-level and organization-level sets of project analysis, management, and improvement strategies based on your own quantitative metrics. These strategies will enable you to determine appropriate objectives and approaches for each project, to manage projects to more successful completion, and to improve your organization's software productivity, speed, and quality by anticipating and capitalizing on change rather than being a reactive victim of change.

# A

# COCOMO II: Assumptions and Phase/Activity Distributions

## A.1   INTRODUCTION

Appendix A defines the particular COCOMO II assumptions about what life-cycle phases and labor categories are covered by its effort and schedule estimates. These and other definitions given in Appendix A were used in collecting all the data to which COCOMO II has been calibrated. If you use other definitions and assumptions, you need to either adjust the COCOMO II estimates or recalibrate its coefficients. (Recalibration techniques are provided in Chapter 4.)

COCOMO II has been developed to be usable by projects employing either waterfall or spiral processes. For these to be reasonably compatible, the waterfall implementation needs to be strongly risk-driven, in order to avoid incurring large amounts of rework not included in spiral-model-based estimates. Fortunately, this was the case for the normative waterfall implementation provided in Chapter 4 of [Boehm 1981] as the underlying process model for COCOMO 81.

The implementation of the spiral model used by COCOMO II also needs an added feature: a set of well-defined common milestones which can serve as the end points between which COCOMO II estimates and actuals are assessed. In 1995, we devoted parts of two COCOMO II Affiliates' workshops to determining such milestones. The result was the set of Anchor Point milestones: Life Cycle Objectives (LCO), Life Cycle Architecture (LCA), and Initial Operational Capability (IOC) [Boehm 1996]. Those milestones were a good fit to key life-cycle project commitment points being used within both our commercial and government contractor Affiliate communities. The LCO and LCA milestones involve concurrent rather than sequential development and elaboration of a system's operational concept, requirements, architecture, prototypes, life-cycle plan, and feasibility rationale. The milestones correspond well with real-life commitment milestones: LCO is roughly equivalent to getting engaged; LCA to getting married; and IOC to having your first child.

These anchor points and the stakeholder win-win extension of the spiral model became the key milestones in our Model-Based (System) Architecting and Software Engineering (MBASE) life-cycle process model [Boehm-Port 1999a; Boehm et al. 1999]. We have also collaborated with one of our Affiliates, Rational, Inc., to ensure the compatibility of MBASE and the Rational Unified Process (RUP). Thus, we have adopted Rational's approach to the four main spiral-oriented phases: Inception, Elaboration, Construction, and Transition. Rational has adopted our definitions of the LCO, LCA, and IOC anchor point milestones defining the entry and exit criteria between the phases [Royce 1998; Kruchten 1999; Jacobson et al. 1999].

Section A.2 proceeds to define the content of the milestones used as endpoints for the waterfall and MBASE/RUP spiral models to which COCOMO II project estimates are related. Section A.3 compares the phase distributions of effort and schedule used by COCOMO II for the waterfall and initial MBASE/RUP spiral process models. Section A.4 defines the activity categories for the Waterfall and MBASE/RUP spiral models, and their content. Section A.5 presents the corresponding effort distributions by activity for each Waterfall and MBASE/RUP phase. Section A.6 covers other COCOMO II assumptions, such as the labor categories considered as "project effort," and the number of person-hours in a person-month. Appendix B then builds upon the phase distributions of effort and schedule to provide an estimation model for incremental development.

## A.2   WATERFALL AND MBASE/RUP PHASE DEFINITIONS

### A.2.1   Waterfall Model Phases and Milestones

Table A.1 defines the milestones used as end points for COCOMO II Waterfall phase effort and schedule estimates. The milestone definitions are the same as those in [Boehm 1981; Table A.1].

A basic risk-orientation is provided with the inclusion of "Identification and resolution of all high-risk development issues" as a Product Design milestone element. However, the other early milestones should have a more risk-driven interpretation. For example, having ". . . specifications validated for . . . feasibility" by the end of the Plans and Requirements phase of a user-interactive system development would imply doing an appropriate amount of user-interface prototyping.

**Table A.1   COCOMO II Waterfall Milestones**

1. *Begin Plans and Requirements Phase.* (Completion of Life-Cycle Concept Review—LCR)
   - Approved, validated system architecture, including basic hardware-software allocations.
   - Approved, validated concept of operation, including basic human-machine allocations.
   - Top-level life-cycle plan, including milestones, resources, responsibilities, schedules, and major activities.

2. *End Plans and Requirements Phase. Begin Product Design Phase.* (Completion of Software Requirements Review—SRR)
   - Detailed development plan—detailed development milestone criteria, resource budgets, organization, responsibilities, schedules, activities, techniques, and products.
   - Detailed usage plan—counterparts of the development plan items for training, conversion, installation, operations, and support.
   - Detailed product control plan—configuration management plan, quality assurance plan, overall V&V plan (excluding detailed test plans).
   - Approved, validated software requirements specifications—functional, performance, and interface specifications validated for completeness, consistency, testability, and feasibility.
   - Approved (formal or informal) development contract—based on the above items.

3. *End Product Design Phase. Begin Detailed Design Phase.* (Completion of Product Design Review—PDR)
   - Verified software product design specification.
   - Program component hierarchy, control and data interfaces through unit* level.
   - Physical and logical data structure through field level.
   - Data processing resource budgets (timing, storage, accuracy).
   - Verified for completeness, consistency, feasibility, and traceability to requirements.
   - Identification and resolution of all high-risk development issues.
   - Preliminary integration and test plan, acceptance test plan, and user's manual.

4. *End Detailed Design Phase. Begin Code and Unit Test Phase.* (Completion of design walk-through or Critical Design Review for unit—CDR)
   - Verified detailed design specification for each unit.
   - For each routine ($\leq 100$ source instructions) within the unit, specifies name, purpose, assumptions, sizing, calling sequence, error exits, inputs, outputs, algorithms, and processing flow.
   - Data base description through parameter/character/bit level.
   - Verified for completeness, consistency, and traceability to requirements and system design specifications and budgets.
   - Approved acceptance test plan.
   - Complete draft of integration and test plan and user's manual.

5. *End Code and Unit Test Phase. Begin Integration and Test Phase.* (Satisfaction of Unit Test criteria for unit—UTC)
   - Verification of all unit computations, using not only nominal values but also singular and extreme values.
   - Verification of all unit input and output options, including error messages.
   - Exercise of all executable statements and all branch options.

*(continued)*

- Verification of programming standards compliance.
- Completion of unit-level, as-built documentation.

6. *End Integration and Test Phase. Begin Implementation Phase.* (Completion of Software Acceptance Review—SAR)
   - Satisfaction of software acceptance test.
   - Verification of satisfaction of software requirements.
   - Demonstration of acceptable off-nominal performance as specified.
   - Acceptance of all deliverable software products: reports, manuals, as-built specifications, data bases.

7. *End Implementation Phase. Begin Operations and Maintenance Phase.* (Completion of System Acceptance Review)
   - Satisfaction of system acceptance test.
   - Verification of satisfaction of system requirements.
   - Verification of operational readiness of software, hardware, facilities, and personnel.
   - Acceptance of all deliverable system products: hardware, software, documentation, training, and facilities.
   - Completion of all specified conversion and installation activities.

8. *End Operations and Maintenance Phase* (via Phaseout).
   - Completion of all items in phaseout plan: conversion, documentation, archiving, transition to new system(s).

---

*A software unit performs a single well-defined function, can be developed by one person, and is typically 100 to 300 source instructions in size.

### A.2.2    MBASE and Rational Unified Process (RUP) Phases and Milestones

Table A.2 defines the milestones used as end points for COCOMO II MBASE/ RUP phase effort and schedule estimates [the content of the Life Cycle Objectives (LCO) and Life Cycle Architecture (LCA) milestones are elaborated in Table A.3]. The definitions of the Inception Readiness Review (IRR) and Product Release Review (PRR) have been added in Table A.2. They ensure that the Inception and Transition phases have milestones at each end between which to measure effort and schedule. The PRR is defined consistently with its Rational counterpart in [Royce 1998; Kruchten 1999]. The IRR was previously undefined; its content focuses on the preconditions for a successful Inception phase.

Figure A.1 shows the relationship of the Waterfall and MBASE/RUP phases and the most likely COCOMO II model to be used in estimating effort and schedule. The milestones have some variation due to the differences in distribution of effort and schedule between the two models.

**Table A.2   MBASE and Rational Unified Software Development Process Milestones**

1. *Inception Readiness Review* (IRR)
   - Candidate system objectives, scope, boundary
     - Key stakeholders identified
   - Committed to support Inception phase
   - Resources committed to achieve successful LCO package
2. *Life-Cycle Objectives Review* (LCO)
   - Life-Cycle Objectives (LCO) Package (see Table A.3)
     - Key elements of Operational Concept, Prototype, Requirements, Architecture, Life-Cycle Plan, Feasibility Rationale
   - Feasibility assured for at least one architecture, using the criteria:
     - Acceptable business case
     - A system developed from the architecture would support the operational concept, be compatible with the prototype, satisfy the requirements, and be buildable within the budgets and schedules in the life cycle plan.
   - Feasibility validated by an Architecture Review Board (ARB)
     - ARB includes project-leader peers, architects, specialty experts, key stakeholders [Marenzano 1995].
     - Key stakeholders concur on essentials, commit to support Elaboration phase
   - Resources committed to achieve successful LCA package
3. *Life-Cycle Architecture Review* (LCA)
   - Life-Cycle Architecture (LCA) Package (see Table A.3)
   - Feasibility assured for selected architecture (see above)
   - Feasibility validated by ARB
     - Stakeholders concur on their success-critical items, commit to support Construction, Transition, and Maintenance phases.
     - All major risks resolved or covered by risk management plan
   - Resources committed to achieve Initial Operational Capability (IOC), life-cycle support
4. *Initial Operational Capability* (IOC)
   - *Software preparation*, including both operational and support software with appropriate commentary and documentation; initial data preparation or conversion; the necessary licenses and rights for COTS and reused software, and appropriate operational readiness testing.
   - *Site preparation*, including initial facilities, equipment, supplies, and COTS vendor support arrangements.
   - *Initial user, operator and maintainer preparation*, including selection, teambuilding, training and other qualification for familiarization usage, operations, or maintenance.
   - Successful Transition Readiness Review
     - Plans, preparations for full conversion, installation, training, and operational cutover
     - *Stakeholders confirm commitment to support Transition and Maintenance phases*
5. *Product Release Review* (PRR)
   - Assurance of successful cutover from previous system for key operational sites
   - Personnel fully qualified to operate and maintain new system
   - Stakeholder concurrence that the deployed system operates consistently with negotiated and evolving stakeholder agreements
   - Stakeholders confirm commitment to support Maintenance phase

**Table A.3     Detailed LCO and LCA Milestone Content**

| Milestone Element | Life-Cycle Objectives (LCO) | Life-Cycle Architecture (LCA) |
|---|---|---|
| Definition of Operational Concept | Top-level system objectives and scope<br>System boundary<br>Environment parameters and assumptions<br>Current system shortfalls<br>Operational concept: key nominal scenarios, stakeholder roles and responsibilities | Elaboration of system objectives and scope by increment<br>Elaboration of operational concept by increment<br>Nominal and key off-nominal scenarios |
| System Prototype(s) | Exercise key usage scenarios<br>Resolve critical risks | Exercise range of usage scenarios<br>Resolve major outstanding risks |
| Definition of System and Software Requirements | Top-level capabilities, interfaces, quality attribute levels, including:<br>Evolution requirements<br>Priorities<br>Stakeholders' concurrence on essentials | Elaboration of functions, interfaces, quality attributes by increment<br>Identification of TBDs (to-be-determined items), evolution requirements<br>Stakeholders' concurrence on their priority concerns |
| Definition of System and Software Architecture | Top-level definition of at least one feasible architecture<br>Physical and logical elements and relationships<br>Choices of COTS and reusable software elements<br>Identification of infeasible architecture options | Choice of architecture and elaboration by increment<br>Physical and logical components, connectors, configurations, constraints<br>COTS, reuse choices<br>Domain-architecture and architectural style choices<br>Architecture evolution parameters |
| Definition of Life-cycle Plan | Identification of life-cycle stakeholders<br>Users, customers, developers, maintainers, interfacers, general public, others<br>Identification of life cycle process model<br>Top-level stages, increments<br>Top-level WWWWWHH* by stage | Elaboration of WWWWWHH for Initial Operational Capability (IOC)<br>Partial elaboration, identification of key TBDs for later increments |
| Feasibility Rationale | Assurance of consistency among elements above via analysis, measurement, prototyping, simulation, etc.<br>Business case analysis for requirements, feasible architectures | Assurance of consistency among elements above<br>Rationale for major options rejected<br>All major risks resolved or covered by risk-management plan within the life-cycle plan |

*WWWWWHH: Why, What, When, Who, Where, How, How Much

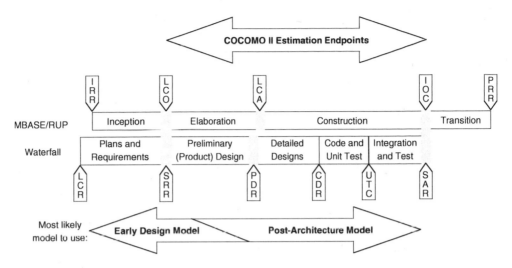

**Figure A.1**   Life-Cycle Phases

## A.3   PHASE DISTRIBUTION OF EFFORT AND SCHEDULE

Provisional phase distributions of effort and schedule are provided below for both the Waterfall and MBASE/RUP process models. These are provisional since not enough calibration data has been collected on phase distributions to date.

The Waterfall phase distribution percentages in Table A.4 are numbers from COCOMO 81 used in USC COCOMO II.2000. The percentages vary as product size varies from 2 KSLOC to 512 KSLOC. The values are taken from the COCOMO 81 Semidetached (average) mode provided in Table 6.8 of [Boehm 1981], except for the Transition phase. This phase was undefined in COCOMO 81 and is set equal to MBASE values in Table A.5. The percentages from PRR to

**Table A.4   Waterfall Phase Distribution Percentages**

| Phase (endpoints) | Effort% | Schedule% |
|---|---|---|
| Plans and Requirements (LCCR-PRR) | 7 (2–15) | 16–24 (2–30) |
| Product Design (PRR-PDR) | 17 | 24–28 |
| Programming (PDR-UTC) | 64–52 | 56–40 |
|    Detailed Design (PDR-CDR) | 27–23 | |
|    Code and Unit Test (CDR-UTC) | 37–29 | |
| Integration and Test (UTC-SWAR) | 19–31 | 20–32 |
| Transition (SWAR-SAR) | 12 (0–20) | 12.5 (0–20) |

**Table A.5      MBASE and RUP Phase Distribution Percentages**

| Phase (end points) | MBASE | | RUP | |
|---|---|---|---|---|
| | Effort% | Schedule% | Effort% | Schedule% |
| Inception (IRR to LCO) | 6 (2–15) | 12.5 (2–30) | 5 | 10 |
| Elaboration (LCO to LCA) | 24 (20–28) | 37.5 (33–42) | 20 | 30 |
| Construction (LCA to IOC) | 76 (72–80) | 62.5 (58–67) | 65 | 50 |
| Transition (IOC to PRR) | 12 (0–20) | 12.5 (0–20) | 10 | 10 |
| Totals: | 118 | 125 | 100 | 100 |

SWAR add up to 100 percent. The percentages for Plans and Requirements and Transition are in addition to the 100 percent of the effort and schedule quantities estimated by COCOMO II.

The MBASE phase distribution percentages in Table A.5 are chosen to be consistent with those provided for the Rational RUP in [Royce 1998] and [Kruchten 1999]. They are rescaled to match the COCOMO II definition that 100 percent of the development effort is done in the Elaboration and Construction phases (between the LCO and IOC milestones, for which most calibration data is available). The corresponding figures for the RUP development cycle are also provided in Table A.5.

### A.3.1   Variations in Effort and Schedule Distributions

The effort and schedule distributions in the Waterfall model vary somewhat by size, primarily reflecting the amount of integration and test required. But the major variations in both the Waterfall model and MBASE/RUP phase effort and schedule quantities come in the phases outside the core development phases (Plans & Requirements and Transition for Waterfall; Inception and Transition for MBASE/RUP).

These large variations are the main reason that the main COCOMO II development estimates do not cover these outer phases (the other strong reason is that calibration data is scanty for the outer phases).

At this time, there is no convenient algorithm for determining whether your Inception phase effort will be nearer to 2 percent than 15 percent and Inception phase schedule will be nearer to 2 percent than 30 percent of the COCOMO II development cost estimates. The best we can offer at this time is Table A.6, which identifies the primary effort and schedule drivers for the Inception and Transition phases.

These are presented in descending order of their effect on Inception phase effort and schedule, and as well as possible in ascending order of their corresponding effect on the Transition phase.

**Table A.6 Inception and Transition Phase Effort and Schedule Drivers**

| Factor | Inception | Transition |
|---|---|---|
| 1. Complexity of LCO issues needing resolution | Very Large | Small |
| 2. System involves major changes in stakeholder roles and responsibilities | Very Large | Large |
| 3. Technical risk level | Large | Some |
| 4. Stakeholder trust level | Large | Considerable |
| 5. Heterogeneous stakeholder communities: Expertise, task nature, language, culture, infrastructure | Large | Large |
| 6. Hardware/software integration | Large | Large |
| 7. Complexity of transition from legacy system | Considerable | Large |
| 8. Number of different installations, classes of installation | Some | Very Large |

**Note:** Order of ratings—Small, Some, Considerable, Large, Very Large

For example, on Factor 1, the stakeholders might enter the Inception phase with a very strong consensus that they wish to migrate some well-defined existing capabilities to a highly feasible client-server architecture. In this case, one could satisfy the LCO criteria with roughly 2 percent each of the development effort and schedule. On the other hand, if the stakeholders entered the Inception phase with strongly conflicting positions on desired capabilities, priorities, infrastructure, etc., it could take up to 15 percent of the development effort and 30 percent of the development schedule to converge to a stakeholder-consensus LCO package.

However, these differences would have a relatively low effect on the amount of effort and schedule it would take to transition the system as defined by the LCO. So the baseline Transition phase percentages of 12 percent added effort and 12.5 percent added schedule would be reasonable initial values to use.

Some of the Inception issues might persist into the Elaboration phase; such persisting issues are the main source of the variations in relative effort and schedule between the Elaboration and Construction phases shown in Table A.5. Thus, if you estimate 30 percent added Inception schedule to achieve a difficult LCO consensus, you may wish to adjust the Elaboration schedule upward from 37.5 percent to something like 42 percent. Factors like your COCOMO II TEAM rating would provide additional total effort and schedule to divide between Elaboration and Construction.

In some cases, a factor can have a strong effect on both the Inception and Transition phases. Factor 2 is an example: If the system's effects involve changes in stakeholder roles and responsibilities (e.g., turf, control, power), the amount of effort and schedule will be increased significantly both in negotiating the changes and implementing them.

Some additional sources of variation in phase distributions are deferred for later versions of COCOMO II. These include phase-dependent effort multipliers (as in Detailed COCOMO 81); effects of language level (reduced Construction effort for very high level languages); and effects of optimizing one's project on development cost, schedule, or quality (partly addressed by CORADMO in Chapter 5).

## A.3.2  Distribution of Effort Across Life Cycle Phases

Figure A.2 shows the Waterfall and MBASE phases for distribution of estimated effort. The Waterfall phase distributions are adapted from those in [Boehm 1981; Table 6.8]. The figure shows that distribution of effort varies by size of the product and the size exponent, $E$. The size exponent $E$ corresponds to the three modes in COCOMO 81. Note that the effort distribution for a small project with a low value for $E$ has the most effort in the Code and Unit Test phase. The top line shows this condition. A large project with a value of $E$ has the most effort concentrated in the Integration and Test phase. This is shown by the bottom line. These distributions of effort are for a Waterfall model project where the development is done in a single sequence through the phases.

The MBASE distribution of effort is taken from Table A.5. The distribution of effort in the table is 72 to 80 percent for the Construction phase which includes

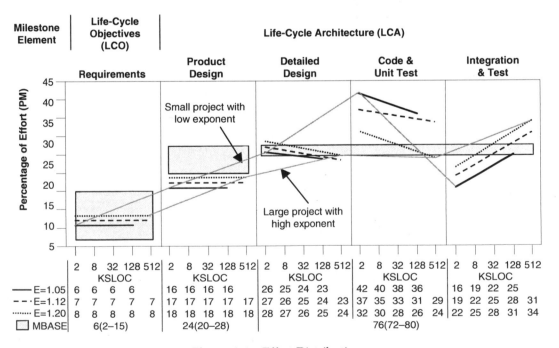

**Figure A.2**   Effort Distribution

Detailed Design, Code and Unit Test, and Integration and Test. The shaded areas in Figure A.2 are approximations of the distribution of the Construction effort.

Contrast the Waterfall distributions with the MBASE/RUP distributions. MBASE/RUP emphasizes planning up front and smaller, repeated iterations to develop the product. This makes the distribution of effort less dependent on size and scale factors. The iterative approach also starts the product integration earlier reducing large-system integration gridlock that can occur if integration is left till the last step (as in the Waterfall model).

### A.3.3   Distribution of Schedule Across Life Cycle Phases

Figure A.3 shows the Waterfall and MBASE phase distribution of estimated schedule. The waterfall distributions are taken from [Boehm 1981; Table 6.8]. As with effort discussed above, schedule varies with size and the scale factor. The two lines bound the range of Waterfall schedule distribution showing a small easy project and a large difficult project.

The MBASE schedule distribution is taken from Table A.5. The shaded areas show the range of distribution for each phase.

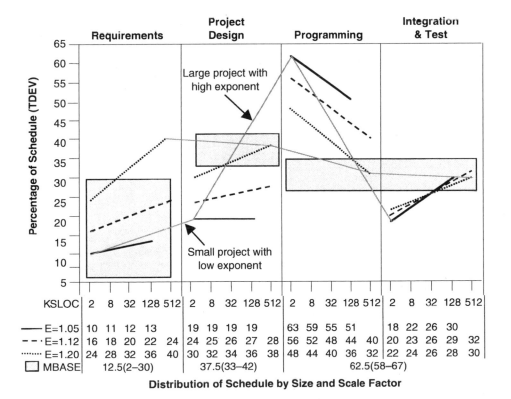

**Figure A.3**   Distribution of Schedule

## A.4    WATERFALL AND MBASE/RUP ACTIVITY DEFINITIONS

### A.4.1    Waterfall Model Activity Categories

The COCOMO II Waterfall model estimates effort for the following eight major activities [Boehm 1981; Table 4.2]:

- *Requirements Analysis*: Determination, specification, review, and update of software functional, performance, interface, and verification requirements.
- *Product Design*: Determination, specification, review, and update of hardware-software architecture, program design, and database design.
- *Programming*: Detailed design, code, unit test, and integration of individual computer program components. Includes programming personnel planning, tool acquisition, database development, component-level documentation, and intermediate level programming management.
- *Test Planning*: Specification, review, and update of product test and acceptance test plans. Acquisition of associated test drivers, test tools, and test data.
- *Verification and Validation*: Performance of independent requirements validation, design V & V, product test, and acceptance test. Acquisition of requirements and design V & V tools.
- *Project Office Functions*: Project-level management functions. Includes project-level planning and control, contract and subcontract management, and customer interface.
- *Configuration Management and Quality Assurance*: Configuration management includes product identification, change control, status accounting, operation of program support library, development and monitoring of end item acceptance plan. Quality assurance includes developing and monitoring project standards, and technical audits of software products and processes.
- *Manuals*: Development and update of users' manuals, operators' manuals, and maintenance manuals.

When the COCOMO II model is used to estimate effort, the estimated effort can be distributed across the major activities. Section A.5 provides the percentage distributions of activity within each phase.

### A.4.2    Waterfall Model Work Breakdown Structure

The COCOMO II Waterfall and MBASE/RUP activity distributions are defined in more detail via work breakdown structures. Table A.7 shows a work breakdown structure outline adapted from [Boehm 1981; Figure 4.6B]. This WBS excludes the requirements-related activities done up to SRR.

**Table A.7    Software Activity Work Breakdown Structure**

1. Management
   1.1. Cost, schedule, performance management
   1.2. Contract Management
   1.3. Subcontract management
   1.4. Customer interface
   1.5. Branch office management
   1.6. Management reviews and audits
2. System Engineering
   2.1. Software Requirements
       2.1.1. Requirements update
   2.2. Software product design
       2.2.1. Design
       2.2.2. Design V & V
       2.2.3. Preliminary design review
       2.2.4. Design update
       2.2.5. Design tools
   2.3. Configuration management
       2.3.1. Program support library
   2.4. End item acceptance
   2.5. Quality assurance
       2.5.1. Standards
3. Programming
   3.1. Detailed design
   3.2. Code and unit test
   3.3. Integration
4. Test and Evaluation
   4.1. Product test
       4.1.1. Plans
       4.1.2. Procedures
       4.1.3. Test
       4.1.4. Reports
   4.2. Acceptance test
       4.2.1. Plans
       4.2.2. Procedures
       4.2.3. Test
       4.2.4. Reports
   4.3. Test support
       4.3.1. Test beds
       4.3.2. Test tools
       4.3.3. Test data
5. Data
   5.1. Manuals

### A.4.3    MBASE/RUP Model Activity Categories

#### A.4.3.1    BACKGROUND

This section defines phase and activity distribution estimators for projects using the life-cycle model provided by USC's Model-Based (System) Architecting and Software Engineering (MBASE) approach and the Rational Unified Process (RUP). Both MBASE and RUP use the same phase definitions and milestones. MBASE has a more explicit emphasis on a stakeholder win-win approach to requirements determination and management. RUP accommodates such an approach but more as an option.

In developing these estimators, we have tried to maintain strong consistency with the published Rational phase and activity distributions in [Royce 1998; Kruchten 1999; and Jacobson et al. 1999], and with the published anchor point/MBASE phase boundary definitions in [Boehm 1996; Boehm-Port 1999a]. We have iterated and merged drafts of the estimators and definitions with Rational.

Our main sources of information on the Rational phase and activity distributions are:

- The common table of default estimators of effort and schedule distribution percentages by phase on page 148 of Royce, page 118 of Kruchten, and page 335 of Jacobson et al.
- The default estimators of total project activity distribution percentages in Table 10.1, page 148 of Royce. These in turn draw on the definitions of the activity categories in Royce's Life-Cycle Phase Emphases (Table 8.1, page 120) and Default Work Breakdown Structure—WBS—(Figure 10.2, pages 144–145).

We and Rational agree that these and the COCOMO table values below cannot fit all project situations, and should be considered as draft values to be adjusted via context and judgement to fit individual projects. As discussed in Section 5.2 on our emerging constructive Phase Schedule and Effort Model (COPSEMO), we have research activities underway to provide stronger guidance on the factors affecting phase and activity distributions.

### A.4.3.2    Phase and Activity Category Definitions

Thus, we have begun with the overall phase and activity distributions in [Royce 1998] and used these to develop a set of default MBASE/RUP phase and activity distributions for use in COCOMO II as a counterpart to those provided for the waterfall model. In the process, we found the need to elaborate a few of the activity-category definitions in Royce's Figure 10.2 (e.g., including configuration management within Environment; adding stakeholder coordination as a Management activity and stakeholder requirements negotiation as a Requirements activity; and including explicit Transition Plan and Evolution Plan activities in

Deployment). We also modified a few definitions and allocations (using "evolution" in place of "maintenance;" splitting "Business case development" and "Business case analysis" between Management and Assessment).

For comparison, we have reproduced Royce's WBS as Table A.8 and provided the counterpart COCOMO II WBS as Table A.9. We have also orthogonal-

---

**Table A.8   Rational Unified Process Default Work Breakdown Structure [Royce, 1998]**

A Management
    AA Inception phase management
        AAA Business case development
        AAB Elaboration phase release specifications
        AAC Elaboration phase WBS* baselining
        AAD Software development plan
        AAE Inception phase project control and status assessments
    AB Elaboration phase management
        ABA Construction phase release specifications
        ABB Construction phase WBS baselining
        ABC Elaboration phase project control and status assessments
    AC Construction phase management
        ACA Deployment phase planning
        ACB Deployment phase WBS baselining
        ACC Construction phase project control and status assessments
    AD Transition phase management
        ADA Next generation planning
        ADB Transition phase project control and status assessments

B Environment
    BA Inception phase environment specification
    BB Elaboration phase environment baselining
        BBA Development environment installation and administration
        BBB Development environment integration and custom toolsmithing
        BBC SCO* database formulation
    BC Construction phase environment maintenance
        BCA Development environment installation and administration
        BCB SCO database maintenance
    BD Transition phase environment maintenance
        BDA Development environment maintenance and administration
        BDB SCO database maintenance
        BDC Maintenance environment packaging and transition

C Requirements
    CA Inception phase requirements development
        CAA Vision specification
        CAB Use case modeling
    CB Elaboration phase requirements baselining
        CBA Vision baselining
        CBB Use case model baselining                                          *(continued)*

**Table A.8** *Continued*

---

    CC Construction phase requirements maintenance
    CD Transition phase requirements maintenance

D Design
    DA Inception phase architecture prototyping
    DB Elaboration phase architecture baselining
        DBA Architecture design modeling
        DBB Design demonstration planning and conduct
        DBC Software architecture description
    DC Construction phase design modeling
        DCA Architecture design model maintenance
        DCB Component design modeling
    DD Transition phase design maintenance

E Implementation
    EA Inception phase component prototyping
    EB Elaboration phase component implementation
        EBA Critical component coding demonstration integration
    EC Construction phase component implementation
        ECA Initial release(s) component coding and stand-alone testing
        ECB Alpha release component coding and stand-alone testing
        ECC Beta release component coding and stand-alone testing
        ECD Component maintenance
    ED Transition phase component maintenance

F Assessment
    FA Inception phase assessment planning
    FB Elaboration phase assessment
        FBA Test modeling
        FBB Architecture test scenario implementation
        FBC Demonstration assessment and release descriptions
    FC Construction phase assessment
        FCA Initial release assessment and release description
        FCB Alpha release assessment and release description
        FCC Beta release assessment and release description
    FD Transition phase assessment
        FDA product release assessment and release descriptions

G Deployment
    GA Inception phase deployment planning
    GB Elaboration phase deployment planning
    GC Construction phase deployment
        GCA User manual baselining
    GD Transition phase deployment
        GDA Product transition to user

*Acronyms
SCO—Software Change Order
WBS—Work Breakdown Structure

**Table A.9 COCOMO II MBASE/RUP Default Work Breakdown Structure**

A Management
    AA Inception phase management
        AAA Top-level Life-Cycle Plan (LCO* version of LCP*)
        AAB Inception phase project control and status assessments
        AAC Inception phase stakeholder coordination and business case development
        AAD Elaboration phase commitment package and review (LCO package preparation and ARB* review)
    AB Elaboration phase management
        ABA Updated LCP with detailed Construction plan (LCA* version of LCP)
        ABB Elaboration phase project control and status assessments
        ABC Elaboration phase stakeholder coordination and business case update
        ABD Construction phase commitment package and review (LCA package preparation and ARB review)
    AC Construction phase management
        ACA Updated LCP with detailed Transition and Maintenance plans
        ACB Construction phase project control and status assessments
        ACC Construction phase stakeholder coordination
        ACD Transition phase commitment package and review (IOC* package preparation and PRB review)
    AD Transition phase management
        ADA Updated LCP with detailed next-generation planning
        ADB Transition phase project control and status assessments
        ADC Transition phase stakeholder coordination
        ADD Maintenance phase commitment package and review (PR* package preparation and PRB* review)

B Environment and Configuration Management (CM)
    BA Inception phase environment/CM scoping and initialization
    BB Elaboration phase environment/CM
        BBA Development environment installation and administration
        BBB Elaboration phase CM
        BBC Development environment integration and custom toolsmithing
    BC Construction phase environment/CM evolution
        BCA Construction phase environment evolution
        BCB Construction phase CM
    BD Transition phase environment/CM evolution
        BDA Construction phase environment evolution
        BDB Transition phase CM
        BDC Maintenance phase environment packaging and transition

C Requirements
    CA Inception phase requirements development
        CAA Operational Concept Description and business modeling (LCO version of OCD*)
        CAB Top-level System and Software Requirements Definition (LCO version of SSRD*)
        CAC Initial stakeholder requirements negotiation
    CB Elaboration phase requirements baselining
        CBA OCD elaboration and baselining (LCA version of OCD)
        CBB SSRD elaboration and baselining (LCA version of SSRD)      *(continued)*

**Table A.9** *Continued*

CC Construction phase requirements evolution
CD Transition phase requirements evolution

D Design
DA Inception phase architecting
DAA Top-level System and Software Architecture Description (LCO version of SSAD*)
DAB Evaluation of candidate COTS* components
DB Elaboration phase architecture baselining
DBA SSAD elaboration and baselining
DBB COTS integration assurance and baselining
DC Construction phase design
DCA SSAD evolution
DCB COTS integration evolution
DCC Component design
DD Transition phase design evolution

E Implementation
EA Inception phase prototyping
EB Elaboration phase component implementation
EBA Critical component implementation
EC Construction phase component implementation
ECA Alpha release component coding and stand-alone testing
ECB Beta release (IOC) component coding and stand-alone testing
ECC Component evolution
ED Transition phase component evolution

F Assessment
FA Inception phase assessment
FAA Initial assessment plan (LCO version; part of LCP*)
FAB Initial Feasibility Rationale Description (LCO version of FRD*)
FAC Inception phase element-level inspections and peer reviews
FAD Business case analysis (part of FRD)
FB Elaboration phase assessment
FBA Elaboration of assessment plan (LCA version; part of LCP)
FBB Elaboration of feasibility rationale (LCA version of FRD)
FBC Elaboration phase element-level inspections and peer reviews
FBD Business case analysis update
FC Construction phase assessment
FCA Detailed test plans and procedures
FCB Evolution of feasibility rationale
FCC Construction phase element-level inspections and peer reviews
FCD Alpha release assessment
FCE Beta release (IOC) assessment
FD Transition phase assessment

G Deployment
GA Inception phase deployment planning (LCO version; part of LCP)
GB Elaboration phase deployment planning (LCA version; part of LCP)

GC Construction phase deployment planning and preparation
   GCA Transition plan development
   GCB Evolution plan development
   GCC Transition preparation
GD Transition phase deployment

*Acronyms
   ARB—Architecture Review Board
   CM—Configuration Management
   COTS—Commercial-Off-The-Shelf
   FRD—Feasibility Rationale Description
   IOC—Initial Operational Capability milestone
   LCA—Life-Cycle Architecture milestone
   LCO—Life-Cycle Objectives milestone
   LCP—Life-Cycle Plan
   OCD—Operational Concept Description
   PR—Product Release milestone
   PRB—Product Release Board
   SSAD—System and Software Architecture Description
   SSRD—System and Software Requirements Definition

---

ized the WBS organization in Table A.9 (e.g., for each phase X, the planning WBS element is AXA and the control element is AXB), and provided more explicit categories corresponding to the Level 2 and 3 project-oriented Key Process Areas in the SEI Capability Maturity model. An exception is Software Quality Assurance, where we agree with Royce that all activities and all people are involved in SQA, and that a separate WBS element for QA is inappropriate.

## A.5   DISTRIBUTION OF EFFORT ACROSS ACTIVITIES

### A.5.1   Waterfall Model Activity Distribution

Tables A.10a through A.10d, adapted from [Boehm 1981; Tables 7.1, 7.2, 7.3], show the distribution of eight major activities (discussed in Section A.4.1) across the estimated project effort per phase. The activity distribution values are interpolated for projects that are between values in the table.

For example, a project with size 128 KSLOC and an exponent of 1.12 would spend 28 percent of its effort in Integration and Test, see Table A.10d Overall Phase Percentage row. From Table A.10d we see that the Requirement Analysis activity takes 2.5 percent of the 28 percent, Product Design takes 5 percent of the 28 percent, Programming takes 39 percent of the 28 percent, and so on. We see that the activity tables break up the estimated effort for a phase into the different activities that occur during the phase.

## Table A.10a  Plans and Requirements Activity Distribution

|  | Size Exponent | | | | | | | | | | | | | |
|---|---|---|---|---|---|---|---|---|---|---|---|---|---|---|
|  | E = 1.05 | | | | E = 1.12 | | | | | E = 1.20 | | | | |
| Size:<br>Overall<br>Phase<br>Percentage | S | I | M | L | S | I | M | L | VL | S | I | M | L | VL |
|  |  |  | 6 |  | 7 | 7 | 7 | 7 | 7 | 8 | 8 | 8 | 8 | 8 |
| Requirements Analysis |  |  | 46 |  | 48 | 47 | 46 | 45 | 44 | 50 | 48 | 46 | 44 | 42 |
| Product Design |  |  | 20 |  | 16 | 16.5 | 17 | 17.5 | 18 | 12 | 13 | 14 | 15 | 16 |
| Programming |  |  | 3 |  | 2.5 | 3.5 | 4.5 | 5.5 | 6.5 | 2 | 4 | 6 | 8 | 10 |
| Test Planning |  |  | 3 |  | 2.5 | 3 | 3.5 | 4 | 4.5 | 2 | 3 | 4 | 5 | 6 |
| V&V |  |  | 6 |  | 6 | 6.5 | 7 | 7.5 | 8 | 6 | 7 | 8 | 9 | 10 |
| Project Office |  |  | 15 |  | 15.5 | 14.5 | 13.5 | 12.5 | 11.5 | 16 | 14 | 12 | 10 | 8 |
| CM/QA |  |  | 2 |  | 3.5 | 3 | 3 | 3 | 2.5 | 5 | 4 | 4 | 4 | 3 |
| Manuals |  |  | 5 |  | 6 | 6 | 5.5 | 5 | 5 | 7 | 7 | 6 | 5 | 5 |

S: 2 KSLOC; I: 8 KSLOC; M: 32 KSLOC; L: 128 KSLOC; VL: 512 KSLOC


## Table A.10b  Product Design Activity Distribution

|  | Size Exponent | | | | | | | | | | | | | |
|---|---|---|---|---|---|---|---|---|---|---|---|---|---|---|
|  | E = 1.05 | | | | E = 1.12 | | | | | E = 1.20 | | | | |
| Size:<br>Overall<br>Phase<br>Percentage | S | I | M | L | S | I | M | L | VL | S | I | M | L | VL |
|  |  |  | 16 |  | 17 | 17 | 17 | 17 | 17 | 18 | 18 | 18 | 18 | 18 |
| Requirements Analysis |  |  | 15 |  | 12.5 | 12.5 | 12.5 | 12.5 | 12.5 | 10 | 10 | 10 | 10 | 10 |
| Product Design |  |  | 40 |  | 41 | 41 | 41 | 41 | 41 | 42 | 42 | 42 | 42 | 42 |
| Programming |  |  | 14 |  | 12 | 12.5 | 13 | 13.5 | 14 | 10 | 11 | 12 | 13 | 14 |
| Test Planning |  |  | 5 |  | 4.5 | 5 | 5.5 | 6 | 6.5 | 4 | 5 | 6 | 7 | 8 |
| V&V |  |  | 6 |  | 6 | 6.5 | 7 | 7.5 | 8 | 6 | 7 | 8 | 9 | 10 |
| Project Office |  |  | 11 |  | 13 | 12 | 11 | 10 | 9 | 15 | 13 | 11 | 9 | 7 |
| CM/QA |  |  | 2 |  | 3 | 2.5 | 2.5 | 2.5 | 2 | 4 | 3 | 3 | 3 | 2 |
| Manuals |  |  | 7 |  | 8 | 8 | 7.5 | 7 | 7 | 9 | 9 | 8 | 7 | 7 |

S: 2 KSLOC; I: 8 KSLOC; M: 32 KSLOC; L: 128 KSLOC; VL: 512 KSLOC

**Table A.10c  Programming Activity Distribution**

| Size: Overall Phase Percentage | Size Exponent | | | | | | | | | | | | | |
|---|---|---|---|---|---|---|---|---|---|---|---|---|---|---|
| | E = 1.05 | | | | E = 1.12 | | | | | E = 1.20 | | | | |
| | S | I | M | L | S | I | M | L | VL | S | I | M | L | VL |
| | 68 | 65 | 62 | 59 | 64 | 61 | 58 | 55 | 52 | 60 | 57 | 54 | 51 | 48 |
| Requirements Analysis | | | 5 | | 4 | 4 | 4 | 4 | 4 | 3 | 3 | 3 | 3 | 3 |
| Product Design | | | 10 | | 8 | 8 | 8 | 8 | 8 | 6 | 6 | 6 | 6 | 6 |
| Programming | | | 58 | | 56.5 | 56.5 | 56.5 | 56.5 | 56.5 | 55 | 55 | 55 | 55 | 55 |
| Test Planning | | | 4 | | 4 | 4.5 | 5 | 5.5 | 6 | 4 | 5 | 6 | 7 | 8 |
| V&V | | | 6 | | 7 | 7.5 | 8 | 8.5 | 9 | 8 | 9 | 10 | 11 | 12 |
| Project Office | | | 6 | | 7.5 | 7 | 6.5 | 6 | 5.5 | 9 | 8 | 7 | 6 | 5 |
| CM/QA | | | 6 | | 7 | 6.5 | 6.5 | 6.5 | 6 | 8 | 7 | 7 | 7 | 6 |
| Manuals | | | 5 | | 6 | 6 | 5.5 | 5 | 5 | 7 | 7 | 6 | 5 | 5 |

S: 2 KSLOC; I: 8 KSLOC; M: 32 KSLOC; L: 128 KSLOC; VL: 512 KSLOC

**Table A.10d  Integration and Test Activity Distribution**

| Size: Overall Phase Percentage | Size Exponent | | | | | | | | | | | | | |
|---|---|---|---|---|---|---|---|---|---|---|---|---|---|---|
| | E = 1.05 | | | | E = 1.12 | | | | | E = 1.20 | | | | |
| | S | I | M | L | S | I | M | L | VL | S | I | M | L | VL |
| | 16 | 19 | 22 | 25 | 19 | 22 | 25 | 28 | 31 | 22 | 25 | 28 | 31 | 34 |
| Requirements Analysis | | | 3 | | 2.5 | 2.5 | 2.5 | 2.5 | 2.5 | 2 | 2 | 2 | 2 | 2 |
| Product Design | | | 6 | | 5 | 5 | 5 | 5 | 5 | 4 | 4 | 4 | 4 | 4 |
| Programming | | | 34 | | 33 | 35 | 37 | 39 | 41 | 32 | 36 | 40 | 44 | 48 |
| Test Planning | | | 2 | | 2.5 | 2.5 | 3 | 3 | 3.5 | 3 | 3 | 4 | 4 | 5 |
| V&V | | | 34 | | 32 | 31 | 29.5 | 28.5 | 27 | 30 | 28 | 25 | 23 | 20 |
| Project Office | | | 7 | | 8.5 | 8 | 7.5 | 7 | 6.5 | 10 | 9 | 8 | 7 | 6 |
| CM/QA | | | 7 | | 8.5 | 8 | 8 | 8 | 7.5 | 10 | 9 | 9 | 9 | 8 |
| Manuals | | | 7 | | 8 | 8 | 7.5 | 7 | 7 | 9 | 9 | 8 | 7 | 7 |

S: 2 KSLOC; I: 8 KSLOC; M: 32 KSLOC; L: 128 KSLOC; VL: 512 KSLOC

The last two activity tables handle the situation where development, Table A.10e or maintenance, Table A.10f is performed as a level of effort. In other words, there is a fixed amount of staff that will be working on the project and the eight major activities are divided among the fixed staffing.

As an example, a maintenance project has 10 staff for 12 months (120 PM), a size of 8 KSLOC, and an exponent of 1.20. From Table A.10f we see that Requirements Analysis will consume 6 percent of the staff's effort or 7.2 PM, Program Design will consume 11 percent of the staff's effort or 13.2 PM, Programming will consume 39 percent of the staff's effort or 46.8 PM, and so on.

### A.5.2    MBASE/RUP Model Activity Distribution Values

Table A.11 shows the resulting COCOMO II MBASE/RUP default phase and activity distribution values. The first two lines show the Rational and COCOMO II schedule percentages by phase. Their only difference is that the Rational percentages sum to 100 percent for the full set of Inception, Elaboration, Construction, and Transition phases (IECT), while COCOMO II counts the core Elaboration and Construction phases as 100 percent. This is done because the scope and duration of the Inception and Transition phases are much more variable, and because less data is available to calibrate estimation models for these phases. For COCOMO II, this means that the current model covering the Elaboration and Construction

**Table A.10e    Development Activity Distribution**

| | Size Exponent | | | | | | | | | | | | | |
| | E = 1.05 | | | | E = 1.12 | | | | | E = 1.20 | | | | |
| Size: | S | I | M | L | S | I | M | L | VL | S | I | M | L | VL |
|---|---|---|---|---|---|---|---|---|---|---|---|---|---|---|
| Requirements Analysis | | | 6 | | 5 | 5 | 5 | 5 | 5 | 4 | 4 | 4 | 4 | 4 |
| Product Design | | | 14 | | 13 | 13 | 13 | 13 | 13 | 12 | 12 | 12 | 12 | 12 |
| Programming | 48 | 47 | 46 | 45 | 45 | 45 | 44.5 | 44.5 | 44.5 | 42 | 43 | 43 | 44 | 45 |
| Test Planning | | | 4 | | 4 | 4 | 4.5 | 5 | 5.5 | 4 | 4 | 5 | 6 | 7 |
| V&V | 10 | 11 | 12 | 13 | 11 | 12 | 13 | 13.5 | 14 | 12 | 13 | 14 | 14 | 14 |
| Project Office | | | 7 | | 8.5 | 8 | 7.5 | 7 | 6.5 | 10 | 9 | 8 | 7 | 6 |
| CM/QA | | | 5 | | 6.5 | 6 | 6 | 6 | 5.5 | 8 | 7 | 7 | 7 | 6 |
| Manuals | | | 6 | | 7 | 7 | 6.6 | 6 | 6 | 8 | 8 | 7 | 6 | 6 |

S: 2 KSLOC; I: 8 KSLOC; M: 32 KSLOC; L: 128 KSLOC; VL: 512 KSLOC

**Table A.10f   Maintenance Activity Distribution**

| | Size Exponent | | | | | | | | | | | | | |
|---|---|---|---|---|---|---|---|---|---|---|---|---|---|---|
| | E = 1.05 | | | | E = 1.12 | | | | | E = 1.20 | | | | |
| Size: | S | I | M | L | S | I | M | L | VL | S | I | M | L | VL |
| Requirements Analysis | | | 7 | | 6.5 | 6.5 | 6.5 | 6 | 6 | 6 | 6 | 6 | 5 | 5 |
| Product Design | | | 13 | | 12 | 12 | 12 | 12 | 12 | 11 | 11 | 11 | 11 | 11 |
| Programming | 45 | 44 | 43 | 42 | 41.5 | 41.5 | 41 | 41 | 41 | 38 | 39 | 39 | 40 | 41 |
| Test Planning | | | 3 | | 3 | 3 | 3.5 | 4 | 4.5 | 3 | 3 | 4 | 5 | 6 |
| V&V | 10 | 11 | 12 | 13 | 11 | 12 | 13 | 13.5 | 14 | 12 | 13 | 14 | 14 | 14 |
| Project Office | | | 7 | | 8.5 | 8 | 7.5 | 7 | 6.6 | 10 | 9 | 8 | 7 | 6 |
| CM/QA | | | 5 | | 6.5 | 6 | 6 | 6 | 5.5 | 8 | 7 | 7 | 7 | 6 |
| Manuals | | | 10 | | 11 | 11 | 10.5 | 10.5 | 10.5 | 12 | 12 | 11 | 11 | 11 |

S: 2 KSLOC; I: 8 KSLOC; M: 32 KSLOC; L: 128 KSLOC; VL: 512 KSLOC

phases is considerably more accurate and robust than we could achieve with counterpart models that would include the Inception and/or Transition phases.

Lines 1 and 2 in Table A.11 show the Rational and COCOMO II phase distributions for the project's schedule in months. Lines 3 and 4 in Table A.11 show the corresponding phase distributions for effort. The sum of the COCOMO II percentages for the total IECT project span is 125 percent for schedule and 118 percent for effort.

Lines 6 to 12 in Table A.11 show the default percentage of effort by activity for each of the MBASE/RUP phases. For example, the Management activities are estimated to consume 14 percent of the effort in the Inception phase, 12 percent in the Elaboration phase, 10 percent in Construction, and 14 percent in Transition. For the total IECT span, the Management activities consume

$$(14\%)(6\%) + (12\%)(24\%) + (10\%)(76\%) + (14\%)(12\%) = 13\%$$

This sum is slightly larger but quite comparable to the IECT percentage of 12 percent derived from Royce's Table 10-1. The WBS definitions in Tables A.8 and A.9 are sufficiently similar that the values in Table A.11 can be applied equally well to both.

These values can be used to determine draft project staffing plans for each of the phases. For example, the 100 KSLOC, all nominal manufacturing control system (MCS) used as an example in Section 2.6 had an estimated development

**Table A.11 COCOMO II MBASE/RUP Phase and Activity Distribution Values**

| | Development | | | | Royce | Total COCOMO II | Total Maint. |
|---|---|---|---|---|---|---|---|
| | Inception | Elaboration | Construction | Transition | | | |
| Rational Schedule | 10 | 30 | 50 | 10 | 100 | | |
| COCOMO II Schedule | 12.5 | 37.5 | 62.5 | 12.5 | | 125 | |
| Rational Effort | 5 | 20 | 65 | 10 | 100 | | |
| COCOMO II Effort | 6 | 24 | 76 | 12 | | 118 | 100 |
| Activity % of phase/IECT | 100 | 100 | 100 | 100 | | 118 | 118 |
| Management | 14 | 12 | 10 | 14 | 12 | 13 | 11 |
| Environment/CM | 10 | 8 | 5 | 5 | 12 | 7 | 6 |
| Requirements | 38 | 18 | 8 | 4 | 12 | 13 | 12 |
| Design | 19 | 36 | 16 | 4 | 18 | 22 | 17 |
| Implementation | 8 | 13 | 34 | 19 | 29 | 32 | 24 |
| Assessment | 8 | 10 | 24 | 24 | 29 | 24 | 22 |
| Deployment | 3 | 3 | 3 | 30 | 6 | 7 | 8 |

effort of 466 PM and an estimated schedule of 26 months. From lines 2 and 4 of Table A.11, we can compute the estimated schedule and effort of the Construction phase as:

$$\text{Schedule: } (26 \text{ Mo.}) (.625) = 16.25 \text{ Mo.}$$
$$\text{Effort: } (466 \text{ PM}) (.76) = 354 \text{ PM}$$

The average staff level of the Construction phase is thus:

$$354 \text{ PM} / 16.25 \text{ Mo.} = 21.8 \text{ persons.}$$

We can then use lines 6 to 12 of Table A.11 to provide a draft estimate of what these 21.8 persons will be doing during the Construction phase. For example, the estimated average number of personnel performing Management activities is:

$$(21.8 \text{ persons}) (.10) = 2.2 \text{ persons}$$

Table A.12 shows the full set of draft activity estimates for the Construction phase.

These staffing estimates can be used for other purposes as well. When multiplied by associated average labor costs for activity categories, they can be used as starting points for project WBS and budget allocations, or for earned values associated with phase deliverables.

It is important to understand that these numbers are just draft starting points for the actual numbers you use to manage your project. Every project will have special circumstances which should be considered in adjusting the draft values (see also [Royce 1998, p. 218], [Kruchten 1999, pp. 118–119], and [Jacobson et al. 1999, p. 336]). For example, an ultra-reliable product will have higher Assessment efforts and costs; a project with a stable environment already in place will have lower up-front Environment efforts and costs. The COCOMO II re-

**Table A.12   Example Staffing Estimate for MCS Construction Phase**

| Activity | % | Ave. Staff |
|---|---|---|
| Total | 100 | 21.8 |
| Management | 10 | 2.2 |
| Environment | 5 | 1.1 |
| Requirements | 8 | 1.7 |
| Design | 16 | 3.5 |
| Implementation | 34 | 7.4 |
| Assessment | 24 | 5.2 |
| Deployment | 3 | 0.7 |

search agenda includes activities to provide further guidelines for adjusting the phase and activity distributions to special circumstances. Even then, however, the estimated phase and activity distribution numbers should be subject to critical review. As with other COCOMO II estimates, the phase and activity distribution estimates should be considered as a stimulus to thought, and not as a substitute for thought.

## A.6   DEFINITIONS AND ASSUMPTIONS

COCOMO II's definitions and assumptions are similar to those for COCOMO 81 [Boehm 1981, pp. 58–61], but with some differences. Here is a summary of similarities and differences:

1. *Sizing.* COCOMO 81 just used Delivered Source Instructions for sizing. COCOMO II uses combinations of Function Points (FP) and Source Lines of Code for the Early Design and Post-Architecture models, with counting rules in [IFPUG 1994] for FP and Chapter 2 for SLOC. The emerging Applications Composition model uses Application Points for sizing, as defined in Section 5.1.

2. *Development Periods Included.* For the Waterfall process model, COCOMO II uses the same milestone endpoints (Software Requirements Review to Software Acceptance Review) as COCOMO 81. For the MBASE/RUP process model, COCOMO II uses the Life Cycle Objectives and Initial Operational Capability milestone as endpoints for counting effort and schedule. Details for both are in Appendix A.2.

3. *Project Activities Included.* For the Waterfall process model, COCOMO II includes the same activities as did COCOMO 81. For the MBASE and RUP process models, the Work Breakdown Structures in Appendix A.4 define the project activities included by phase. For all the models, all software development activities such as documentation, planning and control, and configuration management (CM) are included, while database administration is not. For all the models, the software portions of a hardware-software project are included (e.g., software CM, software project management) but general CM and management are not. Both models have add-on efforts for a front-end phase (Plans and Requirements for COCOMO 81; Inception for (MBASE/RUP). COCOMO II differs from COCOMO 81 in having add-on efforts for a back-end Transition phase, including conversion, installation, and training. As discussed in Appendix A.3 the size of these add-on efforts can vary a great deal, and their effort estimates should be adjusted for particularly small or large add-on endeavors.

4. *Labor Categories Included.* COCOMO 81 and COCOMO II estimates both use the same definitions of labor categories included as direct-charged project

effort vs. overhead effort. Thus, they include project managers and program librarians, but exclude computer center operators, personnel-department personnel, secretaries, higher management, janitors, and so on.

5. *Dollar Estimates.* COCOMO 81 and COCOMO II avoid estimating labor costs in dollars because of the large variations between organizations in what is included in labor costs, e.g., unburdened (by overhead cost), burdened, including pension plans, office rental, and profit margin. Person-months are a more stable quantity than dollars given current inflation rates and international money fluctuations.

6. *Person-month Definition.* A COCOMO PM consists of 152 hours of working time. This has been found to be consistent with practical experience with the average monthly time off because of holidays, vacation, and sick leave. To convert a COCOMO estimate in PM to other units, use the following:

Person-hours: multiply by 152

Person-days: multiply by 19

Person-years: divide by 12

Some implementations, such as USC COCOMO II, provide an adjustable parameter for the number of person-hours per person-month. Thus, if you enter 137 (10 percent less) for this parameter, USC COCOMO II will increase your PM estimate by 10 percent, and calculate an appropriately longer development schedule.

# B

# COCOMO II: Estimating for Incremental Development

## B.1  INTRODUCTION

An incremental development estimation model was developed for Ada CO-COMO in [Boehm-Royce 1989] and expanded into a scheme for subcomponents in [Ligett 1993]. It is available in at least one of the commercial COCOMO implementations, COSTAR [Ligett 2000]. A variant of the incremental model is presented here based on an extension of the MBASE/RUP phase distributions discussed in Appendix A.

Incremental software development is gaining wide acceptance as an approach to handle delivering parts of the software product early. This has several advantages:

- Breaking the project into understandable and manageable pieces—separation of concerns
- Early customer and user review of some product functionality
- Reduction of risk in delivering the wrong product
- Final product integration reduced due to earlier integration work
- More level staffing profile
- Earlier initial capability but a longer schedule and more effort for final capability

There are three development strategies for using incremental development. The first strategy is described as incremental delivery. A portion of the software system capabilities are developed and delivered. This type of development takes the software from requirements all the way through to on-site installation. Succeeding increments use the previous increment's software product to begin development in a way that accommodates user feedback. This strategy has added costs because each increment goes through system testing and delivery, and because later increments may cause significant breakage in the already-installed increments.

The second strategy is incremental development based on builds. A piece of the software product is built in each increment. Each increment is integrated or assembled with the pieces constructed in previous increments. With this strategy each succeeding increment may also cause some of the software built in previous increments to be modified, but the modifications are to a system under development rather than to a system in operational use. Think of this as software that is divided up as pieces of a building. The building is constructed one room at a time, but before people have started to live or work in the rooms completed so far.

The third strategy is described as incremental development where the requirements, software architecture, and critical infrastructure are solidified before work on the application increments begins. Each increment can have multiple modules that proceed through software integration and test, often including friendly-user experimental usage in representative situations. This strategy does not include full system integration and test, customer/user transition, or other later phases. Each increment builds on the software developed in previous increments. An increment's integration and test phase integrates the software from all previous increments, i.e., the entire software is retested. Think of this as software that starts out as the architecture, framework, and infrastructure for a building, and each succeeding increment increases the amount of the building that has been outfitted for particular uses. This strategy is the one described in this appendix.

The primary estimating difference between traditional full and incremental approaches is that the full approach requires a monolithic estimate of effort and schedule which assumes that detailed design, code, integration and test are carried out sequentially for the entire product. The full approach generates uneven levels of effort during different phases. The incremental approach breaks the later phases into a series of increments in which part of the product is developed and tested. This levels-out effort by using overlapping phases to make the level of effort more even.

## B.2  INCREMENTAL DEVELOPMENT MODEL

The traditional full product development schedule is shown at the top of Figure B.1 (see Appendix A.2.2 for a description of each phase and milestone). The lower part of the figure shows the full development broken into three increments. The first increment carries most of the Product Design phase where the product architecture and interfaces are established. Each succeeding increment briefly revisits

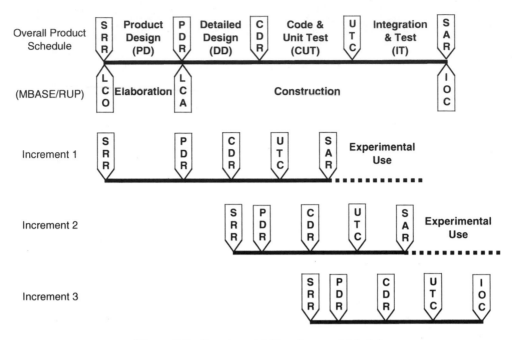

**Figure B.1**   Incremental Development Model

the Product Design phase (about 25 percent of the nominal phase length) for up-dates to the architecture and interfaces.

Increments can start at any milestone, $M_{START}$, from the previous increment. This is discussed in Section B.5. In this example all increments have to start on the same milestone (in reality, project characteristics may make this infeasible). A delay can be introduced if the following increment has to start later than $M_{START}$. The example in Figure B.1 defines $M_{START}$ for succeeding increments to be at the Critical Design Review (CDR) of the previous increment, and for each increment to repeat 25 percent its Product Design activity. Additional parameters in the [Boehm-Royce 1989] model enable these assumptions to be generalized.

Estimation of effort and schedule rely on knowing the requirements for the software project. The incremental estimation model for the MBASE/RUP process assumes that a *full* Life-Cycle Architecture package definition is almost completed before starting on remaining increments. This is reflected by Figure B.1 showing the MBASE/RUP Elaboration phase or the product design phase for the first increment matching the product design phase for the overall product. There is additional work on product design in following increments due to adapting the software product from the previous increment. The process shown in Figure B.1 assumes that the MBASE/RUP Construction phase for each increment is organized into the Waterfall subphases of Detailed Design, Code and Unit Test, and Integration and Test. Other variants can be accommodated via the subphase effort and schedule distribution parameters.

## B.3   INPUTS AND OUTPUTS

Estimation of incremental development requires the following inputs:

- COCOMO II Early Design or Post-Architecture Model scale factor and cost driver ratings
- New software size of each increment
- The percentage of change in software size from all previous increments, called the Adaptation Adjustment Modifier (AAM)
- The starting milestone, $M_{START}$, for each increment after the first
- Any delay-time, $T_{DELAY}$, for starting an increment
- The distribution of effort and schedule for each phase: Product Design (PD), Detailed Design (DD), Code and Unit Test (CUT), and Integration and Test (IT)

The incremental estimation process will be explained by following a simple example. A more detailed example is given in Chapter 3. Using the three-increment development shown in Figure B.1, the inputs are:

| Increment | New Size (KSLOC) | E | Π EM | AAM | $M_{START}$ Milestone | $T_{DELAY}$ (Months) |
|---|---|---|---|---|---|---|
| 1 | $Size_1 = 50$ | 1.15 | 1.0 | 0 | SRR | |
| 2 | $Size_2 = 30$ | 1.15 | 1.0 | 20 | CDR | 0 |
| 3 | $Size_3 = 20$ | 1.15 | 1.0 | 10 | CDR | 0 |
| Total | $Size_T = 100$ | | | | | |

Based on the phase distributions of MBASE discussed earlier, the following percentages will be used:

| Phase | Effort Distribution | Schedule Distribution |
|---|---|---|
| Product Design (PD) | 24% | 38% |
| PD for Increments 2 & 3 | $24\% \times 25\% = 6\%$ | $38\% \times 25\% = 9.5\%$ |
| Detailed Design (DD) | 20% | 17% |
| Code and Unit Test (CUT) | 30% | 23% |
| Integration and Test (IT) | 26% | 22% |

The outputs are the adjusted sizes, estimated effort (PM), and schedule (TDEV) for each phase of each increment. Table B.1 names the output quantities for the example we are about to calculate.

**Table B.1    Incremental Estimation Output**

| Phase | Adj. Size | PD (PM/TDEV) | DD (PM/TDEV) | UTC (PM/TDEV) | IT (PM/TDEV) | Total (PM/TDEV) |
|---|---|---|---|---|---|---|
| Total (T) | $Size_T$ | $PD_T$ | $DD_T$ | $UTC_T$ | $IT_T$ | $PM_T$ |
| Increment 1 | $Size_1$ | $PD_1$ | $DD_1$ | $UTC_1$ | $IT_1$ | $PM_1$ |
| Increment 2 | $Adj. Size_2$ | $PD_2$ | $DD_2$ | $UTC_2$ | $IT_2$ | $PM_2$ |
| Increment 3 | $Adj. Size_3$ | $PD_3$ | $DD_3$ | $UTC_3$ | $IT_3$ | $PM_3$ |

## B.4    ESTIMATION STEPS

As the estimation steps are followed the estimation results will be stored in Table B.2 at the end of this section, in the cells indicated by the terms defined in Table B.1 above.

1. *Compute the size for each increment and the total size.*
    The total size in our example is 100 KSLOC. This is placed in Table B.2 in the $Size_T$ position. The example sets the sizes for Increments 1, 2, and 3 as 50, 30, and 20 KSLOC respectively. Increment 1's size is placed in the results table in the $Size_1$ position. However succeeding increments require that their sizes be adjusted due to reusing the software product from all the previous increments. AAM is applied to the sizes of all previous increments because modification may occur to any code that has already been developed. An increment's size is composed of new code and previous increment's code sizes:

$$Adj. Size_i = Size_i + \left( AAM \times \sum_{j=1}^{i-1} Size_j \right)$$

Recall from the discussion of COCOMO II's reuse model that reuse effort is influenced by a factor called the Adaptation Adjustment Modifier (AAM). *AAM* is based on the percent design modified (*DM*), the code modified (*CM*), the integration and test modified (*IM*), the assessment and assimilation (*AA*), the software understanding (*SU*), and programmer unfamiliarity with the software (*UNFM*), see Section 2.2.4.2. These relationships are repeated below.

$$AAF = 0.4(DM) + 0.3(CM) + 0.3(IM)$$

$$AAM = \frac{[AA + AAF(1 + 0.02(SU)(UNFM))]}{100}, AAF \le 50$$

$$AAM = \frac{[AA + AAF + (SU)(UNFM)]}{100}, AAF > 50$$

To derive the size for the next increment, the sizes from all of the previous increments are summed and adjusted with *AAM* (this is because modifications may effect code from any previous increment). The adjusted sum is then added to the size of the increment to be developed. For the example, *AAM* for Increment 2 (*AAM₂*) is set to 20 percent and to 10 percent for Increment 3 (*AAM₃*); in a real-world scenario, it would be preferable to set *AAM* to the results of the equation above.

$$Adj.\ Size_2 = (AAM_2 \times Size_1) + Size_2 \qquad Adj.\ Size_3 = AAM_3 \times (Size_1 + Size_2)) + Size_3$$
$$= (0.2 \times 50) + 30 \qquad\qquad\qquad\qquad = (0.1 \times (50 + 30)) + 20$$
$$= 40 \qquad\qquad\qquad\qquad\qquad\qquad = 28$$

In the results table, *Adj. Size₂* is set to 40 and *Adj. Size₃* is set to 28. Observe the sum of sizes for all increments is 118 KSLOC compared to the total original product size of 100 KSLOC. This indicates that incremental development increases effort and schedule for achieving the full Initial Operational Capability.*

2. *Determine the total effort and schedule for the total single product.*
    Use COCOMO II to estimate the total effort and schedule and distribute the estimates over the PD, DD, CUT, and IT phases.
    For this example, only the effort will be estimated and placed in the results table. Schedule is estimated in the same manner. The distribution for effort for each phase was given earlier.

$$PM_{Total} = 2.94 \times (100)^{1.15} \times 1.0 = 586.6$$
$$PD_T = 586.6 \times 0.24 = 140.8$$
$$DD_T = 586.6 \times 0.20 = 117.3$$
$$CUT_T = 586.6 \times 0.30 = 176.0$$
$$IT_T = 586.6 \times 0.26 = 152.5$$

3. *Determine Increment 1's estimated effort and schedule.*
    Use the provided COCOMO II parameters, *Size₁*, and phase distributions to estimate effort for Increment 1.

$$PM_{Inc1\ Total} = 2.94 \times (50)^{1.15} \times 1.0 = 264.3$$
$$PD_1 = 264.3 \times 0.24 = 63.4$$
$$DD_1 = 264.3 \times 0.20 = 52.9$$
$$CUT_1 = 264.3 \times 0.30 = 79.3$$
$$IT_1 = 264.3 \times 0.26 = 68.7$$

---

*To make a fair comparison, we'd have to apply some REVL to the full 100-KSLOC project. In practice, the REVL value for single-shot development would be smallest, but the post-IOC effort to modify the operational product to reflect the experimental-use lessons learned during incremental development would be considerably larger.

For only the first increment, Increment 1, the $PD_1$ phase effort is replaced by the Total product phase effort, namely 140.8 PM. This is because the architecture and interfaces for this incremental development strategy have to be defined for all increments in the first increment. Table B.2 now contains $PD_1$, $DD_1$, $CUT_1$, $IT_1$, and $PM_1$ for Increment 1.

4. *Determine the added integration effort.*

Additional effort must be expended to integrate the code in the various increment's (the integration term used here is not the same effort used in each increments I&T phase). Steps 4 and 5 compute this effort and Step 6 uses the computed effort. This step calculates the additional integration effort associated with incremental development by comparing the development of a full product with the development of similarly sized independent products. The full product is the Total product in this example. The independent products are the individual increments using only their sizes without adjustment for reuse of software from previous increments.

Compute the effort and schedule for the remaining increments using new size only (the first increment was done in the previous step).

$$PM_{Inc\,2\,Total} = 2.94 \times (30)^{1.15} \times 1.0 = 146.9 \quad PM_{Inc\,3\,Total} = 2.94 \times (20)^{1.15} \times 1.0 = 92.2$$

These results are intermediate and not stored in the results table. The total additional integration effort is the difference between the full product effort and the sum of the estimated effort for all of the independently estimated Increments.

$$
\begin{aligned}
PM_{Integration} &= PM_{Total} - \Sigma PM_{each\,Increment} \\
&= 586.6 - (264.3 + 146.9 + 92.2) \\
&= 83.2
\end{aligned}
$$

The additional integration effort, $PM_{Integration}$, contains the effort for the full product design, $PD_T$. We have already included the total $PD$ effort as Increment 1's $PD_1$ effort in Step 3. We need to remove the $PD_T$ contribution to $PM_{Integration}$. We do this as next.

The added integration effort, $PM_{Added\,Integration}$, is the integration effort without the added $PD_T$ integration effort. Estimate the $PD$ phase distribution for each remaining increment, the first increment was done in Step 3.

$$
\begin{aligned}
PD_{Inc\,2} &= 146.9 \times 0.24 = 35.3 \\
PD_{Inc\,3} &= 92.2 \times 0.24 = 22.1
\end{aligned}
$$

The additional $PD$ effort is the difference between the full product $PD$ effort and the sum of all independently estimated Increment's $PD$ effort:

$$
\begin{aligned}
PD_{Integration} &= PD_{Total} - \Sigma PD_{each\,Increment} \\
&= 140.8 - (63.4 + 35.3 + 22.1) \\
&= 20.0
\end{aligned}
$$

The added integration effort, $PM_{Added\ Integration}$, is the total integration effort without the added $PD$ integration effort. This represents the additional integration effort for the $DD$, $CUT$, and $IT$ phases.

$$PM_{Added\ Integration} = PM_{Integration} - PD_{Integration}$$

$$= 83.2 - 20.0$$

$$= 63.2$$

*5. Distribute the added integration effort across remaining increments.*

The added integration effort, $PM_{Added\ Integration}$, derived in the previous step, is allocated to all increments after the first. The first increment has nothing to integrate. The allocation is based on each increment's size unadjusted for reuse compared to the sum of all the remaining increment's sizes.

$$Size_{Total\ Remaining} = \Sigma Size_{each\ Increment}$$

$$PM_{Increment\ Added\ Integration} = \frac{Size_{each\ Increment}}{Size_{Total\ Remaining}} \cdot PM_{Added\ Integration}$$

From the example, the added integration effort for Increments 2 and 3 are:

$$Size_{Total\ Remaining} = (30 + 20) = 50$$

$$PM_{Increment\ 2\ Added\ Integration} = \frac{30}{50} \times 63.2 = 37.9 \qquad PM_{Increment\ 3\ Added\ Integration} = \frac{20}{50} \times 63.2 = 25.3$$

*6. Determine all remaining increments' effort and schedule.*

This step picks up from Step 3. Steps 4 and 5 were necessary to derive the additional integration effort in incremental development. The additional integration effort will be used in this step.

Use COCOMO II to estimate the total effort for the remaining increments as was done in Steps 2 and 3. Use the increment's Adj. Size, which is the new size adjusted for reuse.

$$PM_2 = 2.94 \times (40)^{1.15} \times 1.0 = 204.5 \qquad PM_3 = 2.94 \times (28)^{1.15} \times 1.0 = 135.7$$

Add each increment's allocated additional integration effort to its estimated effort.

$$PM_{Increment\ Adjusted} = PM_{Increment} + PM_{Increment\ Added\ Integration}$$

$$PM_{Increment\ 2\ Adjusted} = 204.5 + 37.9 = 240.6 \qquad PM_{Increment\ 3\ Adjusted} = 135.7 + 25.3 = 159.7$$

*7. Distribute each increment's effort and schedule over the phases.*

The adjusted effort for each increment from the previous step is distributed using the phase distribution given in Section B.3. The exception is the distribution for PD, which is a fraction (25 percent) of the PD given in B.3. This is because the requirements and architecture were solidified during the PD phase of Increment

**Table B.2    Incremental Effort Estimation Results**

| Phase | Adj. Size | PD (PM) | DD (PM) | UTC (PM) | IT (PM) | Total (PM) |
|---|---|---|---|---|---|---|
| Total (T) | 100 | 140.8 | 117.3 | 176.0 | 152.5 | 586.6 |
| Increment 1 | 50 | 140.8 | 52.9 | 79.3 | 68.7 | 341.7 |
| Increment 2 | 40 | 14.4 | 48.1 | 72.2 | 62.6 | 197.3 |
| Increment 3 | 28 | 9.6 | 31.9 | 47.9 | 41.5 | 130.6 |

1. The PD phase for the remaining increments consists of checking interfaces and resolving new architectural issues. These distributions are placed in Table B.2.

$$PD_2 = 240.6 \times 0.06 = 14.4 \qquad PD_3 = 159.7 \times 0.06 = 9.6$$
$$DD_2 = 240.6 \times 0.20 = 48.1 \qquad DD_3 = 159.7 \times 0.20 = 31.9$$
$$CUT_2 = 240.6 \times 0.30 = 72.2 \qquad CUT_3 = 159.7 \times 0.30 = 47.9$$
$$IT_2 = 240.6 \times 0.26 = 62.6 \qquad IT_3 = 159.7 \times 0.26 = 41.5$$

*8. Determine resulting cumulative effort and schedule for each increment.*

The results table filled out during the explanation of incremental cost estimating has all the information needed to determine the resulting cumulative effort for the example.

Comparing the total project effort, 586.6 PM, to Increment 1's effort (which includes the PD effort for the entire product), 341.7 PM, it can be seen the effort to reach an initial capability is lower. However the total effort required for all increments is 669.6 PM which is 14 percent higher than the total project effort.

## B.5    INCREMENTAL DEVELOPMENT CONSIDERATIONS

The above example overlapped the different phases at the end of Detailed Design, the Critical Design Review. The degree to which increments overlap is dependent on how much is known about the software product. The more uncertainty characterized by COCOMO drivers such as Architecture and Risk Resolution (RESL), Required Reliability (RELY), Product Complexity (CPLX), and Platform Volatility (PVOL), the less the overlap between increments. This is because change in previous increments causes *unplanned rework* to flow to succeeding increments.

It is reasonable to anticipate additional effort required for phases in succeeding increments that overlap a phase of a previous increment that is undergoing review by the customer or user. This phase is not shown in the example or estimated by the COCOMO II model. This is due to unforeseen installation or initial operational problems, the correction of which may affect the rest of the software product. Such effects may be approximated via either the COCOMO REVL parameter or post-IOC maintenance cost estimates.

# C

# COCOMO Suite: Data Collection Forms and Guidelines

## C.1  INTRODUCTION

Appendix C provides a set of forms and procedures for collecting effort and schedule data for a given software project throughout its life cycle, in a form compatible with the following COCOMO Suite models: COCOMO II, and its emerging extensions COCOTS, COPSEMO, COQUALMO and CORADMO. These data collection or *Software Project Data (SPD)* forms have been kept brief, with minimal definitions, explanations, etc. Please refer to the index and glossary for the definitions of any terms that are unfamiliar. The procedures are oriented around the collection of information and the updating of estimates at the project's life cycle anchor points (see Appendix A). Revising project estimates as each anchor point is achieved provides immediate benefits by furnishing 1) estimates that are more accurate, and 2) current cost-to-complete and schedule-to-complete information. Revised estimates also provide the data needed to perform up-to-date sensitivity, risk and parametric analyses.

Such data collection activities are an integral part of an effective project management process. Information gathered is used in determining whether or not a project is on track relative to original plans built upon initial estimates. When actual cost and schedule performance deviates from plans, new estimates may be in order.

Data collection should not be an additional burden for management. Thus, we have organized COCOMO II data collection to be management-relevant and easy to implement via the electronic forms found on the accompanying CD. For on-going projects, data collection allows you to determine whether or not your performance is on track relative to plans. For completed projects, data collection allows you to develop a database that you can use to more precisely calibrate COCOMO II and the other Suite models to your actual experience. For both types of projects, data collection permits you to use existing knowledge to improve the accuracy of your estimating capabilities.

The data collection forms and procedures provided here enable an organization to develop the core capabilities needed to satisfy the new Level 2 Measurement and Analysis process area called *Activities Performed,* found in the Integrated Capability Maturity Model (CMMI) recently issued at: http://www.sei.cmu.edu/cmm/cmmi/

The activities include: establish measurement objectives; define measures; define data collection and storage procedures; define analysis procedures; collect measurement data; analyze measurement data; store data and results; and communicate results.

## C.2    PROCEDURE FOR PROJECTS

The Software Project Data forms (figures) and corresponding instructions (tables) described below are provided herein as well as on the accompanying CD-ROM. The first form applies to all the Suite models, while numbers two through five apply to COCOMO II; these are also needed, however, as a base for all of the emerging extensions. The remaining forms, six through nine, are specific to each of the extensions of COCOMO II. All the forms can be used either for ongoing or completed projects:

*Form SPD-1: General Information (All Models) (Figure C.1/Table C.1).* Originated at the start of the project, updated at intermediate milestones and completed at the end of the project.

*Form SPD-2a: Phase Summaries (Waterfall-based process) (Figure C.2a/Table C.2a).* Estimated or actual phase information entered at the end of each major phase of the project following a Waterfall-based process. Finalized at the end of the development.

*Form SPD-2b: Phase Summaries (MBASE/RUP-based process) (Figure C.2b/ Table C.2b).* Estimated or actual phase information entered at the end of each major phase of the project following a MBASE/RUP-based process. Finalized at the end of the development.

*Form SPD-3: Component Summaries (Figure C.3/Table C.3).* Component data entered during the start of the project. Completed at the end of the development.

*Form SPD-4: COCOMO II Progress Runs (Figure C.4/Table C.4).* Estimated project cost and schedule data, and ratings for estimating parameters, entered at the end of each major phase of the project.

*Form SPD-5: COCOMO II Project Actuals (Figure C.5/Table C.5).* Actual project cost and schedule data, and final ratings for estimating parameters, collected at the end of the project.

*Form SPD-5a: COCOMO II Project Actuals: Simple Completed Project (Figure C.5a/Table C.5a).* Actual project cost and schedule data, and final ratings for estimating parameters, for *simple* completed projects; collected at the end of the project.

*Form SPD-6a: COCOTS Project Level Data (Figure C.6a/Table C.6a).* Estimated or actual project cost and schedule data, and ratings for estimating parameters; can be entered at the end of each major phase of the project. Finalized at the end of the development.

*Form SPD-6b: COCOTS Assessment Data (Figure C.6b/Table C.6b).* Estimated or actual project cost and schedule data, and ratings for estimating parameters; can be entered at the end of each major phase of the project. Finalized at the end of the development.

*Form SPD-6c: COCOTS Tailoring Data (Figure C.6c/Table C.6c).* Estimated or actual project cost and schedule data, and ratings for estimating parameters; can be entered at the end of each major phase of the project. Finalized at the end of the development.

*Form SPD-6d: COCOTS Glue Code Data (Figure C.6d/Table C.6d).* Estimated or actual project cost and schedule data, and ratings for estimating parameters; can be entered at the end of each major phase of the project. Finalized at the end of the development.

*Form SPD-6e: COCOTS Volatility Data (Figure C.6e/Table C.6e).* Estimated or actual project cost and schedule data, and ratings for estimating parameters; can be entered at the end of each major phase of the project. Finalized at the end of the development.

*Form SPD-7: COPSEMO Detailed MBASE Effort and Schedule Summaries (Figure C.7/Table C.7).* Phase cycles and activity breakdowns.

*Form SPD-8: COQUALMO Defect Summaries (Figure C.8/Table C.8).* Defect introduction and removal data collected by artifact and life cycle phase.

*Form SPD-9: CORADMO RAD Details Summaries (Figure C.9/Table C.9).* Rapid Application Development parameters (CoRADMO Driver Ratings). Project ratings entered during the start of the project. Final ratings reassessed at the end of the development, relying on COPSEMO detailed effort and schedule actuals' data for calibration.

## C.3 GUIDELINES FOR DATA COLLECTION

### C.3.1 New Projects

Projects starting out should consider collecting cost, schedule and error data at the following times during the project's life:

Project Start—develop your initial estimates using the following set of forms:
>*Form SPD-1: General Information*
>*Form SPD-3: Component Summaries*
>*Form SPD-6a: COCOTS Project Level Data*

At the end of Major Project Phases—update your estimates using the following set of forms:
>*Form SPD-2a: Phase Summaries (Waterfall-based process)*
>*Form SPD-2b: Phase Summaries (MBASE/RUP-based process)*
>*Form SPD-3: Component Summaries*
>*Form SPD-4: COCOMO II Progress Runs*
>*Form SPD-6b: COCOTS Assessment Data*
>*Form SPD-6c: COCOTS Tailoring Data*
>*Form SPD-6d: COCOTS Glue Code Data*
>*Form SPD-6e: COCOTS Volatility Data*
>*Form SPD-7: COPSEMO Detailed MBASE Effort and Schedule Summaries*
>*Form SPD-8: COQUALMO Detailed Summaries*
>*Form SPD-9: CORADMO RAD Project Summaries.*

At the end of the development—capture your project actuals using the following forms:
>*Form SPD-2a: Phase Summaries (Waterfall-based process)*
>*Form SPD-2b: Phase Summaries (MBASE/RUP-based process)*
>*Form SPD-5: COCOMO II Project Actuals*
>*Form SPD-6b: COCOTS Assessment Data*
>*Form SPD-6c: COCOTS Tailoring Data*
>*Form SPD-6d: COCOTS Glue Code Data*

*Form SPD-6e: COCOTS Volatility Data*
*Form SPD-7: COPSEMO Detailed MBASE Effort and Schedule Summaries*
*Form SPD-8: COQUALMO Detailed Summaries*
*Form SPD-9: CORADMO RAD Details*

New projects should view data collection as an opportunity. They can use the data to benchmark their progress, develop business cases and calibrate their cost models.

### C.3.2   Completed Projects

In general, it is not possible to reconstruct COCOMO II and other COCOMO Suite milestone runs and detailed phase/activity data from completed projects. If the project was estimated using earlier versions of the model, we suggest that you use our Rosetta stone [Reifer et al. 1999] to convert the data. If they weren't, we suggest that you try to capture as much cost related data as possible using the following forms:

*Form SPD-1: General Information*—Fill out this form as best you can.

*Form SPD-2a: Phase Summaries (Waterfall-based process)*—Complete this form for each major delivery of a Waterfall-based process.

*Form SPD-2b: Phase Summaries (MBASE/RUP-based process)*—Complete this form for each major delivery of a MBASE/RUP-based process.

*Form SPD-3: Component Summaries*—Do the best you can with whatever data you can gather. Use a code counter to collect actuals whenever possible.

*Form SPD-4: COCOMO II Progress Runs*—Fill out this form using any cost- and schedule-to-complete information at your disposal. If no such information exists or is readily available, don't waste your time.

*Form SPD-5: COCOMO II Project Actuals*—Complete this form by sifting through your accounting reports and by inspecting the final product.

*Form SPD-5a: COCOMO II Project Actuals: Simple Completed Projects*—Preferably, this form should be accompanied by Form SPD-1, but it can be used as a one-page total-completed-project data collection form compatible with the data provided for a COCOMO II estimation run.

*Form SPD-6a: COCOTS Project Level Data*—Do the best you can with whatever data you can gather.

*Form SPD-6b: COCOTS Assessment Data*—Do the best you can with whatever data you can gather.

*Form SPD-6c: COCOTS Tailoring Data*—Do the best you can with whatever data you can gather.

*Form SPD-6d: COCOTS Glue Code Data*—Do the best you can with whatever data you can gather. Use a code counter to collect actuals whenever possible.

*Form SPD-6e: COCOTS Volatility Data*—Do the best you can with whatever data you can gather.

*Form SPD-7: COPSEMO Detailed MBASE Effort and Schedule Summaries*—Complete this form by sifting through your accounting reports and applying engineering judgement based on personnel and their tasks or roles.

*Form SPD-8: COQUALMO Detailed Summaries*—Fill out this form as completely as you can using inspection reports, technical review reports, testing results and reports, and software trouble report records as your source.

*Form SPD-9: CORADMO RAD Details Summaries (Figure C.9/Table C.9).* Fill out this form with Rapid Application Development parameters (CoRADMO Driver Ratings).

### C.3.3  Maintenance Projects

COCOMO II also provides you with the capability to develop annual or other periodic maintenance cost estimates based upon the modification of the original COCOMO 81 maintenance model, described in Chapter 2, Section 2.5. We suggest that you use the forms provided when using this model. However, you will want to use actuals and re-rate project attributes collected on *Form SPD-5* when computing the numbers.

## C.4  DATA CONDITIONING

Data conditioning is an essential activity in the software data collection and analysis process. Even when people try to provide the best data they can, there are a number of known problems and subtle sources of misunderstanding that can inject bias into their data. Using such data to calibrate cost models can lead to erroneous results should these and other sources of data contamination not be removed.

### C.4.1   Sources of Data Contamination

Besides the problems of missing data and clerical errors, some of the most common and frequent sources of software data collection problems include:

1. *Inconsistent definitions*—The COCOMO II model defines terms differently than previous models. For example, it uses SLOC (Source Lines of Code) instead of DSI (Delivered Source Instructions) which were used in the original COCOMO model (see Section 2.2.1). An "IF-THEN-ELSE, ELSE IF" pair will now count as a single SLOC instead of two DSI when a terminal semi-colon is used for the counting conventions. As another example, COCOMO uses 152 person hours per PM and assumes casual overtime is not included as part of the burden. If you used something different, the model would generate erroneous answers.

2. *Improper scope*—The COCOMO II model assumes that the project's scope includes certain activities and excludes others. For example, software testing is included while software support to system integration and test is not. As another example, software documentation that is normally generated during the software development life cycle is included while customer unique documentation is not. Again, you would generate erroneous answers if you used the model outside of its proper scope. Appendix A, Section 6, records the major COCOMO II scoping assumptions.

3. *Double-Counting*—Sometimes items are double-counted or taken into account twice using several factors within the model. For example, REVL is used to take into account volatile requirements. However, some people double-dip by improperly rating the Precedentedness or Architecture/Risk Resolution scale factors lower than they should be to take volatility into account. You should understand what the factor ratings involve prior to rating them to avoid making this mistake.

4. *Averaging*—Often, people use average ratings for groupings that extend across subsystems and the project. Because they haven't taken the time to get into the details, they consolidate their estimate and lose fidelity because little differentiation is made between different types of software. You can avoid this problem and greatly improve the accuracy of your estimates by breaking down the project into finer grained components.

5. *Garbage In, Garbage Out*—Another common problem is the use of erroneous assumptions. People often use models to generate quick-and-dirty estimates. They make all sorts of simplifying assumptions in their quest for numbers. One way to avoid problems of this sort is to take a little more time to develop realistic, but simplifying assumptions. This often takes some interaction with both the developer and customer communities.

6. *Observational Bias*—Finally, many people tend to be overly optimistic/ pessimistic when they estimate. Biases either way should be avoided especially when they can become a self-fulfilling prophecy. Use of wide band Delphi in which groups of experts reach consensus on their estimates reduces such biases. However, such group estimates take more time to achieve and may not be practical under some circumstances.

### C.4.2   Data Conditioning Guidelines

The best defense against these problems is to provide those involved in the data collection with a clear set of definitions, automated procedures and examples. Build self-checks whenever possible into your data collection system. For example, you can ask a question in two different ways on two related forms to test the consistency of the answer (e.g., effort, schedule, average staff size). Be careful not to overdo this, however. In addition, such problems can be further avoided by collecting the data close to its source. For example, try to collect labor hours using your time card system. Finally, make data collection a natural part of the way you implement your processes. For example, collect error data as part of your software trouble reporting process. This eliminates the need to use multiple forms and makes it easier to collect the data.

The following additional data conditioning guidelines are recommended for inclusion in your process:

*Data screening*—Each form used should be screened when completed to identify missing, unreasonable and inconsistent entries. For example, a large PM estimate for a small-sized application needs to be checked. As another example, lots of applications experience for a highly unprecedented application seems inconsistent. If the data is collected online, such checks can and should be automated.

*Wide-band Delphi*—Whenever possible, use more than a single person and more than one cost model to base your estimates on. By polling the experts, this approach limits the observational bias natural to estimating to a minimum.

*Online Forms and Counting Conventions*—Put your forms and counting conventions online whenever possible. Make sure that you include plenty of examples to illustrate how to fill out the forms properly and how to count correctly. If possible, construct a web site on your server and make the forms and conventions accessible to all.

*Guard Competitively Sensitive Data with Your Life*—Protect your cost data carefully. Don't allow unauthorized access to the database and guard it against pilfering and pirating. Limit the number of people who have access to the data to those who are responsible for its use and analysis.

*Compare to Industry Benchmarks*—If you can, see how you compare to any published benchmarks. This provides you with yet another check on the reasonableness of your data. The COCOMO II database size, effort, and cost-driver rating distributions in Chapter 4 provide one such source.

---

**Form SPD-1 General Information (All COCOMO Suite Models)**

------------------------------------------------------------------------------------

1. Project Title:                2. Project ID No.          3. Rev No.
4. Date Prepared:             5. Originator:

------------------------------------------------------------------------------------

6. Organization:               7. Project Manager:
8. Customer:                  9. Platform(s):
10. Development type (circle one):    New product    Upgrade    Maintenance & Minor Enhancements

11. Development approach (spiral, waterfall, etc.):
12. Step in the process after which data is collected:

    Waterfall Activity (circle one):
    Start           Requirements      Design             Code & Unit Test
    Integration & Test    Maintenance       Completed

    MBASE Stage (circle one):
    Inception       Elaboration     Construction     Transition     Maintenance

    Development Iteration (which number):

    Other development approach (please explain):

13. Year of expected Initial Operational Capability:

14. Application type (circle one):

    Command and control    MIS                 Simulation
    Communications        Operating Systems     Software Tools
    Diagnostics            Process Control       Testing
    Engineering & Science   Signal Processing     Utilities
    Other (please specify): _____

---

15. COCOMO model (circle one):

    Early design             Post architecture

16. Brief project description:

17. References:

**Figure C.1   Form SPD-1 General Information (All COCOMO Suite Models)**

**Table C.1   Instructions for Form SPD-1: General Information**

| Item | Description |
| --- | --- |
| 1. Project Title | Insert the project name or title. |
| 2. Project ID No. | Identify the project Identification Number using a unique code devised for that purpose. |
| 3. Rev. No. | Insert the revision number starting from 0001. |
| 4. Date prepared | Identify the date when the form was prepared. |
| 5. Originator | Insert the name of the person who completed the form (and phone extension). |
| 6. Organization | Identify the Originator's organization by name. |
| 7. Project Manager | Insert the Project Manager's name (and phone extension). |
| 8. Customer | Identify the customer (and experience in project attributes) |
| 9. Platform | Insert both the host and target (if different) hardware platform and operating system. |
| 10. Development type | Circle the most appropriate development type. |
| 11. Development approach | Insert the most appropriate development paradigm or approach. |
| 12. Step in the process after which data is collected | Based upon your development approach, identify what step in the process you are currently at. |
| 13. Year of expected IOC | Identify the year in which development began in earnest. |
| 14. Application type | Circle the most applicable application type. If there are multiple applications, circle them and put a note in box 19, special factors. |
| 15. COCOMO model | Circle the COCOMO II model in use. |
| 16. Brief project description | Summarize the goals of the project in terms of what products it hopes to deliver. |
| 17. References | Cite references about the project and its progress. These may be customer documents or internal memoranda. |

18. COCOMO II Project Scale Factor Attributes

| | VL | L | N | H | VH | X H | Comments (Including Don't Know) |
|---|---|---|---|---|---|---|---|
| | | | Ratings | | | | |
| Precedentedness (PREC) | | | | | | | |
| Development Flexibility (FLEX) | | | | | | | |
| Architecture/Risk Resolution (RESL) | | | | | | | |
| Team Cohesion (TEAM) | | | | | | | |
| Process Maturity (PMAT) | | | | | | | |

18a. Post-Architecture Project Effort Multiplier Attributes

| | VL | L | N | H | VH | X H | Comments |
|---|---|---|---|---|---|---|---|
| Required Software Reliability (RELY) | | | | | | | |
| Data Base Size (DATA) | | | | | | | |
| Product Complexity (CPLX) | | | | | | | |
| Develop for Reuse (RUSE) | | | | | | | |
| Documentation Match to Life-Cycle Needs (DOCU) | | | | | | | |
| Execution Time Constraint (TIME) | | | | | | | |
| Main Storage Constraint (STOR) | | | | | | | |
| Platform Volatility (PVOL) | | | | | | | |
| Analysis Personnel Capability (ACAP) | | | | | | | |
| Programmer Personnel Capability (PCAP) | | | | | | | |
| Personnel Continuity (PCON) | | | | | | | |
| Applications Experience (APEX) | | | | | | | |
| Personnel Platform Experience (PLEX) | | | | | | | |
| Language & Tool Experience (LTEX) | | | | | | | |
| Use of Software Tools (TOOL) | | | | | | | |
| Multi-Site Development (SITE) | | | | | | | |
| Required Development Schedule (SCED) | | | | | | | |
| Other (USR 1) | | | | | | | |
| Other (USR 2) | | | | | | | |
| Other (USR 3) | | | | | | | |

18b. Early Design Project Effort Multiplier Attributes

| | VL | L | N | H | VH | X H | Comments |
|---|---|---|---|---|---|---|---|
| Product Reliability and Complexity (RCPX) | | | | | | | |
| Required Usability (RUSE) | | | | | | | |
| Platform Difficulty (PDIF) | | | | | | | |
| Personnel Capability (PERS) | | | | | | | |
| Personnel Experience (PREX) | | | | | | | |
| Facilities (FCIL) | | | | | | | |
| Required Development Schedule (SCED) | | | | | | | |

**Figure C.1    Form SPD-1 General Information (cont'd)**

**Table C.1   *Continued***

| 18. Project attributes | Put an "X" in appropriate rating box. For the most, rating guidelines are in Chapters 2 and 3 in the book. If you don't know an answer, say so in the extreme right column of the table. Three "other" parameters are included to allow you to expand the list to include any additional factors that drive cost on your project (e.g., security). Recognize that these factor ratings will be updated at anchor points along with your estimates. |
| --- | --- |

**Form SPD-2a Phase Summaries (Waterfall-based process)**

------------------------------------------------------------------------------------------

1. Project Title:  2. Project ID No.  3. Rev No.
4. Date Prepared:  5. Originator:

------------------------------------------------------------------------------------------

6. Resource Summary by Phase

| Phase # | Name | Mile-stone | Start Date | End Date | P&R | DES | DD | CUT | I&T | Impl | O&M | Total PM | Total M |
|---|---|---|---|---|---|---|---|---|---|---|---|---|---|
| 1 | P&R | | | | | | | | | | | | |
| 2 | DES | | | | | | | | | | | | |
| 3 | DD | | | | | | | | | | | | |
| 4 | CUT | | | | | | | | | | | | |
| 5 | I&T | | | | | | | | | | | | |
| 6 | Impl | | | | | | | | | | | | |
| 7 | O&M | | | | | | | | | | | | |

Phases
P&R — Plans & Requirements    DES — Product Design    DD — Detailed Design    CUT — Code & Unit Test    I&T — Integration & Test    Impl — Implementation    O&M — Operations & Maintenace

Activities
RAA - Requirements Analysis    PDA – Product Design    PA - Programming    TPA - Test Planning    VVA - Verification and Validation    POA - Project Office    CQA - CM/QA    MA - Manuals

7. Error Summary by Phase

| Phase # | Name | Errors Found | | | | | | | | Total Errors Removed | KSLOC at end of Phase |
|---|---|---|---|---|---|---|---|---|---|---|---|
| | | P&R | DES | DD | CUT | I&T | Impl | O&M | Total | | |
| 1 | P&R | | | | | | | | | | |
| 2 | DES | | | | | | | | | | |
| 3 | DD | | | | | | | | | | |
| 4 | CUT | | | | | | | | | | |
| 5 | I&T | | | | | | | | | | |
| 6 | Impl | | | | | | | | | | |
| 7 | O&M | | | | | | | | | | |

8. Other Project Costs by Phase

| Phase # | Name | Mile-stone | Start Date | End Date | RAA | PDA | PA | TPA | VVA | POA | CQA | MA | Total PM | Total M |
|---|---|---|---|---|---|---|---|---|---|---|---|---|---|---|
| 1 | P&R | | | | | | | | | | | | | |
| 2 | DES | | | | | | | | | | | | | |
| 3 | DD | | | | | | | | | | | | | |
| 4 | CUT | | | | | | | | | | | | | |
| 5 | I&T | | | | | | | | | | | | | |
| 6 | Impl | | | | | | | | | | | | | |
| 7 | O&M | | | | | | | | | | | | | |

**Figure C.2a   Form SPD-2a Phase Summaries (Waterfall-based process)**

**Table C.2a   Instructions for Form SPD-2a: Phase Summaries (Waterfall-based process)**

| Item | Description |
|---|---|
| 1. Project Title | Insert the project name or title. |
| 2. Project ID No. | Identify the project Identification Number using a unique code devised for that purpose. |
| 3. Rev. No. | Insert the revision number starting from 0001. |
| 4. Date prepared | Identify the date when the form was prepared. |
| 5. Originator | Insert the name of the person who completed the form (and phone extension). |
| 6. Resource Summary by Phase | Start by inserting the phases of your life cycle in the left most column. Then, enter the anchor points for the phase. Next, insert the start and end dates for the phase. Then, enter the number of person-months (PM) for each of the following activities: RA (Requirements Analysis) DES (Design) CUT (Code and Unit Test) I&T (software Integration & Test) Blank (for any activity you wish to collect resources) Finally, summarize the PM and duration by phase. |
| 7. Error Summary by Phase | Start by inserting the phases of your life cycle in the left most column. Then, enter the names for the anchor points for the phase. Next, insert the start and end dates for the phase. Then, enter the number of errors found by designated activity and total by phase. Next, insert the number of errors removed by phase. Finally, identify the SLOC (Source Line of Code) count estimated during the phase or the actual. Backfire to get this count if you are using object, feature or function points to size your system. |
| 8. Other Project Costs by Phase | Start by inserting the phases of your life cycle in the left most column. Then, enter the anchor points for the phase. Next, insert the start and end dates for the phase. Finally, enter the dollars expended for travel, materials, training, documentation and other non-labor costs in the appropriate column. |

**Form SPD-2b Phase Summaries (MBASE/RUP process)**

--------------------------------------------------------------------------------

1. Project Title:     2. Project ID No.     3. Rev No.
4. Date Prepared:     5. Originator:

--------------------------------------------------------------------------------

6. Resource Summary by Phase

| # | Phase Name | Anchor Points | Start Date | End Date | MGT | ENV | REQ | DES | Impl | ASS | DEP | Total PM | Total M |
|---|---|---|---|---|---|---|---|---|---|---|---|---|---|
| 1. | Incpt. | | | | | | | | | | | | |
| 2 | Elab. | | | | | | | | | | | | |
| 3. | Cnst. | | | | | | | | | | | | |
| 4. | Trns. | | | | | | | | | | | | |
| | | | | | | | | | | | | | |

Activities
MGT – Management     ENV – Environment incl. CM     REQ – Requirements incl. Bus. Modeling     DES – Design     Impl – Implementation     ASS – Assessment incl. Test, QA, R/D V&V     DEP – Deployment

Phases
Incpt. – Inception     Elab. – Elaboration     Cnst. – Construction     Trns. – Transition

7. Error Summary by Phase

| | Phase (above) | Errors Found | | | | | | | | Errors Removed | KSLOC |
|---|---|---|---|---|---|---|---|---|---|---|---|
| # | Phase Name | MGT | ENV | REQ | DES | Impl | ASS | DEP | Total Errors | | |
| 1. | Incpt. | | | | | | | | | | |
| 2 | Elab. | | | | | | | | | | |
| 3. | Cnst. | | | | | | | | | | |
| 4. | Trns. | | | | | | | | | | |

8. Other Project Costs by Phase

| # | Phase Name | Anchor Points | Start Date | End Date | MGT | ENV | REQ | DES | Impl | ASS | DEP | Total PM | Total M |
|---|---|---|---|---|---|---|---|---|---|---|---|---|---|
| 1. | Incpt. | | | | | | | | | | | | |
| 2 | Elab. | | | | | | | | | | | | |
| 3. | Cnst. | | | | | | | | | | | | |
| 4. | Trns. | | | | | | | | | | | | |
| | | | | | | | | | | | | | |

Activities
MGT – Management     ENV – Environment incl. CM     REQ – Requirements incl. Bus. Modeling     DES – Design     Impl – Implementation     ASS – Assessment incl. Test, QA, R/D V&V     DEP – Deployment

Phases
Incpt. – Inception     Elab. – Elaboration     Cnst. – Construction     Trns. – Transition

**Figure C.2b    Form SPD-2b Phase Summaries (MBASE/RUP process)**

**Table C.2b** **Instructions for Form SPD-2b: Phase Summaries (MBASE/RUP-based process)**

| Item | Description |
|---|---|
| 1. Project Title | Insert the project name or title. |
| 2. Project ID No. | Identify the project Identification Number using a unique code devised for that purpose. |
| 3. Rev. No. | Insert the revision number starting from 0001. |
| 4. Date prepared | Identify the date when the form was prepared. |
| 5. Originator | Insert the name of the person who completed the form (and phone extension). |
| 6. Resource Summary by Phase | Start by confirming the phases of your life cycle (Inception, Elaboration, Construction and Transition) in the left most column; if other names as used, please provide them along with a mapping to the MBASE/RUP phase names.<br>Then, enter the anchor points for the phase.<br>Next, insert the start and end dates for the phase.<br>Then, enter the number of person-months (PM) for each of the following activities:<br>    MGT (Management)<br>    ENV (Environment incl. CM)<br>    REQ (Requirements incl. Bus. Modeling)<br>    DES ( Design)<br>    Impl (Implementation)<br>    ASS (Assessment incl. Test, QA, R/D V&V)<br>    DEP (Deployment<br>Finally, summarize the PM and duration by phase. |
| 7. Error Summary by Phase | Start as in 6, above.<br>Then, enter the names for the anchor points for the phase.<br>Next, insert the start and end dates for the phase.<br>Then, enter the number of errors found by designated activity and total by phase.<br>Next, insert the number of errors removed by phase.<br>Finally, identify the SLOC (Source Line of Code) count estimated during the phase or the actual. Backfire to get this count if you are using object, feature or function points to size your system. |
| 8. Other Project Costs by Phase | Start as in 6, above.<br>Then, enter the anchor points for the phase.<br>Next, insert the start and end dates for the phase.<br>Finally, enter the dollars expended for travel, materials, training, documentation and other non-labor costs in the appropriate column. |

## Form SPD-3 Component Summaries

1. Project Title:                    2. Project ID No.              3. Rev No.
4. Date Prepared:                  5. Originator:

6. Type of components (circle one):

   Software applications     Software programs     Software packages     Software builds
   Other:_____

7. Component size (Source Lines Of Code (SLOC))

| Component | REVL (%) | New SLOC | Adapted SLOC | AAF | SU (%) | AA (%) | UNFM | Reused SLOC |
|---|---|---|---|---|---|---|---|---|
| 1. | | | | | | | | |
| 2. | | | | | | | | |
| 3. | | | | | | | | |
| 4. | | | | | | | | |
| 5. | | | | | | | | |
| 6. | | | | | | | | |
| 7. | | | | | | | | |
| 8. | | | | | | | | |
| 9. | | | | | | | | |
| 10. | | | | | | | | |
| 11. | | | | | | | | |
| 12. | | | | | | | | |
| 13. | | | | | | | | |
| 14. | | | | | | | | |
| 15. | | | | | | | | |
| 16. | | | | | | | | |
| TOTAL | | | | | | | | |

| REVL — Requirements Evolution and Volatility | AAF — Adaptation Adjustment Factor | SU — Software Understanding | AA — Assessment and Assimilation | UNFM - Unfamiliarity |
|---|---|---|---|---|

8. SLOC Counting Conventions (circle one):
          Logical SLOC                  Physical SLOC (carriage returns)
          Non-blank, Non-comment SLOC     Physical SLOC (terminal semi-colons)

          COCOMO II SLOC (Section 2.2.1)     Other

9. Programming language(s):
   Primary language:
   Secondary language:

10. Percentage of code that was generated/translated automatically:
    Generator/translator used:

**Figure C.3   Form SPD-3 Component Summaries**

**Table C.3   Instructions for Form SPD-3: Component Summaries**

| Item | Description |
|---|---|
| 1. Project Title | Insert the project name or title. |
| 2. Project ID No. | Identify the project Identification Number using a unique code devised for that purpose. |
| 3. Rev. No. | Insert the revision number starting from 0001. |
| 4. Date prepared | Identify the date when the form was prepared. |
| 5. Originator | Insert the name of the person who completed the form (and phone extension). |
| 6. Type of component | Circle or describe under "other" the type of components that you are estimating (or counting). |
| 7. Component size (SLOC) | Summarize by component the number of new, adapted and reused SLOCs by component and the factors that influence derivation of equivalent size (i.e., AAF, SU, AA, UNFM, and number of requirements). Definitions for these factors are found in the glossary and chapter 2 of this book. |
| 8. SLOC counting conventions | Circle or describe under "other" the conventions used to count SLOCs. |
| 9. Programming language | Name your primary and secondary programming languages. |
| 10. Percentage of code automatically generated | Insert the percentage of code (actual or estimated/total size) and the name of the generator/translator used. |

11. Adapted code assumptions by component:

| Component | % Design Modified (DM) | % Code Modified (CM) | % Integration Modified (IM) | AAF [AAF = 0.4(DM) + 0.3(CM) + 0.3 (IM)] |
|---|---|---|---|---|
| 1. | | | | |
| 2. | | | | |
| 3. | | | | |
| 4. | | | | |
| 5. | | | | |
| 6. | | | | |
| 7. | | | | |
| 8. | | | | |
| 9. | | | | |
| 10. | | | | |
| 11. | | | | |
| 12. | | | | |
| 13. | | | | |
| 14. | | | | |
| 15. | | | | |
| 16. | | | | |

12. Object, feature or unadjusted function points assumed per component:

| Component | Language | Backfiring ratio (SLOCs per FP) | Unadjusted Function Points |
|---|---|---|---|
| 1. | | | |
| 2. | | | |
| 3. | | | |
| 4. | | | |
| 5. | | | |
| 6. | | | |
| 7. | | | |
| 8. | | | |
| 9. | | | |
| 10. | | | |
| 11. | | | |
| 12. | | | |
| 13. | | | |
| 14. | | | |
| 15. | | | |
| 16. | | | |
| TOTAL | | | |

13. Additional details:

**Figure C.3  Form SPD-3 Component Summaries (cont'd)**

**Table C.3**  *Continued*

| 11. Adapted code assumptions by component | For each component listed, identify the assumptions used to develop your AAF (i.e., percent design, code and integration modified) in the appropriate column. |
| 12. Object, feature or unadjusted function points assumed per component | For each component listed, identify the number of object, feature or unadjusted function points assumed in the appropriate column; include the component languages and associated backfiring ratios (the SLOCs per function point by language). |
| 13. Additional details | Provide any additional information that sheds light on the hierarchy, relationship and size of your components. |

**Form SPD-4 COCOMO II Progress Runs**

----------------------------------------------------------------------

1. Project Title:              2. Project ID No.                3. Rev No.
4. Date Prepared:              5. Originator:

----------------------------------------------------------------------

6. Starting Point:
7. Ending Point:
8. Progress Summary Information

| Milestone/ Anchor Point | Run No. | Date | Cost-to-Complete (PM) | Schedule-to-Complete (Months) | Remarks |
|---|---|---|---|---|---|
| | | | | | |
| | | | | | |
| | | | | | |
| | | | | | |
| | | | | | |
| | | | | | |
| | | | | | |
| | | | | | |
| | | | | | |

9. Component Information

| Component | Total ESLOC | Composite SF Rating | Composite EAF | Estimated Effort | SCED | Estimated Schedule |
|---|---|---|---|---|---|---|
| 1. | | | | | | |
| 2. | | | | | | |
| 3. | | | | | | |
| 4. | | | | | | |
| 5. | | | | | | |
| 6. | | | | | | |
| 7. | | | | | | |
| 8. | | | | | | |
| 9. | | | | | | |
| 10. | | | | | | |
| 11. | | | | | | |
| 12. | | | | | | |
| 13. | | | | | | |
| 14. | | | | | | |
| 15. | | | | | | |
| 16. | | | | | | |
| TOTAL | | | | | | |

**Figure C.4    Form SPD-4 COCOMO II Progress Runs**

**Table C.4   Instructions for Form SPD-4: COCOMO II Progress Runs**

| Item | Description |
|------|-------------|
| 1. Project Title | Insert the project name or title. |
| 2. Project ID No. | Identify the project Identification Number using a unique code devised for that purpose. |
| 3. Rev. No. | Insert the revision number starting from 0001. |
| 4. Date prepared | Identify the date when the form was prepared. |
| 5. Originator | Insert the name of the person who completed the form (and phone extension). |
| 6. Starting point | Identify the point in the life cycle where the run starts. |
| 7. Ending point | Identify the point in the life cycle where the run ends. |
| 8. Progress information | Summarize by anchor point and date the results of the runs in terms of both your cost-to-complete (in PM) and schedule-to-complete (in months). List each run if you have more than one per date. Put amplifying details in the remark column. |
| 9. Component information | Summarize the following information derived by run by component in the appropriate columns: Total ESLOC (Equivalent SLOC) used for the run; The composite SF (Scale Factor) rating; The composite EAF (Effort Adjustment Factor); The total estimated effort in PM; The SCED adjustment made (if any); The total estimated effort. At the bottom of the columns, summarize the entries. |

**Form SPD-5 COCOMO II Project Actuals**

--------------------------------------------------------------------------------

1. Project Title:                    2. Project ID No.                    3. Rev No.
4. Date Prepared:                    5. Originator:

--------------------------------------------------------------------------------

6. Actual cost data
   Total no. of person-months:          Total no. of calendar months:
   Total no. of SLOC:                   Total no. of defects:

7. Lessons learned summary

8. Component size (SLOC)

|  | | | | Totals | | | |
| Component | Estimated SLOC | Actual SLOC | Adapted SLOC | Reused SLOC | Gen. SLOC | Trans. SLOC | No. of Requirements. |
|---|---|---|---|---|---|---|---|
| 1. | | | | | | | |
| 2. | | | | | | | |
| 3. | | | | | | | |
| 4. | | | | | | | |
| 5. | | | | | | | |
| 6. | | | | | | | |
| 7. | | | | | | | |
| 8. | | | | | | | |
| 9. | | | | | | | |
| 10. | | | | | | | |
| 11. | | | | | | | |
| 12. | | | | | | | |
| 13. | | | | | | | |
| 14. | | | | | | | |
| 15. | | | | | | | |
| 16. | | | | | | | |
| 17. | | | | | | | |
| 18. | | | | | | | |
| 19 | | | | | | | |
| 20. | | | | | | | |
| 21. | | | | | | | |
| 22. | | | | | | | |
| TOTAL | | | | | | | |

**Figure C.5   Form SPD-5 COCOMO II Project Actuals**

**Table C.5   Instructions for Form SPD-5: COCOMO II Project Actuals**

| Item | Description |
| --- | --- |
| 1. Project Title | Insert the project name or title. |
| 2. Project ID No. | Identify the project Identification Number using a unique code devised for that purpose. |
| 3. Rev. No. | Insert the revision number starting from 0001. |
| 4. Date prepared | Identify the date when the form was prepared. |
| 5. Originator | Insert the name of the person who completed the form (and phone extension). |
| 6. Actual cost data | Tabulate the following four actuals based upon your records:<br>Total number of person months expended on the project<br>Total number of SLOCs developed on the project<br>Total number of calendar months consumed by the project<br>Total number of defects made (and corrected) on the project |
| 7. Lessons learned summary | Summarize the five most important lessons learned on the project. Provide amplifying detail in a lessons learned report as appropriate. |
| 8. Component size | Summarize the total number of estimated, actual, adapted, reused, generated and translated SLOCs and requirements upon which they were based in the appropriate columns by component. Total the columns at the bottom of the table. |

9.  Project attributes

|  | Ratings | | | | | | Comments (Including Don't Know) |
|---|---|---|---|---|---|---|---|
|  | VL | L | N | H | VH | XH |  |
| Precedentedness (PREC) |  |  |  |  |  |  |  |
| Development flexibility (FLEX) |  |  |  |  |  |  |  |
| Architecture/risk resolution (RESL) |  |  |  |  |  |  |  |
| Team cohesion (TEAM) |  |  |  |  |  |  |  |
| Process maturity (PMAT) |  |  |  |  |  |  |  |
| Required reliability (RELY) |  |  |  |  |  |  |  |
| Data base size (DATA) |  |  |  |  |  |  |  |
| Product complexity (CPLX) |  |  |  |  |  |  |  |
| Develop for reuse (RUSE) |  |  |  |  |  |  |  |
| Documentation match to life-cycle needs (DOCU) |  |  |  |  |  |  |  |
| Execution time constraint (TIME) |  |  |  |  |  |  |  |
| Main storage constraint (STOR) |  |  |  |  |  |  |  |
| Platform volatility (PVOL) |  |  |  |  |  |  |  |
| Analyst capability (ACAP) |  |  |  |  |  |  |  |
| Programmer capability (PCAP) |  |  |  |  |  |  |  |
| Personnel continuity (PCON) |  |  |  |  |  |  |  |
| Applications experience (APEX) |  |  |  |  |  |  |  |
| Platform experience (PLEX) |  |  |  |  |  |  |  |
| Language & tool experience (LTEX) |  |  |  |  |  |  |  |
| Use of software tools (TOOL) |  |  |  |  |  |  |  |
| Multi-site development (SITE) |  |  |  |  |  |  |  |
| Required development schedule (SCED) |  |  |  |  |  |  |  |
| Other |  |  |  |  |  |  |  |

10. Actual Resource Summary by Phase

| Milestone/ Anchor Point | Effort (PM) at Completion | Schedule (months) at Completion |
|---|---|---|
| 1. |  |  |
| 2. |  |  |
| 3. |  |  |
| 4. |  |  |
| 5. |  |  |
| 6. |  |  |
| 7. |  |  |
| 8. |  |  |
| 9. |  |  |
| 10 |  |  |
| TOTAL |  |  |

**Figure C.5    Form SPD-5 COCOMO II Project Actuals (cont'd)**

**Table C.5**   *Continued*

| Item | Description |
|---|---|
| 9.  Project attributes | Develop a composite rating for the COCOMO II scale factors and effort multipliers based upon project actuals. |
| 10. Actual Resource Summary by Phase | Summarize the actual effort and schedule expended by phase. Total across all phases at the bottom of the table. |

### Form SPD-5a COCOMO II Project Actuals: Simple Completed Project

---

1. Project Title:                2. Project ID No.                3. Rev No.
4. Date Prepared:                5. Originator:                   6. Organization:

---

7.  Starting Milestone:               8.  Ending Milestone:
9.  Total no. of person-months:       10. Total no. of calendar months:
11. Equivalent SLOC:                  12. Total no. of SLOC reused:
13. Non-trivial defects detected:     14. Defect detection starting milestone:

15. Project attribute ratings

| | VL | L | N | H | VH | XH | Comments (Including Don't Know) |
|---|---|---|---|---|---|---|---|
| Precedentedness (PREC) | | | | | | | |
| Development flexibility (FLEX) | | | | | | | |
| Architecture/risk resolution (RESL) | | | | | | | |
| Team cohesion (TEAM) | | | | | | | |
| Process maturity (PMAT) | | | | | | | |
| Required reliability (RELY) | | | | | | | |
| Data base size (DATA) | | | | | | | |
| Product complexity (CPLX) | | | | | | | |
| Develop for reuse (RUSE) | | | | | | | |
| Documentation match to life-cycle needs (DOCU) | | | | | | | |
| Execution time constraint (TIME) | | | | | | | |
| Main storage constraint (STOR) | | | | | | | |
| Platform volatility (PVOL) | | | | | | | |
| Analyst capability (ACAP) | | | | | | | |
| Programmer capability (PCAP) | | | | | | | |
| Personnel continuity (PCON) | | | | | | | |
| Applications experience (APEX) | | | | | | | |
| Platform experience (PLEX) | | | | | | | |
| Language & tool experience (LTEX) | | | | | | | |
| Use of software tools (TOOL) | | | | | | | |
| Multi-site development (SITE) | | | | | | | |
| Required development schedule (SCED) | | | | | | | |
| Other | | | | | | | |

16. Special project characteristics or lessons learned:

**Figure C.5a    Form SPD-5a COCOMO II Project Actuals: Simple Completed Project**

**Table C.5a  Instructions for Form SPD-5a: COCOMO II Actuals: Simple Completed Project**

| Item | Description |
| --- | --- |
| 1. Project Title | Insert the project name or title. |
| 2. Project ID No. | Identify the project Identification Number using a unique code devised for that purpose. |
| 3. Rev. No. | Insert the revision number starting from 0001. |
| 4. Date prepared | Identify the date when the form was prepared. |
| 5. Originator | Insert the name of the person who completed the form (and phone extension). |
| 6. Organization | Identify the Originator's organization by name. |
| 7. Starting Milestone | Identify the project milestone after which data is collected. |
| 8. Ending Milestone | Identify the project milestone after which data is no longer collected. |
| 9. Total no. of person-months | Total number of person-months expended on the project. |
| 10. Total no. of calendar months | Total number of calendar months consumed by the project. |
| 11. Equivalent SLOC | Report the total equivalent SLOC developed for the project (defined in Chapter 2). |
| 12. Total no. of SLOC reused | Report the total SLOC reused for the project (defined in Chapter 2). |
| 13. Non-trivial defects detected | Total number of non-trivial defects reported and tracked on the project. |
| 14. Defect detection starting milestone | Identify the project milestone after which defect detection data is collected. |
| 15. Project attributes | Put an "X" in appropriate rating box. For the most, rating guidelines are in Chapters 2 and 3 in the book. If you don't know an answer, say so in the extreme right column of the table. An "other" parameter is included to allow you to expand the list to include any additional factors that drive cost on your project (e.g., security). Recognize that these factor ratings will be updated at anchor points along with your estimates. |
| 16. Special project characteristics or lessons learned | Explain those special factors or characteristics that you believe influence your cost estimate or cost history, and record any major lessons learned on either cost estimation or productivity improvement. |

**Form SPD-6a COCOTS Project Level Data**

--------------------------------------------------------------------------------------------------------

1.  Project Title:                          2.  Project ID No.                          3.  Rev No.
4.  Date Prepared:                          5.  Originator:

--------------------------------------------------------------------------------------------------------

6.  Project Domain (circle one):

> *Core System Functionality*
>     Operational, Mission Critical
>     Operational, Non-mission Critical
>     Support
> *Communications, Navigation, and Surveillance*
>     Operational, Mission Critical
>     Operational, Non-mission Critical
>     Support
> *Administrative*
>     Operational, Business Critical
>     Operational, Non-business Critical
>     Support
> *Other (describe):*

7.  Where does COTS assessment occur in life cycle?:

8.  Delivery Scheduling (circle one):

| Delivery to one location, no ongoing maintenance | Delivery to one location, maintenance ongoing | Delivery to multiple locations, no ongoing maintenance | Delivery to multiple locations, maintenance ongoing |

9.  Schedule Duration (calendar months):

10. Project Total Effort (person-months):
        Development_____
        Maintenance_____

11. Standard Person-month(hours/person-month):

12. Project Total Delivered Source Code (SLOC):

**Figure C.6a     Form SPD-6a COCOTS Project Level Data**

**Table C.6a    Instructions for Form SPD-6a: COCOTS Project Level Data**

| Item | Description |
|---|---|
| 1. Project Title | Insert the project name or title. |
| 2. Project ID No. | Identify the project Identification Number using a unique code devised for that purpose. |
| 3. Rev. No. | Insert the revision number starting from 0001. |
| 4. Date prepared | Identify the date when the form was prepared. |
| 5. Originator | Insert the name of the person who completed the form (and phone extension). |
| 6. Project Domain | Circle or describe under "other" the general application domain of your system. |
| 7. Where does COTS assessment occur in life cycle? | Indicate when COTS products are assessed prior to selection (e.g., pre-, during, or post requirements definition?). |
| 8. Delivery Scheduling | Circle the item that best describes how the system is to be delivered for final acceptance test. |
| 9. Schedule Duration | Insert the overall number of months from the start of the project to final delivery, or to the end of the last phase being reported. |
| 10. Project Total Effort | Insert the overall effort accrued to the project during development and/or during maintenance. |
| 11. Standard Person-month | Insert the number of effective work hours you include in a person-month (e.g., 160 hrs?; 152 hrs?). |
| 12. Project Total Delivered Source Code | Insert the total size of the project including new and glue code (but by definition excluding the size of the COTS products themselves). |

13. SLOC Count Type (circle one):

| Logical | Physical (semicolons) | Physical (carriage returns) | Non-commented/ Non-blank | Other: |

14. Programming Languages

| Language | Percentage of Total SLOC |
|---|---|
|  |  |
|  |  |
|  |  |
|  |  |
|  |  |
|  |  |
|  |  |
|  |  |
|  |  |
|  |  |

15. Total System Function Points:

16. System Architecture (circle as needed):

| Pipe & Filter | Distributed | Main/Subroutine | Event Based |
|---|---|---|---|
| Multithreaded | Blackboard/Single Layer or General Repository | Closed Loop Feedback Control | Real Time |
| Rule-based | Transactional Database Centric | Layered | Other: |

17. System Architecting Process (describe):

**Figure C.6a    Form SPD-6a COCOTS Project Level Data (cont'd)**

**Table C.6a**   *Continued*

| Item | Description |
|------|-------------|
| 13. SLOC Count Type | Circle or describe under "other" your definition of a single source line of code. |
| 14. Programming Languages | Identify the languages used in the system and the percentage of total SLOC reported in item #13 that each represents. |
| 15. Total System Function Points | Insert the size of the system as determined in Function Points. |
| 16. System Architecture | Circle the item (or items) that best describe the underlying architecture of your system. |
| 17. System Architecting Process | Describe how or the activities that were performed to arrive at the architecture identified in item #16. |

**Form SPD-6b COCOTS Assessment Data**

------------------------------------------------------------------------------------------------

1. Project Title:               2. Project ID No.           3.  Rev No.
4. Date Prepared:               5. Originator:              5a. COTS Class:

------------------------------------------------------------------------------------------------

*Initial Filtering Effort by COTS class*
6. Total number of COTS candidates filtered:
7. Total initial filtering effort (person-months):
8. Average filtering effort per COTS candidate (person-months):

*Attribute Assessment Effort by COTS class*
9. Total number of COTS products assessed:
10. Total number COTS products selected/integrated:
11. Total attribute assessment effort (person-months):
12. Assessment Schedule duration (calendar months):
13. Assessment Effort per attribute:

| Attribute | Effort | | | | | | | |
|---|---|---|---|---|---|---|---|---|
| | U | EL | VL | L | N | H | VH | EH |
| Correctness | | | | | | | | |
| Availability/Robustness | | | | | | | | |
| Security | | | | | | | | |
| Product Performance | | | | | | | | |
| Understandability | | | | | | | | |
| Ease of Use | | | | | | | | |
| Version Compatibility | | | | | | | | |
| Intercomponent Compatibility | | | | | | | | |
| Flexibility | | | | | | | | |
| Installation/Upgrade Ease | | | | | | | | |
| Portability | | | | | | | | |
| Functionality | | | | | | | | |
| Price | | | | | | | | |
| Maturity | | | | | | | | |
| Vendor Support | | | | | | | | |
| Training | | | | | | | | |
| Vendor Concessions | | | | | | | | |
| Other1: | | | | | | | | |
| Other2: | | | | | | | | |

U — dont know              EL — no effort           VL — <1 per-hr          L — 1 per-hr<X<1 per-day
N — 1 per-day<X<1 per-wk    H — 1 per-wk<X<1 per- mt   VH — 1 per-mt<X<3 per-mt   VH — 1 per-mt<X<N per-yrs

**Figure C.6b    Form SPD-6b COCOTS Assessment Data**

**Table C.6b   Instructions for Form SPD-6b: COCOTS Assessment Data**

| Item | Description |
| --- | --- |
| 1. Project Title | Insert the project name or title. |
| 2. Project ID No. | Identify the project Identification Number using a unique code devised for that purpose. |
| 3. Rev. No. | Insert the revision number starting from 0001. |
| 4. Date prepared | Identify the date when the form was prepared. |
| 5. Originator | Insert the name of the person who completed the form (and phone extension). |
| 5a. COTS Class | Indicate the functional class of COTS products for which you are supplying data (e.g., GUIs, databases, OS, drivers, etc.) |
| 6. Total number of COTS candidates filtered | Insert the number of COTS products in the current class that were considered during initial product winnowing or filtering. |
| 7. Total initial filtering effort | Insert the total effort expended to winnow or filter COTS products in the current class down to the set of products that went through detailed assessment. |
| 8. Average filtering effort per COTS candidate | Insert the average effort expended to filter a given COTS product within the current class of COTS products. |
| 9. Total number of COTS products assessed | Insert the number of COTS products in the current class that went through detailed assessment before the final set of COTS products were selected for integration. |
| 10. Total number of COTS products selected/ integrated | Insert the number of COTS products in the current class that were finally integrated. |
| 11. Total attribute assessment effort | Insert the total effort expended to assess COTS products in the current class to arrive at the final set of products that were actually selected for integration. |
| 12. Assessment Schedule duration | Insert the overall number of months from the start of COTS product assessment until final selection for the current class of products. |
| 13. Assessment Effort per attribute | Check the box that most closely captures the amount of effort expended assessing the COTS products in the current class in terms of each given product attribute. |

## Form SPD-6c COCOTS Tailoring Data

------------------------------------------------------------------------

1. Project Title:          2. Project ID No.          3. Rev No.
4. Date Prepared:         5. Originator:             5a. COTS Class:

------------------------------------------------------------------------

*Tailoring Effort by COTS class*

6. Total number of COTS components tailored:
7. Total tailoring effort (person-months):
8. Tailoring schedule duration (calendar months):

*Tailoring Activity Complexity by COTS class*

| Tailoring Activities & Aids | Individual Activity & Aid Complexity Ratings | | | | | Corre-sponding Points |
|---|---|---|---|---|---|---|
| | Very Low (point value = 1) | Low (point value = 2) | Nominal (point value = 3) | High (point value = 4) | Very High (point value = 5) | |
| Parameter Specification | Zero to 50 parms to be initialized. | 51 to 100 parms to be initialized. | 101 to 500 parms to be initialized. | 501 to 1000 parms to be initialized. | 1001 or more parms to be initialized. | ------- |
| Script Writing | Menu-driven; 1 to 5 line scripts; 1 to 5 scripts needed. | Menu-driven; 6 to 10 line scripts; 6 to 15 scripts needed. | Handwritten; 11 to 25 line scripts; 16 to 30 scripts needed. | Handwritten; 26 to 50 line scripts; 31 to 50 scripts needed. | Handwritten; 51 or more line scripts; 51 or more scripts needed. | ------- |
| I/O Report & GUI Screen Specification & Layout | Automated or standard templates used; 1 to 5 reports/screens needed. | Automated or standard templates used; 6 to 15 reports/screens needed. | Automated or standard templates used; 16 to 25 reports/screens needed. | Handwritten or custom-designed; 26 to 50 reports/screens needed. | Handwritten or custom-designed; 51 or more reports/screens needed. | ------- |
| Security/Access Protocol Initialization & Set-up | 1 security level; 1 to 20 user profiles; 1 input screen/user. | 2 security levels 21 to 50 user profiles; 2 input screens/user. | 3 security levels 51 to 75 user profiles; 3 input screens/user. | 4 security levels 76 to 100 user profiles; 4 input screens/user. | 5 or more security levels 101 or more user profiles; 5 or more input screens/user. | ------- |
| Availability of COTS Tailoring Tools | Tools were highly useful. | Tools were very useful. | Tools were moderately useful. | Tools were somewhat useful. | No tools available. | ------- |

Total Point Score = _____

| Very Low | Low | Nominal | High | Very High |
|---|---|---|---|---|
| Point total is between 5 and 10. | Point total is between 11 and 15. | Point total is between 16 and 20. | Point total is between 21 and 25. | Point total is between 26 and 30. |

9. Aggregate complexity rating (circle one):    VL   L   N   H   VH

**Figure C.6c    Form SPD-6c COCOTS Tailoring Data**

**Table C.6c   Instructions for Form SPD-6c: COCOTS Tailoring Data**

| Item | Description |
| --- | --- |
| 1. Project Title | Insert the project name or title. |
| 2. Project ID No. | Identify the project Identification Number using a unique code devised for that purpose. |
| 3. Rev. No. | Insert the revision number starting from 0001. |
| 4. Date prepared | Identify the date when the form was prepared. |
| 5. Originator | Insert the name of the person who completed the form (and phone extension). |
| 5a. COTS Class | Indicate the functional class of COTS products for which you are supplying data (e.g., GUIs, databases, OS, drivers, etc.) |
| 6. Total number of COTS components tailored | Insert the number of COTS products in the current class that were tailored as part of integration into the larger system. |
| 7. Total tailoring effort | Insert the total effort expended to tailor COTS products in the current class as part of integration into the larger system. |
| 8. Assessment Schedule duration | Insert the overall number of months from start to completion of tailoring activities for all COTS components in the current class of products. |
| 9. Aggregate complexity rating | 1) Going row by row in the complexity table, rate each item in column 1 by the criteria in columns 2 through 6; record the corresponding points associated with your rating for that item in column 7. 2) Add the points in column 7 to determine the total point score. 3) Use that score to determine the final aggregate complexity rating from the lower rating table. |

**Form SPD-6d COCOTS Glue Code Data**

---

1. Project Title:                2. Project ID No.                     3. Rev No.
4. Date Prepared:                5. Originator:                        5a. COTS Class:

---

6.  Number COTS components with Glue Code:
7.  Functions provided by these COTS components (circle as needed):

| Spreadsheet | Communications | Message Handling | Word Processing | User Display |
| CASE Environment | Scheduling | Database | Diagnostics | Mathematical Utilities |
| Signal Processing | Compiler | Other: | | |

8. Glue Code integration nature: % new integration_____ %
   upgrade/refresh_____

9. Glue Code schedule duration (calendar months):
10. Total Glue Code effort (person-months):
11. Glue Code SLOC:
12. Glue Code SLOC count type (circle one):

| Logical | Physical (semicolons) | Physical (carriage returns) | Non-commented/ Non-blank | Other: |

13. Glue Code Programming Languages

| Language | Percentage of Total Glue SLOC | Language | Percentage of Total Glue SLOC |
|----------|-------------------------------|----------|-------------------------------|
|          |                               |          |                               |
|          |                               |          |                               |
|          |                               |          |                               |
|          |                               |          |                               |
|          |                               |          |                               |
|          |                               |          |                               |
|          |                               |          |                               |
|          |                               |          |                               |
|          |                               |          |                               |
|          |                               |          |                               |

14. Total Glue Code Function Points:

15. Percentage rework Glue Code (CREVOL): SLOC:_____     UFP:_____

**Figure C.6d     Form SPD-6d COCOTS Glue Code Data**

**Table C.6d   Instructions for Form SPD-6d: COCOTS Glue Code Data**

| Item | Description |
|---|---|
| 1. Project Title | Insert the project name or title. |
| 2. Project ID No. | Identify the project Identification Number using a unique code devised for that purpose. |
| 3. Rev. No. | Insert the revision number starting from 0001. |
| 4. Date prepared | Identify the date when the form was prepared. |
| 5. Originator | Insert the name of the person who completed the form (and phone extension). |
| 5a. COTS Class | Indicate the functional class of COTS products for which you are supplying data (e.g., GUIs, databases, OS, drivers, etc.) |
| 6. Number COTS components with Glue Code | Insert the number of COTS products in the current class for which you are reporting Glue Code data. |
| 7. Functions provided by these COTS components | Circle or describe under "other" the general functions being supplied by the COTS components in the current class. |
| 8. Glue Code integration nature | Insert the percentage of overall glue code written for the current class of products that represents new integration and/or an up grade or refresh effort. |
| 9. Glue Code Schedule duration | Insert the overall number of months from start to completion of glueware coding activities for all COTS components in the current class of products. |
| 10. Total Glue Code effort | Insert the total effort expended to write Glue Code for COTS products in the current class as part of integration into the larger system. |
| 11. Glue Code SLOC | Insert the total size of the Glue Code written for the current class of COTS products. |
| 12. SLOC Count Type | Circle or describe under "other" your definition of a single source line of Glue Code. |
| 13. Glue Code Programming Languages | Identify the languages used in the Glue Code and the percentage of Glue SLOC reported in item #12 that each represents. |
| 14. Total Glue Code Function Points | Insert the size of the Glue Code as determined in Function Points for the current class of COTS products. |
| 15. Percentage rework Glue Code (CREVOL) | Insert the percentage of Glue Code and/or Function Points that had to be reworked due to requirements evolution and/or COTS component upgrade for the current class of products. |

16. Glue Code Project Scale Factor Attribute

| | VL | L | N | H | VH | Comments (Including Don't Know) |
|---|---|---|---|---|---|---|
| | | | Ratings | | | |
| Application Architectural Engineering (AAREN) | | | | | | |

17. Glue Code Project Effort Multiplier Attributes

| | VL | L | N | H | VH | Comments |
|---|---|---|---|---|---|---|
| COTS Integrator Experience with Product (ACIEP) | | | | | | |
| COTS Integratot Personnel Capability (ACIPC) | | | | | | |
| Integrator Experience with COTS Integration Processes (AXCIP) | ▓ | | | | | |
| Integrator Personnel Continuity (APCON) | | | | | | |
| COTS Product Maturity (ACPMT) | | | | | | |
| COTS Supplier Product Extenstion Willingness (ACSEW) | ▓ | | | | | |
| COTS Product Interface Complexity (APCPX) | ▓ | | | | | |
| COTS Supplier Product Support (ACPPS) | ▓ | | | | | |
| COTS Supplier Provided Training and Documentation (ACPTD) | | | | | | |
| Constraints on System/subsystem Reliability (ACREL) | ▓ | | | | | |
| Application Interface Complexity (AACPX) | ▓ | | | | | |
| Constraints on System/subsystem Technical Performance (ACPER) | ▓ | ▓ | | | | |
| System Portability (ASPRT) | ▓ | ▓ | | | | |

**Figure C.6d    Form SPD-6d COCOTS Glue Code Data (cont'd)**

**Table C.6d**   *Continued*

| Item | Description |
|------|-------------|
| 16. Glue Code Project Scale Factor Attribute | Put an "X" in appropriate rating box. Rating guidelines appear in the detailed COCOTS data collection survey found on the accompanying CD-ROM. If you don't know an answer, say so in the extreme right column of the table. Recognize that this factor rating will be updated at anchor points along with your estimates. |
| 17. Glue Code Project Effort Multiplier Attributes | Put an "X" in appropriate rating box. (Follow the guidelines for item #16.) |

**Form SPD-6e COCOTS Volatility Data**

---------------------------------------------------------------------------------------

1. Project Title:          2. Project ID No.          3. Rev No.
4. Date Prepared:          5. Originator:

---------------------------------------------------------------------------------------

6. Application effort *excluding* effort due to COTS integration (person-months):

7. Percentage application rework effort due to requirements evolution *excluding* rework effort directly related to COTS integration (%):

8. Percentage application rework effort due to COTS product volatility (%):

9. COCOMO II Project Scale Factor Attributes

| | VL | L | N | H | VH | X H | Comments (Including Don't Know) |
|---|---|---|---|---|---|---|---|
| Precedentedness (PREC) | | | | | | | |
| Development Flexibility (FLEX) | | | | | | | |
| Architecture/Risk Resolution (RESL) | | | | | | | |
| Team Cohesion (TEAM) | | | | | | | |
| Process Maturity (PMAT) | | | | | | | |

Ratings

**Figure C.6e    Form SPD-6e COCOTS Volatility Data**

**Table C.6e   Instructions for Form SPD-6e: COCOTS Volatility Data**

| Item | Description |
|---|---|
| 1. Project Title | Insert the project name or title. |
| 2. Project ID No. | Identify the project Identification Number using a unique code devised for that purpose. |
| 3. Rev. No. | Insert the revision number starting from 0001. |
| 4. Date prepared | Identify the date when the form was prepared. |
| 5. Originator | Insert the name of the person who completed the form (and phone extension). |
| 6. Application effort *excluding* effort due to COTS integration | Insert the total effort expended to develop the system minus that effort directly related to integration of COTS products. |
| 7. Percentage application rework effort due to requirements evolution *excluding* rework effort directly related to COTS integration | Insert the percentage of application effort that represents rework that had to be done due to requirements evolution (REVOL) minus rework effort directly related to integration of COTS products. |
| 8. Percentage application rework effort due to COTS product volatility | Insert the percentage of application effort that represents rework that had to be done due to requirements evolution directly related to integration of COTS products and/or due to COTS component upgrades. |
| 9. COCOMO II Project Scale Factor Attributes | Put an "X" in appropriate rating box. For the most, rating guidelines are in Chapters 2 and 3 in the book. If you don't know an answer, say so in the extreme right column of the table. Recognize that these factor ratings will be updated at anchor points along with your estimates. |

## Form SPD-7 COPSEMO Details Summaries

--------------------------------------------------------------------------------

1. Project Title:               2. Project ID No.               3. Rev No.
4. Date Prepared:               5. Originator:

--------------------------------------------------------------------------------

6. Cycles and total effort and schedule per phase

| Phase # | Name | Number of Cycles | Start Date | End Date | Tota l PM | Total M |
|---------|------|------------------|------------|----------|-----------|---------|
| 1. | Incpt. | | | | | |
| 2 | Elab. | | | | | |
| 3. | Cnst. | | | | | |
| 4. | Trns. | | | | | |

7. Effort per Activity per Cycle per Phase

| Phase # | Name | Cycle # | Start Date | End Date | MGT | ENV | REQ | DES | Impl | ASS | DEP | Total PM | Total M |
|---------|------|---------|------------|----------|-----|-----|-----|-----|------|-----|-----|----------|---------|
| 1. | Incpt. | 1. | | | | | | | | | | | |
| | | | | | | | | | | | | | |
| | | | | | | | | | | | | | |
| | | | | | | | | | | | | | |
| | | | | | | | | | | | | | |
| | | | | | | | | | | | | | |
| | | | | | | | | | | | | | |
| | | | | | | | | | | | | | |

**Activities**
MGT – Management   ENV – Environment incl. CM   REQ – Requirements incl. Bus. Modeling   DES – Design   Impl – Implementation   ASS – Assessment incl. Test, QA, R/D V&V   DEP – Deployment

**Phases**
Incpt. – Inception   Elab. – Elaboration   Cnst. – Construction   Trns. – Transition

8. Persons per Activity per Cycle per Phase

| Phase # | Name | Cycle # | Start Date | End Date | MGT | ENV | REQ | DES | Impl | ASS | DEP | Total PM | Total M |
|---------|------|---------|------------|----------|-----|-----|-----|-----|------|-----|-----|----------|---------|
| 1. | Incpt. | 1. | | | | | | | | | | | |
| | | | | | | | | | | | | | |
| | | | | | | | | | | | | | |
| | | | | | | | | | | | | | |
| | | | | | | | | | | | | | |
| | | | | | | | | | | | | | |
| | | | | | | | | | | | | | |
| | | | | | | | | | | | | | |

**Figure C.7   Form SPD-7 COPSEMO Details Summaries**

**Table C.7   Instructions for Form SPD-7: COPSEMO Details Summaries**

| Item | Description |
|------|-------------|
| 1. Project Title | Insert the project name or title. |
| 2. Project ID No. | Identify the project Identification Number using a unique code devised for that purpose. |
| 3. Rev. No. | Insert the revision number starting from 0001. |
| 4. Date prepared | Identify the date when the form was prepared. |
| 5. Originator | Insert the name of the person who completed the form (and phone extension). |
| 6. Cycles and total effort and schedule per phase | Start by confirming the phases of your life cycle (Inception, Elaboration, Construction and Transition) in the left most columns; if other names as used, please provide them along with a mapping to the MBASE/RUP phase names. |
| | Enter the number of cycles or iterations within each phase. A cycle or iteration does not have to do all the activities, but does have clear start and finish times and be delineated by some concrete criteria. |
| | Next, insert the start and end dates for the phase. |
| | Finally, summarize the effort (number of person months, PM) and duration (months; M) by phase. The effort is also shown on Figure C-2b Phase Summaries (MBASE/RUP process). |
| 7. Effort per Activity per Cycle per Phase | Start by entering the phase (Inception, Elaboration, Construction and Transition) and the cycle number in the left most columns. |
| | Next, insert the start and end dates for the cycle or iteration. |
| | Then, enter the number of person-months (PM) for each of the following activities for the cycle: |
| |     MGT (Management) |
| |     ENV (Environment incl. CM) |
| |     REQ (Requirements incl. Bus. Modeling) |
| |     DES ( Design) |
| |     Impl (Implementation) |
| |     ASS (Assessment incl. Test, QA, R/D V&V) |
| |     DEP (Deployment |
| | Finally, summarize the effort (number of person-months; PM) and duration (months; M) by cycle. |
| 8. Persons per Activity per Cycle per Phase | Start by entering the phase (Inception, Elaboration, Construction and Transition) and the cycle number in the left most columns. |
| | Next, insert the start and end dates for the cycle or iteration. |
| | Then, enter the number of persons and at what level (e.g., 1 @ FT, 2 @ .5 FT) for each of each activity as listed above for the cycle. |
| | Finally, summarize the effort (number of person-months; PM) and duration (months; M) by cycle. |

## Form SPD-8 COQUALMO Details Summaries

-----------------------------------------------------------------------------------------------

1. Project Title:              2. Project ID No.              3. Rev No.
4. Date Prepared:              5. Originator:

-----------------------------------------------------------------------------------------------

6.  Defect Introduction by Stage and Artifact

Number of Defects Introduced

|  | Inception (WF P&R) | Elaboration (WF PD) | Construction (WF P+I+T) | Transition | Don't Know |
|---|---|---|---|---|---|
| No. of Requirements Defects |  |  |  |  |  |
| No. of Design Defects |  |  |  |  |  |
| No. of Code Defects |  |  |  |  |  |
| No. of Rework Defects |  |  |  |  |  |

TOTAL

7.  Defect Removal by Stage and Artifact

Number of Defects Removed

|  | Inception (WF P&R) | Elaboration (WF PD) | Construction (WF P+I+T) | Transition | Don't Know |
|---|---|---|---|---|---|
| No. of Requirements Defects |  |  |  |  |  |
| No. of Design Defects |  |  |  |  |  |
| No. of Code Defects |  |  |  |  |  |
| No. of Rework Defects |  |  |  |  |  |

TOTAL

8.  Defect Identification by Severity and Artifact

Number of Defects Found

|  | Critical | High | Medium | Low | None | Don't Know |
|---|---|---|---|---|---|---|
| No. of Requirements Defects |  |  |  |  |  |  |
| No. of Design Defects |  |  |  |  |  |  |
| No. of Code Defects |  |  |  |  |  |  |
| No. of Rework Defects |  |  |  |  |  |  |

TOTAL

9. Number of Open Trouble Reports (Liens) At Product Delivery:

**Figure C.8    Form SPD-8 COQUALMO Details Summaries**

**Table C.8    Instructions for Form SPD-8: COQUALMO Details Summaries**

| Item | Description |
|---|---|
| 1. Project Title | Insert the project name or title. |
| 2. Project ID No. | Identify the project Identification Number using a unique code devised for that purpose. |
| 3. Rev. No. | Insert the revision number starting from 0001. |
| 4. Date prepared | Identify the date when the form was prepared. |
| 5. Originator | Insert the name of the person who completed the form (and phone extension). |
| 6. Defect introduction by stage and and artifact [Note: COQUALMO only addresses non-trivial (Critical, High and Medium Severity) defects (see chapter 5, section 5); thus, report only non-trivial defects unless other wise specified.] | Identify the number of defects introduced by artifact (row) and phase (column). If you don't know, place an "X" in the appropriate column. Summarize your answers at the bottom of the table. "WF P&R" stands for Waterfall process Plans and Requirements phase; "WF PD" stands for Waterfall process Preliminary Design phase; and "WF P+I+T" stands for Waterfall process Programming, Integration and Test phase |
| 7. Defect removal by stage and artifact | Insert the number of defects removed by artifact (row) and stage (column). |
| 8. Defect identification by severity and artifact | Identify the number of defects found by artifact (row) and severity (column). If you don't know, place an "X" in the appropriate column. Summarize your answers at the bottom of the table. |
| 9. Number of Open Trouble Reports (Liens) At Product Delivery | Identify the total number of known liens (open trouble reports) upon delivery. This number should include any patches that were made that you plan to fix in operations. |

## 10. Defect Removal Capability Rating Scales

### Automated Analysis

| | Very Low | Low | Nominal | High | Very High | Extra High | Dont Know |
|---|---|---|---|---|---|---|---|
| Rating Scale | Simple compiler syntax checking | Basic compiler capabilities for static module-level code analysis, syntax type-checking. | All of the above, plus some compiler extensions for static module and inter-module level code analysis, syntax, type-checking. Basic requirements and design consistency, traceability checking. | All of the above, plus intermediate-level module and inter-module code syntax and semantic analysis. Simple requirements /design view consistency checking. | All of the above, plus more elaborate requirements /design view consistency checking. Basic distributed-processing and temporal analysis, model checking, symbolic execution. | All of the above, plus formalized* specification and verification. Advanced distributed processing and temporal analysis, model checking, symbolic execution\n\n*Consistency-checkable pre-conditions and post-conditions, but not mathematical theorems. | |
| Your Rating | | | | | | | |

### Peer Reviews

| | Very Low | Low | Nominal | High | Very High | Extra High | Dont Know |
|---|---|---|---|---|---|---|---|
| Rating Scale | No peer review | Ad-hoc informal walkthroughs Minimal preparation, no follow-up. | Well-defined sequence of preparation, review, minimal follow-up. Informal review roles and procedures. | Formal review roles with all participants well-trained and procedures applied to all products using basic checklists*, follow up. | Formal review roles with all participants well-trained and procedures applied to all product artifacts & changes (formal change control boards). Basic review checklists*, root cause analysis. Formal follow-up. Use of historical data on inspection rate, preparation rate, fault density. | Formal review roles and procedures for fixes, change control. Extensive review checklists*, root cause analysis. Continuous review process improvement. User/Customer involvement, Statistical Process Control. | |
| Your Rating | | | | | | | |

* Checklists are lists of things to look for or to check against (e.g. Fagan's exit criteria)

### Execution Testing and Tools

| | VL | Low | Nominal | High | VH | EH | Dont Know |
|---|---|---|---|---|---|---|---|
| Rating Scale | No testing | Ad-hoc testing and debugging. Basic text-based debugger. | Basic unit test, integration test, system test process. Basic test data management, problem tracking support. Test criteria based on checklists. | Well-defined test sequence tailored to organization (acceptance, alpha, beta, flight, etc.) test. Basic test coverage tools, test support system. Basic test process management. | More advanced test tools, test data preparation, basic test oracle support, distributed monitoring and analysis, assertion checking. Metrics-based test process management. | Highly advanced tools for test oracles, distributed monitoring and analysis, assertion checking. Integration of automated analysis and test tools. Model-based test process management. | |
| Your Rating | | | | | | | |

**Figure C.8 Form SPD-8 COQUALMO Details Summaries (cont'd)**

**Table C.8**   *Continued*

| Item | Description |
|------|-------------|
| 10. Defect Removal Capability Rating Scales | Rate the defect removal capability using three relatively orthogonal profiles each with six levels of increasingly better removal capability. *Automated Analysis*—rates the ability to automatically analyze life cycle artifacts for defects. |
| | *Peer Reviews*—rates the effectiveness of peer reviews used to identify defects early in the life cycle. |
| | *Execution Testing and Tools*—rates the ability to find errors using automated execution testing techniques and tools. |

**Form SPD-9 CORADMO Details Summaries**

--------------------------------------------------------------------------------------

1. Project Title:          2. Project ID No.          3. Rev No.
4. Date Prepared:          5. Originator:

--------------------------------------------------------------------------------------

6.   CORADMO Driver Ratings (attributes)

| | VL | L | N | H | VH | X H | Comments (Including Don't Know) |
|---|---|---|---|---|---|---|---|
| Reuse and Very High Level Languages (RVHL) | | | | | | | |
| Development Process Reengineering and Streamlining (DPRS) | | | | | | | |
| Collaboration Efficiency (CLAB) | | | | | | | |
| Architecture/Risk Resolution (RESL) | | | | | | | |
| Prepositioning Assets (PPOS) | | | | | | | |

7.   Brief descriptions of RAD approaches and tools:

**Figure C.9    Form SPD-9 CORADMO Details Summaries**

**Table C.9    Instructions for Form SPD-9: CORADMO Details Summaries**

| Item | Description |
|---|---|
| 1. Project Title | Insert the project name or title. |
| 2. Project ID No. | Identify the project Identification Number using a unique code devised for that purpose. |
| 3. Rev. No. | Insert the revision number starting from 0001. |
| 4. Date prepared | Identify the date when the form was prepared. |
| 5. Originator | Insert the name of the person who completed the form (and phone extension). |
| 6. CORADMO Driver Ratings (attributes) | Put an "X" in appropriate rating box. The rating definitions and guidelines for CORADMO are in Chapter 5 of the book. RESL should be the same as the rating for your project as shown on SPD-1. If you don't know an answer, say so in the extreme right column of the table. |
| 7. Brief descriptions of RAD approaches and tools | Summarize the RAD approaches and tools applied in this project. |

# D

# COCOMO II and USC-CSE
# Affiliate ProgramS

## D.1  INTRODUCTION

The COCOMO II Affiliates' program is a special option within the overall USC-CSE Affiliates' program. COCOMO II Affiliates obtain early access to COCOMO II calibration updates; to emerging extensions such as COCOTS, CORADMO, and COPROMO; and to associated tools such as code counters for newer programming languages. They participate in Affiliates' workshops to collaboratively prioritize and refine the definition of COCOMO II model updates and emerging extensions, and to compare experiences on the maturity and utility of emerging estimation-related technology. They obtain preferential access to USC-CSE researchers for COCOMO II-related questions.

The overall USC-CSE Affiliates' program extends this mode of operation to include CSE's other main research areas: Model-Based (System) Architechting and Software Engineering (MBASE), software architectures, and WinWin requirements negotiation groupware and techniques.

A copy of the application to become an Affiliate is available on the CD that accompanies this book. Alternatively, you may call our administrator at (213) 740-5703 or email us at CSE@sunset.usc.edu.

## D.2 PRIMARY BENEFITS

As an Affiliate, members of your organization are invited to attend as our guests conferences and workshops on topics in software project management and software cost estimation. Such technical meetings and focused workshops, which often include tutorials, provide the Affiliates organizations' leading-edge personnel with valuable lessons, insights and the latest versions of COCOMO II tools and extensions.

In the event that someone from an Affiliates' organization could not participate in these conferences or workshops but desires a copy of the proceedings, the Center is more than happy to provide it. Most of the material is initially posted on the Affiliates-only web site.

The Center also makes available standardized code counters for all of the generally available programming languages. This code counters can be used freely within an Affiliates organization. Since they are provided in source code form they can, be tailored as needed.

The most valuable benefit, however, may be the technical support in cost modeling and estimating that is available only to Affiliates. The support has been likened to that provided by commercial estimating packages, but is provided by our researchers directly.

## D.3. ADDITIONAL BENEFITS

Organizations that wish to take advantage of the other research areas that CSE is involved in can become full Affiliates which provides access to *all* technical conferences, not just those limited to project management and cost estimation. They enjoy technical support on tools and in areas such as MBASE, software architecture, and WinWin. They have the opportunity to assess technology maturity and to benchmark their relative capabilities across the full spectrum of emerging software engineering technologies. They obtain additional benefits such as a free annual one-day visit by a CSE researcher, and opportunities to collaborate on joint research projects.

## D.4 LEVELS OF AFFILIATION

There are different levels of affiliation, each with different costs. For small organizations, those with under $100 M/year sales or budget, the fee is $5000. For COCOMO II Affiliation, the fee is $15,000 per year. For full affiliation, the fee is $25,000 per year. For non-U.S. organizations, only full affiliation at $40,000 per year is available.

## D.5    CURRENT AFFILIATES

Finally, to highlight the opportunities available to our Affiliates for mutually beneficial interaction with other top-notch organizations within their industries, we present here those members that currently enjoy the benefits of the USC-SCE Affiliates' program:

*Commercial Industry*
Automobile Club of Southern California, C-bridge, EDS, Fidelity, GroupSystems.com, Hughes Network Systems, Lucent, Microsoft, Motorola, Rational, Sun, Telcordia, Xerox.

*Aerospace Industry*
Boeing, Draper Labs, GDE Systems, Litton, Lockheed Martin, Northrop Grumman, Raytheon/East, Raytheon/West, SAIC, TRW.

*Government*
FAA, USAF Rome Lab, US Army Research Labs, US Army TACOM.

*FFRDCs and Consortia*
Aerospace Corporation, IDA, SEI, SPC.

*International Members*
Chung-Ang University (Korea).

# E

# USC COCOMO II.2000
# Software Reference Manual

---

**CHAPTER 1: INTRODUCTION**

## 1.1   WHAT IS COCOMO?

COCOMO (COnstructive COst MOdel) is a screen-oriented, interactive software package that assists in budgetary planning and schedule estimation of a software development project. Through the flexibility of COCOMO, a software project manager (or team leader) can develop a model (or multiple models) of projects in order to identify potential problems in resources, personnel, budgets, and schedules both before and while the potential software package is being developed.

The COCOMO software package is based upon the software cost and schedule estimation model: COnstructive COst MOdel version II (COCOMO II). This is the newly revised version of the original COnstructive COst MOdel (COCOMO) first published by Dr. Barry Boehm in his book *Software Engineering Economics*, Prentice-Hall (1981), and Ada COCOMO (1989) predecessors. The current model is described in *Software Cost Estimation with COCOMO II*, (Prentice-Hall) [Boehm et al. 2000]

The primary objectives of the COCOMO II.2000 effort are:

- To develop a software cost and schedule estimation model tuned to the life cycle practices of the 21$^{st}$ century.
- To develop software cost database and tool support capabilities for continuous model improvement.
- To provide a quantitative analytic framework, and set of tools and techniques for evaluating the effects of software technology improvements on software life cycle costs and schedules.

The full COCOMO II model includes three stages. Stage 1 supports estimation of prototyping or applications composition efforts. Stage 2 supports estimation in the Early Design stage of a project, when less is known about the project's cost drivers. Stage 3 supports estimation in the Post-Architecture stage of a project.

This version of USC COCOMO II implements stage 3 formulas to estimate the effort, schedule, and cost required to develop a software product. It also provides the breakdown of effort and schedule into software life-cycle phases and activities from both the Waterfall model and the Mbase Model. The Mbase model is fully described in *Software Cost Estimation with COCOMO II*.

### 1.1.1    Effort Estimation Equation

Estimate effort with:

$$ PM = \prod_{i=1}^{17} (EM_i) \cdot A \cdot \left[ \left( 1 + \frac{REVL}{100} \right) \cdot Size \right]^{(0.91 + 0.01 \sum_{j=1}^{5} SF_j)} + \left( \frac{ASLOC \cdot \left( \frac{AT}{100} \right)}{ATPROD} \right) $$

where

$$ Size = KNSLOC + \left[ KASLOC \cdot \left( \frac{100 - AT}{100} \right) \right. $$

$$ \cdot \left. \frac{\left( AA + SU + 0.4 \cdot DM + 0.3 \cdot CM + 0.3 \cdot IM \right)}{100} \right] $$

$$ B = 0.91 + 0.01 \sum_{j=1}^{5} SF $$

(EQ 1-1)

| Symbol | Description |
|---|---|
| A | Constant, currently calibrated as 2.45 |
| AA | Assessment and assimilation |
| ADAPT | Percentage of components adapted (represents the effort required in understanding software) |
| AT | Percentage of components that are automatically translated |
| ATPROD | Automatic translation productivity |
| REVL | Breakage: Percentage of code thrown away due to requirements volatility |
| CM | Percentage of code modified |
| DM | Percentage of design modified |
| EM | Effort Multipliers: RELY, DATA, CPLX, RUSE, DOCU, TIME, STOR, PVOL, ACAP, PCAP, PCON, APEX, PLEX, LTEX, TOOL, SITE |
| IM | Percentage of integration and test modified |
| KASLOC | Size of the adapted component expressed in thousands of adapted source lines of code |
| KNSLOC | Size of component expressed in thousands of new source lines of code |

| Symbol | Description |
|--------|-------------|
| PM | Person Months of estimated effort |
| SF | Scale Factors: PREC, FLEX, RESL, TEAM, PMAT |
| SU | Software understanding (zero if DM = 0 and CM = 0) |

### 1.1.2 Schedule Estimation Equation

Determine time to develop (TDEV) with an estimated effort, PM, that excludes the effect of the SCED effort multiplier:

$$TDEV = \left[3.67 \times (\overline{PM})^{(0.28 + 0.2 \times (b - 1.91))}\right] \cdot \frac{SCED\%}{100}$$

(EQ 1-2)

$$B = 0.91 + 0.01 \sum_{j=1}^{5} SF_j$$

| Symbol | Description |
|--------|-------------|
| PM | Person Months of estimated effort from Early Design or Post-Architecture models (excluding the effect of the SCED effort multiplier) |
| SF | Scale Factors: PREC, FLEX, RESL, TEAM, PMAT |
| TDEV | Time to develop |
| SCED | Schedule |
| SCED% | The compression / expansion percentage in the SCED effort multiplier |

### 1.1.3 Scale Factors

Equation 1-2 defines the exponent, B, used in Equation 1-1. Table 1-1 provides the rating levels for the COCOMO II scale drivers. The selection of scale drivers is based on the rationale that they are a significant source of exponential variation on a project's effort or productivity variation. Each scale driver has a range of rating levels, from Very Low to Extra High. Each rating level has a weight, W, and the specific value of the weight is called a scale factor. A project's scale factors, $W_i$, are summed across all of the factors, and used to determine a scale exponent, B, via the following formula:

$$B = 0.91 + 0.01 \times \sum_{j=1}^{5} SF_j$$

(EQ 1-3)

For example, if scale factors with an Extra High rating are each assigned a weight of (0), then a 100 KSLOC project with Extra High ratings for all factors will have $SF_j = 0$, $B = 1.01$, and a relative effort $E = 100^{1.01} = 105$ PM. If scale factors with Very Low rating are each assigned a weight of (5), then a project with Very Low (5) ratings for all factors will have $SF_j = 5$, $B = 1.26$, and a relative effort $E = 331$ PM. This represents a large variation, but the increase involved in a one-unit change in one of the factors is only about 4.7%.

**Table 1-1   Scale Factors for COCOMO II Early Design and Post-Architecture Models**

| Scale Factors (SF$_j$) | Very Low | Low | Nominal | High | Very High | Extra High |
|---|---|---|---|---|---|---|
| PREC | thoroughly unprecedented | largely unprecedented | somewhat unprecedented | generally familiar | largely familiar | thoroughly familiar |
| FLEX | rigorous | occasional relaxation | some relaxation | general conformity | some conformity | general goals |
| RESL [1] | little (20%) | some (40%) | often (60%) | Generally (75%) | mostly (90%) | full (100%) |
| TEAM | very difficult interactions | some difficult interactions | basically cooperative interactions | largely cooperative | highly cooperative | seamless inter-actions |
| PMAT | Weighted average of "Yes" answers to CMM Maturity Questionnaire | | | | | |

### 1.1.4   Sizing Methods

#### SLOC: LINES OF CODE COUNTING RULES

In COCOMO II, the logical source statement has been chosen as the standard line of code. Defining a line of code is difficult due to conceptual differences involved in accounting for executable statements and data declarations in different languages. The goal is to measure the amount of intellectual work put into program development, but difficulties arise when trying to define consistent measures across different languages. Breakage due to change of requirements also complicates sizing. To minimize these problems, the Software Engineering Institute (SEI) definition checklist for a logical source statement is used in defining the line of code measure. The Software Engineering Institute (SEI) has developed this checklist as part of a system of definition checklists, report forms and supplemental forms to support measurement definitions [Park 1992] [Goethert et al. 1992].

Figure 1-1 shows a portion of the definition checklist as it is being applied to support the development of the COCOMO II model. Each checkmark in the "Includes" column identifies a particular statement type or attribute included in the definition, and vice-versa for the excludes. Other sections in the definition clarify statement attributes for usage, delivery, functionality, replications and development status. There are also clarifications for language specific statements for ADA, C, C++, CMS-2, COBOL, FORTRAN, JOVIAL and Pascal.

Some changes were made to the line-of-code definition that departs from the default definition provided in [Park 1992]. These changes eliminate categories of software, which are generally small sources of project effort. Not included in the definition are commercial-off-the-shelf software (COTS), government-furnished software (GFS), other products, language support libraries and operating systems, or other commercial libraries. Code generated with source code generators is not included though measurements will be taken with and without generated code to support analysis.

---

[1] % significant module interfaces specified, percentages are the subjective weighted average of 1 and % significant risks eliminated.

## Definition Checklist for Source Statements Counts

Definition name:   Logical Source Statements     Date: _____

_____ (basic definition)     Originator:  COCOMO.II _____

| Measurement unit | | Physical source lines | | | | |
|---|---|---|---|---|---|---|
| | | Logical source statements | ☑ | | | |
| Statement type | Definition ☑ | Data Array | | | Includes | Excludes |
| *When a line or statement contains more than one type, classify it as the type with the highest precedence.* | | | | | | |
| 1 Executable | Order of precedence → | | 1 | | ☑ | |
| 2 Nonexecutable | | | | | | |
| 3   Declarations | | | 2 | | ☑ | |
| 4   Compiler directives | | | 3 | | ☑ | |
| 5   Comments | | | | | | |
| 6      On their own lines | | | 4 | | | ☑ |
| 7      On lines with source code | | | 5 | | | ☑ |
| 8      Banners and non-blank spacers | | | 6 | | | ☑ |
| 9      Blank (empty) comments | | | 7 | | | ☑ |
| 10     Blank lines | | | 8 | | | ☑ |
| 11 | | | | | | |
| 12 | | | | | | |
| How produced | Definition ☑ | Data array | | | Includes | Excludes |
| 1 Programmed | | | | | ☑ | |
| 2 Generated with source code generators | | | | | | ☑ |
| 3 Converted with automated translators | | | | | ☑ | |
| 4 Copied or reused without change | | | | | ☑ | |
| 5 Modified | | | | | ☑ | |
| 6 Removed | | | | | | ☑ |
| 7 | | | | | | |
| 8 | | | | | | |
| Origin | Definition ☑ | Data array | | | Includes | Excludes |
| 1 New work: no prior existence | | | | | ☑ | |
| 2 Prior work: taken or adapted from | | | | | | |
| 3   A previous version, build, or release | | | | | ☑ | |
| 4   Commercial, off-the-shelf software (COTS), other than libraries | | | | | | ☑ |
| 5   Government furnished software (GFS), other than reuse libraries | | | | | | ☑ |
| 6   Another product | | | | | | ☑ |
| 7   A vendor-supplied language support library (unmodified) | | | | | | ☑ |
| 8   A vendor-supplied operating system or utility (unmodified) | | | | | | ☑ |
| 9   A local or modified language support library or operating system | | | | | | ☑ |
| 10  Other commercial library | | | | | | ☑ |
| 11  A reuse library (software designed for reuse) | | | | | ☑ | |
| 12  Other software component or library | | | | | ☑ | |
| 13 | | | | | | |
| 14 | | | | | | |

**Figure 1-1**   Definition Checklist for Source Statements Counts

The "COCOMO II line-of-code definition" can be calculated in several ways. One way is to use the software program, Amadeus[Amadeus 1994] [Selby et al. 1991]. Another software program is Code Count, which is ailable from the Center for Software Engineering website under category Tools.

### 1.1.5    FP: Counting with Unadjusted Function Points

The function point cost estimation approach is based on the amount of functionality in a software project and a set of individual project factors [Behrens 1983][Kunkler 1985] [IFPUG 1994]. Function points are useful estimators since they are based on information that is available early in the project life cycle. A brief summary of function points and their calculation in COCOMO II is as follows.

Function points measure a software project by quantifying the information processing functionality associated with major external data input, output, or file types. Five user function types should be identified as defined in the Table 1-2.

Each instance of these function types is then classified by complexity level. The complexity levels determine a set of weights, which are applied to their corresponding function counts to determine the Unadjusted Function Points quantity. This is the Function Point sizing metric used by COCOMII. The usual Function Point procedure involves assessing the degree of influence (DI) of fourteen application characteristics on the software project determined according to a rating scale of 0.0 to 0.05 for each characteristic. The 14 ratings are added together, and added to a base level of 0.65 to produce a general characteristics adjustment factor that ranges from 0.65 to 1.35.

Each of these fourteen characteristics, such as distributed functions, performance, and reusability, thus have a maximum of 5% contribution to estimated effort. This is inconsistent with COCOMO experience; thus COCOMO.II uses Unadjusted Function Points for sizing, and applies its reuse factors, cost driver effort multipliers, and exponent scale factors to this sizing quantity.

### Table 1-2    User Function Types

| | |
|---|---|
| External Input (Inputs) | Count each unique user data or user control input type that (i) enters the external boundary of the software system being measured and (ii) adds or changes data in a logical internal file. |
| External Output (Outputs) | Count each unique user data or control output type that leaves the external boundary of the software system being measured. |
| Internal Logical File (Files) | Count each major logical group of user data or control information in the software system as a logical internal file type. Include each logical file (e.g., each logical group of data) that is generated, used, or maintained by the software system. |
| External Interface Files (Interfaces) | Files passed or shared between software systems should be counted as external interface file types within each system. |
| External Inquiry (Queries) | Count each unique input-output combination, where an input causes and generates an immediate output, as an external inquiry type. |

### 1.1.6   AAF: Adaptation Adjustment Factors

#### ADAPTATION OF EXISTING CODE

COCOMO is not only capable of estimating the cost and schedule for a development started from "scratch", but it is also able to estimate the cost and schedule for products that are built upon already existing code. Adaptation considerations have also been incorporated into COCOMO, where an estimate for KSLOC will be calculated. This value will be substituted in place of the SLOC found in the equations already discussed. This adaptation of code utilizes an additional set of equations that are used to calculate the final count on source instructions and related cost and schedule. These equations use the following values as components:

- Adapted Source Lines of Code (ASLOC). The number of source lines of code adapted from existing software used in developing the new product.
- Percent of Design Modification (DM). The percentage of the adapted software's design that received modification to fulfill the objectives and environment of the new product.
- Percent of Code Modification (CM). The percentage of the adapted software's code that receives modification to fulfill the objectives and environment of the new product.
- Percent of Integration Required for Modified Software (IM). The percentage of effort needed for integrating and testing of the adapted software in order to combine it into the new product.
- Percentage of reuse effort due to Software Understanding (SU).
- Percentage of reuse effort due to Assessment and Assimilation (AA).
- Programmer Unfamiliarity with Software (UNFM)

These components are brought together in Figure 1-6. The AAF is the adaptation adjustment factor. The AAF is the calculated degree to which the adapted software will affect overall development.

### 1.1.7   Effort Multipliers

There are a number of contributing factors to a project's delivery time and effort. Development productivity was found to be affected by additional factors that were found to fall under the headings: product attributes, platform attributes, personnel attributes, and project attributes.

*Product attributes* refer to the constraints and requirements placed upon the project to be developed. These included

- Required software reliability (RELY)
- Database size (DATA)
- Documentation match to life-cycle needs (DOCU)
- Product complexity (CPLX)
- Required Reusability (RUSE)

*Platform attributes* refer to the limitations placed upon development effort by the hardware and operating system being used to run the project. These limitations are listed below.

- Execution time constraint (TIME)
- Main storage constraint (STOR)
- Platform volatility (PVOL)

*Personnel attributes* refer to the level of skills that are possessed by the personnel. The skills in question are general professional ability, programming ability, experience with the development environment and familiarity with the project's domain. These skills are characterized below.

- Analyst capabilities (ACAP)
- Applications experience (APEX)
- Programmer capabilities (PCAP)
- Platform experience (PLEX)
- Programming language experience (LTEX)
- Personnel Continuity (PCON)

*Project attributes* refer to the constraints and conditions under which project development takes place. The issues that affect development are:

- Use of software tools (TOOL)
- Multisite Development (SITE)

These 16 factors are incorporated into calculating an estimated effort and schedule. Each of the factors has associated with it up to six ratings. These ratings are *very low, low, nominal, high, very high,* and *extra high*. Each rating has a corresponding real number based upon the factor and the degree to which the factor can influence productivity. A rating less than 1 denotes a factor that can decrease the schedule and effort. A rating greater than 1 denotes a factor that extends the schedule or effort. Lastly, a rating equal to 1 does not extend nor decrease the schedule and effort (this rating is called *nominal*).

These 16 factors (or effort multipliers) are incorporated into the schedule and effort estimation formulas by multiplying them together (see Figure 1-7 for the COCOMO dialog box). The numerical value of the $i^{th}$ adjustment factor (there are 16 of them) is called $EM_i$ and their product is called the adjustment factor or EAF. The actual effort, $PM_{total}$ is the product of the nominal effort times the EAF (see Figure 1-2).

$$PMtotal = (SCED) \times PMnominal \times \prod_{i=1}^{18} EMi$$

**Figure 1-2**   Estimate Development Effort

In addition to the 16 EAF factors there are two user defined factors named USR1 and USR2. Their initial values are all set to 1. They may be redefined by using the Parameters-User Defined EAF menu item.

A final effort multiplier, Required Development Schedule (SCED) is treated separately as it operates at the overall project level rather than potentially varying from module to module.

## 1.2  NAVIGATING COCOMO

This software is a stand-alone software system intended for a single user. The software is user interactive in that it attempts to interface well with a user's needs, using extensive mouse interaction wherever possible.

On the screen in Figure 1-3 is the CLEF (Component Level Estimation Form). This is where all of the entered information will be displayed. The top of the screen shows all of the subfunctions which the user may call. The choices appear in pop down menus according to the major headings of Project, Model, and Phase.

In order to efficiently use COCOMO, you must become familiar with the Component Level Estimating Form (CLEF). The different sections that are to be discussed have been given a corresponding number. These sections are given a descriptive label as a point of reference as well as a summary of their contents and functions.

The sections found in Figure 1-3 and their descriptions are as follows:

1. **Main Menu bar**—This area contains the menu selection of the main functions of COCOMO. These selections are *File, View, Edit, Parameters, Calibrate, Phase Distribu-*

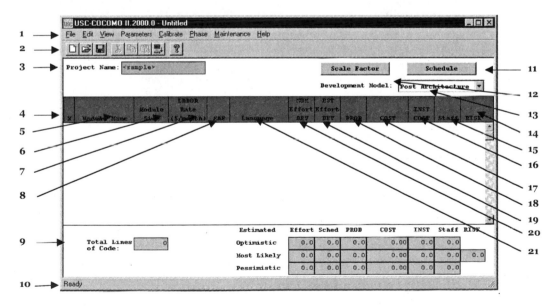

**Figure 1-3**  COCOMO CLEF

*tion* and *Help*. File, View, Edit, Parameters, Calibrate, and Phase Distribution are discussed in Chapters 2, 3, 4, 5, and 6 respectively. Help is the selection used to receive on-line assistance with the available functions.

2. **Tool bar**—This area contains image buttons like other windows applications for New Project, Open Project, Save Project, Delete Module, Copy & Paste, Insert clipboard content, Insert a module, and About functions.

3. **Project Name**—This editable field displays the name of the currently displayed project. To edit the name click twice upon this field and proceed to edit name. Upon completion of editing press the "Return" key. The Default name of a new project is " example"

4. **X**—This column is reserved for identifying a module. Pressing upon this field for a given module will mark the desired module. Marking is denoted by an x that appears in this column. Only one module can be marked at a time. Modules are marked in order to perform module deletion, cutting, copying or pasting.

5. **Module Name Column**—This column is used to house the name of each module located in the Module Area. The module name can be changed by clicking twice on the desired module name box and entering the changes into the module name field. Upon completion of editing press "Return".

6. **Module Size (SLOC) Column**—This column is used to house the SLOC of each module located in the Module Area. The value for SLOC can be computed in one of three ways. One, the value can be entered directly in the SLOC field as shown in Figure 1-4. Two, by using the function point model as shown in Figure 1-5. Three, by using Adaptation Adjustment Factor as shown in Figure 1-6. Upon completion click on OK. There is a limit to the range of input. The inputted value for SLOC must be within the range 0—9,999,999. The language of implementation of each module is initially unspecified, but may be set here.

   **Note**—COCOMO is not calibrated for Total SLOC < 2000.

7. **Labor Rate Column**—This column contains the amount of money at which a developer working on a particular module would be paid per month. The labor rate can be edited by clicking on the corresponding Labor Rate box and entering the new value via the edit area. The range on labor rate is between $0 and $99,999.

8. **Effort Adjustment Factor (EAF) Column**—This column displays the product of the cost drivers for each specific module. By clicking on this field a dialog box appears (see Figure 1-7). This box displays all of the cost drivers, inter cost drivers and their current ratings. The cost drivers are divided into the groupings: *Product, Platform, Personnel* and *Project*. The inter cost drivers are rated as 0%, 25%, 50%, and 75 %. The ratings for each multiplier can be changed by cycling through the available ratings until the desired rating is displayed. As the cost driver ratings are changed the total product of the cost drivers is displayed in the upper right hand corner of the dialog box along with the module name. The final rating of a cost driver is calculated using this formula for the interpolation.

   Final rating = (Next cost driver rating—Current cost driver rating) * Current inter cost driver / 100

   COCOMO supports two different models, called Early Design and Post Architecture. The Early Design model is supposed to be used at the earliest phase of a software project. The Post Architecture Model applies once a software architecture has

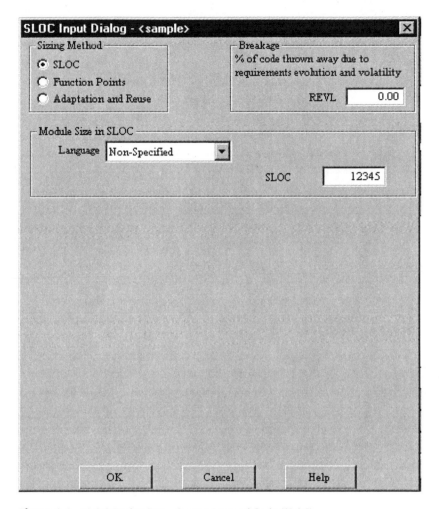

**Figure 1-4**   SLOC Dialog Box—Source Lines of Code (SLOC)

been formulated. In terms of the COCOMO program, the Early Design Model differs from the Post Architecture Model in its use of Effort Adjustment Factors. The Early Design Model considers only seven pre-defined effort adjustment factors (including schedule SCHED). Only six are shown in Figure 1-7. The Post Architecture Model makes use of seventeen pre-defined effort adjustment factors and sixteen of these are shown in Figure 1-8. Each of the models can be specified by selecting it using the button in the upper right portion of the COCOMO main screen.

9. **Totals Area**—This area houses the calculated results of all of the modules combined. Within this area is the total SLOC count for the module, the total nominal effort (PM), the total nominal productivity (SLOC/PM), the total estimated effort (EST PM), the total estimated productivity (Prod), the total estimated project cost, the esti-

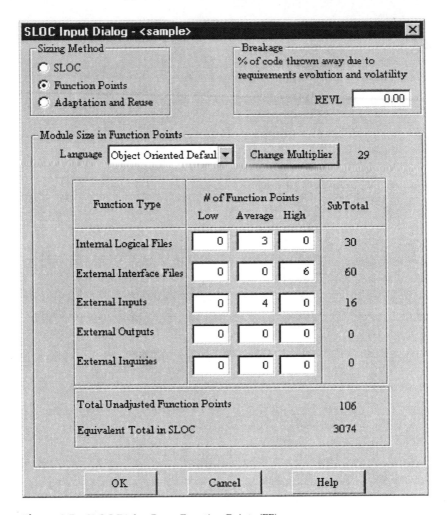

**Figure 1-5**  SLOC Dialog Box—Function Points (FP)

mated cost per instruction, the total estimated FSWP and the total estimated schedule for project completion (see each individual column for more information). The latter six quantities have not only a most likely estimate but also an optimistic estimate (no less than this, 90% of the time) and a pessimistic estimate (no greater than this, 90% of the time).

10. **Status bar**—This window displays a short definition of the column headings clicked upon and also displays a short description of the result of the last function initiated by the user.

11. **Schedule Button**—This button displays the Schedule Dialog Box as shown in Figure 1-9.

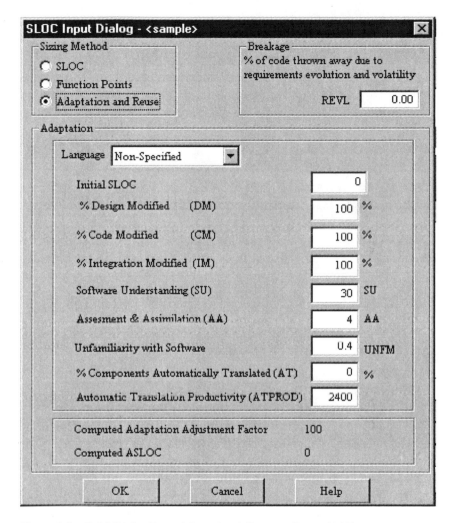

**Figure 1-6** SLOC Dialog Box—Adaptation Adjustment Factor (AAF)

12. **Scale Factor Button**—This button displays the Scale Factor Dialog Box as shown in Figure 1-10.

13. **Model Selection button**—This button displays COCOMO II Post Architecture and Early Design Model. One of the Models can be selected and applied to the project.

14. **Risk Column**—This column contains the Total risk level for each specific module. By clicking on this field a dialog box appears (see Figure 1-11). This box displays all of the risk levels for the chosen module. The total risk of a module is computed as:

total_risk=schedule_risk+product_risk+personnel_risk+process_risk+platform_risk +reuse_risk;

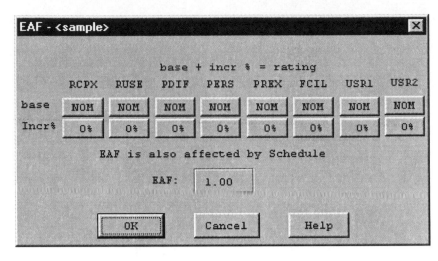

**Figure 1-7**  EAF Dialog Box—Early Design

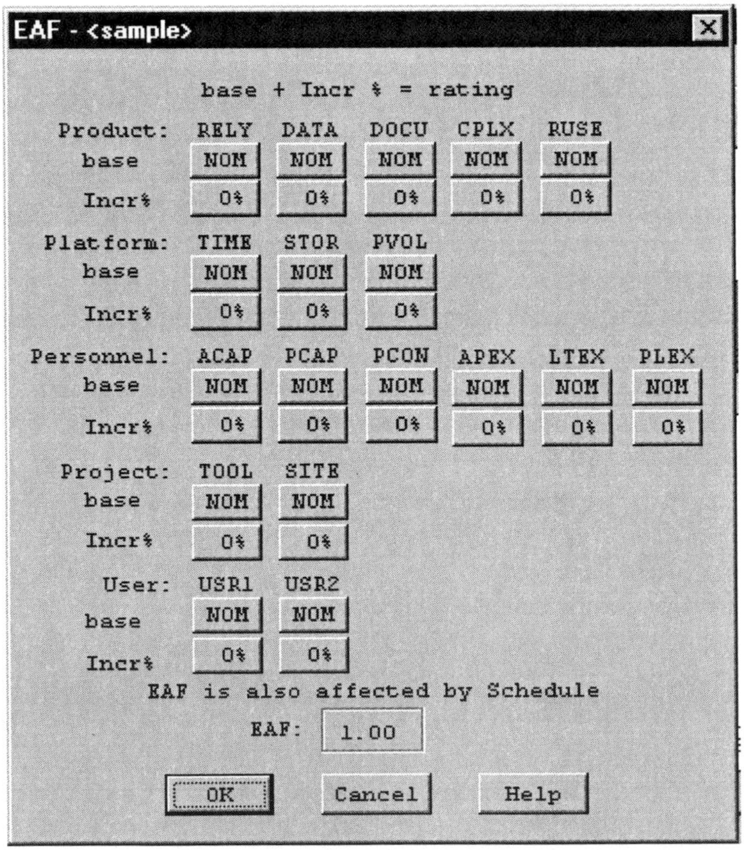

**Figure 1-8**  EAF Dialog Box—Post Architecture

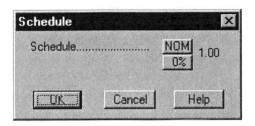

**Figure 1-9**   Schedule Dialog Box

total risk of a module=total_risk/373.*100.;

For the definitions of schedule risk, product risk, platform risk, personnel risk, process risk, and reuse risk, see [Madachy 1997].

15. **Staff (FSWP) Column**—This column houses the calculated most likely estimate for the number of full-time developers that would be needed to complete a module in the estimated development time.

16. **Instruction Cost Column**—This column contains the calculated most likely cost per instruction. This number is calculated from Cost/SLOC in each module.

17. **Cost Column**—This column contains the calculated most likely estimate of the development cost for a particular module.

18. **Productivity (PROD) Column**—This column contains the calculated result of the module's individual SLOC divided by the module's most likely effort estimate.

19. **Estimated Person-Month (EST PM) Column**—This column holds the module's most likely effort estimate obtained from multiplying Effort Adjustment Factor (EAF) by Nominal Person Month (NOM PM).

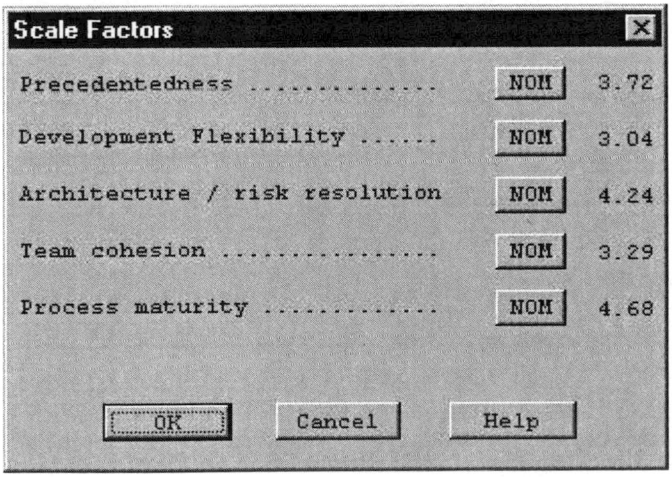

**Figure 1-10**   Scale Factor Dialog Box

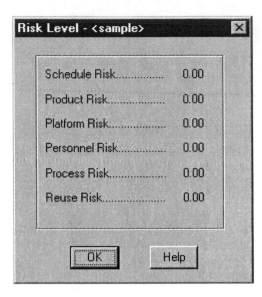

**Figure 1-11**  Risk Level Dialog Box

20. **Nominal Person-Month (NOM PM) Column**—This column holds the module's most likely effort estimate without incorporating the Effort Adjustment Factors (EAF).
21. **Languages**—This column indicates the development language for the module. Its value is set by clicking on the SLOC. The initial value is unspecified.

## 1.3  BEGIN USING COCOMO

To begin entering a new module, either click on the "Add Module" button on the Tool bar or on the pulldown menu item(Edit I Add Module). At this point, a new module will appear in the CLEF with all values set to their respective defaults. Double click upon the module name field in order to give the new module a name. Upon typing the module name press "Return." A value for SLOC and Labor rate may also be given by clicking on the respective field and editing appropriately (see Figure 1-12).

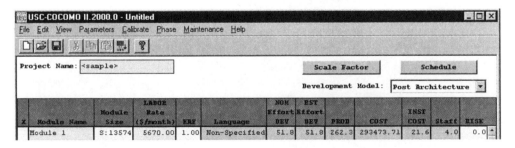

**Figure 1-12**  Create Sample Module and give values to SLOC and Labor Rate

| | | | EST | Sched | PROD | COST | INST | FSWP | RISK |
|---|---|---|---|---|---|---|---|---|---|
| Total SLOC: | 7000 | Optimistic | 20.0 | 9.5 | 350.2 | 0.00 | 0.0 | 2.1 | |
| Effort (PM): | 25.0 | Most Likely | 25.0 | 10.2 | 280.2 | 0.00 | 0.0 | 2.4 | 0.0 |
| Productivity: | 280.2 | Pessimistic | 31.2 | 11.0 | 224.1 | 0.00 | 0.0 | 2.8 | |

Project File : C:\cocomo\test.est Is Loaded

**Figure 1-13**   Totals area after calculations have been completed

*NOTE*—In order to change any of the editable fields, just click on the desired field twice and begin editing the field. Upon completing editing, either hit the "Return" key, or click on OK. All of the final results can be found at the bottom of the CLEF in the Totals area (see Figure 1-13).

## 1.4   OBTAINING COCOMO

To download COCOMO, you should enter this in a web browser:

http://sunset.usc.edu/COCOMOII/cocomo.html

and scroll down to the section labeled **COCOMO II Downloads (Software and Documentation)**

or

ftp://ftp.usc.edu/pub/soft_engineering/COCOMOII/

where you will see files:

c2000windows.zip, usersman.ps, usersman.pdf, modelman.ps, modelman.pdf

### CHAPTER 2: FILE MENU

The COCOMO file types include: project file, model file, report file, calibration file, and comma separated values (csv) file. The first three are discussed here. The others are discussed in later chapters.

The project file in COCOMO stores a project's data, which include project name, project scale factors, project schedule constraint, module name, SLOC, labor rate, effort adjustment factors (EAF), and COCOMO related calculation results. The COCOMO system gives all project files an ".est" extension.

Regarding the model file, as we mentioned in chapter one, COCOMO incorporates predictor factors, or cost driver attributes, which are grouped into four categories: software product attributes, platform attributes, personnel attributes, and project attributes. Each of these cost driver attributes determines a multiplying factor, which estimates the effect of the attribute in software development effort. There are also two user defined EAF factors plus the project-level required development schedule EAF factor. Besides these cost drivers, COCOMO also has scale factors. These multiplying factors and effort estimating equations constitute the model of a project. As we said previously, COCOMO has assigned default values and equations for the annually calibrated default model. Each time a COCOMO project is created, its effort estimate is based on the default parameter values. COCOMO provides flexibility in changing the values of multiplying factors, effort estimating equation, or schedule estimating equation. Adjusted parameter values are stored in the est file, but may also be saved in a model file. Upon saving this model file, these altered values can be applied to another project by loading the saved model file. The COCOMO system gives all model files a ".mod" extension.

The report file is a summary report of the COCOMO project. This report contains all entered and calculated values of a project. These files are given a ".rpt" extension.

The File menu option will enable you to create, retrieve, save, or print COCOMO files.

To select the File menu and its options, click on File with the mouse. The File menu will appear as Figure 2-1.

## 2.1   NEW

The  New option creates a new project file in the COCOMO working window, replacing any previous project file in the working window.

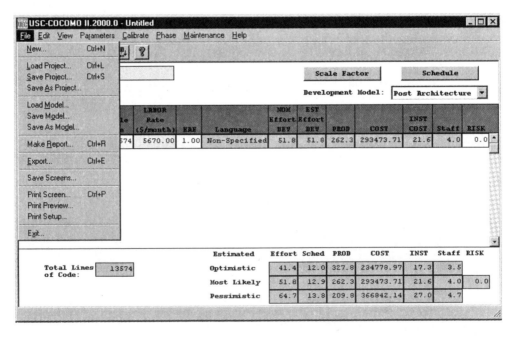

**Figure 2-1**   File Menu

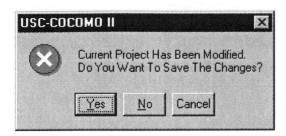

**Figure 2-2** Warning Dialog Box

### To Create a New Working File

1. Choose New from the File menu with mouse.

   The working window will now be clear; the previous project file in the working window has been removed.

   **Note:** New can be selected anytime; however, if the previous project file or model file has been modified, a warning dialog box will appear and requests confirmation. (as seen in Figure 2-2)

2. If the modifications on the previous file are not to be saved, choose Yes, otherwise choose No. If the No is selected, a Save File dialog will appear. (See Save Project and Save Model respectively)

## 2.2  LOAD PROJECT

The Load Project option is used to retrieve a project file as well as loading it on the working window.

### To Retrieve or Load a Project File

1. Choose Load Project from the File menu with the mouse.
2. If a previous project file has been modified in the working window, the dialog box as in Figure 2-3 will appear.
3. If the previous project file is to be saved, choose Yes, then a Save File dialog box will appear. (See Save Project). If the modified file is not to be saved, choose No.
4. The Load Project dialog box will appear as seen in Figure 2-4.

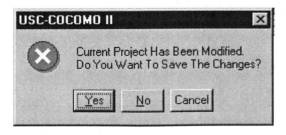

**Figure 2-3**  Warning Dialog Box

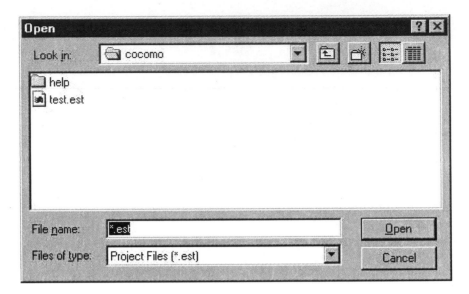

**Figure 2-4**   Load Project Dialog Box

The file name of a COCOMO project has a default format with ".est" as an extension. With this window, the desired project file can be selected from the Files scroll list for loading. If the desired project file does not exist in the scroll list, it is necessary to choose an appropriate directory.

5. Choose desired directory for file loading
6. When the desired file is shown on the Files list, click it, and click the "OK" button to initiate project loading.
7. After a project file is loaded, its file name will be displayed on the PROJECT FILE field at upper left corner on the working window, and all modules and related items will be displayed in the CLEF area. If the number of modules is beyond the window scope, the scroll bar can be used to look at all items.

## 2.3   SAVE PROJECT

The Save Project option is used to store the results of the current COCOMO project as a file with ".est" extension.

### To Store the Results of Current Project

1. Choose Save Project from the File menu with the mouse. If the current project is loaded from a previously stored project file, the Save Project will overwrite the same project file with the current project.
2. If the current project is a new one, i.e., being created by the New command, the Project Save dialog box will appear, as seen in Figure 2-5.

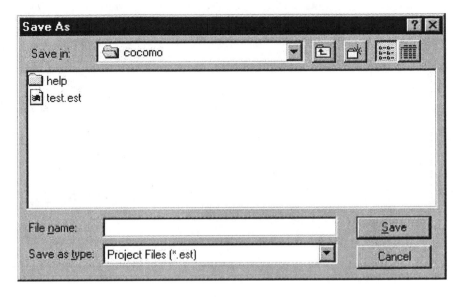

**Figure 2-5**   Save Project Dialog Box

3. Look at the Files scroll window. If the file saving is to update (overwrite) a existing project file, the desired filename should be found in the Files scroll list. If the filename can not be found from current list, change the directory from the Directories scroll list until the desired filename is being shown. When the desired filename is on the list, click it.

4. If the file saving is to store a new project file, choose the desired directory, then type in a new filename.

5. After the desired filename is selected or inputted, click the OK button to initiate project saving.

## 2.4   SAVE AS PROJECT

The Save As Project option is to store the current project as a COCOMO project file, which has a file name different from current file.

### To Store Current Project With Different File Name

1. Choose Save As Project from the File menu with the mouse.

2. The Save Project dialog box will appear, as seen in Figure 2-6.

3. Look at the Files scroll window. If the file saving is to update (overwrite) a existing project file, the desired filename should be found in the Files scroll list. If the filename can not be found from current list, change the directory from the Directories scroll list until the desired filename is being shown. When the desired filename is on the list, click it.

4. If the file saving is to store a new project file, choose the desired directory, then type in a new filename in the SELECTION box.

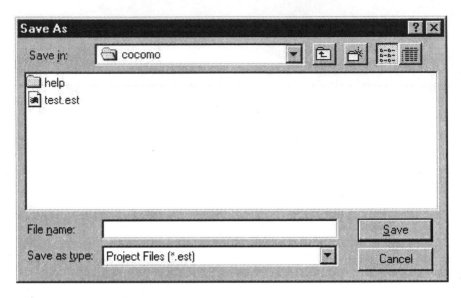

**Figure 2-6**   Save Project Dialog Box

5. After the desired filename is selected or inputted, click the OK button to initiate project saving. After a project file is saved, the project file name will be displayed on the PROJECT FILE field at the upper left corner of the working window.

## 2.5   LOAD MODEL

The Load Model command is used when a specific model, in which the values of multiplying factors and scale factors are different from the COCOMO default model, is to be applied to the current project.

The Load Model option is used to retrieve a model file as well as loading it for the current project.

### To Retrieve or Load a Model File

1. Choose Load Model from the File menu.
2. If a previous model has been modified in the current project, the dialog box in Figure 2-7 will appear.
3. If the previous model file is to be saved, choose Yes, then a Save Model dialog box will appear. (See Save Model). If the modified model is not to be saved, choose No.
4. The Load Model dialog box will appear as seen in Figure 2-8.

   The file name of a COCOMO model has a default format with ".mod" as an extension. With this window, the desired model file can be selected from the Files scroll

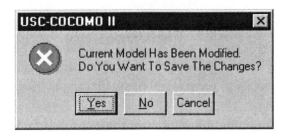

**Figure 2-7**   Warning Dialog Box

list for loading. If the desired model file does not exist in the scroll list, look for it in the other directories.

5. Choose desired directory for file loading
6. When the desired file is shown on the Files list, click it, and click the "OK" button to initiate model loading.
7. After a model file is loaded, its file name will be displayed on the MODEL FILE field at upper left corner on the working window, and the related costs of current project will be recalculated and shown on the working window.

## 2.6   SAVE MODEL

The Save Model option is used to store the results of the current COCOMO model as a file with ".mod" extension.

**Figure 2-8**   Load Model Dialog Box

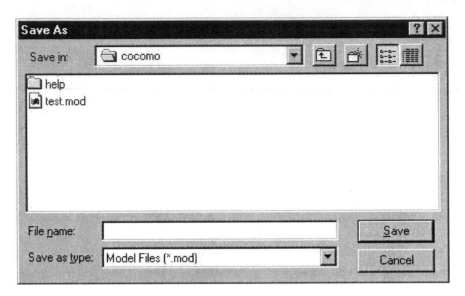

**Figure 2-9**   Save Model Dialog Box

### To Store the Results of Current Model

1. Choose Save Model from the File menu. If the current model is loaded from a previously stored model file, the Save Model will overwrite the same model file with the current model.

2. If the current model is a new one, the Save Model dialog box will appear, as seen in Figure 2-9.

3. Look at the Files scroll window. If the file saving is to update (overwrite) a existing model file, the desired filename should be found in the Files scroll list. If the filename can not be found from current list, change the directory from the Directories scroll list until the desired filename is being shown. When the desired filename is on the list, click it.

4. If the file saving is to store a new model file, choose the desired directory, then type in the filename.

5. After the desired filename is selected or inputted, click the OK button to initiate model saving.

## 2.7   SAVE AS MODEL

The Save As Model option is to store the current model as a COCOMO model file, which has a file name different from current model.

### To Store Current Model With different File Name

1. Choose Save As Model from the File menu.

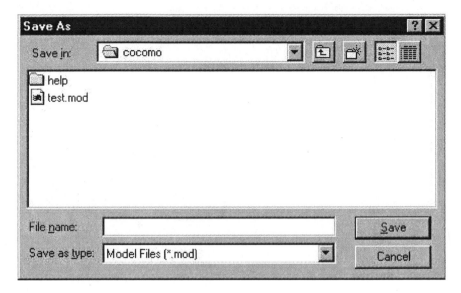

**Figure 2-10**   Save As Model Dialog Box

2. The Save Model dialog box will appear, as seen in Figure 2-10.
3. Look at the Files scroll window. If the file saving is to update (overwrite) a existing model file, the desired filename should be found in the Files scroll list. If the filename can not be found from current list, change the directory from the Directories scroll list until the desired filename is being shown. When the desired filename is on the list, click it.
4. If the file saving is to store a new model file, choose the desired directory, then type in the filename in the SELECTION box.
5. After the desired filename is selected or inputted, click the OK button to initiate model saving. After a model file is saved, the project file name will be displayed on the MODEL FILE field at the upper left corner of the working window.

## 2.8   MAKE REPORT

The Make Report option creates a COCOMO report in the form of a text file for printing. In Post Architecture mode the text file contains ALL of the COCOMO parameter values and all of the input values. In Early Design mode only those parameters that affect Early Design are included.

### To Create Project Report

1. Choose Make Report from the File menu.
2. The Make Report dialog box will appear, as seen in Figure 2-11.

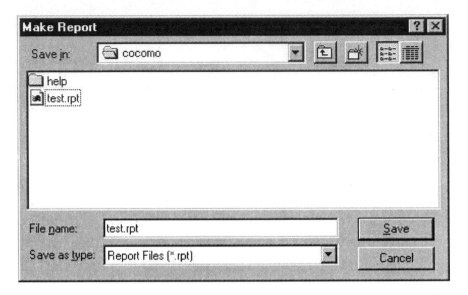

**Figure 2-11**   Make Report Dialog Box

3. Look at the Files scroll window. If the file saving is to update (overwrite) a existing report file, the desired filename should be found in the Files scroll list. If the file-name can not be found from current list, change the directory from the Directories scroll list until the desired filename is shown. When the desired filename is on the list, click it.

4. If the file saving is to store a new report file, choose the desired directory, then type in the filename.

5. Choose desired directory for file saving: Look at the filter input box. The path found in this box represents the directory where the report file is going to be saved. This path will be changed after each directory change. To change the directory, click the appropriate directory choice from the Directories scroll list, then click the "Filter" button.

6. After the desired filename is selected or inputted, click the OK button to initiate report file saving.

7. To print a COCOMO project report, execute the local commands for your system in order to send the file for printing.

## 2.9   EXPORT

The Export option lets you select a directory to write files that can be imported into Excel. This option only works in Post Architecture mode, and only deals with the waterfall model and the corresponding phase distributions.

COCOMO Import & Analyze Tool is an Excel template which automates the process of importing the Comma Separated Values (CSV) files, produced by the COCOMO File |

Export command. This command produces two sheets: Main, which contains Project and Module information, and Phases, which contains the phase distribution information. DO NOT rename those worksheets.

The template automates the process of generating charts which are useful for software project management. Though the template produces many useful charts, it is still possible to perform your own analysis of the COCOMO data. However to do that you must have a detailed knowledge of Excel and become familiar with the format of the csv files produced by COCOMO. Note that Excel does not permit you to open two workbooks with the same name, even if the workbooks are in different folders. To open the second workbook, you can either close the current workbook, or rename it. However it is recommended that you do not rename cocomo.xls

Step 1: Start Excel and import the files generated by COCOMO

Click on Import COCOMO Files. The Browse For Folder dialog box will appear. Select the folder containing the Comma-Separated Values Files (CSV) generated by USC-COCOMO. If COCOMO Import&Analyze can find the files it is looking for (Main.csv and Phases.csv) it will open each file, read its contents and place it in the appropriate worksheet.

Step 2: Generate Charts

Once the sheets 'Main' and 'Phases' have been correctly initialized, you can generate meaningful analyses of the data, with the click of a button. Specific help on each chart is given below.

If the sheet corresponding to the chart you are trying to create has been already created, then the existing sheet will be activated, and get the input focus. If you want to overwrite the existing sheet, you will have to delete it by selecting the Delete Sheet command from the Edit menu.

### Performing your own analyses

The charts that the COCOMO Import and Analyze tool can generate for you are just a subset of what you can do with the data imported into the 'Main' and 'Phases' sheets. COCOMO Import and Analyze Tool provides you with maximum flexibility by:

Copying the relevant parts of 'Main' and 'Phases' sheets into the sheet for the purpose of the generation of graphs; Using references to the values entered in 'Main' and 'Phases sheets, so that if you update the values in those sheets, the changes will be reflected in all the other 'calculated' sheets, as well as the charts. Note however, that if you introduce changes in any calculated sheet, the changes wont be carried over to Main or Phases; Allowing you to change some values. In particular, the sheets 'Project Cumulative Cost' and 'Project Cost per Phase' allow you to enter the Cost per Person-Month per Phase. The provided value is just an average computed from the COCOMO values. However you can use the value which reflects more accurately your organizational process.

If you click on the button marked Delete All Generated Sheets, and you select OK, all the 'calculated' sheets will be deleted. If you introduce changes to one of the 'calculated' sheets, and to prevent the sheet from being deleted, it is recommended that you rename the sheet.

The 'Menu' sheet is protected to avoid accidental displacement of the various buttons. It also disables resizing rows and columns, as well as selecting a range of cells. If you need to make changes to the 'Menu' sheet, toggle the 'Protect Sheet/Unprotect Sheet from the Protection command under the Tools menu.

## Chart Explanations

### Project Schedule per Phase

This chart is useful for determining the total calendar time required for the completion of the project.

COCOMO computes the schedule as the calendar time in months from the determination of a product's requirements baseline to the completion of an acceptance activity certifying that the product satisfies its requirements. Time spent in requirements is computed as an additional 20%.

### Cost per Phase

This chart is useful for determining the cumulative cost as the project moves from one phase to another. It also displays the milestones between the phases (using the assumption of the Waterfall Model).

To obtain the Cost per Phase, given that the COCOMO computes only the Effort per Phase, it is necessary to compute the average Cost per Person-Month as Total Cost for entire project (excluding requirements) / Total Effort in Person-Months. Effort for requrements is assumed at an additional 7% of the Total Effort, and with the same Cost per Person-Month as the overall project. If your organization uses other Costs per Person-Month, you can use those values instead.

### Cumulative Cost

This chart is useful for determining the cumulative cost of a project over time. It also displays the milestones between the phases (using the assumption of the Waterfall Model).

To obtain the Cost per Phase, given that the COCOMO computes only the Effort per Phase, it is necessary to compute the average Cost per Person-Month as Total Cost for entire project (excluding requirements) / Total Effort in Person-Months. Effort for requirements is assumed at an additional 7% of the Total Effort, and with the same Cost per Person-Month as the overall project. If your organization uses other Costs per Person-Month, you can use those values instead.

### Cost per Module

This chart is useful for determining the cost of every module, and comparing which modules are accounting for the highest part of the cost. The cost of the entire project is the sum of the costs of the individual modules. Since these are only estimates, error bars are used to display the range within which the actual cost will fall, with a very high probability. COCOMO generates only the Optimistic (as 0.8xMost Likely) and the Pessimistic bound (as 1.25xMost Likely) for the cost of the entire project. The Optimistic/Pessimistic bounds on the cost estimates of the individual modules are similarly computed. This assumes that the error on the cost estimate for the entire project is the sum of the errors on the cost of the component modules. You can modify the Optimistic/Pessimistic bounds on the individual modules to match your organizational experience. The error bars will be adjusted accordingly.

### Effort
Project Effort per Phase

This chart displays how the total effort for the overall project is distributed across phases.

The Effort percentages computed by COCOMO, that are displayed under 'Percentage' exclude the effort spent on requirements. However, the percentages displayed on the chart include the effort spent on Requirements, hence the slight difference.

### Effort per Phase and Module
This chart displays the effort spent on every module, during the phases of the project. It can be used to quickly identify the modules which are the most effort-intensive. Effort for requirements is assumed at an additional 7% of the Total Effort.

### Staffing
Project Personnel per Schedule. This chart displays the staffing levels of the project over its duration. The cutoff points between the various phases are also clearly displayed. Staffing levels are assumed to remain constant during a given phase, and to experience a sharp increase/decrease at the beginning/end of a phase.

### Project Personnel per Phase
This chart displays the staffing levels of the project during the various phases. Staffing levels are assumed to remain constant during a given phase, and to experience a sharp increase/decrease at the beginning/end of a phase.

### Personnel per Module
This chart displays the staffing requirements for every module. It is useful for identifying the most labor intensive modules, and to appropriately plan for the staffing of teams which are typically responsible for modules within the project.

### Activity
Project Activity per Phase. This chart displays the effort spent by activity during the project lifetime. The activities correspond to the ones associated with a waterfall model.

The effort spent per activity is computed as a percentage from the total effort spent during a phase. Refer to the EFFORT (%) section of the 'Phases' sheet to view the percentages used. The same percentages are used for the overall project, and for the individual modules. If you think from your organizational experience that some modules may require different activity distribution than others you can recompute the effort spent by activity for those modules.

### Project Personnel per Activity and Phase
This chart displays the personnel required for every activity during each phase of the project. The activities correspond to the ones associated with a waterfall model.

The personnel required for every activity is computed from the effort spent per activity. The effort spent per activity is computed as a percentage from the total effort spent during a phase. Refer to the EFFORT (%) section of the 'Phases sheet to view the percentages used. The same percentages are used for the overall project, and for the individual modules. If you think from your organizational experience that some modules may require different activity distribution than others, you can re-compute the effort spent by activity for those modules.

## General Assumptions

The general assumptions behind COCOMO are briefly listed below.

For all the analyses, it is assumed that the waterfall model is used; in particular, a phase does not start until the previous one has been completed.

COCOMO treats the effort and the schedule spent on plans and requirements as separate from the effort and the schedule spent on the other phases (Product Design, Programming, Integration and Test).

The Effort percentages computed by COCOMO, exclude the effort spent on requirements

COCOMO computes the schedule as the calendar time in months from the determination of a product's requirements baseline to the completion of an acceptance activity certifying that the product satisfies its requirements. Time spent in requirements is computed as an additional 20%.

COCOMO uses a single labor rate for a given module within the project, and therefore, does not use Cost per Person-Month for a phase. To compute the cumulative cost per phase, or over time, the Average Cost per Person-Month is computed as Total Cost for entire project (excluding requirements) / Total Effort in Person-Months (excluding requirements)

Total Effort = Effort (Product Design) + Effort (Programming) + Effort (Integration and Test)

Effort for requirements is assumed at an additional 7% of the Total Effort, and with the same Cost per Person-Month as the overall project

## Known Problems

If the project does not have any cost information (I.e., cost-related data has not been entered and defaults to zero), some charts may be incorrectly displayed, and some cells may have a 'Division by Zero' error.

For unusually large COCOMO data sets, e.g. 50 modules, the predefined graphs may not display correctly. However, by disabling the labeling of the data points, resizing the graphs, you may be able to achieve an acceptable display.

### To Export

1. Choose Export from the File menu.
2. The Export dialog box will appear, as seen in Figure 2-12.
3. When you click on OK, a dialog box appears if Main.csv and Phases.csv already exist, as shown in Figure 2-13.
4. If Yes is selected, COCOMO saves two files(main.csv and phase.csv) in the chosen directory. If No is selected, these files will not be replaced.

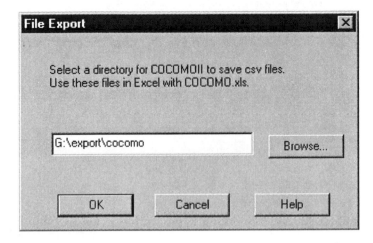

**Figure 2-12**   File Export Dialog Box

## 2.10   SAVE SCREENS

The Save Screens option allows the user to save the image of any COCOMO window.

### To Save Screens

1. Choose Save Screens from the File menu.
2. The Save Screens dialog box will appear, as seen in Figure 2-14.
3. Follow the directions on the dialog box.

## 2.11   PRINT SCREEN

The Print Screen option prints the screen of the main COCOMO window.

### To Print Screen

1. Choose Print Screen from the File menu.

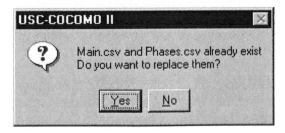

**Figure 2-13**   Subsequent File Export Dialog Box

**Figure 2-14**  Save Screens Dialog Box

2. The Print Screen dialog box will appear, as seen in Figure 2-15.
3. The Name of the printer can be selected from the dropdown list. Alternatively, you can print to a file by clicking on the Print to file checkbox.
4. Properties of the printer can be set by clicking on the Properties button.
5. The Print range can be All or Pages (e.g. from 1 to 3).

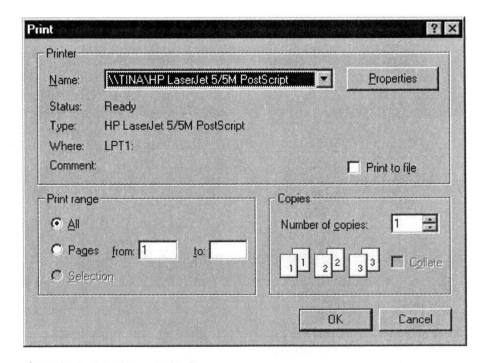

**Figure 2-15**  Print Screen Dialog Box

    **6.** The Number of copies can be selected by clicking the up and down arrows, or by typing a number directly.

    **7.** Select OK when finished to print or select Cancel to not print.

## 2.11   PRINT PREVIEW

The Print Preview option displays that which will appear when printed, if Print Screen is selected from the File menu.

### To Preview what is to be printed

    **1.** Choose Print Preview from the File menu.

    **2.** The Print Preview dialog box will appear, as seen in Figure 2-16.

    **3.** Select the Print button to print.

    **4.** The Next Page button to advance to the next Page.

    **5.** The Zoom In button zooms in, and the Zoom Out button becomes enabled so that the user can zoom out.

    **6.** The Close button closes the Print Preview dialog.

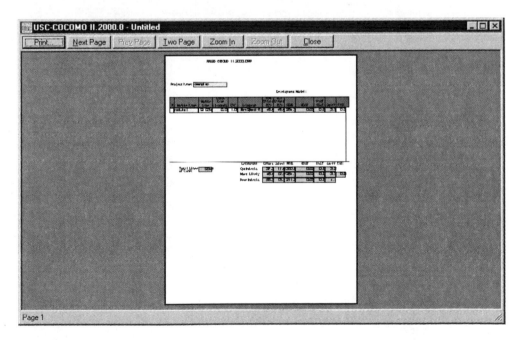

**Figure 2-16**   Print Preview Dialog Box

## 2.12    PRINT SETUP

The Print Setup option allows the user to set up printing.

### To set up Printing

1.  Choose Print Setup from the File menu.
2.  The Print Setup dialog box will appear, as seen in Figure 2-17.
3.  The Name of the printer can be selected from the dropdown list.
4.  Properties of the printer can be set by clicking on the Properties button.
5.  The Size and Source of the paper can be selected from the dropdown lists.
6.  The Network button can be selected to connect to a printer on a network.
7.  Select OK when finished to print or select Cancel to not print.

## 2.13    EXIT

The Exit option leaves the COCOMO system.

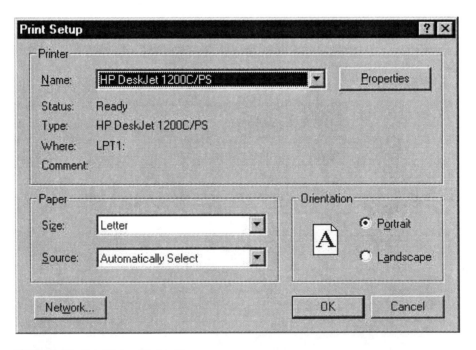

**Figure 2-17**    Print Setup Dialog Box

**To Exit COCOMO**

1. Choose Exit from the File menu with the mouse.
2. This causes your system to terminate the COCOMO program.

---

### CHAPTER 3:   EDIT MENU

The Edit Menu option supplies several useful commands, which will enable you to establish a project more conveniently.

To select the Edit menu and its options, click on Edit with the mouse, then the Edit menu will appear as Figure 3-1.

---

### 3.1   ADD MODULE

The Add Module option adds a new module to the project that is currently being worked upon by the user. This Add Module function can be done by pressing the Add Module button in the Tool bar area.

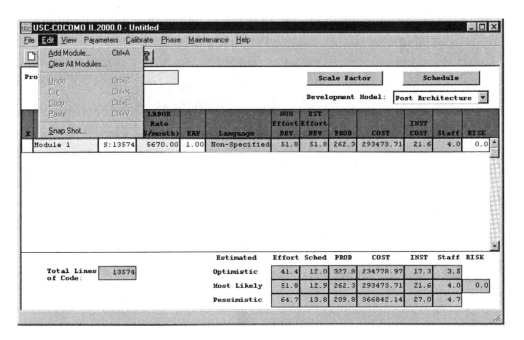

**Figure 3-1**   Edit Menu

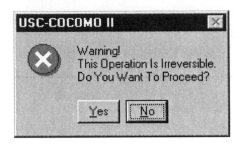

**Figure 3-2**    Warning Dialog Box

## 3.2    CLEAR ALL MODULE

The Clear All option erases all modules of the current project on the working window.

### To Erase All Modules of Current Project

1. Choose Clear from the Edit menu.

   During the execution of the Clear command, if some changes have occurred on the currently viewed project and have not been saved, the warning dialog box will appear as Figure 3-2.

2. If you really want to clear, click Yes. If not, click No.

3. After Clear, all modules of current project will disappear.

## 3.3    SNAPSHOT

The Snapshot option enables users to compare the effort estimation change for a project so that he/she can decide to apply the change or not. This function makes COCOMO more convenient and powerful for software project decision analyses.

The Snapshot command stores the current set of modules, effort adjustment factors and all other data associated with a project. At a later time this data can be restored.

### To Compare the Overall Change of a Project

1. Choose Snapshot from the Edit menu. The Snapshot dialog box will initially appear as Figure 3-3.

   In the dialog box, the lower section represents the current results for the project. The upper section is previously snapped results. The current project can be snapped by clicking upon the Snap button. After completing this action the upper and lower section of the Snapshot window will contain identical information. At this point changes can be made to the current project values after clicking upon the Done button.

2. Upon completing the modification of the project values, a comparison can be made between the previously snapped project and the modified project by clicking again upon Snapshot option in the Edit menu.

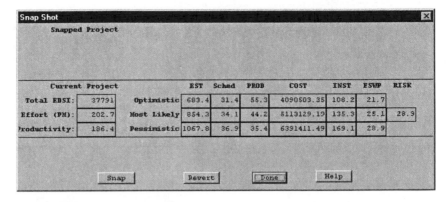

**Figure 3-3**  Snapshot Dialog Box-1

3. Now the values in the upper part of the window will likely be different from the current values, in the lower part. To restore the upper values, click on Revert. The two sets of values are interchanged.
4. When finished, click the Done button.

## 3.4  UNDO

The Undo option retracts the previous cut or paste done on a module.

### To Retract Previous Cut/Paste for a Module

1. Choose Undo from the Edit menu with the mouse.
2. The changed module will go back to its previous status; see Figure 3-4.

| Snapped Project | | EST | Sched | PROB | COST | INST | FSWP | RISK |
|---|---|---|---|---|---|---|---|---|
| Total EBSI: | 37791 | Optimistic | 683.4 | 31.4 | 55.3 | 4090503.35 | 108.2 | 21.7 | |
| Effort (PM): | 202.7 | Most Likely | 854.3 | 34.1 | 44.2 | 5113129.19 | 135.3 | 25.1 | 28.9 |
| Productivity: | 186.4 | Pessimistic | 1067.8 | 36.9 | 35.4 | 6391411.49 | 169.1 | 28.9 | |
| Current Project | | EST | Sched | PROB | COST | INST | FSWP | RISK |
| Total EBSI: | 40035 | Optimistic | 735.3 | 32.3 | 54.4 | 4354135.25 | 108.8 | 22.8 | |
| Effort (PM): | 216.7 | Most Likely | 919.1 | 35.0 | 43.6 | 5442669.06 | 135.9 | 26.3 | 28.9 |
| Productivity: | 184.7 | Pessimistic | 1148.9 | 37.9 | 34.9 | 6803336.32 | 169.9 | 30.3 | |

Snap    Revert    Done    Help

**Figure 3-4**  Snapshot Dialog Box-2

## 3.5   CUT

The Cut option copies a module into the cut buffer and removes it from the current project. The cut module can be used for Paste.

### To Cut a Module and Remove It From the CLEF

1. Check the module which is to be cut. The Check boxes for modules are located in the leftmost column of the CLEF area. Place the mouse in the box just to the left of the module name, and click.
2. Choose Cut from the Edit menu with the mouse.
3. The cut module disappears.

## 3.6   COPY

The Copy option copies a module. The copied module can be used for Paste.

### To Copy a Module

1. Check the module which is to be copied. The Check boxes for modules are located in the leftmost column of the CLEF area.
2. Choose Copy from the Edit menu with the mouse.
3. The cross sign in the check box disappears.

## 3.7   PASTE

The Paste option pastes a previously copied or cut module in the CLEF.

### To Paste a Previously Copied or Cut Module

1. Check the module above which the previously copied or cut module is to be pasted. The Check boxes for modules are located in the leftmost column of CLEF area.
2. Choose Paste from the Edit menu with the mouse.
3. The pasted module appears at the checked position, and the modules lower than it were pushed one row down.
4. If there is no module checked, the Paste will attach the previously copied or cut module at the end.

   Note that the Edit/Paste command works exactly like the Edit/Paste command in Microsoft Word, with the exception that instead of highlighting a module one first clicks on the X in the leftmost column.

### CHAPTER 4:   PARAMETERS MENU

The Parameters menu option will enable you to look at, or change the values of effort adjustment factors, scale factors and effort/schedule estimating equations factors for the current project.

To choose the Parameters menu and its options, click on Parameters with the mouse. The Parameters menu will appear as Figure 4-1.

## 4.1   POST ARCHITECTURE MODEL

### 4.1.1   Product

The Product option displays five cost drivers: RELY, DATA, DOCU, CPLX, and RUSE and their corresponding ratings and multiplier values. Select Product from the Parameters menu with the mouse. The Product Dialog Box will appear as Figure 4-2.

To modify these values, go straight to those edit boxes and type new values. When finished with the modification, click the OK button.

### 4.1.2   Platform

The Platform option displays three cost drivers: TIME, STOR and PVOL, and their corresponding ratings and multiplier values.

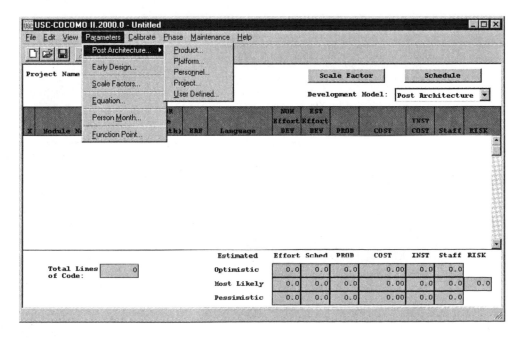

**Figure 4-1**   Parameters Menu

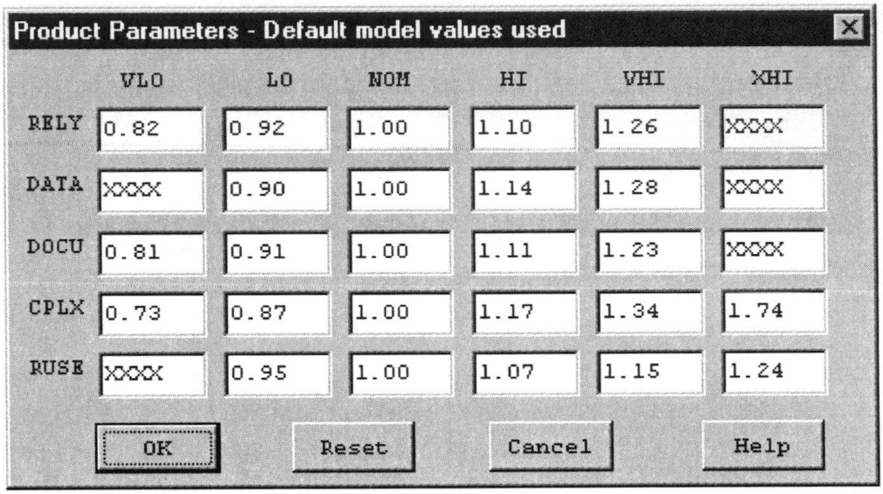

**Product Parameters - Default model values used**                    ☒

|      | VLO | LO | NOM | HI | VHI | XHI |
|------|-----|-----|-----|-----|-----|-----|
| RELY | 0.82 | 0.92 | 1.00 | 1.10 | 1.26 | XXXX |
| DATA | XXXX | 0.90 | 1.00 | 1.14 | 1.28 | XXXX |
| DOCU | 0.81 | 0.91 | 1.00 | 1.11 | 1.23 | XXXX |
| CPLX | 0.73 | 0.87 | 1.00 | 1.17 | 1.34 | 1.74 |
| RUSE | XXXX | 0.95 | 1.00 | 1.07 | 1.15 | 1.24 |

[ OK ]      [ Reset ]      [ Cancel ]      [ Help ]

**Figure 4-2**    Product Dialog Box

Select Platform from the Parameters menu with the mouse. The Platform Dialog Box will appear as Figure 4-3.

To modify these values, go straight to those edit boxes and type new values. When finished with the modification, click the OK button.

### 4.1.3   PERSONNEL

The Personnel option displays six cost drivers: ACAP, AEXP, PCAP, PEXP, LTEX, and PCON and their corresponding ratings and multiplier values.

Select Personnel from the Parameters menu with the mouse. The Personnel Dialog Box will appear as Figure 4-4.

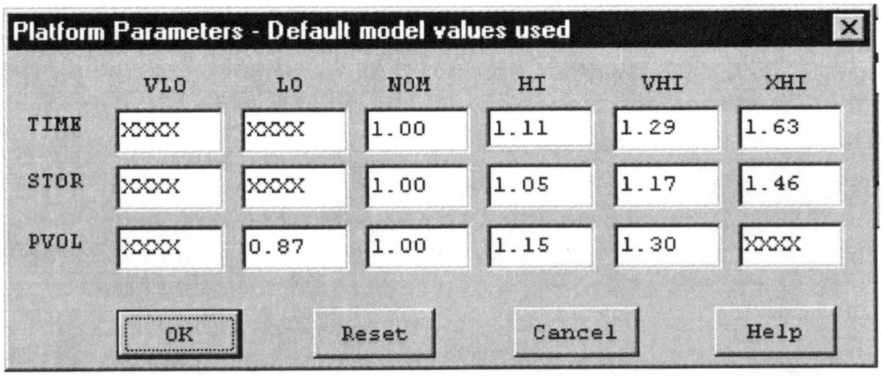

**Platform Parameters - Default model values used**                    ☒

|      | VLO | LO | NOM | HI | VHI | XHI |
|------|-----|-----|-----|-----|-----|-----|
| TIME | XXXX | XXXX | 1.00 | 1.11 | 1.29 | 1.63 |
| STOR | XXXX | XXXX | 1.00 | 1.05 | 1.17 | 1.46 |
| PVOL | XXXX | 0.87 | 1.00 | 1.15 | 1.30 | XXXX |

[ OK ]      [ Reset ]      [ Cancel ]      [ Help ]

**Figure 4-3**    Platform Dialog Box

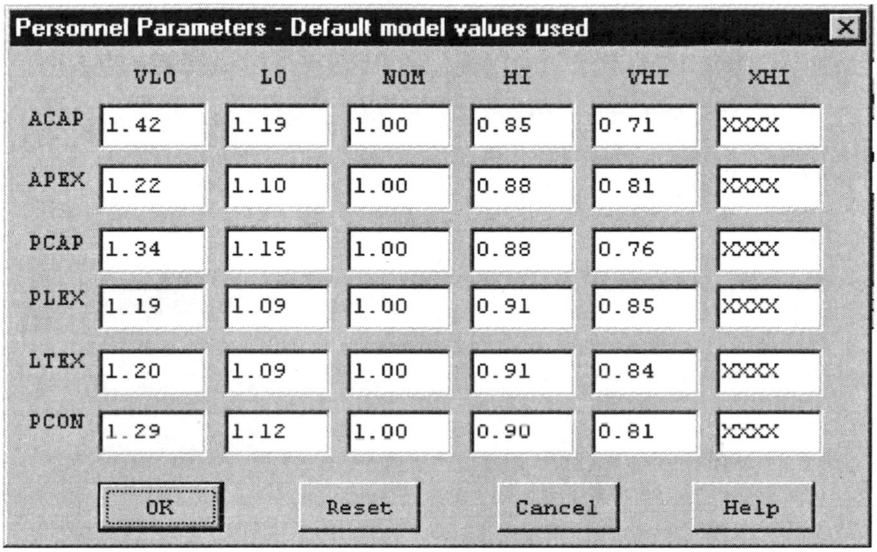

**Personnel Parameters - Default model values used**

| | VLO | LO | NOM | HI | VHI | XHI |
|---|---|---|---|---|---|---|
| ACAP | 1.42 | 1.19 | 1.00 | 0.85 | 0.71 | XXXX |
| APEX | 1.22 | 1.10 | 1.00 | 0.88 | 0.81 | XXXX |
| PCAP | 1.34 | 1.15 | 1.00 | 0.88 | 0.76 | XXXX |
| PLEX | 1.19 | 1.09 | 1.00 | 0.91 | 0.85 | XXXX |
| LTEX | 1.20 | 1.09 | 1.00 | 0.91 | 0.84 | XXXX |
| PCON | 1.29 | 1.12 | 1.00 | 0.90 | 0.81 | XXXX |

OK      Reset      Cancel      Help

**Figure 4-4**  Personnel Dialog Box

To modify these values, go straight to those edit boxes and type new values. When finished with the modification, click the OK button.

### 4.1.4  Project

The Project option displays three cost drivers: TOOL, SCED, and SITE and their corresponding ratings and multiplier values.

Select Project from the Parameters menu with the mouse. The Project Dialog Box will appear as Figure 4-5.

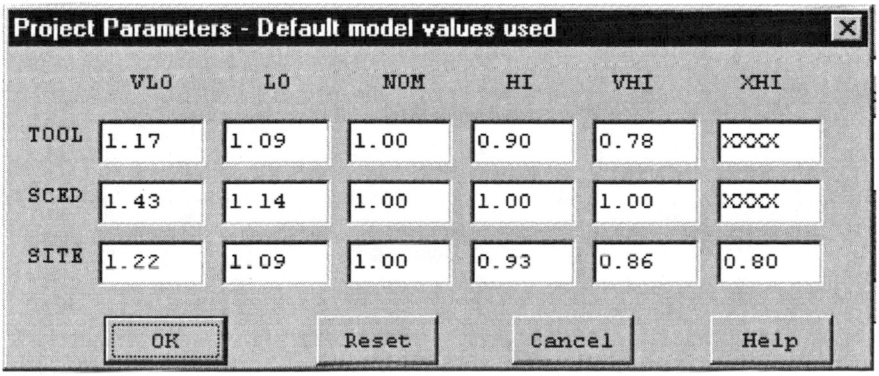

**Project Parameters - Default model values used**

| | VLO | LO | NOM | HI | VHI | XHI |
|---|---|---|---|---|---|---|
| TOOL | 1.17 | 1.09 | 1.00 | 0.90 | 0.78 | XXXX |
| SCED | 1.43 | 1.14 | 1.00 | 1.00 | 1.00 | XXXX |
| SITE | 1.22 | 1.09 | 1.00 | 0.93 | 0.86 | 0.80 |

OK      Reset      Cancel      Help

**Figure 4-5**  Project Dialog Box

To modify these values, go straight to those edit boxes and type new values. When finished with the modification, click the OK button.

### 4.1.5  User Defined EAF

The User Defined EAF option displays two cost driver: USR1 and USR2, and their corresponding ratings and multipliers.

Select User EAF from the Parameters menu with the mouse. The User EAF Dialog Box will appear as Figure 4-6.

To modify these values, go straight to those edit boxes and type new values. When finished with the modification, click the OK button.

## 4.2  EARLY DESIGN MODEL

The Early Design model supports only seven Effort Adjustment factors, plus two user defined factors as shown below in Figure 4-7.

## 4.3  SCALE FACTORS

The Scale Factors option displays five development attributes: PREC, FLEX, RESL, TEAM and PMAT, and their corresponding ratings and values. Select Scale Factors from the Parameters menu with the mouse. The Scale Factor Dialog Box will appear as Figure 4-8.

To modify these values, go straight to those edit boxes and type new values. When finished with the modification, click OK button.

## 4.4  EQUATION

The Equation options displays effort and schedule equations. Select Equation from the Parameters menu. The Equation Dialog Box will appear as in Figure 4-9.

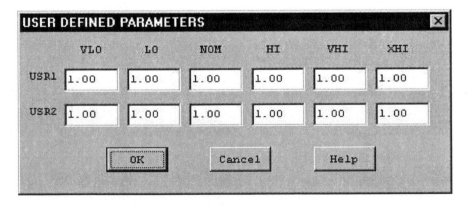

**Figure 4-6**  User Defined EAF Dialog Box

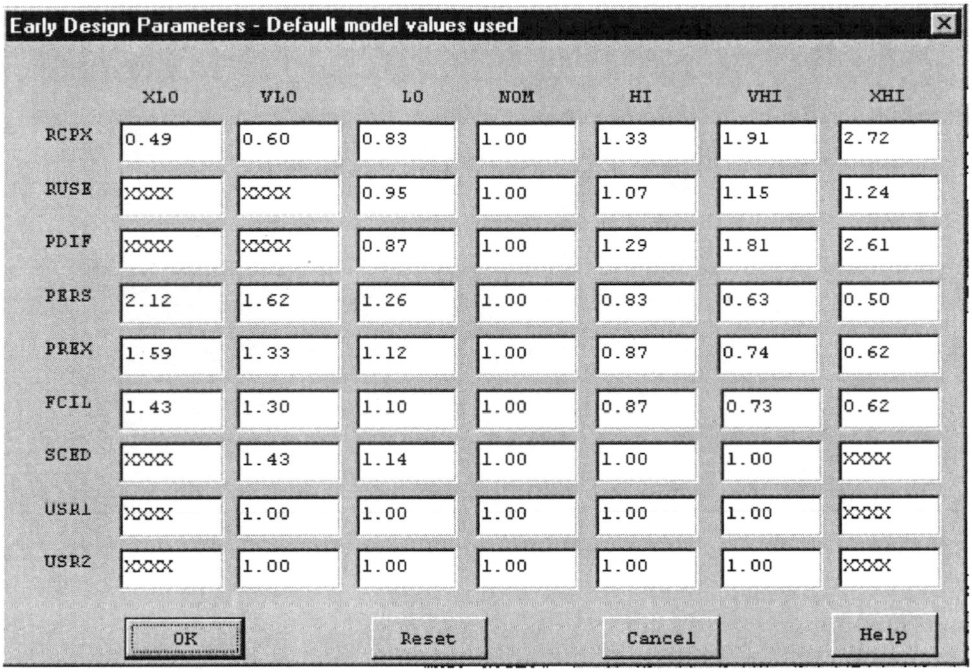

Early Design Parameters - Default model values used

| | XLO | VLO | LO | NOM | HI | VHI | XHI |
|---|---|---|---|---|---|---|---|
| RCPX | 0.49 | 0.60 | 0.83 | 1.00 | 1.33 | 1.91 | 2.72 |
| RUSE | XXXX | XXXX | 0.95 | 1.00 | 1.07 | 1.15 | 1.24 |
| PDIF | XXXX | XXXX | 0.87 | 1.00 | 1.29 | 1.81 | 2.61 |
| PERS | 2.12 | 1.62 | 1.26 | 1.00 | 0.83 | 0.63 | 0.50 |
| PREX | 1.59 | 1.33 | 1.12 | 1.00 | 0.87 | 0.74 | 0.62 |
| FCIL | 1.43 | 1.30 | 1.10 | 1.00 | 0.87 | 0.73 | 0.62 |
| SCED | XXXX | 1.43 | 1.14 | 1.00 | 1.00 | 1.00 | XXXX |
| USR1 | XXXX | 1.00 | 1.00 | 1.00 | 1.00 | 1.00 | XXXX |
| USR2 | XXXX | 1.00 | 1.00 | 1.00 | 1.00 | 1.00 | XXXX |



**Figure 4-7** Early Design Model—EAF Dialog Box

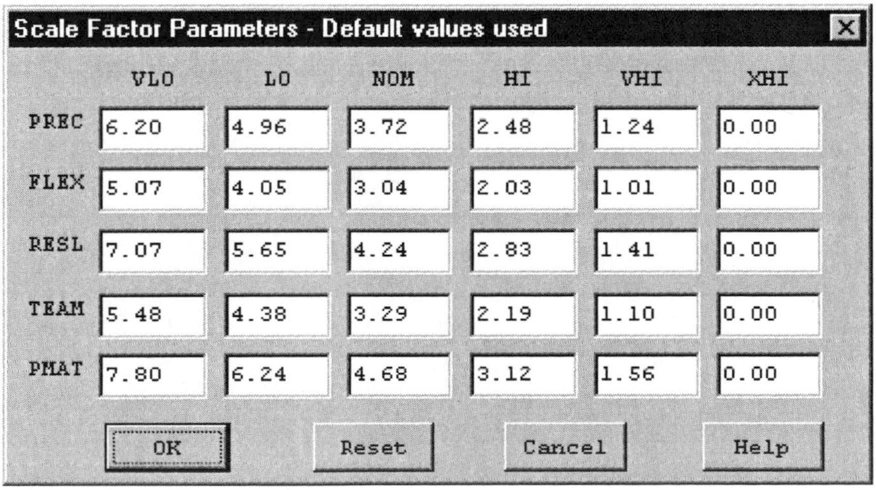

Scale Factor Parameters - Default values used

| | VLO | LO | NOM | HI | VHI | XHI |
|---|---|---|---|---|---|---|
| PREC | 6.20 | 4.96 | 3.72 | 2.48 | 1.24 | 0.00 |
| FLEX | 5.07 | 4.05 | 3.04 | 2.03 | 1.01 | 0.00 |
| RESL | 7.07 | 5.65 | 4.24 | 2.83 | 1.41 | 0.00 |
| TEAM | 5.48 | 4.38 | 3.29 | 2.19 | 1.10 | 0.00 |
| PMAT | 7.80 | 6.24 | 4.68 | 3.12 | 1.56 | 0.00 |



**Figure 4-8** Scale Factors Dialog Box

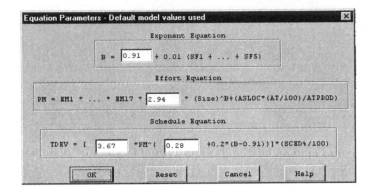

**Figure 4-9**   Equation Dialog Box

To modify these values, go straight to those edit boxes and type new values. When finished with the modification, click the OK button.

## 4.5   PERSON MONTH

It is possible to vary the number used to calculate person months. Figure 4-10 shows the dialog box.

## 4.5   FUNCTION POINT

This command causes a dialog box to appear that permits alteration of the Function Point complexity weights (see Figure 4-11).

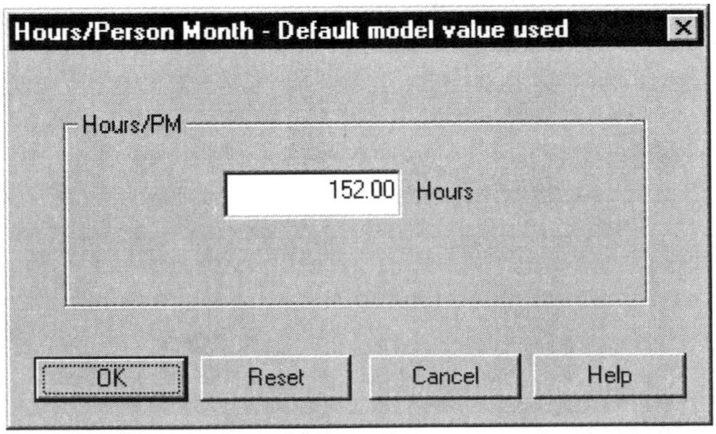

**Figure 4-10**   Dialog Box for Person Month

**Function Point - Default model values used**                    ☒

| Function Type | Low | Average | High |
|---|---|---|---|
| Internal Logical Files | 7 | 10 | 15 |
| External Interface Files | 5 | 7 | 10 |
| External Inputs | 3 | 4 | 6 |
| External Outputs | 4 | 5 | 7 |
| External Inquiries | 3 | 4 | 6 |

[ OK ]   [ Reset ]   [ Cancel ]   [ Help ]

**Figure 4-11**   Dialog Box for Function Point Complexity Weights

---

## CHAPTER 5:   CALIBRATE MENU

COCOMO II now has the ability to archive your own software project data (see Figure 5-1). Using this data, COCOMO II will compute various coefficients and exponents involved in the effort and schedule equations. This will make your COCOMO II estimates even more reliable.

Each software project to be archived is described as a complete COCOMO II project. It may include multiple modules, each with their own SLOC estimate and EAF factors. In addition, a software project consists of a name, date/time, actual effort and actual schedule. The actual effort and actual schedule must be supplied by the COCOMO II user. En-

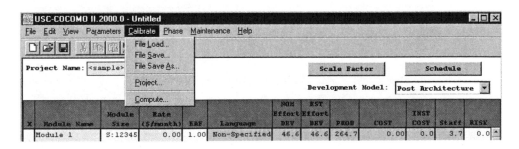

**Figure 5-1**   Calibrate Menu

tering revised values for effort and schedule are always possible. Effort is given in units of person/months. Schedule is given in units of months.

## 5.1    FILE LOAD

The Calibrate File Load option is used to retrieve a calibration project file as well as loading all project data on the working project window (Figure 5-2).

## 5.2    FILE SAVE

The Calibrate File Save command saves the current calibration data in the file whose name was previously identified using File Save As. If a previous Save As has not been performed, the File Save As dialog box will open (shown in Figure 5-3).

## 5.3    FILE SAVE AS

The Calibrate File Save As command stores the current calibration data as a *.cal file, which has a different file name from the current file. This command works precisely the same as the File Save As for *.est and *.mod files (see Figure 5-4).

## 5.4    PROJECT

A windows appears (shown in Figure 5-5) which displays the archived project data.

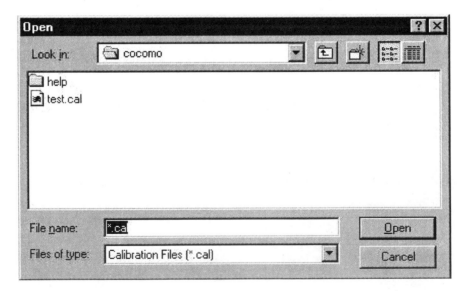

**Figure 5-2**    Load Calibration Dialog Box

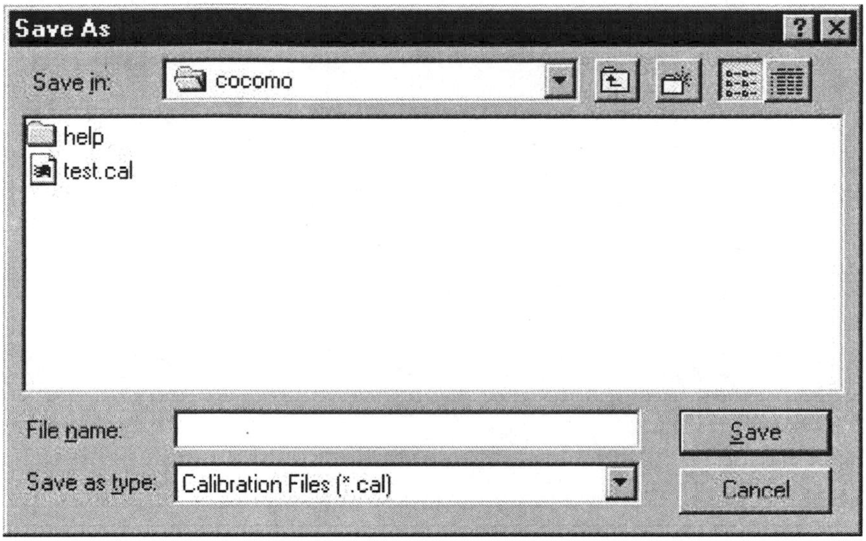

**Figure 5-3**   Save Calibration Dialog Box

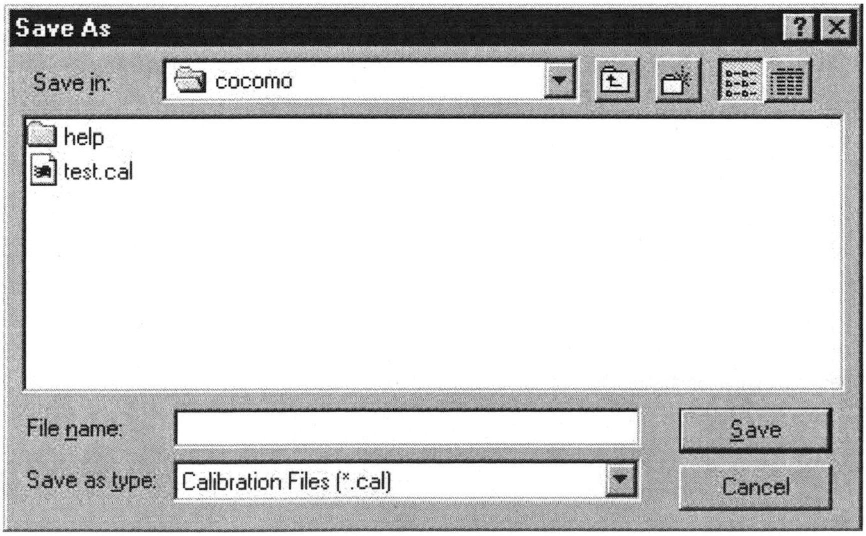

**Figure 5-4**   Save As Calibration Dialog Box

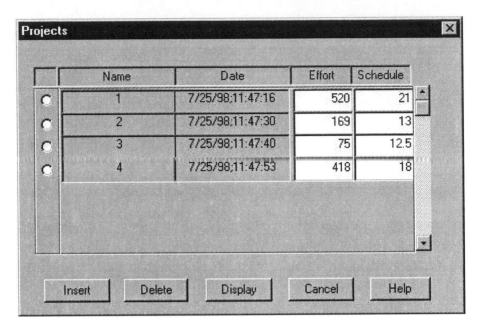

**Figure 5-5**   Projects Dialog Box

- To remove the window, click on Cancel.
- To delete an existing entry, first place an x at the leftmost end of the row and click on Delete. A warning box appears as shown in Figure 5-6.
- To display the entire set of values for an archived project, click on Display. Since the display of an archived project eliminates the display of any existing CLEF data, a warning message appears as shown in Figure 5-7.
- To insert a new archived project from the CLEF, click on Insert.

## 5.5   COMPUTE

This command takes all of the data that has been archived and uses it to compute new constant and exponent values for the effort equation and similarly for the schedule equation. There are two options to calibrate equation parameters. One is the Constant Term and the

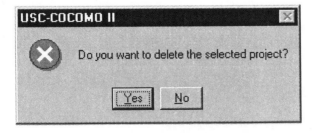

**Figure 5-6**   Delete Warning Dialog

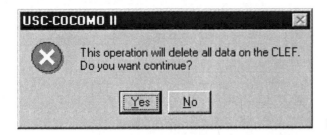

**Figure 5-7**   Display Warning Dialog

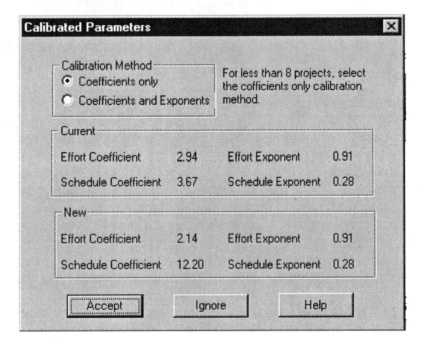

**Figure 5-8**   Compute Dialog Box

other one is Development Mode. Those two options are explained below in detail. They are displayed in this window and compared to the values currently used by COCOMO II. To get COCOMO II to use these values, click on Accept, as shown Figure 5-8.

---

### CHAPTER 6:   PHASE DISTRIBUTION

The Phase Distribution is one of the main menu selections. Its function is to display a breakdown of the software effort and schedule into the phases of the development cycle. COCOMO II offers support for two different development cycles, the *waterfall model* and the *mbase model*. The waterfall model consists of the phases: plans & requirements, design, programming and integration & test. These phases are described as follows:

Plans & Requirements—In this phase, a statement for the required functions, interfaces and performance is created. These expectations are used to define the capabilities of the software product as expressed by representatives of all interested parties.

Product Design—In this phase, a hardware/software architecture, control structure and data structure for the product are defined. A draft of the user's manual and test plans are also created during this phase.

Programming—In this phase, the design of the previous phase is implemented in the creation of complete sets of software components.

Integration & Test—In this phase, the various software components are brought together in order to achieve a properly functioning software product composed of loosely coupled modules. The requirements as defined in the first phase are used to determine the fitness of the delivered product.

The Mbase model is an implementation of the spiral model. A well-defined set of common milestones serve as the endpoints between which COCOMO II estimates and actuals are counted. These milestones consist of the phases inception, elaboration, construction and transition. *Inception* covers the period of time from Inception Readiness Review (IRR) to the definition of Life Cycle Objectives (LCO). *Elaboration* covers the period of time from LCO to Life Cycle Architecture (LCA). *Construction* spans the time from LCA to Initial Operational Capability (IOC). The final phase is *Transition* which covers the time from IOC to Product Release Review (PRR).

In either the waterfall model or the Mbase model, the phase distribution menu has two selections: project phase distribution and module phase distribution. The project phase distribution allows the user to view the development phases for the entire project all together or individually. The module phase distribution allows the user to view the development phases for a particular module either all together or individually. These two variations of phase distribution are discussed further in this chapter.

## 6.1  WATERFALL MODEL—PROJECT PHASE DISTRIBUTION

In order to view the phase distribution of an entire project, the user can click on the Waterfall Project Phase Distribution button under the Phase Distribution menu (see Figure 6-1). Four formats for viewing will appear in another menu: overall phase, plan & requirements, programming, and integration & test. Each of these menu selections will be discussed in later sections. The phase distribution of plan & requirements, programming and integration & test are broken down into sub-phases. These phases include: requirements analysis, product design, programming, test planning, verification & validation, project office, CM/QA, and manuals. For each of these sub-phases the percentage of the phase, the estimated effort, the estimated schedule, and the estimated FSWP are displayed. A description of each of these sub-phases follows:

Requirements analysis: Determination, specification review and update of software functional, performance, interface, and verification requirements.

Product Design: Determination, specification, review and update of hardware-software architecture, program design, and database design.

Programming: Detailed design, code, unit test, and integration of individual computer program components. Includes programming personnel planning, tool acquisitions,

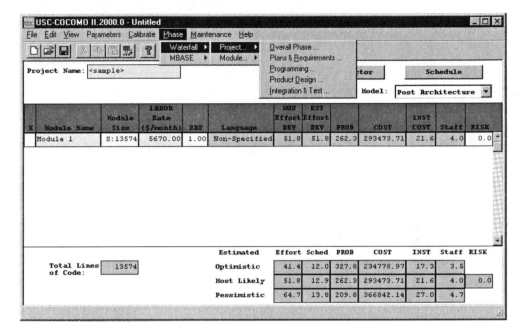

**Figure 6-1**   Waterfall Phase Distribution Sub-menu

database development, component level documentation, and intermediate level programming management.

Test Planning: Specification, review, and update of product test and acceptance test plans. Acquisition of associated test drivers, test tools, and test data.

Verification & Validation(V&V): Performance of independent requirements validation, design V&V, product test, and acceptance test. Acquisition of requirements and design V&V tools. "Are we building the product right?" and "are we building the right product?"

Project Office Functions: Project level management functions. Includes project level planning and control, contract and subcontract management, and customer interface.

Configuration Management and Quality Assurance (CM/QA): Configuration management includes product identification, change control, status accounting, operation of program support library, development and monitoring of end item acceptance plan. Quality assurance includes development and monitoring of project standards, and technical audits of software products and processes.

Manuals: Development and update of users' manuals, operators' manuals and maintenance manuals.

### 6.1.1   Waterfall Overall Project Phase

The overall phase distribution allows the user to view an entire project's estimated effort, schedule and number of personnel needed for phase completion. Upon clicking on "Overall Phase," a window will be displayed showing the phase breakdown of the current project in COCOMO (see Figure 6-2). This window displays the project name, project SLOC,

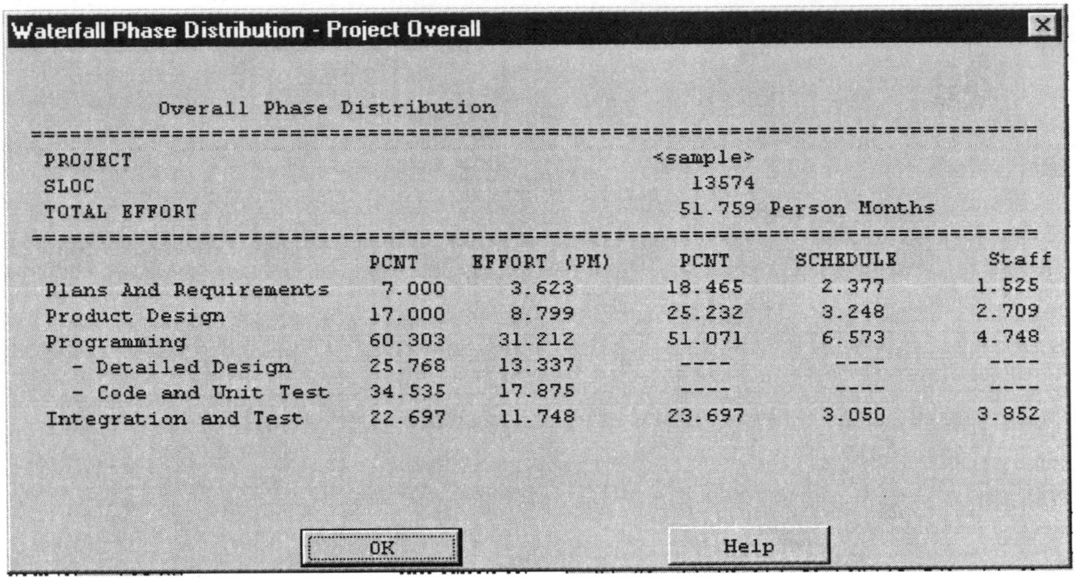

**Figure 6-2**   Waterfall Phase Distribution Window Displaying Overall Phase Distribution

and the total estimated effort for the project. This information can be seen in the upper left corner of the window.

In addition, each phase of the project's development cycle is represented by the estimated effort, the estimated schedule and the estimated number of personnel needed for phase completion. Again looking at Figure 6-2, the information has been separated into columns. The first column displays the phase name. The second column displays the percentage that the corresponding phase takes in the estimated effort. The third column displays the estimated effort for each phase. The fourth column displays the percentage of the estimated schedule that is dedicated to the corresponding phase's completion. The fifth column displays the estimated schedule for phase completion. And the last column displays the estimated number of personnel needed for phase completion (FSWP).

Note: The programming phase has been broken down into two additional phases: "Detailed Design" and "Code and Unit Test." The detailed design is a follow-up to the product design phase. In this sub phase, those points developed in the product design are elaborated to a point necessary to breakdown agreed functions into units necessary for coding. The code and unit test sub-phases house the actual coding effort of the individual units of code. The testing of these units (upon completion) is also encompassed within this sub phase.

### 6.1.2   Waterfall Plans and Requirements Project Phase

The plans and requirements phase distribution allows the user to view the components of this particular phase. When the Plans and Requirements distribution is chosen from the Project Phase distribution menu, the window shown in Figure 6-3 is displayed. This window displays the following information: project name, the total project SLOC, the total es-

```
┌─────────────────────────────────────────────────────────────────────────┐
│ Waterfall Phase Distribution - Project Plans & Requirements           [X] │
├─────────────────────────────────────────────────────────────────────────┤
│                                                                           │
│  =======================================================================  │
│   Life Cycle Phase                  Plans And Requirements                │
│   Life Cycle Effort                                 3.623 Person Months   │
│   Life Cycle Schedule                               2.377 Months          │
│  =======================================================================  │
│                             PCNT       EFFORT (PM)   SCHEDULE      Staff   │
│   Requirements Analysis     46.768     1.694         2.377         0.713   │
│   Product Design            16.616     0.602         2.377         0.253   │
│   Programming               3.732      0.135         2.377         0.057   │
│   Test Planning             3.116      0.113         2.377         0.048   │
│   Verification and Validation  6.616   0.240         2.377         0.101   │
│   Project Office            14.268     0.517         2.377         0.218   │
│   CM/QA                     3.000      0.109         2.377         0.046   │
│   Manuals                   5.884      0.213         2.377         0.090   │
│                                                                           │
│                                                                           │
│              ┌──────────────────┐        ┌──────────────────┐             │
│              │       OK         │        │      Help        │             │
│              └──────────────────┘        └──────────────────┘             │
└─────────────────────────────────────────────────────────────────────────┘
```

**Figure 6-3**   Waterfall Plans and Requirements Phase window for the overall project

timated project effort, and the total estimated project schedule. In addition the window displays the estimated effort for the activities of requirements analysis, product design, programming, test planning, verification & validation, project office, CM/QA, and manuals. These activity estimates are accompanied with a percentage of the phase effort that they encompass, the estimated effort, schedule and FSWP for the activity's completion as shown in Figure 6-3. To exit from this window click the OK button.

### 6.1.3   Waterfall Programming Project Phase

The programming phase distribution allows the user to view the components of this particular phase. When the Programming distribution is chosen from the Project Phase distribution menu, the window shown in Figure 6-4 is displayed. This window displays the following information: project name, the total project SLOC, the total estimated project effort, and the total estimated project schedule. In addition the window displays the estimated effort for the activities of requirements analysis, product design, programming, test planning, verification & validation, project office, CM/QA, and manuals. These activities are accompanied with a percentage of the phase effort that they encompass, the estimated effort, schedule and FSWP for the activity's completion as shown in Figure 6-4. To exit from this window click the OK button.

### 6.1.4   Waterfall Product Design Project Phase

The product design phase distribution allows the user to view the components of this particular phase. When the Product Design distribution is chosen from the Project Phase distribution menu, the window shown in Figure 6-5 is displayed. This window dis-

```
┌──────────────────────────────────────────────────────────────────────────────┐
│ Waterfall Phase Distribution - Project Programming                        [X] │
├──────────────────────────────────────────────────────────────────────────────┤
│                                                                                │
│  ==============================================================================│
│    Life Cycle Phase                                Programming                 │
│    Life Cycle Effort                                31.212 Person Months       │
│    Life Cycle Schedule                               6.573 Months              │
│  ==============================================================================│
│                           PCNT        EFFORT (PM)   SCHEDULE       Staff        │
│    Requirements Analysis   4.000        1.248         6.573        0.190        │
│    Product Design          8.000        2.497         6.573        0.380        │
│    Programming            56.500       17.635         6.573        2.683        │
│    Test Planning           4.616        1.441         6.573        0.219        │
│    Verification and Validation 7.616    2.377         6.573        0.362        │
│    Project Office          6.884        2.149         6.573        0.327        │
│    CM/QA                   6.500        2.029         6.573        0.309        │
│    Manuals                 5.884        1.836         6.573        0.279        │
│                                                                                │
│                  ┌─────────────┐              ┌─────────────┐                  │
│                  │     OK      │              │    Help     │                  │
│                  └─────────────┘              └─────────────┘                  │
└──────────────────────────────────────────────────────────────────────────────┘
```

**Figure 6-4**    Waterfall Phase Project Programming Window for the Overall Project

```
┌──────────────────────────────────────────────────────────────────────────────┐
│ Waterfall Phase Distribution - Project Product Design                     [X] │
├──────────────────────────────────────────────────────────────────────────────┤
│                                                                                │
│  ==============================================================================│
│    Life Cycle Phase                                Product Design              │
│    Life Cycle Effort                                 8.799 Person Months       │
│    Life Cycle Schedule                               3.248 Months              │
│  ==============================================================================│
│                           PCNT        EFFORT (PM)   SCHEDULE       Staff        │
│    Requirements Analysis  12.500        1.100         3.248        0.339        │
│    Product Design         41.000        3.608         3.248        1.111        │
│    Programming            12.616        1.110         3.248        0.342        │
│    Test Planning           5.116        0.450         3.248        0.139        │
│    Verification and Validation 6.616    0.582         3.248        0.179        │
│    Project Office         11.768        1.035         3.248        0.319        │
│    CM/QA                   2.500        0.220         3.248        0.068        │
│    Manuals                 7.884        0.694         3.248        0.214        │
│                                                                                │
│                  ┌─────────────┐              ┌─────────────┐                  │
│                  │     OK      │              │    Help     │                  │
│                  └─────────────┘              └─────────────┘                  │
└──────────────────────────────────────────────────────────────────────────────┘
```

**Figure 6-5**    Waterfall Model Product Design Window for the Overall Project

plays the following information: project name, the total project SLOC, the total estimated project effort, and the total estimated project schedule. In addition the window displays the estimated effort for the activities of requirements analysis, product design, programming, test planning, verification & validation, project office, CM/QA, and manuals These activity estimates are accompanied with a percentage of the phase effort that they encompass, the estimated effort, schedule and FSWP for the activity's completion as shown in Figure 6-5. To exit from this window click the OK button.

### 6.1.5   Waterfall Integration and Test Project Phase

The integration & test phase distribution allows the user to view the components of this particular phase. When the Integration and Test distribution is chosen from the Project Phase distribution menu, the window shown in Figure 6-6 is displayed. This window displays the following information: project name, the total project SLOC, the total estimated project effort, and the total estimated project schedule. In addition the window displays the estimated effort for the activities of requirements analysis, product design, programming, test planning, verification & validation, project office, CM/QA, and manuals. These activity estimates are accompanied with a percentage of the phase effort that they encompass the estimated effort, schedule and FSWP for the activity's completion as shown in Figure 6-6. To exit from this window click the OK button.

| 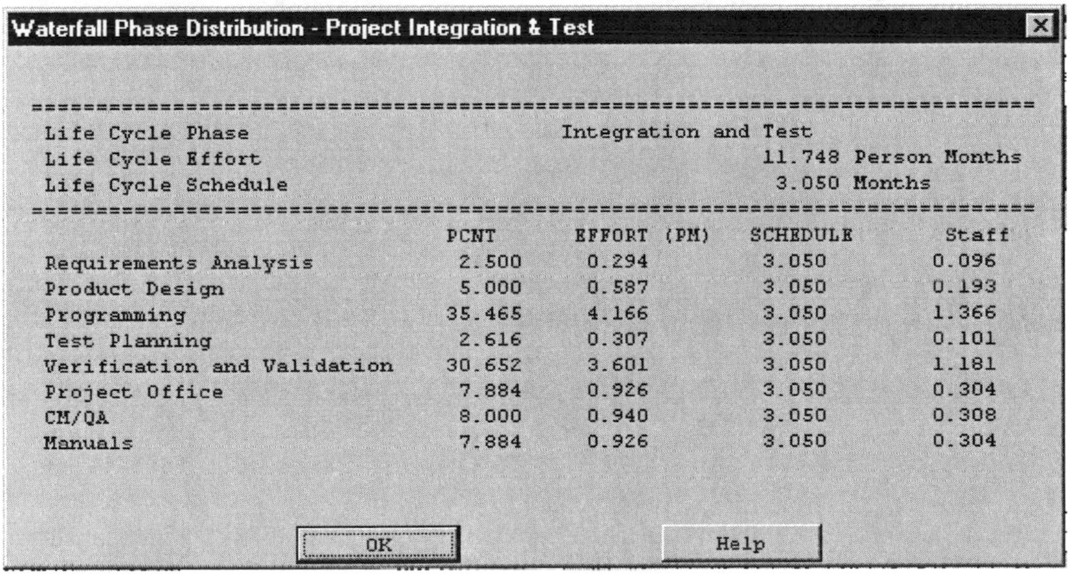 Waterfall Phase Distribution - Project Integration & Test | | | | |
|---|---|---|---|---|
| Life Cycle Phase | | Integration and Test | | |
| Life Cycle Effort | | | 11.748 Person Months | |
| Life Cycle Schedule | | | 3.050 Months | |
| | PCNT | EFFORT (PM) | SCHEDULE | Staff |
| Requirements Analysis | 2.500 | 0.294 | 3.050 | 0.096 |
| Product Design | 5.000 | 0.587 | 3.050 | 0.193 |
| Programming | 35.465 | 4.166 | 3.050 | 1.366 |
| Test Planning | 2.616 | 0.307 | 3.050 | 0.101 |
| Verification and Validation | 30.652 | 3.601 | 3.050 | 1.181 |
| Project Office | 7.884 | 0.926 | 3.050 | 0.304 |
| CM/QA | 8.000 | 0.940 | 3.050 | 0.308 |
| Manuals | 7.884 | 0.926 | 3.050 | 0.304 |
| OK | | | Help | |

**Figure 6-6**   Waterfall Model Integration and Test Window for the Overall Project

## 6.2    WATERFALL MODEL—MODULE PHASE DISTRIBUTION

For the waterfall model there are four formats for viewing that will appear in another menu: overall phase, plan & requirements, programming, and integration & test (see Figure 6-7). Each of these menu selections will be discussed in the upcoming sections. The phase distribution of plan & requirements, programming and integration & test are broken down into activities. These activities include: requirements analysis, product design, programming, test planning, verification & validation, Module office, CM/QA, and manuals. For each of these activities, the percentage of the phase, the estimated effort, the estimated schedule, and the estimated FSWP is displayed. A description of each of these activities follows:

> Requirements analysis: Determination, specification review and update of software functional, performance, interface, and verification requirements.

> Product Design: Determination, specification, review and update of hardware-software architecture, program design, and database design.

> Programming: Detailed design, code, unit test, and integration of individual computer program components. Includes programming personnel planning, tool acquisitions, database development, component level documentation, and intermediate level programming management.

> Test Planning: Specification, review, and update of product test and acceptance test plans. Acquisition of associated test drivers, test tools, and test data.

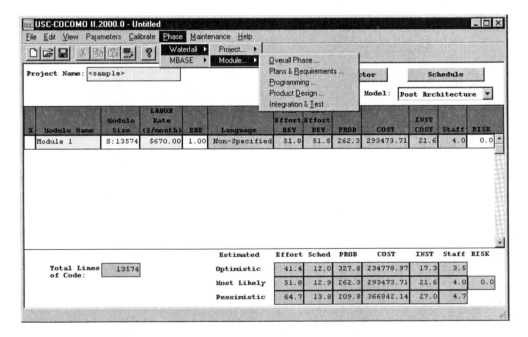

**Figure 6-7**    Phase Distribution Module Sub-menu

Verification & Validation(V&V): Performance of independent requirements validation, design V&V, product test, and acceptance test. Acquisition of requirements and design V&V tools. "Are we building the product right?" and "are we building the right product?"

Module Office Functions: Module level management functions. Includes Module level planning and control, contract and subcontract management, and customer interface.

Configuration Management and Quality Assurance (CM/QA): Configuration management includes product identification, change control, status accounting, operation of program support library, development and monitoring of end item acceptance plan. Quality assurance includes development and monitoring of Module standards, and technical audits of software products and processes.

Manuals: Development and update of users' manuals, operators' manuals and maintenance manuals.

In order to view the phase distribution of an entire Module, the user can click on the Module Phase Distribution button under the Phase Distribution menu. When choosing any of the views of phase distribution, you will be confronted with a module selection window (see Figure 6-8). At this point, you may choose which module is to be viewed by clicking on the desired module name, which will be highlighted after the click. Click the OK button in order to initiate phase distribution of the chosen module.

### 6.2.1   Waterfall Overall Module Phase

The overall phase distribution allows the user to view an entire Module's estimated effort, schedule and number of personnel needed for phase completion. Upon clicking on "Overall Phase," a window will be displayed showing the phase breakdown four formats for viewing will appear in another menu: overall phase, plan & requirements, programming, and integration & test (see Figure 6-9). To exit from this window click the OK button.

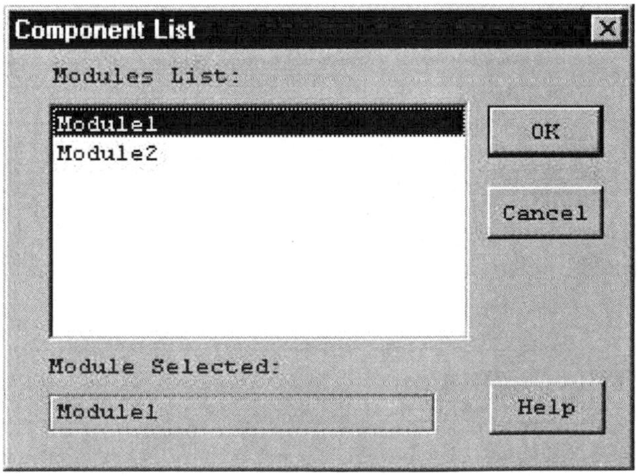

**Figure 6-8**   Module selection window

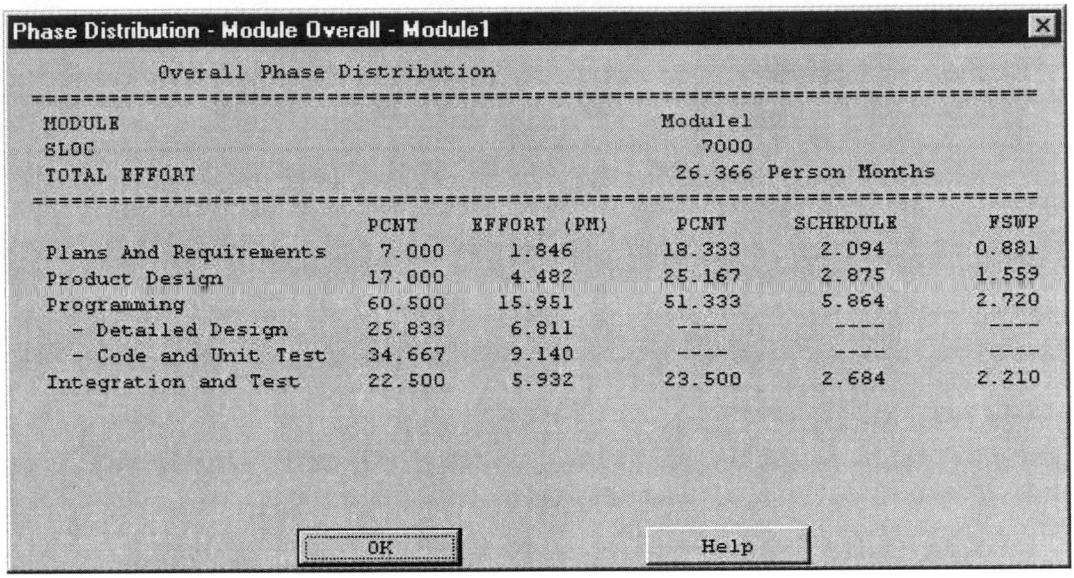

```
Phase Distribution - Module Overall - Module1                              [X]
             Overall Phase Distribution
================================================================================
   MODULE                                  Module1
   SLOC                                      7000
   TOTAL EFFORT                             26.366 Person Months
================================================================================
                         PCNT    EFFORT (PM)    PCNT    SCHEDULE      FSWP
   Plans And Requirements  7.000    1.846      18.333    2.094       0.881
   Product Design         17.000    4.482      25.167    2.875       1.559
   Programming            60.500   15.951      51.333    5.864       2.720
     - Detailed Design    25.833    6.811      ----      ----        ----
     - Code and Unit Test 34.667    9.140      ----      ----        ----
   Integration and Test   22.500    5.932      23.500    2.684       2.210




              ┌──────────────┐              ┌──────────────┐
              │      OK       │              │     Help      │
              └──────────────┘              └──────────────┘
```

**Figure 6-9**   Phase Distribution window displaying a sample Module's overall phase distribution

In addition, each phase of the Module's development cycle is represented by the estimated effort, the estimated schedule and the estimated number of personnel needed for phase completion. Again looking at Figure 6-9, the information has been separated into columns. The first column displays the phase name. The second column displays the percentage that the corresponding phase takes in the estimated effort. The third column displays the estimated effort for each phase. The fourth column displays the percentage of the estimated schedule that is dedicated to the corresponding phase's completion. The fifth column displays the estimated schedule for phase completion. And the last column displays the estimated number of personnel needed for phase completion (FSWP).

Note: The programming phase has been broken down into two additional phases: "Detailed Design" and "Code and Unit Test." The detailed design is a follow-up to the product design phase. In this sub phase, those points developed in the product design are elaborated to a point necessary to breakdown agreed functions into units necessary for coding. The code and unit test sub phase houses the actually coding effort of the individual units of code. The testing of these units (upon completion) is also encompassed within this sub phase.

### 6.2.2   Waterfall Plans and Requirements Module Phase

The plans and requirements phase distribution allows the user to view the components of this particular phase. When the Plans and Requirements distribution is chosen from the Module Phase distribution menu, the window shown in Figure 6-10 is displayed. This window displays the following information: Module name, the total Module SLOC, the total estimated Module effort, and the total estimated Module schedule. In addition the window displays the activities requirements analysis, product design, programming, test planning, verification & validation, Module office, CM/QA, and manuals. These activity estimates are accompanied with a percentage of the phase effort that they encompass, the estimated effort, schedule and FSWP for the activity's completion as shown in Figure 6-10. To exit from this window click the OK button.

### 6.2.3   Waterfall Programming Module Phase

The programming phase distribution allows the user to view the components of this particular phase. When the Programming distribution is chosen from the Module Phase distribution menu, the window shown in Figure 6-11 is displayed. This window displays the following information: Module name, the total Module SLOC, the total estimated
Module effort, and the total estimated Module schedule. In addition the window displays the activity's requirements analysis, product design, programming, test planning, verification & validation, Module office, CM/QA, and manuals. These activity estimates are accompanied with a percentage of the phase effort that they encompass, the estimated effort, schedule and FSWP for the activity's completion as shown in Figure 6-11. To exit from this window click the OK button.

### 6.2.4   Waterfall Product Design Module Phase

The product design phase distribution allows the user to view the components of this particular phase. When the Product Design distribution is chosen from the Module Phase distribution menu, the window shown in Figure 6-12 is displayed. This window displays the following information: Module name, the total Module SLOC, the total estimated Module effort, and the total estimated Module schedule. In addition the window displays the activities requirements analysis, product design, programming, test planning, verification &

---

**Phase Distribution - Module Plans & Requirements - Module1**                                       ☒

```
=================================================================================
   Life Cycle Phase                       Plans And Requirements
   Life Cycle Effort                                    1.846 Person Months
   Life Cycle Schedule                                  2.094 Months
=================================================================================
```

|                            | PCNT   | EFFORT (PM) | SCHEDULE | FSWP  |
|----------------------------|--------|-------------|----------|-------|
| Requirements Analysis      | 46.833 | 0.864       | 2.094    | 0.413 |
| Product Design             | 16.583 | 0.306       | 2.094    | 0.146 |
| Programming                | 3.667  | 0.068       | 2.094    | 0.032 |
| Test Planning              | 3.083  | 0.057       | 2.094    | 0.027 |
| Verification and Validation| 6.583  | 0.122       | 2.094    | 0.058 |
| Project Office             | 14.333 | 0.265       | 2.094    | 0.126 |
| CM/QA                      | 3.000  | 0.055       | 2.094    | 0.026 |
| Manuals                    | 5.917  | 0.109       | 2.094    | 0.052 |

[      OK      ]                    [     Help     ]

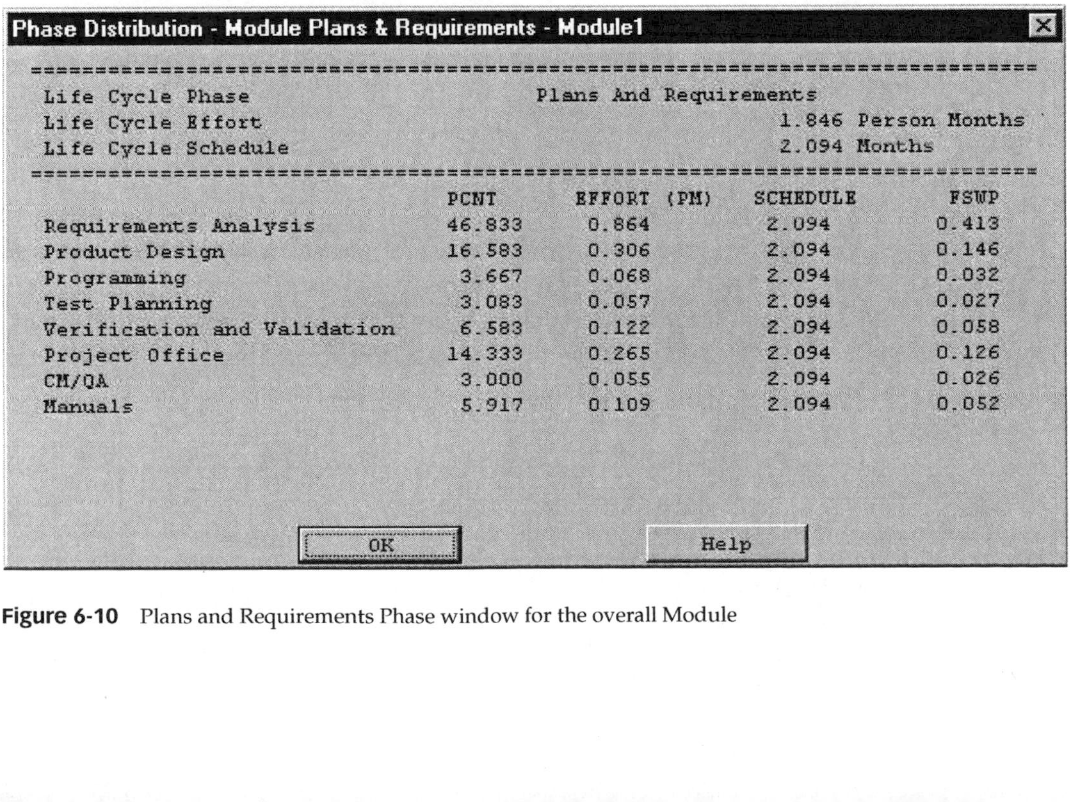

**Figure 6-10**   Plans and Requirements Phase window for the overall Module

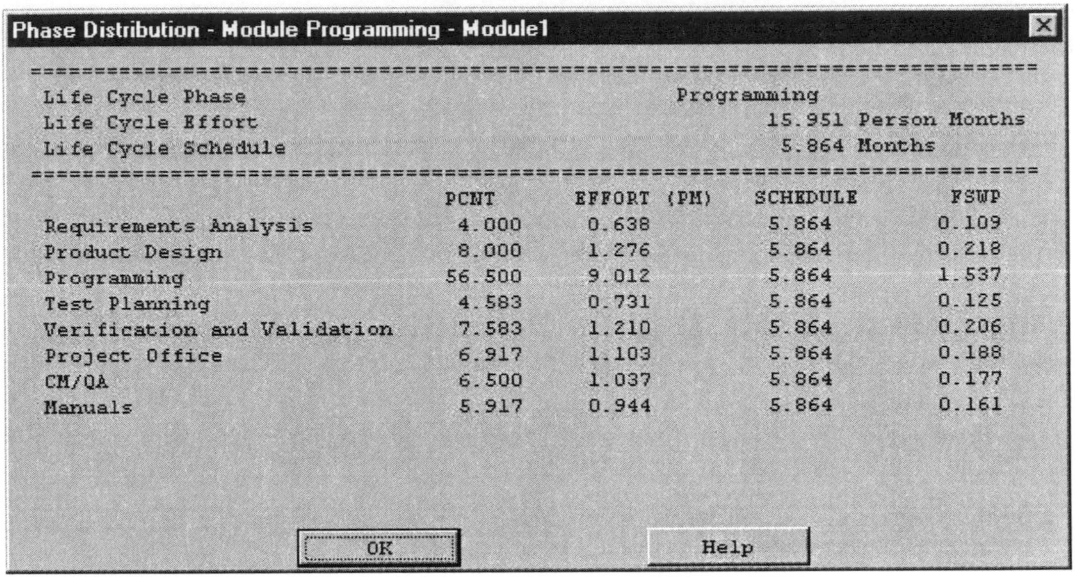

```
┌──────────────────────────────────────────────────────────────────────────┐
│ Phase Distribution - Module Programming - Module1                      [X] │
├──────────────────────────────────────────────────────────────────────────┤
│ ==========================================================================  │
│    Life Cycle Phase                            Programming                  │
│    Life Cycle Effort                           15.951 Person Months         │
│    Life Cycle Schedule                          5.864 Months                │
│ ==========================================================================  │
│                             PCNT      EFFORT (PM)   SCHEDULE      FSWP       │
│    Requirements Analysis    4.000     0.638         5.864         0.109      │
│    Product Design           8.000     1.276         5.864         0.218      │
│    Programming             56.500     9.012         5.864         1.537      │
│    Test Planning            4.583     0.731         5.864         0.125      │
│    Verification and Validation 7.583 1.210          5.864         0.206      │
│    Project Office           6.917     1.103         5.864         0.188      │
│    CM/QA                    6.500     1.037         5.864         0.177      │
│    Manuals                  5.917     0.944         5.864         0.161      │
│                                                                             │
│              ┌─────────────┐              ┌─────────────┐                   │
│              │     OK      │              │    Help     │                   │
│              └─────────────┘              └─────────────┘                   │
└──────────────────────────────────────────────────────────────────────────┘
```

**Figure 6-11**    Programming Phase window for the overall Module

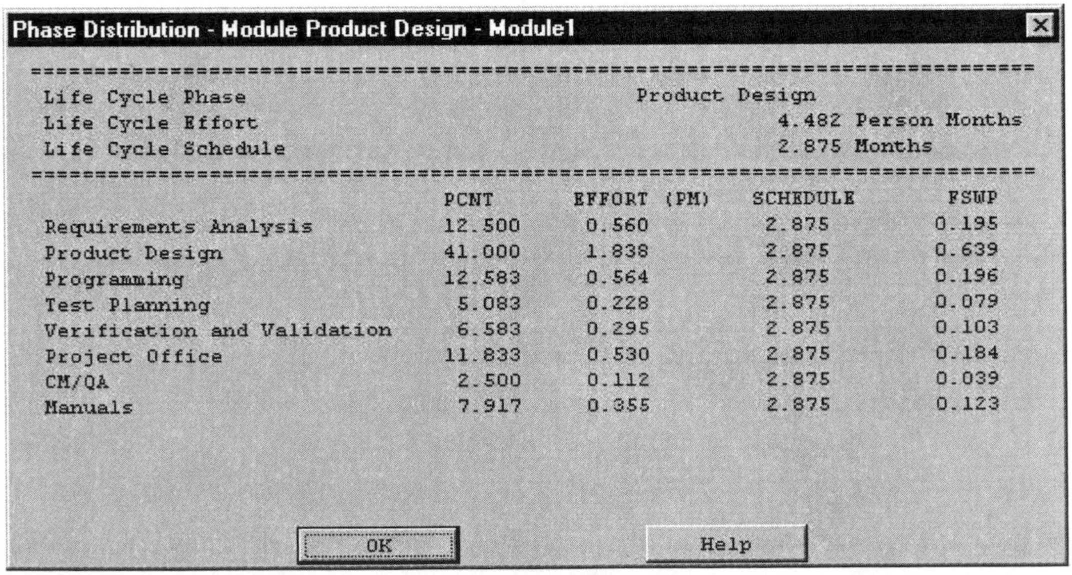

```
┌──────────────────────────────────────────────────────────────────────────┐
│ Phase Distribution - Module Product Design - Module1                   [X] │
├──────────────────────────────────────────────────────────────────────────┤
│ ==========================================================================  │
│    Life Cycle Phase                          Product Design                 │
│    Life Cycle Effort                          4.482 Person Months           │
│    Life Cycle Schedule                        2.875 Months                  │
│ ==========================================================================  │
│                             PCNT      EFFORT (PM)   SCHEDULE      FSWP       │
│    Requirements Analysis   12.500     0.560         2.875         0.195      │
│    Product Design          41.000     1.838         2.875         0.639      │
│    Programming             12.583     0.564         2.875         0.196      │
│    Test Planning            5.083     0.228         2.875         0.079      │
│    Verification and Validation 6.583 0.295          2.875         0.103      │
│    Project Office          11.833     0.530         2.875         0.184      │
│    CM/QA                    2.500     0.112         2.875         0.039      │
│    Manuals                  7.917     0.355         2.875         0.123      │
│                                                                             │
│                                                                             │
│              ┌─────────────┐              ┌─────────────┐                   │
│              │     OK      │              │    Help     │                   │
│              └─────────────┘              └─────────────┘                   │
└──────────────────────────────────────────────────────────────────────────┘
```

**Figure 6-12**    Product Design window for the overall Module

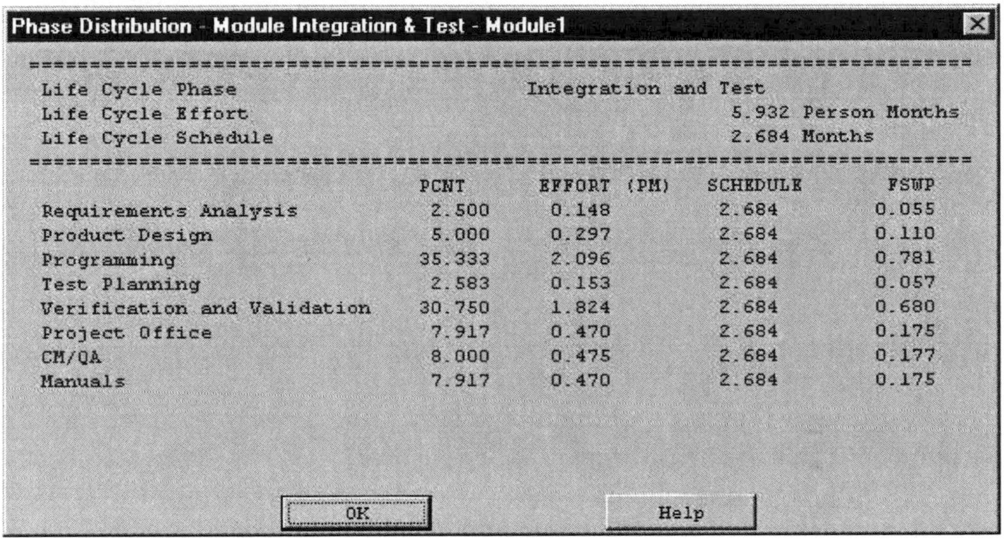

```
Phase Distribution - Module Integration & Test - Module1                    ☒
=====================================================================================
   Life Cycle Phase                        Integration and Test
   Life Cycle Effort                                      5.932 Person Months
   Life Cycle Schedule                                    2.684 Months
=====================================================================================
                                PCNT      EFFORT (PM)   SCHEDULE      FSWP
   Requirements Analysis        2.500      0.148         2.684        0.055
   Product Design               5.000      0.297         2.684        0.110
   Programming                 35.333      2.096         2.684        0.781
   Test Planning                2.583      0.153         2.684        0.057
   Verification and Validation 30.750      1.824         2.684        0.680
   Project Office               7.917      0.470         2.684        0.175
   CM/QA                        8.000      0.475         2.684        0.177
   Manuals                      7.917      0.470         2.684        0.175



                      ┌──────────────┐      ┌──────────────┐
                      │      OK      │      │     Help     │
                      └──────────────┘      └──────────────┘
```

**Figure 6-13**   Waterfall Integration & Test window for the overall Module

validation, Module office, CM/QA, and manuals. These activity estimates are accompanied with a percentage of the phase effort that they encompass, the estimated effort, schedule and FSWP for the activity's completion as shown in Figure 6-12. To exit from this window click the OK button.

### 6.2.5   Waterfall Integration and Test Module Phase

The integration & test phase distribution allows the user to view the components of this particular phase. When the Integration and Test distribution is chosen from the Module Phase distribution menu, the window shown in Figure 6-13 is displayed. This window displays the following information: Module name, the total Module SLOC, the total estimated Module effort, and the total estimated Module schedule. In addition the window displays the activities requirements analysis, product design, programming, test planning, verification & validation, Module office, CM/QA, and manuals. These activity estimates are accompanied with a percentage of the phase effort that they encompass, the estimated effort, schedule and FSWP for the activity's completion as shown in Figure 6-13. To exit from this window click the OK button.

## 6.3   MBASE MODEL—PROJECT PHASE DISTRIBUTION

Figures 6-14 through 6-23 show the screens that appear when the MBASE model is chosen.

### 6.3.1 MBASE Model Project Overall Phase
In Figure 6-14  below you see the screen that results from the MBASE Model Project Overall menu item.

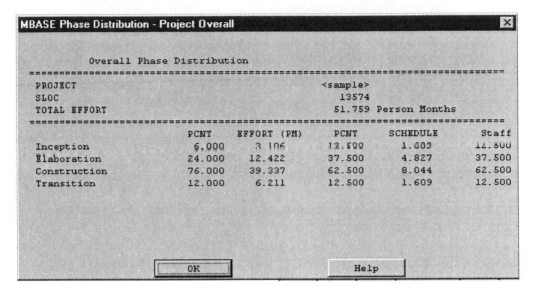

```
MBASE Phase Distribution - Project Overall                              [X]


        Overall Phase Distribution
========================================================================
PROJECT                                   <sample>
SLOC                                       13574
TOTAL EFFORT                               51.759 Person Months
========================================================================

                PCNT     EFFORT (PM)   PCNT     SCHEDULE     Staff
Inception       6.000      3.106       12.500    1.609      12.500
Elaboration     24.000    12.422       37.500    4.827      37.500
Construction    76.000    39.337       62.500    8.044      62.500
Transition      12.000     6.211       12.500    1.609      12.500



                  [      OK      ]              [    Help    ]
```

**Figure 6-14**   MBASE Model Project Overall

## 6.3.2   MBASE Model Project Inception

In Figure 6-15 below see the screen that results from the MBASE Model Project Inception menu item.

```
MBASE Phase Distribution - Project Inception (IRR to LCO)               [X]


========================================================================
  Life Cycle Phase                          Inception
  Life Cycle Effort                          3.106 Person Months
  Life Cycle Schedule                        1.609 Months
========================================================================
                        PCNT     EFFORT (PM)   SCHEDULE     Staff
  Requirements Capture  38.000     1.180        1.609       0.734
  Analysis and Design   19.000     0.590        1.609       0.367
  Implementation         8.000     0.248        1.609       0.154
  Test                   8.000     0.248        1.609       0.154
========================================================================
  Management            14.000     0.435        1.609       0.270
  Environment           10.000     0.311        1.609       0.193
  Deployment             3.000     0.093        1.609       0.058


                  [      OK      ]              [    Help    ]
```

**Figure 6-15**   MBASE Model Project Inception

### 6.3.3. MBASE Model Project Elaboration

In Figure 6-16 below you see the screen that results from the MBASE Model Project Elaboration menu item.

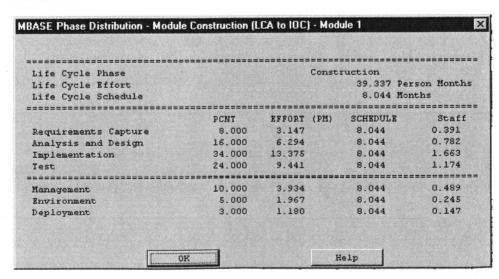

**Figure 6-16** MBASE Model Project Elaboration

### 6.3.4 MBASE Model Project Construction

In Figure 6-17 below you see the screen that results from the MBASE Model Project Construction menu item.

**MBASE Phase Distribution - Module Construction (LCA to IOC) - Module 1**

| Life Cycle Phase | | Construction | | |
|---|---|---|---|---|
| Life Cycle Effort | | 39.337 Person Months | | |
| Life Cycle Schedule | | 8.044 Months | | |

| | PCNT | EFFORT (PM) | SCHEDULE | Staff |
|---|---|---|---|---|
| Requirements Capture | 8.000 | 3.147 | 8.044 | 0.391 |
| Analysis and Design | 16.000 | 6.294 | 8.044 | 0.782 |
| Implementation | 34.000 | 13.375 | 8.044 | 1.663 |
| Test | 24.000 | 9.441 | 8.044 | 1.174 |
| Management | 10.000 | 3.934 | 8.044 | 0.489 |
| Environment | 5.000 | 1.967 | 8.044 | 0.245 |
| Deployment | 3.000 | 1.180 | 8.044 | 0.147 |

OK        Help

**Figure 6-17** MBASE Model Project Construction

### 6.3.5 MBASE Model Project Transition

In Figure 6-18 below you see the screen that results from the MBASE Model Project Transition menu item.

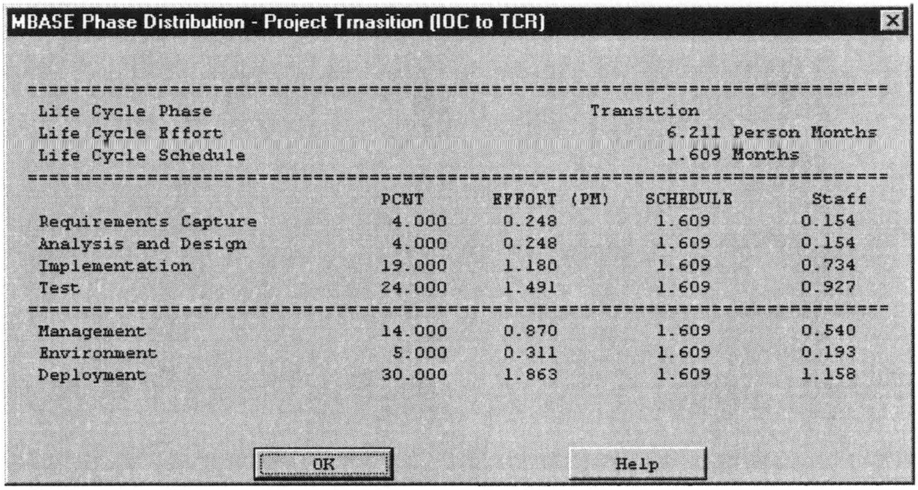

```
MBASE Phase Distribution - Project Trnasition (IOC to TCR)                  [X]


==========================================================================
    Life Cycle Phase                          Transition
    Life Cycle Effort                             6.211 Person Months
    Life Cycle Schedule                           1.609 Months
==========================================================================
                            PCNT     EFFORT (PM)   SCHEDULE    Staff
    Requirements Capture    4.000      0.248        1.609       0.154
    Analysis and Design     4.000      0.248        1.609       0.154
    Implementation         19.000      1.180        1.609       0.734
    Test                   24.000      1.491        1.609       0.927
==========================================================================
    Management             14.000      0.870        1.609       0.540
    Environment             5.000      0.311        1.609       0.193
    Deployment             30.000      1.863        1.609       1.158



                  [      OK      ]            [    Help    ]
```

**Figure 6-18** MBASE Model Project Transition

## 6.4 MBASE MODEL—MODULE PHASE DISTRIBUTION

### 6.4.1 MBASE Model Module Overall Phase

In Figure 6-19 below you see the screen that results from the MBASE Model Module Overall phase menu item.

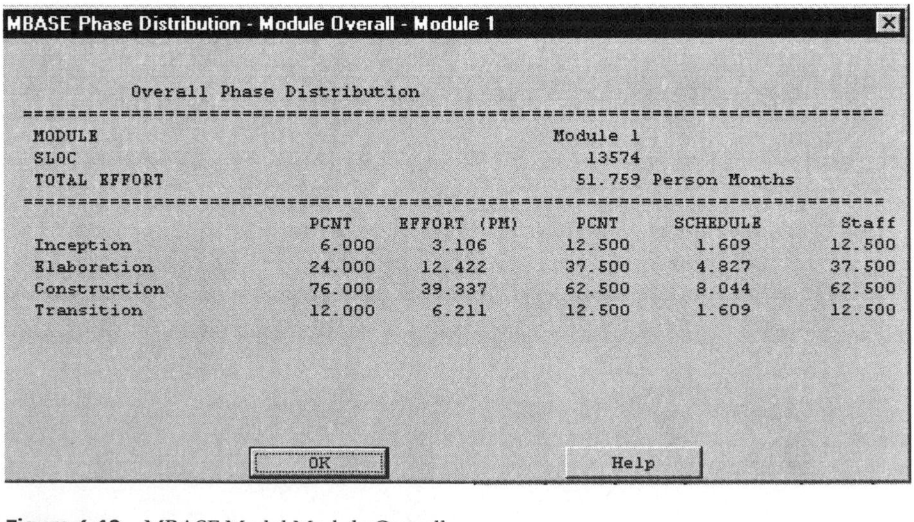

```
MBASE Phase Distribution - Module Overall - Module 1                        [X]


        Overall Phase Distribution
==========================================================================
    MODULE                                    Module 1
    SLOC                                       13574
    TOTAL EFFORT                              51.759 Person Months
==========================================================================
                    PCNT    EFFORT (PM)    PCNT     SCHEDULE     Staff
    Inception       6.000      3.106      12.500     1.609      12.500
    Elaboration    24.000     12.422      37.500     4.827      37.500
    Construction   76.000     39.337      62.500     8.044      62.500
    Transition     12.000      6.211      12.500     1.609      12.500




                  [      OK      ]            [    Help    ]
```

**Figure 6-19** MBASE Model Module Overall

### 6.4.2 MBASE Model Module Inception Phase

In Figure 6-20 below you see the screen that results from the MBASE Model Module Inception Phase window.

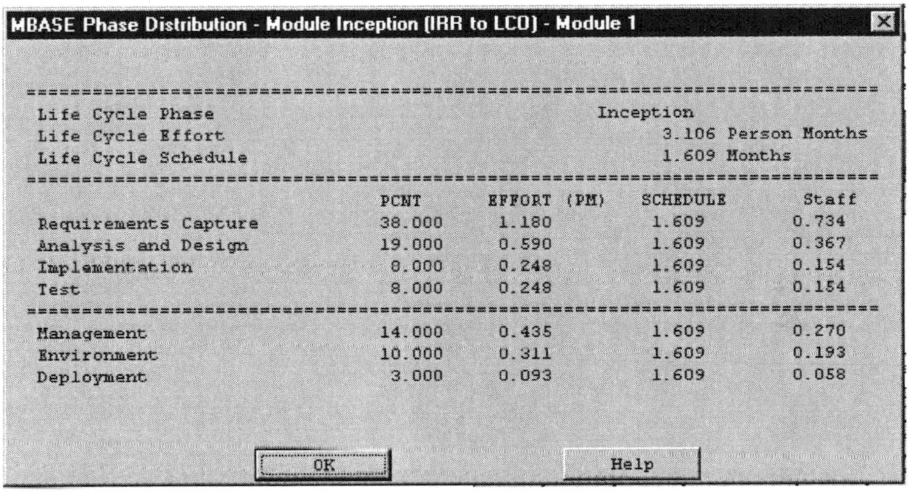

```
MBASE Phase Distribution - Module Inception (IRR to LCO) - Module 1          [X]

==================================================================
    Life Cycle Phase                        Inception
    Life Cycle Effort                        3.106 Person Months
    Life Cycle Schedule                      1.609 Months
==================================================================
                         PCNT    EFFORT (PM)   SCHEDULE    Staff
    Requirements Capture  38.000   1.180         1.609      0.734
    Analysis and Design   19.000   0.590         1.609      0.367
    Implementation         8.000   0.248         1.609      0.154
    Test                   8.000   0.248         1.609      0.154
==================================================================
    Management            14.000   0.435         1.609      0.270
    Environment           10.000   0.311         1.609      0.193
    Deployment             3.000   0.093         1.609      0.058


                 [    OK    ]              [  Help  ]
```

**Figure 6-20** MBASE Model Module Inception

### 6.4.3 MBASE Model Module Elaboration Phase

In Figure 6-21 below you see the screen that results from the MBASE Model Module Elaboration Phase window.

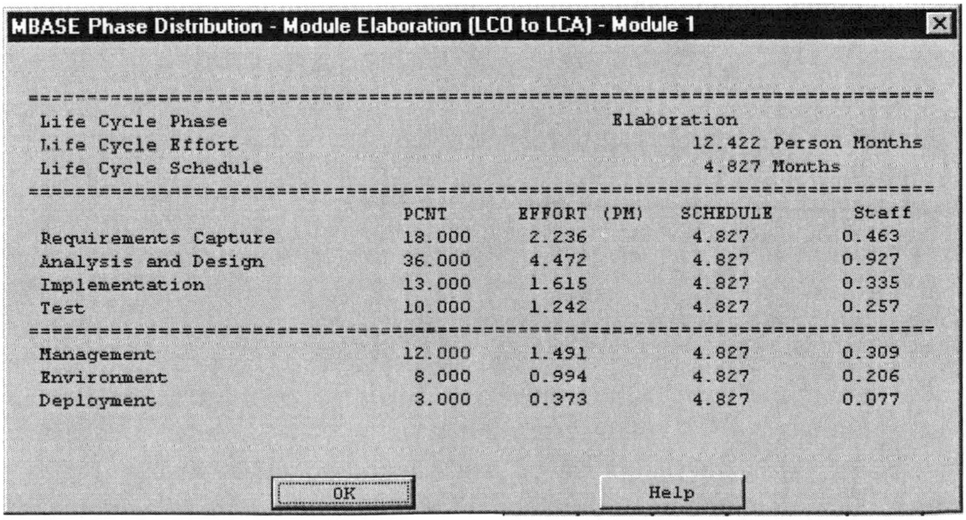

```
MBASE Phase Distribution - Module Elaboration (LCO to LCA) - Module 1          [X]

==================================================================
    Life Cycle Phase                        Elaboration
    Life Cycle Effort                       12.422 Person Months
    Life Cycle Schedule                      4.827 Months
==================================================================
                         PCNT    EFFORT (PM)   SCHEDULE    Staff
    Requirements Capture  18.000   2.236         4.827      0.463
    Analysis and Design   36.000   4.472         4.827      0.927
    Implementation        13.000   1.615         4.827      0.335
    Test                  10.000   1.242         4.827      0.257
==================================================================
    Management            12.000   1.491         4.827      0.309
    Environment            8.000   0.994         4.827      0.206
    Deployment             3.000   0.373         4.827      0.077


                 [    OK    ]              [  Help  ]
```

**Figure 6-21** MBASE Model Module Elaboration

### 6.4.4    MBASE Model Module Construction Phase

In Figure 6-22 below you see the screen that results from the MBASE Model Module Construction Phase window.

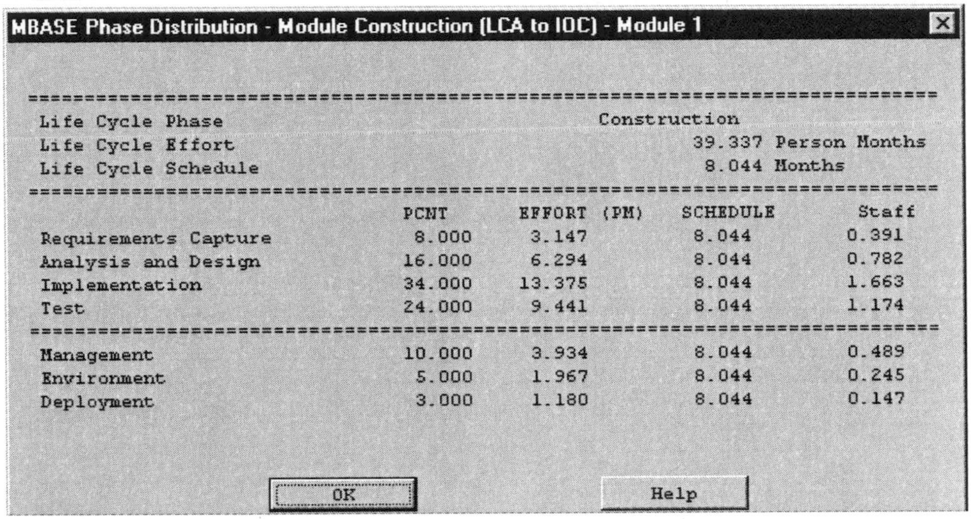

```
MBASE Phase Distribution - Module Construction (LCA to IOC) - Module 1          [X]

=================================================================================
  Life Cycle Phase                              Construction
  Life Cycle Effort                                39.337 Person Months
  Life Cycle Schedule                               8.044 Months
=================================================================================
                        PCNT        EFFORT (PM)    SCHEDULE       Staff
  Requirements Capture  8.000        3.147          8.044         0.391
  Analysis and Design   16.000       6.294          8.044         0.782
  Implementation        34.000      13.375          8.044         1.663
  Test                  24.000       9.441          8.044         1.174
=================================================================================
  Management            10.000       3.934          8.044         0.489
  Environment            5.000       1.967          8.044         0.245
  Deployment             3.000       1.180          8.044         0.147


                [       OK       ]              [    Help    ]
```

**Figure 6-22**   MBASE Model Module Construction

### 6.4.5    MBASE Model Module Transition Phase

In Figure 6-23 below you see the screen that results from the MBASE Model Module Transition Phase window.

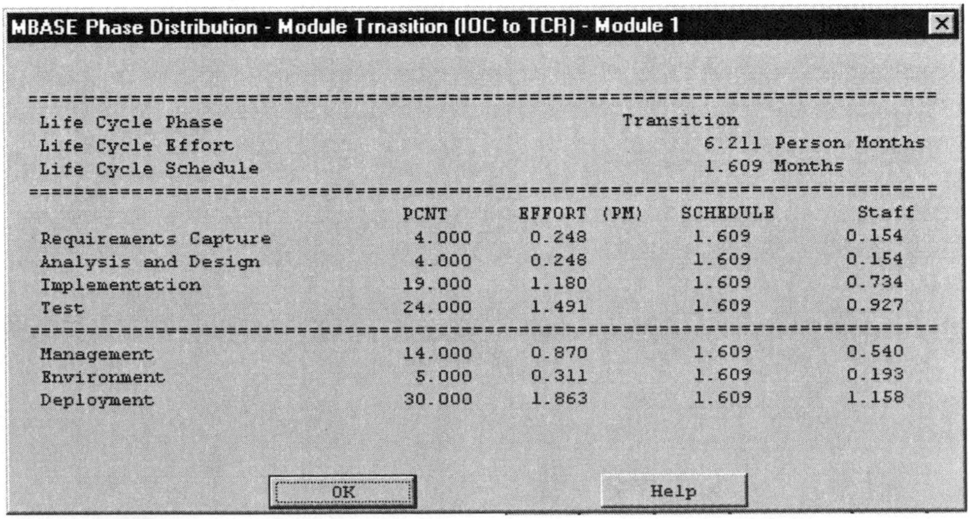

```
MBASE Phase Distribution - Module Trnasition (IOC to TCR) - Module 1            [X]

=================================================================================
  Life Cycle Phase                              Transition
  Life Cycle Effort                                 6.211 Person Months
  Life Cycle Schedule                               1.609 Months
=================================================================================
                        PCNT        EFFORT (PM)    SCHEDULE       Staff
  Requirements Capture   4.000       0.248          1.609         0.154
  Analysis and Design    4.000       0.248          1.609         0.154
  Implementation        19.000       1.180          1.609         0.734
  Test                  24.000       1.491          1.609         0.927
=================================================================================
  Management            14.000       0.870          1.609         0.540
  Environment            5.000        0.311          1.609         0.193
  Deployment            30.000       1.863          1.609         1.158


                [       OK       ]              [    Help    ]
```

**Figure 6-23**   MBASE Model Module Transition

## CHAPTER 7:   MAINTENANCE

Maintenance is one of the menu selections in the menu bar that can be accessed by either clicking upon "Maintenance" in the menu bar or pressing Meta+M. Its function is to calculate and display an estimate of the effort and cost necessary to maintain a post development software product for a user-defined number of years (maximum five years). Maintenance encompasses the process of modifying existing operational software while leaving its primary functions intact. This process excludes the following types of activities:

- Major re-design and re-development (more than 50% new code) of a new software product performing substantially the same functions
- Design and development of a sizeable (more than 20% of the source instructions comprising the existing product) interfacing software package which requires relatively little redesigning of the existing product
- Data processing system operations, data entry, and modification of values in the database

Maintenance does include the following types of activities:

- Re design and re-development of small portions of an existing software product
- Design and development of small interfacing software packages, which require some redesign of the existing software product
- Modification of the software product's code, documentation, or database structure

Maintenance effort and costs are determined by essentially the same cost driver attributes used to determine the software development costs and effort (exceptions are the RELY, SCED and MODP factors which will be discussed in greater detail later in this chapter). The maintenance calculations are heavily based upon the Maintenance change Factor (MCF) and the Maintenance Adjustment Factor (MAF). The MCF is similar to the Annual change Traffic in COCOMO81, except that maintenance periods other than a year can be used (see EQ 7-1).

**Maintenance Change Factor (EQ 7-1)**

$$MCF = \frac{Size\ Added\ +\ Size\ Modified}{Base\ Code\ Size}$$

The initial maintenance size is obtained in one to two ways. The first equation in EQ 7-2 is used when the base code size is known and percentage of change to the base code is known. The second equation in EQ 7-2 is used when the fraction of code added or modified to the existing base code during the maintenance period is known.

**Initial Maintenance Size (EQ 7-2)**

$$(Size)_M = (Base\ Code\ Size) \times MCF \times MAF$$

$$(Size)_M = (SizeAdded\ +\ SizeModified) \times MAF$$

As shown in EQ 7-2, the initial maintenance size estimate is adjusted with a Maintenance Adjustment Factor (see EQ 7-3).

$$MAF = 1 + \left(\frac{SU}{100} \times UNFM\right)$$

The resulting maintenance effort estimation formula is the same as the COCOMO II Post Architecture development model (see EQ 7-4).

**Maintenance Effort (EQ 7-4)**

$$PM_M = A \times (Size_M)^B \times \prod_{i=1}^{17} EM_i$$

As stated previously, three cost drivers for maintenance differ from development. Those cost drivers are software reliability (RELY), modern programming practices (MODP) and schedule (SCED). The reason for the change in MODP, RELY is that increased investment in software reliability and use of modern programming practices during software development have a strong positive effect upon the maintenance stage. The SCED attribute is controlled by the number of years value entered by the user. As a result the SCED driver is no longer editable in the EAF window, but is calculated from the user inputted value for number of years when the maintenance function is engaged. For more information on these cost drivers please refer to the introduction of this manual.

The Maintenance menu option offers sub-menu with a maintenance effort estimation for either an entire project or an individual module (see Figure 7-1). These separate options are discussed in section 7.1 and 7.2.

## 7.1 PROJECT MAINTENANCE

In order to view the maintenance estimation calculations for an entire project, the user can click on Project under the Maintenance menu (see Figure 7-1). Upon clicking upon this selection a window will appear displaying the current value of the Scale Factor. Clicking on this button produces a window with the individual scale factors, each of which is independently editable (see Figure 7-2).

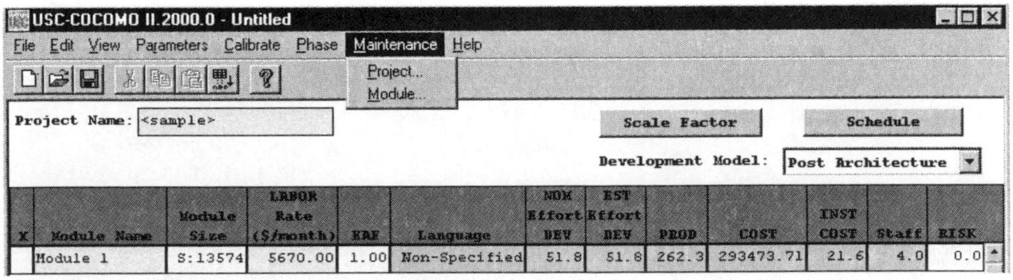

**Figure 7-1** Maintenance sub-menu

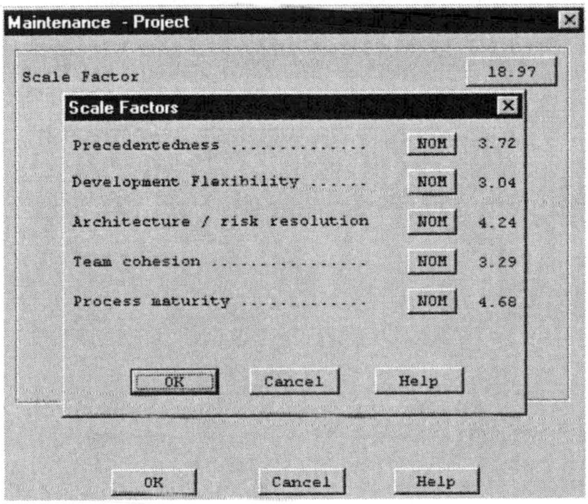

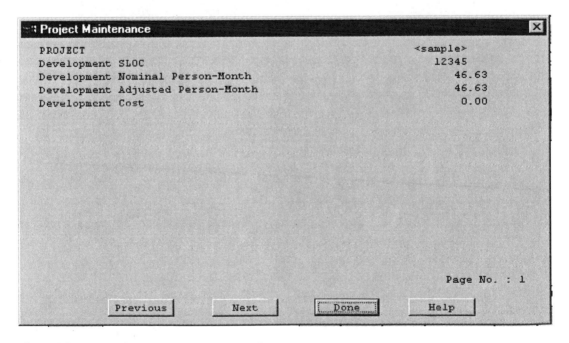

**Figure 7-2**   Project Maintenance Dialog Box

The scale factors can be changed by clicking upon the corresponding scale factor button. This action will result in the appearance of an EAF dialog box where the cost driver ratings can be changed as described in the introduction (see Figure 7-3)

Upon completing the adjustment of the scale factors click the OK button and a series of screens appear with maintenance information as shown in Figures 7-3 and 7-4. Or click the Cancel button to return to the CLEF without viewing maintenance estimations.

**Figure 7-3**   Project Maintenance window (page 1)

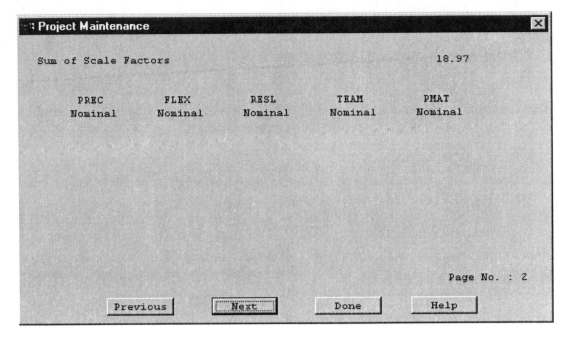

**Figure 7-4**    Project Maintenance window (page 2)

The second page of the maintenance window can be seen by clicking upon the Next button. It contains the settings for the 16 cost drivers, SCED is not applicable (see Figure 7-4).

The third page of the maintenance window contains the effort and cost estimation for the next N number of years (as defined by the user). With each year is listed the KDSI (EDSI * $10^3$), the nominal effort for development (PM nom), the actual effort for maintenance (PM maint), the number of full time software personnel necessary to maintain the project for the year (FSWP), the number of instructions that are to be maintained be per personnel(KDSI/FSWP) and the total cost for maintenance for the year (see Figure 7-5).

The fourth window of the maintenance window contains the cumulative figures for effort and cost for maintenance for the total number of years (see Figure 7-6). This first displays the total number of effort estimated for maintenance, then sums the effort of development and maintenance together. It also displays the total cost of maintenance of the project and then displays the summed total cost of development and maintenance for the entire project.

Note—Each individual page can be seen by cycling through the pages pressing either the Previous or Next buttons as needed.

## 7.2   MODULE MAINTENANCE

In order to view the maintenance estimation calculations for an entire module, the user can click on Module under the Maintenance menu (see Figure 7-1). Upon clicking upon this selection a window will appear displaying the current module names. Choose only

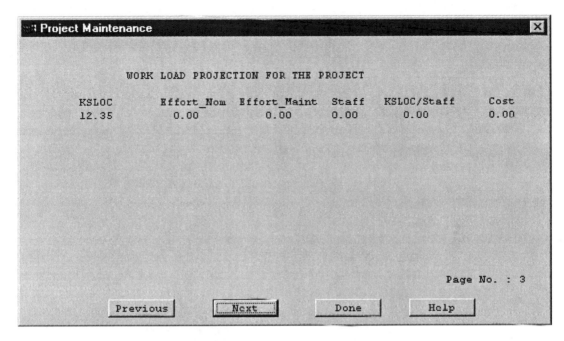

**Figure 7-5**   Project Maintenance window (page 3)

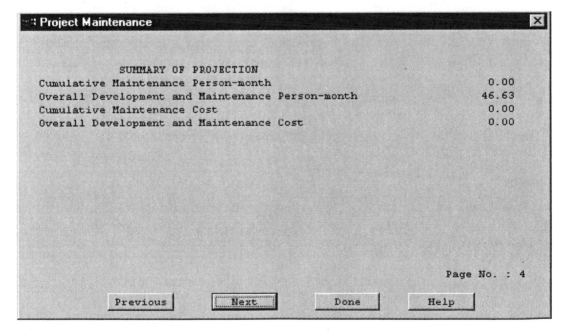

**Figure 7-6**   Project Maintenance window (page 4)

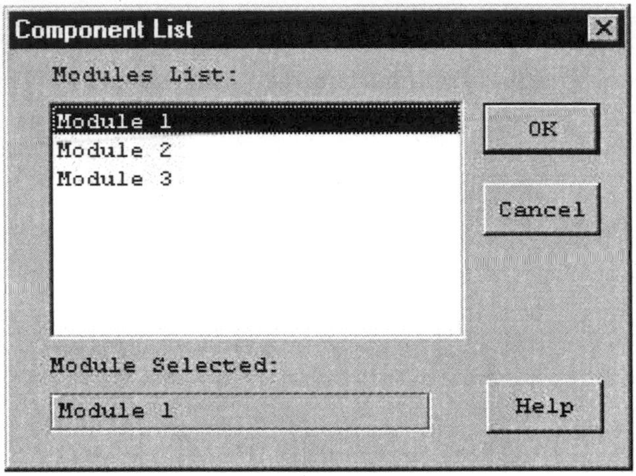

**Component List**                    [X]

Modules List:

| Module 1 | | OK |
|----------|--|----|
| Module 2 | | |
| Module 3 | | Cancel |

Module Selected:

| Module 1 | Help |
|----------|------|

**Figure 7-7**    Module Selection window

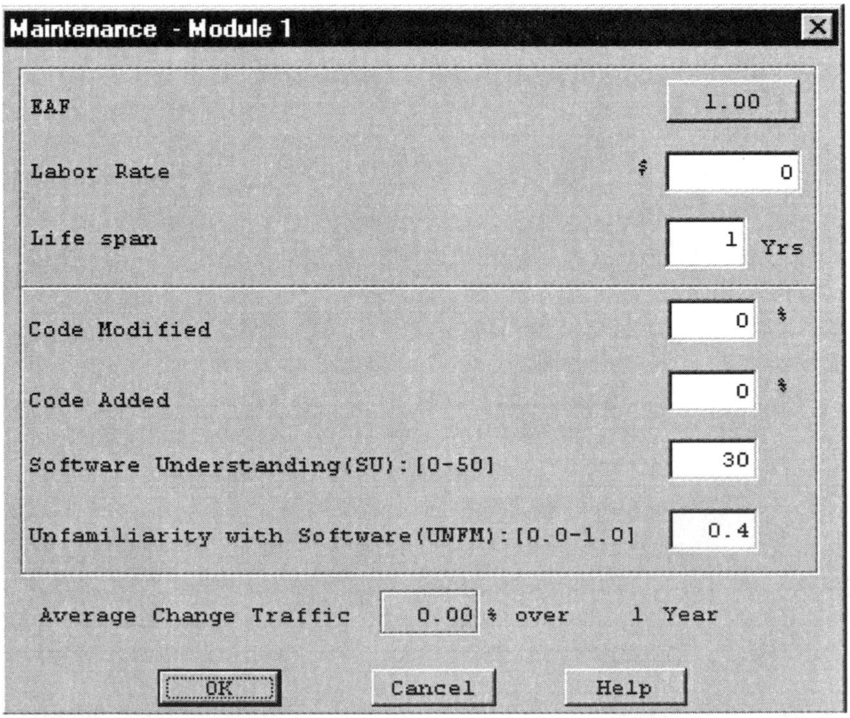

**Maintenance  - Module 1**                    [X]

| EAF | | 1.00 |
|-----|--|------|
| Labor Rate | $ | 0 |
| Life span | | 1 Yrs |

| Code Modified | | 0 % |
|---------------|--|-----|
| Code Added | | 0 % |
| Software Understanding(SU):[0-50] | | 30 |
| Unfamiliarity with Software(UNFM):[0.0-1.0] | | 0.4 |

Average Change Traffic    0.00 % over    1 Year

OK      Cancel      Help

**Figure 7-8**    Module Maintenance Dialog Box

one of the modules by highlighting the appropriate module name and then clicking upon OK (see Figure 7-7).

Upon exiting the module selection window, another window will be appear that displays, the selected module name, an EAF button, an editable labor rate field, editable number of years of maintenance field, an editable percent of added source instructions field per year of maintenance and an editable percent of modified source instructions field per year of maintenance (see Figure 7-8).

The EAF rate can be changed by clicking upon the corresponding button. This action will result in the appearance of an EAF dialog box where the cost driver ratings can be changed as described in the introduction (see Figure 7-9).

Upon completing the adjustment of the cost drivers click the OK button or click the Cancel button to return to the CLEF without viewing maintenance estimations.

After exiting the EAF dialog box, you will be returned to the Module Maintenance Dialog box to continue inputting the editable values.

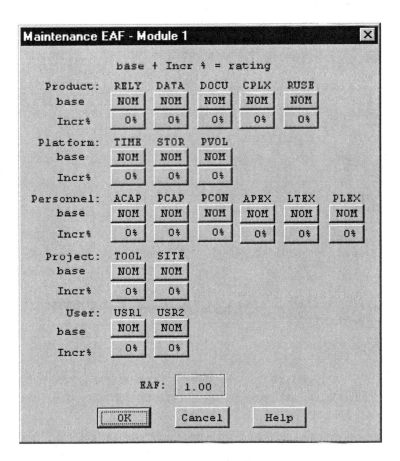

**Figure 7-9**   Module Maintenance EAF Dialog Box

Click upon the OK button upon completion of editing the displayed fields or click upon the Cancel button if no changes are desired to the default values (if more assistance, the Help button is available to receive on-line assistance).

When the OK button is clicked in the Module Maintenance Dialog Box, a window displaying the first of four pages that contains the module name, the current development mode, the total number of source instructions for development of the module (EDSI) hat is loaded in the CLEF, the nominal effort of the module, the actual effort of the module, the development cost, the inputted maintenance labor rate, the inputted percent of code added during maintenance per year, the inputted percent of code modified during maintenance per year (see Figure 7-10) and the calculated annual change traffic.

The second page of the maintenance window can be seen by clicking upon the Next button. It contains the settings for the 16 cost drivers, SCED is not applicable (see Figure 7-11).

The third page of the maintenance window contains the effort and cost estimation for the next N number of years (as defined by the user). With each year is a listed the KDSI (EDSI * $10^3$), the nominal effort for development (PM nom), the actual effort for maintenance (PM maint), the number of full time software personnel necessary to maintain the module for the year (FSWP), the number of instructions that are to be maintained be per personnel(KDSI/FSWP) and the total cost for maintenance for the year (see Figure 7-12).

The fourth window of the maintenance window contains the cumulative figures for effort and cost for maintenance for the total number of years (see Figure 7-13). This first displays the total number of effort estimated for maintenance, then sums the effort of de-

```
┌──────────────────────────────────────────────────────────────────────┐
│ ┊ Module Maintenance - Module 1                                    [X] │
├──────────────────────────────────────────────────────────────────────┤
│  MODULE                                                     Module 1    │
│  Development SLOC                                              13574     │
│  Development Nominal Person-Month                             72.81      │
│  Development Adjusted Person-Month                           345.28      │
│  Development Cost                                        1957717.90      │
│  Maintenance Labor Rate                                        0.00      │
│  Percentage Added                                             0.00%      │
│  Percentage Modified                                          0.00%      │
│  Maintenance Software Understanding                           30.00      │
│  Unfamiliarity with the Software                               0.40      │
│                                                                          │
│  Annual Change Traffic                                        0.00%      │
│                                                                          │
│                                                                          │
│                                                                          │
│      ┌───────────┐    ┌───────────┐   ┌┄┄┄┄┄┄┄┄┐   ┌───────────┐         │
│      │ Previous  │    │   Next    │   ┊  Done  ┊   │   Help    │         │
│      └───────────┘    └───────────┘   └┄┄┄┄┄┄┄┄┘   └───────────┘         │
└──────────────────────────────────────────────────────────────────────┘
```

**Figure 7-10**   Module Maintenance window (page 1)

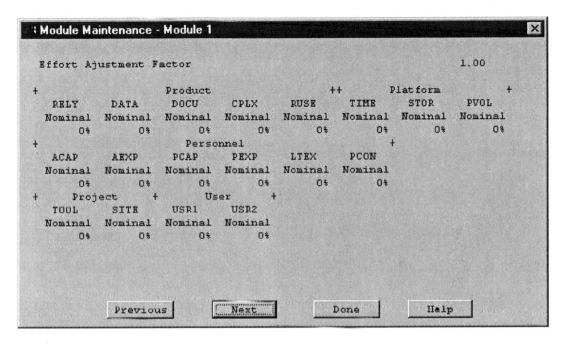

**Figure 7-11**   Module Maintenance window (page 2)

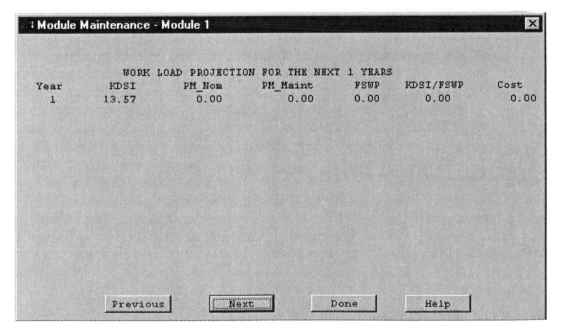

**Figure 7-12**   Module Maintenance window (page 3)

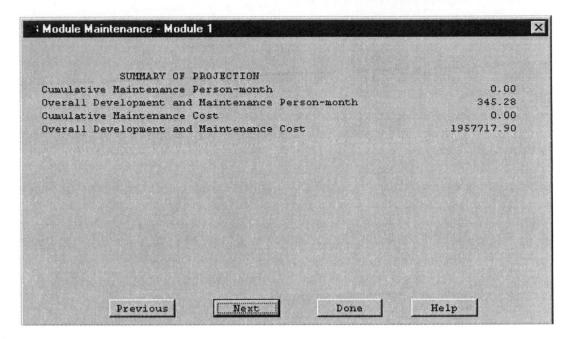

**Figure 7-13**   Module Maintenance window (page 4)

velopment and maintenance together. It also displays the total cost of maintenance of the module and then displays the summed total cost of development and maintenance for the entire module.

Note—Each individual page can be seen by cycling through the pages pressing either the Previous or Next buttons as needed.

## S/W REFERENCE REFERENCES

Amadeus (1994), Amadeus Measurement System User's Guide, Version 2.3a, Amadeus Software Research, Inc., Irvine, California, July 1994.

Behrens, C. (1983), "Measuring the Productivity of Computer Systems Development Activities with Function Points," *IEEE Transactions on Software Engineering*, November 1983.

Boehm, B. (1981), *Software Engineering Economics*, Prentice Hall.

Boehm, Abts, Brown, Chulani, Clark, Horowitz, Madachy, Reifer, and Steece (2000), *Software Cost Estimation with COCOMO II*, Prentice Hall.

Boehm, B. and W. Royce (1989), "Ada COCOMO and the Ada Process Model," *Proceedings, Fifth COCOMO Users' Group Meeting*, Software Engineering Institute, Pittsburgh, PA, November 1989.

Boehm et al. (1995), "Cost Models for future Software Life Cycle Process: COCOMO 2.0", Annals of Software Engineering Special Volume on Software Process and Product Measurement, J.D Arther and S.M. Henry, Eds., J.C. Baltzer AG, Science Publishers, Amsterdam, The Netherlands, Vol 1, pp. 45—60.

Chidamber, S. and C. Kemerer (1994), "A Metrics Suite for Object Oriented Design," *IEEE Transactions on Software Engineering*, (to appear 1994).

Goethert, W., E. Bailey, M. Busby (1992), "Software Effort and Schedule Measurement: A Framework for Counting Staff Hours and Reporting Schedule Information." CMU/SEI-92-TR-21, Software Engineering Institute, Pittsburgh, PA.

IEPUG (1994), *IFPUG Function Point Counting Practices: Manual Release 4.0*, International Function Point Users' Group, Westerville, OH.

Kunkler, J. (1985), "A Cooperative Industry Study on Software Development/Maintenance Productivity," Xerox Corporation, Xerox Square — XRX2 52A, Rochester, NY 14644, Third Report, March 1985.

Madachy, J. Raymond (1997), "Heuristic Risk Assessment Using Cost Factors," *IEEE Software*, May/June 1997, pp. 51-59.

Park R. (1992), "Software Size Measurement: A Framework for Counting Source Statements," CMU/SEI-92-TR-20, Software Engineering Institute, Pittsburgh, PA.

Selby, R., A. Porter, D. Schimidt and J. Berney (1991), "Metric-Driven Analysis and Feedback systems for Enabling Empirically Guided Software Development," Proceedings of the Thirteenth International Conference on Software Engineering (ICSE 13), Austin, TX, May 13-16, 1991, pp. 288-298.

## S/W REFERENCE APPENDIX A: ACCELERATOR KEYS

|  |  | Windows |
|---|---|---|
| File |  | Alt+F |
| New | N | Ctrl+N |
| Load Project | L | Ctrl+L |
| Save Project | S | Ctrl+S |
| Save As Project | A | Ctrl+A |
| Load Model | O |  |
| Save Model | V |  |
| Save As Model | E |  |
| Make Report | R |  |
| Exit | X |  |
| **View** |  | Alt+V |
| **Edit** |  | Alt+E |
| Add Module | A | Ctrl+A |
| Clear All Modules | L |  |
| Snapshot | S |  |
| Undo | U | Ctrl+Z |
| Cut | T | Ctrl+X |
| Copy | C | Ctrl+C |
| Paste | P | Ctrl+V |
| **Parameters** |  | Alt+R |
| Product | P |  |
| Platform | L |  |
| Personnel | N |  |
| Project | J |  |
| User EAF | U |  |
| Scale Factor | S |  |
| Equation | E |  |
| Person Month | M |  |
| **Calibrate** |  | Alt+C |
| File Load | L |  |
| File Save | S |  |
| File Save As | A |  |
| Project | P |  |
| Compute | C |  |

|  | Windows |
| --- | --- |
| **Phase** | Alt+P |
| **Waterfall Project & Module** | P |
| Overall Phase | O |
| Plans & Requirement | R |
| Programming | P |
| Product Design | D |
| Integration & Test | I |
| **MBASE Project & Module** |  |
| Overall Phase | O |
| Inception (IRR to LCO) | I |
| Elaboration (LCO to LCA) | E |
| Construction (LCA to IOC) | C |
| Transition (IOC to TCR) | T |
| **Help** | Alt+H |
| On Application | No |
| On Version | No |
| COCOMO II |  |
| User's Manual | C |
| Using Help | U |
| About USC-COCOMO II | A |

## S/W REFERENCE APPENDIX B: FUNCTION POINT VALUES

| Language | Value |
|---|---|
| Ada 83 | 71 |
| AI Shell | 49 |
| APL | 32 |
| Assembly, Basic | 320 |
| Assembly, Macro | 213 |
| Basic, ANSI | 64 |
| Basic, Compiled | 49 |
| Basic, Interpreted | 32 |
| C | 128 |
| Cobol 85, ANSI | 91 |
| First Generation | 320 |
| Forth | 49 |
| Fortran77 | 107 |
| Fourth Generation | 20 |
| Fifth Generation | 5 |
| High Level | 91 |
| Lisp | 64 |
| Modula 2 | 80 |
| Object Oriented | 29 |
| Pascal | 91 |
| Procedural | 105 |
| PowerBuilder | 16 |
| Prolog | 64 |
| Query Default | 13 |
| Report Generator | 80 |
| Second Generation | 107 |
| Spreadsheet Default | 6 |
| Third Generation | 80 |
| Machine Code | 640 |
| Access | 38 |
| Ada 95 | 49 |
| C++ | 53 |
| Database Default | 40 |
| Fortran 95 | 71 |

| Language | Value |
| --- | --- |
| HTML 3.0 | 15 |
| Java | 53 |
| Perl | 21 |
| Visual Basic 5.0 | 29 |
| Visual C++ | 34 |
| Simulation Default | 46 |
| UNIX Shell | 21 |
| USR_1 | 1 |
| USR_2 | 1 |
| USR_3 | 1 |
| USR_4 | 1 |
| USR_5 | 1 |

# F

# Contents of Accompanying CD-ROM

## F.1  INTRODUCTION

Appendix F describes the contents of the CD-ROM that accompanies the book. Sections F.2 through F.9 provide detailed information about the contents of the CD as though it were being explored in a breadth-first search through the displayed screens. Section F.10 describes the most significant files at the outermost directory level of the CD.

In order to use the CD you need to be running Windows 95 or higher, and for some files a browser like Internet Explorer 4.0 or Netscape 3.0. Your system should have at least 8MB of available RAM. For the spreadsheet models and support software you must have Excel 5.0 or higher or a spreadsheet capable of reading such ".xls" files. Everything else that is needed is either described on the relevant screens or provided on the CD.

## F.2  TOP-LEVEL SCREEN

The top-level screen of the CD provides an "Introduction and Mapping to Book", and a greeting (video clip) and a book overview (video clip and presentation) by Barry Boehm. There are also links to submenus which allow one to install USC COCOMO II.2000, as explained in Section F.3; provide access to the USC

COCOMO II.2000 Manuals; the spreadsheet models that are extensions of COCOMO II; Tutorials; commercial COCOMO II–based estimation tools and training; data collection forms; and Affiliation information.

In addition, there is a section with information on using the CD which explains how to use the CD including the navigation approach for accessing the contents of the CD. It provides more detailed explanations of the contents of the CD, and repeats some of the README.txt information.

The main page of the CD, and every subpage, has an Exit ICON, always positioned in the lower right corner. Activating this button/ICON will exit the CD ROM player software and return the user to other running programs on his/her computer.

Since most of the documents included on the CD are in PDF, a compatible version of Acrobat Reader is provided on the CD. The icon for installing Acrobat Reader is provided along the bottom of the main screen. All the videos are provided as ".mpg" files for which a compatible media player is required. A media player is a default accessory of most Windows 95 and later systems.

## F.3 INSTALL USC COCOMO II.2000

This link on the similarly named submenu initiates a self-install program to install the USC COCOMO II.2000 program files, which include USC COCOMO II.exe, COCOMO_ charts.xls and the USC COCOMO II.2000 help files. The installation file is a little over 3MB in size, but requires up to 12MB of available temporary disk memory to complete the installation process. The final program files occupy about 4MB after installation.

COCOMO_charts.xls is a spreadsheet-based tool designed to produce most of the typical graphs that management likes to see for Waterfall development lifecycles. Its instructions are shown on the first tab of the workbook.

The USC COCOMO II.2000 help files are HTML representations of the tool's online help, covering both the operation of the software itself and the COCOMO II model.

## F.4 COCOMO II.2000 MANUALS

The COCOMO II.2000 Manuals submenu screen provides access to the USC COCOMO II.2000 Software Reference Manual (PDF format); a Model Definition Manual (PDF format), based primarily on the same information as Chapter 2 of the book; and a link to the Center for Software Engineering's COCOMO website, http://sunset.usc.edu/research/COCOMOII/cocomo.html. The COCOMO website also has postscript (PS) versions of these manuals.

## F.5   THE COCOMO SUITE—EXTENSIONS AND COMPANION TOOLS

This companion submenu screen provides access to the currently implemented extensions to COCOMO II.2000 and companion tools like the stand-alone copy of COCOMO_charts.xls. COCOMO_charts is a 283KB MS Excel program that uses macros to accomplish many of its tasks. While not strictly an implementation of a model in its own right, it is included to assure an unaltered version is always available.

### F.5.1   COPSEMO Spreadsheet Models

This submenu provides access to a COPSEMO Summary document, a COPSEMO_README.txt file, COPSEMO.xls which implements the four-phase model described in Chapter 5; a COPSEMO "user manual" document, and a COPSEMO percentage determination aide worksheet.

### F.5.2   CORADMO Spreadsheet Models

This submenu provides access to a CORADMO Summary document; a CORADMO_README.txt file; CORADMO.xls which implements the Rapid Application Development schedule and effort model described in Chapter 5; a CORADMO "user manual" document; and a CORADMO driver determination aide worksheet.

### F.5.3   COPROMO Spreadsheet Models

This submenu provides access to a COPROMO Summary document; a COPROMO_README.txt file; COPROMO_03.xls which implements the productivity improvement estimation model described in Chapter 5; a COPROMO "user manual" document; and a COPROMO model instruction and description document.

### F.5.4   Homepages of COCOMO II.2000 Suite and CodeCount™

The last entry in this submenu provides links to the USC-CSE COCOMO II Suite web page and directly to the CodeCount page. The USC-CSE COCOMO II Suite page provides overviews and links to the most current versions of the extensions and the CodeCount™ toolset. The CodeCount toolset automates the collection of source code sizing information. It is only available via the world wide web.

## F.6   TUTORIALS

The Tutorials submenu screen provides access to several kinds of tutorial material: an interactive use of COCOMO and several of its extensions, and support for the COCOMO examples from Chapter 3 of the book.

"My 1st COCOMO Run" is a user-interactive tutorial. It walks the user through the creation of a simple COCOMO estimate, the generation of a few charts (using COCOMO_charts.xls), and the use of COPSEMO and CORADMO.

The Transaction Processing System (TPS) example from Chapter 3 is supported with a video overview, the video presentation support slides, and the USC COCOMO II.2000 estimate files TPS.est (6.63kb) and TPS1.est (6.63kb).

The Airborne Radar System (ARS) example from Chapter 3 is supported with a video overview, the video presentation support slides, and the USC COCOMO II.2000 estimate files ars_breadboard_9.est (5.44kb), ars_top_level_7.est (5.43kb), and ars_detailed_9.est (14.1kb).

The last entry on this submenu will start a copy of COCOMO II.2000 on the extensions that is fully installed on the CD itself. With this capability it is possible to follow along with the tutorials even if the COCOMO II.2000 software has not been installed on the system running the CD.

## F.7   COMMERCIAL COCOMO II.2000-BASED TOOLS

The Commercial COCOMO II.2000-Based Tools and Training submenu screen provides both information and working demonstration copies of commercial implementations of COCOMO II which have been assessed as faithful to the COCOMO II.2000 model. They are COSTAR from SoftStar Systems, Cost Xpert from Marotz, and SoftwareCost Calculator from SoftwareCost.com. It also lists training vendors who have at least one course on COCOMO II.

For each tool vendor, there is 1) a copy of their company's homepage and one tool introduction or explanation page, complete with graphics, etc.; and 2) a demonstration or evaluation copy of their software that was provided to us for this purpose; and/or 3) a link to their web address.

The COSTAR entry includes the "About COSTAR" HTML file as well as image files, COSTAR trial version [5.5], and the COSTAR homepage HTML file with image files. Also provided is the current (at time of printing) version of SoftStar Systems' Calico, a "calibration" tool that is available for free.

The Cost Xpert entry includes the "About Cost Xpert" HTML file with image files, the "About Marotz" HTML file with image files, and a self-install file for Cost Xpert – version 2.1.

The SoftwareCost Calculator entry only has a link to SoftwareCost.com's home page because the tool is a web-based tool.

## F.8    DATA COLLECTION FORMS

The Data Collection Forms submenu screen provides all the forms from Appendix C, as well as stand-alone versions of questionnaires that have been developed to gather calibration data for COCOMO II.2000 and its extensions.

Each table and figure from Appendix C is available as a separate PDF file. This was done to make it easier to get the individual forms or instructions since many are used repeatedly during the course of a project.

The Full Questionnaires are "stand-alone" in that they both define all the items being asked for and provide assistance for how to evaluate the information one has about a given project. There are questionnaires for 1) COCOMO II Cost Estimation 2) COQUALMO, 3) COPSEMO data gathering, 4) CORADMO data gathering, and 5) COCOTS.

## F.9    AFFILIATION

The Affiliation submenu screen provides information on becoming an Affiliate of the Center for Software Engineering, including benefits, costs, and an application.

## F.10    CD TOP-LEVEL DIRECTORY HIGHLIGHTS

There are two important files at this level: COCOMOII.2000-CD.exe and Readme.txt. The latter file brings up the main control program for the CD. It is also identified as the "autorun" file.

# Acronyms & Glossary

**3GL**   Third-Generation Language

**4GL**   Fourth-Generation Language

**A**   Linear coefficient for the effort equation that can be calibrated

**AA**   Percentage of reuse effort due to assessment and assimilation

**AAF**   Adaptation Adjustment Factor, a component of the overall Adaptation Adjustment Multiplier for reuse sizing, including the effects of Design Modified, Code Modified, and Integration Modified factors (COCOMO Reuse model).

**AAM**   Adaptation Adjustment Multiplier for reuse sizing (COCOMO Reuse model)

**ACAP**   Analyst Capability cost driver

**ACT**   Annual Change Traffic (used in COCOMO 81)

**APEX**   Applications Experience cost driver

**API**   Application Program Interface

**Application volatility**   COTS integration cost source in COCOTS, resulting from the use of COTS products which may experience multiple or frequent product releases or upgrades during system development

**ARB**   Architecture Review Board

**ASLOC**   Adapted Source Lines of Code, used in reuse sizing (COCOMO Reuse model)

**AT**   Automated Translation

**ATPROD**   Automatic translation productivity

**B**   The scaling base-exponent for the effort equation that can be calibrated

**Black Box COTS**   Internal code modifications to COTS product not allowed

**C**   Linear coefficient for the schedule equation that can be calibrated

**C**   Construction phase (MBASE/RUP development process)

**C**   Construction phase subscript (MBASE/RUP development process)

**CASE**   Computer Aided Software Engineering

**CCB**   Change Control Board

**CD**   Commercial technology and DoD general practice

**CDR**   Critical Design Review milestone (Waterfall development process)

**CII**   COCOMO II.2000

**CM**   Percentage of code modified during reuse (COCOMO Reuse model)

**CM**   Code Modified (COCOMO Reuse model)

**CM**   Configuration Management

**CMM**   Capability Maturity Model

**COCOMO**   Constructive Cost Model; refers collectively to COCOMO 81 and COCOMO II

**COCOMO 81**   The original version of the Constructive Cost Model, published in 1981

**COCOMO II**   The revised version of the Constructive Cost Model, first released in 1997

**COCOMO II.1997**   The original year 1997 calibration of the revised Constructive Cost Model

**COCOMO II.2000**   The year 2000 calibration of the revised Constructive Cost Model

**COCOMO Suite**   The collection of estimation models (including COCOMO itself) being developed to extend and enhance the coverage and utility of COCOMO: COCOTS, COPROMO, COPSEMO, COQUALMO and CORADMO

**COCOTS**   Constructive COTS cost model

**COPROMO**   Constructive Productivity improvement Model

**COPSEMO**   Constructive Phased Schedule & Effort Model

**COQUALMO**   Constructive Quality Model

**CORADMO**   Constructive RAD cost Model

**Cost Driver**   A particular characteristic of the software development that has a multiplicative effect of increasing or decreasing the amount of development effort, e.g., required product reliability, execution time constraints, project team application experience

**COTS**   Commercial-off-the-shelf

**COTS assessment**   COTS integration cost source in COCOTS: the activity of determining the appropriateness or feasibility of using specific COTS products to fulfill required system functions

**COTS attribute**   Characteristic of a COTS package or associated products and services; evaluated and used in comparing alternative products as input into a buy/no buy decision

**COTS qualifying**   See COTS assessment

**COTS tailoring**   COTS integration cost source in COCOTS: the activity associated with setting or defining shell parameters or configuration options available for a COTS product, but which do not require modification of COTS source code, including defining I/O report formats, screens, etc.

**CPLX**   Product Complexity cost driver

**CSTB**   Computer Science and Telecommunications Board

**D**   The scaling base-exponent for the schedule equation that can be calibrated

**DATA**   Database Size cost driver

**DBMS**   Database Management System

**DI**   Degree of Influence

**DI**   Defect Introduction or Number of Defects Introduced

**DIR**   Defect Introduction Rate

**DM**   Percentage of design modified during reuse (COCOMO Reuse model)

**DOCU**   Documentation Match to Lifecycle Needs cost driver

**DR**   Defect Removal or Number of Defects Removed

**Dres**   Number of Residual Defects

**DRF**   Defect Removal Fraction

**DSI**   Deliverable Source Instructions

**E**   Elaboration phase (MBASE/RUP development process)

**E**   Elaboration phase subscript (MBASE/RUP development process)

**E**   The scaling exponent for the schedule equation that can be calibrated

**EAF**   Effort Adjustment Factor—product of effort multipliers

**EDA**   Exploratory Data Analysis

**EDCS**   Evolutionary Design of Complex Software technology

**EHART**   Embedded, High Assurance, Real Time [baseline application domain]

**EK**   Both EDCS & KBSA (KG & KD)

**EM**   Effort Multiplier; a value associated with a specific Cost Driver

**ESLOC**   Equivalent Source Lines of Code

**F**    Scaling exponent for the schedule equation

**FCIL**    Facilities

**FFRDC**    Federally Funded Research and Development Center

**FLEX**    Development Flexibility scale driver

**FP**    Function Points

**FSP**    Full-time Software Personnel

**GFE**    Government Furnished Equipment (see GFS and GOTS)

**GFS**    Government Furnished Software (see GFE and GOTS)

**Glue code**    COTS integration cost source in COCOTS: software developed in-house and composed of 1) code needed to facilitate data or information exchange between the COTS/NDI component and the system or other COTS/NDI component into which it is being integrated, 2) code needed to connect or "hook" the COTS/NDI component into the system or other COTS/NDI component but does not necessarily enable data exchange, and 3) code needed to provide required functionality missing in the COTS/NDI component *and* which depends upon or must interact with the COTS/NDI component

**GOTS**    Government-off-the-shelf (see GFE and GFS)

**GUI**    Graphical User Interface

**H**    High rating

**I**    Inception phase (MBASE/RUP development process)

**I**    Inception phase subscript (MBASE/RUP development process)

**ICASE**    Integrated Computer Aided Software Environment; used in Applications Composition projects

**IECT**    Inception, Elaboration, Construction, and Transition phases for the MBASE/RUP lifecycle model

**IFPUG**    International Function Point Users Group

**IM**    Integration Modified: percentage of integration and test redone during reuse (COCOMO Reuse model)

**Integration code**    See Glue code

**IOC**    Initial Operational Capability milestone (MBASE/RUP development process)

**IRR**    Initial Readiness Review milestone (MBASE/RUP development process)

**ISPA**    International Society of Parametric Analysts

**K**    See both KD and KG

**KASLOC**    Thousands of Adapted Source Lines of Code (COCOMO Reuse model)

**KB**    Knowledge Base

**KBSA**  Knowledge Based Software Assistant technology

**KD**  KBSA Project Decision Support (SE decision assistant concept) (+CD)

**KESLOC**  Thousands of Equivalent Source Lines of Code (COCOMO Reuse model)

**KG**  KBSA Applications Generators including KB domain engineering (+CD)

**KNCSS**  Thousands of Non-Commented Source Statements

**KSLOC**  Thousands (K) of Source Lines of Code

**L**  Low rating

**LCA**  Life-cycle Architecture milestone (MBASE/RUP development process)

**LCO**  Life-cycle Objectives milestone (MBASE/RUP development process)

**LCR**  Life-cycle Concept Review milestone (MBASE/RUP development process)

**LEXP**  Programming Language Experience, used in COCOMO 81

**LOC**  Lines of Code

**LTEX**  Language and Tool Experience cost driver

**M**  Months

**MAF**  Maintenance Adjustment Factor; used to account for software understanding and unfamiliarity effects (COCOMO Reuse and Maintenance models)

**MBASE**  Model-Based (System) Architecting and Software Engineering

**MCF**  Maintenance Change Factor: fraction of legacy code modified or added (COCOMO Maintenance model)

**Mo**  Months

**MODP**  Modern Programming Practices, used in COCOMO 81

**MOTS**  Modified-off-the-shelf (see White Box COTS)

**N**  Nominal rating

**NDI**  Non-developmental item; software available from some source other than the organization developing the system into which the NDI component is to be integrated; the source can be commercial, private, or public sector, just so long as the procuring organization expended no resources on the NDI component's initial development. Source code is usually available for an NDI component, which may or may not be able to function as a stand-alone item

**NIST**  National Institute of Standards and Technology

**NOP**  New Object Points

**NOTS**  Not-off-the-shelf

**OS**  Operating Systems

**OTS**  Off-the-shelf

**PCAP**  Programmer Capability cost driver

**PCON**  Personnel continuity cost driver

**PDIF**   Platform Difficulty: composite cost driver for Early Design model

**PDR**   Product Design Review milestone (Waterfall development process)

**PERS**   Personnel Capability: composite cost driver for Early Design model

**PL**   Product Line

**PLEX**   Platform Experience cost driver

**PM**   Person-Months; a person month is the amount of time one person spends working on the software development project for one month; in COCOMO normally assumed to be 152 person-hours.

**PM$_{AUTO}$**   Person-months effort from automatic translation activities

**PM$_{NS}$**   Person-months estimated without the SCED cost driver (Nominal Schedule)

**PMAT**   Process Maturity scale driver

**PR**   Productivity Range

**PREC**   Project Precedentedness scale driver

**PRED(X)**   Prediction Accuracy: percentage of estimates within X% of the actuals

**PREX**   Personnel Experience: composite cost driver for Early Design model

**PROD**   Productivity rate

**PSE**   Phase Schedule and Effort

**PVOL**   Platform Volatility cost driver

**QAF**   Quality Adjustment Factor

**RAD**   Rapid Application Development; applies to both schedule and effort

**RCPX**   Product Reliability and Complexity: composite cost driver for Early Design model

**RELY**   Required Software Reliability cost driver

**Reuse software**   Reusable software components built in-house, or obtained from outside, and for which the source code is available

**RESL**   Architecture and known Risk Resolution scale driver

**REVL**   Requirements Evolution and Volatility: percentage size adjustment factor from requirements evolution or requirements volatility

**ROI**   Return on Investment

**ROTS**   Research-off-the-shelf

**RUP**   Rational Software Corporation's Unified Process (see VSDP)

**RUSE**   Developed for Reusability cost driver

**RVOL**   Requirements Volatility, used in COCOMO 81

**SAR**   Software Acceptance Review milestone (Waterfall development process)

**Scale Factor**   A particular characteristic of the software development that has an exponential effect of increasing or decreasing the amount of development effort, e.g., precedentedness, process maturity

**SCED**   Required Development Schedule: project-level cost driver

**SCED%**   Required Schedule Compression percentage

**SECU**   Classified Security Application, used in Ada COCOMO

**SEI**   Software Engineering Institute

**SF**   Scale Factor; a value for a specific rating of a Scale Driver

**SITE**   Multi-site Development cost driver

**SLOC**   Source Lines of Code

**SM**   Schedule Multiplier

**SRR**   Software Requirements Review milestone (Waterfall development process)

**STOR**   Main Storage Constraint cost driver

**SU**   Percentage of reuse effort due to software understanding (COCOMO Reuse model)

**SW-CMM**   Software Capability Maturity Model

**T&E**   Test and Evaluation

**TCR**   Transition Completion Review milestone (MBASE/RUP development process)

**TDEV**   Software development time (in months)

**TEAM**   Development Team cooperation and cohesion scale driver

**TIME**   Execution Time Constraint cost driver

**TOOL**   Use of Software Tools cost driver

**TURN**   Computer Turnaround Time, used in COCOMO 81

**UNFM**   Programmer Unfamiliarity; factor used in reuse and maintenance estimation (COCOMO Reuse and Maintenance models)

**USAF/ESD**   U.S. Air Force Electronic Systems Division

**USDP**   Unified Software Development Process; Rational Software Corp.'s Unified Process (see RUP)

**UTC**   Unit Test Completion milestone (Waterfall development process)

**Var**   Variance

**VEXP**   Virtual Machine Experience, used in COCOMO 81

**VH**   Very High rating

**VIF**   Variance Inflation Factor

**VIRT**   Virtual Machine Volatility, used in COCOMO 81

**VL**  Very Low rating

**VMVH**  Virtual Machine Volatility: Host; used in Ada COCOMO

**VMVT**  Virtual Machine Volatility: Target; used in Ada COCOMO

**White Box COTS**  Some internal code modifications to COTS product performed; if the vendor does not support the modifications, it is no longer considered COTS by COCOMO/COCOTS definitions, but rather adapted software (see MOTS)

**XH**  Extra High rating

# References

Banker et al. 1991. R. Banker, R. Kauffman, and R. Kumar, "An Empirical Test of Object-Based Output Measurement Metrics in a Computer Aided Software Engineering (CASE) Environment," *Journal of Management Information Systems*, Winter 1991–92, 8 (3) pp. 127–150.

Banker et al. 1994. R. D. Banker, H. Chang, C. Kemerer, "Evidence on Economies of Scale in Software Development," *Information and Software Technology*, 1994, pp. 275–282.

Behrens 1983. C. Behrens, "Measuring the Productivity of Computer Systems Development Activities with Function Points," *IEEE Transactions on Software Engineering*, November 1983.

Boehm et al. 1984. B. Boehm, T. Gray, and T. Seewaldt, "Prototyping vs. Specifying: A Multi-Project Experiment," *IEEE Transactions on Software Engineering*, May 1984, pp. 133–145.

Boehm et al. 1995. B. Boehm, B. Clark, E. Horowitz, C. Westland, R. Madachy, and R. Selby, "Cost Models for Future Software Software Life Cycle Processes: COCOMO 2.0," *Annals of Software Engineering* 1 (1995), pp. 57–94.

Boehm 1996. B. Boehm, "Anchoring the Software Process," IEEE *Software*, July 1996.

Boehm et al. 1998. B. W. Boehm, A. Egyed, D. Port, A. Shah, J. Kwan, and R. Madachy, "A Stakeholder Win-Win Approach to Software Engineering Education," *Annals of Software Engineering* 6(1998) 295–321.

Boehm et al. 1998a. B. Boehm, M. Kellner, and D. Perry (eds.), *Proceedings, ISPW 10: Process Support of Software Product Lines*, IEEE Computer Society, 1998.

Boehm et al. 1999. B. Boehm, D. Port, A. Egyed, and M. Abi-Antoun, "The MBASE Life Cycle Architecture Package: No Architecture is an Island," in P. Donohoe (ed.), *Software Architecture*, Kluwer, 1999, pp. 511–528.

Boehm, et al. 1999a. B. Boehm, A.W. Brown, and P. Bose, "KBSA Life Cycle Evaluation," Air Force Research Laboratory Report AFRL-IF-RS-TR-1999-225, October 1999.

Boehm 1981. B. Boehm, *Software Engineering Economics*, Prentice Hall, Englewood Cliffs, N.J., 1981.

Boehm 1983. B. Boehm, "The Hardware/Software Cost Ratio: Is It a Myth?" *Computer 16*(3), March 1983, pp. 78–80.

Boehm 1985. B. Boehm, "COCOMO: Answering the Most Frequent Questions," In Proceedings, First COCOMO Users' Group Meeting, Wang Institute, Tyngsboro, MA, May 1985.

Boehm 1989. B. Boehm, *Software Risk Management*, IEEE Computer Society Press, Los Alamitos, CA, 1989.

Boehm 1996. B. Boehm, "Anchoring the Software Process," IEEE *Software,* July 1996.

Boehm 1999. B. Boehm, "Making RAD Work for Your Project," Extended version of March 1999 IEEE Computer column; *USC Technical Report* USC-CSE-99-512

Boehm-Royce 1989. B. Boehm, and W. Royce, "Ada COCOMO and the Ada Process Model," Proceedings, Fifth COCOMO Users' Group Meeting, Software Engineering Institute, Pittsburgh, PA, November 1989.

Boehm-Port 1999a. B. Boehm, and D. Port, "Escaping the Software Tar Pit: Model Clashes and How to Avoid Them," *ACM Software Engineering Notes,* Jan. 1999, pp. 36–48.

Boehm-Port 1999b. B. Boehm, and D. Port, "When Models Collide: Lessons in Software Systems Analysis," *IT Professional*, Jan./Feb. 1999, pp. 49–56.

Box-Tiao 1973. G. Box, and G. Tiao, *Bayesian Inference in Statistical Analysis,* Addison-Wesley, 1973.

Briand et al. 1992. L. C. Briand, V. R. Basili, and W. M. Thomas, "A Pattern Recognition Approach for Software Engineering Data Analysis," *IEEE Transactions on Software Engineering*, Vol. 18, No. 11, November 1992.

Chidamber-Kemerer 1994. S. Chidamber, and C. Kemerer, "A Metrics Suite for Object-Oriented Design," *IEEE Trans. SW Engr.* 20(6) June 1994, pp. 476–493.

Chulani et al. 1997. Sunita Devnani-Chulani, Brad Clark, Barry Boehm, "Calibration Results of COCOMOII.1997," 22nd Software Engineering Workshop, NASA-Goddard, December 1997.

Chulani et al. 1998. S. Chulani, B. Clark, B. Boehm and B. Steece, "Calibration Approach and Results of the COCOMO II Post Architecture Model," 20th Annual Conference of the International Society of Parametric Analysts (ISPA) and the 8th

Annual Conference of the Society of Cost Estimating and Analysis (SCEA), June '98.

Chulani et al. 1999. S. Chulani, B. Boehm, B. Steece, "From Multiple Regression to Bayesian Analysis for COCOMO II," 21st Annual Conference of the International Society of Parametric Analysts (ISPA) and the 9th Annual Conference of the Society of Cost Estimating and Analysis (SCEA), Best paper in Software track and overall joint conference, June 1999.

Chulani 1997a. S. Chulani, "Modeling Software Defect Introduction," California Software Symposium, Irvine, CA, Nov '97.

Chulani 1997b. S. Chulani, "Results of Delphi for the Defect Introduction Model—Sub-Model of the Cost/Quality Model Extension to COCOMO II," Technical Report, USC-CSE-97-504, 1997, Computer Science Department, University of Southern California, Center for Software Engineering, Los Angeles, CA 90089-0781.

Chulani 1999. S. Chulani, "Bayesian Analysis of Software Cost and Quality Models," Ph.D. Dissertation, University of Southern California, http://sunset.usc.edu/TechRpts/Dissertations/Schulani.pdf, May 1999.

Clark 1999. B. Clark, "Effects of Process Maturity on Development Effort," IEEE *Software*, 2000 (to appear).

Cook-Weisberg 1994. D. Cook and Sanford Weisberg, *An Introduction to Regression Graphics*, Wiley Series, 1994.

Cuelenaere et al. 1987. A. M. Cuelenaere, M. J. van Genuchten and F. J. Heemstra, "Calibrating Software Cost Estimation Model: Why and How," *Information and Software Technology,* 29 (10), pp. 558–567, 1987.

CSTB 1993. Computer Science and Telecommunications Board (CSTB) National Research Council, *Computing Professionals: Changing Needs for the 1990's*, National Academy Press, Washington, D.C., 1993.

Devenny 1976. T. Devenny, "An Exploratory Study of Software Cost Estimating at the Electronic Systems Division," Thesis No. GSM/SM/765-4, Air Force Institute of Technology, Dayton, OH.

Edgar 1982. J. D. Edgar, "Controlling Murphy: How to Budget for Program Risk," *Concepts*, Summer 1982, pp. 60–73.

Flowers 1996. S. Flowers, *Software Failure: Management Failure*, John Wiley and Sons, 1996.

Gelman et al. 1995. A. Gelman, J. Garlin, H. Stern, and D. Rubin, *Bayesian Data Analysis*, Chapman Hall, 1995.

Gerlich-Denskat 1994. R. Gerlich, and U. Denskat, "A Cost Estimation Model for Maintenance and High Reuse," Proceedings, ESCOM 1994, Ivrea, Italy.

Glass 1998. R. Glass, *Software Runaways*, Prentice Hall, 1996.

Goethert et al. 1992. W. Goethert, E. Bailey, M. Busby, "Software Effort and Schedule Measurement: A Framework for Counting Staff Hours and Reporting

Schedule Information." CMU/SEI-92-TR-21, Software Engineering Institute, Pittsburgh, PA.

Goudy 1987. R. Goudy, "COCOMO-Based Personnel Requirements Model," Proceedings, Third COCOMO Users' Group Meeting, Software Engineering Institute, Pittsburgh, PA, November 1987.

Gulledge-Hutzler 1993. T. R. Gulledge, and W. P. Hutzler, Analytical Methods in Software Engineering Economics, 1993, Springer-Verlag.

Hall 1998. E. Hall, *Managing Risk*, Addison Wesley, 1998.

Hayes-Zubrow 1995. W. Hayes and D. Zubrow, "Moving on Up: Data and Experience Doing CMM-Based Process Improvement," SEI Technical Report CMU/SEI-95-TR-008, August 1995.

Helmer 1966. O. Helmer, *Social Technology*, Basic Books, New York, 1966.

Henderson-Sellers 1996. B. Henderson-Sellers, *Object Oriented Metrics—Measures of Complexity*, Prentice Hall, 1996.

Hocking-Pendleton 1983. R. R. Hocking, and O. J. Pendleton, "The Regression Dilemma," *Communications in Statistics A*, V. 12 (1983), 497–527.

IFPUG 1994. *Function Point Counting Practices: Manual Release 4.0*, International Function Point Users' Group, Blendonview Office Park, 5008-28 Pine Creek Drive, Westerville, OH 43081-4899.

Jacobson et al. 1997. I. Jacobson, M. Griss, and P. Jonsson, *Software Reuse*, Addison Wesley, 1997.

Jacobson et al. 1999. I. Jacobson, G. Booch, and J. Rumbaugh, *The Unified Software Development Process*, Addison Wesley Longman, Reading, MA, 1999.

Jeffery-Low 1990. D. R. Jeffery, and G. C. Low, "Calibrating estimation tools for software development," *Software Engineering Journal*, 5 (4), pp. 215–22, 1990.

Johnson 1988. E. J. Johnson, "Expertise and Decision under Uncertainty: Performance and Process," *The Nature of Expertise*, Editors Chi, Glaser, Farr, Lawrence Earlbaum Associates, 1988.

Jones 1975. C. Jones, "Programming Defect Removal," Proceedings, GUIDE 40, 1975.

Jones 1996. C. Jones, *Applied Software Measurement, Assuring Productivity and Quality*, McGraw-Hill, New York, 1996.

Jones 1998. C. Jones, "The Impact of Poor Quality and Cancelled Projects on the Software Labor Shortage," *SPR, Inc. Technical Report*, Burlington, MA, October 11, 1998.

Judge-Griffiths 1993. G. G. Judge, W. Griffiths, R. C. Hill, *Learning and Practicing Econometrics*, Wiley, 1993.

Kauffman-Kumar 1993. R. Kauffman, and R. Kumar, "Modeling Estimation Expertise in Object Based ICASE Environments," *Stern School of Business Report*, New York University, January 1993.

Kemerer 1987. C. F. Kemerer, "An Empirical Validation of Software Cost Estimation Models," *Communications of the ACM*, Volume 30, Number 5, May 1987.

Kitchenham-Taylor 1984. B. A. Kitchenham, and N. R. Taylor, "Software Cost Models," *ICL Technical Journal*, May 1984.

Kominski 1991. R. Kominski, *Computer Use in the United States: 1989*, Current Population Reports, Series P-23, No. 171, U.S. Bureau of the Census, Washington, D.C., February 1991.

Kruchten 1999. P. Kruchten, *The Rational Unified Process: An Introduction*, Addison-Wesley, 1999.

Kunkler 1983. J. Kunkler, "A Cooperative Industry Study on Software Development/Maintenance Productivity," Xerox Corporation, Xerox Square—XRX2 52A, Rochester, NY 14644, Third Report, March 1985.

Leamer 1978. E. E. Leamer, *Specification Searches, Ad hoc Inference with Nonexperimental Data*, Wiley Series, 1978.

Ligett 1993. D. Ligett, "Extensions to Incremental Development COCOMO," Proceedings, Eighth International Forum on COCOMO and Software Cost Modeling, Software Engineering Institute, Carnegie Mellon University, Pittsburg, PA, October 6–8, 1993

Ligett 2000. D. Ligett, Costar Cost Estimation tool available from SoftStar Systems, *http://www.SoftStarSystems.com*. A trial version is available on the included CD-ROM.

Madachy 1995. R. Madachy, *System Dynamics and COCOMO: Complementary Modeling Paradigms*, Proceedings of the Tenth International Forum on COCOMO and Software Cost Modeling, SEI, Pittsburgh, PA, October 1995.

Madachy 1996. R. Madachy, *System Dynamics Modeling of an Inspection-Based Process*, Proceedings of the Eighteenth International Conference on Software Engineering, IEEE Computer Society Press, Berlin, Germany, March 1996.

Madachy 1997. R. Madachy, *Heuristic Risk Assessment Using Cost Factors*, IEEE *Software*, May 1997.

Madachy-Boehm 2001. R. Madachy, and B. Boehm, *Software Process Dynamics*, IEEE Computer Society, Washington D.C., 2001.

Maier 1998. M. Maier, "Architecting Principles for Systems-of-Systems," *Systems Engineering* (1) 4 (1998), pp. 267–284.

Marenzano 1995. J. Marenzano, "System Architecture Validation Review Findings," in D. Garlan, ed., ICSE17 Architecture Workshop Proceedings, CMU, Pittsburgh, PA 1995.

McGarry et al. 1998. J. McGarry, E. Bailey, D. Card, J. Dean, F. Hall, C. Jones, B. Layman, and G. Stark, *Practical Software Measurement: A Foundation for Objective Project Management*, Office of the Under Secretary of Defense for Acquisition and Technology, Version 3.1A, April 17, 1998. Available at http://www. psmsc.com

Mullet 1976. G. M. Mullet, "Why Regression Coefficients Have the Wrong Sign," *Journal of Quality Technology*, 1976.

Miyazaki-Mori 1985. Y. Miyazaki and K. Mori, "COCOMO Evaluation and Tailoring," Proceedings, ICSE 8, IEEE-ACM-BCS, London, August 1985, pp. 292–299.

Park et al. 1994. R. Park, W. Goethert, and J. Webb, "Software Cost and Schedule Estimating: A Process Improvement Initiative," CMU/SEI-94-SR-03, Software Engineering Institute, Pittsburgh, PA.

Park 1992. R. Park, "Software Size Measurement: A Framework for Counting Source Statements." CMU/SEI-92-TR-20, Software Engineering Institute, Pittsburgh, PA, 1992.

Paulk et al. 1995. M. Paulk, C. Weber, B. Curtis, and M. Chrissis, *The Capability Maturity Model: Guidelines for Improving the Software Process*, Addison-Wesley, 1995.

Pfleeger 1991. S. Pfleeger, "Model of Software Effort and Productivity," *Information and Software Technology* 33 (3), April 1991, pp. 224–231.

Poulin 1997. Jeffrey S. Poulin, *Measuring Software Reuse, Principles, Practices and Economic Models*, Addison Wesley, 1997.

Parikh-Zvegintzov 1983. G. Parikh and N. Zvegintzov, "The World of Software Maintenance," Tutorial on Software Maintenance, *IEEE Computer Society Press*, pp. 1–3.

Reifer et al. 1999. D. Reifer, B. Boehm, and S. Chulani, "The Rosetta Stone: Making COCOMO Estimates Work With COCOMO II," *Crosstalk, The Journal of Defense Engineering*, February 1999.

Reifer 1997a. D.J. Reifer, *Practical Software Reuse*, John Wiley and Sons, 1997.

Reifer 1997b. D.J. Reifer, *Tutorial Software Management (5th Edition)*, IEEE Computer Society Press, 1997.

Royce 1990. R. Royce, "TRW's Ada Process Model for Incremental Development of Large Software Systems," Proceedings, ICSE 12, Nice, France, March 1990.

Royce 1998. R. Royce, *Software Project Management A Unified Framework*, Addison-Wesley, Reading, MA, 1998.

Rubin 1999. H. Rubin, *Software Productivity and Quality Issues and the U.S. IT Workforce Shortage*, META Group, Stamford, CT, 1999.

Ruhl-Gunn 1991. M. Ruhl and M. Gunn, "Software Reengineering: A Case Study and Lessons Learned," NIST Special Publication 500-193, Washington, DC, September 1991.

Selby et al. 1991. R. Selby, A. Porter, D. Schmidt and J. Berney, "Metric-Driven Analysis and Feedback Systems for Enabling Empirically Guided Software Development," Proceedings of the Thirteenth International Conference on Software Engineering (ICSE 13), Austin, TX, May 13–16, 1991, pp. 288–298.

Selby 1988. R. Selby, "Empirically Analyzing Software Reuse in a Production Environment," In *Software Reuse: Emerging Technology,* W. Tracz (Ed.), IEEE Computer Society Press, 1988., pp. 176–189.

Shepperd-Schofield 1997. M. Shepperd and C. Schofield, "Estimating Software Project Effort Using Analogies," IEEE Transactions on Software Engineering, Vol. 23, No. 11, November 1997.

Snee, 1977. R. Snee, "Validation of Regression Models: Methods and Example," *Technometrics*, Vol. 19, No. 4, November 1977.

Standish 1995. The Standish Group, "Chaos," Standish Group Report, 1995.

Stensrud 1998. E. Stensrud, "Estimating with Enhanced Object Points vs. Function Points," *Proceedings, 13th COCOMO/SCM Forum*, USC, October 1998.

Silvestri-Lukasiewicz 1991. G. Silvestri and J. Lukasiewicz, "Occupational Employment Projections," *Monthly Labor Review* 114(11), November 1991, pp. 64–94.

USC-CSE 1997a. "COCOMO II Model Definition Manual," Computer Science Department, University of Southern California, Center for Software Engineering, Los Angeles, CA 90089-0781, 1997.

USC-CSE 1997b. *Proceedings*, 1997 CSE Focused Workshop on Rapid Application Development, Computer Science Department, University of Southern California. Center for Software Engineering, Los Angeles, CA 90089-0781, 1997

Vicinanza et al. 1991. S. Vicinanza, T. Mukhopadhyay, and M. Prietula, "Software Effort Estimation: An Exploratory Study of Expert Performance, *Information Systems* 2, pp. 243–262, 1991.

Weisberg 1985. S. Weisberg, *Applied Linear Regression*, 2nd Ed., John Wiley and Sons, New York, 1985.

# Index

# About the CD-ROM

The CD-ROM included with *Software Cost Estimation with COCOMO II* contains the following:

The COCOMO II.2000 CD-ROM allows you to install or use COCOMO II.2000 software along with the book or the tutorials on the CD-ROM. This CD-ROM also contains the following useful information:

- Video introduction message from Dr. Barry Boehm
- The book overview by Dr. Barry Boehm
- COCOMO II.2000 manuals in PDF
- Implementations of COCOMO II.2000 Extensions including documentation
- Tutorials with videos, their presentations and example files
- Various commerical demonstration or evaluation copies of COCOMO II-based tools
- Data collection forms
- Affiliation information
- Links for COCOMO II related web sites
- Adobe Acrobat Reader installation package for PDF files on the CD

This CD-ROM has both software and hardware system requirements. For further information, see Readme.txt on the CD.

The CD-ROM can be used on Microsoft Windows® 95/98/NT®.

*License Agreement*

Use of the software accompanying *Software Cost Estimation with COCOMO II* is subject to terms of the License Agreement and Limited Warranty, found on the previous two pages.

*Technical Support*

Prentice Hall does not offer technical support for any of the programs on the CD-ROM. However, if the CD-ROM is damaged, you may obtain a replacement copy by sending an email that describes the problem to disc_exchange@ prenhall.com.

# COCOMO II.2000 Effort Equations

$$PM = A \times Size^E \times \prod_{i=1}^{n} EM_i + PM_{Auto}$$

$$E = B + 0.01 \times \sum_{j=1}^{5} SF_j$$

$$PM_{Auto} = \frac{Adapted\ SLOC \times \left(AT / 100\right)}{ATPROD}$$

| Symbol | Description |
|---|---|
| A | Effort coefficient that can be calibrated |
| AT | Percentage of the Adapted SLOC that is re-engineered by automatic translation |
| ATPROD | Automatic translation productivity |
| B | Scaling base-exponent for Effort that can be calibrated |
| E | Scaling exponent for Effort |
| EM | Effort Multipliers: seven (7) for the Early Design and seventeen (17) for the Post-Architecture modes |
| PM | Person Months effort from developing new and adapted code |
| $PM_{Auto}$ | Person Months effort from automatic translation activities |
| SF | Five (5) Scale Factors |
| SLOC | Source Lines of Code |

# COCOMO II.2000 Schedule Equations

$$TDEV = [C \times (PM_{NS})^F] \times \frac{SCED\%}{100}$$

$$F = D + 0.2 \times [E - B]$$

| Symbol | Description |
|---|---|
| B | The scaling base-exponent for the effort equation |
| C | Schedule coefficient that can be calibrated |
| D | Scaling base-exponent for Schedule that can be calibrated |
| E | The scaling exponent for the effort equation |
| F | Scaling exponent for Schedule |
| $PM_{NS}$ | Person Months estimated without the SCED cost driver (Nominal Schedule) and without $PM_{Auto}$ |
| SCED% | Required Percentage of Schedule Compression relative to Nominal Schedule |
| TDEV | Time to Develop in calendar months |